Andreas Uhl · Christoph Busch ·
Sébastien Marcel · Raymond Veldhuis
Editors

Handbook of Vascular Biometrics

Editors
Andreas Uhl
Department of Computer Science
University of Salzburg
Salzburg, Austria

Sébastien Marcel
Swiss Center for Biometrics
Research and Testing
Idiap Research Institute
Martigny, Switzerland

Christoph Busch
Hochschule Darmstadt
Darmstadt, Germany

Raymond Veldhuis
Faculty of EEMCS
University of Twente
Enschede, The Netherlands

https://doi.org/10.1007/978-3-030-27731-4

Foreword

The Handbook of Vascular Biometrics is essential reading for anyone involved in biometric identity verification, be they students, researchers, practitioners, engineers or technology consultants.

In June 1983 following the theft and fraudulent use of my chequebook & guarantee card, I started vascular scanning work colleagues at Kodak Ltd.'s Annesley plant in the UK. It was only after I had scanned my first set of identical twins and examined the resulting traces was I convinced that I had invented or more accurately discovered a very secure and private way of verifying the identity of individuals. On that June evening, vascular biometrics was born and I envisioned how the technique could be applied to digitally secure the possessions, authorship and transactions of individuals. What I didn't appreciate then was just how long it would take for vascular biometric techniques to go mainstream.

I submitted my design and results to Kodak Ltd.'s product opportunities panel, they liked my proposal but Eastman Kodak sought biometric experts' opinions before agreeing to a development project. The experts concluded that there was no need for vascular biometrics as fingerprint, voice and signature would predominate. Eastman Kodak stopped the nascent project. I secured a release for my technology and signed a development agreement with the UK's National Research Development Corporation (NRDC). The NRDC's formal patent application based on my DIY provisional application was hit by a UK Ministry of Defence secrecy order; we could only file in secret in friendly NATO countries. Something I'd built on my kitchen table at home was now Top Secret!

After the secrecy order was lifted, I showed the system at Barclay's TechMart exhibition in Birmingham and Kodak Ltd. started talks with the NRDC to smuggle vascular biometric development in through the back door. Work started at Kodak's Ltd.'s. Harrow Research facilities, I was temporarily assigned from manufacturing to research to work with Dr. Andrew Green, we built a vein scanner and arranged for it to be production engineered and manufactured at the Kodak camera plant in Stuttgart Germany and we just had to convince Eastman Kodak to agree. I was dispatched to Rochester to show the system with Brian Goodwin a colleague from Annesley. It was well received, but senior Eastman Kodak executives wanted me to forgo any license fees from NRDC; they didn't want me to profit from Kodak's involvement and their earlier mistake, so I declined their offer.

During this time, I was sponsored by the NRDC and Kodak Ltd. to attend various conferences and working groups. I visited a few conferences and met the attendees. I listen to their enthusiasm for biometrics but I had misgivings; I was unhappy with the State & Big Business holding users' biometric data. Increasingly, I was meeting Police Officers and Home Office officials looking into biometrics for managing society; they were interested in video surveillance, border controls and access to social security payments, etc. My view was that the wholesale use by the State of biometric systems and data would enslave us all. These officials were well-intentioned but were not interested in the long-term consequences on society of their actions. I feared that the consequences of Government-sponsored development of biometrics would be the descent into a Big Brother controlled surveillance society.

I published my views on biometric privacy on the vein biometric homepage which I started in 1993 and called for the development of worn biometric solutions like a biowatch where people owned and controlled their own biometric systems and data. I also shared my biometric libertarian views in various chat groups during the 1990s and as a result, I was invited to speak at the 1999 biometric summit in Washington DC. Meanwhile, the NRDC had sparked no commercial success in trying to license vein biometric technology—they hadn't in my opinion undertaken sufficient testing to prove beyond doubt the viability of vascular biometrics.

In my 1999 Washington talk entitled "A third way for biometrics" (still viewable via Google), I called for biometric companies to stop producing "Big Brother" solutions but rather to develop personal systems and particularly personal private worn vascular systems that the people owned and controlled themselves. My talk was followed by a review of biometrics modalities by IBG (The International biometrics group)—their view was that vascular biometrics didn't have sufficient information content to become a viable solution, a damning conclusion that stymied me from raising any further investment in vascular biometric development. We now know that vascular patterns are far better and have more entropy than fingerprints but this is only after millions of investment and millions of vein scans.

Today, vascular biometrics is going mainstream given the number of actual and planned products and services incorporating vascular scanning and the amount of global research and development activity being applied to this technology.

In this first edition of the Handbook of Vascular Biometrics, the authors provide an excellent authoritative and comprehensive review of the current state of the art providing students, scientists and engineers with detailed insights into the diverse field of vascular biometrics. The handbook reviews major algorithmic approaches in the recognition toolchain together with information on available datasets, public competitions, open-source software resources and template protection schemes. Their in-depth investigations, accompanied by comprehensive experimental evaluations, provide the reader with theoretical and empirical explanations of fundamental and current research. A key feature of the handbook is its strong focus on reproducible research. Moreover, the handbook contains detailed analysis including performance figures, results and source code including descriptions of proposed methods with detailed instructions on how to build, code and reproduce the experiments.

The Handbook is intended for a broad readership. The first part provides a description of the state of the art in vascular biometrics including a vast bibliography. Further chapters provide detailed open-source material for the hardware and software construction of vascular biometric devices and thus support graduate students starting to work on this topic or researchers aiming to build their own devices. Subsequent parts delve deeper into research topics and are aimed at the more advanced reader, and are focussed in particular on graduate and Ph.D. students as well as junior researchers.

The second part of the handbook concentrates on commercially available solutions particularly hand-based vascular systems. This section contains contributions from both Fujitsu and Hitachi, on palm and finger vein systems and the diverse applications to which they are applied. Additional chapters focus on large-scale finger vein identification systems and particularly address the minimisation of computational cost plus investigate the use of recent semantic segmentation work with convolutional neural networks for finger vein vasculature structure extraction.

The third part of the handbook focuses on eye-based vascular biometrics, i.e. retina and sclera recognition and covers a wide range of topics, including the examination of both medical and biometric devices for fundus imaging. This section includes a discussion of retinal diseases and their potential impact on retina recognition accuracy.

The final part of the handbook covers topics related to security and privacy including securing systems against presentation attack (PAD) techniques. Subsequent chapters deal with biometric template protection schemes, in particular, cancellable biometric schemes including reviews of classical cancellable transforms. Finally, a proposed methodology to quantify the amount of discriminatory information from the application of classical binarisation feature extraction is discussed as a complement to traditional EER benchmarking.

The handbook contains invited as well as contributed chapters, which all underwent rigorous reviewing procedures prior to their inclusion.

Clifton Village Nottingham — Joe Rice
May 2019

Preface

Biometrics refers to the recognition of individuals based on their physiological or behavioural characteristics or traits. In this sense, biometrics may be seen to be as old as mankind itself. The possibility to automatise the recognition process and let computers and attached capture devices perform this task has led to the successful development and deployment of numerous biometric technologies. Vascular biometrics have emerged in recent years and are perceived as an attractive, yet still unexplored from many perspectives, alternative to more established biometric modalities like face recognition or fingerprint recognition, respectively. As the name suggests, vascular biometrics are based on vascular patterns, formed by the blood vessel structure inside the human body. While some vascular recognition systems have seen significant commercial deployment (e.g. finger vein and palm vein recognition in financial services and to secure personal devices), others remain niche products to current date (e.g. wrist, retina and sclera recognition). In any case, there is significant commercial and scientific interest in these approaches, also documented by an increasing number of corresponding scientific publications.

In this first edition of the Handbook of Vascular Biometrics, we address the current state of the art in this field. In addition, we intend to provide students, scientists and engineers with a detailed insight into diverse advanced topics in the various fields of vascular biometrics. In-depth investigations, accompanied by comprehensive experimental evaluations, provide the reader with theoretical and empirical explanations of fundamental and current research topics. Furthermore, research directions, open questions and issues yet to be solved are pointed out.

Editors from this first edition would like to thank Mr. Joseph Rice, the inventor of vein recognition and of the concept of wearable wrist vein biometrics, for the Foreword.

Objectives

Selected chapters and topics cover a wide spectrum of research on vascular biometrics; however, the handbook is intended to complement existing literature in the field, and as a pre-requisite for acceptance, each chapter was required to contain a percentage of at least 25–30% novel content as compared to earlier published work. As a key feature, this handbook has a strong focus on reproducible research (RR). All contributions aim to meet the following conditions:

- Experiments should relate to publicly available datasets as a first requirement for RR.
- System scores generated with proposed methods should be openly available as a second requirement for RR.

Additionally, the sharing of plots or performance figures, open-source code of the proposed methods and detailed instructions to reproduce the experiments was strongly encouraged.

Key objectives, which this book is focused on, are as follows:

- Provision of an extended overview of the state of the art in vascular biometrics.
- Guidance and support for researchers in the field regarding the design of capture devices and software systems by providing open-source material in the respective fields.
- Detailed investigations of advanced topics in vascular biometrics ranging from questions related to security and privacy to support for developing efficient large-scale systems.
- A comprehensive collection of references on vascular biometrics.

Audience

The handbook is divided into four parts comprising a total of 17 chapters. Parts, distinct groups of chapters as well as single chapters are meant to be fairly independent and also self-contained, and the reader is encouraged to study only relevant parts or chapters.

This book is intended for a broad readership. The first part provides a description of the state of the art in vascular biometrics including a vast bibliography on the topic. Thus, this part addresses readers wishing to gain an overview of vascular biometrics. Further chapters in the first part provide detailed open-source material for hardware and software construction and thus support graduate students starting to work on this topic or researchers aiming to build their own devices. Subsequent parts delve deeper into research topics and are aimed at the more advanced reader, in particular, graduate and Ph.D. students as well as junior researchers.

Organisation

The handbook contains invited as well as contributed chapters, which all underwent a rigorous 3-round reviewing procedure. The reviewing process for each chapter was led by one of the editors and was based on two independent reviews.

Part I: Introduction

Chapter 1 of the handbook, by Andreas Uhl, *State of the Art in Vascular Biometrics*, provides a comprehensive discussion of the state of the art in vascular biometrics, covering hand-oriented techniques (finger vein, palm vein, (dorsal) hand vein and wrist vein recognition) as well as eye-oriented techniques (retina and sclera recognition). For all these vascular approaches, we discuss commercial capture devices (also referred to as sensors) and systems, major algorithmic approaches in the recognition toolchain, available datasets, public competitions and open-source software, template protection schemes, presentation attacks and presentation attack detection, sample quality assessment, mobile acquisition and acquisition on the move, and finally eventual disease impact on recognition and template privacy issues. The chapter provides more than 350 references in the respective areas.

The second and third chapters provide detailed descriptions of research-oriented, non-commercial finger vein sensors. Chapter 2, by Raymond Veldhuis, Luuk Spreeuwers, Bram Ton and Sjoerd Rozendal, *A High-Quality Finger Vein Dataset Collected Using a Custom-Designed Capture Device*, describes the transillumination scanner used to acquire the UTFVP dataset, one of the first publicly available finger vein datasets and provides experimental recognition results based on publicly available software. The last part of the chapter highlights a new sensor type capable of acquiring finger vein data from three different perspectives (using three NIR cameras). Chapter 3, by Christof Kauba, Bernhard Prommegger and Andreas Uhl, *OpenVein—An Open-Source Modular Multipurpose Finger Vein Scanner Design*, describes a three-finger scanner capable of acquiring transillumination as well as reflected light finger vein data which can be equipped with near-infrared LEDs as well as with near-infrared laser modules. All details regarding the two scanner devices, including technical drawings of all parts, models of the 3D printed parts, control board schematics, the microcontroller firmware, the capturing software, parts lists as well as assembly and set-up instructions, are available as open-source data to facilitate the re-construction by interested readers. Finally, the openly available PLUSVein-FV3 finger vein data set is described. Chapter 4, by Christof Kauba and Andreas Uhl, *An Available Open-Source Vein Recognition Framework*, presents PLUS OpenVein, a full-fledged vein recognition open-source software framework implemented in MATLAB. It contains various well-established and state-of-the-art vein enhancement, feature extraction and template comparison schemes. Moreover, it contains tools to evaluate the recognition performance and provides functions to perform feature- and score-level fusion. To round up, the chapter exemplary describes the conduct of an experimental evaluation on the UTFVP dataset (Chap. 2) using the introduced software framework.

Part II: Hand and Finger Vein Biometrics

The second part of the handbook exclusively focuses on hand-based vascular biometrics, i.e. palm vein and finger vein recognition, respectively. The first two chapters are contributed from the two major commercial players in the filed, i.e. the Japanese companies Fujitsu and Hitachi, respectively. Chapter 5, by Takashi Shinzaki, *Use case of Palm Vein Authentication,* contributed by Fujitsu, describes the diverse application areas in which the contactless Fujitsu palm vein recognition technology is deployed, ranging from device login authentication to access control systems and financial services. Chapter 6, by Mitsutoshi Himaga and Hisao Ogota, *Evolution of Finger Vein Biometric Devices in Terms of Usability*, contributed by Hitachi, describes the evolution of Hitachi's finger vein readers with particular emphasis on usability aspects, highlighting the latest walk-through-style finger vein entrance gates.

The subsequent chapters in this part are devoted to more research-oriented topics. Chapter 7, by Simon Kirchgasser, Christof Kauba and Andreas Uhl, *Towards Understanding Acquisition Conditions Influencing Finger Vein Recognition*, investigates the potential impact of different environmental as well as physiological acquisition conditions on finger vein recognition performance. Although based on a dataset of limited size, the insights gained in this chapter might help to improve finger vein recognition systems in the future by explicitly compensating problematic acquisition conditions. Chapter 8, by Ehsaneddin Jalilian and Andreas Uhl, *Improved CNN-Segmentation-Based Finger Vein Recognition Using Automatically Generated and Fused Training Labels*, investigates the use of recent semantic segmentation convolutional neural networks for finger vein vasculature structure extraction. In particular, the role of training data is highlighted and it is proposed to fuse automatically and manually generated training labels. In Chap. 9, by Benedikt-Alexander Mokroß, Pawel Drozdowski, Christian Rathgeb and Christoph Busch, *Efficient Identification in Large-Scale Vein Recognition Systems Using Spectral Minutiae Representations*, the authors focus on large-scale finger vein identification systems and particularly address the issue of minimising computational cost. Based on a spectral minutiae feature representation, efficient indexing and template comparison schemes are proposed and evaluated. Finally, Chap. 10, by Bernhard Prommegger, Christof Kauba and Andreas Uhl, *Different Views on the Finger—Score-Level Fusion in Multi-Perspective Finger Vein Recognition*, investigates multi-perspective finger vein recognition, i.e. comprising views all around the finger's longitudinal axis, captured using a self-developed rotating multi-perspective finger vein capture device. Besides evaluating the performance of the single views, several score-level fusion experiments involving different fusion strategies are carried out in order to determine the best performing set of views (in terms of recognition accuracy) while minimising the overall number of views involved.

Part III: Sclera and Retina Biometrics

The third part of the handbook focuses on eye-based vascular biometrics, i.e. retina and sclera recognition, respectively. Corresponding to the lesser extent of available literature for these modalities, only three chapters could be included in this part of the book.

Chapter 11, by Lukáš Semerád and Martin Drahanský, *Retinal Vascular Characteristics*, is devoted to retina recognition and covers a wide range of topics. After describing a set of medical and biometric devices for fundus imaging, retinal diseases are discussed exhibiting a potential impact on retina recognition accuracy. For some of these diseases, automated detection algorithms are proposed and evaluated. Additional topics covered are the determination of biometric information content in retinal data and a description of how to generate synthetic fundus imagery (corresponding datasets are released to the public). Chapter 12, by Arathi Arakala, Stephen Davis and K. J. Horadam, *Vascular Biometric Graph Comparison: Theory and Performance,* also covers retina recognition technology, but only as one example for the application of vascular biometric graph comparison, which is also applied to wrist vein, palm vein and hand vein data. This chapter also discusses template protection techniques for this type of feature representation based on anchors (i.e. small connected subgraphs). Chapter 13, by Peter Rot, Matej Vitek, Klemen Grm, Žiga Emeršič, Peter Peer and Vitomir Štruc, *Deep Sclera Segmentation and Recognition*, covers sclera recognition by proposing a sequential combination of deep learning-based segmentation and recognition, respectively. In addition to extensive experimental validation and comparison, the authors also provide a new public dataset including a per-pixel markup of various eye parts, gaze direction and gender labels.

Part IV: Security and Privacy in Vascular Biometrics

The fourth part of the handbook covers topics related to security and privacy aspects of vascular biometrics; in this part, only hand-based vascular modalities are considered (in fact, the attention is restricted entirely to finger vein technology).

Chapter 14, by Jascha Kolberg, Marta Gomez-Barrero, Sushma Venkatesh, Raghavendra Ramachandra and Christoph Busch, *Presentation Attack Detection for Finger Recognition*, deals with Presentation Attack Detection (PAD) techniques. However, contrasting the many papers available dealing with PAD for finger vein recognition systems, this paper uses finger vein imaging of fingerprint artefacts to counter fingerprint PA by using a dual imaging approach.

The subsequent chapters deal with biometric template protection schemes, in particular with cancellable biometric schemes for finger vein recognition. Chapter 15, by Vedrana Krivokuća and Sébastien Marcel, *On the Recognition Performance of BioHash-Protected Finger Vein Templates*, applies BioHashing to finger vein templates generated by classical binarisation feature extraction and evaluates the resulting recognition performance. Chapter 16, by Simon Kirchgasser, Christof Kauba and Andreas Uhl, *Cancellable Biometrics for Finger Vein Recognition—Application in the Feature Domain*, applies the classical cancellable transforms, i.e. block re-mapping and block warping, also to binary features as in Chap. 15 and evaluates the impact on recognition performance and unlinkability. Finally, Chap. 17, by Vedrana Krivokuća, Marta Gomez-Barrero, Sébastien Marcel, Christian Rathgeb and Christoph Busch, *Towards Measuring the Amount of Discriminatory Information in Finger Vein Biometric Characteristics Using a Relative Entropy Estimator*, proposes a methodology to quantify the amount of discriminatory information in features again resulting from classical binarisation feature extraction like in the two chapters before. The derived metric is suggested to be used as a complement to the EER in benchmarking the discriminative capabilities of different biometric systems.

Salzburg, Austria — Andreas Uhl
Darmstadt, Germany — Christoph Busch
Martigny, Switzerland — Sébastien Marcel
Enschede, The Netherlands — Raymond Veldhuis

Acknowledgements

Research work reported in this book has received funding from the European Union's Horizon 2020 research and innovation programme under grant agreements No. 700259 (PROTECT) and No. 690907 (IDENTITY). The work was also funded by the Austrian Research Promotion Agency, FFG KIRAS project AUTFingerATM under grant No. 864785. Furthermore, this book has also received funding from the Norwegian IKTPLUSS SWAN project, from the Swiss Center for Biometrics Research and Testing, and from the University of Twente. We acknowledge financial support by the Open Access Publication Fund of the University of Salzburg.

Contents

Part I Introduction

1 **State of the Art in Vascular Biometrics** 3
Andreas Uhl

2 **A High-Quality Finger Vein Dataset Collected Using a Custom-Designed Capture Device** 63
Raymond Veldhuis, Luuk Spreeuwers, Bram Ton and Sjoerd Rozendal

3 **OpenVein—An Open-Source Modular Multipurpose Finger Vein Scanner Design** 77
Christof Kauba, Bernhard Prommegger and Andreas Uhl

4 **An Available Open-Source Vein Recognition Framework** 113
Christof Kauba and Andreas Uhl

Part II Hand and Finger Vein Biometrics

5 **Use Case of Palm Vein Authentication** 145
Takashi Shinzaki

6 **Evolution of Finger Vein Biometric Devices in Terms of Usability** 159
Mitsutoshi Himaga and Hisao Ogata

7 **Towards Understanding Acquisition Conditions Influencing Finger Vein Recognition** 179
Simon Kirchgasser, Christof Kauba and Andreas Uhl

8 **Improved CNN-Segmentation-Based Finger Vein Recognition Using Automatically Generated and Fused Training Labels** 201
Ehsaneddin Jalilian and Andreas Uhl

9 Efficient Identification in Large-Scale Vein Recognition Systems Using Spectral Minutiae Representations 225
Benedikt-Alexander Mokroß, Pawel Drozdowski, Christian Rathgeb and Christoph Busch

10 Different Views on the Finger—Score-Level Fusion in Multi-Perspective Finger Vein Recognition 261
Bernhard Prommegger, Christof Kauba and Andreas Uhl

Part III Sclera and Retina Biometrics

11 Retinal Vascular Characteristics 309
Lukáš Semerád and Martin Drahanský

12 Vascular Biometric Graph Comparison: Theory and Performance 355
Arathi Arakala, Stephen Davis and K. J. Horadam

13 Deep Sclera Segmentation and Recognition 395
Peter Rot, Matej Vitek, Klemen Grm, Žiga Emeršič, Peter Peer and Vitomir Štruc

Part IV Security and Privacy in Vascular Biometrics

14 Presentation Attack Detection for Finger Recognition 435
Jascha Kolberg, Marta Gomez-Barrero, Sushma Venkatesh, Raghavendra Ramachandra and Christoph Busch

15 On the Recognition Performance of BioHash-Protected Finger Vein Templates 465
Vedrana Krivokuća and Sébastien Marcel

16 Cancellable Biometrics for Finger Vein Recognition—Application in the Feature Domain 481
Simon Kirchgasser, Christof Kauba and Andreas Uhl

17 Towards Measuring the Amount of Discriminatory Information in Finger Vein Biometric Characteristics Using a Relative Entropy Estimator 507
Vedrana Krivokuća, Marta Gomez-Barrero, Sébastien Marcel, Christian Rathgeb and Christoph Busch

Index 527

Part I
Introduction

Chapter 1
State of the Art in Vascular Biometrics

Andreas Uhl

Abstract The investigation of vascular biometric traits has become increasingly popular during the last years. This book chapter provides a comprehensive discussion of the respective state of the art, covering hand-oriented techniques (finger vein, palm vein, (dorsal) hand vein and wrist vein recognition) as well as eye-oriented techniques (retina and sclera recognition). We discuss commercial sensors and systems, major algorithmic approaches in the recognition toolchain, available datasets, public competitions and open-source software, template protection schemes, presentation attack(s) (detection), sample quality assessment, mobile acquisition and acquisition on the move, and finally eventual disease impact on recognition and template privacy issues.

Keywords Vascular biometrics · Finger vein recognition · Hand vein recognition · Palm vein recognition · Retina recognition · Sclera recognition · Near-infrared

1.1 Introduction

As the name suggests, vascular biometrics are based on vascular patterns, formed by the blood vessel structure inside the human body.

Historically, Andreas Vesalius already suggested in 1543 that the vessels in the extremities of the body are highly variable in their location and structure. Some 350 years later, a professor of forensic medicine at Padua University, Arrigo Tamassia, stated that no two vessel patterns seen on the back of the hand seem to be identical in any two individuals [23].

This pattern has to be made visible and captured by a suitable biometric scanner device in order to be able to conduct biometric recognition. Two parts of the human body (typically not covered by clothing in practical recognition situations) are the major source to extract vascular patterns for biometric purposes: The human

A. Uhl (✉)
Department of Computer Sciences, University of Salzburg, Jakob-Haringer-Str. 2, 5020 Salzburg, Austria
e-mail: uhl@cs.sbg.ac.at

A. Uhl et al. (eds.), *Handbook of Vascular Biometrics*, Advances in Computer Vision and Pattern Recognition, https://doi.org/10.1007/978-3-030-27731-4_1

hand [151, 275] (used in *finger vein* [59, 120, 234, 247, 250, 300] as well as in *hand/palm/wrist vein* [1, 226] recognition) and the human eye (used in *retina* [97, 166] and *sclera* [44] recognition), respectively.

The imaging principles used, however, are fairly different for those biometric modalities. Vasculature in the human hand is at least covered by skin layers and also by other tissue types eventually (depending on the vasculatures' position depth wrt. skin surface). Therefore, Visible Light (VIS) imaging does not reveal the vessel structures properly.

1.1.1 Imaging Hand-Based Vascular Biometric Traits

In principle, high-precision imaging of human vascular structures, including those inside the human hand, is a solved problem. Figure 1.1a displays corresponding vessels using a Magnetic Resonance Angiography (MRA) medical imaging device, while Fig. 1.1b shows the result of applying hyperspectral imaging using a STEMMER IMAGING device using their Perception Studio software to visualise the data captured in the range 900–1700 nm. However, biometric sensors have a limitation in terms of their costs. For practical deployment in real-world authentication solutions, the technologies used to produce the images in Fig. 1.1 are not an option for this reason. The solution is much simpler and thus more cost-effective Near-Infrared (NIR) imaging.

Joe Rice (the author of the Foreword of this Handbook) patented his NIR-imaging-based "Veincheck" system in the early 1980s which is often seen as the birth of hand-based vascular biometrics. After the expiry of that patent, Hitachi, Fujitsu and Techsphere launched security products relying on vein biometrics (all holding various patents in this area now). Joe Rice is still involved in this business, as he is partnering with the Swiss company BiowatchID producing wrist vein-based mobile recognition technology (see Sect. 1.2).

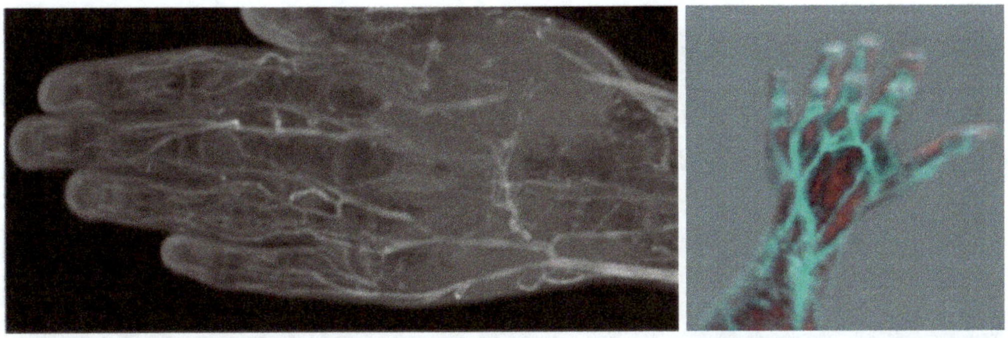

(a) Magnetic Resonance Angiography (MRA) (b) Hyper-spectral Imaging

Fig. 1.1 Visualising hand vascular structures

The physiological background of this imaging technique is as follows. The haemoglobin in the bloodstream absorbs NIR light. The haemoglobin is the pigment in the blood which is primarily composed of iron, which carries the oxygen. Haemoglobin is known to absorb NIR light. This is why vessels appear as dark structures under NIR illumination, while the surrounding tissue has a much lower light absorption coefficient in that spectrum and thus appears bright. The blood in veins obviously contains a higher amount of deoxygenated haemoglobin as compared to blood in arteries. Oxygenated and deoxygenated haemoglobin absorb NIR light equally at 800 nm, whereas at 760 nm absorption is primarily from deoxygenated haemoglobin while above 800 nm oxygenated haemoglobin exhibits stronger absorption [68, 161]. Thus, the vascular pattern inside the hand can be rendered visible with the help of an NIR light source in combination with an NIR-sensitive image sensor. Depending on the used wavelength of illumination, either both or only a single type of vessels is captured predominantly.

The absorbing property of *deoxygenated* haemoglobin is also the reason for terming these hand-based modalities as finger *vein* and hand/palm/wrist *vein* recognition, while it is actually never demonstrated that it is really only veins and not arteries that are acquired by the corresponding sensors. Finger vein recognition deals with the vascular pattern inside the human fingers (this is the most recent trait in this class, and often [126] is assumed to be its origin), while hand/palm/wrist vein recognition visualises and acquires the pattern of the vessels of the central area (or wrist area) of the hand. Figure 1.2 displays example sample data from public datasets for palm vein, wrist vein and finger vein.

The positioning of the light source relative to the camera and the subject's finger or hand plays an important role. Here, we distinguish between *reflected light* and *transillumination* imaging. Reflected light means that the light source and the camera are placed on the same side of the hand and the light emitted by the source is reflected back to the camera. In transillumination, the light source and the camera are on the opposite side of the hand, i.e. the light penetrates skin and tissue of the hand before it is captured by the camera. Figure 1.3 compares these two imaging principles for the backside of the hand. A further distinction is made (mostly in reflected light imaging)

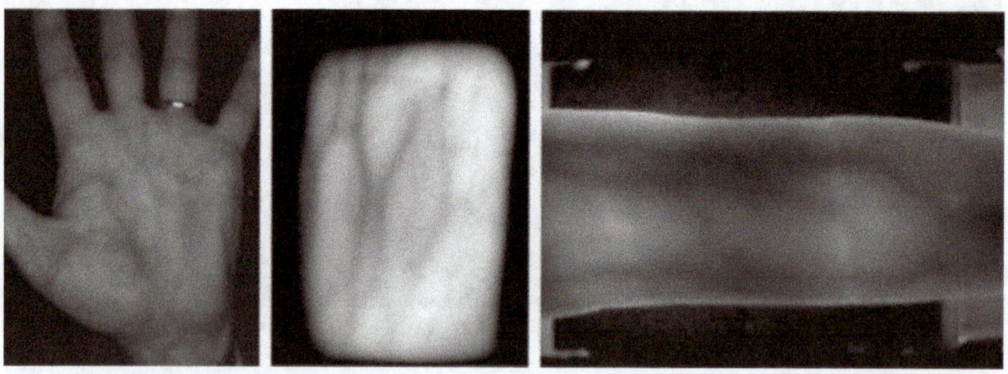

(a) Vera Palm Vein (b) PUT Wrist Vein (c) SDUMLA Finger Vein

Fig. 1.2 Example sample data

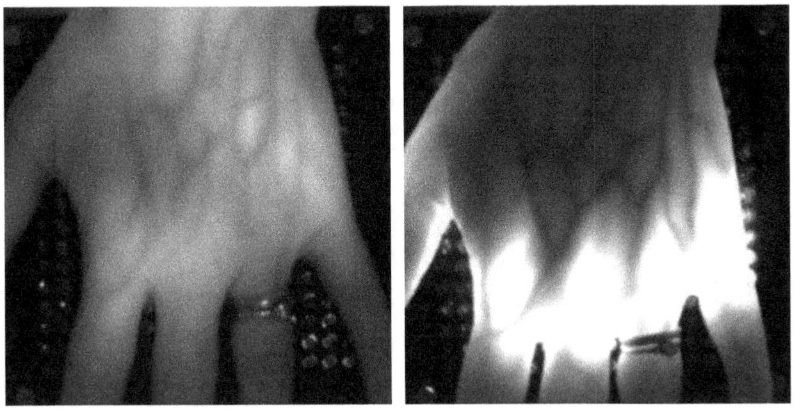

(a) Reflected light (b) Transillumination

Fig. 1.3 Example sample data: PROTECTVein hand veins

whether the *palmar* or *ventral* (i.e. inner) side of the hand (or finger) is acquired, or if the *dorsal* side is subject to image acquisition. Still, also in transillumination imaging, it is possible to discriminate between palmar and dorsal acquisition (where in palmar acquisition, the camera is placed so to acquire the palmar side of the hand while the light is positioned at the dorsal side). Acquisition for wrist vein recognition is limited to reflected light illumination of the palmar side of the wrist.

1.1.2 Imaging Eye-Based Vascular Biometric Traits

For the eye-based modalities, VIS imaging is applied to capture vessel structures. The retina is the innermost, light-sensitive layer or "coat", of shell tissue of the eye. The optic disc or optic nerve head is the point of exit for ganglion cell axons leaving the eye. Because there are no rods or cones covering the optic disc, it corresponds to a small blind spot in each eye. The ophthalmic artery bifurcates and supplies the retina via two distinct vascular networks: The choroidal network, which supplies the choroid and the outer retina, and the retinal network, which supplies the retina's inner layer. The bifurcations and other physical characteristics of the inner retinal vascular network are known to vary among individuals, which is exploited in retina recognition. Imaging this vascular network is accomplished by *fundus photography*, i.e. capturing a photograph of the back of the eye, the fundus (which is the interior surface of the eye opposite the lens and includes the retina, optic disc, macula, fovea and posterior pole). Specialised fundus cameras as developed for usage in ophthalmology (thus being a medical device) consist of an intricate microscope (up to 5$\times$ magnification) attached to a flash-enabled camera, where the annulus-shaped illumination passes through the camera objective lens and through the cornea onto the retina. The light reflected from the retina passes through the un-illuminated hole in the doughnut-shaped illumination system. Illumination is done with white light and acquisition is done either in full colour or employing a green-pass filter

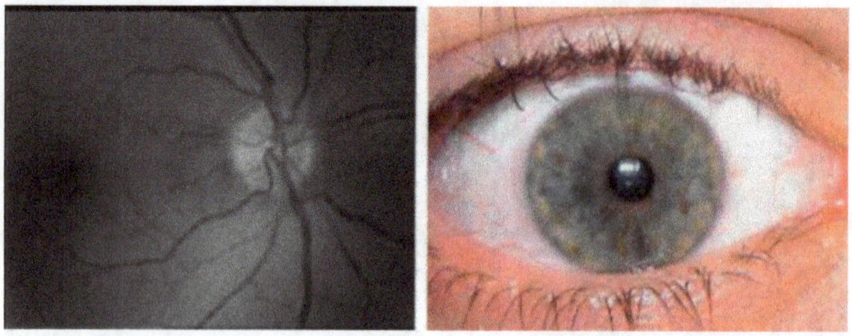

(a) VARIA - Retina (b) UBIRISv1 - Sclera

Fig. 1.4 Example sample data

($\approx$540–570 nm) to block out red wavelengths resulting in higher contrast. In medicine, fundus photography is used to monitor, e.g. macular degeneration, retinal neoplasms, choroid disturbances and diabetic retinopathy.

Finally, for sclera recognition, high-resolution VIS eye imagery is required in order to properly depict the fine vessel network being present. Optimal visibility of the vessel network is obtained from two off-angle images in which the eyes look into two directions. Figure 1.4 displays example sample data from public datasets for retina and sclera biometric traits.

1.1.3 Pros and Cons of Vascular Biometric Traits

Vascular biometrics exhibit certain advantages as compared to other biometric modalities as we shall discuss in the following. However, these modalities have seen commercial deployments to a relatively small extent so far, especially when compared to fingerprint or face recognition-based systems. This might be attributed to some disadvantages also being present for these modalities, which will be also considered subsequently. Of course, not all advantages or disadvantages are shared among all types of vascular biometric modalities, so certain aspects need to be discussed separately and we again discriminate between hand- and eye-based traits.

- Advantages of hand-based vascular biometrics (finger, hand, and wrist vein recognition): Comparisons are mostly done against fingerprint and palmprint recognition (and against techniques relying on hand geometry to some extent).
  - Vascular biometrics are expected to be insensitive to skin surface conditions (dryness, dirt, lotions) and abrasion (cuts, scars). While the imaging principle strongly suggests this property, so far no empirical evidence has been given to support this.
  - Vascular biometrics enable contactless sensing as there is no necessity to touch the acquiring camera. However, in finger vein recognition, all commercial systems and almost all other sensors being built require the user to place the finger directly on some sensor plate. This is done to ensure position normalisation

to some extent and to avoid the camera being dazzled in case of a mal-placed finger (in the transillumination case, the light source could directly illuminate the sensing camera).
- Vascular biometrics are more resistant against forgeries (i.e. spoofing, presentation attacks) as the vessels are only visible in infrared light. So on the one hand, it is virtually impossible to capture these biometric traits without user consent and from a distance and, on the other hand, it is more difficult to fabricate artefacts to be used in presentation attacks (as these need to be visible in NIR).
- Liveness detection is easily possible due to detectable blood flow. However, this requires NIR video acquisition and subsequent video analysis and not much work has been done to actually demonstrate this benefit.

• Disadvantages

- In transillumination imaging (as typically applied for finger veins), the capturing devices need to be built rather large.
- Images exhibit low contrast and low quality overall caused by the scattering of NIR rays in human tissue. The sharpness of the vessel layout is much lower compared to vessels acquired by retina or sclera imaging. Medical imaging principles like Magnetic Resonance Angiography (MRA) produce high-quality imagery depicting vessels inside the human body; however, these imaging techniques have prohibitive cost for biometric applications.
- The vascular structure may be influenced by temperature, physical activity, as well as by ageing and injuries/diseases; however, there is almost no empirical evidence that this applies to vessels inside the human hand (see for effects caused by meteorological variance [317]). This book contains a chapter investigating the influence of varying acquisition conditions on finger vein recognition to lay first foundations towards understanding these effects [122].
- Current commercial sensors do not allow to access, output and store imagery for further investigations and processing. Thus, all available evaluations of these systems have to rely on a black-box principle and only commercial recognition software of the same manufacturer can be used. This situation has motivated the construction of many prototypical devices for research purposes.
- These modalities cannot be acquired from a distance (which is also an advantage in terms of privacy protection), and it is fairly difficult to acquire them on the move. While at least the first property is beneficial for privacy protection, the combination of both properties excludes hand-based vascular biometrics from free-flow, on-the-move-type application scenarios. However, at least for on-the-move acquisition, advances can be expected in the future [164].

• Advantages of eye-based vascular biometrics (sclera and retina recognition): Comparisons are mostly done against iris, periocular and face recognition.

- As compared to iris recognition, there is no need to use NIR illumination and imaging. For both modalities, VIS imaging is used.

  - As compared to periocular and face recognition, retina and sclera vascular patterns are much less influenced by intended (e.g. make-up, occlusion like scarfs, etc.) and unintended (e.g. ageing) alterations of the facial area.
  - It is almost impossible to conduct presentation attacks against these modalities—entire eyes cannot be replaced as suggested by the entertainment industry (e.g. "Minority Report"). Full facial masks cannot be used for realistic sclera spoofing.
  - Liveness detection should be easily possible due to detectable blood flow (e.g. video analysis of retina imagery) and pulse detection in sclera video.
  - Not to be counted as an isolated advantage, but sclera-related features can be extracted and fused with other facial related modalities given the visual data is of sufficiently high quality.

- Disadvantages
  - Retina vessel capturing requires to illuminate the background of the eye which is not well received by users. Data acquisition feels like ophthalmological treatment.
  - Vessel structure/vessel width in both retina [171] and sclera [56] is influenced by certain diseases or pathological conditions.
  - Retina capturing devices originate from ophthalmology and thus have a rather high cost (as it is common for medical devices).
  - Currently, there are no commercial solutions available that could prove the practicality of these two biometric modalities.
  - For both modalities, data capture is not possible from a distance (as noted before, this can also be seen as an advantage in terms of privacy protection). For retina recognition, data acquisition is also definitely not possible on-the-move (while this could be an option for sclera given top-end imaging systems in place).

In the subsequent sections, we will discuss the following topics for each modality:

- Commercial sensors and systems;
- Major algorithmic approaches for preprocessing, feature extraction, template comparison and fusion (published in high-quality scientific outlets);
- Used datasets (publicly available), competitions and open-source software;
- Template protection schemes;
- Presentation attacks, presentation attack detection techniques and sample quality;
- Mobile acquisition and acquisition on the move.

(a) Hitachi (b) Mofiria (c) YannanTech

Fig. 1.5 Commercial finger vein sensors

1.2 Commercial Sensors and Systems

1.2.1 Hand-Based Vascular Traits

The area of commercial systems for hand-based vein biometrics is dominated by the two Japanese companies Hitachi and Fujitsu which hold patents for many technical details of the corresponding commercial solutions. This book contains two chapters authored by leading personnel of these two companies [88, 237]. Only in the last few years, competitors have entered the market. Figure 1.5 displays the three currently available finger vein sensors. As clearly visible, the Hitachi sensor is based on a pure transillumination principle, while the other two sensors illuminate the finger from the side while capturing is conducted from below (all sensors capture the palmar side of the finger). Yannan Tech has close connections to a startup from Peking University.

With respect to commercial hand vein systems, the market is even more restricted. Figure 1.6 shows three variants of the Fujitsu PalmSecure system: The "pure" sensor (a), the sensor equipped with a supporting frame to stabilise the hand and restrict the possible positions relative to the sensor (b) and the sensor integrated into a larger device for access control (integration done by a Fujitsu partner company) (c). When comparing the two types of systems, it gets clear that the PalmSecure system can be configured to operate in touchless/contactless manner (where the support frame is suspected to improve in particular genuine comparison scores), while finger vein scanners all require the finger to be placed on the surface of the scanner. While this would not be required in principle, this approach limits the extent of finger rotation and guarantees a rather correct placement of the finger relative to the sensors' acquisition device. So while it is understandable to choose this design principle, the potential benefit of contactless operation, especially in comparison to fingerprint scanners, is lost.

Techsphere,[1] being in the business almost right from the start of vascular biometrics, produces dorsal hand vein readers. BiowatchID,[2] a recent startup, produces a bracelet that is able to read out the wrist pattern and supports various types of

[1] http://www.vascularscanner.com/.

[2] https://biowatchid.com/.

(a) Fujitsu (b) Fujitsu (c) Sensometrix

Fig. 1.6 Commercial hand vein sensors

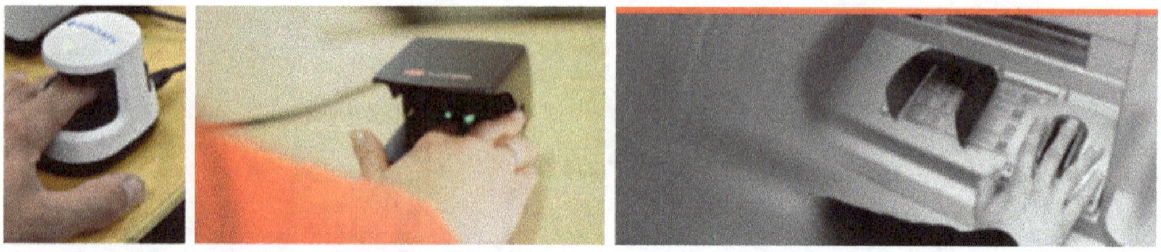

(a) Barclays (b) Homebanking BPH Bank (c) Fingervein ATM

Fig. 1.7 Finger vein recognition in banking

authentication solutions. Contrasting to a stationary sensor, this approach represents a per-se mobile solution permanently attached to the person subject to authentication.

Although hand vein-based sensors have been readily available for years, deployments are not seen as frequently as compared to the leading biometric modalities, i.e. face and fingerprint recognition. The most widespread application field of finger vein recognition technology can be observed in finance industry (some examples are illustrated in Fig. 1.7). On the one hand, several financial institutions offer their clients finger vein sensors for secure authentication in home banking. On the other hand, major finger vein equipped ATM roll-outs have been conducted in several countries, e.g. Japan, Poland, Turkey and Hong Kong. The PalmSecure system is mainly used for authentication on Fujitsu-built devices like laptops and tablets and in access control systems.

1.2.2 *Eye-Based Vascular Traits*

For vascular biometrics based on retina, commercialisation has not yet reached a mature state (in contrast, first commercial systems have disappeared from the market). Starting very early, the first retina scanners were launched in 1985 by the company EyeDentify and subsequently the company almost established a monopoly in this area. The most recent scanner is the model ICAM 2001, and it seems that this apparatus can still be acquired.[3] In the first decade of this century, the company

---

[3] http://www.raycosecurity.com/biometrics/EyeDentify.html.

Retica Systems Inc. even provided some insight into their template structure called retina code ("Multi-Radius Digital Pattern",[4] website no longer active), which has been analysed in earlier work [67]. The proposed template seemed to indicate a low potential for high variability (since the generation is not explained in detail, a reliable statement on this issue is not possible of course). Recall that Retica Systems Inc. claimed a template size of 20–100 bytes, whereas the smallest template investigated in [67] had 225 bytes and did not exhibit sufficient inter-class variability. Deployment of retina recognition technology has been seen mostly in US governmental agencies like CIA, FBI, NASA,[5] which is a difficult business model for sustainable company development (which might represent a major reason for the low penetration of this technology).

For sclera biometrics, the startup EyeVerify (founded 2012) termed their sclera recognition technology "Eyeprint ID" for which the company also acquired the corresponding patent. After the inclusion of the technology into several mobile banking applications, the company was acquired by Ant Financial, the financial services arm of Alibaba Group in 2016 (their website http://eyeverify.com/ is no longer active).

1.3 Algorithms in the Recognition Toolchain

Typically, the recognition toolchain consists of several distinct stages, most of which are identical across most vascular traits:

1. Acquisition: Commercial sensors are described in Sect. 1.2, while references to custom developments are given in the tables describing publicly available datasets in Sect. 1.4. The two chapters in this handbook describing sensor technologies provide further details on this topic [113, 258].
2. Image quality assessment: Techniques for this important topic (as required to assess sample quality to demand another acquisition process in case of poor quality or to conduct quality-weighted fusion) are described in Sect. 1.6 for all considered vascular modalities separately.
3. Preprocessing: Typically describes low-level image processing techniques (including normalisation and a variety of enhancement techniques) to cope with varying acquisition conditions, poor contrast, noise and blur. These operations depend on the target modality and are typically even sensor specific. They might also be conducted after the stage mentioned subsequently, but do often assist in RoI determination so that in most cases, the order as suggested here is the typical one.
4. Region of Interest (RoI) determination: This operation describes the process to determine the area in the sample image which is further subjected to feature extraction. In finger vein recognition, the actual finger texture has to be determined, while in palm vein recognition in most cases a rectangular central area

---

[4] http://www.retica.com/site/images/howitworks.pdf.

[5] https://www.bayometric.com/retinal-vs-iris-recognition/.

of the palm is extracted. For hand and wrist vein recognition, respectively, RoI extraction is hardly consistently done across different methods; still, the RoI is concentrated to contain visual data corresponding to hand tissue only. For retina recognition, the RoI is typically defined by the imaging device and is often a circle of normalised radius around the blind spot. In sclera recognition, this process is of highest importance and is called sclera segmentation, as it segments the sclera area from iris and eyelids.

5. Feature extraction: The ultimate aim of feature extraction is to produce a compact biometric identifier, i.e. the biometric template. As all imagery involving vascular biometrics contain visualised vascular structure, there are basically two options for feature extraction: First, feature extraction directly employs extracted vessel structures, relying on binary images representing these structures, skeletonised versions thereof, graph representations of the generated skeletons or using vein minutiae in the sense of vessel bifurcations or vessel endings. The second option relies on interpreting the RoI as texture patch which is used to extract discriminating features, in many cases key point-related techniques are employed. Deep-learning-based techniques are categorised into this second type of techniques except for those which explicitly extract vascular structure in a segmentation approach. A clear tendency may be observed: The better the quality of the samples and thus the clarity of the vessel structure, the more likely it is to see vein minutiae being used as features. In fundus images with their clear structure, vessels can be identified with high reliability, thus, vessel minutiae are used in most proposals (as fingerprint minutiae-based comparison techniques can be used). On the other hand, sclera vessels are very fine-grained and detailed structures which are difficult to explicitly extract from imagery. Therefore, in many cases, sclera features are more related to texture properties rather than to explicit vascular structure. Hand-based vascular biometrics are somewhat in between, so we see both strategies being applied.
6. Biometric comparison: Two different variants are often seen in literature: The first (and often more efficient) computes distance among extracted templates and compares the found distance to the decision threshold for identifying the correct user, and the second approach applies a classifier to assign a template to the correct class (i.e. the correct user) as stored in the biometric database. This book contains a chapter on efficient template indexing and template comparison in large-scale vein-based identification systems [178].

In most papers on biometric recognition, stages (3)–(5) of this toolchain are presented, discussed, and evaluated. Often, those papers rely on some public (or private) datasets and do not discuss sensor issues. Also, quality assessment is often left out or discussed in separate papers (see Sect. 1.6). A minority of papers discusses certain stages in isolated manner, as also evaluation is more difficult in this setting (e.g. manuscripts on sensor construction, as also contained in this handbook [113, 258], sample quality (see Sect. 1.6), or RoI determination (e.g. on sclera segmentation [217])). In the following, we separately discuss the recognition toolchain of the considered vascular biometric traits and provide many pointers into literature.

A discussion and comparison of the overall recognition performance of vascular biometric traits turns out to be difficult. First, no major commercial players take part in open competitions in this field (contrasting to e.g. fingerprint or face recognition), so the relation between documented recognition accuracy as achieved in these competitions and claimed performance of commercial solutions is not clear. Second, many scientific papers in the field still conduct experiments on private datasets and/or do not release the underlying software for independent verification of the results. As a consequence, many different results are reported and depending on the used dataset and the employed algorithm, reported results sometimes differ by several orders of magnitude (among many examples, see e.g. [114, 258]). Thus, there is urgent need for reproducible research in this field to enable a sensible assessment of vascular traits and a comparison to other biometric modalities.

1.3.1 Finger Vein Recognition Toolchain

An excellent recent survey covering a significant number of manuscripts in the area of finger vein recognition is [234]. Two other resources provide an overview of hand-based vascular biometrics [151, 275] (where the latter is a monograph) including also finger vein recognition, and also less recent or less comprehensive surveys of finger vein recognition do exist [59, 120, 247, 250, 300] (which still contain a useful collection and description of work in the area).

A review of finger vein *preprocessing* techniques is provided in [114]. A selection of manuscripts dedicated to this topic is discussed as follows. Yang and Shi [288] analyse the intrinsic factors causing the degradation of finger vein images and propose a simple but effective scattering removal method to improve visibility of the vessel structure. In order to handle the enhancement problem in areas with vasculature effectively, a directional filtering method based on a family of Gabor filters is proposed. The use of Gabor filter in vessel boundary enhancement is almost omnipresent: Multichannel Gabor filters are used to prominently protrude vein vessel information with variances in widths and orientations in images [298]. The vein information in different scales and orientations of Gabor filters is then combined together to generate an enhanced finger vein image. Grey-Level Grouping (GLG) and Circular Gabor Filters (CGF) are proposed for image enhancement [314] by using GLG to reduce illumination fluctuation and improve the contrast of finger vein images, while the CGF strengthens vein ridges in the images. Haze removal techniques based on the Koschmieder's law can approximatively solve the biological scattering problem as observed in finger vein imagery [236]. Another, yet related approach, is based on a Biological Optical Model (BOM [297]) specific to finger vein imaging according to the principle of light propagation in biological tissues. Based on BOM, the light scattering component is properly estimated and removed for finger vein image restoration.

Techniques for *RoI determination* are typically described in the context of descriptions of the entire recognition toolchain. There are hardly papers dedicated to this

Table 1.1 Finger vein feature extraction techniques focussing on vascular structure

Method class	References
Binary vascular structure	[32, 130, 174, 175, 244, 248, 326]
Binary vascular structure with deformation/rotation compensation	[76, 94, 163, 203, 209, 299]
Binary vascular structure using semantic segmentation CNNs	[91, 100–102]
Minutiae	[84, 148, 293]

issue separately. A typical example is [287], where an inter-phalangeal joint prior is used for finger vein RoI localisation and haze removal methods with the subsequent application of Gabor filters are used for improving visibility of the vascular structure. The determination of the finger boundaries using a simple 20×4 mask is proposed in [139], containing two rows of one followed by two rows of -1 for the upper boundary and a horizontally mirrored one for the lower boundary. This approach is further refined in [94], where the finger edges are used to fit a straight line between the detected edges. The parameters of this line are then used to perform an affine transformation which aligns the finger to the centre of the image. A slightly different method is to compute the orientation of the binarised finger RoI using second-order moments and to compensate for the orientation in rotational alignment [130].

The vast majority of papers in the area of finger vein recognition covers the toolchain stages (3)–(5). The systematisation used in the following groups the proposed schemes according to the employed type of features. We start by first discussing feature extraction schemes focusing at the vascular structures in the finger vein imagery, see Table 1.1 for a summarising overview of the existing approaches.

Classical techniques resulting in a binary layout of the vascular network (which is typically used as template and is subject to correlation-based template comparison employing alignment compensation) include *repeated line tracking* [174], *maximum curvature* [175], *principle curvature* [32], *mean curvature* [244] and *wide line detection* [94] (where the latter technique proposes a finger rotation compensating template comparison stage). A collection of these features (including the use of spectral minutiae) has also been applied to the dorsal finger side [219] and has been found to be superior to global features such as ordinal codes. Binary finger vein patterns generated using these techniques have been extracted from both the dorsal and palmar finger sides in a comparison [112].

The simplest possible binarisation strategy is adaptive local binarisation, which has been proposed together with a Fourier-domain computation of matching pixels from the resulting vessel structure [248]. Matched filters as well as Gabor filters with subsequent binarisation and morphological post-processing have also been suggested to generate binary vessel structure templates [130]. A repetitive scanning of the images in steps of 15 degrees for strong edges after applying a Sobel edge detector is proposed in combination with superposition of the strong edge responses and subsequent thinning [326]. A fusion of the results when applying this process to several samples leads to the final template.

The more recent techniques focusing on the entire vascular structure take care of potential deformations and misalignment of the vascular network. A matched filtering at various scales is applied to the sample [76], and subsequently local and global characteristics of enhanced vein images are fused to obtain an accurate vein pattern. The extracted structure is then subjected to a geometric deformation compensating template comparison process. Also, [163] introduces a template comparison process, in which a finger-shaped model and non-rigid registration method are used to correct a deformation caused by the finger-posture change. Vessel feature points are extracted based on curvature of image intensity profiles. Another approach considers two levels of vascular structures which are extracted from the orientation map-guided curvature based on the valley- or half valley-shaped cross-sectional profile [299]. After thinning, the reliable vessel branches are defined as vein backbone, which is used to align two images to overcome finger displacement effects. Actual comparison uses elastic matching between the two entire vessel patterns and the degree of overlap between the corresponding vein backbones. A local approach computing vascular pattern in corresponding localised patches instead of the entire images is proposed in [209], template comparison is done in local patches and results are fused. The corresponding patches are identified using mated SIFT key points. Longitudinal rotation correction in both directions using a predefined angle combined with score-level fusion is proposed and successfully applied in [203].

A different approach not explicitly leading to a binary vascular network as template is the employment of a set of Spatial Curve Filters (SCFs) with variations in curvature and orientation [292]. Thus the vascular network consists of vessel curve segments. As finger vessels vary in diameters naturally, a Curve Length Field (CLF) estimation method is proposed to make weighted SCFs adaptive to vein width variations. Finally, with CLF constraints, a vein vector field is built and used to represent the vascular structure used in template comparison.

Subsequent work uses vein minutiae (vessel bifurcations and endings) to represent the vascular structure. In [293], it is proposed to extract each bifurcation point and its local vein branches, named tri-branch vein structure, from the vascular pattern. As these features are particularly well suited to identify imposter mismatches, these are used as first stage in a serial fusion before conducting a second comparison stage using the entire vascular structure. Minutiae pairs are the basis of another feature extraction approach [148], which consists of minutiae pairing based on an SVD-based decomposition of the correlation-weighted proximity matrix. False pairs are removed based on an LBP variant applied locally, and template comparison is conducted based on average similarity degree of the remaining pairs. A fixed-length minutiae-based template representation originating in fingerprint recognition, i.e. minutiae cylinder codes, have also been applied successfully to finger vein imagery [84].

Finally, semantic segmentation convolutional neural networks have been used to extract binary vascular structures subsequently used in classical binary template comparison. The first documented approach uses a combination of vein pixel classifier and a shallow segmentation network [91], while subsequent approaches rely on fully fledged deep segmentation networks and deal with the issue of training data generation regarding the impact of training data quality [100] and a joint training

Table 1.2 Finger vein feature extraction techniques **not** focussing on vascular structure

Method class	References
Texture descriptors	[11, 31, 114, 138, 139, 157, 279, 289, 290]
Learned binary codes	[78, 280]
Deep learning (entire toolchain) learning subject classes	[30, 40, 60, 98, 144, 228]
Deep learning (entire toolchain) learning sample similarity	[89, 284]

with manually labelled and automatically generated training data [101]. This book contains a chapter extending the latter two approaches [102].

Secondly, we discuss feature extraction schemes interpreting the finger vein sample images as texture image without specific vascular properties. See Table 1.2 for a summarising overview of the existing approaches.

An approach with main emphasis on alignment conducts a fuzzy contrast enhancement algorithm as first stage with subsequent mutual information and affine transformation-based registration technique [11]. Template comparison is conducted by simple correlation assessment. LBP is among the most prominent texture-oriented feature extraction schemes, also for finger vein data. Classical LBP is applied before a fusion of the results of different fingers [290] and the determination of personalised best bits from multiple enrollment samples [289]. Another approach based on classical LBP features applies a vasculature-minutiae-based alignment as first stage [139]. In [138], a Gaussian HP filter is applied before a binarisation with LBP and LDP. Further texture-oriented feature extraction techniques include correlating Fourier phase information of two samples while omitting the high-frequency parts [157] and the development of personalised feature subsets (employing a sparse weight vector) of Pyramid Histograms of Grey, Texture and Orientation Gradients (PHGTOG) [279]. SIFT/SURF keypoints are used for direct template comparison in finger vein samples [114]. A more advanced technique, introducing a deformable finger vein recognition framework [31], extracts PCA-SIFT features and applies bidirectional deformable spatial pyramid comparison.

One of the latest developments is the development usage of learned binary codes of learned binary codes. The first variant [78] is based on multidirectional pixel difference vectors (which are basically simple co-occurrence matrices) which are mapped into low-dimensional binary codes by minimising the information loss between original codes and learned vectors and by conducting a Fisher discriminant analysis (the between-class variation of the local binary features is maximised and the within-class variation of the local binary features is minimised). Each finger vein image is represented as a histogram feature by clustering and pooling these binary codes. A second variant [280] is based on a subject relation graph which captures correlations among subjects. Based on this graph, binary templates are transformed in an optimisation process, in which the distance between templates from different subjects is maximised and templates provide maximal information about subjects.

The topic of learned codes naturally leads to the consideration of *deep learning techniques* in finger vein recognition. The simplest approach is to extract features from certain layers of pretrained classification networks and to feed those features into a classifier to determine vein pattern similarity to result in a recognition scheme [40, 144]. A corresponding dual-network approach based on combining a Deep Belief Network (FBF-DBN) and a Convolutional Neural Network (CNN) and using vessel feature point image data as input is introduced in [30].

Another approach to apply traditional classification networks is to train the network with the available enrollment data of certain classes (i.e. subjects). A model of a reduced complexity, four-layered CNN classifier with fused convolutional-subsampling architecture for finger vein recognition is proposed for this [228], besides a CNN classifier of similar structure [98]. More advanced is a lightweight two-channel network [60] that has only three convolution layers for finger vein verification. A mini-RoI is extracted from the original images to better solve the displacement problem and used in a second channel of the network. Finally, a two-stream network is presented to integrate the original image and the mini-RoI. This approach, however, has significant drawbacks in case new users have to be enrolled as the networks have to be re-trained, which is not practical.

A more sensible approach is to employ fine-tuned pretrained models of VGG-16, VGG-19, and VGG-face classifiers to determine whether a pair of input images belongs to the same subject or not [89]. Thus, authors eliminated the need for training in case of new enrollment. Similarly, a recent approach [284] uses several known CNN models (namely, light CNN (LCNN), LCNN with triplet similarity loss function, and a modified version of VGG-16) to learn useful feature representations and compare the similarity between finger vein images.

Finally, we aim to discuss certain specific topics in the area of finger vein recognition. It has been suggested to incorporate user individuality, i.e. user role and user gullibility, into the traditional cost-sensitive learning model to further lower misrecognition cost in a finger vein recognition scheme [301]. A study on the individuality of finger vein templates [304] analysing large-scale datasets and corresponding imposter scores showed that at least the considered finger vein templates are sufficiently unique to distinguish one person from another in such large scale datasets. This book contains a chapter [128] on assessing the amount of discriminatory information in finger vein templates. *Fusion* has been considered in multiple contexts. Different feature extractions schemes have been combined in score-level fusion [114] as well as feature-level fusion [110], while the recognition scores of several fingers have also been combined [290] ([318] aims to identify the finger suited best for finger vein recognition). Multimodal fusion has been enabled by the development of dedicated sensors for this application context, see e.g. for combined fingerprint and finger vein recognition [140, 222]. A fusion of finger vein and finger image features is suggested in [130, 302], where the former technique uses the vascular finger vein structure and normalised texture which are fused into a feature image from which block-based texture is extracted, while the latter fuses the vascular structure binary features at score level with texture features extracted by Radon transform and

Gabor filters. Finger vein feature comparison scores (using phase-only correlation) and finger geometry scores (using centroid contour distance) are fused in [10].

A topic of current intensive research is template comparison techniques (and suited feature representations) enabling the compensation of finger rotation and finger deformation [76, 94, 163, 203, 204, 299]. Somewhat related is the consideration multi-perspective finger vein recognition, where two [153] and multiple [205] perspectives are fused to improve recognition results of single-perspective schemes. A chapter in this handbook contains the proposal of a dedicated three-view finger vein scanner [258], while an in-depth analysis of multi-perspective fusion techniques is provided in another one [206].

1.3.2 Palm Vein Recognition Toolchain

Palm vein recognition techniques are reviewed in [1, 226], while [151, 275] review work on various types of hand-based vein recognition techniques including palm veins. The palm vein recognition toolchain has different requirements compared to the finger vein one, which is also expressed by different techniques being applied. In particular, finger vein sensors typically require the finger to be placed directly on the sensor (not contactless), while palm vein sensors (at least the more recent models) often facilitate a real contactless acquisition. As a consequence, the variability with respect to relative position between hand and sensor can be high, and especially the relative position of sensor plane and hand plane in 3D space may vary significantly causing at least affine changes in the textural representation of the palm vein RoI imagery. Also, RoI extraction is less straightforward compared to finger veins; however, in many cases we see techniques borrowed from palmprint recognition (i.e. extracting a central rectangular area defined by a line found by connecting inter-phalangeal joints). However, it has to be pointed out that most public palm vein datasets do not exhibit these positional variations so that recognition results of many techniques are quite well, but many of these cannot be transferred to real contactless acquisition. We shall notice that the amount of work attempting to rely on the vascular structure directly is much lower, while we see more papers applying local descriptors compared to the finger vein field, see Table 1.3 for an overview of the proposed techniques.

Table 1.3 Palm vein feature extraction techniques

Method class	References
Binary vasculature structure	[141, 154, 277]
Models of vascular structure	[9, 263]
Local descriptors	[72, 108, 133, 172, 173, 187, 193, 266, 286, 320, 325]
Discriminant analysis and CNNs	[57, 309]

We start by describing approaches targeting the *vascular structure*. Based on an area maximisation strategy for the RoI, [154] propose a novel parameter selection scheme for Gabor filters used in extracting the vascular network. A directional filter bank involving different orientations is designed to extract the vein pattern [277]; subsequently, the Minimum Directional Code (MDC) is employed to encode the line-based vein features. The imbalance among vessel and non-vessel pixels is considered by evaluating the Directional Filtering Magnitude (DFM) and considered in the code construction to obtain better balance of the binary values. A similar idea based on 2-D Gabor filtering [141] proposes a robust directional coding technique entitled "VeinCode" allowing for compact template representation and fast comparison. The "Junction Points" (JP) set [263], which is formed by the line segments extracted from the sample data, contains position and orientation information of detected line segments and is used as feature. Finally, [9] rely on their approach of applying the Biometric Graph Matching (BGM) to graphs derived from skeletons of the vascular network. See a chapter in this book for a recent overview of this type of methodology [8].

Another group of papers applies *local descriptors*, obviously with the intention to achieve robustness against positional variations as described before. SIFT features are extracted from registered multiple samples after hierarchical image enhancement and feature-level fusion is applied to result in the final template [286]. Also, [133] applies SIFT to binarised patterns after enhancement, while [193] employs SIFT, SURF and Affine-SIFT as feature extraction to histogram equalised sample data. An approach related to histogram of gradients (HOG) is applied in [72, 187], where after the application of matched filters localised histograms encoding vessel directions (denoted as "histogram of vectors") are generated as features. It is important to note that this work is based on a custom sensor device which is able to apply reflected light as well as transillumination imaging [72]. Another reflected light palm vein sensor prototype is presented in [238]. After a scaling normalisation of the RoI, [172, 173] apply LBP and LDP for local feature encoding. An improved mutual foreground LBP method is presented [108] in which the LBP extraction process is restricted to neighbourhoods of vessels only by first extracting the vascular network using the principle curvature approach. Multiscale vessel enhancement is targeted in [320, 325] which is implemented by a Hessian-phase-based approach in which the eigenvalues of the second-order derivative of the normalised palm vein images are analysed and used as features. In addition, a localised Radon transform is used as feature extraction and (successfully) compared to the "Laplacianpalm" approach (which finds an embedding that preserves local information by basically computing a local variant of PCA [266]).

Finally, a wavelet scattering approach is suggested [57] with subsequent Spectral Regression Kernel Discriminant Analysis (SRKDA) for dimensionality reduction of the generated templates. A ResNet CNN [309] is proposed for feature extraction on a custom dataset of palm vein imagery with preceding classical RoI detection.

Several authors propose to apply *multimodal recognition* combining palmprint and palm vein biometrics. In [79], a multispectral fusion of multiscale coefficients of image pairs acquired in different bands (e.g. VIS and NIR) is proposed. The reconstructed images are evaluated in terms of quality but unfortunately no recognition experimentation is conducted. A feature-level fusion of their techniques applied to palm vein and palmprint data is proposed in [187, 263, 266]. The mentioned ResNet approach [309] is also applied to both modalities with subsequent feature fusion.

1.3.3 (Dorsal) Hand Vein Recognition Toolchain

There are no specific review articles on (dorsal) hand vein recognition, but [151, 275] review work on various types of hand-based vein recognition techniques. Contrasting to the traits discussed so far, there is no commercial sensor available dedicated to acquire dorsal hand vein imagery. Besides the devices used to capture the publicly available datasets, several *sensor prototypes* have been constructed. For example, [35] use a hyperspectral imaging system to identify the spectral bands suited best to represent the vessel structure. Based on PCA applied to different spectral bands, authors were able to identify two bands which optimise the detection of the dorsal veins. Transillumination is compared to reflected light imaging [115] in a recognition context employing several classical recognition toolchains (for most configurations the reflected light approach was superior due to the more uniform illumination—light intensity varies more due to changing thickness of the tissue layers in transillumination). With respect to preprocessing, [316] propose a combination of high-frequency emphasis filtering and histogram equalisation, which has also been successfully applied to finger vein data [114].

Concerning feature extraction, Table 1.4 provides an overview of the existing techniques. We first discuss techniques relying on the extracted *vascular structure*. Lee et al. [143] use a directional filter bank involving different orientations to extract vein patterns, and the minimum directional code is employed to encode line-based vein features into a binary code. Explicit background treatment is applied similar to the techniques used in [277] for palm veins. The knuckle tips are used as key points for the image normalisation and extraction of the RoI [131]. Comparison scores are generated by a hierarchical comparison score from the four topologies of triangulation in the binarised vein structures, which are generated by Gabor filtering.

Classical *vessel minutiae* are used as features in [271], while [33] adds dynamic pattern tree comparison to accelerate recognition performance to the minutiae repre-

Table 1.4 Hand vein feature extraction techniques

Method class	References
Binary vessel structure	[131, 143]
Minutiae (points and network)	[33, 86, 93, 271, 307, 310]
Local texture descriptors	[28, 92, 150, 168, 249, 262, 267, 270, 311]
CNN-based feature extraction	[144]

sentation. A fixed-length minutiae-based representation originating from fingerprint biometrics, i.e. spectral minutiae [82], is applied successfully to represent dorsal hand vein minutiae in a corresponding recognition scheme. Biometric graph comparison, as already described before in the context of other vascular modalities, is also applied to graphs constructed from skeletonised dorsal hand vascular networks. Zhang et al. [310] extend the basic graph model consisting of the minutiae of the vein network and their connecting lines to a more detailed one by increasing the number of vertices, describing the profile of the vein shape more accurately. PCA features of patches around minutiae are used as templates in this approach, and thus this is an approach combining vascular structure information with local texture description. This idea is also followed in [93], however, employing different technologies: A novel shape representation methodology is proposed to describe the geometrical structure of the vascular network by integrating both local and holistic aspects and finally combined with LPB texture description. Also, [307] combine geometry and appearance methods and apply these to the Bosphorus dataset which is presented the first time in this work. [86] use an ICA representation of the vascular network obtained by thresholding-based binarisation and several post-processing stages.

Texture-oriented feature extraction techniques are treated subsequently. Among them, again key point-based schemes are the most prominent option. A typical toolchain description including the imaging device used, image processing methods proposed for geometric correction, region of interest extraction, image enhancement and vein pattern segmentation, and finally the application of SIFT key point extraction and comparison with several enrollment samples is described in [267]. Similarly, [150] uses contrast enhancement with subsequent application of SIFT in the comparison stage. Hierarchical key points' selection and mismatch removal is required due to excessive key point generation caused by the enhancement procedure. SIFT with improved key point detection is proposed [262] as the NIR dorsal hand images do not contain many key points. Also, an improved comparison stage is introduced as compared to traditional SIFT key point comparison. Another approach to improve the key point detection stage is taken by [311], where key points are randomly selected and using SIFT descriptors an improved, fine-grained SIFT descriptor comparison is suggested. Alternatively, [249] conduct key point detection by Harris-Laplace and Hessian-Laplace detectors and SIFT descriptors, and corresponding comparison is applied. [270] propose a fusion of multiple sets of SIFT key points which aims at reducing information redundancies and improving the discrimination power, respectively. Different types of key points are proposed to be used by [92], namely, based on Harris corner-ness measurement, Hessian blob-ness measurement and detection of curvature extrema by operating the DoG detector on a human vision inspired image representation (so-called oriented gradient maps).

Also, other types of texture descriptors have been used. A custom acquisition device and LBP feature description is proposed in [268]. Gabor filtering using eight encoding masks is proposed [168] to extract four types of features, which are derived from the magnitude, phase, real and imaginary components of the dorsal hand vein image after Gabor filtering, respectively, and which are then concatenated into feature histograms. Block-based pattern comparison introduced with a Fisher linear discriminant adopts a "divide and conquer" strategy to alleviate the effect of noise and to enhance the discriminative power. A localised (i.e. block-based) statistical texture descriptor denoted as "Gaussian membership function" is employed in [28]. Also, classical CNN architectures have been suggested for feature extraction [144].

Dual-view acquisition has been introduced [215, 216, 315] resulting in a 3D point cloud representations of hand veins. Qi et al. [215, 216] propose a 3D point cloud registration for multi-pose acquisition before the point cloud matching vein recognition process based on a kernel correlation method. In [315], both the 3D point clouds of hand veins and knuckle shape are obtained. Edges of the hand veins and knuckle shape are used as key points instead of other feature descriptors because they are representing the spatial structure of hand vein patterns and significantly increase the amount of key points. A kernel correlation analysis approach is used to register the point clouds.

Multimodal fusion techniques have been used, e.g. [86] use dorsal hand veins as well as palm veins while [28] fuse palmprint, palm–phalanges print and dorsal hand vein recognition. The knuckle tips have been used as key points for the image normalisation and extraction of region of interest in [131]. The comparison subsystem combines the dorsal hand vein scheme [131] and the geometrical features consisting of knuckle point perimeter distances in the acquired images.

1.3.4 Wrist Vein Recognition Toolchain

There are no specific review articles on wrist vein recognition, but [151, 275] review work on various types of hand-based vein recognition techniques. Overall, the literature on wrist vein recognition is sparse. A low-cost device to capture wrist vein data is introduced [195] with good results when applying standard recognition techniques to the acquired data as described subsequently. Using vascular pattern-related feature extraction, [177] propose the fusion of left and right wrist data; a classical preprocessing cascade is used and binary images resulting from local and global thresholding are fused for each hand. A fast computation of cross-correlation comparison of binary vascular structures with shift compensation is derived in [186]. Another low-cost sensor device is proposed in [221]. Experimentation with the acquired data reveals Log Gabor filtering and a sparse representation classifier to be the best of 10 considered techniques. The fixed-length spectral minutiae representation has been identified to work well on minutiae extracted from the vascular pattern [82].

With respect to texture-oriented feature representation, [49] employs a preprocessing consisting of adaptive histogram equalisation and enhancement using a discrete Meyer wavelet. Subsequently, LBP is extracted from patches with subsequent BoF representation in a spatial pyramid.

1.3.5 Retina Recognition Toolchain

Survey-type contributions on retina recognition can be found in [97, 166] where especially the latter manuscript is a very recent one. Fundus imagery exhibits very different properties as compared to the sample data acquired from hand-related vasculature as shown in Fig. 1.4a. In particular, the vascular network is depicted with high clarity and with far more details with respect to the detailed representation of fine vessels. As the vessels are situated at the surface of the retina, illumination does not have to penetrate tissue and thus no scattering is observed. This has significant impact on the type of feature representations that are mainly used—as the vascular pattern can be extracted with high reliability, the typical features used as templates and in biometric comparisons are based on vascular minutiae. On the other hand, we hardly see texture-oriented techniques being applied. With respect to alignment, only rotational compensation needs to be considered, in case the head or the capturing instrument (in case of mobile capturing) is being rotated. Interestingly, retina recognition is not limited to the authentication of human beings. Barron et al. [15] investigate retinal identification of sheep. The influence of lighting and different human operators is assessed for a commercially available retina biometric technology for sheep identification.

As fundus imaging is used as an important diagnostic tool in (human) medicine (see Sect. 1.8), where the vascular network is mainly targeted as the entity diagnosis is based on, a significant corpus of medical literature exists on techniques to reliably extract the vessel structure (see [260] for a performance comparison of publicly available retinal blood vessel segmentation methods). A wide variety of techniques has been developed, e.g.

- Wavelet decomposition with subsequent edge location refinement [12],
- 2-D Gabor filtering and supervised classification of vessel outlines [241],
- Ridge-based vessel segmentation where the direction of the surface curvature is estimated by the Hessian matrix with additional pixel grouping [245],
- Frangi vessel enhancement in a multiresolution framework [26],
- Application of matched filters, afterwards a piecewise threshold probing for longer edge segments is conducted on the filter responses [90],
- Neural network-based pixel classification after application of edge detection and subsequent PCA [240],
- Laplace-based edge detection with thresholding applied to detected edges followed by a pixel classification step [259],
- Wavelet transform and morphological post-processing of detail sub-band coefficients [137], and
- Supervised multilevel deep segmentation networks [180].

Also, the distinction among arterial and venous vessels in the retina has been addressed in a medical context [95], which could also exploited by using this additional label in vascular pattern comparison.

When looking at techniques for the recognition toolchain, one of the exceptions not relying on vascular minutiae is represented by an approach relying on Hill's algorithm [25] in which fundus pixels are averaged in some neighbourhood along scan circles, typically centred around the blind spot. The resulting waveforms (extracted from the green channel) are contrast-enhanced and post-processed in Fourier space. Combining these data for different radii lead to "retina codes" as described in [67]. Another texture-oriented approach [169] applies circular Gabor filters and iterated spatial anisotropic smoothing with subsequent application of SIFT key point detection and matching. A Harris corner detector is used to detect feature points [54], and phase-only correlation is used to determine and compensate for rotation before comparing the detected feature points.

All the techniques described in the following rely on an accurate determination of the *vascular network* as first stage. In a hybrid approach, [261] combine vascular and non-vascular features (i.e. texture–structure information) for retina-based recognition. The entire retinal vessel network is extracted, registered and finally subject to similarity assessment [85], and a strong focus on a scale, rotation and translation compensating comparison of retinal vascular network is set by [127]. In [13], an angular and radial partitioning of the vascular network is proposed where the number of vessel pixels is recorded in each partition and the comparison of the resulting feature vector is done in Fourier space. In [66], retinal vessels are detected by an unsupervised method based on direction information. The vessel structures are co-registered via a point set alignment algorithm and employed features also exploit directional information as also used for vessel segmentation. In [182], not the vessels but the regions surrounded by vessels are used and characterised as discriminating entities. Features of the regions are compared, ranging from simple statistical ones to more sophisticated characteristics in a hierarchical similarity assessment process.

All subsequent techniques rely on the extraction of *retinal minutiae*, i.e. vessel bifurcations, crossings and endings, respectively. In most cases, the vascular pattern is extracted from the green channel after some preprocessing stages, with subsequent scanning of the identified vessel skeleton for minutiae [145, 191, 285] and a final minutiae comparison stage. An important skeleton post-processing stage is the elimination of spurs, breakages and short vessels as described in [61]. The pure location of minutiae is augmented by also considering relative angles to four neighbouring minutiae in [207]. Biometric Graph Matching, relying on the spatial graph connecting two vessel minutiae points by a straight line of certain length and angle, has also been applied to retinal data [134]. In [22], only minutiae points from major blood vessels are considered (to increase robustness). Features generated from these selected minutiae are invariant to rotation, translation and scaling as inherited from the applied geometric hashing. A graph-based feature points' comparison followed by pruning of wrongly matched feature points is proposed in [190]. Pruning is done based on a Least-Median-Squares estimator that enforces an affine transformation geometric constraint.

The actual information content of retinal data has been investigated in some detail [232], with particular focus set on minutiae-type [103, 232] and vessel-representation-type templates [7], respectively.

1.3.6 Sclera Recognition Toolchain

An excellent survey of sclera recognition techniques published up to 2012 can be found in [44]. Sclera recognition is the most difficult vascular trait as explained subsequently. While imaging can be done with traditional cameras, even from a distance and on the move, there are distinct difficulties in the processing toolchain: (i) sclera segmentation involves very different border types and non-homogeneous texture and is thus highly non-trivial especially when considering off-angle imagery and (ii) the fine-grained nature of the vascular pattern and its movement in several layers when the eye is moving makes feature extraction difficult in case of sensitivity against these changes. As a consequence, rather sophisticated and involved techniques have been developed and the recognition accuracy, in particular under unconstraint conditions, is lower as compared to other vascular traits. Compared to other vascular traits, a small number of research groups have published on sclera recognition only. This book contains a chapter on using deep learning techniques in sclera segmentation and recognition, respectively [229].

A few papers deal with a restricted part of the recognition toolchain. As *gaze detection* is of high importance for subsequent segmentation and the determination of the eventual off-angle extent, [3] cover this topic based on the relative position of iris and sclera pixels. This relative position is determined on a scan line connecting the two eye corners. After pupil detection, starting from the iris centre, flesh-coloured pixels are scanned to detect eyelids. Additionally, a Harris corner detector is applied and the centroid of detected corners is considered. Fusing the information about corners and flesh-coloured pixels in a way to look for the points with largest distance to the pupil leads to the eye corners.

Also, *sclera segmentation* (as covered in the corresponding challenges/competitions, see Sect. 1.4) has been investigated in isolated manner. Three different feature extractors, i.e. local colour-space pixel relations in various colour spaces as used in iris segmentation, Zernike moments, and HOGs, are fused into a two-stage classifier consisting of three parallel classifiers in the first stage and a shallow neural net as second stage in [217]. Also, deep-learning-based semantic segmentation has been used by combining conditional random fields and a classical CNN segmentation strategy [170].

Subsequent papers comprise the entire sclera recognition toolchain. Crihalmeanu and Ross [37] introduce a novel algorithm for segmentation based on a normalised sclera index measure. In the stage following segmentation, line filters are used for vessel enhancement before extracting SURF key points and vessel minutiae. After multi-scale elastic registration using these landmarks, direct correlation between extracted sclera areas is computed as biometric comparison. Both [2, 4] rely on gaze detection [3] to guide the segmentation stage, which applies a classical integro-differential operator for iris boundary detection, while for the sclera–eyelid boundary the first approach relies on fusing a non-skin and low saturation map, respectively. After this fusion, which involves an erosion of the low saturation map, the convex hull is computed for the final determination of the sclera area. The second approach fuses multiple colour space skin classifiers to overcome the noise factors introduced through acquiring sclera images such as motion, blur, gaze and rotation. For coping with template rotation and distance scaling alignment, the sclera is divided into two sections and Harris corner detection is used to compute four internal sclera corners. The angles among those corners are normalised to compensate for rotation, and the area is resized to a normalised number of pixels. For feature extraction, CLAHE enhancement is followed by Gabor filtering. The down-sampled magnitude information is subjected to kernel Fisher discriminant analysis, and the resulting data are subjected to Mahalanobis cosine similarity determination for biometric template comparison. Alkassar et al. [5] set the focus on applying sclera recognition on the move at a distance by applying the methodology of [2, 4] to corresponding datasets. Fuzzy C-means clustering sclera segmentation is proposed by [43]. For enhancement, high-frequency emphasis filtering is done followed by applying a discrete Meyer wavelet filtering. Dense local directional patterns are extracted subsequently and fed into a bag of features template construction. Also, active contour techniques have been applied in the segmentation stage as follows. A sclera pixel candidate selection is done after iris and glare detection by looking for pixels which are of non-flesh type and exhibit low saturation. Refinement of sclera region boundaries is done based on Fourier active contours [322]. A binary vessel mask image is obtained after Gabor filtering of the sclera area. The extracted skeleton is used to extract data for a line descriptor (using length and angle to describe line segments). After sclera region registration using RANSAC, the line segment information is used in the template comparison process. Again, [6] use the integro-differential operator to extract the iris boundary. After a check for sufficient sclera pixels (to detect eventually closed eyes) by determination of the number of non-skin pixels, an active contours approach is used for the detection of the sclera-eyelid boundary. For feature extraction, Harris corner and edge detections are applied and the phase of Log Gabor filtering of a patch centred around the Harris points is used as template information. For biometric comparison, alignment is conducted to the centre of the iris and by applying RANSAC to the Harris points.

Oh et al. [188] propose a *multi-trait fusion* based on score-level fusion of periocular and binary sclera features, respectively.

1.4 Datasets, Competitions and Open-Source Software

1.4.1 Hand-Based Vascular Traits

Finger vein recognition has been the vascular modality that has been researched most intensively in the last years, resulting in the largest set of public datasets available for experimentation and reproducible research as displayed in Table 1.5. The majority is acquired in palmar view, but especially in more recent years also dorsal view is available. All datasets are imaged using the transillumination principle. As a

Table 1.5 Finger vein datasets available for research (typically upon written request)

Name	Dors/palm	Subjects	Fingers	Images	Sess.	Year	Scanner
THU-FVFDT [302]	Palmar	610	2	6540	2	2009	*Tsinghua Proto*
SDUMLA-HMT [305]	Palmar	106	6	3816	1	2010	*Wuhan Proto*
HKPU-FID [130]	Palmar	156	4	6264	2	2011	*HKPU Proto*
UTFVP [255]	Palmar	60	6	1440	2	2013	*Twente Proto*
MMCBNU_6000 [152]	Palmar	100	6	6000	1	2013	*Chonbuk Proto*
CFVD [313]	Palmar	13	6	1345	2	2013	*Shandong Proto*
FV-USM [10]	Palmar	123	4	5940	2	2013	*Sains Proto*
VERA FV Spoof [254]	Palmar+spoof	110	2	440	2	2014	*Twente Proto*
PMMDB-FV [233]	Dorsal	20	4	240	1	2017	*PLUSVein-V2*
PLUSVein-V3 [111]	Dorsal+palmar	60	6	7200	1	2018	*PLUS OpenVein*
SCUT-SFVD [213]	Palmar+spoof	100	6	7200	1	2018	*SCUT-FV Proto*

significant limitation, the largest number of individuals that is reflected in all these datasets is 610 (THU-FVFDT), while all the others do not even surpass 156 individuals. This is not enough for predicting behaviour when applied to large-scale or even medium-scale populations.

There are also "Semi-public" datasets, i.e. these can only be analysed in the context of a visit at the corresponding institutions, including GUC45 [81], GUC-FPFV-DB [225] and GUC-Dors-FV-DB [219] (where the former are palmar and the latter is a dorsal dataset, respectively). A special case is the (large-scale) datasets of Peking University, which are only partially available, but can be interfaced by the RATE[6] (Recognition Algorithm Test Engine), which has also been used in the series of (International) Finger Vein Recognition Contests (ICFVR/FVRC/PFVR) [281, 282, 303, 312]. This series of contests demonstrated the advances made in this field, e.g. the winner of 2017 improved the EER from 2.64 to 0.48% compared to the winner of 2016 [312].

The datasets publicly available for hand vein recognition are more diverse as shown in Table 1.6. Palmar, dorsal and wrist datasets are available, and we also find reflected light as well as transillumination imaging being applied. However, again,

[6] http://rate.pku.edu.cn/.

Table 1.6 Hand vein datasets available for research (typically upon written request)

Name	Images	Subjects	Img/hand	Dors/palm/wrist	Resolution	Illumination	Camera
CIE/PUT [107]	2400	50	12	Palmar/wrist	1280 × 960	Reflected light	Low-cost USB
UC3M [194]	348	29	6	Wrist	640 × 480	Reflected light	NIR low cost
Vera Palm Vein [252]	2200	110	5	Palmar	580 × 680	Reflected light	No details given
Bosphorus Hand Vein [307]	1575	100	3	Dorsal	300 × 240	Reflected light	Monochrome NIR CCD
CASIA Multispectral [79]	7200	100	18	Palmar	660 × 550	Reflected light	Multispectral device
Tecnocampus Hand Image [62]	6000	100	12	Palmar/dorsal	640 × 480	Reflected light	NIR, VIS and thermal
PROTECTVein [115]	2400	40	15	Palmar/dorsal	3264 × 2448	Refl. and transill.	Nexus 5 smartphone
PROTECTVein [115]	2400	40	15	Palmar/dorsal	720 × 720	Refl. and transill.	NIR IDS

the maximal number of subjects covered in these datasets is 110, and thus the same limitations as with finger vein data do apply.

VeinPLUS [73] is a semi-public hand vein dataset (reflected light and transillumination, resolution of 2784 × 1856 pixels with RoI of 500 × 500 pixels). To the best of the authors' knowledge, no public open competition has been organised in this area.

1.4.2 Eye-Based Vascular Traits

For retina recognition, the availability of public fundus image datasets is very limited as shown in Table 1.7. Even worse, there are only two datasets (i.e. VARIA and RIDB) which contain more than a single image per subject. The reason is that the other datasets originate from a medical background and are mostly used to investigate techniques for vessel segmentation (thus, the availability of corresponding segmentation ground truth is important). The low number of subjects (20 for RIDB) and low number of images per subjects (233 images from 139 subjects for VARIA) makes the modelling of intra-class variability a challenging task (while this is not possible at all for the medical datasets, for which this has been done by introducing distortions to the images to simulate intra-class variability [67]).

The authors are not aware of any open or public competition for retina biometrics.

For sclera-based biometrics, sclera segmentation (and recognition) competitions have been organised 2015–2018[7] (SSBC'15 [45], SSRBC'16 [46], SSERBC'17 [48], SSBC'18 [47]) based on the SSRBC Dataset (2 eyes of 82 individuals, RGB, 4 angles)

[7] https://sites.google.com/site/ssbc2k18/.

Table 1.7 Retina datasets (fundus imagery) available for research (typically upon written request)

Name	Subjects	Eyes	Images	Resolution	Biometric/medical	Seg. ground tr.	Year	Scanner
VARIA [191]	139	139	233	768 × 584	Biometric	No	2006	TopCon NW-100
RIDB [261]	20	20	100	1504 × 1000	Biometric	No	2016	TopCon TRC 50EX
DRIVE [245]	40	40	40	768 × 584	Medical	20 imgs	2004	Canon CR5
STARE [90]	400	400	400	605 × 700	Medical	40 imgs	2003	TopCon TRV-50
HRF [26]	45	45	45	3504 × 2336	Medical	Yes	2013	Canon CR-1

for which segmentation ground truth is being prepared. However, this dataset is not public and only training data are made available to participants of these competitions. Apart from this dataset, no dedicated sclera data are available and consequently, most experiments are conducted on the VIS UBIRIS datasets: UBIRIS v1 [201] and UBIRIS v2 [202].

Synthetic sample data has been generated for several biometric modalities including fingerprints (generated by SFinGe [160] and included as an entire synthetic dataset in FVC2004 [159]) and iris (generated from iris codes using genetic algorithms [69] or entirely synthetic [38, 327]), for example. The background is to generate (large-scale) realistic datasets without the requirements of human enrollment avoiding all eventual pitfalls with respect to privacy regulations and consent forms. Also, for vascular structures, synthetic generation has been discussed and some interesting results have been obtained. The general synthesis of blood vessels (more from a medical perspective) is discussed in [276] where Generative Adversarial Networks (GANs) are employed. The synthesis of fundus imagery is discussed entirely with a medical background [24, 36, 64, 75] where again the latter two papers rely on GAN technology. Within the biometric context, finger vein [87] as well as sclera [42] data synthesis has been discussed and rather realistic results have been achieved.

Open-source or free software is a scarce resource in the field of vascular biometrics, a fact that we aim to improve on with this book project. In the context of the (medical) analysis of retinal vasculature, retinal vessel extraction software based on wavelet-domain techniques has been provided: The ARIA Matlab package based on [12] and a second MATLAB software package termed `mlvessel`[8] based on the methods described in [241].

For finger vein recognition, B. T. Ton[9] provides MATLAB implementations of Repeated Line Tracking [174], Maximum Curvature [175], and the Wide Line Detector [94] (see [255] for results) and a collection of related preprocessing techniques

[8] http://www.retina.iv.fapesp.br.

[9] available on MATLAB Central: http://www.mathworks.nl/matlabcentral/fileexchange/authors/57311.

(e.g. region detection [139] and normalisation [94]). These implementations are the nucleus for both of the subsequent libraries/SDKs.

The "Biometric Vein Recognition Library[10]" is an open-source tool consisting of a series of plugins for bob.bio.base, IDIAP's open-source biometric recognition platform. With respect to (finger) vein recognition, this library implements Repeated Line Tracking [174], Maximum Curvature [175] and the Wide Line Detector [94], all with the Miura method used for template comparison. For palm vein recognition,[11] a local binary pattern-based approach is implemented.

Finally, the "PLUS OpenVein Finger- and Hand-Vein SDK[12]" is currently the largest open-source toolbox for vascular-related biometric recognition and is a feature extraction and template comparison/evaluation framework for finger and hand vein recognition implemented in MATLAB. A chapter in this book [116] is dedicated to a detailed description of this software.

1.5 Template Protection

Template protection schemes are of high relevance when it comes to the security of templates in biometric databases, especially in case of database compromise. As protection of biometric templates by classical encryption does not solve all associated security concerns (as the comparison has to be done after the decryption of templates and thus, these are again exposed to eventual attackers), a large variety of template protection schemes has been developed. Typically, these techniques are categorised into *Biometric Crypto Systems* (BCS), which ultimately target on the release of a stable cryptographic key upon presentation of a biometric trait and *Cancelable Biometrics* (CB), where biometric sample or template data are subjected to a key-dependent transformation such that it is possible to revoke a template in case it has been compromised [227]. According to [99], each class of template protection schemes can be further divided into two subclasses. BCS can either be *key binding* (a key is obtained upon presentation of the biometric trait which has before been bound to the biometric features) or *key generating* (the key is generated directly from the biometric features often using informed quantisation techniques). CB (also termed feature transformation schemes) can be subdivided into *salting* and *non-invertible transformations* [99]. If an adversary gets access to the key used in the context of the salting approach, the original data can be restored by inverting the salting method. Thus, the key needs to be handled with special care and stored safely. This drawback of the salting approaches can be solved by using non-invertible transformations as they are based on the application of one-way functions which cannot be reversed. In this handbook, two chapters are devoted to template protection schemes for finger vein recognition [121, 129] and both fall into the CB category.

---

[10] https://www.idiap.ch/software/bob/docs/bob/bob.bio.vein/stable/index.html.

[11] https://pypi.org/project/bob.palmvein/.

[12] http://www.wavelab.at/sources/OpenVein-SDK/.

Vein-based biometrics subsumes some of the most recent biometric traits. It is therefore not surprising that template protection ideas which have been previously developed for other traits are now being applied to vascular biometric traits, without developments specific for the vascular context. For example, in case we consider vascular minutiae points as features, techniques developed for fingerprint minutiae can be readily applied, like the fuzzy vault approach or techniques relying on fixed-length feature descriptors like spectral minutiae and minutiae cylinder codes. In case binary data representing the layout of the vascular network are being used as feature data, the fuzzy commitment scheme approach is directly applicable.

1.5.1 Hand-Based Vascular Traits

Starting the discussion with *finger vein recognition*, we find classical signal-domain CB schemes being applied, like block re-mapping and image warping [199]. Spectral minutiae representations [82] are subjected to binarisation and subsequently fed into Bloom filters to result in a CB scheme, thereby avoiding position correction during template comparison as required by many techniques based on vascular structure representation [71]. We find techniques, which apply both CB and BCS: After applying a set of Gabor filters for feature extraction and subsequent dimensionality reduction using PCA, a CB scheme close to *Bio-Hashing* is used employing random projections. The obtained coefficients are binarised and subjected to a Fuzzy Commitment Scheme (FCS), which is a particular CBS approach based on helper data. This approach is used to secure medical data on a smart card [294]. A second approach combining CB and BCS is suggested in [296], where bio-hashing is applied to features generated by applying Gabor filters and subsequent LDA. The binary string is then subjected to FCS and also to a fuzzy vault scheme (where the binary string is somewhat artificially mapped into points used in the vault). Another approach to combine CB and BCS is proposed in [149], where finger vein minutiae are extracted and random projections are used to achieve revocability and dimensionality reduction. Afterwards, a so-called deep belief network architecture learns irreversible templates. Minutiae-based feature representations suffer from the drawback that they are no fixed-length representations (which is a prerequisite for the application of several template protection schemes)—techniques developed in the context of fingerprint minutiae representations have been transferred to vein minutiae representations, i.e. vein minutiae cylinder codes [84] and vein spectral minutiae representations [82].

A direct application of FCS to finger vein binary data is demonstrated in [83]. In a similar approach, [63] also apply the FCS, but they tackle the issue of bias in the binary data (as non-vein pixels are in clear majority as compared to vein pixels) by applying no vein detection but a simple thresholding scheme using the median. For FCS error correction, this approach applies product codes. A BCS approach based on quantisation is proposed in [278]: Based on multiple samples per subject (i.e. class), features with low intra-class scatter and high inter-class scatter (found by Fisher Discriminant

Analysis (FDA)) are generated, which are finally subjected to a quantisation-based key generation where the quantisation parameters (helper data) depend on the distribution of the generated stable features. Another quantisation-based BCS is proposed in [29], where vein intersection points are located by considering a neighbourhood connectivity criteria, after Gabor-based enhancement with subsequent thresholding. However, the generation of a stable key is not discussed as it is just suggested to use a subset of the identified feature points as key material.

A multimodal CB scheme combining fingerprint and finger vein features uses a minutiae-based fingerprint feature set and an image-based finger vein feature set (obtained after Gabor filtering and subsequent application of LDA) [295]. Those features are fused in three variants and subjected to bio-hashing. An enhanced partial discrete Fourier transform (EP-DFT, omitting key-controlled parts of the DFT transform matrix) ensures non-invertability of the transform.

For *palm vein recognition*, in [34], palmprint templates are hashed with a set of pseudo-random keys to obtain a unique code called palmhash (basically the CB bio-hashing approach). FDA is applied to palm vein images; the FDA data are projected to a randomly generated orthogonal basis (Gram-Schmidt orthogonalisation) and subsequent thresholding results in a binary vector. A template-free key generation framework is suggested in [80], where local derivative patterns are used for feature extraction and a quantisation-based approach is used to generate keys, although a sufficiently detailed description is missing. An alternative approach being discussed is based on PalmSecure templates, which are processed in cooperation with iCognize GmbH. In [200], the palm vein data itself act as a key to encrypt a template database of independent biometric traits—however, no information about used vein features or how stability is achieved is given.

A multimodal template protection approach involving both *hand and palm vein data* suggests to fuse feature sets of both modalities [135, 136] (where stable vein points extracted from multiple enrollment samples act as feature sets) to create a fuzzy vault where chaff points are added as in the original scheme. However, the use of dual encryption involving both AES and DES in the second paper remains entirely unclear.

1.5.2 Eye-Based Vascular Traits

For eye-based vascular traits, not many template protection schemes have been proposed so far. For *retina recognition*, [167] applies a fuzzy vault scheme to secure retina minutiae. To account for weaknesses revealed in the fuzzy vault scheme due to non-uniformities in biometric data, a two-factor authentication is proposed using an additional password, to harden the BCS. In [192], minutiae of retina vessels are transformed in polar representation which have been computed from the gradient of intensity and eigenvalues of second-order derivatives. A quantisation-based BCS is applied to have only a single minutia in a spatial tile. These data are used as an encryption key, while the template is a random nonce—the encrypted data are generated by applying the quantised polar minutiae data as the key.

In the context of *sclera recognition*, [189] proposes a CB scheme based on a region indicator matrix which is generated using an angular grid reference frame. For binary feature template generation, a random matrix and a Local Binary Pattern (LBP) operator are utilised. Subsequently, the template is manipulated by user-specific random sequence attachment and bit shifting which enables normalised Hamming distance comparison to be used in the comparison stage.

1.6 Presentation Attacks and Detection, and Sample Quality

1.6.1 Presentation Attack Detection

One advantage of hand-based veins over other biometric traits is the fact that they are embedded *inside* the human body, as opposed to traits like fingerprints or faces. Moreover, vein images cannot be acquired from a distance without the subject noticing the capturing process. However, despite the claims of being resistant against inserting artefacts into the sensor to mimic real users, vein-based authentication turned out to be vulnerable to Presentation Attacks (PA) (experimentally shown using printed artefacts [252, 254]). Also, [27] presents some examples of how to produce spoofing artefacts for a dorsal hand vein scanner, however, without giving any quantitative results. Still, this work is the first one addressing this issue.

These demonstrated attacks triggered work on PA Detection (PAD) techniques and consequently in 2015, the first competition on countermeasures to finger vein spoofing attacks took place [253] (providing the IDIAP finger vein Spoofing-Attack Finger Vein Database consisting of real and fake finger vein images). The competition baseline algorithm looks at the frequency domain of finger vein images, exploiting the bandwidth of the vertical energy signal of real finger vein images, which is different for fakes ones. Three teams participated in this competition. The first team (GUC) uses Binarised Statistical Image Features (BSIF) [253]. They represent each pixel as a binary code. This code is obtained by computing the pixel's response to a filter that is learned using statistical properties of natural images [253]. The second team (B-Lab) uses monogenic-scale space-based global descriptors employing the Riesz transform. This is motivated by the fact that local object appearance and shape within an image can be represented as a distribution of local energy and local orientation information. The best approach (team GRIP-PRIAMUS) utilises local descriptors, i.e. Local Binary Patterns (LBP), and Local-Phase Quantisation (LPQ) and Weber Local Descriptors (WLD). They distinguish between full and cropped images. LBPs and LPQ/WLD are used to classify full and cropped images, respectively.

However, countermeasures to finger vein PA were/are already developed prior or independent to this competition. In 2013, the authors of [183] introduced a fake finger vein image detection based upon Fourier, and Haar and Daubechies wavelet transforms. For each of these features, the score of spoofing detection was computed. To decide whether a given finger vein image is fake or real, an SVM was used to combine the three features.

The authors of [251] propose windowed dynamic mode decomposition (W-DMD) to be used to identify spoofed finger vein images. DMD is a mathematical method to extract the relevant modes from empirical data generated by non-linear complex fluid flows. While DMD is classically used to analyse a set of image sequences, the W-DMD method extracts local variations as low-rank representation inside a single still image. It is able to identify spoofed images by capturing light reflections, illuminations and planar effects.

Texture-based PAD techniques have been proven to be applicable to the imagery in the FV-Spoofing-Attack database [253] independent of the above-referenced competition, in particular, baseline LBP [220]. Inspired by the success of basic LBP techniques [181, 253] in finger vein PAD and the availability of a wide variety of LBP extensions and generalisations in the literature, [123] has empirically evaluated different features obtained by using these more recent LBP-related feature extraction techniques for finger vein spoofing detection. Additionally, the steerable pyramid is used to extract features subsequently used for FV spoofing detection [220].

Steerable pyramids are a set of filters in which a filter of arbitrary orientation is synthesised as a linear combination of a set of basis functions. This enables the steerable pyramids scheme to compute the filter response at different orientations. This scheme shows consistent high performance for the finger vein spoofing detection problem and outperforms many other texture-classification-based techniques. The approach is compared to techniques from [252], including two LBP variants, and to quality-based approaches computing block-wise entropy, sharpness and standard deviation. Qiu et al. [213] employ total variation regularisation to decompose original finger vein images into structure and noise components, which represent the degrees of blurriness and the noise distribution. Subsequently, a block local binary pattern descriptor is used to encode both structure and noise information in the decomposed components, the histograms of which are fed into an SVM classifier.

Finally, image quality measures have been proposed for finger vein PAD. A detection framework based on Singular Value Decomposition (SVD) is proposed in a rather confused paper [181]. The authors utilise the fact that one is able to extract geometrical finger edge information from infrared finger images. Finger vein images are classified based on Image Quality Assessment (IQA) without giving any clear indication about the actual IQA used and any experimental results. In [21], the authors successfully apply general-purpose non-reference image quality metrics to discriminate real finger vein images from fake ones. Subsequent work [242] additionally applies natural scene statistics and looks into the issue of cross-sensor and cross-subject finger vein presentation attack detection. However, it is often cumbersome to identify and/or design texture descriptors suited for a specific task in this context. As a consequence, generative techniques like deep learning employing Convolutional Neural Networks (CNNs) have been successfully applied to discriminate real from spoofed biometric finger vein data [185, 214, 223, 224].

In contrast to all finger vein PAD techniques reviewed so far (which are based on still images and exploit corresponding texture properties), [27] already realise that analysing single still images is not able to exploit liveness signs. Thus, in this work, it is suggested to look into differences of features in adjacent frames, however, without giving any concrete features or experimental results. A custom-designed 2D transillumination NIR-laser scanner [142] is used for finger vein liveness detection based on extracting parameters from laser speckle image sequences (e.g. average speckle intensity). The technique proposed by [218] aims also at liveness detection and relies on LED-NIR video data. In this approach, motion magnification is employed to magnify the subtle motion of finger veins caused by blood flow. A motion magnitude derived from the optical flow between the first and the last frame in the captured video is used to determine liveness of the subject. This book contains a chapter [125] on using finger vein PAD to secure fingerprint sensors.

In addition to the publicly available IDIAP VERA Finger Vein Spoofing Database used in the competition mentioned above, we have another finger vein spoofing dataset available: The SCUT-SFVD: A Finger Vein Spoofing/Presentation Attack Database.[13]

There is less work on PAD for hand vein-based systems. PCA and power spectrum estimation of an autoregressive model are used [269] to detect artefacts resulting from printouts and from wearing coloured gloves. A dorsal hand vein dataset with artefacts produced by acquiring vein imagery with a smartphone camera has been created where the smartphones' display has been inserted into the sensor [196]. Histogram of Oriented Gradients (HOG) turned out to deliver good results for discriminating real from fake samples [20]. The same group has also established the PALMSpoof dataset including three different types of palm vein artefacts including such generated by display and print attacks. In [18], a noise residual image is obtained by subtracting the denoised image from the acquired image. The local texture features extracted from the noise residual image are then used to detect the presentation attack by means of a trained binary support vector machine classifier. Additionally, in [19], statistical features computed from the distributions of pixel intensities, sub-band wavelet coefficients, and the grey-level co-occurrence matrix are used to discriminate original and fake samples. In addition to these private PAD datasets, the publicly available IDIAP VERA Spoofing Palm Vein dataset[14] is available to assess PAD technology.

Liveness detection based on speckle analysis in retinal imagery is proposed in [235], but we actually doubt that there is really a corresponding realistic threat vector in retinal imaging (except for mobile self-capturing). For sclera-based recognition, neither PAD techniques nor liveness detection has been addressed so far.

---

[13]https://github.com/BIP-Lab/SCUT-SFVD.

[14]https://www.idiap.ch/dataset/vera-spoofingpalmvein.

1.6.2 *Biometric Sample Quality—Hand-Based Vascular Traits*

Biometric sample quality is important in many aspects. The probably most important application case is to request another sample data capturing in case sample quality turns out to be too low. Moreover, quality is important for various types of fusion approaches by rating authentication based on low-quality samples as less reliable. There are strong connections to presentation attacks, as the quality of PA artefacts is often questionable, as also illustrated by the use of quality measures to counter PA. ISO/IEC 29794 standard contains definitions for face, fingerprint and iris biometric sample quality. However, for vascular biometrics, no such standardisation exists yet. Thus, in the following, we review the available literature on this topic for vascular biometric traits. It is clear that quality assessment techniques applicable in the targeted biometric context need to be non-reference, i.e. without considering any "original" image in the assessment (as this original not even exists). An issue specific to vascular biometrics is the distinction among techniques being applied to the sample image as it is (we denote those as "a priori") from techniques which analyse the vascular network after extraction (denoted as "a posteriori", as for these techniques the vessels need to be segmented first, thus imposing significantly higher computational cost, and being feature extraction specific moreover).

We start the discussion by reviewing work on finger vein image quality assessment. A non-vein specific extension of SNR incorporating human visual system properties is proposed in [165] and combined with a contrast score and finger vein specific measures like area and finger shifting score [156]. It is not really obvious why the evaluation is done with respect to human inspection. Highly vein specific (and applicable in principle to most vein-based biometric traits) is a suggested quality measure based on the curvature in Radon space [212] (which is applied a priori), which is later combined with an assessment of connectivity, smoothness and reliability of the binary vein structures (applied a posteriori) [210]. Based on the NIR sample images, [305] use image contrast, information content and capacity to filter out low-quality finger vein images, and a very similar approach is taken by [291]. These entities are also combined in a fusion scheme termed "triangular norm" [198] combining these a priori measures into a single (weighted) one.

Another a posteriori approach is proposed by [283], in which, after extracting vessels using a Gabor filter, thick major vessels and short minor vessels construct the hierarchical structure of the finger vein network. This structure is modelled by a hierarchical Gaussian energy distribution which is used to assess the hierarchical quality of the vessel network. Also, [184] is based on an a posteriori approach, in which the quality of a finger vein image is measured by using the number of detected vein points in relation to the depth of the vein profile, which allows individual variations of vein density to be considered for quality assessment.

Learning-based schemes are employed to binary vessel structure images (so to be applied a posteriori) both by [321] and [208, 211], where the former is based on support vector regression and the latter on a CNN approach. Both approaches share the disadvantage of requiring a significant amount of (manually labelled) training data. A quality-driven fusion approach for vein structure and skin texture is suggested by [96].

For *palm and hand vein image quality*, respectively, the available literature is less extensive. However, most approaches suggested for finger vein quality assessment as discussed before can be transferred to palm and hand vein imagery. A fusion of clarity and brightness uniformity is suggested for palm vein data in [274]. Another quality notion for palm vein images [104], being much more specific, addresses one of the problems in contactless acquisition, i.e. the differences in camera–object distance and the resulting defocus blur. Corresponding quality is assessed by combining the Tenengrad sharpness measure [158] with a classical image quality metric (SSIM [265]), which is applied to pairs of images of different distances. Authors were able to show a clear relation of the assessment results with recognition accuracy. Natural scene statistics have also been used to assess the quality of palm vein imagery [272]. For dorsal hand vein images, [264] introduces a quality-specific vein recognition system, which uses the “CFISH score” in adaptively selecting LBP-based feature extraction according to high or low quality of the samples. The CFISH score is computed as weighted average from wavelet detail sub-bands’ mean energy and variance, thus representing image sharpness.

1.6.3 Biometric Sample Quality—Eye-Based Vascular Traits

In the context of *retina images’ quality* (quality of fundus images), work has exclusively been done in a medical context. Thus, it is important to discriminate among techniques addressing general quality (and thus potentially relevant for biometrics’ use) and techniques which specifically address quality related to the detection of certain diseases (which might not be suited in a biometric context). For example “..., an image with dark regions might be considered of good quality for detecting glaucoma but of bad quality for detecting diabetic retinopathy” [70]. However, it turns out that the quality measures considered are not really pathology-specific and could be all employed in retina biometrics in principle.

Without stating a clear diagnostic aim, local sharpness as well as illumination measures are combined into a four-stage measure [16] which has been validated on a ground truth provided by three ophthalmologists and three ophthalmic nurses with special training in and considerable experience of fundus photography, respectively.

In [70], fundus image quality is defined as “characteristics of an image that allow the retinopathy diagnosis by a human or software expert” (thus, it is focused on the vasculature of the retina). In this work, a thorough discussion of retina quality measures developed until 2009 is given. Authors propose a scale-invariant measure based on the density of extracted vessels; thus, it is only applicable after vascular structure has been detected (so it is an a posteriori measure). These features are combined with RGB histograms used in earlier work on retinal image quality. The work in [306], being quite similar, aims to determine, whether the quality of a retinal image is sufficient for computer-based diabetic retinopathy screening. Authors combine vessel density, histogram, co-occurrence matrix as well as local edge width and gradient magnitude-based features, respectively. Evaluation is done with respect to the ground truth (four quality grades) as provided by two optometrists.

As diagnostic aims, [197] define glaucoma and diabetic retinopathy. The proposed technique maps diagnosis-relevant criteria—inspired by diagnosis procedures based on the advise of an eye expert—to quantitative and objective features related to image quality. Independent from segmentation methods, global clustering and the consideration of inter-cluster differences are used to determine structural contrast which implies the recognisability of distinct anatomical structures. This measure is combined with local sharpness based on gradient magnitude and texture features (three Haralick features are used) for classification. Ground truth for quality staging is provided by three human observers including one eye expert.

In [257], first it is determined if the clinically most relevant area (the region around the macula) is distorted by areas of very dark and/or very light areas. Subsequently, if the image exhibits sufficient clinically relevant context, three different types of focus measures, i.e. wavelet-based ones, Chebyshev moment-based focus features, and a measure based on computing the difference between the original and a median-filtered version of the image, are fused into a common feature representation and classified (the Matlab Fuzzy Logic Toolbox is used).

Köhler et al. [124] present a quality metric to quantify image noise and blur and its application to fundus image quality assessment. The proposed metric takes the vessel tree visible on the retina (as determined by the Frangi's vesselness criterion) as guidance to determine an image quality score. Vessel-containing patches are weighted more strongly in this scheme. The performance of this approach is demonstrated by correlation analysis with the full-reference metrics Peak-Signal-to-Noise Ratio (PSNR) and structural similarity (SSIM) for artificially degraded data. For real data, the metric correlates reasonably to a human observer. Finally, a deep learning framework has been applied recently to train a network [230] to rate fundus images into "accept" and "reject" classes, based on a set of 3428 fundus images labelled correspondingly by three human experts and evaluated on 3572 other images leading to perfect separation.

For *sclera image quality grading*, the major focus of work done so far is on image sharpness/edge clarity. After a blink detection approach based on a Sobel filter, [324] evaluates the strength of responses to a spatial domain high-pass filter for the detection of blurred images, while [5] introduces a four-class quality grading scheme based on the response to a Laplacian edge operator. An a posteriori approach also involving segmentation and feature quality is introduced in [323].

1.7 Mobile and On-the-Move Acquisition

The application of biometric recognition systems in mobile scenarios and acquisition of sample data on-the-move raises some problems compared to the stationary use of such systems. This is true in general and thus also applies to vascular biometrics. First of all, mobile devices are typically restricted in terms of available resources, e.g. in terms of power provision and available computational capacity. Therefore, applied algorithms need to be low-cost and have to be executed on embedded systems typically. In addition, the acquisition process in both settings is more unconstrained (more degrees of freedom for the placement of the biometric trait and varying environmental conditions) compared to the stationary case, causing several recognition performance issues (see e.g. challenges in contactless hand vein systems [65, 109, 179]). Eventually, the authentication process is unsupervised, enabling presentation attacks [162]. Furthermore, the mobile system might not be a trusted platform, especially if the authentication is performed on the user's smartphone. This opens the door for all kinds of insertion and replay attacks to the biometric system. Hence, there is a need for presentation attack detection systems as well as methods to prove the authenticity and integrity of the biometric sample that has been captured.

1.7.1 Hand-Based Vascular Traits

In medical imaging, vein visualisation using mobile devices is a current topic of research. In [106], the available technology for subcutaneous vein detection is reviewed and low-cost mobile health solution using near-infrared spectroscopy is proposed.

Several papers deal with low-power and low-complexity implementations without looking into the sample acquisition process. Thus, no mobile capturing is foreseen, and the focus is on an implementation potentially suited for a mobile deployment. A low-complexity finger vein recognition algorithm is reported to be implemented on a DSP platform [147], but while actual power consumption is reported, the actual DSP system is not revealed. A modified thermal webcam is used for image acquisition in the three papers subsequently listed. FPGA implementations of hand vein [58] as well as finger vein [117, 118] recognition algorithms are reported, where the latter paper uses an NIR LED array for transillumination imaging, while the other two use the same device for reflected light acquisition.

However, work has been done to develop custom devices for mobile vein capturing: A device almost the size of an SLR camera has been constructed which enables both fingerprint and finger vein capturing [140]. Also, the concept of using smartwatches or similar devices for vein capturing has been suggested, i.e. Samsung has presented an idea involving a smartwatch with built-in NIR illumination[15] and associated capturing of dorsal hand veins, while the startup BioWatchID[16] acquire wrist veins with their bracelet technology.

[15]https://www.patentlymobile.com/2016/02/samsung-invents-a-new-user-id-system-for-smartwatches-using-hand-vein-patterns.html.

[16]https://biowatchid.com/wrist-vein-biometric-technology/.

Of course, smartphones have been considered as potential authentication devices for hand-related vascular biometrics. However, we face significant challenges. First, smartphones typically do not operate in the NIR domain (although sensors are able to capture NIR rays). Second, smartphones do not offer NIR-type illumination required for reflected light illumination as well as transillumination. In the VIS domain, recent work [14] reports on using current smartphones to capture hand imagery and using geometrical features for authentication. While this does not seem to be possible for vein-related authentication, still we find work pointing into this direction. In fact, Hitachi[17] claims to be able to enable "high-precision finger vein authentication" based on the RGB images users take with their smartphone. Also, the mobile App VeinSeek[18] claims to emphasise vein structure using a common smartphone. Personal experience shows that some benefits can be observed for dorsal hand veins, while for palmar veins we were not able to observe a positive effect when using this tool. While the entire idea seems to be slightly obscure at first sight, there is indeed work [243] which explains RGB-based vein visualisation enhancement from RGB images by exact RGB reflection modelling, Wiener filtering and additional post-processing. However, this idea can be only applied to superficial vascular structures. Wrist vein recognition using VIS smartphone imagery is proposed in [132], where shallow neural network structures and PCA are applied to the RoI. However, experiments are restricted to a small dataset consisting of Caucasian ethnicity subjects only.

When looking at NIR smartphone-based capturing, there are different approaches to solve the issues discussed before. The first observation is that Fujitsu managed to minimise their PalmSecure sensor significantly, so that the F-pro sensor variant can be used as authentication device for the Fujitsu V535 tablet. Thus, we might expect the deployment of this sensor generation in smartphones. In the context of finger vein recognition, reflected light illumination has been investigated [308] as it is clear that transillumination cannot be implemented in smartphones. As expected, this illumination variant decreases the recognition accuracy for finger vein biometrics.

In a medical patient identification context, several variants to visualise dorsal hand veins have been investigated in [65]. In any case, external NIR illumination is used, image acquisition is done either with a smartphone (with NIR-blocking filter in place) or an external night-vision webcam used as a smartphone plug-in. Contrasting to this simple solution, a custom-built plug-on finger vein acquisition device [239] based on reflection-based imaging has been developed. Experimentation reveals rather low contrast, especially in difficult lighting conditions. An NIR illumination module attached to a smartphone with removed NIR-blocking filter[19] is proposed [53] to capture dorsal hand veins. In this context, the authors investigate challenge–response protocols based on pulsed illumination intensity changes to secure the capturing process against replay attacks.

Also, dedicated NIR-imaging smartphone prototypes (or components thereof) including NIR illumination have been developed. SONY already came up with a

---

[17] http://social-innovation.hitachi/us/case_studies/finger_vein_smartphone/.

[18] https://www.veinseek.com/.

[19] www.eigenimaging.com.

finger vein capturing smartphone in 2009 [231], while another research-oriented prototype has been presented 7 years later [17].

Finally, also 3D imaging was discussed to generate representations involving vessel structures. Simulating a corresponding smartphone depth sensor, a KinectV2 [319] has been used to capture the dorsal hand side to generate such datasets. However, the actual processing of the Kinect data and the conducted biometric comparisons are not described in sufficient detail. Last but not least, there are rumours that Apple might go for "Vein ID[20]" for their next-generation iPhones, which could be based on depth sensing as well.

The only work suggesting a kind-of on-the-move acquisition for hand-related vascular technology is a prototype proposed by Hitachi [164], who introduce a finger vein device which captures five fingers concurrently using a kind of side transillumination, where the NIR rays not penetrating the fingers do not directly enter the camera system. The proposed system is said to operate in a walk-through style, while this is not entirely clear from the description.[21]

1.7.2 Eye-Based Vascular Traits

For eye-based vascular biometric techniques, much less work can be identified. With respect to retina imaging, traditional fundus cameras are large, expensive stationary medical devices. Only recently, there is a trend to consider also mobile variants. A prototype of a handheld, portable fundus camera is introduced in [105], where also the quality of the acquired fundus images is compared to a standard, stationary device. A commercial solution following the same path is offered by OPTOMED.[22] While the latter devices require a person to operate the portable capturing device, [246] propose a self-capturing device providing user feedback to optimise the acquired data.

To reduce costs, also the use of smartphones in fundus imaging has been discussed (see [77] for an overview of corresponding ideas). A common approach is the manual positioning of a lens in front of eye and the subsequent capturing of the lens with a smartphone [119, 146]. More professional though is the direct attachment of an imaging device to the smartphone (which can be rather large [155]), an approach for which several commercial solutions do exists, e.g. as provided by Volk[23] or Remidio.[24] The D-EYE system excels by its small-scale device being magnetically attached to an iPhone.[25]

[20]https://mobileidworld.com/vein-id-iphone-905154/.

[21]http://social-innovation.hitachi/us/case_studies/advanced-finger-vein-authentication-technology-opens-doors-for-you/.

[22]https://www.optomed.com/.

[23]https://volk.com/index.php/volk-products/ophthalmic-cameras/volk-inview.html.

[24]http://remidio.com/nm-fundus-on-phone/.

[25]https://www.d-eyecare.com/.

It has to be noted that all these reported solutions for mobile fundus photography (i.e. retina capturing) have not been discussed in the context of retina biometrics but in the medical imaging context. Nevertheless, these developments could render retina biometrics less intrusive and thus more realistic. Capturing on-the-move can be ruled out for retina biometrics as the illumination of the retina requires a focused and precise illumination process.

Last but not least, in the context of sclera recognition, the topic of mobile capturing has not been sufficiently addressed yet. The only work in this direction that we are aware of [2] applies sclera segmentation and recognition technology to UBIRIS v2 [202] data and titles this work as "... Captured On-The-Move and At-A-Distance" as the UBIRIS v2 data have been captured under these conditions. However, it is out of question that sclera recognition can be performed on datasets acquired by common smartphones [5] (e.g. when focussing on MICHE I [50, 52] and MICHE II [51] datasets as done in [5]).

1.8 Disease Impact on Recognition and (Template) Privacy

This section is devoted to a relatively unexplored field. For other modalities, e.g. fingerprints, it is better known and documented that certain diseases [55] and different age groups [176, 256] impact on recognition performance.

For hand-based vascular biometric traits, knowledge about certain diseases which influence the vessels' position and structure does exist [83], e.g. Arteriovenous Malformation (AVM) and the Hypothenar Hammer Syndrome (HHS). Also, it is known that certain injuries, including the insertion of small soft plastic tubes (Venflon) into venous vessels in the context of stationary medicamentation, can cause a change in the vessels' layout and thickness. However, there is neither theoretical nor empirical evidence that these effects might or might not actually degrade vascular-based recognition performance.

For eye-based vascular biometric traits, the situation is somewhat similar, but the argumentation is more indirect. As there exist certain diseases which can be diagnosed from fundus imagery (see e.g. [41] for a survey including several diseases which obviously affect retinal vasculature like diabetic retinopathy) and sclera images ([56] reports a sclera-vessel-based screening for cardiovascular diseases), those diseases also could eventually impact on corresponding recognition accuracy. Also, in this area, there is no evidence in favour or against this hypothesis.

Extraction of privacy-related information from biometric templates is one of the main motivations to establish template protection schemes. For example, it is well known that gender information can be extracted from facial or gait-related biometric samples and even templates [74], also fingerprints are known to reveal gender information.[26] Other privacy-related attributes include age, ethnicity and of course various types of medically relevant information.

---

[26] https://www.forensicmag.com/article/2015/11/identifying-gender-fingerprint.

For vascular biometrics, corresponding research is in its infancy. The extent of privacy-threatening information that can be potentially extracted also significantly depends on the type of data to be analysed. If we consider sample data (which is hardly ever stored in an operational biometric system, at least not online, except for recent deep-learning-based schemes relying on assessment of sample data pairs or triples), the threat of extracting such information illegitimately is much higher compared to looking at templates. Also, for templates, a representation of the vascular network based on the binary structure reveals much more information compared to a minutiae-based or even texture-property-based representation.

Having discussed diseases affecting the vascular layout above, it is obvious that information about these diseases can/could/might be extracted from corresponding sample data or templates, respectively. For finger vein sample data, it has been additionally shown [39] that gender as well as 2–4 age classes can be determined with high accuracy (>95%) based on typical preprocessing and the application of LBP. For dorsal hand vein data, [273] reports that feature representation based on vessel structure, PCA, LBP and SIFT do not allow to correctly discriminate male and female subjects. However, the authors propose to apply a feature learning scheme based on an unsupervised sparse feature learning model and achieve a classification accuracy of up to 98%.

One important aspect to be considered in this area is the lack of public datasets with metadata suited for corresponding analyses as well as reproducible research work. This should be considered when establishing datasets in the future.

1.9 Conclusion and Outlook

The structure of human vasculature is a suited identifier to be used in biometric systems. Currently, we have seen exploitation of this observation in the context of hand- and eye-oriented vascular biometric recognition.

For the hand-oriented modalities (i.e. finger vein, palm vein, (dorsal) hand vein and wrist vein recognition), several undisputed advantages over fingerprint recognition do exist; however, we still see several open issues being present, also inhibiting further widespread deployments. For example, the promise of contactless operation has been made, but many current system (especially in finger vein recognition) users need to touch the capturing devices, often for good reasons. Furthermore, contrasting to other biometric modalities, current commercial sensors do not allow to output captured sample data, which prohibits further progress and open competition in the area. Potential users planning a deployment cannot rely on large-scale public evaluation of the technology, and they have to rely on data provided by the companies producing sensors and corresponding recognition software—public evaluation would certainly increase trust in this technology. Last but not least, there is a huge gap in the quality of extracted vascular structures comparing currently used biometric technology (reflected light or transillumination NIR imaging) and techniques that are used in medical imaging for similar purposes (e.g. magnetic resonance angiography or similar). Thus, a further increase in sample quality while keeping sensor costs low is still an important challenge.

For the eye-oriented modalities (i.e. retina and sclera recognition), future does not seem to be as promising as many obstacles still exist. Retina recognition suffers from the highly intrusive sample acquisition process (while the quality of the acquired vascular structures is the best of all vascular modalities considered, allowing for very accurate recognition) and the high cost of (medical) stationary sensors. Eventually, recent developments in mobile retina capturing might become game changers for this modality. Sclera recognition does not have obvious advantages as compared to face recognition in terms of applicability and security, and good quality sample data are difficult to acquire from a distance or on the move. Eventually, similar as for periocular recognition, there is potential to be employed in a multimodal setting of facial biometric characteristics, as acquisition can be done in the visible domain.

Acknowledgements This work has received funding from the European Union's Horizon 2020 research and innovation programme under grant agreement No. 700259. The work was also funded by the Austrian Research Promotion Agency, FFG KIRAS project AUTFingerATM under grant No. 864785.

References

1. Agha AMJ, George LE (2014) Palm veins recognition and verification system: design and implementation. LAP Lambert Academic Publishing, Germany
2. Alkassar S, Woo WL, Dlay SS, Chambers JA (2016) A novel method for sclera recognition with images captured on-the-move and at-a-distance. In: 4th International workshop on biometrics and forensics (IWBF'16), pp 1–6
3. Alkassar S, Woo WL, Dlay SS, Chambers JA (2016) Efficient eye corner and gaze detection for sclera recognition under relaxed imaging constraints. In: 24th European signal processing conference, EUSIPCO 2016, Budapest, Hungary, 29 Aug–2 Sept 2016, pp 1965–1969
4. Alkassar S, Woo WL, Dlay SS, Chambers JA (2016) Enhanced segmentation and complex-sclera features for human recognition with unconstrained visible-wavelength imaging. In: International conference on biometrics, ICB 2016, Halmstad, Sweden, 13–16 June 2016, pp 1–8
5. Alkassar S, Woo WL, Dlay SS, Chambers JA (2017) Sclera recognition: on the quality measure and segmentation of degraded images captured under relaxed imaging conditions. IET Biom 6(4):266–275
6. Alkassar S, Woo WL, Dlay SS, Chambers JA (2017) Robust sclera recognition system with novel sclera segmentation and validation techniques. IEEE Trans Syst Man Cybern: Syst 47(3):474–486
7. Arakala A, Culpepper JS, Jeffers J, Turpin A, Boztas S, Horadam KJ, McKendrick AM (2009) Entropy of the retina template. In: Advances in biometrics: international conference on biometrics (ICB'09), volume 5558 of Springer LNCS, pp 1250–1259
8. Arakala A, Davis S, Horadam KJ (2019) Vascular biometric graph comparison: theory and performance. In: Uhl A, Busch C, Marcel S, Veldhuis R (eds) Handbook of vascular biometrics. Springer Science+Business Media, Boston, MA, USA, pp 355–394
9. Arakala A, Hao H, Davis SA, Horadam KJ (2015) The palm vein graph—feature extraction and matching. In: ICISSP 2015—Proceedings of the 1st international conference on information systems security and privacy, ESEO, Angers, Loire Valley, France, 9–11 February, 2015, pp 295–303

10. Asaari MSM, Rosdi BA, Suandi SA (2014) Fusion of band limited phase only correlation and width centroid contour distance for finger based biometrics. Expert Syst Appl 41(7):3367–3382
11. Banerjee A, Basu S, Basu S, Nasipuri M (2018) ARTeM: a new system for human authentication using finger vein images. Multimed Tools Appl 77(5):5857–5884
12. Bankhead P, Scholfield CN, McGeown JG, Curtis TM (2012) Fast retinal vessel detection and measurement using wavelets and edge location refinement. PLoS ONE 7(3):e32435
13. Barkhoda W, Tab FA, Amiri MD, Nouroozzadeh M (2011) Retina identification based on the pattern of blood vessels using fuzzy logic. EURASIP J Adv Sig Proc 2011:113
14. Barra S, De Marsico M, Nappi M, Narducci F, Ricci D (2018) A hand-based biometric system in visible light for mobile environments. Inf Sci
15. Barron UG, Corkery G, Barry B, Butler F, McDonnell K, Ward S (2008) Assessment of retinal recognition technology as a biometric method for sheep identification. Comput Electron Agric 60(2):156–166
16. Bartling H, Wanger P, Martin L (2009) Automated quality assessment of digital fundus photography. Acta Ophthalmol 87(6):643–647
17. Bazrafkan S, Nedelcu T, Costache C, Corcoran P (2016) Finger vein biometric: smartphone footprint prototype with vein map extraction using computational imaging techniques. In: Proceedings of the IEEE international conference on consumer electronics (ICCE'16), pp 512–513
18. Bhilare S, Kanhangad V (2018) Securing palm-vein sensors against presentation attacks using image noise residuals. J Electron Imaging 27:053028
19. Bhilare S, Kanhangad V, Chaudhari N (2018) A study on vulnerability and presentation attack detection in palmprint verification system. Pattern Anal Appl 21(3):769–782
20. Bhilare S, Kanhangad V, Chaudhari N (2017) Histogram of oriented gradients based presentation attack detection in dorsal hand-vein biometric system. In: Fifteenth IAPR international conference on machine vision applications (MVA'17), pp 39–42
21. Bhogal APS, Söllinger D, Trung P, Hämmerle-Uhl J, Uhl A (2017) Non-reference image quality assessment for fingervein presentation attack detection. In: Proceedings of 20th Scandinavian conference on image analysis (SCIA'17), volume 10269 of Springer lecture notes on computer science, pp 184–196
22. Bhuiyan A, Akter Hussain Md., Mian AS, Wong TY, Ramamohanarao K, Kanagasingam Y (2017) Biometric authentication system using retinal vessel pattern and geometric hashing. IET Biom 6(2):79–88
23. Black S (2018) All that remains: a life in death. Doubleday
24. Bonaldi L, Menti E, Ballerini L, Ruggeri A, Trucco E (2016) Automatic generation of synthetic retinal fundus images: vascular network. Procedia Comput Sci 90:54–60. In: 20th Conference on medical image understanding and analysis (MIUA 2016)
25. Borgen H, Bours P, Wolthusen SD (2008) Visible-spectrum biometric retina recognition. In: International conference on intelligent information hiding and multimedia signal processing (IIH-MSP'08), pp 1056–1062
26. Budai A, Bock R, Maier A, Hornegger J, Michelson G (2013) Robust vessel segmentation in fundus images. Int J Biomed Imaging 2013:ID 154860
27. Cao G, Pan J, Qin B, Du G (2009) The anti-spoofing study of vein identification system. In: International conference on computational intelligence and security (CIS'09), vol 02, pp 357–360
28. Chaudhury G, Srivastava S, Bhardwaj S, Bhargava S (2016) Fusion of palm-phalanges print with palmprint and dorsal hand vein. Appl Soft Comput 47:12–20
29. Chavez-Galaviz J, Ruiz-Rojas J, Garcia-Gonzalez A (2015) Embedded biometric cryptosystem based on finger vein patterns. In: 12th International conference on electrical engineering, computing science and automatic control, CCE 2015, Mexico City, Mexico, 28–30 Oct 2015, pp 1–6
30. Chen C, Zhendong W, Zhang J, Li P, Azmat F (2017) A finger vein recognition algorithm based on deep learning. Int J Embed Syst 9(3):220–228

31. Chen Q, Yang L, Yang G, Yin Y, Meng X (2017) DFVR: deformable finger vein recognition. In: 2017 IEEE International conference on acoustics, speech and signal processing, ICASSP 2017, New Orleans, LA, USA, 5–9 Mar 2017, pp 1278–1282
32. Choi JH, Song W, Kim T, Lee S-R, Kim HC (2009) Finger vein extraction using gradient normalization and principal curvature. Proc SPIE 7251:9
33. Chuang S-J (2018) Vein recognition based on minutiae features in the dorsal venous network of the hand. Signal Image Video Process 12(3):573–581
34. Connie T, Teoh A, Goh M, Ngo D (2005) PalmHashing: a novel approach for cancelable biometrics. Inf Process Lett 93:1–5
35. Cortés F, Aranda JM, Sánchez-Reillo R, Meléndez J, López F (2009) Spectral selection for a biometric recognition system based on hand veins detection through image spectrometry. In: BIOSIG 2009—Proceedings of the special interest group on biometrics and electronic signatures, 17–18 Sept 2009 in Darmstadt, Germany, pp 81–92
36. Costa P, Galdran A, Ines Meyer M, Niemeijer M, Abramoff M, Mendonça AM, Campilho AJC (2018) End-to-end adversarial retinal image synthesis. IEEE Trans Med Imaging 37(3):781–791
37. Crihalmeanu S, Ross A (2012) Multispectral scleral patterns for ocular biometric recognition. Pattern Recognit Lett 33(14):1860–1869
38. Cui J, Wang Y, Huang JZ, Tan T, Sun Z (2004) An iris image synthesis method based on PCA and super-resolution. In: Proceedings of the 17th international conference on pattern recognition, 2004. ICPR 2004, vol 4, pp 471–474
39. Damak W, Trabelsi RB, Masmoudi AD, Sellami D, Nait-Ali A (2016) Age and gender classification from finger vein patterns. In: Intelligent systems design and applications—16th international conference on intelligent systems design and applications (ISDA 2016) held in Porto, Portugal, 16–18 Dec 2016, pp 811–820
40. Das R, Piciucco E, Maiorana E, Campisi P (2019) Convolutional neural network for finger-vein-based biometric identification. IEEE Trans Inf Forensics Secur 14(2):360–373
41. Das S, Malathy C (2018) Survey on diagnosis of diseases from retinal images. J Phys: Conf Ser 1000(1):012053
42. Das A, Mondal P, Pal U, Blumenstein M, Ferrer MA (2016) Sclera vessel pattern synthesis based on a non-parametric texture synthesis technique. In: Raman B, Kumar S, Roy P, Sen D (eds) Proceedings of international conference on computer vision and image processing, volume 460 of Advances in intelligent systems and computing. Springer, pp 241–250
43. Das A, Pal U, Ballester MAF, Blumenstein M (2014) A new efficient and adaptive sclera recognition system. In: IEEE Symposium on computational intelligence in biometrics and identity management (CIBIM'14), pp 1–8
44. Das A, Pal U, Blumenstein M, Ballester MAF (2013) Sclera recognition—a survey. In: Second IAPR Asian conference on pattern recognition (ACPR'13), pp 917–921
45. Das A, Pal U, Ferrer MA, Blumenstein M (2015) SSBC 2015: sclera segmentation benchmarking competition. In: IEEE 7th international conference on biometrics theory, applications and systems, BTAS 2015, Arlington, VA, USA, 8–11 Sept 2015
46. Das A, Pal U, Ferrer MA, Blumenstein M (2016) SSRBC 2016: sclera segmentation and recognition benchmarking competition. In: International conference on biometrics, ICB 2016, Halmstad, Sweden, 13–16 June 2016
47. Das A, Pal U, Ferrer MA, Blumenstein M, Stepec D, Rot P, Emersic Z, Peer P, Struc V (2018) SSBC 2018: sclera segmentation benchmarking competition. In: 2018 International conference on biometrics, ICB 2018, Gold Coast, Australia, 20–23 Feb 2018, pp 303–308
48. Das A, Pal U, Ferrer MA, Blumenstein M, Stepec D, Rot P, Emersic Z, Peer P, Struc V, Aruna Kumar SV, Harish BS (2017) SSERBC 2017: sclera segmentation and eye recognition benchmarking competition. In: 2017 IEEE international joint conference on biometrics, IJCB 2017, Denver, CO, USA, 1–4 Oct 2017, pp 742–747
49. Das A, Pal U, Ferrer-Ballester MA, Blumenstein M (2014) A new wrist vein biometric system. In: 2014 IEEE symposium on computational intelligence in biometrics and identity management, CIBIM 2014, Orlando, FL, USA, 9–12 Dec 2014, pp 68–75

50. De Marsico M, Nappi M, Narducci F, Proença H (2018) Insights into the results of MICHE I—Mobile Iris CHallenge Evaluation. Pattern Recognit 74:286–304
51. De Marsico M, Nappi M, Proença H (2017) Results from MICHE II—Mobile Iris CHallenge Evaluation II. Pattern Recognit Lett 91:3–10
52. De Marsico M, Nappi M, Riccio D, Wechsler H (2015) Mobile Iris CHallenge Evaluation (MICHE)-I, biometric iris dataset and protocols. Pattern Recognit Lett 57:17–23. Mobile Iris CHallenge Evaluation part I (MICHE I)
53. Debiasi L, Kauba C, Prommegger B, Uhl A (2018) Near-infrared illumination add-on for mobile hand-vein acquisition. In: 2018 IEEE 9th international conference on biometrics theory, applications and systems (BTAS). Los Angeles, California, USA, pp 1–9
54. Dehghani A, Ghassabi Z, Moghddam H, Moin M (2013) Human recognition based on retinal images and using new similarity function. EURASIP J Image Video Process 2013:58
55. Drahansky M, Dolezel M, Urbanek J, Brezinova E, Kim T-H (2012) Influence of skin diseases on fingerprint recognition. J Biomed Biotechnol 2012:Article ID 626148
56. Elhussieny N, El-Rewaidy H, Fahmy AS (2016) Low cost system for screening cardiovascular diseases in large population: preliminary results. In: 13th International IEEE symposium on biomedical imaging (ISBI'18)
57. Elnasir S, Mariyam Shamsuddin S, Farokhi S (2015) Accurate palm vein recognition based on wavelet scattering and spectral regression kernel discriminant analysis. J Electron Imaging 24(1):013031
58. Eng PC, Khalil-Hani M (2009) FPGA-based embedded hand vein biometric authentication system. In: TENCON 2009—2009 IEEE region 10 conference, pp 1–5
59. Fadhil RI, George LE (2017) Finger vein identification and authentication system. LAP Lambert Academic Publishing, Germany
60. Fang Y, Qiuxia W, Kang W (2018) A novel finger vein verification system based on two-stream convolutional network learning. Neurocomputing 290:100–107
61. Fatima J, Syed AM, Akram MU (2013) Feature point validation for improved retina recognition. In: IEEE Workshop on biometric measurements and systems for security and medical applications, 2013, pp 13–16
62. Faundez-Zanuy M, Mekyska J, Font-Aragonès X (2014) A new hand image database simultaneously acquired in visible, near-infrared and thermal spectrums. Cogn Comput 6(2):230–240
63. Favre M, Picard S, Bringer J, Chabanne H (2015) Balancing is the key—performing finger vein template protection using fuzzy commitment. In: ICISSP 2015–Proceedings of the 1st international conference on information systems security and privacy, ESEO, Angers, Loire Valley, France, 9–11 Feb 2015, pp 304–311
64. Fiorini S, De Biasi M, Ballerini L, Trucco E, Ruggeri A (2014) Automatic generation of synthetic retinal fundus images. In: Giachetti A (ed) Smart tools and apps for graphics—Eurographics Italian chapter conference. The Eurographics Association
65. Fletcher RR, Raghavan V, Zha R, Haverkamp M, Hibberd PL (2014) Development of mobile-based hand vein biometrics for global health patient identification. In: IEEE Global humanitarian technology conference (GHTC 2014), pp 541–547
66. Frucci M, Riccio D, di Baja GS, Serino L (2018) Using direction and score information for retina based person verification. Expert Syst Appl 94:1–10
67. Fuhrmann T, Hämmerle-Uhl J, Uhl A (2009) Usefulness of retina codes in biometrics. In: Advances in image and video technology: proceedings of the 3rd Pacific-Rim symposium on image and video technology, PSIVT '09, volume 5414 of Lecture notes in computer science, Tokyo, Japan, Jan 2009. Springer, pp 624–632
68. Fuksis R, Greitans M, Nikisins O, Pudzs M (2010) Infrared imaging system for analysis of blood vessel structure. Elektronika IR Elektrotechnika 97(1):45–48
69. Galbally J, Ross A, Gomez-Barrero M, Fierrez J, Ortega-Garcia J (2013) Iris image reconstruction from binary templates: an efficient probabilistic approach based on genetic algorithms. Comput Vis Image Underst 117(10):1512–1525
70. Giancardo L, Meriaudeau F, Karnowski TP, Chaum E, Tobin K (2010) Quality assessment of retinal fundus images using elliptical local vessel density. In: New developments in biomedical engineering. IntechOpen

71. Gomez-Barrero M, Rathgeb C, Li G, Ramachandra R, Galbally J, Busch C (2018) Multi-biometric template protection based on bloom filters. Inf Fusion 42:37–50
72. Greitans M, Pudzs M, Fuksis R (2010) Palm vein biometrics based on infrared imaging and complex matched filtering. In: Multimedia and security workshop, ACM MM&Sec 2010, Roma, Italy, 9–10 Sept 2010, pp 101–106
73. Gruschina A (2015) VeinPLUS: a transillumination and reflection-based hand vein database. In: Proceedings of the 39th annual workshop of the Austrian association for pattern recognition (OAGM'15), 2015. arXiv:1505.06769
74. Guan Y, Wei X, Li Ch-T (2014) On the generalization power of face and gait in gender recognition. Int J Digit Crime Forensics 6(1)
75. Guibas JT, Virdi TS, Li PS (2017) Synthetic medical images from dual generative adversarial networks. arXiv:1709.01872
76. Gupta P, Gupta P (2015) An accurate finger vein based verification system. Digit Signal Process 38:43–52
77. Haddock LJ, Qian C (2015) Smartphone technology for fundus photography. Retin Phys 12(6):51–58
78. Haiying Liu L, Yang GY, Yin Y (2018) Discriminative binary descriptor for finger vein recognition. IEEE Access 6:5795–5804
79. Hao Y, Sun Z, Tan T (2007) Comparative studies on multispectral palm image fusion for biometrics. Comput Vis-ACCV 2007:12–21
80. Harmer K, Howells G (2012) Direct template-free encryption key generation from palm-veins. In: 2012 Third international conference on emerging security technologies, Lisbon, Portugal, 5–7 Sept 2012, pp 70–73
81. Hartung D (2012) Vascular pattern recognition and its application in privacy–preserving biometric online–banking system. PhD thesis, PhD dissertation, Gjovik University College,
82. Hartung D, Aastrup Olsen M, Xu H, Thanh Nguyen H, Busch C (2012) Comprehensive analysis of spectral minutiae for vein pattern recognition. IET Biom 1(1):25–36
83. Hartung D, Busch C (2009) Why vein recognition needs privacy protection. In: Fifth international conference on intelligent information hiding and multimedia signal processing (IIH-MSP'09), pp 1090–1095
84. Hartung D, Tistarelli M, Busch C (2013) Vein minutia cylinder-codes (V-MCC). In: International conference on biometrics, ICB 2013, June 4–7 2013, Madrid, Spain, pp 1–7
85. Hatanaka Y, Tajima M, Kawasaki R, Saito K, Ogohara K, Muramatsu C, Sunayama W, Fujita H (2017) Retinal biometrics based on iterative closest point algorithm. In: 2017 39th Annual international conference of the IEEE engineering in medicine and biology society (EMBC), Jeju Island, South Korea, 11–15 July 2017, pp 373–376
86. Heenaye M, Khan M (2012) A multimodal hand vein biometric based on score level fusion. Procedia Eng 41:897–903. In: International symposium on robotics and intelligent sensors 2012 (IRIS 2012)
87. Hillerström F, Kumar A, Veldhuis R (2014) Generating and analyzing synthetic finger vein images. In: Proceedings of the international conference of the biometrics special interest group (BIOSIG'14), Sept 2014, pp 121–132
88. Himaga M, Ogota H (2019) Evolution of finger vein biometric devices in terms of usability. In: Uhl A, Busch C, Marcel S, Veldhuis R (eds) Handbook of vascular biometrics. Springer Science+Business Media, Boston, MA, USA, pp 159–178
89. Hong HG, Lee MB, Park KR (2017) Convolutional neural network-based finger-vein recognition using NIR image sensors. Sensors 17(6):1297
90. Hoover A, Kouznetsova V, Goldbaum M (2000) Locating blood vessels in retinal images by piece-wise threhsold probing of a matched filter response. IEEE Trans Med Imaging 19(3):203–210
91. Huafeng Q, ElYacoubi MA (2017) Deep representation-based feature extraction and recovering for finger-vein verification. IEEE Trans Inf Forensics Secur 12(8):1816–1829
92. Huang D, Tang Y, Wang Y, Chen L, Wang Y (2015) Hand-dorsa vein recognition by matching local features of multisource keypoints. IEEE Trans Cybern 45(9):1823–1837

93. Huang D, Zhu X, Wang Y, Zhang D (2016) Dorsal hand vein recognition via hierarchical combination of texture and shape clues. Neurocomputing 214:815–828
94. Huang B, Dai Y, Li R, Tang D, Li W (2010) Finger-vein authentication based on wide line detector and pattern normalization. In: 2010 20th International conference on pattern recognition (ICPR). IEEE, pp 1269–1272
95. Huang F, Dashtbozorg B, Tan T, ter Haar Romeny BM (2018) Retinal artery/vein classification using genetic-search feature selection. Comput Methods Programs Biomed 161:197–207
96. Huang Z, Kang W, Wu Q, Zhao J, Jia W (2016) A finger vein identification system based on image quality assessment. In: Chinese conference on biometric recognition (CCBR'16), volume 9967 of Springer lecture notes in computer science, pp 244–254
97. Islam R, Abdul Goffar Khan M (2012) Retina recognition: secure biometric authentication system—an approach to implement the eye recognition system using artificial neural networks. LAP Lambert Academic Publishing, Germany
98. Itqan KS, Radzi S, Gong FG, Mustafa N, Wong YC, Mat ibrahim M (2016) User identification system based on finger-vein patterns using convolutional neural network. ARPN J Eng Appl Sci 11(5):3316–3319
99. Jain AK, Nandakumar K, Nagar A (2008) Biometric template security. EURASIP J Adv Signal Process 1–17:2008
100. Jalilian E, Uhl A (2018) Finger-vein recognition using deep fully convolutional neural semantic segmentation networks: the impact of training data. In: Proceedings of the IEEE 10th international workshop on information forensics and security (WIFS 2018), Hong Kong, pp 1–8
101. Jalilian E, Uhl A (2019) Enhanced segmentation-CNN based finger-vein recognition by joint training with automatically generated and manual labels. In: Proceedings of the IEEE 5th international conference on identity, security and behavior analysis (ISBA 2019), IDRBT, pp 1–8
102. Jalilian E, Uhl A (2019) Improved CNN-segmentation based finger-vein recognition using automatically generated and fused training labels. In: Uhl A, Busch C, Marcel S, Veldhuis R (eds) Handbook of vascular biometrics. Springer Science+Business Media, Boston, MA, USA, pp 201–224
103. Jeffers J, Arakala A, Horadam KJ (2010) Entropy of feature point-based retina templates. In: 20th International conference on pattern recognition (ICPR'10), pp 213–216
104. Jiaqiang W, Ming Y, Hanbing Q, Bin L (2013) Analysis of palm vein image quality and recognition with different distance. In: 2013 Fourth international conference on digital manufacturing automation, pp 215–218
105. Jini K, Lu H, Sun Z, Cheng C, Ye J, Qian D (2017) Telemedicine screening of retinal diseases with a handheld portable non-mydriatic fundus camera. BMC Ophthalmol 17:89
106. Juric S, Flis V, Debevc M, Holzinger A, Zalik B (2014) Towards a low-cost mobile subcutaneous vein detection solution using near-infrared spectroscopy. Sci World J, page ID 365902
107. Kabacinski R, Kowalski M (2011) Vein pattern database and benchmark results. Electron Lett 47(20):1127–1128
108. Kang W, Qiuxia W (2014) Contactless palm vein recognition using a mutual foreground-based local binary pattern. IEEE Trans Inf Forensics Secur 9(11):1974–1985
109. Kanhangad V, Kumar A, Zhang D (2011) Contactless and pose invariant biometric identification using hand surface. IEEE Trans Image Process 20(5):1415–1424
110. Kauba C, Piciucco E, Maiorana E, Campisi P, Uhl A (2016) Advanced variants of feature level fusion for finger vein recognition. In: Proceedings of the international conference of the biometrics special interest group (BIOSIG'16), Darmstadt, Germany, pp 1–12
111. Kauba C, Prommegger B, Uhl A (2018) Focussing the beam—a new laser illumination based data set providing insights to finger-vein recognition. In: 2018 IEEE 9th International conference on biometrics theory, applications and systems (BTAS). Los Angeles, California, USA, pp 1–9
112. Kauba C, Prommegger B, Uhl A (2018) The two sides of the finger—an evaluation on the recognition performance of dorsal vs. palmar finger-veins. In: Proceedings of the international

conference of the biometrics special interest group (BIOSIG'18), Darmstadt, Germany, pp 1–8
113. Kauba C, Prommegger B, Uhl A (2019) OpenVein—an open-source modular multi-purpose finger-vein scanner design. In: Uhl A, Busch C, Marcel S, Veldhuis R (eds) Handbook of vascular biometrics. Springer Science+Business Media, Boston, MA, USA, pp 77–112
114. Kauba C, Reissig J, Uhl A (2014) Pre-processing cascades and fusion in finger vein recognition. In: Proceedings of the international conference of the biometrics special interest group (BIOSIG'14), Darmstadt, Germany
115. Kauba C, Uhl A (2018) Shedding light on the veins—reflected light or transillumination in hand-vein recognition. In: Proceedings of the 11th IAPR/IEEE international conference on biometrics (ICB'18), Gold Coast, Queensland, Australia, pp 1–8
116. Kauba C, Uhl A (2019) An available open source vein recognition framework. In: Uhl A, Busch C, Marcel S, Veldhuis R (eds) Handbook of vascular biometrics. Springer Science+Business Media, Boston, MA, USA, pp 113–144
117. Khalil-Hani M, Eng PC (2010) FPGA-based embedded system implementation of finger vein biometrics. In: IEEE Symposium on industrial electronics and applications (ISIEA'10), pp 700–705
118. Khalil-Hani M, Eng PC (2011) Personal verification using finger vein biometrics in FPGA-based system-on-chip. In: 7th International conference on electrical and electronics engineering (ELECO'11), pp II-171–II-176
119. Khanamiri HN, Nakatsuka A, El-Annan J (2017) Smartphone fundus photography. J Vis Exp 125:55958
120. Kharabe S, Nalini C (2018) Survey on finger-vein segmentation and authentication. Int J Eng Technol 7(1–2):9–14
121. Kirchgasser S, Kauba C, Uhl A (2019) Cancellable biometrics for finger vein recognition—application in the feature level domain. In: Uhl A, Busch C, Marcel S, Veldhuis R (eds) Handbook of vascular biometrics. Springer Science+Business Media, Boston, MA, USA, pp 481–506
122. Kirchgasser S, Kauba C, Uhl A (2019) Towards understanding acquisition conditions influencing finger-vein recognition. In: Uhl A, Busch C, Marcel S, Veldhuis R (eds) Handbook of vascular biometrics. Springer Science+Business Media, Boston, MA, USA, pp 179–200
123. Kocher D, Schwarz S, Uhl A (2016) Empirical evaluation of LBP-extension features for finger vein spoofing detection. In: Proceedings of the international conference of the biometrics special interest group (BIOSIG'16), Darmstadt, Germany, p 8
124. Köhler T, Budai A, Kraus MF, Odstrcilik J, Michelson G, Hornegger J (2013) Automatic no-reference quality assessment for retinal fundus images using vessel segmentation. In: Proceedings of the 26th IEEE international symposium on computer-based medical systems, pp 95–100
125. Kolberg J, Gomez-Barrero M, Venkatesh S, Ramachandra R, Busch C (2019) Presentation attack detection for finger recognition. In: Uhl A, Busch C, Marcel S, Veldhuis R (eds) Handbook of vascular biometrics. Springer Science+Business Media, Boston, MA, USA, pp 435–464
126. Kono M, Ueki H, Umemura S (2002) Near-infrared finger vein patterns for personal identification. Appl Opt 41(35):7429–7436
127. Köse C, Ikibas C (2011) A personal identification system using retinal vasculature in retinal fundus images. Expert Syst Appl 38(11):13670–13681
128. Krivokuca V, Gomez-Barrero M, Marcel S, Rathgeb C, Busch C (2019)Towards measuring the amount of discriminatory information in fingervein biometric characteristics using a relative entropy estimator. In: Uhl A, Busch C, Marcel S, Veldhuis R (eds) Handbook of vascular biometrics. Springer Science+Business Media, Boston, MA, USA, pp 507–526
129. Krivokuca V, Marcel S (2019) On the recognition performance of BioHash-protected fingervein templates. In: Uhl A, Busch C, Marcel S, Veldhuis R (eds) Handbook of vascular biometrics. Springer Science+Business Media, Boston, MA, USA, pp 465–480

130. Kumar A, Zhou Y (2012) Human identification using finger images. IEEE Trans Image Process 21(4):2228–2244
131. Kumar A, Venkata Prathyusha K (2009) Personal authentication using hand vein triangulation and knuckle shape. IEEE Trans Image Process 18(9):2127–2136
132. Kurban OC, Niyaz O, Yildirim T (2016) Neural network based wrist vein identification using ordinary camera. In: International symposium on innovations in Intelligent SysTems and Applications, INISTA 2016, Sinaia, Romania, 2–5 Aug 2016, pp 1–4
133. Ladoux P-O, Rosenberger C, Dorizzi B (2009) Palm vein verification system based on SIFT matching. In: Advances in biometrics, third international conference, ICB 2009, Alghero, Italy, 2–5 June 2009. Proceedings, pp 1290–1298
134. Lajevardi SM, Arakala A, Davis SA, Horadam KJ (2013) Retina verification system based on biometric graph matching. IEEE Trans Image Process 22(9):3625–3635
135. Lalithamani N, Sabrigiriraj M (2015) Dual encryption algorithm to improve security in hand vein and palm vein-based biometric recognition. J Med Imaging Health Inform 5(3):545–551
136. Lalithamani N, Sabrigiriraj M (2015) Palm and hand vein-based fuzzy vault generation scheme for multibiometric cryptosystem. Imaging Sci J 63(2):111–118
137. Leandro JJG, Cesar RM, Jelinek HF (2001) Blood vessels segmentation in retina: preliminary assessment of the mathematical morphology and of the wavelet transform techniques. In: Proceedings of Brazilian symposium on computer graphics, image processing and vision, (SIBGRAPI-01), Florianopolis, Brazil, pp 84–90
138. Lee EC, Jung H, Kim D (2011) New finger biometric method using near infrared imaging. Sensors 11(3):2319–2333
139. Lee EC, Lee HC, Park KR (2009) Finger vein recognition using minutia-based alignment and local binary pattern-based feature extraction. Int J Imaging Syst Technol 19(3):179–186
140. Lee HC, Park KR, Kang BJ, Park SJ (2009) A new mobile multimodal biometric device integrating finger vein and fingerprint recognition. In: Proceedings of the 4th international conference on ubiquitous information technologies applications, pp 1–4
141. Lee J-C (2012) A novel biometric system based on palm vein image. Pattern Recognit Lett 33(12):1520–1528
142. Lee J, Moon S et al (2017) Imaging of the finger vein and blood flow for anti-spoofing authentication using a laser and a mems scanner. Sensors 17(4):925
143. Lee J-C, Lo T-M, Chang C-P (2016) Dorsal hand vein recognition based on directional filter bank. Signal Image Video Process 10(1):145–152
144. Li X, Huang D, Wang Y (2016) Comparative study of deep learning methods on dorsal hand vein recognition. In: Chinese conference on biometric recognition (CCBR'16). Springer, pp 296–306
145. Lin T, Zheng Y (2003) Node-matching-based pattern recognition method for retinal blood vessel images. Opt Eng 42(11):3302–3306
146. Lin S-J, Yang C-M, Yeh P-T, Ho T-C (2014) Smartphone fundoscopy for retinopathy of prematurity. Taiwan J Ophthalmol 4(2):82–85
147. Liu Z, Song S (2012) An embedded real-time finger-vein recognition system for mobile devices. IEEE Trans Consum Electron 58(2):522–527
148. Liu F, Yang G, Yin Y, Wang S (2014) Singular value decomposition based minutiae matching method for finger vein recognition. Neurocomputing 145:75–89
149. Liu Y, Ling J, Liu Z, Shen J, Gao C (2018) Finger vein secure biometric template generation based on deep learning. Soft Comput 22(7):2257–2265
150. Li F, Zhang T, Liu Y, Wang G (2017) Hand-dorsa vein recognition based on scale and contrast invariant feature matching. IEICE Trans 100-D(12):3054–3058
151. Luo H, Fa-Xin Y, Pan J-S, Chu S-C, Tsai P-W (2010) A survey of vein recognition techniques. Inf Technol J 9(6):1142–1149
152. Lu Y, Xie SJ, Yoon S, Wang Z, Park DS (2013) An available database for the research of finger vein recognition. In: 2013 6th International congress on image and signal processing (CISP), vol 1. IEEE, pp 410–415

153. Lu Y, Yoon S, Park DS (2014) Finger vein identification system using two cameras. Electron Lett 50(22):1591–1593
154. Ma X, Jing X, Huang H, Cui Y, Junsheng M (2017) Palm vein recognition scheme based on an adaptive gabor filter. IET Biom 6(5):325–333
155. Maamari RN, Keenan JD, Fletcher DA, Margolis T (2014) A mobile phone-based retinal camera for portable wide field imaging. Br J Ophthalmol 98:438–441
156. Ma H, Cui FP, Oluwatoyin P (2013) A non-contact finger vein image quality assessment method. In: Measurement technology and its application, volume 239 of *Applied mechanics and materials*. Trans Tech Publications, pp 986–989
157. Mahri N, Suandi SAS, Rosdi BA (2010) Finger vein recognition algorithm using phase only correlation. In: 2010 International workshop on emerging techniques and challenges for hand-based biometrics (ETCHB). IEEE, pp 1–6
158. Maier A, Niederbrucker G, Stenger S, Uhl A (2012) Efficient focus assessment for a computer vision-based Vickers hardness measurement system. J Electron Imaging 21:021114
159. Maio D, Maltoni D, Cappelli R, Wayman JL, Jain AK (2004) FVC2004: third fingerprint verification competition. In: ICBA, volume 3072 of LNCS. Springer, pp 1–7
160. Maltoni D, Maio D, Jain AK, Prabhakar S (2009) Synthetic fingerprint generation. Handbook of fingerprint recognition, pp 271–302
161. Mancini DM, Bolinger L, Li H, Kendrick K, Chance B, Wilson JR (1994) Validation of near-infrared spectroscopy in humans. J Appl Physiol 77(6):2740–2747
162. Marcel S, Nixon MS, Li SZ (eds) (2014) Handbook of biometric anti-spoofing. Springer
163. Matsuda Y, Miura N, Nagasaka A, Kiyomizu H, Miyatake T (2016) Finger-vein authentication based on deformation-tolerant feature-point matching. Mach Vis Appl 27(2):237–250
164. Matsuda Y, Miura N, Nonomura Y, Nagasaka A, Miyatake T (2017) Walkthrough-style multi-finger vein authentication. In: Proceedings of the IEEE international conference on consumer electronics (ICCE'17), pp 438–441
165. Ma H, Wang K, Fan L, Cui F (2013) A finger vein image quality assessment method using object and human visual system index. In: Proceedings of the third Sino-foreign-interchange conference on intelligent science and intelligent data engineering (IScIDE'12), pages 498–506. Springer
166. Mazumdar JB, Nirmala SR (2018) Retina based biometric authentication system: a review. Int J Adv Res Comput Sci 9(1)
167. Meenakshi VS, Padmavathi G (2009) Security analysis of hardened retina based fuzzy vault. In: 2009 International conference on advances in recent technologies in communication and computing, pp 926–930
168. Meng Z, Gu X (2014) Hand vein identification using local gabor ordinal measure. J Electron Imaging 23(5):053004
169. Meng X, Yin Y, Yang G, Xi X (2013) Retinal identification based on an improved circular gabor filter and scale invariant feature transform. Sensors 13(7):9248–9266
170. Mesbah R, McCane B, Mills S (2017) Conditional random fields incorporate convolutional neural networks for human eye sclera semantic segmentation. In: 2017 IEEE International joint conference on biometrics, IJCB 2017, Denver, CO, USA, 1–4 Oct 2017, pp 768–773
171. Miri M, Amini Z, Rabbani H, Kafieh R (2017) A comprehensive study of retinal vessel classification methods in fundus images. J Med Signals Sens 7(2):59–70
172. Mirmohamadsadeghi L, Drygajlo A (2014) Palm vein recognition with local texture patterns. IET Biom 3(4):198–206
173. Mirmohamadsadeghi L, Drygajlo A (2011) Palm vein recognition with local binary patterns and local derivative patterns. In: 2011 International joint conference on biometrics (IJCB). IEEE, pp 1–6
174. Miura N, Nagasaka A, Miyatake T (2004) Feature extraction of finger-vein patterns based on repeated line tracking and its application to personal identification. Mach Vis Appl 15(4):194–203
175. Miura N, Nagasaka A, Miyatake T (2007) Extraction of finger-vein patterns using maximum curvature points in image profiles. IEICE Trans Inf Syst 90(8):1185–1194

176. Modi SK, Elliott SJ, Whetsone J, Kim H (2007) Impact of age groups on fingerprint recognition performance. In: IEEE Workshop on automatic identification advanced technologies, pp 19–23
177. Mohamed C, Akhtar Z, Boukezzoula N-E, Falk TH (2017) Combining left and right wrist vein images for personal verification. In: Seventh international conference on image processing theory, tools and applications, IPTA 2017, Montreal, QC, Canada, 28 Nov–1 Dec 2017, pp 1–6
178. Mokroß B-A, Drozdowski P, Rathgeb C, Busch C (2019) Efficient identification in large-scale vein recognition systems using spectral minutiae representations. In: Uhl A, Busch C, Marcel S, Veldhuis R (eds) Handbook of vascular biometrics. Springer Science+Business Media, Boston, MA, USA, pp 225–260
179. Morales A, Ferrer MA, Kumar A (2011) Towards contactless palmprint authentication. IET Comput Vis 5:407–416
180. Mo J, Zhang L (2017) Multi-level deep supervised networks for retinal vessel segmentation. Int J Comput Assist Radiol Surg 12(12):2181–2193
181. Mythily B, Sathyaseelan K (2015) Measuring the quality of image for fake biometric detection: application to finger vein. In: National conference on research advances in communication, computation, electrical science and structures (NCRACCESS), pp 6–11
182. Nazari P, Pourghassem H (2017) A novel retina-based human identification algorithm based on geometrical shape features using a hierarchical matching structure. Comput Methods Programs Biomed 141:43–58
183. Nguyen DT, Park YH, Shin KY, Kwon SY, Lee HC, Park KR (2013) Fake finger-vein image detection based on Fourier and wavelet transforms. Digit Signal Process 23(5):1401–1413
184. Nguyen DT, Park YH, Shin KY, Park KR (2013) New finger-vein recognition method based on image quality assessment. KSII Trans Internet Inf Syst 7(2):347–365
185. Nguyen DT, Yoon HS, Pham TD, Park KR (2017) Spoof detection for finger-vein recognition system using NIR camera. Sensors 17(10):2261
186. Nikisins O, Eglitis T, Anjos A, Marcel S (2018) Fast cross-correlation based wrist vein recognition algorithm with rotation and translation compensation. In: International workshop on biometrics and forensics (IWBF'18), pp 1–7
187. Nikisins O, Eglitis T, Pudzs M, Greitans M (2015) Algorithms for a novel touchless bimodal palm biometric system. In: International conference on biometrics (ICB'15), pp 436–443
188. Oh K, Oh B-S, Toh K-A, Yau W-Y, Eng H-L (2014) Combining sclera and periocular features for multi-modal identity verification. Neurocomputing 128:185–198
189. Oh K, Toh K (2012) Extracting sclera features for cancelable identity verification. In: 5th IAPR International conference on biometrics (ICB'12), pp 245–250
190. Ong EP, Xu Y, Wong DWK, Liu J (2015) Retina verification using a combined points and edges approach. In: 2015 IEEE International conference on image processing, ICIP 2015, Quebec City, QC, Canada, 27–30 Sept 2015, pp 2720–2724
191. Ortega M, Penedo MG, Rouco J, Barreira N, Carreira MJ (2009) Personal verification based on extraction and characterization of retinal feature points. J Vis Lang Comput 20(2):80–90
192. Pabitha M, Latha L (2013) Efficient approach for retinal biometric template security and person authentication using noninvertible constructions. Int J Comput Appl 69(4):28–34
193. Pan M, Kang W (2011) Palm vein recognition based on three local invariant feature extraction algorithms. In: 6th Chinese conference on biometric recognition, CCBR 2011, Beijing, China, 3–4 Dec 2011. Proceedings, pp 116–124
194. Pascual JES, Uriarte-Antonio J, Sanchez-Reillo R, Lorenz MG (2010) Capturing hand or wrist vein images for biometric authentication using low-cost devices. In: Proceedings of the sixth international conference on intelligent information hiding and multimedia signal processing (IIH-MSP 2010), pp 816–819
195. Pascual JES, Uriarte-Antonio J, Sánchez-Reillo R, Lorenz MG (2010) Capturing hand or wrist vein images for biometric authentication using low-cost devices. In: Sixth international conference on intelligent information hiding and multimedia signal processing (IIH-MSP 2010), Darmstadt, Germany, 15–17 Oct 2010, Proceedings, pp 318–322

196. Patil I, Bhilare S, Kanhangad V (2016) Assessing vulnerability of dorsal hand-vein verification system to spoofing attacks using smartphone camera. In: IEEE International conference on identity, security and behavior analysis (ISBA'16), pp 1–6
197. Paulus J, Meier J, Bock R, Hornegger J, Michelson G (2010) Automated quality assessment of retinal fundus photos. Int J Comput Assist Radiol Surg 5(6):557–564
198. Peng J, Li Q, Niu X (2014) A novel finger vein image quality evaluation method based on triangular norm. In Tenth international conference on intelligent information hiding and multimedia signal processing (IIHMSP'14), pp 239–242
199. Piciucco E, Maiorana E, Kauba C, Uhl A, Campisi P (2016) Cancelable biometrics for finger vein recognition. In: Proceedings of the 1st workshop on sensing, processing and learning for intelligent machines (SPLINE 2016), Aalborg, Denmark, pp 1–6
200. Prasanalakshmi B, Kannammal A (2010) Secure cryptosystem from palm vein biometrics in smart card. In: The 2nd international conference on computer and automation engineering (ICCAE'10), vol 1, pp 653–657
201. Proenca H, Alexandre LA (2005) UBIRIS: a noisy iris image database. In: Roli F, Vitulano S (eds) Image analysis and processing—ICIAP 2005, vol 3617. Lecture notes on computer science, Sept 2005, Cagliari, Italy, pp 970–977
202. Proenca H, Filipe S, Santos R, Oliveira J, Alexandre LA (2010) The UBIRIS.v2: a database of visible wavelength images captured on-the-move and at-a-distance. IEEE Trans Pattern Anal Mach Intell 32(8):1529–1535
203. Prommegger B, Kauba C, Linortner M, Uhl A (2019) Longitudinal finger rotation—deformation detection and correction. IEEE Trans Biom Behav Identity Sci 1(2):123–138
204. Prommegger B, Kauba C, Uhl A (2018) Longitudinal finger rotation—problems and effects in finger-vein recognition. In: Proceedings of the international conference of the biometrics special interest group (BIOSIG'18), Darmstadt, Germany, pp 1–11
205. Prommegger B, Kauba C, Uhl A (2018) Multi-perspective finger-vein biometrics. In: 2018 IEEE 9th International conference on biometrics theory, applications and systems (BTAS). Los Angeles, California, USA, pp 1–9
206. Prommegger B, Kauba C, Uhl A (2019) Different views on the finger—score level fusion in multi-perspective finger vein recognition. In: Uhl A, Busch C, Marcel S, Veldhuis R (eds) Handbook of vascular biometrics. Springer Science+Business Media, Boston, MA, USA, pp 261–308
207. Qamber S, Waheed Z, Akram MU (2012) Personal identification system based on vascular pattern of human retina. In: Cairo international biomedical engineering conference (CIBEC'12), pp 64–67
208. Qin H, El-Yacoubi MA (2018) Deep representation for finger-vein image-quality assessment. IEEE Trans Circuits Syst Video Technol 28(8):1677–1693
209. Qin H, Qin L, Xue L, He X, Chengbo Y, Liang X (2013) Finger-vein verification based on multi-features fusion. Sensors 13(11):15048–15067
210. Qin H, Chen Z, He X (2018) Finger-vein image quality evaluation based on the representation of grayscale and binary image. Multim Tools Appl 77(2):2505–2527
211. Qin H, El Yacoubi M (2015) Finger-vein quality assessment by representation learning from binary images. In: International conference on neural information processing (ICONIP'15), volume 9489 of Springer LNCS, pp 421–431
212. Qin H, Li S, Kot AC, Qin L (2012) Quality assessment of finger-vein image. In: Proceedings of the 2012 Asia Pacific signal and information processing association annual summit and conference
213. Qiu X, Kang W, Tian S, Jia W, Huang Z (2018) Finger vein presentation attack detection using total variation decomposition. IEEE Trans Inf Forensics Secur 13(2):465–477
214. Qiu X, Tian S, Kang W, Jia W, Wu Q (2017) Finger vein presentation attack detection using convolutional neural networks. In: Chinese conference on biometric recognition (CCBR'17), volume 10568 of Springer lecture notes in computer science, pp 296–305
215. Qi Y, Zhou Y, Zhou C, Hu X, Hu X (2016) 3D feature array involved registration algorithm for multi-pose hand vein authentication. In: International conference on biometrics, ICB 2016, Halmstad, Sweden, 13–16 June 2016, pp 1–7

216. Qi Y, Zhou Y, Zhou C, Hu X, Hu X (2016) Vein point cloud registration algorithm for multi-pose hand vein authentication. In: IEEE International conference on identity, security and behavior analysis, ISBA 2016, Sendai, Japan, 29 Feb–2 Mar 2016, pp 1–6
217. Radu P, Ferryman JM, Wild P (2015) A robust sclera segmentation algorithm. In: IEEE 7th International conference on biometrics theory, applications and systems, BTAS 2015, Arlington, VA, USA, 8–11 Sept 2015, pp 1–6
218. Raghavendra R, Avinash M, Marcel S, Busch C (2015) Finger vein liveness detection using motion magnification. In: Proceedings of the seventh IEEE international conference on biometrics: theory, applications and systems (BTAS'15)
219. Raghavendra R, Busch C (2015) Exploring dorsal finger vein pattern for robust person recognition. In: 2015 International conference on biometrics (ICB), pp 341–348
220. Raghavendra R, Busch C (2015) Presentation attack detection algorithms for finger vein biometrics: a comprehensive study. In: 11th International conference on signal-image technology internet-based systems (SITIS'15), pp 628–632
221. Raghavendra R, Busch C (2016) A low cost wrist vein sensor for biometric authentication. In: Proceedings of the 2016 IEEE international conference on imaging systems and techniques (IST)
222. Raghavendra R, Raja KB, Surbiryala J, Busch C (2014) A low-cost multimodal biometric sensor to capture finger vein and fingerprint. In: 2014 IEEE International joint conference on biometrics (IJCB). IEEE, pp 1–7
223. Raghavendra R, Raja KB, Venkattesh S, Busch C (2018) Fingervein presentation attack detection using transferable features from deep convolutional networks. In: Deep learning in biometrics, pp 97–104
224. Raghavendra R, Raja K, Venkatesh S, Busch C (2017) Transferable deep convolutional neural network features for fingervein presentation attack detection. In: Proceedings of the 5th international workshop on biometrics and forensics (IWBF'17), Coventry, United Kingdom, pp 1–6
225. Raghavendra R, Surbiryala J, Raja K, Busch C (2014) Novel finger vascular pattern imaging device for robust biometric verification. In: Proceedings of the 2014 IEEE conference on imaging systems and techniques (IST 2014)
226. Rahul RC, Cherian M, Mohan M (2015) Literature survey on contactless palm vein recognition. Int J Comput Sci Trends Technol (IJCST) 3(5)
227. Rathgeb C, Uhl A (2011) A survey on biometric cryptosystems and cancelable biometrics. EURASIP J Inf Secur 3:2011
228. Razdi SA, Hani MK, Bakhteri R (2016) Finger-vein biometric identification using convolutional neural network. Turk J Electr Eng Comput Sci 24(3):1863–1878
229. Rot P, Vitek M, Grm K, Emersic Z, Peer P, Struc V (2019) Deep sclera segmentation and recognition. In: Uhl A, Busch C, Marcel S, Veldhuis R (eds) Handbook of vascular biometrics. Springer Science+Business Media, Boston, MA, USA, pp 395–434
230. Saha S, Fernando B, Cuadros J, Xiao D, Kanagasingam Y (2018) Automated quality assessment of colour fundus images for diabetic retinopathy screening in telemedicine. J Digit Imaging 31(6):869–878
231. Sato H (2009) Finger vein verification technology for mobile apparatus. In: Proceedings of the international conference on security and cryptography (SECRYPT'09), pp 37–41
232. Semerad L, Drahansky M (2015) Biometric entropy of retina. In: 2015 International conference on information and digital technologies, pp 302–304
233. Sequeira AF, Ferryman J, Chen L, Galdi C, Dugelay J-L, Chiesa V, Uhl A, Prommegger B, Kauba C, Kirchgasser S, Grudzien A, Kowalski M, Szklarski L, Maik P, Gmitrowicz P (2018) Protect multimodal DB: a multimodal biometrics dataset envisaging border control. In: Proceedings of the international conference of the biometrics special interest group (BIOSIG'18), Darmstadt, Germany, pp 1–8
234. Shaheed K, Liu H, Yang G, Qureshi I, Gou J, Yin Y (2018) A systematic review of finger vein recognition techniques. Information 9:213

235. Shaydyuk NK, Cleland T (2016) Biometric identification via retina scanning with liveness detection using speckle contrast imaging. In: IEEE International Carnahan conference on security technology, ICCST 2016, Orlando, FL, USA, 24–27 Oct 2016, pp 1–5
236. Shi Y, Yang J, Yang J (2012) A new algorithm for finger-vein image enhancement and segmentation. Inf Sci Ind Appl 4(22):139–144
237. Shinzaki T (2019) Use case of palm vein authentication. In: Uhl A, Busch C, Marcel S, Veldhuis R (eds) Handbook of vascular biometrics. Springer Science+Business Media, Boston, MA, USA, pp 145–158
238. Sierro A, Ferrez P, Roduit P (2015) Contact-less palm/finger vein biometric. In: BIOSIG 2015—Proceedings of the 14th international conference of the biometrics special interest group, 9–11 Sept 2015, Darmstadt, Germany, pp 145–156
239. Sierro A, Ferrez P, Roduit P (2015) Contact-less palm/finger vein biometrics. In: Proceedings of the international conference of the biometrics special interest group (BIOSIG'15), pp 145–156
240. Sinthanayothin C, Boyce JF, Cook HL, Williamson TH (1999) Automated localisation of the optic disc, fovea, and retinal blood vessels from digital colour fundus images. Br J Ophthalmol 83:902–910
241. Soares JVB, Leandro JJG, Cesar-Jr RM, Jelinek HF, Cree MJ (2006) Retinal vessel segmentation using the 2-D gabor wavelet and supervised classification. IEEE Trans Med Imaging 25(9):1214–1222
242. Söllinger D, Trung P, Uhl A (2018) Non-reference image quality assessment and natural scene statistics to counter biometric sensor spoofing. IET Biom 7(4):314–324
243. Song JH, Kim C, Yoo Y (2015) Vein visualization using a smart phone with multispectral wiener estimation for point-of-care applications. IEEE J Biomed Health Inform 19(2):773–778
244. Song W, Kim T, Kim HC, Choi JH, Kong H-J, Lee S-R (2011) A finger-vein verification system using mean curvature. Pattern Recognit Lett 32(11):1541–1547
245. Staal JJ, Abramoff MD, Niemeijer M, Viergever MA, van Ginneken B (2004) Ridge based vessel segmentation in color images of the retina. IEEE Trans Med Imaging 23(4):501–509
246. Swedish T, Roesch K, Lee IK, Rastogi K, Bernstein S, Raskar R (2015) eyeSelfie: self directed eye alignment using reciprocal eye box imaging. ACM Trans Graph 34(4)
247. Syazana-Itqan K, Syafeeza AR, Saad NM, Hamid NA, Saad WHBM (2016) A review of finger-vein biometrics identification approaches. Indian J Sci Technol 9(32)
248. Tagkalakis F, Vlachakis D, Megalooikonomou V, Skodras A (2017) A novel approach to finger vein authentication. In: 14th IEEE International symposium on biomedical imaging, ISBI 2017, Melbourne, Australia, 18–21 Apr 2017, pp 659–662
249. Tang Y, Huang D, Wang Y (2012) Hand-dorsa vein recognition based on multi-level keypoint detection and local feature matching. In: Proceedings of the 21st international conference on pattern recognition, ICPR 2012, Tsukuba, Japan, 11–15 Nov 2012, pp 2837–2840
250. Ting E, Ibrahim MZ (2018) A review of finger vein recognition system. J Telecommun Electron Comput Eng 10(1–9):167–171
251. Tirunagari S, Poh N, Bober M, Windridge D (2015) Windowed DMD as a microtexture descriptor for finger vein counter-spoofing in biometrics. In: IEEE International workshop on information forensics and security (WIFS), Nov 2015, pp 1–6
252. Tome P, Marcel S (2015) On the vulnerability of palm vein recognition to spoofing attacks. In: The 8th IAPR international conference on biometrics (ICB), May 2015
253. Tome P, Raghavendra R, Busch C, Tirunagari S, Poh N, Shekar BH, Gragnaniello D, Sansone C, Verdoliva L, Marcel S (2015) The 1st competition on counter measures to finger vein spoofing attacks. In: International conference on biometrics (ICB'15), May 2015, pp 513–518
254. Tome P, Vanoni M, Marcel S (2014) On the vulnerability of finger vein recognition to spoofing attacks. In: Proceedings of the international conference of the biometrics special interest group (BIOSIG'14), Sept 2014, pp 111–120

255. Ton BT, Veldhuis RNJ (2013) A high quality finger vascular pattern dataset collected using a custom designed capturing device. In: International conference on biometrics, ICB 2013. IEEE
256. Uhl A, Wild P (2009) Comparing verification performance of kids and adults for fingerprint, palmprint, hand-geometry and digitprint biometrics. In: Proceedings of the 3rd IEEE international conference on biometrics: theory, application, and systems 2009 (IEEE BTAS'09). IEEE Press, pp 1–6
257. Veiga D, Pereira C, Ferreira M, Gonçalves L, Monteiro J (2014) Quality evaluation of digital fundus images through combined measures. J Med Imaging 1:014001
258. Veldhuis R, Spreeuwers L, Ton B, Rozendal S (2019) A high quality finger vein dataset collected using a custom designed capture device. In: Uhl A, Busch C, Marcel S, Veldhuis R (eds) Handbook of vascular biometrics. Springer Science+Business Media, Boston, MA, USA, pp 63–76
259. Vermeer KA, Vos FM, Lemij HG, Vossepoel AM (2004) A model based method for retinal blood vessel detection. Comput Biol Med 34:209–219
260. Vostatek P, Claridge E, Uusitalo H, Hauta-Kasari M, Fält P, Lensu L (2017) Performance comparison of publicly available retinal blood vessel segmentation methods. Comput Med Imaging Graph 55:2–12
261. Waheed Z, Akram MU, Waheed A, Khan MA, Shaukat A, Ishaq M (2016) Person identification using vascular and non-vascular retinal features. Comput Electr Eng 53:359–371
262. Wan H, Chen L, Song H, Yang J (2017) Dorsal hand vein recognition based on convolutional neural networks. In: 2017 IEEE International conference on bioinformatics and biomedicine, BIBM 2017, Kansas City, MO, USA, 13–16 Nov 2017, pp 1215–1221
263. Wang J-G, Yau W-Y, Suwandy A (2008) Feature-level fusion of palmprint and palm vein for person identification based on a "junction point" representation. In: Proceedings of the international conference on image processing, ICIP 2008, 12–15 Oct 2008, San Diego, California, USA, pp 253–256
264. Wang J, Wang G (2017) Quality-specific hand vein recognition system. IEEE Trans Inf Forensics Secur 12(11):2599–2610
265. Wang Z, Bovik AC, Sheikh HR, Simoncelli EP (2004) Image quality assessment: from error visibility to structural similarity. IEEE Trans Image Process 13(4):600–612
266. Wang J-G, Yau W-Y, Suwandy A, Sung E (2008) Person recognition by fusing palmprint and palm vein images based on "Laplacianpalm" representation. Pattern Recognit 41(5):1514–1527
267. Wang Y, Zhang K, Shark L-K (2014) Personal identification based on multiple keypoint sets of dorsal hand vein images. IET Biom 3(4):234–245
268. Wang Y, Xie W, Xiaojie Y, Shark L-K (2015) An automatic physical access control system based on hand vein biometric identification. IEEE Trans Consum Electron 61(3):320–327
269. Wang Y, Zhang D, Qi Q (2016) Liveness detection for dorsal hand vein recognition. Pers Ubiquit Comput 20(3):447–455
270. Wang Y, Fan Y, Liao W, Li K, Shark L-K, Varley MR (2012) Hand vein recognition based on multiple keypoints sets. In: 5th IAPR International conference on biometrics, ICB 2012, New Delhi, India, 29 Mar–1 Apr 2012, pp 367–371
271. Wang L, Leedham G, Cho DSY (2008) Minutiae feature analysis for infrared hand vein pattern biometrics. Pattern Recognit 41(3):920–929
272. Wang C, Sun X, Dong W, Zhu Z, Zheng S, Zeng X (2017) Quality assessment of palm vein image using natural scene statistics. In: Computer vision—second CCF Chinese conference, CCCV 2017, Tianjin, China, 11–14 Oct 2017, Proceedings, Part II, pp 248–255
273. Wang J, Wang G, Pan Z (2018) Gender attribute mining with hand-dorsa vein image based on unsupervised sparse feature learning. IEICE Trans 101-D(1):257–260
274. Wang C, Zeng X, Sun X, Dong W, Zhu Z (2017) Quality assessment on near infrared palm vein image. In: 2017 32nd Youth academic annual conference of Chinese association of automation (YAC), pp 1127–1130

275. Wilson C (2010) Vein pattern recognition: a privacy-enhancing biometric. CRC Press, Boca Raton, FL, US
276. Wolterink JM, Leiner T, Isgum I (2018) Blood vessel geometry synthesis using generative adversarial networks. In: 1st Conference on medical imaging with deep learning (MIDL 2018)
277. Wu KS, Lee J-C, Lo T-M, Chang K-C, Chang C-P (2013) A secure palm vein recognition system. J Syst Softw 86(11):2870–2876
278. Wu Z, Tian L, Li P, Ting W, Jiang M, Wu C (2016) Generating stable biometric keys for flexible cloud computing authentication using finger vein. Inf Sci 433–434:431–447
279. Xi X, Yang G, Yin Y, Meng X (2013) Finger vein recognition with personalized feature selection. Sensors 13(9):11243–11259
280. Xi X, Yang L, Yin Y (2017) Learning discriminative binary codes for finger vein recognition. Pattern Recognit 66:26–33
281. Xian R, Li W (2014) Performance evaluation of finger-vein verification algorithms in PFVR2014. In: Chinese conference on biometric recognition (CCBR'14), volume 8833 of Springer LNCS, pp 244–251
282. Xian R, Ni L, Li W (2015) The ICB-2015 competition on finger vein recognition. In: International conference on biometrics, ICB 2015, Phuket, Thailand, 19–22 May 2015, pp 85–89
283. Xie SJ, Zhou B, Yang JC, Lu Y, Pan Y (2013) Novel hierarchical structure based finger vein image quality assessment. In: Proceedings of the Chinese conference on biometric recognition (CCBR'13), volume 8232 of Springer lecture notes in computer science, pp 266–273
284. Xie C, Kumar A (2018) Finger vein identification using convolutional neural network and supervised discrete hashing. Pattern Recognit Lett
285. Xu Z, Guo X, Hu X, Chen X, Wang Z (2006) The identification and recognition based on point for blood vessel of ocular fundus. In: Proceedings of the 1st IAPR international conference on biometrics (ICB'06), number 3832 in Lecture notes on computer science, pp 770–776
286. Yan X, Kang W, Deng F, Qiuxia W (2015) Palm vein recognition based on multi-sampling and feature-level fusion. Neurocomputing 151:798–807
287. Yang J, Shi Y (2012) Finger-vein roi localization and vein ridge enhancement. Pattern Recognit Lett 33(12):1569–1579
288. Yang J, Shi Y (2014) Towards finger-vein image restoration and enhancement for finger-vein recognition. Inf Sci 268:33–52
289. Yang G, Xi X, Yin Y (2012) Finger vein recognition based on a personalized best bit map. Sensors 12:1738–1757
290. Yang Y, Yang G, Wang S (2012) Finger vein recognition based on multi-instance. Int J Digit Content Technol Appl 6(11):86–94
291. Yang L, Yang G, Yin Y, Xiao R (2013) Finger vein image quality evaluation using support vector machines. Opt Eng 52(2):027003
292. Yang J, Shi Y, Jia G (2017) Finger-vein image matching based on adaptive curve transformation. Pattern Recognit 66:34–43
293. Yang L, Yang G, Xi X, Meng X, Zhang C, Yin Y (2017) Tri-branch vein structure assisted finger vein recognition. IEEE Access 5:21020–21028
294. Yang W, Wang S, Jiankun H, Guanglou Z, Chaudhry J, Adi E, Valli C (2018) Securing mobile healthcare data: a smart card based cancelable finger-vein bio-cryptosystem. IEEE Access 06:36939–36947
295. Yang W, Wang S, Jiankun H, Zheng G, Valli C (2018) A fingerprint and finger-vein based cancelable multi-biometric system. Pattern Recognit 78:242–251
296. Yang W, Hu J, Wang S (2013) A finger-vein based cancellable bio-cryptosystem. In: 7th International conference network and system security, NSS 2013, Madrid, Spain, 3–4 June 2013. Proceedings, pp 784–790
297. Yang J, Shi Y, Yang J (2012) Finger-vein image restoration based on a biological optical model. In: New trends and developments in biometrics. InTech
298. Yang J, Yang J (2009) Multi-channel gabor filter design for finger-vein image enhancement. In: Fifth international conference on image and graphics, 2009. ICIG'09. IEEE, pp 87–91

299. Yang L, Yang G, Yin Y, Xi X (2017) Finger vein recognition with anatomy structure analysis. IEEE Trans Circuits Syst Video Technol
300. Yang L, Yang G, Yin Y, Zhou L (2014) A survey of finger vein recognition. In: Chinese conference on biometric recognition (CCBR'14, volume 8833 of Springer LNCS, pp 234–243
301. Yang L, Yang G, Yin Y, Zhou L (2016) User individuality based cost-sensitive learning: a case study in finger vein recognition. In: International conference on biometrics, ICB 2016, Halmstad, Sweden, 13–16 June 2016, pp 1–8
302. Yang W, Yu X, Liao Q (2009) Personal authentication using finger vein pattern and finger-dorsa texture fusion. In: Proceedings of the 17th ACM international conference on multimedia. ACM, pp 905–908
303. Ye Y, Ni L, Zheng H, Liu S, Zhu Y, Zhang D, Xiang W, Li W (2016) FVRC2016: the 2nd finger vein recognition competition. In: International conference on biometrics, ICB 2016, Halmstad, Sweden, 13–16 June 2016
304. Ye Y, Zheng H, Ni L, Liu S, Li W (2016) A study on the individuality of finger vein based on statistical analysis. In: International conference on biometrics, ICB 2016, Halmstad, Sweden, 13–16 June 2016, pp 1–5
305. Yin Y, Liu L, Sun X (2011) SDUMLA-HMT: a multimodal biometric database. In: The 6th Chinese conference on biometric recognition (CCBR 2011), volume 7098 of Springer lecture notes on computer science, pp 260–268
306. Yu H, Agurto C, Barriga S, Nemeth SC, Soliz P, Zamora G (2012) Automated image quality evaluation of retinal fundus photographs in diabetic retinopathy screening. In: 2012 IEEE Southwest symposium on image analysis and interpretation, pp 125–128
307. Yuksel A, Akarun L, Sankur B (2011) Hand vein biometry based on geometry and appearance methods. IET Comput Vis 5(6):398–406
308. Zhang C, Liu Z, Liu Y, Su F, Chang J, Zhou Y, Zhao Q (2015) Reflection-type finger vein recognition for mobile applications. J Opt Soc Korea 19(5):467–476
309. Zhang L, Cheng Z, Shen Y, Wang D (2018) Palmprint and palmvein recognition based on DCNN and A new large-scale contactless palmvein dataset. Symmetry 10(4):78
310. Zhang R, Huang D, Wang Y (2016) Textured detailed graph model for dorsal hand vein recognition: a holistic approach. In: International conference on biometrics, ICB 2016, Halmstad, Sweden, 13–16 June 2016, pp 1–7
311. Zhang R, Huang D, Wang Y, Wang Y (2015) Improving feature based dorsal hand vein recognition through random keypoint generation and fine-grained matching. In: International conference on biometrics, ICB 2015, Phuket, Thailand, 19–22 May 2015, pp 326–333
312. Zhang Y, Huang H, Zhang H, Ni L, Xu W, Ahmed NU, Ahmed MdS, Jin Y, Chen Y, Wen J, Li W (2017) ICFVR 2017: 3rd international competition on finger vein recognition. In: 2017 IEEE International joint conference on biometrics, IJCB 2017, Denver, CO, USA, 1–4 Oct 2017, pp 707–714
313. Zhang C, Li X, Liu Z, Zhao Q, Xu H, Su F (2013) The CFVD reflection-type finger-vein image database with evaluation baseline. In: Biometric recognition. Springer, pp 282–287
314. Zhang J, Yang J (2009) Finger-vein image enhancement based on combination of gray-level grouping and circular gabor filter. In: International conference on information engineering and computer science, 2009. ICIECS 2009. IEEE, pp 1–4
315. Zhang Q, Zhou Y, Wang D, Hu X (2013) Personal authentication using hand vein and knuckle shape point cloud matching. In: IEEE Sixth international conference on biometrics: theory, applications and systems, BTAS 2013, Arlington, VA, USA, 29 Sept–2 Oct 2013, pp 1–6
316. Zhao J, Tian H, Xu W, Li X (2009) A new approach to hand vein image enhancement. In: Second International Conference on Intelligent Computation Technology and Automation, 2009. ICICTA'09, vol 1. IEEE, pp 499–501
317. Zheng H, Xu Q, Ye Y, Li W (2017) Effects of meteorological factors on finger vein recognition. In: IEEE International conference on identity, security and behavior analysis, ISBA 2017, New Delhi, India, 22–24 Feb 2017, pp 1–8

318. Zheng H, Ye Y, Ni L, Liu S, Li W (2016) Which finger is the best for finger vein recognition? In: 8th IEEE International conference on biometrics theory, applications and systems, BTAS 2016, Niagara Falls, NY, USA, 6–9 Sept 2016, pp 1–5
319. Zhong H, Kanhere SS, Chou CT (2017) VeinDeep: smartphone unlock using vein patterns. In: IEEE International conference on pervasive computing and communications (PerCom'17), pp 2–10
320. Zhou Y, Kumar A (2011) Human identification using palm-vein images. IEEE Trans Inf Forensics Secur 6(4):1259–1274
321. Zhou L, Gongping Yang L, Yang YY, Li Y (2015) Finger vein image quality evaluation based on support vector regression. Int J Signal Process Image Process Pattern Recognit 8:211–222
322. Zhou Z, Du EY, Thomas NL, Delp EJ (2012) A new human identification method: sclera recognition. IEEE Trans Syst Man Cybern Part A 42(3):571–583
323. Zhou Z, Du EY, Thomas NL, Delp EJ (2013) A comprehensive approach for sclera image quality measure. IJBM 5(2):181–198
324. Zhou Z, Du EY, Thomas NL (2010) A comprehensive sclera image quality measure. In: 11th International conference on control, automation, robotics vision, pp 638–643
325. Zhou Y, Kumar A (2010) Contactless palm vein identification using multiple representations. In: Fourth IEEE international conference on biometrics: theory applications and systems, BTAS 2010, Washington, DC, USA, 27–29 Sept 2010, pp 1–6
326. Zou H, Zhang B, Tao Z, Wang X (2016) A finger vein identification method based on template matching. J Phys Conf Ser 680:012001
327. Zuo J, Schmid NA, Chen X (2007) On generation and analysis of synthetic iris images. IEEE Trans Inf Forensics Secur 2(1):77–90

Chapter 2
A High-Quality Finger Vein Dataset Collected Using a Custom-Designed Capture Device

Raymond Veldhuis, Luuk Spreeuwers, Bram Ton and Sjoerd Rozendal

Abstract High-quality finger vein datasets available for the research community are still relatively scarce; therefore, we collected a set of finger vein images of high resolution and a known pixel density. Furthermore, this is the first dataset which contains the age, gender and handedness of the participating data subjects as metadata. This dataset has been collected using a custom-designed biometric capture device. The various aspects of designing this biometric capture device are addressed in this chapter. New insights and continuing work on the design of better capture devices have led to novel ideas which are presented in this chapter. To justify the importance of this dataset, performance figures in terms of EER of several well-established algorithms using this dataset and an existing dataset are compared side by side.

Keywords Finger vein capture device · Finger vein data set · 3D finger vein reconstruction

2.1 Introduction

The vascular or vein pattern of the finger is advertised as a promising new biometric characteristic. Biometric recognition based on finger vein patterns is characterised by very low error rates, good presentation attack resistance and a user convenience that is equivalent to that of fingerprint recognition. Though this new form of biometrics is already commercially deployed, it still lacks a strong scientific base. This is due to

R. Veldhuis · L. Spreeuwers (✉) · B. Ton
Data Science Group, Faculty of EEMCS, University of Twente, Enschede, The Netherlands
e-mail: l.j.spreeuwers@utwente.nl

R. Veldhuis
e-mail: r.n.j.veldhuis@utwente.nl

B. Ton
e-mail: b.t.ton@alumnus.utwente.nl

S. Rozendal
University of Twente, Enschede, Netherlands
e-mail: s.p.rozendal@student.utwente.nl

A. Uhl et al. (eds.), *Handbook of Vascular Biometrics*, Advances in Computer Vision and Pattern Recognition, https://doi.org/10.1007/978-3-030-27731-4_2

industrial protectiveness, which restricts the ability to verify claimed performances. In order to compare existing algorithms, a standardised testing method is needed and more datasets should be made available to researchers.

In order to stimulate the academic research on vascular pattern recognition, this chapter will present a finger vascular pattern dataset which has recently been made available to other researchers [17]. The presented dataset is unique in its kind as it provides high-resolution images together with demographics about the data subjects. Another contribution of this chapter is the performance verification of several published algorithms using both the newly collected dataset and an existing dataset collected by the Peking University [12].

Our dataset has been collected using a custom-designed capture device. The various aspects of designing this capture device are also covered in this chapter.

In the remainder of this chapter, first a brief overview is provided of finger vein acquisition techniques and systems in Sect. 2.2. Next, the custom-designed capture device is described in detail (Sect. 2.3), followed by the dataset (Sect. 2.4). In Sect. 2.5, results of various finger vein recognition algorithms on the database are presented. Section 2.6 presents the next-generation finger vein scanner currently under development at the University of Twente: a more compact design with 3D capabilities and other enhancements. Section 2.7 presents conclusions and in Sect. 2.8 future work is described.

2.2 Overview of Finger Vein Acquisition Systems

2.2.1 Types of Sensors

We first briefly summarise the different types of sensors for finger vein recognition and then present our own design. Devices that capture the vascular pattern inside a finger are based on the fact that the haemoglobin inside the veins has a higher absorption of Near-Infrared Light (NIR light) than the surrounding tissue. This means that the vascular pattern inside a finger can be captured by a device that is sensitive to NIR light. The veins have to be made visible with NIR light, but there are multiple possibilities to illuminate the finger. The main types that are found in existing devices are shown in Fig. 2.1.

The illumination with the light reflection method is on the same side as the camera. This allows the device to be more compact. During operation, the user of the device can still see his finger. The disadvantage of this method is that the image sensor mainly captures the reflected light from the surface of the finger, because the light shallowly penetrates the skin. Hence, this method gives images with low contrast between tissue and veins. The light transmission method does deliver high-contrast vascular pattern images, because the light passes through the finger and no reflections of the surface are captured. The illumination is at the other side of the finger relative to the camera. The disadvantage of this method is that the user has to put his finger into the device such that he cannot see his finger anymore, which can cause discomfort. The third illumination type is side lighting method. This method still allows an open

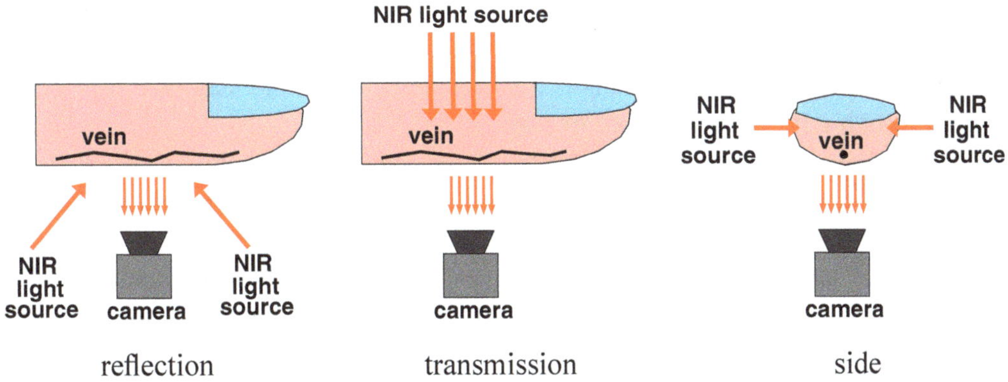

Fig. 2.1 Reflection, transmission and side illumination acquisition

device such that the user can see his finger. The light sources are placed on either one side or both sides of the finger. NIR light goes through the sides of the finger and scatters there, before it is captured by the image sensor. This method does allow for high-contrast images. However, the sides of the finger are overexposed in the images.

Some examples of commercially available sensors and sensors developed by academics are presented in Sects. 2.2.2 and 2.2.3. For a more complete overview, please refer to Chap. 3 of this book.

2.2.2 *Commercial Sensors*

There are several devices on the market for vascular pattern recognition. The market leader in finger vein capture devices is Hitachi. They have developed multiple systems that are capable of capturing finger vein images using light transmission or side illumination. Hitachi claims that it has a False Non-Match Rate (FNMR) of 0.01% at a False Match Rate (FMR) of 0.0001% [3, 4]. However, it is hard to verify these claims, because the devices and image data are not accessible.

Another company that builds finger vein capture devices is Mofiria, a daughter company of Sony. This company also produces various devices among which one using light transmission, but where the finger is placed sideways on the sensor. They claim an FNMR of 0.1% at an FMR of 0.0001% [15], but again these are closed devices and data are not accessible.

2.2.3 *Sensors Developed by Academics*

At several universities, research into finger vein recognition is performed and acquisition devices were developed. Examples are the finger vein scanner devices developed by the Civil Aviation University of China [21] and the University of Electronic Science and Technology [9]. The latter device also has the capability of making 3D recordings of finger veins. A more recent sensor, developed at the Norwegian

Biometrics Laboratory (NBL), allows simultaneous capturing of both finger vein patterns and fingerprints [13]. This is a closed sensor, and the user has to place his finger through a hole inside the device.

The device developed at the University of Twente, which is described in the subsequent sections, is also an example of this group of finger vein acquisition devices. The huge advantage of these devices, developed by academics, is that they are usually open devices, the image data is accessible and datasets are made available to the research community. This enables us to evaluate and compare various methods for finger vein recognition.

2.3 University of Twente Finger Vein Capture Device

A custom transillumination device type has been designed to capture the finger vascular pattern [18, 19]. This type of capture device has been chosen for its simplicity, robustness and the fact that external light interferences have little influence on the captured images. A downside of this type of capture device is the reduced user convenience because the finger is partially obscured during the capture process. All finger vascular pattern capture devices are based on the fact that blood has a higher absorbency than surrounding tissue in the near-infrared spectrum. A schematic cross section of the capture device can be seen in Fig. 2.2. The USB lightbox is responsible for regulating the individual LED intensities and is encapsulated in the capture device for the ease of portability. The overview also shows the slanted mirror indicated in green and the top plate containing the eight LEDs. The total length of the realised capture device is 50 cm, and the maximum height is 15 cm.

The constructed capture device consists of three main components: a light source, a camera and a mirror. These components will be described briefly in the successive paragraphs.

Light source This the most important part of the capture device since it determines the intensity of the captured image. Eight SFH4550 near-infrared LEDs produced by Osram with a wavelength of 850 nm are used to transilluminate the finger. This LED type has been chosen because it has a small angle of half intensity, which means more power can be directed into the finger. Each individual LED intensity is regulated using a simple control loop in such a way that a uniform intensity along

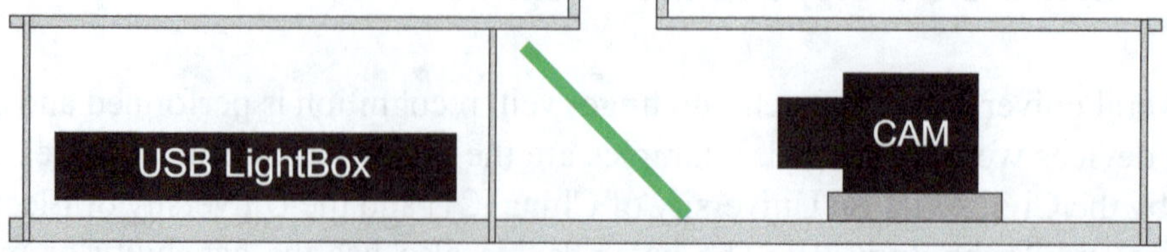

Fig. 2.2 Schematic cross section of the capture device

the finger is obtained in the captured image. This control loop is also necessary to cope with varying thicknesses along the finger and between various biometric data subjects. The benefit of this simple control loop can be seen in Fig. 2.3. It clearly shows the over- and underexposure in the non-regulated case.

Camera The camera used to capture the images is a BCi5 monochrome CMOS camera with firewire interface produced by C-Cam technologies. The camera has been fitted with a Pentax H1214-M machine vision lens with a focal length of 12 mm. This lens is fitted with a B+W 093 infrared filter which has a cutoff wavelength of 930 nm. The filter is used to block out any interfering visible light. The camera is used in 8-bit mode with a resolution of 1280 × 1024 pixels.

Mirror To minimise the height of the capture device, a mirror is used so the camera can be placed horizontally. An NT41-405 first surface mirror produced by Edmund Optics has been used for this purpose. The reason for choosing a first surface mirror is to avoid distortions in the captured image. A conventional mirror has its

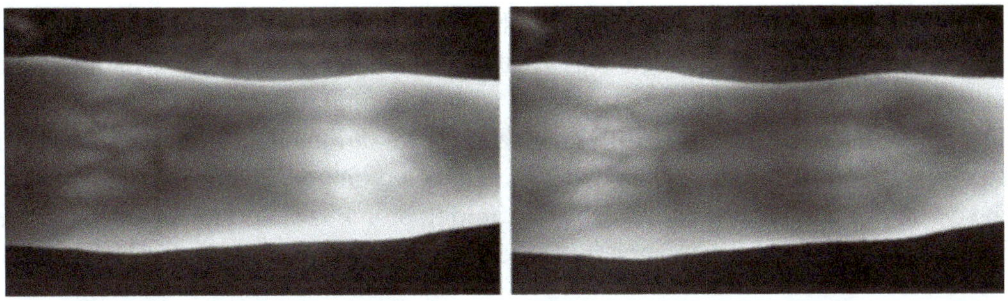

(a) Eight equal LED intensities (b) LED intensities regulated by control loop

Fig. 2.3 Benefit of the control loop to adjust the individual LED intensities

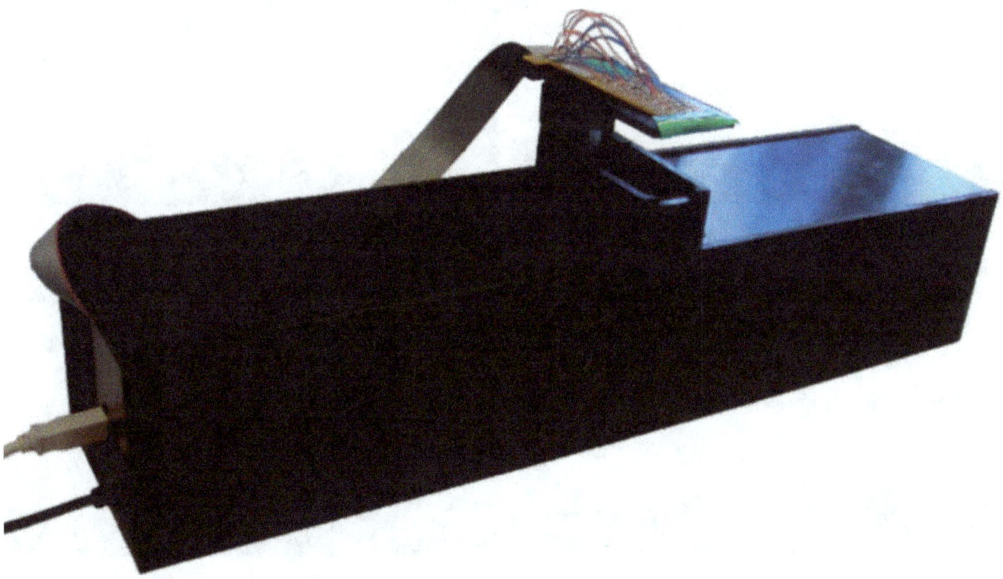

Fig. 2.4 Realised finger vascular pattern capture device

reflective layer protected by glass. The refractive indices of glass and air differ which means distortions will occur in the captured image. The final constructed capture device can be seen in Fig. 2.4.

2.4 Description of Dataset

The University of Twente Finger Vein Pattern (UTVP) dataset contains 1440 finger vascular pattern images in total which have been collected from 60 volunteering subjects at our university during the 2011–2012 academic year. Images were captured in two identical sessions with an average time-lapse of 15 days. For each data subject, the vascular pattern of the index, ring and middle finger of both hands has been collected twice at each session. This means that each individual finger has been captured four times in total. The captured images have a resolution of 672×380 pixels and have a pixel density of 126 pixels per centimetre (ppcm). The images are stored using the lossless 8-bit greyscale Portable Network Graphics (PNG) format. The percentage of male data subjects was 73%, and the percentage of right-handed data subjects was 87%. The dataset represents a young population with 82% of the data subjects falling in the age range of 19–30, and the remaining data subjects were older than this. A set of sample images from the collected dataset can be seen in Fig. 2.5. The quality of the collected images varies among biometric capture subjects, but the variation in quality of the images from the same biometric capture subject is small.

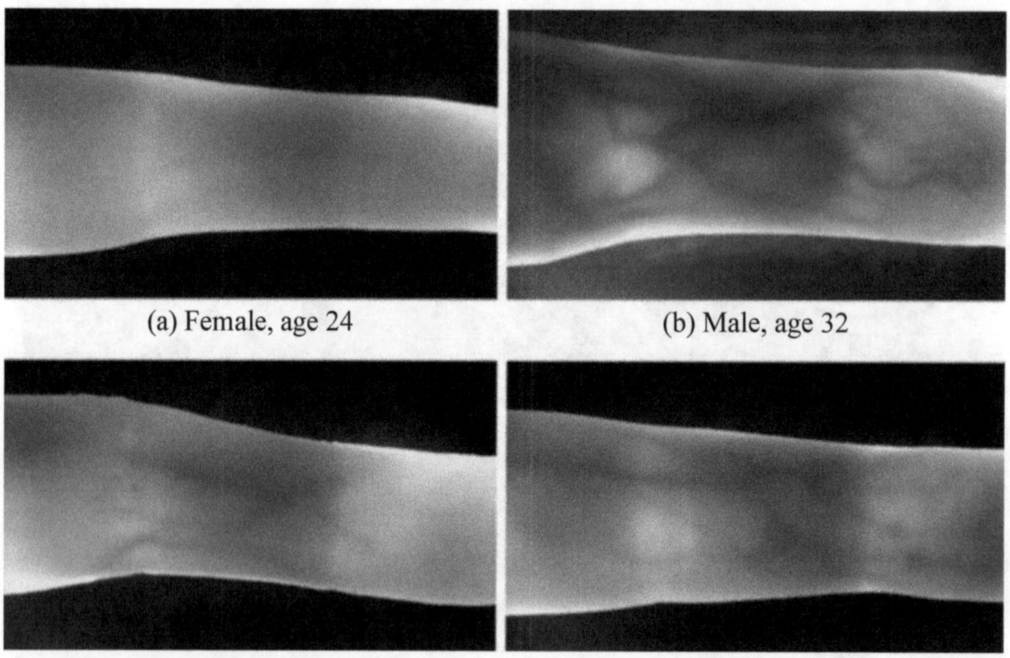

(a) Female, age 24 (b) Male, age 32

(c) Male, age 20 (d) Female, age 31

Fig. 2.5 Sample images of the left-hand ring finger from the collected dataset

The width of the visible blood vessels ranges from 4–20 pixels which, using a pixel density of 126 pixels per centimetre, corresponds to vessel widths of approximately 0.3–1.6 mm. The pixel density was determined by placing a piece of flat graph paper at exactly the same position as the finger and counting the number of pixels per centimetre in the recorded image. This resulted in a pixel density of 126 pixels per centimetre.

The UTVP dataset is available from the University of Twente by completing an online download request and license agreement, see [17].

2.5 Results

2.5.1 Performance Analysis

To illustrate and rank the quality of the collected dataset, the performance of a few published algorithms was evaluated. These algorithms have been applied to our collected dataset and the V4 finger vein database from the Peking University [12] which has been used as a reference. The performance of the algorithms is measured in terms of Equal Error Rate (EER). The experiments also investigate the merit of Adaptive Histogram Equalisation (AHE) as a preprocessing step. Each directory of the Peking dataset contains between four and eight images of the same finger. For the experiments only directories containing exactly eight images have been used, this accounts for 153 directories out of the available 200 directories. For this dataset, it is not known which fingers belong to the same subject.

For both datasets, 10% of the fingers have been used for tuning the various parameters of the algorithms. For the Peking dataset, the valid directories are sorted ascending by filename and the first 10% are used for parameter tuning. For our dataset, 10% of the *fingers* have been selected by taking the first finger of the first data subject, the second finger of the second data subject … the first finger of the seventh data subject. This method of selecting the training set has been chosen to get a larger variation in the quality of the vascular pattern images. The other 90% of both datasets have been used to determine the actual performance of the algorithms.

The exact number comparison trials done for both the parameter tuning and the actual determination of the performance are given in Table 2.1.

For all of these experiments, fingers were treated as identical individual biometric samples, for example, left-hand index fingers were compared with right-hand middle fingers. Two performance experiments are done per dataset, one with and one without adaptive histogram equalisation as preprocessing step. This preprocessing step is done using MATLAB's `adapthisteq()` function with the default parameters' set. The effect of applying an adaptive histogram equalisation to a vascular pattern image can be seen in Fig. 2.6.

To ensure that only image regions containing finger are compared with each other a binary mask is used. This mask is created by first determining the edges of the

Table 2.1 Number of mated and non-mated comparison trials performed

Dataset	# fingers	Mated	Non-mated
Parameter tuning			
Peking	15	420	6720
UTFVP	35	210	9520
Actual performance experiment			
Peking	138	3864	604,992
UTFVP	325	1950	842,400

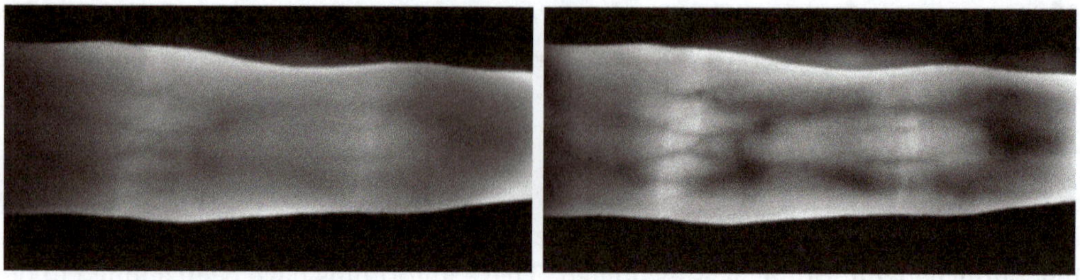

(a) Original image (b) Adaptive Histogram Equalisation

Fig. 2.6 Effect of Adaptive Histogram Equalisation

finger in the image using the method described by Lee et al. [8] and then filling in the area between these edges.

The edges detected in the previous step are used to normalise the image using the method described by Huang et al. [5]. This method tries to estimate a rotation and a translation based on the detected finger edges. After these parameters have been estimated, they are used to define an affine image transformation which aligns the finger to the centre of the image. This affine transformation is also applied to the binary mask.

The output of each of the algorithms, except the normalised cross-correlation, is a binary template indicating the position of a blood vessel. Two binary templates are compared with each other by using the method described by Miura et al. [10]. An incidental side effect of using the binary finger region mask is that the shape of the finger is also indirectly taken into account when comparing two templates.

The final verification results are shown in Table 2.2 which indicates that our dataset performs significantly better in all cases and that adaptive histogram equalisation is beneficial in most of the cases. The results presented here have been independently replicated by Vanoni et al. [20].

The two methods proposed by Miura et al. have been tested by other researchers using their own collected datasets. One of them is Huang et al. [5] who has achieved an EER of 2.8% for the maximum curvature method and an EER of 5% for the repeated line tracking method. Another one is Choi et al. [2] who have achieved an EER of 3.6% for the maximum curvature method. The last one is Kumar and Zhou [7] who achieved an EER of 8.3% for the repeated line tracking method and

Table 2.2 Performance expressed in terms of EER (%) of several algorithms for both datasets, both with and without Adaptive Histogram Equalisation (AHE) as a preprocessing step

	EER (%)					
	Original paper	Best reported	Peking		UTFVP	
			No AHE	With AHE	No AHE	With AHE
Normalised cross-correlation[a]	0.0	–	14.7	9.8	3.1	1.9
Maximum curvature[b]	0.0	2.7[e]	1.2	1.3	0.4	0.4
Repeated line tracking[c]	0.2	5.0[f]	6.8	5.9	0.9	1.2
Principal curvature[d]	0.4	–	2.7	2.2	0.8	0.4
Wide line detector[e]	0.9	–	4.7	2.7	1.5	0.9

[a] See [6]
[b] See [11]
[c] See [10]
[d] See [2]
[e] See [5]
[f] See [7]

achieved an EER of 2.7% for the maximum curvature method. The mentioned EERs from Kumar and Zhou are the average EER of the middle and index fingers. The best reported performance figures for these two methods are mentioned in Table 2.2 as well. Our MATLAB implementation of these algorithms can be found in [16].

2.6 Next-Generation Finger Vein Scanner

2.6.1 Overview

Since the design of the described finger vein scanner, we developed a second version of the finger vein scanner with new capabilities, see Fig. 2.7 [14]. The scanner is much more compact and is built using cheaper components: it uses Raspberry Pi processing boards and cameras. This new scanner has been designed in such a way as to support further research in various ways. It supports multiple NIR LED strips that can be positioned in a semicircle from 0° to 180°. It also supports three cameras, thus allowing for 3D finger vein reconstruction. Currently, we are investigating optimal illumination and settings of the cameras and 3D finger vein reconstruction.

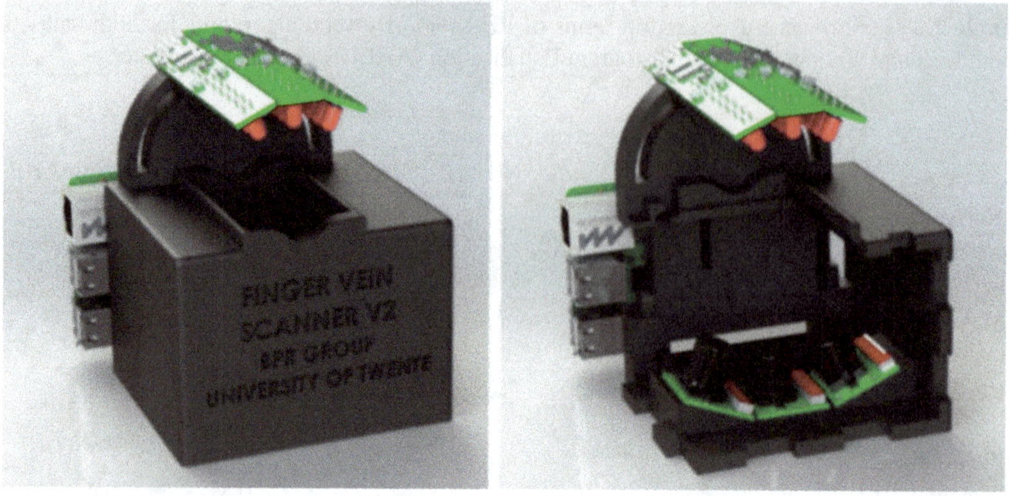

Fig. 2.7 Second-generation finger vein scanner of the University of Twente. It has three cameras for 3D recordings and multiple adjustable LED strips

2.6.2 *Illumination Control*

The setup with multiple LED strips that can be rotated up to 180° allows for various illumination methods. It supports both transmission and side illumination. Reflection is not supported, however. Care was taken to position the LED strip with respect to the finger position and the opening for the finger with below it the infrared filter, such that as little as possible infrared light can "leak" around the finger. The new setup inherited the advanced control over the intensity of each individual LED from the previous version of the scanner, enabling a more homogeneous illumination and adjustment to the properties of the finger (e.g. thick and thin fingers). In Fig. 2.8, a comparison is made between images recorded using the first- and second-generation finger vein scanner of the University of Twente. The images of the new scanner show much less overexposure at the boundaries of the fingers.

We are currently investigating various ways to optimise illumination ranging from illumination from different angles and multiple LED strips to refined control of the LED intensities and combination of multiple images with different illumination.

2.6.3 *3D Reconstruction*

The advantage of 3D recordings is that if fingers are slightly rotated, causing a deformation of the finger vein pattern, this deformation can be compensated for. Another possibility is direct comparison of 3D finger vein patterns. Using the three cameras in the new scanner, we used stereo reconstruction to recover the 3D vein patterns. A preliminary result of 3D finger vein reconstruction using this second-generation finger vein scanner is shown in Fig. 2.9 [1].

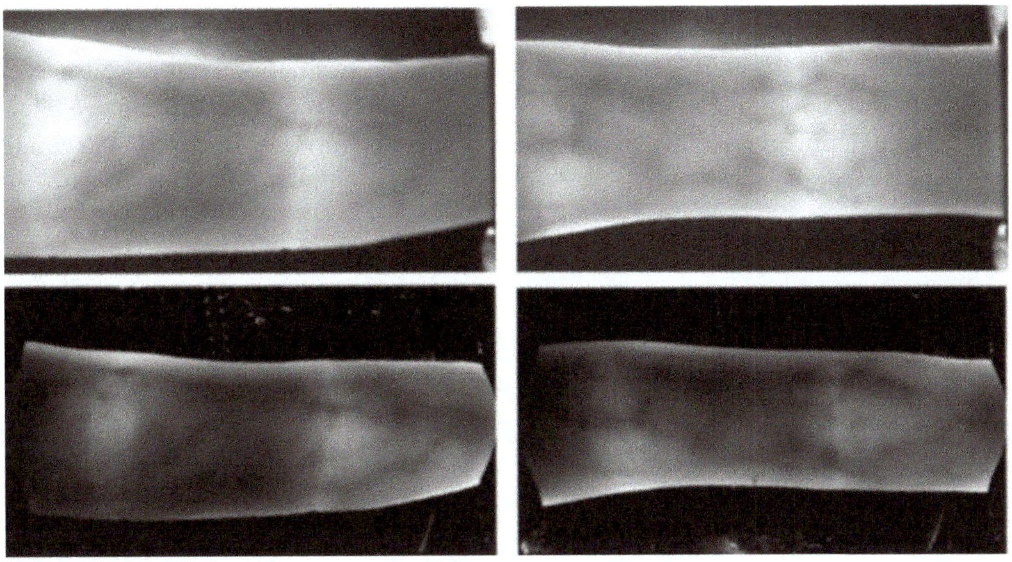

Fig. 2.8 Comparison between images of the same fingers captured by the first (top)- and second (bottom)-generation finger vein scanners. The images captured by the new scanner show less overexposure near the boundaries of the fingers

Fig. 2.9 Preliminary 3D finger vein reconstruction using new vein scanner

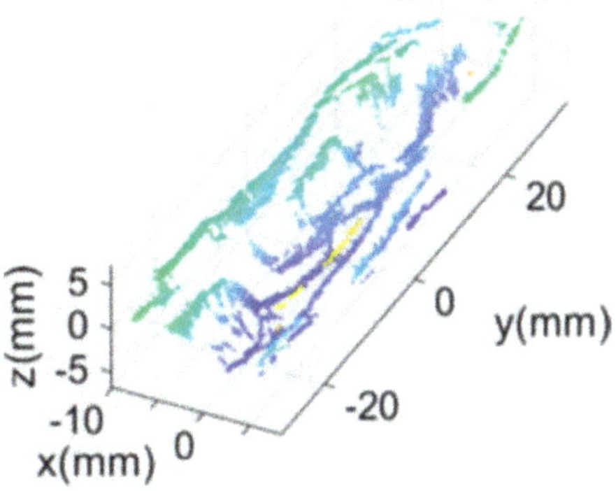

Careful observation shows that the veins at the sides of the fingers are somewhat above the veins in the middle of the finger, i.e. they follow the curvature of the surface of the finger. This is to be expected, because only the veins at the surface of the finger can be visualised using this technique.

2.7 Conclusions

A finger vascular pattern dataset containing 1440 high-quality images is presented to the research community. Despite the low number of 60 data subjects which participated, the major contribution of this dataset is the addition of demographic data such as gender, age, and handedness. Another contribution is the high quality of the captured images and the known pixel density of the images. Furthermore, the data is collected in two identical sessions with a time lapse of approximately 2 weeks. Because of the high quality of the captured images, our dataset can pave the way for the research of high-security cooperative applications. The performance evaluation using existing algorithms has shown that equal error rates down to 0.4% can be achieved by using our dataset.

2.8 Future Work

The use of the vascular pattern of the finger as a biometric is still not as mature as other biometric traits such as 2D face recognition. To reach an equal maturity, more research is needed.

Future research should include the collection of larger datasets including 3D data, together with demographic data of the data subjects. These larger datasets will enable researchers to report performance figures with a higher confidence. It will also enable the research of factors such as age, gender and ethnicity on the performance. The research community would also greatly benefit from standardised testing methods and datasets.

The biometric performance can further be improved by fusing other finger traits such as traditional fingerprints, the crease pattern of the finger and the shape of the finger. An advantage of finger shape is that it is already present in the captured image.

The current control loop which adjusts the LED intensities is still rather crude and leaves space for further improvements in terms of speed and image intensity uniformity. Preliminary results have shown that the relation between the intensity in the captured image and the intensity of the LEDs is as good as linear.

Finally, 3D scanning techniques allow compensation of distortions of the finger vein pattern caused by rotation of the finger. Also, direct 3D finger vein comparison is an interesting subject for further research.

References

1. Bunda S (2018) 3D point cloud reconstruction based on the finger vascular pattern. Bachelor's thesis, University of Twente, Netherlands
2. Choi J, Song W, Kim T, Lee S, Kim H (2009) Finger vein extraction using gradient normalization and principal curvature. In: Niel KS, Fofi D (eds) Image processing: machine vision applications II, SPIE-IS&T Electronic Imaging, vol 7251. SPIE. https://doi.org/10.1117/12.810458
3. Hitachi Ltd. (2018) Finger vein reader. http://www.hitachi.co.jp/products/it/veinid/global/products/embeddeddevicesr.html
4. Hitachi Ltd. (2018) USB finger vein biometric authentication unit. http://www.hitachi.co.jp/products/it/veinid/global/products/embeddeddevicesu.html
5. Huang B, Dai Y, Li R, Tang D, Li W (2010) Finger-vein authentication based on wide line detector and pattern normalization. In: 20th International conference on pattern recognition, pp 1269–1272. https://doi.org/10.1109/ICPR.2010.316
6. Kono M, Ueki H, Umemura S (2002) Near-infrared finger vein patterns for personal identification. Appl Opt 41(35):7429–7436. https://doi.org/10.1364/AO.41.007429

7. Kumar A, Zhou Y (2012) Human identification using finger images. IEEE Trans Image Process 21(4):2228–2244. https://doi.org/10.1109/TIP.2011.2171697
8. Lee E, Lee H, Park K (2009) Finger vein recognition using minutia-based alignment and local binary pattern-based feature extraction. Int J Imaging Syst Technol 19(3):179–186. https://doi.org/10.1002/ima.20193
9. Ma Z, Fang L, Duan J, Xie S, Wang Z (2016) Personal identification based on finger vein and contour point clouds matching. In: IEEE International conference on mechatronics and automation, pp 1983–1988
10. Miura N, Nagasaka A, Miyatake T (2004) Feature extraction of finger vein patterns based on iterative line tracking and its application to personal identification. Syst Comput Jpn 35:61–71. https://doi.org/10.1002/scj.v35:7
11. Miura N, Nagasaka A, Miyatake T (2005) Extraction of finger-vein patterns using maximum curvature points in image profiles. In: IAPR conference on machine vision applications, vol 9, pp 347–350. http://b2.cvl.iis.u-tokyo.ac.jp/mva/proceedings/CommemorativeDVD/2005/papers/2005347.pdf
12. Peking University (2013) PKU finger vein database. http://rate.pku.edu.cn
13. Raghavendra R, Raja KB, Surbiryala J, Busch C (2014) A low-cost multimodal biometric sensor to capture finger vein and fingerprint. In: IEEE International joint conference on biometrics, pp 1–7. https://doi.org/10.1109/BTAS.2014.6996225
14. Rozendal S (2017) Redesign of a finger vein scanner. Bachelor's thesis, University of Twente, Netherlands
15. Sony Corporation (2009) Sony develops compact sized, high speed, high accuracy finger vein authentication technology dubbed "mofiria". https://www.sony.net/SonyInfo/News/Press/200902/09-016E/index.html
16. Ton B (2012, 2017) MATLAB implementation of Miura et al. vein extraction methods. University of Twente, Netherlands. https://www.mathworks.com/matlabcentral/fileexchange/35716-miura-et-al-vein-extraction-methods
17. Ton B, Veldhuis R (2012) University of Twente Finger Vascular Pattern (UTFVP) dataset. https://www.utwente.nl/en/eemcs/ds/downloads/utfvp/
18. Ton BT (2012) Vascular pattern of the finger: biometric of the future? sensor design, data collection and performance verification. Master's thesis, University of Twente
19. Ton BT, Veldhuis RNJ (2013) A high quality finger vascular pattern dataset collected using a custom designed capturing device. In: 2013 International conference on biometrics (ICB), pp 1–5. https://doi.org/10.1109/ICB.2013.6612966
20. Vanoni M, Tome P, Shafey LE, Marcel S (2014) Cross-database evaluation using an open finger vein sensor. In: Workshop on biometric measurements and systems for security and medical applications, pp 30–35. https://doi.org/10.1109/BIOMS.2014.6951532
21. Yang J, Shi Y, Yang J (2011) Personal identification based on finger-vein features. Comput Hum Behav 27:1565–1570

Chapter 3
OpenVein—An Open-Source Modular Multipurpose Finger Vein Scanner Design

Christof Kauba, Bernhard Prommegger and Andreas Uhl

Abstract One of the main prerequisites in finger vein research is the availability of comprehensive, available finger vein datasets. In order to capture such datasets, a biometric scanner device tailored to capture the vascular patterns is essential. A sophisticated scanner design is the key to achieve a good image quality, robustness against external influences and finally to arrive at a competitive recognition performance. In this chapter, a fully open-source, modular and multipurpose finger vein scanner design is proposed. Two novel finger vein scanners are derived from this basic design. Both are able to capture reflected light and light transmission illuminated images from the dorsal as well as the palmar side. Three fingers are captured at once. The first scanner is based on widely used near-infrared LEDs as its light source, the second one on near-infrared laser modules. Despite their advantages in touchless operation, near-infrared laser modules have hardly been used in finger vein recognition so far. Our scanner design has proven to accomplish an excellent recognition performance using common finger vein recognition schemes. All details regarding the two scanner devices, including technical drawings of all parts, models of the 3D printed parts, control board schematics, the microcontroller firmware, the capturing software, parts list as well as assembly and setup instructions, are available free of charge for research purposes. This should facilitate interested researchers to rebuild such a scanner device for capturing finger vein data on their own.

Keywords Finger vein scanner · Open-source biometric sensor device · Light transmission · Reflected light · Open finger vein dataset · Dorsal · Palmar · Scanner assembly details

---

C. Kauba (✉) · B. Prommegger · A. Uhl
Department of Computer Sciences, University of Salzburg, Jakob-Haringer-Str. 2, 5020 Salzburg, Austria
e-mail: ckauba@cs.sbg.ac.at

B. Prommegger
e-mail: bprommeg@cs.sbg.ac.at

A. Uhl
e-mail: uhl@cs.sbg.ac.at

A. Uhl et al. (eds.), *Handbook of Vascular Biometrics*, Advances in Computer Vision and Pattern Recognition, https://doi.org/10.1007/978-3-030-27731-4_3

3.1 Introduction

Vascular pattern based biometrics, as a new and emerging biometric trait, deals with the patterns formed by the blood vessels located inside the human body, i.e. it is an internal biometric trait. These vascular patterns are not visible to the naked eye, thus a specifically designed capturing device, usually denoted as biometric scanner or biometric sensor, is necessary to sample this biometric [16]. The haemoglobin contained in the blood flowing through the vessels has a higher light absorption coefficient within the near-infrared (NIR) spectrum than the surrounding tissue. Hence, the vascular patterns can be rendered visible as dark lines in the captured images with the help of NIR illumination and NIR-sensitive cameras but not by using commodity off-the-shelf digital cameras as they usually have a built-in NIR blocking filter. The most common body parts considered include fingers [7, 27, 28, 32, 39], hands [6, 8, 36, 37, 42] and also wrists [21]. In the following, we will focus on the recognition of vascular patterns inside the human fingers, commonly denoted as finger vein recognition.

Finger vein scanner devices are already equipped in commercial products, like automated teller machines (ATMs) in Japan [10], for authentication of bank customers in Poland [9], for securing online banking transactions at home in the UK [29] and as an alternative to fingerprint-based authentication systems in general. Almost all commercial-off-the-shelf (COTS) finger vein scanner devices do not permit access to the captured finger vein images. Instead, they only provide a biometric template, encoded in a proprietary format defined by the manufacturer of the scanner device, which can only be used within the software framework provided by the manufacturer. This situation leads to a vendor lock-in, which is not desired for the operator. Moreover, it makes recognition performance evaluations possible, but these biometric templates do neither allow for the development of biometric template protection and biometric workload reduction schemes (see Chap. 12) nor enable a systematic evaluation of the template's properties in regards to external influences and changes in the vein pattern (robustness evaluation). Hence, these templates and the COTS scanners are only of little use in biometric research.

An important requirement for doing research on any biometric trait is the availability of comprehensive datasets. However, the number of finger vein datasets available to the research community is limited and there is still a lack of large, available finger vein databases. In order to establish a dataset that is of value for research purposes, a finger vein scanner that provides access to the raw vein images is essential. The design of such a scanner device is a crucial point if it comes to image quality, robustness against external influences, user convenience and consequently to a good recognition performance. Only a specifically designed finger vein scanner is able to provide high-quality vein images enabling a competitive recognition performance. The main contribution of this chapter is our proposed design of two open-source, multipurpose finger vein scanners. Both scanners are based on the same modular design. They are one of the first finger vein scanners (besides the scanner proposed by Raghavendra et al. in [26]) that are able to capture three fingers at once in order to speed up the data acquisition process and to minimise longitudinal pose variations (see [23] for an in-depth discussion of the problems due to longitudinal finger rotation). Both are equipped with a light transmission (also called transillumination) as well as a reflected light illuminator allowing to capture light transmission and reflected light images. Hence, these scanners are the first ones that are able to capture both reflected light and light transmission images. Both scanners capture high-resolution and high-quality finger vein images providing a high recognition performance. Furthermore, both of the mainly used views of the finger, dorsal and palmar, can be captured. The two scanners only differ in the type of transillumination light source: the first scanner utilises NIR light-emitting diodes (LEDs) while the second one is based on NIR laser modules. NIR laser modules are not common in finger vein recognition despite the advantages they offer. They enable an increased range of vertical finger movement while preserving a good image contrast and quality compared to LEDs which is especially important if touchless operation is desired.

Our proposed scanner design is fully open source. All of the housing parts and mounting brackets are either 3D-printed or laser-cut plywood parts and can be reproduced with low expenditure. While this chapter covers all the important design key points and describes each of the scanner parts, all technical details of the scanner together with detailed assembly and setup instructions are available in a public repository. This includes part lists, data sheets of the individual parts, technical drawings of the housing parts, models of the 3D printed parts, the schematics and board layout of the illumination controller, the firmware of the illumination controller and the capturing software. By open sourcing all details of our proposed scanner design, other researchers working in the field of finger vein biometrics can benefit from our design. They can get and/or make all the parts needed to construct a finger vein scanner based on our design, follow the instructions and assemble the scanner on their own which enables them to capture high-quality finger vein images and facilitate their own research. The use of our proposed scanner design and the reproduction of the finger vein scanner itself is free of charge for research purposes. The modular design of the scanner allows to exchange, modify and improve the individual parts easily. With the help of other researchers we are confident that our scanner design will continue to improve over time.

The second advantage that comes with a fully open-source scanner design is the ability to establish a large, publicly available finger vein dataset. We already established a finger vein dataset captured using the two scanners based on our design which is available for research purposes [34]. This dataset confirms the decent recognition performance that can be achieved using a scanner based on our design. For more details, see [12, 13]. Together with other researchers and research institutions, we plan to extend this dataset in order to establish a comprehensive, publicly available finger vein dataset for research purposes. Researchers already owning a scanner based on our design and interested in a collaboration can contribute to the dataset by providing us their captured finger vein samples. Such an extensive, collaborative dataset will stimulate the research on finger vein biometrics. Moreover, large finger vein datasets are vital in order to develop and test finger vein indexing schemes, template protection schemes and runtime efficient identification schemes.

The rest of this chapter is organised as follows: Sect. 3.2 gives an overview on the basic design principles of finger vein scanners, followed by a review of commercial finger vein scanners and related research on finger vein scanners as well as datasets. Section 3.3 discusses all important details and individual parts of our proposed finger vein scanner design. Section 3.4 presents our open finger vein dataset captured using the scanners built according to our design. Section 3.5 concludes this chapter together with an outlook on future work, especially on further improving the scanner design and extending our open finger vein dataset.

3.2 Finger Vein Scanners

Finger vein recognition belongs to vascular pattern based biometrics. As the name suggests, these biometrics are based on the vascular pattern, formed by the blood vessel structure inside the human body. Finger vein recognition deals with the vascular pattern inside the human fingers. This pattern has to be made visible and captured by a suitable biometric scanner device in order to enable biometric recognition. The deoxinated haemoglobin in the blood flowing through the blood vessels absorbs light within the NIR spectrum while the surrounding tissue has a much lower light absorption coefficient within that spectrum. Thus, the vascular pattern can be rendered visible with the help of an NIR light source in combination with an NIR-sensitive image sensor.

Consequently, the most important parts of a finger vein scanner are an NIR light source and an NIR-sensitive image sensor or camera. The NIR light source usually consists of NIR LEDs (light-emitting diodes) with a light emission peak wavelength between 750 and 950 nm. In addition to the NIR camera and the NIR light source, either an NIR pass-through filter or an optically opaque box to reduce the influence of ambient light is beneficial. To assist the capture subject in positioning of the finger, most finger vein scanners contain some kind of finger positioning support or finger guide unless they are meant for fully touchless operation.

3.2.1 *Light Source Positioning*

Two types of illumination are distinguished, based on the relative positioning of the image sensor, the finger and the illuminator: light transmission, also called transillumination and reflected light. Figure 3.1 shows both variants.

Light transmission: the image sensor and the illuminator are placed on opposite sides of the finger. The light penetrates the skin on the side of the finger next to the illuminator, runs through the finger tissue, where it gets reflected, refracted, dispersed, scattered and absorbed. A fraction of the emitted light emerges on the opposite side of the finger and gets captured by the image sensor. As the light has to travel through the whole finger, higher light intensities are needed compared to reflected light, thus

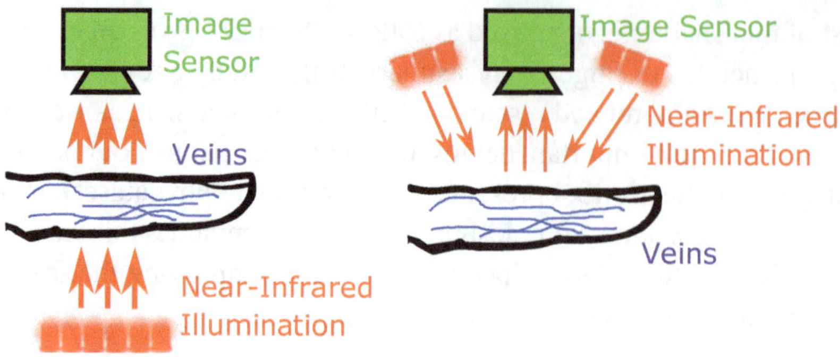

Fig. 3.1 Light source and image sensor positioning, left: light transmission, right: reflected light. Reflected light enables smaller scanner devices while light transmission renders more details of the vascular pattern visible due to the higher penetration depth inside the finger tissue

leading to higher power consumption. Due to the placement of the illuminator and the image sensor opposite to each other, the scanner devices are bigger compared to reflected light ones. Note that the positioning of the image sensor and the illuminator perpendicular to each other (in an angle of 90°) is sometimes called light dispersion. We consider this still as light transmission as it is just a kind of light transmission caused due to scattering and refraction. The light travels sideways through the finger and the fraction of the light which is emitted on the image sensor side of the finger gets captured.

Reflected light: the image sensor and the illuminator are placed on the same side of the finger, either dorsal or palmar. The light originates from the illuminator, a small part gets reflected directly at the finger's surface, the remaining part penetrates the skin and tissue and gets reflected, refracted and scattered there. The fraction of the light emerging at the same side of the finger is captured by the image sensor. Reflected light based scanners need less light intensity. Thus, they have a lower power consumption and can be built in a smaller manner as the light source and image sensor are positioned next to each other. However, the penetration depth of the light is lower than for light transmission, and thus less details of the vascular patterns become visible. Nevertheless, in finger vein recognition, light transmission is used almost exclusively.

3.2.2 *Two Main Perspectives of the Finger—Dorsal and Palmar*

The main perspectives or views from which the finger is captured are dorsal and palmar (also called ventral). Dorsal images are taken from the back or dorsal side of the hand while palmar images are taken from the palm or bottom side of the hand. Figure 3.2 shows both capturing perspectives. Of course there are several more views around the finger that could be captured like the side views, but finger vein

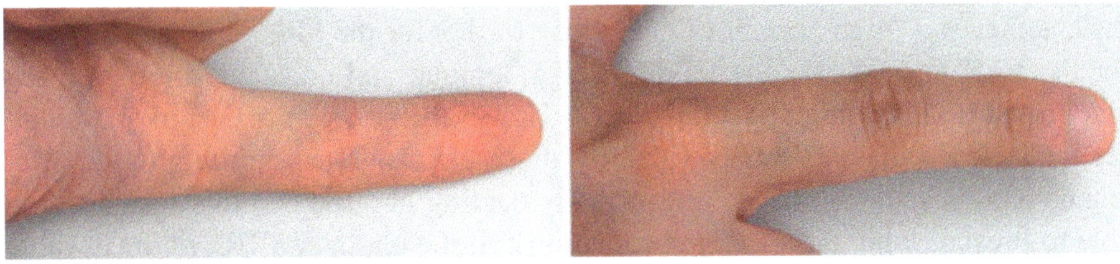

Fig. 3.2 Two main perspectives on the finger. Left: palmar view, right: dorsal view

recognition mainly deals with palmar images, with some exceptions where the dorsal view is used.

3.2.3 Commercial Finger Vein Scanners

Here we present some common COTS finger vein scanners. As in finger vein recognition, light transmission in combination with palmar images is used almost exclusively, so all COTS scanners are based on this set-up as well (some COTS scanners have the light source and the camera arranged perpendicular to each other which the manufacturers call light dispersion). As motivated in the introduction, the COTS scanners do not provide access to the captured vein images but only output a template encoded in a proprietary format. Figure 3.3 shows some widely used COTS finger vein scanners. The major two companies providing finger vein authentication solutions are Hitachi Ltd. and Mofiria Ltd. Their technologies are patented and non-disclosed. Hence, not many details are known about these scanners, except that they are based on the light transmission principle and capture palmar images. The M2-FingerVein™ reader [52] is basically a rebranded version of the original Hitachi H-1 (or PCT-KCUA011) USB finger vein scanner [51]. According to the M2SYS website, it "scans the inner surface of the finger", is "resistant to criminal temper-

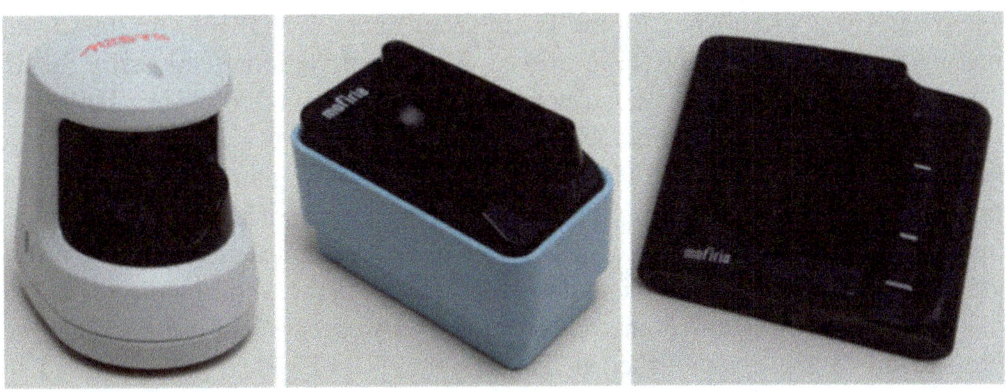

Fig. 3.3 COTS finger vein scanners, from left to right: M2SYS M2-FingerVein™ reader, Mofiria FVA-U4ST, Mofiria FVA-U3SX

ing", achieves a "high accuracy", "less than 0.01% for the FRR, less than 0.0001% for the FAR and 0% for the FTE", uses a "unique and constant" biometric trait and provides "fast authentication speed". However, the scanner design and details are undisclosed making it hard to verify those claims. The scanner provides "fast authentication speed" indeed but especially bearing in mind that this scanner is not able to prevent longitudinal finger rotation [23], the claimed FRR and FAR values are doubtful. Moreover, it has been shown that commercial scanners are susceptible to presentation attacks [30], hence the claim "resistant to criminal tempering" might only refer to tempering with the scanner hardware and authentication software. The Mofiria FVA-U3SX [57] and the FVA-U4ST [58] are based on Mofiria's "unique reflective dispersion method" and an "automatic finger position adjustment ensures both comfortable usability and high accuracy authentication without firmly fixing the finger position on the unit" according to their respective data sheets. Both are small, fast and comfortable USB-powered finger vein scanners that provide two enrolment methods. The FVA-U3SX has an electrostatic sensor to detect the presence of the finger on the scanner. Note the compact size of all the commercial scanners and the semi- or full-open scanner housing. Scanners built in an open manner have been shown to increase the capture subjects' acceptance and convenience.

3.2.4 Finger Vein Prototype Scanners and Datasets in Research

Due to the fact that almost all COTS finger vein scanners do not provide access to the raw finger vein images and that the datasets established by the commercial companies are non-disclosed, researchers began to construct their own finger vein scanners and established several finger vein datasets. Table 3.1 gives an overview of several available as well as unpublished finger vein datasets in chronological order. It lists the number of subjects and fingers per subject that were captured, the total number of images contained in the dataset, the number of capturing sessions, the image resolution and the scanner used to capture the images. The first publicly available finger vein dataset was established by the Peking University (PKU) [11] in 2008 using their own prototype scanner (*PKU Proto*). The Seoul National University (SNU) [15] established the first non-contact finger vein dataset in 2009. They built their own touchless prototype scanner (*SNU Proto*). The dataset was captured using two different scanners, an LED and a laser-based one. The Norwegian Biometrics Laboratory collected the GUC45 [5], a multi-modal database comprising finger vein, finger knuckle and fingerprint images using their two prototype scanners (*GUC Proto 1* and *GUC Proto* 2) in 2009. This database is only available semi-publicly, i.e. that visitors at the Norwegian Biometrics Laboratory can access and use the database. The second database established in 2009 is the THU-FVFDT [40] provided by the University of Tsinghua, captured using their self-designed prototype scanner (*Tsinghua Proto*). It contains finger vein as well as finger dorsal texture images. In 2010, the SDUMLA-HMT [41], a multi-modal biometric database including finger

Table 3.1 Finger vein datasets acquired for research purposes

Name	Dors/palm	Avail.	Subjects	Fingers	Images	Sessions	Year	Scanner
PKU [11]	Palmar	Yes	5208	4	50,700	1	2008	PKU Proto
SNU-LP-FV [15]	Palmar	No	10	1	200	1	2009	SNU Proto
GUC45 [5]	Palmar	Semi	45	10	10080	12	2009	GUC Proto 1/2
THU-FVFDT [40]	Palmar	Yes	610	2	6540	2	2009	Tsinghua Proto
SDUMLA-HMT [41]	Palmar	Yes	106	6	3816	1	2010	Wuhan Proto
HKPU-FID [16]	Palmar	Yes	156	4	6264	2	2011	HKPU Proto
KTDeaduk-FV [17]	Palmar	No	30	8	2400	1	2011	KTDeaduk Proto
S-EMB-Laser-FV [18]	Palmar	No	100	6	6000	1	2012	Shandong EL Proto
UTFVP [32]	Palmar	Yes	60	6	1440	2	2013	Twente Proto
MMCBNU_6000 [19]	Palmar	Yes	100	6	6000	1	2013	Chonbuk Proto
CFVD [43]	Palmar	Yes	13	6	1345	2	2013	Shandong Proto
Shandong. Univ [38]	Palmar	No	34	6	4080	2	2013	Wuhan Proto
FV-USM [1]	Palmar	Yes	123	4	5940	2	2013	Sains Proto
VERA FV-Spoof [30]	Palmar	Yes	110	2	440	2	2014	Twente Proto
GUC-FPFV-DB [25]	Palmar	No	41	6*	1500	1	2014	GUC-FPFV Proto
GUC-Dors-FV-DB [24]	Dorsal	Semi	125	4	5000	1	2015	GUC-Dors Proto
PMMDB-FV [33]	Dorsal	Yes	20	4	240	1	2017	PLUSVein-V2
PLUSVein-FV3 [12]	Dorsal	Yes	60	6	3600	1	2018	PLUS OpenVein

vein images, was released by the University of Shandong. They utilised a custom prototype scanner provided by the University of Wuhan (*Wuhan Proto*) during their finger vein data collection. In 2011, the HKPU finger vein database [16] captured using their own prototype scanner (*HKPU Proto*) was released by the Hong Kong Polytechnical University. The KTDeaduk-FV finger vein database [17] was collected by the KT Daeduk Research Center in Korea in cooperation with the Korea Science Academy of KAIST in 2011 too. This database was captured with their own prototype scanner (*KTDeaduk Proto*). It has not been published so far. The Shandong University acquired a finger vein dataset using their prototype embedded finger vein scanner (*Shandong EL Proto*). This dataset has not been published though. In 2013, several finger vein databases have been established. The University of Twente published the UTFVP finger vein database [32], captured with the help of their prototype scanner (*Twente Proto*). The Chonbuk University in South Korea used their prototype scanner (*Chonbuk Proto*) to establish the MMCBNU_6000 finger vein database [19]. The Shandon University released the CFVD [43], the first reflected light finger vein database acquired using their prototype scanner (*Shandong Proto*). The Shandong University established a second finger vein database [38] using a prototype scanner provided by the University of Wuhan (*Wuhan Proto*) but did not make this database available. The FV-USM database [1] published by the University of Sains in Malaysia was acquired using their custom-designed scanner (*Sains Proto*) and also released in 2013. In 2014, the Idiap Research Institute in Switzerland established the first finger vein spoofing attack database, VERA Finger Vein Spoofing [30] using the same scanner design as it has been used to capture the UTFVP (*Twente Proto*). The Norwegian Biometrics Laboratory designed another finger vein scanner prototype (*GUC-FPFV Proto*), able to capture fingerprint and finger vein images at the same time. In 2014, they captured the GUC-FPFV-DB [25] but they did not make it available * in Table 3.1 indicates that for most but not for all subjects 6 fingers have been captured as there are subjects with less than 6 captured fingers. In 2015, the Norwegian Biometrics Laboratory designed another finger vein scanner which captures dorsal images (*GUC-Dors Proto*) and created the first dorsal finger vein database [24]. Again they did not fully release this database for the research community. It is only semi-public, i.e. available for visitors at the Norwegian Biometrics Laboratory. In 2017, together with our partners from the PROTECT project the team at PLUS (Paris Lodron University of Salzburg) established a multi-modal biometric database PMMDB [33]. Among other biometric traits, this database contains dorsal finger vein images captured with the predecessor of our proposed scanner design (*PLUSVein-V2*), and is publicly available. Our most recent finger vein database is the PLUSVein-FV3 [12], captured using the scanner design presented in this chapter (*PLUS OpenVein*). This database is publicly available as well. Note that except the GUC-Dors-FV-DB [24] established by the Norwegian Biometrics Laboratory, the PMMDB-FV [33] and the PLUSVein-FV3 dataset [12], which have been captured by members of PLUS, all finger vein datasets are palmar ones. Figure 3.4 shows some example images for the available finger vein datasets (except for PKU and CFVD). We will not go into further details about the databases but focus on the corresponding scanner devices in the following.

Table 3.2 gives some details about the scanners that were used to acquire the finger vein databases listed in Table 3.1, including the equipped camera, focal length of the lens (column: lens), additional filter, the illuminator peak wavelength (column: illumin., note that all illuminators except the one of the *SNU Proto*, the *Shandong EL Proto* and the *PLUS OpenVein* are LED based) as well as if the illuminator is a reflected light or light transmission type (column: r/t) as far as the information is available for the respective finger vein scanner device (– in the table indicates that this information is not available). All of the listed finger vein scanners except the *Shandong Proto* and our proposed scanner *PLUS OpenVein* (which is able to use both reflected light as well as light transmission) use light transmission to capture the images. The *PKU Proto* scanner consists of a 1/3-in. greyscale CMOS camera and an advanced illumination control system using an LED-based illuminator. Apart

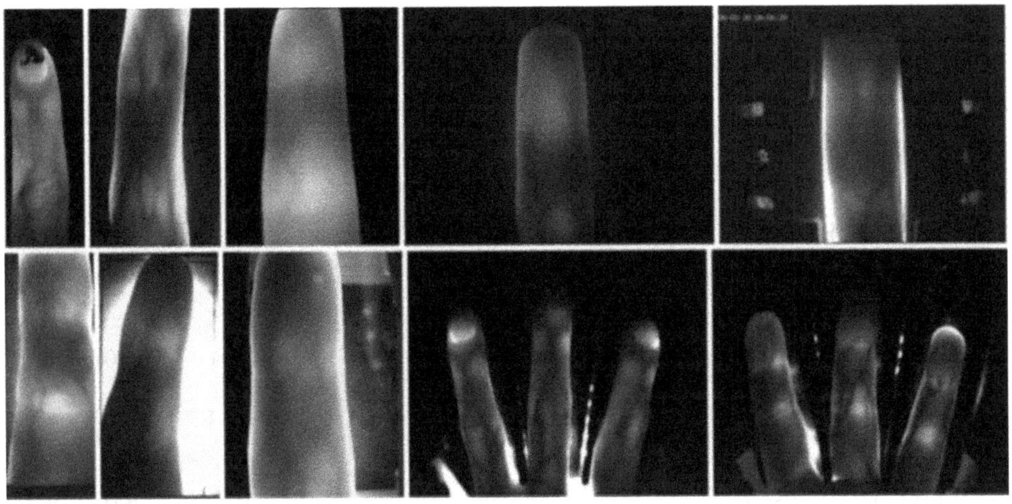

Fig. 3.4 Example images from several available finger vein datasets, left-to-right, top-to-bottom row (all images have been rotated such that the finger is in vertical position pointing upwards): PMMDB-FV, UTFVP, MMCBNU_6000, FV-USM, THU-FVFDT, VERA FV-Spoofing, HKPU-FID, SDUMLA-HMT, PLUSVein-FV3 dorsal, PLUSVein-FV3 palmar

from those details there is no additional information about the camera, the LEDs or the equipped infrared filter available. There are two variants of the touchless scanner prototype developed by the Seoul National University, *SNU Proto*. This touchless scanner should prevent the cross-contamination of skin diseases. The first one is based on conventional 850 nm LEDs as light source, the second one is based on an 830 nm NIR laser. The NIR lasers are manufactured by Lasiris Laser in StokerYale, Canada. A laser line generator lens (E43-475 from Edmund optics in Singapore) with a fixed pan angle is added in order to generate a line laser from the spot laser. This should enable a uniform illumination along the finger. Both scanners are based on light transmission and use a GF 038B NIR CCD Camera from ALLIED Vision Technologies, Germany. The camera is equipped with an additional IR-pass filter. The first two scanner prototypes developed by the Norwegian Biometrics Laboratory in 2009, *GUC Proto* 1 and *GUC Proto* 2 both use a CCD camera in combination with an NIR-pass filter. 850 nm LEDs and 940 nm LEDs are used in the first and second scanners, respectively. Besides this basic information, also the arrangement of the LEDs, their view range and the physical design of the scanners are described in the respective papers. The *Tsinghua Proto* uses two arrays of 890 nm LEDs, one mounted above the top-left and the other one above the top-right of the finger. It has two cameras, one located at the bottom of the device (below the finger), equipped with an IR filter with a cut-off wavelength of 1000 nm to capture the finger vein images and another camera situated on the top of the device (above the finger) to capture the dorsal texture images. The *Wuhan Proto* scanner is based on a near-infrared CCD camera including an additional NIR-pass filter with a wavelength of 900 nm. The light source consists of 790 nm LEDs. The scanner device has a groove in the shell of the device used to guide the finger's orientation. No detailed information about the camera and the illumination control is available. The *HKU Proto* scanner

Table 3.2 Finger vein scanners that were used to acquire the datasets in Table 3.1—means that the information was not available

Name	Camera	Resolution	Lens (mm)	Filter	Illumin.	r/t
PKU Proto	1/3–in. CMOS cam	512 × 384	–	IR filter	–	t
SNU Proto	GF 038B NIR, AVT	768 × 492	–	IR-pass filter	830/850	t
GUC Proto 1	CCD camera	512 × 240	–	NIR-pass filter	850 nm	t
GUC Proto 2	CCD camera	512 × 240	–	NIR-pass filter	940 nm	t
Tsinghua Proto	industrial camera	720 × 576	–	IR filter 1000 nm	890 nm	t
Wuhan Proto	NIR CCD camera	320 × 240	–	NIR-pass 900 nm	790 nm	t
HKPU Proto	NIR camera	512 × 256	–	NIR-pass filter	850 nm	t
KTDeaduk Proto	–	640 × 480	–	NIR-pass 750 nm	850 nm	t
Shandong EL Proto	NIR camera	580 × 600	–	NIR-pass 800 nm	808 nm	t
Twente Proto	C-Cam BCi5	1280 × 1024	12	B+W 093 930 nm	850 nm	t
Chonbuk Proto	cam w. NIR filter rem.	640 × 480	–	NIR-pass filter	850 nm	t
Shandong Proto	–	640 × 480	–	NIR-pass 850 nm	850 nm	r
Sains Proto	Sony PSEye cam	640 × 480	–	IR-pass filter	850 nm	t
GUC-FPFV Proto	DMK 22BUC03 CMOS	744 × 480	8	none	870 nm	t
GUC-Dors Proto	monochrome CMOS	744 × 480	8	none	920 nm	t
PLUSVein-V2	IDS UI-ML1240-NIR	1280 × 1024	9	none	850 nm	t
PLUS OpenVein	IDS UI-ML1240-NIR	1280 × 1024	9	NIR-pass 850 nm	multiple	t+r

exposes the dorsal side to NIR frontal illuminators consisting of LEDs with a peak wavelength of 850 nm. It has two cameras, an NIR camera in combination with an NIR filter to capture the vein images and one webcam to capture the finger texture. It does neither use a finger guide nor pegs to align the finger, so it can be regarded as semi-touchless device. Again, there are no details about the specific type of camera, LEDs or NIR filter available. The *KTDaeduk Proto* scanner is equipped with a CCD camera, including an additional NIR passing filter with a cut-off wavelength of 750 nm, located at the bottom of the device. A hot mirror is used to be able to mount the camera horizontally, and thus to reduce the height of the device. The NIR illuminator is located at the top of the device, above the dorsal side of the finger, and based on 850 nm LEDs. In addition, the scanner has a finger guidance to assist the capture subject in positioning his finger correctly. The *Shandong EL Proto* is the main part of an embedded finger vein recognition system. It is based on the light transmission principle but uses three NIR laser diodes with a peak wavelength of 808 nm instead of LEDs due to their stronger permeability and higher optical output power compared to LEDs. The scanner is equipped with a monochromatic NIR camera and an additional NIR-pass filter with a cut-off frequency of 800 nm to block daylight. A plate of 10 mm thick, transparent acryl is located above the NIR laser diodes to serve as a platform for positioning the finger and to remove uneven illumination. The whole scanner/finger vein recognition system is controlled by a DSP based mainboard. The *Twente Proto* is the best documented scanner so far. Its light source consists of 8 Osram SFH4550 LEDs (the same type we use for the reflected light illuminator) with a peak wavelength of 850 nm, situated on top of the dorsal side of the finger. Each LED is intensity controlled individually by a simple control loop to achieve a uniform illumination intensity along the finger. The camera is a C-Cam BCi5 monochrome CMOS camera, fitted with a Pentax H1214-M machine vision lens having a focal length of 12 mm. An additional infrared filter with a cut-off wavelength of 930 nm (type B+W 093) is mounted on the lens. The scanner device uses an Edmund Optics NT41-405 first surface mirror to minimise the height of the scanner. However, this scanner device is still quite bulky. Detailed information about the scanner design can be found in the Master's thesis of Ton [31]; however, based solely on the published details it is not possible to construct a ready-to-use scanner in a straightforward way. The *Twente Proto* scanner is described in Chap. 5 [35] of this book. Section 6 of Chap. 5 [35] also presents a novel finger vein acquisition device proposed by the University of Twente. This new version of the scanner is much more compact compared to the *Twente Proto* one. It is based on a Raspberry Pi as processing board and three Raspberry Pi camera modules as image sensors. It consists of three NIR LED strips that can be positioned in a semicircle from 0–180°. Thus, this scanner is able to capture multi-perspective finger vein images (cgf. Chap. 13 [22]) and allows for 3D finger vein reconstruction. The team at the University of Twente is currently investigating the optimal illumination and settings for the 3D finger vein reconstruction. The *Chonbuk Proto* scanner is equipped with a camera including an additional infrared light passing filter and an array of 850 nm infrared LEDs located above the finger. The camera is a modified COTS camera where the NIR blocking filter was replaced by an NIR pass-through filter. It has a finger holder with a hole in the backside of the scanner serving as a finger placement unit. This prototype scanner is quite small with a size of 68 × 54 × 101 mm. The *Shandong Proto* is the only scanner prototype besides out PLUS OpenVein scanner that is based on reflected light. It consists of a camera, an NIR pass-through filter with a cut-off wavelength of 850 nm and an NIR light source based on 850 nm LEDs. This is the only information that is available for this prototype scanner. The *Sains Proto* scanner has three units of 850 nm NIR LEDs, placed in a row on the top section of the scanner, serving as light source. A Sony PSEye camera is mounted at the bottom section of the scanner. It does not use any pegs or finger guides. The capture subject has to touch the back wall of the scanner with their finger only. The *GUC-FPFV Proto* scanner is able to capture finger vein and fingerprint images at once. It is designed to be a low-cost device, consisting of a DMK 22BUC03 monochrome CMOS camera, fitted with a T3Z0312CS 8 mm lens and an LED-based illuminator made of 40 Vishey Semiconductors TSSF5210 870 nm NIR LEDs. The scanners have additional physical structures made of aluminium foil to channel and focus the luminous flux in order to provide enough light intensity to penetrate the whole finger. The scanner device has a size of 180 × 110 × 70 mm. The *GUC-Dors Proto* scanner is designed to capture dorsal finger vein images. It uses the same camera and lens as the *GUC-FPFV Proto* (DMK 22BUC03 monochrome CMOS camera, fitted with a T3Z0312CS 8 mm lens) but 920 nm LEDs instead of 850 nm ones. The light source is placed 10 mm away from the finger placement holder and the camera is placed 100 mm away from the finger. This is the only information available about that scanner, not even an image is depicted in the paper. The *PLUSVein-V2* scanner is also designed to capture dorsal finger vein images but could be easily used to capture palmar images as well. It is based on an IDS Imaging UI-ML-1240NIR NIR-enhanced industrial camera fitted with a Fujifilm HF9HA-1B 9 mm lens (the same as in our design of the *PLUS OpenVein* scanner). No additional NIR pass-through filter is used, instead the scanner is embedded in a wooden box to block the ambient light. The light transmission illuminator consists of 8 Osram SFH 4253-Z 850 nm LEDs. Each LED is brightness controlled individually by an automatic brightness control algorithm in order to achieve an optimal illumination along the finger.

For most of the above-mentioned finger vein scanner prototypes, except the *Twente Proto*, only very few details are available. Thus, it is not possible to reproduce those scanners in a straightforward manner. Our *PLUS OpenVein* scanner is the first finger vein scanner that is able to capture both reflected light and light transmission images. Moreover, it is designed to capture dorsal as well as palmar images. Most important though: its design is fully open source. Our scanner design is explained in detail in the following section.

3.3 PLUS OpenVein Finger Vein Scanner

This section presents our proposed, fully open-source finger vein scanner design, called PLUS OpenVein. At first, the advantages of our scanner design and the differences to existing finger vein scanners are discussed, followed by a detailed explanation of the individual scanner parts. The finger vein scanner design consists of the following main components: an NIR-enhanced camera together with a lens and an NIR pass-through filter, an NIR light transmission illuminator including an illuminator bracket, an NIR reflected light illuminator, an illuminator control board, a finger placement unit and a modular wooden housing. The functional interaction of each of the individual scanner parts, specified by the scanner design, is as important as the choice of each of the individual parts in order to achieve a good finger vein image quality, and consequently a high recognition performance.

3.3.1 Advantages and Differences to Existing Designs

The following list summarises the main advantages and differences of the proposed design over the existing ones presented in Sect. 3.2.4:

- Modular and easy to reproduce design: Most finger vein scanners in research do not place any importance on enabling changes of their individual parts. The PLUS OpenVein is a modular finger vein scanner design, i.e. its individual parts can be replaced, modified and improved easily. All of the housing parts and mounting brackets are either 3D-printed or laser-cut plywood parts. One the one hand, this enables each researcher owning a 3D printer to reproduce the scanner (the laser-cut parts can also be reproduced using a jigsaw). On the other hand, it is easy to modify and improve those parts to individual needs as only the 3D models have to be edited.
- Dorsal/palmar images as well as light transmission/reflected light: although it is easy to capture dorsal images using a scanner meant to capture palmar ones by simply turning the finger around, it is hard to maintain the same longitudinal rotation angle at each capture. Moreover, all exisiting finger vein scanner designs exhibit either light transmission or reflected light only. Our finger vein scanner design is a multipurpose one as it is able to capture dorsal as well as palmar (by rotating the hand 180° around its longitudinal axis), with the finger placement unit especially shaped to prevent unwanted longitudinal finger rotation [23] and achieve a defined finger position for each image capture. Furthermore, it is equipped with two types of illuminators, a light transmission as well as a reflected light one, to acquire palmar and dorsal finger vein images during a single acquisition.
- Three fingers are captured simultaneously: All COTS scanners as well as all research prototype scanners listed in Table 3.2 capture only one finger at a time. The PLUS OpenVein scanner design is the first proposed finger vein scanner that is designed to capture three fingers (index, middle and ring finger) at once to speed up the data acquisition process.
- NIR laser module based scanner version: NIR laser modules exhibit several advantages over NIR LEDs, especially in contactless operation as described in Sect. 3.3.3.2. However, all COTS finger vein scanners as well as the majority of scanners used in research are based on NIR LEDs. We derived two versions of our PLUS OpenVein finger vein scanner design, one is based on a standard NIR LED light transmission illuminator while the second one is based on an NIR laser module illuminator. Both scanners are derived from the same basic structure and differ only in their illuminator, the illuminator control board and the illuminator bracket.
- Finger placement unit to prevent finger misplacement: In [23], we showed that longitudinal finger rotation can easily occur with most types of finger vein scanners and has a severe impact on the recognition performance too. Bearing that in mind, we designed our finger placement unit to prevent most possible kinds of finger misplacements, especially longitudinal finger rotation. This finger placement unit is described in Sect. 3.3.6.

- Open-source scanner design: As mentioned in Sect. 3.2.4, not many details are available for most of the finger vein scanner designs in research, apart from a few exceptions (e.g. the design of Ton [31]). Our scanner design is the first true open-source one. All technical details of the scanner parts, the data sheets, the software as well as more detailed descriptions and instructions for constructing and setting up the scanner can be found in our public repository: http://www.wavelab.at/sources/PLUS-OpenVein, making it a fully open-source scanner design. Our license agreement permits the free of charge use, modifications and reproduction finger vein scanners based on our design for research and non-profit purposes.
- The main disadvantage of our scanner design is its higher price compared to other designs which are based on low-cost camera modules, like the new Twente Proto [35], the *GUC-FPFV Proto* [25], the *GUC-Dors Proto* [24] and the one proposed in [26]. On the one hand, the high-quality industrial NIR enhanced camera allows for a higher image quality and contrast compared to the low-cost cameras. On the other hand, the camera module can be easily replaced by any other suitable camera module thanks to our modular design, effectively reducing the total costs of the scanner device to the same level as other low-cost scanner devices. Hence, in practice, this is not really a disadvantage.

Figure 3.5 shows both of the scanners fully assembled and with the right and front side of the scanner half open including labelled parts. The outside dimensions of the LED version and the laser module based scanner are 146 × 175 × 258 mm and 146 × 175 × 306 mm, respectively. Each individual scanner part together with its advantages over similar designs and the design decisions is explained in the following.

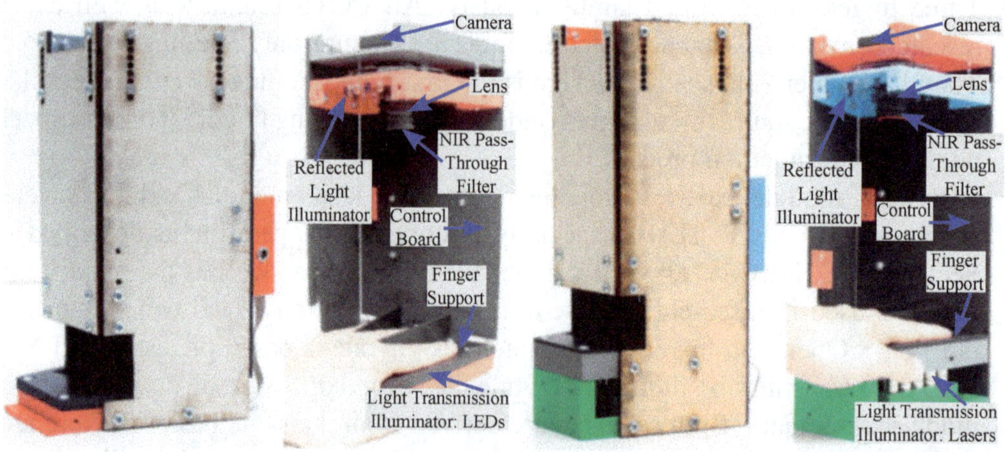

Fig. 3.5 PLUS OpenVein finger vein scanner, left: LED version, right: laser module version

3.3.2 Image Sensor, Lens and Additional Filter

The IDS Imaging UI-ML1240-NIR camera [60] was chosen as image sensor. It has a max. resolution of 1280 × 1024 pixels and a max. frame rate of 25 fps. It is based on the EV76C661ABT CMOS monochrome image sensor, having a colour depth of 8 bit, a max. resolution of 1.31 megapixels, with a pixel size of 5.3 µm and a sensor diagonal of 1/1.84 in. The main advantage of this camera compared to modified webcams and other visible light cameras is that it is an NIR-enhanced industrial camera. It is specifically designed to achieve a high quantum efficiency within the NIR spectrum. Note the higher quantum efficiency within 800–900 nm of the NIR version compared to the monochrome one, both depicted in Fig. 3.6 left. This wavelength range includes the peak wavelengths of our NIR LEDs (850 nm) and NIR laser modules (808 nm) equipped in the light transmission illuminator. Most COTS and consumer cameras that are designed for the visible wavelength spectrum are sensitive in the NIR spectrum too, but they are equipped with NIR blocking filters in order to avoid unwanted colour effects caused by NIR light (the sunlight contains an NIR wavelength spectrum part too which would stain the images blue to violet). The NIR blocking filter can be removed, enabling the camera to capture NIR images, but those modified cameras are less sensitive than a special NIR-enhanced camera. Due to its increased NIR sensitivity, an NIR-enhanced camera achieves a higher image contrast in the NIR spectrum than a visible wavelength one. On the contrary, a special NIR-enhanced industrial camera is several orders of magnitude more expensive than a modified webcam solution, posing a disadvantage for this type of camera in terms of costs. However, advantages in terms of image quality predominated, and thus the use of an NIR-enhanced camera was the preferred option for our finger vein scanner design. Note that the camera holder bracket can be modified for the use of different camera models easily.

The camera is equipped with a Fujifilm HF9HA-1B 9 mm fixed focal lens [50]. The lens has a manual iris and is C-Mount compatible. The short focal length of 9 mm

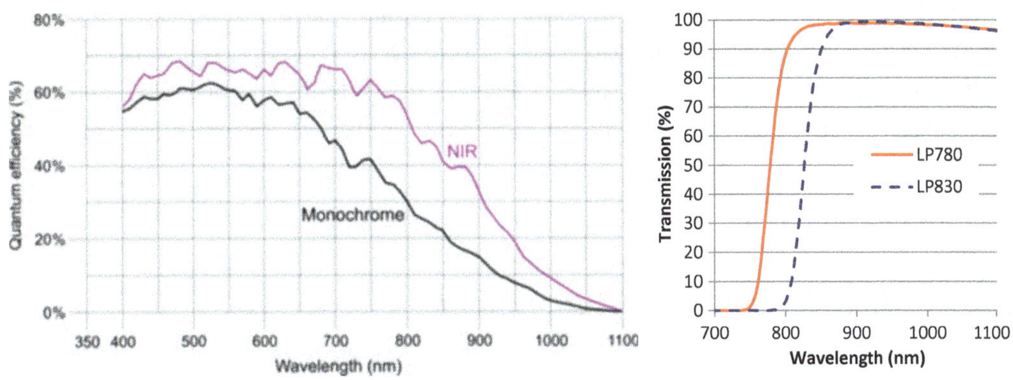

Fig. 3.6 Left: quantum efficiency charts for the UI-ML-1240-NIR (black line) and the UI-ML-1240-M (purple line), taken from the data sheet [60], right: filter chart for the MIDOPT FIL LP780/27 (solid red line) and LP830/27 (dashed blue line) NIR pass-through filter

is necessary to maintain a short distance between the camera and the finger which is desired in order to reduce the overall size of the scanner device. A lens with an increased focal length has less image distortions but requires a larger distance from the finger, thus increasing the overall size of the scanner. A shorter focal length reduces the minimum distance to the finger but increases the image distortions, especially at the image boundaries. Thus, we decided to use a 9 mm focal length as the best trade-off between the distance to the finger, i.e. the overall scanner dimensions, and the image distortions introduced by the lens itself. A MIDOPT FIL LP830/27 [56] and a MIDOPT FIL LP780/27 [55] NIR pass-through filter for the LED and the laser-based version of the scanner, respectively, are mounted on top of the lens. The filter chart of the LP830, depicted in Fig. 3.6 right as dashed blue line, fits well with the emission spectrum (cf. Fig. 3.9) of the NIR LEDs (peak wavelength of 860 nm) and the filter chart of the LP780 (solid red line in Fig. 3.6) fits well with the NIR laser modules (peak wavelength of 808 nm). This additional NIR pass-through filter helps to reduce the influence of ambient light and further improves the quality of the vein images. Currently, the wooden scanner housing is still needed for stability reasons, to comply with safety regulations for the laser-based version of the scanner and to further reduce the influence of the ambient light in case of direct sunlight shining on the scanner. For the next, slightly improved version of the scanner design, the NIR pass-through filters will be replaced by the MIDOPT BN850 Narrow Near-IR Bandpass Filter [54] and the MIDOPT BN810 Narrow Near-IR Bandpass Filter [53] for the LED version of the scanner and the laser module version of the scanner, respectively. These filters are more effective in reducing the ambient light's influence and enable the removal of the wooden scanner housing without impacting the image quality for indoor use of the scanner and at least a reduction of the housing's side plates dimensions if outdoor use is desired. On the other hand, the NIR pass-through filter increases the total costs of the scanner, especially the narrow bandpass filter. If the scanner is used in indoor environments only, where the influence of ambient light can be controlled, it is possible to refrain from using and NIR pass-through filter for cost reasons. To achieve an optimal image quality, we recommend to use the additional NIR pass-through filter though.

The last part of the camera assembly is the camera holder bracket, depicted in Fig. 3.7 together with the camera, the lens and the NIR pass-through filter, which is mounted on the very top of the scanner. The camera holder bracket is again a custom-developed, 3D-printed part which can be easily modified for mounting different cameras.

3.3.3 Light Transmission Illuminator

There are two different versions of the light transmission illuminator: one based on NIR LEDs and the other one based on NIR laser modules. The scanner equipped with the laser modules is bigger due to the larger size of the laser module based illuminator compared to the LED-based one and due to the minimal distance of

Fig. 3.7 Camera holder bracket (left), IDS NIR-enhanced camera + Fujifilm 9 mm lens and NIR pass-through filter (right)

about 30 mm between the laser modules and the finger surface which is necessary to adjust the optimal focal length of the laser modules. Both illuminators consist of three stripes, one stripe underneath each finger. These stripes are mounted with the help of a custom-developed, 3D-printed, illuminator bracket, depicted in Fig. 3.8 top for the LED version (the two parts are then screwed together to hold the LEDs in place) and Fig. 3.8 bottom for the laser module based version. This bracket is located underneath the finger placement unit.

3.3.3.1 LED-Based Version

The LED-based light transmission illuminator has three stripes consisting of 8 Osram SFH-4253-Z SMD LEDs [65] each. The stripes are depicted in Fig. 3.8 top-right. The LEDs have a radiation half-angle of ±60°, a peak wavelength of 860 nm and a max. radiant intensity of 13 mW/sr. The emission spectrum of the LEDs is depicted in Fig. 3.9 left. These LEDs were chosen as their peak wavelength is within the recommended wavelength band for vascular pattern recognition and because they are standard, low-cost electronic components. They are placed in a distance of 7.5 mm next to each other, which has been determined to be the optimal distance during our tests in order to provide a sufficient and uniform illumination along the finger. Each LED can be brightness controlled separately and independently from the other LEDs in order to achieve an optimal image contrast. The health and safety requirements for NIR LEDs are defined in the IEC-62471 standard on "Photobiological safety of lamps and lamp systems" [3]. The standard defines limits in terms of radiation intensity and duration to prevent Corneal Hazard as well as Retinal Thermal Hazard. The Renesas Electronics application note AN1737 [67] shows an example calculation for an LED similar to the ones equipped in our scanner design, a distance of the LED and eyes of 200 mm and a radiation duration of 10 s. In this case, the safety factor for the Corneal and the Retinal Thermal Hazard is 4×10^6 and 2×10^5, respectively, i.e.

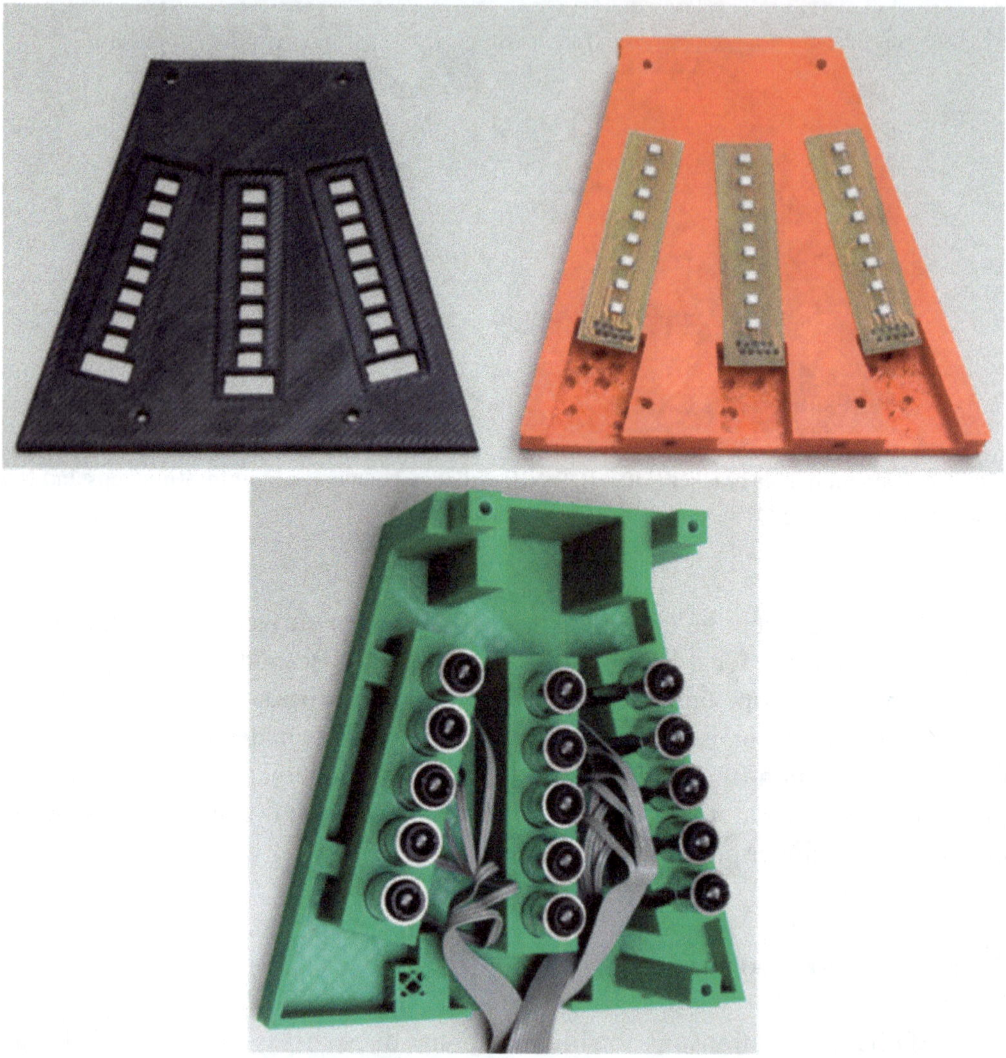

Fig. 3.8 Illuminator mounting bracket, top: LED version (two parts) + single LED stripes, bottom: laser version including the laser modules

the radiation level is at least 10^5 times below the critical limit. Moreover, our scanner housing prevents any direct exposure of the eye to the LED radiation. Hence, our scanner complies with the health and safety regulations.

3.3.3.2 Laser Module Based Version

The second version of the light transmission illuminator is based on laser modules instead of LEDs and consists of three stripes of five laser diodes [46] including an adjustable constant-current laser diode driver PCB [45] and a TO-18 housing with a focus adjustable lens [44] for each of the laser modules (the combination of laser diode + control PCB + housing is denoted as laser module or laser). The laser diodes

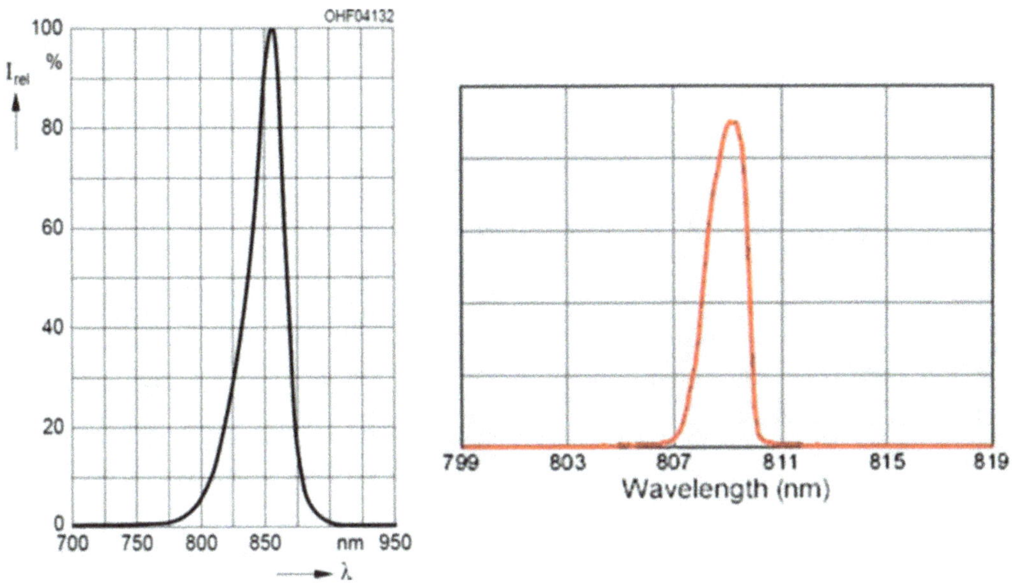

Fig. 3.9 Emission spectrum of the light transmission illuminator NIR LEDs (left) and the NIR laser modules (right), taken from the data sheet [65]

are TO-18 type (diameter 5.6 mm), and have a peak wavelength of 808 nm and an optical output power of 300 mW. These laser diodes belong to Class 3B according to the IEC 60825-1 standard [4]. The guidelines on laser health and safety require that any direct exposure to the laser beam has to be avoided for this laser class. To be compliant with these regulations, the housing of the scanner design is built in a way to ensure that no exposure of the eyes to the laser beam is possible. The emission spectrum of the laser diodes can be seen in Fig. 3.9 right. Note that their emission spectrum is narrower than the spectrum of the LEDs facilitating the use of narrow bandpass filters instead of NIR longpass filters, leading to further attenuation of the ambient light. The main advantages of the laser diodes/laser modules over the LEDs are their higher optical output power and their narrow radiation half-angle. This enables a higher degree of vertical finger movement without degrading the image quality, which is especially important if a full touchless operation is desired. The broad radiation half-angle of the LEDs leads to over-illuminated areas at the finger outline while the contrast in the vein regions is decreased as soon as the finger is not placed directly on top of the illuminator. Due to the narrow radiation half-angle of the laser modules (note that the laser diodes itself do not have such a narrow radiation angle, instead the focus adjustable lens included in the housing makes such a narrow angle possible), the main part of the luminous flux stays inside the centre regions of the finger (where most of the veins are) and thus the contrast in these regions remains stable if the finger is moved upwards (away from the illuminator). Figure 3.10 shows a comparison between the LED (left) and the laser module (right) based scanner. It can be clearly seen that for the LED version the contrast gets lower the further away the finger is from the illuminator while it remains high for the laser module based version. The disadvantage of using laser modules instead of LEDs is

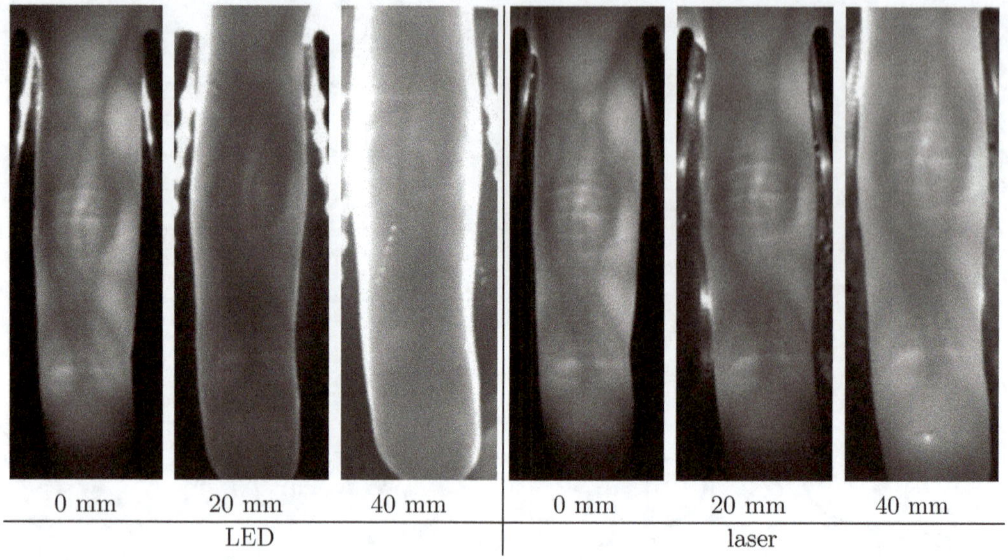

Fig. 3.10 Finger vein images captured with our scanners showing illumination issues due to vertical finger movement (0, 20 and 40 mm away from the scanner surface): note the bright areas along the finger boundaries and the reduced contrast of the vein region the further away the finger gets from the scanner surface for the LED scanner images (left) compared to the laser scanner ones (right) (image originally published in [12], © 2018 IEEE)

their high price. A single laser module is about 15–20 times more expensive than a single LED. In non-contactless operation, the image quality of the laser modules is only slightly better compared to LEDs. Hence, for the current version of the scanner, we recommend the LED-based version to cut down costs. If the scanner design is adopted towards a touchless version, laser modules are the preferred option.

3.3.4 Reflected Light Illuminator

The reflected light illuminator is composed of three different types of LEDs, 850 nm (Osram SFH 4550 LEDs [66] with a radiation half-angle of ±3° and a max. radiant intensity of 700 mW/sr), 950 nm (Vishay Semiconductors CQY 99 [69] with a radiation half-angle of ±22° and a max. radiant intensity of 35 mW/sr) and warm white daylight ones (Luckylight 504WC2E-W6-3PC [61] with a radiation half-angle of ±15° and a typical luminous intensity of 23000 mcd), eight pieces each. These three types of LEDs are all standard, low-cost electronic parts. The two NIR types have peak wavelengths that are within the recommended spectrum for vascular pattern recognition and the warm white daylight one is commonly used in many different applications. The LEDs are mounted in a circle on the reflected light illuminator bracket (depictedn in Fig. 3.11), situated on top of the scanner device around the camera lens. The LEDs are arranged in an alternating manner, i.e. each 850 nm LED is followed by a 950 nm one, then a warm white one, then a 850 nm one and so on.

Fig. 3.11 Reflected light illuminator: 850, 950 nm and warm white daylight LEDs are arranged in an alternating manner around a circle. The camera lens is put through the circular hole in the middle of the bracket

This design turned out to be optimal in terms of uniform illumination regardless which of the three illuminators is turned on. Each of the 850 nm and the 950 nm eight tuples of LEDs can be brightness controlled separately, but not each individual LED. The warm white daylight LEDs can only be turned on at a fixed intensity (no brightness control). The reflected light illuminator enables the capturing of reflected light finger vein images. The warm white daylight LEDs are mainly meant for use during adjusting and testing and not during finger vein image acquisition. However, they can be utilised to capture additional finger texture images.

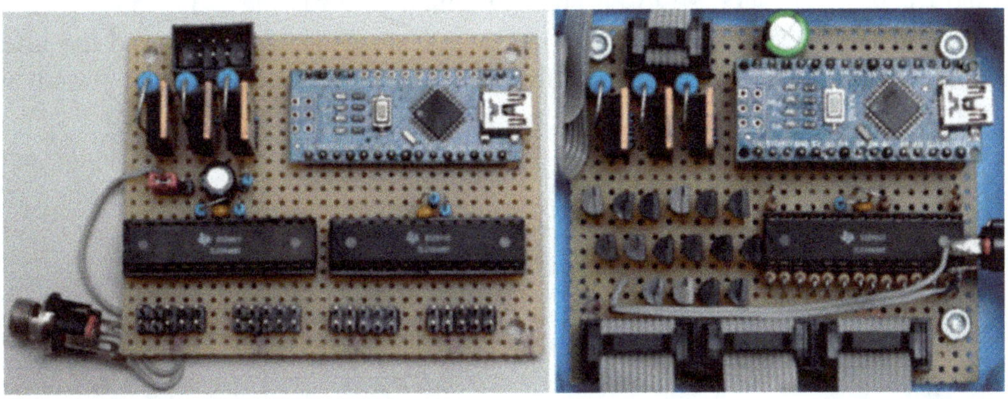

Fig. 3.12 Illuminator brightness control board prototype, left: LED version, right: laser module version

3.3.5 Illuminator Brightness Control Board

Figure 3.12 (left: LED version, right: laser module version) shows an image of the first prototype brightness control PCB board built using THT (through-hole-technology) parts. The final version is based on SMD (surface-mounted device) parts. Its two main components are an Arduino Nano board [48] and a Texas Instruments TLC59401/TLC5940PWP [68] (the THT version of the board uses the old version, the TLC5940). The Arduino Nano is a complete, breadboard-friendly microcontroller development board based on the Microchip ATmega328P microcontroller [63], including an integrated USB to UART converter and several external components necessary to operate the ATmega328P. The ATmega328P offers several built-in components, like analog and digital outputs, timers, UART, I2C, SPI Interface, etc. Most important for our application are the six PWM outputs and the UART interface. More details on the ATmega328P can be found in the data sheet [62]. The Texas Instruments TLC5940 is an integrated 16-channel LED driver with dot correction and greyscale PWM control enabling a convenient brightness control of LEDs without the need for external components like dropping resistors. Each output can be controlled separately (4096 steps) and has a drive capability of 120 mA. It operates as a constant-current sink and the desired current can be set using only one external resistor. It is controlled using a serial data interface. As every single LED of the three stripes of eight LEDs each (24 LEDs in total) is desired to be controlled individually, two of these TLC5940 are equipped on the LED version of the control board as each TLC5940 has 16 outputs. In Fig. 3.13, a schematic overview of the control board is depicted. The control board is connected to the PC over the USB interface. The data sent over USB is converted to UART compatible data, received by the Arduino Nano (or the ATmega328P to be precise) which controls the 2 TLC5940s. Each output of the TLC5940 is directly connected to an LED. The LED and the laser module version differ. The laser modules exhibit a higher current consumption than

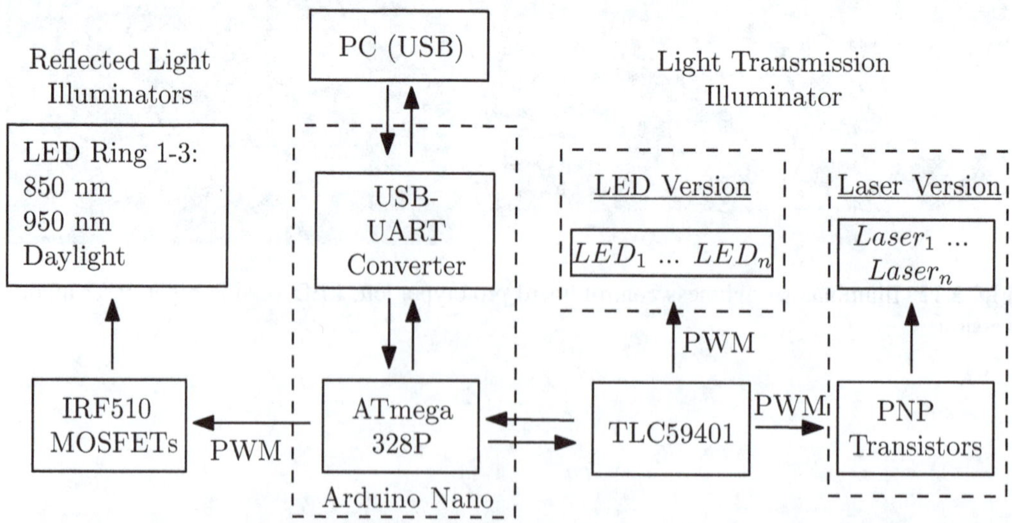

Fig. 3.13 Schematic structure of the control PCB

the LEDs that would exceed the maximum of 120 mA provided by the TLC5940. Thus, external PNP transistors (CDIL BC327-25 [49] for the THT version of the board and ON Semiconductor BC808-25 SMD [64] for the final SMD version) in combination with suitable base dropping resistors are added. The laser modules are not directly connected to the TLC5940 but to the PNP transistors. The laser module version has only one TLC5940 as there are 15 laser modules in total (compared to the LED version with 24 LEDs). Furthermore, two of the PWM outputs on the Arduino Nano board are used to brightness control the reflected light illuminator. One digital output is utilised to turn the warm white daylight reflected light illuminator on and off. There are additional N-Channel MOSFETs (International Rectifier IRF510 [70] for the THT version and Alpha&Omega Semiconductor AO3418 [47] for the final SMD version) and dropping resistors on both versions of the control board for the reflected light illuminators. The complete schematic and board layout as well as all data sheets for the final SMD version can be found in our public repository.

3.3.5.1 Arduino Firmware

The Arduino Nano or to be more precise the ATmega328P microcontroller on which it is based can be programmed in several different programming languages and development environments. We decided to use C++ together with the Arduino IDE to be able to utilise all the convenient Arduino libraries. There is a library for the TLC5940 included in the Arduino framework. Using this library the TLC5940 can be easily interfaced and controlled. It handles the serial protocol of the TLC5940 and setting/receiving of the brightness level values. It uses two out of the three internal timers of the ATmega328P, so if the TLC5940 library is utilised, only two of the six available PWM outputs on the Arduino Nano remain available for use (thus, we went on without being able to brightness control the warm white daylight reflected light in order to avoid adding another external hardware part). We implemented a simple protocol to interface each of the individual LEDs/laser modules as well as the reflected light illuminators, to set a whole stripe at once and to turn off all illuminators again. The Arduino Nano is recognised as USB serial port on the PC and a fixed-length text-based serial protocol, allowing for easy debugging, is used to send the command to the brightness control board. Details about the protocol as well as the brightness control board firmware can be found in our repository.

3.3.6 Finger Placement Unit

To provide an intuitive interaction with the scanner device and to help the capture subject at positioning their fingers correctly, the scanner has a finger guide or a finger placement unit. As the scanner captures the index, middle and ring fingers simultaneously, it is important that all three fingers are aligned with the underneath illumination stripes. This is especially important for the LED version of the scanner in order to avoid overexposed areas along the finger outline (refer to Sect. 3.3.3.2 for details on the advantages of the lasers over the LEDs). The finger placement unit, depicted in Fig. 3.14, is a custom-developed, 3D-printed part with three elliptically shaped grooves, each with a rectangular hole in the centre of the groove which is situated above the location where the LEDs or laser modules are placed. These grooves guide the capture subject at placing their fingers correctly and enable a natural and comfortable finger placement position during the capturing process, regardless if the fingers are placed in palmar or dorsal direction. Moreover, the finger placement unit was designed to prevent most kinds of finger misplacement, including tilts, planar finger rotation, horizontal shifts and especially longitudinal finger rotation by requiring the capture subject to place their finger flat on the placement unit with the fingers aligned to the grooves. In addition, the placement unit has two walls in between the index and middle and the middle and ring finger, respectively. These walls in combination with the shape of the grooves lead to a slightly spread position of the fingers, which makes an easy segmentation of the single fingers possible. Moreover, they block the diffuse light emitted sideways from the fingers which would otherwise lead to overexposed areas along the finger boundaries. In order to arrive at an optimal size and shape of the finger positioning support we performed several tests with male and female subjects, different age groups and different ethnicities (European, Asian, African). The current design is suitable for a broad range of people, especially for the average European and also for most adult Asian people. However, there might be some modifications necessary for younger Asian people with small hands/fingers. As it is a 3D-printed part, these adjustments to better suit different groups of people can be done easily. Note that adjustments have to be made to the LED/laser mounting brackets (see Sect. 3.3.3) too if the finger placement unit is changed.

3.3.7 *Housing Parts*

The housing for the PLUS OpenVein finger vein scanner was designed for two reasons. The first version of the scanner did not include an NIR pass-through filter, thus the housing was necessary to shield the scanner from the ambient light and improve the image contrast. Second, the wooden housing serves as a frame for mounting all the brackets and parts and putting the whole scanner assembly together. The housing consists of four wooden parts: two side panels, one front panel and one back panel which are connected using 3D-printed mounting brackets. The parts for the LED-based version are shown in Fig. 3.15. The laser module based version ones are not shown but only differ in their height (which are larger than the LED ones). There is an additional 3D-printed housing to accommodate the brightness control PCB which is mounted on the backplane (depicted in Fig. 3.5). The wooden parts are cut out of 4 mm plywood using a laser cutter. The current version of the scanner includes an NIR pass-through filter, so the wooden housing is mainly for stability and mounting reasons (except if the scanner is exposed to direct sunlight, then the

Fig. 3.14 Finger placement unit: the finger-shaped grooves guide the capture subject in placing their fingers correctly. The walls are blocking diffuse emitted light from adjacent fingers, the light transmission illuminators are placed underneath the rectangular holes

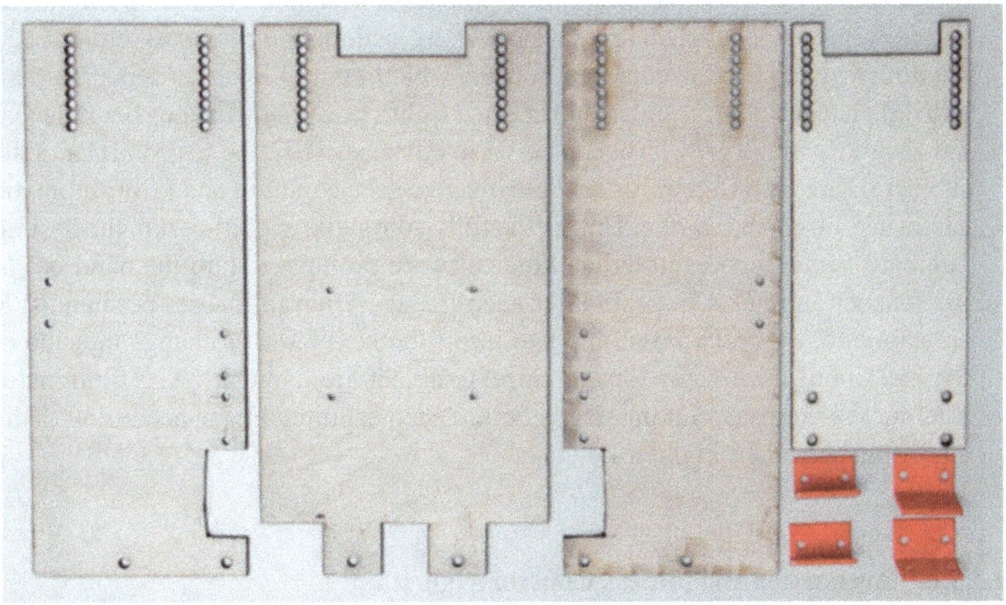

Fig. 3.15 Housing parts of the LED-based scanner

housing is necessary to reduce the influence of the ambient light too). As studies showed that the capture subjects' acceptance and convenience is higher for scanner devices built in a semi-open or fully open manner, we are planning to design a second version of the housing which has smaller side and front panels (semi-open design).

3.3.8 Capturing Software

So far, all the hardware parts of the scanner including the brightness controller firmware have been described. There is still one important thing missing, the scanner control software for capturing actual finger vein images. Our control software is based on the IDS Imaging uEye Software Suite [59] as the image sensor is an IDS camera. Their framework is available for Windows- and Linux-based operating systems. We implemented our capturing software for Windows using C# and Microsoft Visual Studio 2015. A screenshot of the capturing software can be seen in Fig. 3.16. Its functionality can be divided into four main parts:

1. Initial scanner calibration: During initial scanner calibration the LED/laser module centres are set with the help of 3D-printed calibration sticks. This is essential for the automated brightness control algorithm to work correctly.
2. Setting camera parameters: Here several camera parameters, e.g. frame rate, white balance, gain, pixel clock, exposure time, etc. can be set.
3. Controlling the illumination sources: the light sources (light transmission and reflected light) can be either be controlled manually and individually or automatically. The manual control is only meant for troubleshooting purposes and tests while usually the automatic brightness control is applied.
4. Image capturing: The image capturing process is designed to be semi-automated and convenient for a typical finger vein data collection. Some general settings, e.g. the directory to save the captured images, which kind of images (dorsal/palmar, left/right hand, light transmission/reflected light), how many images per kind and the desired average grey level can be set in advance. Then the session ID and the subject ID are set. Afterwards a single image can be captured or a fully automatic capturing run can be started. During the fully automatic capturing run, the desired number of images is captured and the software prompts to pull the hand out of the scanner and put it in again after each image. After all images per hand/side are captured, the software prompts to insert the next hand or change the side of the hand until all images for the current subject are captured. The illuminator brightness is adjusted automatically before each captured image according to the algorithm described in the following.

3.3.8.1 Automated Brightness Control Algorithm

In order to achieve an optimal image contrast especially in the vein regions, an automatic brightness control algorithm was developed. This algorithm controls each of the single light transmission illuminator LEDs/laser modules as well as the reflected light illuminators as a whole. After several tests with different image qualities and image contrast metrics, we opted for a simple, iterative algorithm based on a comparison against a target grey level. This algorithm works as follows: at first, the LED/laser centres have to be configured once as described below. This includes the determination of the area of influence for each LED/laser, which is the area in the image a single LED/laser illuminates (defined by a circle with a certain radius). Then all LEDs/lasers are set to an initial intensity level/brightness value which is half of their maximum intensity (I_{max}). The live image of the camera is analysed and the current grey level within the area of influence of each LED/laser is determined ($GL_{current}$) and compared against the set target grey level (GL_{target}). The new brightness value is then set according to $I_{n+1} = I_n + I_{corr}$, where I_{n+1} is the new intensity level, I_n is the current intensity level and $I_{corr} = \frac{GL_{target} - GL_{current}}{GL_{max}} \cdot \frac{I_{max}}{2 \cdot n}$, where GL_{max} is the maximum grey value and n is the current iteration. The iteration stops if either the target grey level GL_{target} has been reached or if no more intensity change is possible. The algorithm finishes in at most $log_2(I_{max})$ iterations. Thus, it is fast enough for real-time applications while preserving a good performance in terms of uniform image contrast.

3.4 PLUSVein-FV3 Finger Vein Dataset

To demonstrate the high recognition performance that can be achieved by using our proposed scanner design, we established a dataset using both of our scanners, the LED-based version and the laser-based one. This dataset has already been published [12] and is available at: http://www.wavelab.at/sources/PLUSVein-FV3/. The first version contained dorsal finger vein images captured from 60 subjects, 6 fingers

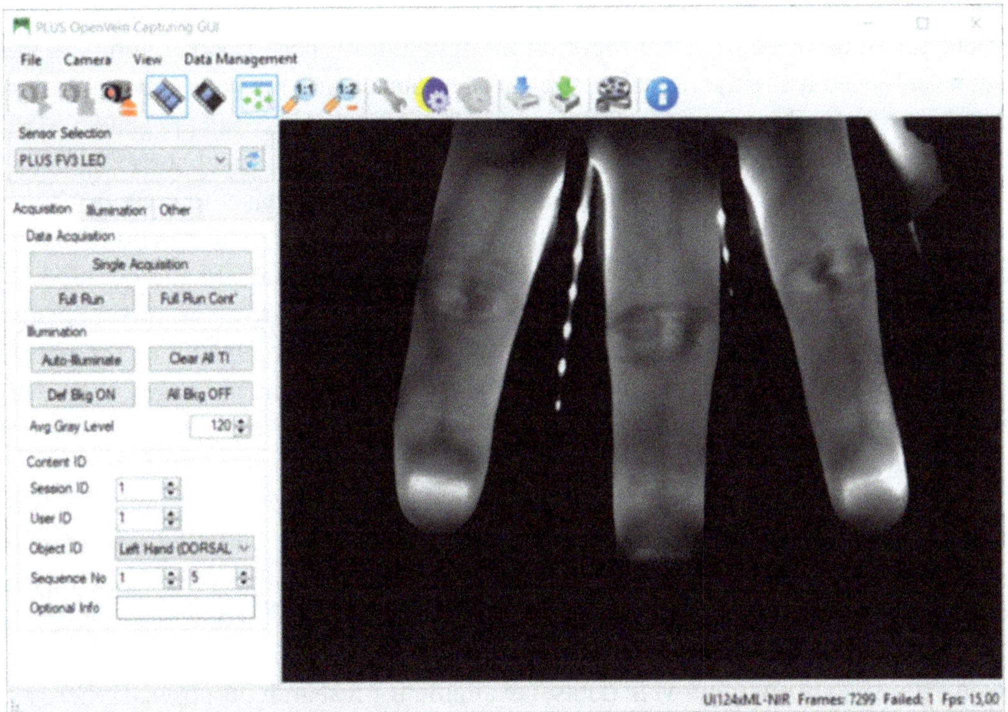

Fig. 3.16 Main window of the PLUS OpenVein finger vein capturing software

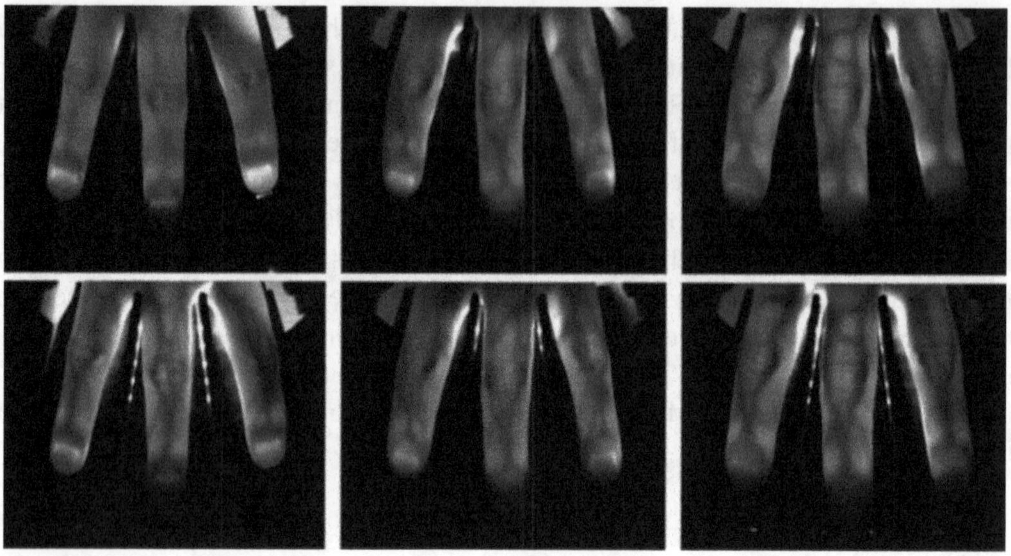

Fig. 3.17 PLUSVein-FV3 example images, top: laser module based scanner, bottom: LED-based scanner

per subject and 5 images per finger in one session, summing up to a total of 3600 images from 360 individual fingers (1800 per scanner). Our scanners capture three fingers at once, so the 3600 images are actually extracted from 1200 raw finger vein images which were separated into three images corresponding to each individual finger. Those single finger images have a resolution of 420×1024 pixels and are stored in 8-bit greyscale png format. Some example images are shown in Fig. 3.17. In our previous work [12], we reported the recognition performance numbers that can be achieved using the dorsal images of our dataset, and thus our scanner design. We arrived at EERs as low as 0.028% and 0.111% for MC [20]/PC [2] and a SIFT-based approach [14], respectively, with these simple but well-established finger vein recognition schemes. In the meanwhile, we extended the dataset to contain palmar finger vein images captured from the same subjects too. Thus, it now includes a total of 7200 images, 1800 per scanner and per view (palmar/dorsal). In another recently published work [13], we compared the performance of palmar versus dorsal images. We showed that the best view in terms of recognition accuracy depends on the feature extraction algorithm, resulting in EER of 0.08% for the palmar images using MC and an EER of 0.08% for the dorsal images using SIFT. These performance figures approve the sophisticated and deliberate design of our finger vein scanners.

We are still extending our dataset in-house. The most recent version consists of about 100 subjects so far. The main reason for open sourcing our finger vein scanner design was to help other researchers working in the field of finger vein biometrics by sharing our custom-developed scanner design with them. The second most important reason is that we are interested in collaborations to extend our dataset and evolve it to an extensive, open finger vein dataset available for research purposes. If there are several reproductions of the scanner based on our design out there, every researcher having such a scanner device at hand and interested in participating could just provide the captured vein images and we will then include them in a new release of the open finger vein dataset.

We are currently discussing options for a suitable online platform to handle such a collaboration efficiently as well as trying to clarify the legal aspects (the consent forms have to include the right to merge the single datasets together which of course includes sharing the finger vein data with other partners in different countries and under different legislations) of sharing the finger vein images. We are confident that these two issues can be resolved soon.

3.5 Conclusion

This chapter proposes a new finger vein scanner design. After the introduction, the basic principle of a finger vein scanner is outlined, followed by a review on commercial finger vein scanners, available research finger vein datasets and the corresponding finger vein scanners used to establish these datasets. The main contribution of this chapter are the details about our fully open-source, modular, multipurpose finger vein scanner design. Our finger vein scanner design is based on commercial-off-the-shelf parts, a custom-developed brightness control board and custom-designed 3D-printed parts as well as laser-cut plywood parts. It is modular as each individual part can be replaced, modified and improved easily. This scanner is the first finger vein scanner that is able to capture reflected light as well as light transmission images. Moreover, it is able to capture three fingers at once (index, middle and ring finger) from the dorsal and palmar view (by rotating the hand around 180°). Thus, we call it a multipurpose finger vein scanner. Two different versions of the basic design are presented, one based on a conventional NIR LED illuminator, the second one based on NIR laser modules. Laser modules have not gotten much attention in finger vein recognition so far, despite their advantages especially if it comes to touchless operation. All the individual parts are described together with their design decisions. Our scanner design is fully open source: all technical details of the scanner design, including data sheets, parts lists, technical drawings and 3D models of the housing parts, firmware and software together with detailed assembly and setup instructions can be found in a public repository: http://www.wavelab.at/sources/PLUS-OpenVein. The use of our scanner design and the reproduction of the finger vein scanner according to our design is free of charge for research purposes. Thanks to our fully open-source design, other researchers can easily reproduce our scanner and utilise this scanner for their own finger vein data collection, meaning they are no longer dependent from publicly available datasets. Moreover, they can contribute their modifications and improvements to our scanner design as well. To confirm the decent recognition performance that can be achieved using our scanner design, we established a dataset using our two scanners. This dataset currently contains 7200 images from 360 individual fingers and is publicly available for research purposes at: http://www.wavelab.at/sources/PLUSVein-FV3.

3.5.1 Future Work

Although the current scanner design has been proven to be competitive in terms of recognition accuracy and usability, we still strive to improve it. The first improvement will be a rather small one. We will replace the NIR pass-through filter with an NIR bandpass filter for both versions of the scanner. This helps in further reducing the influence of the ambient light and is advantageous if it comes to the next improvement. The next change to the scanner design will include a removal of the side plates and the front plate to arrive at a more open or at least semi-open design. Scanners designed in an open manner have been shown to increase the capture subjects' acceptability and convenience. Instead of removing the side plates completely we are thinking of making them only half of their current width such that the scanner becomes semi-open while still retaining its mechanical stability. The second improvement we are currently working on is the integration of the capturing software on a Raspberry Pi microcomputer as a first step towards a stand-alone, embedded finger vein scanner device which only requires an external power source but no additional PC for acquiring the images. The next step towards this stand-alone design is an additional touchscreen display, mounted at the front plate of the scanner device, connected to the Raspberry Pi and used to control the whole data acquisition process. Thanks to our fully open-source design, other researchers can contribute their modifications and improvements to our scanner design too.

Furthermore, we plan to establish a comprehensive, publicly available finger vein dataset for research purposes. Researchers who are interested in a contribution to this new finger vein dataset can simply build a scanner based on our open-source design, acquire finger vein images on their own and then contribute to the dataset by providing us their captured finger vein data. Such an extensive, available, collaborative finger vein dataset will be beneficial for the whole finger vein research community and is vital in order to achieve further progress in finger vein recognition. We are currently also extending the first version of our already available finger vein dataset in-house. Together with our partners and other researchers who are willing to contribute and build a scanner based on our design, we are confident that we will establish a comprehensive, open finger vein dataset from which the whole finger vein research community will benefit.

Acknowledgements This project has received funding from the European Union's Horizon 2020 research and innovation program under grant agreement No. 700259, project PROTECT—Pervasive and UseR Focused BiomeTrics BordEr ProjeCT.

References

1. Asaari MSM, Suandi SA, Rosdi BA (2014) Fusion of band limited phase only correlation and width centroid contour distance for finger based biometrics. Expert Syst Appl 41(7):3367–3382
2. Choi JH, Song W, Kim T, Lee SR, Kim HC (2009) Finger vein extraction using gradient normalization and principal curvature. Proc SPIE 7251:9. https://doi.org/10.1117/12.810458
3. Commission IE et al (2006) IEC 62471: 2006. IEC Photobiological safety of lamps and lamp systems, Geneva
4. Commission IE et al (2007) Safety of laser products-part 1: equipment classification and requirements. IEC 60825–1
5. Daniel H (2012) Vascular pattern recognition and its application in privacy–preserving biometric online–banking system. PhD thesis, PhD dissertation, Gjovik University College
6. Eng PC, Khalil-Hani M (2009) Fpga-based embedded hand vein biometric authentication system. In: TENCON 2009 IEEE region 10 conference, pp 1–5
7. Fadhil RI, George LE (2017) Finger vein identification and authentication system. LAP Lambert Academic Publishing, Germany
8. Fletcher RR, Raghavan V, Zha R, Haverkamp M, Hibberd PL (2014) Development of mobile-based hand vein biometrics for global health patient identification. In: IEEE global humanitarian technology conference (GHTC 2014), pp 541–547
9. Hitachi Group, Corp (2018) Finger vein technology for Bank BPH (Poland)—Hitachi Europe News. http://www.hitachi.eu/en-gb/case-studies/finger-vein-technology-bank-bph-poland. Accessed 20 June 2018
10. Hitachi-Omron Terminal Solutions, Corp (2018) Taiwan's CTBC bank adopts finger vein authentication solution for ATMs—Hitachi News. http://www.hitachi-omron-ts.com/news/pdf/201607-001.pdf. Accessed 20 June 2018
11. Huang B, Dai Y, Li R, Tang D, Li W (2010) Finger-vein authentication based on wide line detector and pattern normalization. In: 20th international conference on pattern recognition (ICPR) 2010. IEEE, pp 1269–1272
12. Kauba C, Prommegger B, Uhl A (2018) Focussing the beam—a new laser illumination based data set providing insights to finger-vein recognition. In: Proceedings of the IEEE 9th international conference on biometrics: theory, applications, and systems (BTAS2018), Los Angeles, California, USA, pp 1–9
13. Kauba C, Prommegger B, Uhl A (2018) The two sides of the finger—dorsal or palmar—which one is better in finger-vein recognition? In: Proceedings of the international conference of the biometrics special interest group (BIOSIG'18), Darmstadt, Germany
14. Kauba C, Reissig J, Uhl A (2014) Pre-processing cascades and fusion in finger vein recognition. In: Proceedings of the international conference of the biometrics special interest group (BIOSIG'14), Darmstadt, Germany
15. Kim J, Kong HJ, Park S, Noh S, Lee SR, Kim T, Kim HC (2009) Non-contact finger vein acquisition system using NIR laser. In: Sensors, cameras, and systems for industrial/scientific applications X, vol 7249. International Society for Optics and Photonics
16. Kumar A, Zhou Y (2012) Human identification using finger images. IEEE Trans Image Process 21(4):2228–2244
17. Lee EC, Jung H, Kim D (2011) New finger biometric method using near infrared imaging. Sensors 11(3):2319–2333
18. Liu Z, Song S (2012) An embedded real-time finger-vein recognition system for mobile devices. IEEE Trans Consum Electron 58(2):
19. Lu Y, Xie SJ, Yoon S, Wang Z, Park DS (2013) An available database for the research of finger vein recognition. In: 6th international congress on image and signal processing (CISP), 2013 , vol 1. IEEE, pp 410–415
20. Miura N, Nagasaka A, Miyatake T (2007) Extraction of finger-vein patterns using maximum curvature points in image profiles. IEICE Trans Inf Syst 90(8):1185–1194

21. Pascual JES, Uriarte-Antonio J, Sanchez-Reillo R, Lorenz MG (2010) Capturing hand or wrist vein images for biometric authentication using low-cost devices. In: Proceedings of the sixth international conference on intelligent information hiding and multimedia signal processing (IIH-MSP 2010), pp 816–819
22. Prommeger B, Kauba C, Uhl A (2019) A different view on the finger–multi-perspective score level fusion in finger-vein recognition. In: Uhl A, Busch C, Marcel S, Veldhuis R (eds) Handbook of vascular biometrics. Springer Science+Business Media, Boston, MA, USA, pp 395–434
23. Prommegger B, Kauba C, Uhl A (2018) Longitudinal finger rotation—problems and effects in finger-vein recognition. In: Proceedings of the international conference of the biometrics special interest group (BIOSIG'18), Darmstadt, Germany
24. Raghavendra R, Busch C (2015) Exploring dorsal finger vein pattern for robust person recognition. In: 2015 international conference on biometrics (ICB), pp 341–348. https://doi.org/10.1109/ICB.2015.7139059
25. Raghavendra R, Raja KB, Surbiryala J, Busch C (2014) A low-cost multimodal biometric sensor to capture finger vein and fingerprint. In: IEEE international joint conference on biometrics (IJCB), 2014. IEEE, pp 1–7
26. Raghavendra R, Venkatesh S, Raja K, Busch C (2018) A low-cost multi-finger vein verification system. In: proceedings of international conference on imaging systems and techniques (IST 2018), Karkow, Poland
27. Shaheed K, Liu H, Yang G, Qureshi I, Gou J, Yin Y (2018) A systematic review of finger vein recognition techniques. Information 9:213
28. Ting E, Ibrahim M (2018) A review of finger vein recognition system. J Telecommun Electron Comput Eng 10(1–9):167–171
29. Today BT (2014) Uk banking customers ready for finger biometrics authentication. Biom Technol Today 2014(9):3–12. 10.1016/S0969-4765(14)70138-9 http://www.sciencedirect.com/science/article/pii/S0969476514701389
30. Tome P, Vanoni M, Marcel S (2014) On the vulnerability of finger vein recognition to spoofing. In: IEEE international conference of the biometrics special interest group (BIOSIG). URL http://publications.idiap.ch/index.php/publications/show/2910
31. Ton B (2012) Vascular pattern of the finger: biometric of the future? sensor design, data collection and performance verification. Master's thesis, University of Twente
32. Ton B, Veldhuis R (2013) A high quality finger vascular pattern dataset collected using a custom designed capturing device. In: International conference on biometrics, ICB 2013. IEEE. URL http://doc.utwente.nl/87790/
33. University of Reading (2017) PROTECT multimodal DB dataset. http://projectprotect.eu/dataset/
34. University of Salzburg (2018) PLUSVein-FV3 finger-vein data set. http://www.wavelab.at/sources/PLUSVein-FV3
35. Veldhuis R, Spreeuwers L, Ton B, Rozendal S (2019) A high quality finger vein dataset collected using a custom designed capture device. In: Uhl A, Busch C, Marcel S, Veldhuis R (eds) Handbook of vascular biometrics. Springer Science+Business Media, Boston, MA, USA, pp 145–158
36. Wang J, Wang G (2017) Quality-specific hand vein recognition system. IEEE Trans Inf Forensics Secur 12(11):2599–2610
37. Watanabe M, Endoh T, Shiohara M, Sasaki S (2005) Palm vein authentication technology and its applications. In: Proceedings of the biometric consortium conference, Citeseer, pp 19–21
38. Xi X, Yang G, Yin Y, Meng X (2013) Finger vein recognition with personalized feature selection. Sensors 13(9):11243–11259
39. Yang L, Yang G, Yin Y, Zhou L (2014) A survey of finger vein recognition. In: Chinese conference on biometric recognition (CCBR'14), vol 8833. Springer LNCS, pp 234–243
40. Yang W, Yu X, Liao Q (2009) Personal authentication using finger vein pattern and finger-dorsa texture fusion. In: Proceedings of the 17th ACM international conference on Multimedia. ACM, pp 905–908

41. Yin Y, Liu L, Sun X (2011) Sdumla-hmt: a multimodal biometric database. In: Biometric recognition, pp 260–268
42. Yuksel A, Akarun L, Sankur B (2011) Hand vein biometry based on geometry and appearance methods. IET Comput Vis 5(6):398–406
43. Zhang, C., Li, X., Liu, Z., Zhao, Q., Xu, H., Su, F.: The cfvd reflection-type finger-vein image database with evaluation baseline. In: Biometric recognition. Springer, pp 282–287

Online References and Data Sheets

44. Aliexpress (2018) 10x focusable 1230 metal housing w lens for TO-18 5.6 mm laser diode LD product page. https://www.aliexpress.com/item/10x-Focusable-1230-Metal-Housing-w-Lens-for-TO-18-5-6mm-Laser-Diode-LD/32665828682.html?spm=a2g0s.9042311.0.0.27424c4drx8E2d. Accessed 20 June 2018
45. Aliexpress (2018) Double IC two road ACC circuit laser diode driver board 650 nm 2.8–5 v adjustable constant current 0-390 mA 780 nm 808 nm 980 nm laser product page. https://www.aliexpress.com/item/Double-IC-Two-Road-ACC-Circuit-laser-Dode-Driver-Board-650nm-2-8-5v-Adjustable-Constant/32818824875.html?spm=a2g0s.9042311.0.0.27424c4drx8E2d. Accessed 20 June 2018
46. Aliexpress: TO-18 300 mW 808 nm NIR laser diode product page. https://www.aliexpress.com/item/5Pcs-lot-High-Quality-808nm-300mW-High-Power-Burning-Infrared-Laser-Diode-Lab/32272128336.html?spm=a2g0s.9042311.0.0.27424c4drx8E2d. Accessed 20 June 2018
47. Alpha & Omega Semiconductor (2018) AO3418 30V N-Channel MOSFET SMD data sheet. http://aosmd.com/pdfs/datasheet/AO3418.pdf. Accessed 20 June 2018
48. Arduino LLC: Arduino Nano manual. https://www.arduino.cc/en/uploads/Main/ArduinoNanoManual23.pdf. Accessed 20 June 2018
49. Continental Device India Limited (2018) BC327-25 PNP TO-92 silicon planar epitaxal transistor data sheet. http://pdf.datasheetcatalog.com/datasheet_pdf/continental-device-india-limited/BC327_to_BC338-40.pdf. Accessed 20 June 2018
50. Corporation, F.: Fujifilm HF9HA-1B product page. http://www.fujifilmusa.com/products/optical_devices/machine-vision/2-3-15/hf9ha-1b/index.html. Accessed 20 June 2018
51. Corporation H (2018) Hitachi H-1 finger-vein scanner product page. http://www.hitachi.co.jp/products/it/veinid/global/products/embedded_devices_u.html. Accessed 20 June 2018
52. Corporation M (2018) M2SYS M2-finger-vein reader product page. http://www.m2sys.com/finger-vein-reader/. Accessed 20 June 2018
53. Corporation M (2018) MIDOPT BN810 810 nm narrow near-IR bandpass filter product page. http://midopt.com/filters/bn810/. Accessed 20 June 2018
54. Corporation M (2018) MIDOPT BN850 850 nm narrow near-IR bandpass filter product page. http://midopt.com/filters/bn850/. Accessed 20 June 2018
55. Corporation M (2018) MIDOPT LP780 NIR pass-through filter product page. http://midopt.com/filters/lp780/. Accessed 20 June 2018
56. Corporation M (2018) MIDOPT LP830 NIR pass-through filter product page. http://midopt.com/filters/lp830/. Accessed 20 June 2018
57. Corporation M (2018) Mofiria FVA-U3SXE finger vein reader data sheet. https://www.mofiria.com/wp/wp-content/uploads/2017/08/FVA-U3SXE.pdf. Accessed 20 June 2018
58. Corporation M (2018) Mofiria FVA-U4BT finger vein reader data sheet (FVA-U4ST is the same device except for the USB instead of Bluetooth connection). https://www.mofiria.com/wp/wp-content/uploads/2017/08/FVA-U4BT_E.pdf. Accessed 20 June 2018
59. IDS Imaging Development Systems GmbH (2018) uEye software suite product and download page. https://de.ids-imaging.com/download-ueye-win32.html. Accessed 20 June 2018

60. IDS Imaging Development Systems GmbH (2018) UI-ML1240-NIR NIR-enhanced industrial camera data sheet. https://de.ids-imaging.com/IDS/datasheet_pdf.php?sku=AB00184. Accessed 20 June 2018
61. Lucky Light Electronics Co., Ltd. (2018) 504WC2E-W6-3PC 5 mm round with flange type warm white LED technical data sheet. https://www.luckylight.cn/media/component/data-sheet/504WC2E-W6-3PC.pdf. Accessed 20 June 2018
62. Microchip Corporation (2018) Microchip AVR ATmega328P 8-bit microcontroller full data sheet. http://ww1.microchip.com/downloads/en/DeviceDoc/ATmega328_P%20AVR%20MCU%20with%20picoPower%20Technology%20Data%20Sheet%2040001984A.pdf. Accessed 20 June 2018
63. Microchip Corporation (2018) Microchip AVR ATmega328P 8-bit microcontroller product page. https://www.microchip.com/wwwproducts/en/ATmega328P. Accessed 20 June 2018
64. ON Semiconductor (2018) BC808 PNP SMD general purpose transistor data sheet. http://www.onsemi.com/pub/Collateral/BC808-25LT1-D.PDF. Accessed 20 June 2018
65. Osram Opto Semiconductors AG (2018) Osram SFH-4253-Z 850 nm NIR SMD LED data sheet. https://media.osram.info/media/resource/hires/osram-dam-2496162/SFH%204253.pdf. Accessed: 20 June 2018
66. Osram Opto Semiconductors AG (2018) Osram SFH-4550 850 nm high power infrared LED data sheet. https://dammedia.osram.info/media/resource/hires/osram-dam-5580407/SFH%204550_EN.pdf. Accessed 20 June 2018
67. Renesas Electronics (2019) Application Note AN1737—eye safety for proximity sensing using infrared light-emitting diodes. https://www.renesas.com/eu/en/doc/application-note/an1737.pdf. Accessed 20 Jan 2019
68. Texas Instruments Corporation (2018) Texas instruments TLC59401 16-channel LED driver with dot correction and greyscale PWM control data sheet. http://www.ti.com/lit/ds/sbvs137/sbvs137.pdf. Accessed 20 June 2018
69. Vishay Semiconductor (2018) TSUS540 series infrared emitting diode, 950 nm, GaAs data sheet. https://www.vishay.com/docs/81056/tsus5400.pdf. Accessed 20 June 2018
70. Vishay Siliconix (2018) IRF510 Hexfet power MOSFET T0-220 data sheet. https://www.vishay.com/docs/91015/sihf510.pdf. Accessed 20 June 2018

Chapter 4
An Available Open-Source Vein Recognition Framework

Christof Kauba and Andreas Uhl

Abstract An available recognition toolkit is one of the basic requirements for conducting research in finger- and hand vein recognition. Currently, there is only one comprehensive, open-source, software package available, which includes a full finger vein recognition toolkit. We present a novel, full fledged vein recognition software framework implemented in MATLAB. Our PLUS OpenVein software package contains various well-established and state-of-the-art vein enhancement, feature extraction and comparison schemes. Moreover, it contains tools to evaluate the recognition performance and provides functions to perform feature- and score-level fusion. It is fully open source and available free of charge for research and non-commercial purposes. This vein recognition framework has already been used in several papers and can be a valuable tool for other researchers working in vein recognition.

Keywords Finger vein recognition · Hand vein recognition · Open-source software · Vein recognition software · Performance evaluation

4.1 Introduction

Vascular pattern-based biometrics are an emerging biometric trait due to their various advantages over other biometric traits. Vascular pattern-based biometrics deal with the patterns formed by the blood vessels located inside the human body, where the patterns inside the human fingers and hands are the most widely used body parts. This is commonly denoted as finger- and hand vein recognition. In order to conduct research on any biometric trait, there are two important prerequisites: the availability of datasets for training and testing and the availability of a complete

C. Kauba (✉) · A. Uhl
Department of Computer Sciences, University of Salzburg, Jakob-Haringer-Str. 2, 5020 Salzburg, Austria
e-mail: ckauba@cs.sbg.ac.at

A. Uhl
e-mail: uhl@cs.sbg.ac.at

A. Uhl et al. (eds.), *Handbook of Vascular Biometrics*, Advances in Computer Vision and Pattern Recognition, https://doi.org/10.1007/978-3-030-27731-4_4

biometric recognition tool chain tailored to the specific biometric trait to be able to conduct recognition performance evaluations.

Regarding the first requirement, the availability of datasets, there are already several publicly available finger- and hand vein data sets like the UTFVP [45], the HKPU [22], the SDUMLA-HMT [52] and the FV-USM [3]. Regarding open finger vein sensors, besides the sensor presented by Ton [44] and Raghavendra et al. [36], we propose an open- source finger vein scanner design which is available free of charge for research purposes in Chap. 3 [13] of this book. This enables every researcher to capture his own data set with a reproduction of a scanner based on our design. Hence, it is easily possible to meet the first requirement by either obtaining one of the publicly available datasets or by capturing a new one.

Prior to publishing any new results in vein recognition, regardless if they are from a proposed enhancement scheme or a new feature extraction approach, the second important requirement is the implementation of a complete biometric recognition tool chain. This tool chain includes the following five major steps/modules: The first one is parsing the dataset and reading the images according to the subject, finger/hand and image ID. The second step is preprocessing in order to enhance the quality of the vein patterns. The next step is the feature extraction itself, where feature vectors or biometric templates, encoding the relevant details of the vein patterns are extracted from the preprocessed images. During the subsequent comparison step, two templates are compared against each other and a comparison score is calculated. The last step is the performance evaluation, where certain performance figures and plots describing the recognition performance of the evaluated approach are generated. These results are a vital part in assessing the performance of a new vein recognition scheme and publishing a paper without reporting recognition performance results hardly makes sense. Another important aspect is that it should be easy to include a new recognition scheme in the existing tool chain in order to evaluate its recognition performance. Of course, it is always possible to combine all the individual parts and implement this tool chain from scratch for conducting the performance evaluation. However, it is more convenient if there is a tool chain provided and only the new part has to be included in the existing tool chain. Moreover, if the tool chain provides standardised test protocols it helps in enabling a common basis for the performance evaluation and makes the results easier to compare.

For several parts of the recognition tool chain, there are a few publicly available implementations available, especially for the feature extraction and comparison step. There is only one full featured vein recognition library, which is part of the BOB library, written in Python, combining all the necessary steps, available. Even this library, which is described in the following subsection, does neither include more recent vein recognition schemes, nor a comprehensive set of vein tailored enhancement schemes. BOB provides such a tool chain where the test protocols are included and a new recognition scheme can be easily added by adhering to the specified interface. Although Python and especially some freely available Python modules provide several image processing operations, many researchers prefer MATLAB instead of other programming languages to test their new approaches. MATLAB provides many common image processing operations out of the box and is easy to use and debug.

In this chapter, we present a new full fledged, open-source, vein recognition framework, called PLUS OpenVein Toolkit which is written in MATLAB. This framework includes a full vein recognition tool chain, consisting of image reading, preprocessing, feature extraction, comparison and performance evaluation. Its design enables an easy integration of new recognition schemes and allows for flexible combinations of different preprocessing and feature extraction schemes. It supports several commonly used hand- and finger vein datasets out of the box while it is straightforward to include the support for new ones. There are 11 vein specific preprocessing as well as 13 feature extraction and comparison approaches included. The whole framework is available free of charge for research and non-commercial purposes. In addition, we would encourage every interested researcher to contribute their own work to extend and improve the whole framework.

The rest of this chapter is structured as follows: Sect. 4.2 discusses related work on publicly available vein recognition software. The software framework, its history, licensing, the directory structure as well as the contained external components are explained in Sect. 4.3. The vein recognition schemes included in our OpenVein toolkit are listed and described in Sect. 4.4. Section 4.5 gives some exemplary baseline results of the toolkit's application on the UTFVP dataset. Section 4.6 summarises this chapter together with an outlook on future work.

4.2 Related Work

Bram Ton provided several finger vein recognition methods as MATLAB implementations on MATLAB Central.[1] These implementations include the following feature extraction methods: Maximum Curvature, proposed by Miura et al. [32], Repeated Line Tracking, also proposed by Miura et al. [31], Principal Curvature, proposed by Choi et al. [6] and the Wide Line Detector as proposed by Huang et al. [8]. The comparison scheme used by Miura et al. in [31, 32] is also contained. In addition, the finger region detection method proposed by Lee et al. [23] and the finger normalisation method proposed by Huang et al. [8] are included too. However, there is no surrounding framework combining all those individual parts and forming a whole vein recognition tool chain (e.g. to read all the images of a whole dataset and to evaluate the recognition performance). We included all the schemes implemented and provided by Bram Ton in our software framework. The respective links can be found in Sect. 4.3.3.

The Bob toolbox[2] [1, 2], which "is a signal-processing and machine learning toolbox originally developed by the Biometrics Security and Privacy Group, and the Research and Development Engineers at Idiap, in Switzerland." contains a biometric

[1] https://www.mathworks.com/matlabcentral/.

[2] https://www.idiap.ch/software/bob/.

vein recognition library.[3] This library is based on their open-source biometric recognition platform, using the base types and techniques provided by the bob.bio.base package.[4] The bob.bio.vein package contains several finger vein preprocessing and feature extraction/comparison schemes as well as performance evaluation tools and supports a few publicly available vein datasets. It is written in Python and uses several Python libraries like NumPi[5] and SciPi.[6] The implemented vein preprocessing methods include fixed cropping, masking and padding, histogram equalisation, finger normalisation as proposed by Huang et al. [8], finger masking as proposed by Kono [21], finger masking as proposed by Lee et al. [23] and a Watershed segmentation-based finger masking. The provided feature extraction methods consist of: an LBP based approach [30], Miura et al.'s Maximum Curvature [32] and Repeated Line Tracking [31] method, a normalised cross-correlation method as proposed by Kono [21], Choi et al.'s Principal Curvature [6] and the Wide Line Detector proposed by Huang et al. [8]. The comparison algorithms include a simple cross-correlation based method, a Hamming distance-based approach and the cross-correlation approach suggested by Miura et al. [31, 32]. The bob.bio.vein software runs automated biometric recognition experiments where a certain dataset, preprocessor, feature extractor and comparison algorithm are selected. The results can be saved and several evaluation metrics and plots can be generated. Score-level fusion is supported too. The UTFVP [45] and the Vera Fingervein database [43] are supported out of the box. A new or custom data set can be easily defined following their interface specification. Furthermore, the software package is able to perform a grid-based best parameter search and utilise parallel processing.

Our provided PLUS OpenVein Toolkit vein recognition framework is an all-in-one solution, providing a complete biometric recognition tool chain from reading the input vein images to outputting the performance figures and results. It includes 11 vein specific preprocessing and image enhancement schemes together with some more generic ones. Thirteen different feature extraction methods together with the respective comparison schemes are implemented or included, ranging from several well-established ones to more recent state-of-the-art ones like DTFPM [27] and ASAVE [51]. Moreover, several evaluation protocols are available together with some widely used performance figures and plots. It is able to process finger- as well as hand vein images. Furthermore, basic feature- and score-level fusion tools as well as image contrast and vein image quality assessment schemes are provided as well. It supports a variety of different finger- and hand vein datasets. All those individual parts are bundled in an easy and convenient to use MATLAB-based vein recognition framework, which is available free of charge. The included schemes are described in the following section.

---

[3] https://www.idiap.ch/software/bob/docs/bob/bob.bio.vein/master/index.html.

[4] https://gitlab.idiap.ch/bob/bob.bio.base.

[5] http://www.numpy.org/.

[6] http://www.scipy.org/.

4.3 PLUS OpenVein Toolkit

This subsection gives a general overview of the vein recognition framework, including its structure and main components as well as its terms of use and where to obtain it.

Figure 4.1 shows the design of a typcial biometric recognition system, including the biometric trait which is to be captured, the biometric capture device and the recognition tool chain. Our PLUS OpenVein Toolkit vein recognition framework resembles the software parts, i.e. the whole recognition tool chain part of the figure. The corresponding methods are shown in Fig. 4.2. The whole framework is implemented in MATLAB. At the time of writing, MATLAB version 2016a–2018b are supported. Compatibility to new releases will be reported on our website. MATLAB is widely used in academia as it enables quick and easy prototyping as well as platform independence. MATLAB itself is neither open source nor free of charge. However, many research institutions already licensed MATLAB so there will be no additional costs for them. Moreover, student licenses for MATLAB are available at a very reasonable price. Futhermore, there is the free and open source alternative to MATLAB, called GNU Octave.[7] Note that the toolkit has not been tested in Octave and is not guaranteed to run with Octave.

The vein recognition framework started as a finger vein recognition tool in the scope of a proseminar project back in 2013 which was done by Christof Kauba and Jakob Reissig. At first, only MC, RLT and WLD were contained as feature extraction methods, based on the publicly available code provided by B.T. Ton on MATLAB Central. Then a SIFT-based feature extraction method [14] and several preprocessing methods have been implemented. From there on it started to grow and include several other feature extraction and preprocessing schemes as well as convenience code for automated execution based on settings files before we finally decided to provide it to the research community as an open-source framework. The PLUS OpenVein Toolkit vein recognition framework is available[8] free of charge for research and non-commercial purposes. It is covered under the New BSD Licence.[9] By downloading and using our framework you agree to our terms of use, especially to cite one of our papers [11, 13] if results obtained with the help of our recognition framework are published. Further usage instructions, a detailed description of the individual parts and a link to our git repository can be found on the website. The framework is still being improved and extended and we encourage every interested researcher to contribute to our open-source framework.[10] It has already been used in numerous publications (sorted by date of publication):

---

[7] http://www.gnu.org/software/octave/.

[8] Can be downloaded at: http://www.wavelab.at/sources/OpenVein-Toolkit/.

[9] https://opensource.org/licenses/BSD-3-Clause.

[10] The source code is hosted on our gitlab server: https://gitlab.cosy.sbg.ac.at/ckauba/openvein-toolkit.

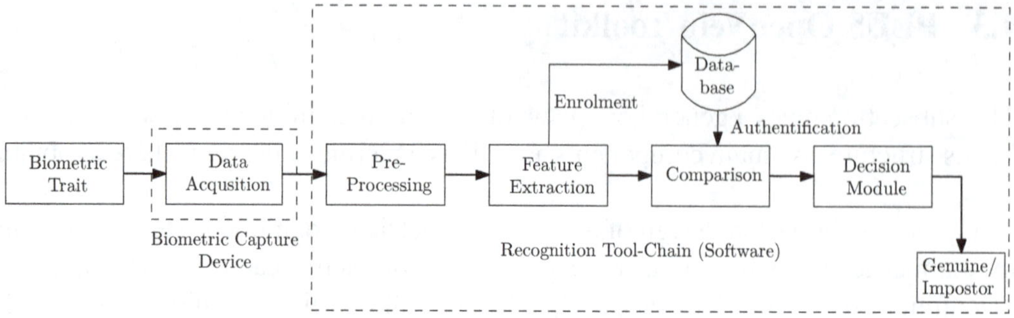

Fig. 4.1 Biometric recognition system

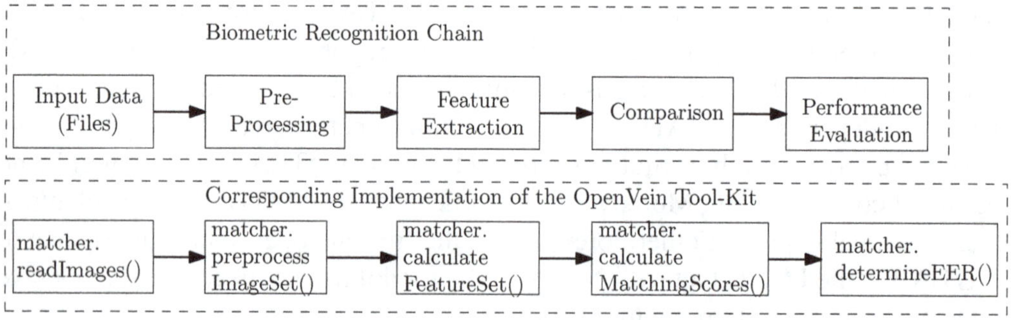

Fig. 4.2 Implementation of the different processing steps by the PLUS OpenVein Toolkit

- Kauba, C., Reissig, J., Uhl, A.: Pre-processing cascades and fusion in finger vein recognition (2014) [14]
- Kauba, C., Uhl, A.: Sensor Ageing Impact on Finger-Vein Recognition (2015) [16]
- Kauba, C., Uhl, A.: Robustness Evaluation of Hand Vein Recognition Systems (2015) [15]
- Kauba, C.: Impact of Sensor Ageing on Finger-Image based Biometric Recognition Systems. Master's thesis (2015) [9]
- Kauba, C., Piciucco, E., Maiorana, E., Campisi, P., Uhl, A.: Advanced Variants of Feature Level Fusion for Finger Vein Recognition (2016) [10]
- Kauba, C., Uhl, A.: Shedding Light on the Veins—Reflected Light or Transillumination in Hand-Vein Recognition (2018) [18]
- Kauba, C., Uhl, A.: Robustness of Finger-Vein Recognition (2018) [17]
- Kauba, C., Prommegger, B., Uhl, A.: Focussing the Beam—A New Laser Illumination Based Data Set Providing Insights to Finger-Vein Recognition (2018) [11]
- Kauba, C., Prommegger, B., Uhl, A.: The Two Sides of the Finger—An Evaluation on the Recognition Performance of Dorsal versus Palmar Finger-Veins (2018) [12]
- Prommegger, B., Kauba, C., Uhl, A.: Multi-Perspective Finger-Vein Biometrics (2018) [34]
- Prommegger, B., Kauba, C., Uhl, A.: Longitudinal Finger Rotation—Problems and Effects in Finger-Vein Recognition (2018) [33]

- Kirchgasser, S., Kauba, C., Uhl, A.: Towards Understanding Acquisition Conditions Influencing Finger-Vein Recognition (2019) [20]
- Prommeger, B., Kauba, C., Uhl, A.: A Different View on the Finger—Multi-Perspective Score Level Fusion in Finger-Vein Recognition (2019) [35].

4.3.1 Directory Structure

Figure 4.3 shows a schematic overview of the vein recognition framework. The main file is `Matcher.m`, which contains most of the program logic, including the pre-processing, feature extraction, comparison execution functions. The "matcher" is actually a MATLAB object, also storing the input images, the extracted features, the comparison scores and the results. Some parts of the recognition schemes are directly implemented in `Matcher.m`, but most of the schemes are called as external functions, implemented in distinct .m files. These .m files are organised in the following subdirectories:

- Automation: several scripts for batch automation, automated testing of setting files, etc.
- EEREvaluation: functions to determine the performance figures and plots.
- FeatureExtraction: most of the self-contained feature extraction functions, like the ones provided by Bram Ton.
- FeatureLevelFusion: tools to perform feature-level fusion and evaluate fusion results.
- GUI: graphical user interface related stuff.
- Matching: different comparison functions, e.g. the Miura matcher.
- Preprocessing: various preprocessing functions for vein images.
- Quality Assessment: a few general image contrast metrics as well as vein specific quality metrics.
- ScoreLevelFusion: tools and functions to perform (simple) score-level fusion.
- Settings: contains the settings files for various datasets.
- UtilityFunctions: several helper functions, e.g. for handling ini files, progress bar, plotting SIFT key-points.
- vl_feat: directory where to put the vl_feat sources.

Besides these directories, there are several other directories inside the main directory, e.g. `Matsuda16` and `ASAVE`. These recognition schemes contain feature extraction as well as comparison methods and it is not obvious how to separate these parts so we decided to put all the stuff necessary for the scheme in one directory, named according to the method. As this is neither feature extraction only, nor comparison only, the directories are located inside the main directory instead. More details on the implemented recognition and evaluation schemes can be found in Sect. 4.4.

Each step of the program execution can be called manually. To run the whole recognition tool chain at once, including reading of the vein images, preprocess-

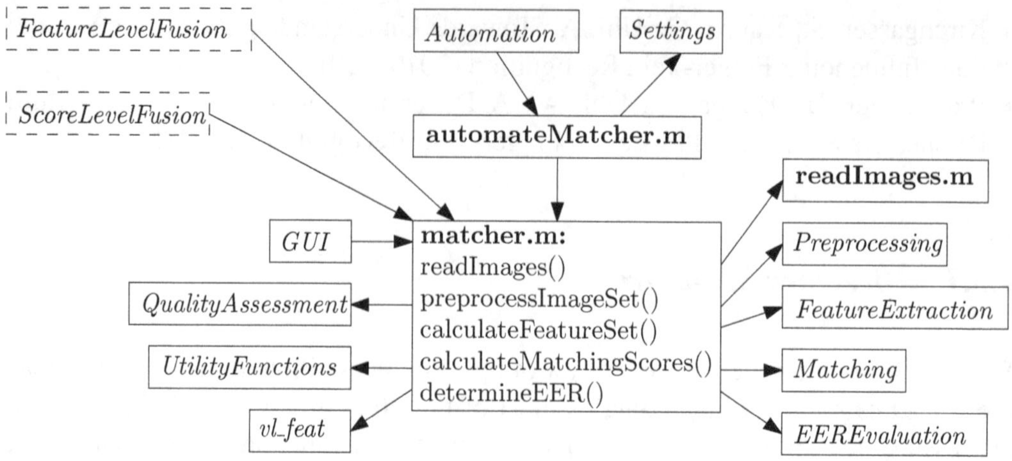

Fig. 4.3 Schematic overview of the PLUS OpenVein Toolkit, MATLAB files are **bold** font, directory names are *italics* font

ing, feature extraction, comparison and performance determination, we provide the `automateMatcher()` function/script, which has to be called with the paths to the input images and the desired settings file, which is described in Sect. 4.3.2. During each of the steps, a progress bar with the current progress and the estimated remaining time is shown. After all the steps are finished, the results (plots and EER/FMR values) are displayed.

4.3.2 Settings Files

Several settings files for the supported datasets are provided in the `Settings` subdirectory. There is an example settings file in this directory, called `settingsExample.ini`, which lists all possible options (excluding all parameters of the different preprocessing, feature extraction and comparison methods) together with a short explanation. All the important parameters and options are controlled via these settings files and by automatically generating settings files, various different settings can be tested in batch processing for parameter tuning. The settings are grouped according to general settings, preprocessing settings, feature extraction settings, optional post-processing settings, comparison settings and results settings. Optionally, most of these options can be passed to `automateMatcher` as additional input arguments, overwriting the parameters defined in the settings file. The settings are described in more detail in the readme file of the PLUS OpenVein Toolkit.

4.3.3 External Dependencies

Our framework contains several external dependencies. The following ones are not included in the sources of the framework and have to be downloaded separately and then put into the respective subdirectories:

- vl_feat: mainly used to provide a SIFT implementation, the MATLAB version can be found at [68].
- MASI Fusion: implements the STAPLE/STAPLER and COLLATE fusion algorithms. The MATLAB version is available at [62].
- ARIA Vessels Library: used to perform the IUWT feature extraction, a MATLAB implementation is freely available at [57].

Furthermore, several schemes and functions have not been implemented by ourselves. Instead, publicly available implementation have been used. These implementations are already contained in the framework:

- MC, WLD, RLT vein network extraction methods: these implementations are provided by Bram Ton and are available on MATLAB Central [65] and [67].
- PC: For principal curvature [6] another implementation of Bram Ton is used.
- LeeRegion, HuangNormalise: these implementations are provided by Bram Ton and are available on MATLAB Central [66] and [64].
- Retinex: a publicly available MATLAB implementation of Brian Funt, Florian Ciurea, and John McCann is utilised. It can be found at [59].
- SUACE: The implementation provided by the original authors of [4] is used. It is available on github: [56].
- Adaptive thresholding: an implementation by Guanglei Xiong, which is available at [69] is used.
- Gaussian filtering: an implementation by F. van der Heijden, available as part of the Image Edge Enhancing Coherence Filter Toolbox [60] is used.
- Frangi filtering and Hessian filtering: an implementation by D. Kroon, also available as part of the Image Edge Enhancing Coherence Filter Toolbox [60] is utilised.
- Histogram distances: For several of the included histogram comparison distances the implementation by Boris Schauerte, available at [63] are used.
- EER/DET plots: For determining the EER and other performance figures as well as for creating the ROC/DET plots, modified versions of the functions contained in the BioSecure framework are utilised. The original implementation can be found at: [61].
- Ini file handling: The open source ini library for MATLAB by Primoz Cermelj is utilised, available at: [58].

For several basic image processing as well as morphological image operations, functions provided by MATLAB's image processing toolbox are utilised. All the other vein specific preprocessing, feature extraction and comparison schemes that are included within the PLUS OpenVein Toolkit and not listed above are custom re-implementations done by the authors. Some smaller helper functions and methods are not implemented by the authors, but again publicly available implementations have been utilisied. These are not listed above, however, the information regarding the original author and the copyright notice can be found in the respective source code files. More details about each individual implementation can be found in the source code files of the respective scheme.

4.4 Included Vein Recognition Schemes

In this section, the reading of the input datasets, preprocessing, feature extraction, comparison and performance evaluations schemes which are implemented and/or included in our PLUS OpenVein Toolkit are listed and described, including references to their original publications. Some of those methods are custom re-implementations done by the authors of the PLUS OpenVein Toolkit while for others, publicly available implementations or the original authors' implementations have been used if available. Section 4.3.3 lists the details about the schemes which are used from external sources and have not been implemented by ourselves.

4.4.1 Input File Handling/Supported Datasets

Instead of acquiring the biometric data directly from the capture device, this data is read from the file system in the form of images. The handling of the image files (getting all files in a directory, reading the images and storing them in an in-memory cell array for further use) is done in `readImages.m`. Parsing of the file names (subject, finger/hand and sample ID) is based on regular expressions. A new dataset can be easily added by adding a new case to the switch-case clause in `readImages.m`, providing a suitable regular expression for parsing the file name. Currently, the following commonly used hand- and finger vein dataset are supported by our vein recognition framework[11]:

- UTFVP [45],
- SDUMLA-HMT [52],
- FV-USM [3],
- HKPU [22],
- VERA FingerVein Spoofing [43],
- VERA PalmVein [42],
- PLUSVein-FV3 [12],

[11] Supported means that the files are read and partitioned into subjects/fingers/samples correctly but not necessarily that optimised settings files for each single one of them exist.

- PLUSVein-3D-FV [35],
- PROTECT Hand-/ Finger-/ and Wrist Vein [46].

4.4.2 Preprocessing

This subsection lists the included preprocessing schemes, grouped according to vein tailored ones at first, followed by general image processing ones. The names in brackets are the names as used in the toolkit. All of the mentioned preprocessing schemes can be combined in any order and more than once (a list of methods and parameters has to be provided in the settings file), e.g. CLAHE followed by Zhao09, followed by Zhang09, followed by CLAHE, followed by Resize. Different parameters for each preprocessing scheme can be used each time it is applied. The order and the parameters are configured in the settings file.

Finger Masking (LeeRegion)

Lee et al. [23] proposed a simple method to localise the finger region and mask out the background. In general, the finger region is brighter than the background. Thus, to detect the finger outline, the image is convolved with a custom mask containing lines of 1 and -1 values (different order for upper and lower outline). Afterwards, all pixels above the detected upper boundary and below the detected lower boundary are masked out by setting their value to 0 (black).

Finger Rotation Compensation Normalisation (HuangNormalise)

Huang et al. [8] use a normalisation method based on the finger outline and the finger baseline as the first step of their finger vein recognition approach. They utilised an active contour model to detect the finger outline. Afterwards, the baseline of the finger is estimated as a straight line by calculating the midpoints between the points of the top and bottom outline of the finger using the least squares method. The angle between the finger baseline and the horizontal line is then determined and the image is transformed such that the finger baseline is horizontal. The transformation is done by the nearest sampling method. In our implementation, the LeeRegion method is used to detect the finger outline instead of the active contour model.

High-Frequency Emphasis Filtering (Zhao09)

Zhao et al. [54] utilised high-frequency emphasis filtering in combination with histogram equalisation for improving hand vein images. High-frequency Emphasis Filtering (HFEF) is applied in the frequency domain, hence at first the Fourier transform of the input vein images is computed. The HFE is computed based on an offset and a fixed multiplicative factor together with a Butterworth high-pass filter. Then the inverse Fourier transform is computed to obtain the enhanced image. Finally, a simple global histogram equalisation is applied to further improve the image contrast. Instead of this global histogram equalisation, we use CLAHE in our implementation.

Grey Level Grouping with Circular Gabor Filtering (Zhang09)

A combination of Grey Level Grouping and circular Gabor filters was proposed by Zhang and Yang [53] in the context of finger vein image enhancement. At first, they applied Grey Level Grouping to reduce illumination fluctuations and improve the contrast of the finger vein images. Then a circular Gabor filter is used to further enhance the visibility of the vein ridges in the images. In contrast to usual Gabor filters, which have a certain direction, Circular Gabor Filters (CGF) are omnidirectional. A CGF is essentially a 2D band pass filter whose passband looks like a circle and which is suitable for edge detection in arbitrary directions. Hence, vein lines in arbitrary directions are captured without distortion by this type of Gabor filter. The authors only use the real part of the Gabor filter output, thus arriving at an even-symmetric circular Gabor filter. Instead of Grey Level Grouping, we apply CLAHE again as the first step in our implementation.

Multichannel Gabor Filtering for Finger Vein Image Enhancement (Yang09)

Yang and Yang [50] proposed a finger vein enhancement scheme based on multi-channel Gabor filters in different scales and orientations. The input vein image is filtered by various different Gabor filters and the outputs of the individual filters are then combined to a final enhanced vein image using a simple reconstruction rule where a pixel value at a certain position is set to the index of the Gabor filter with the lowest output value. The Gabor filters are designed in a way that their period is twice the vein width and at least the orientation of one of the filters should be orthogonal to the vein lines. Four orientations with different centre frequencies turned out to achieve the best enhancement results.

A New Algorithm for Finger Vein Image Enhancement and Segmentation (Shi12)

The vein image enhancement scheme proposed by Shi et al. [38] is based on Koschmieder's law to reduce light scattering effects and on a bank of even Gabor filters to further enhance the visible vein patterns. At first, an anisotropic diffusion method together with an averaging filter is used to generate a smoothed finger vein image. This image in combination with the assumption that the extinction coefficient and the thickness of the skin tissue are used to solve the Koschmieder's law equation with respect to the undistorted vein image. This image is then further enhanced by applying a bank of even-symmetric Gabor filters. The final output image is obtained by combining the responses of each single Gabor filter using a multi-scale multiplication rule to further suppress unwanted information.

Finger Vein Image Restoration Based on a Biological Optical Model (Yang12)

Instead of Koschmieder's law, Yang et al. [49] proposed another vein enhancement scheme based on a Biological Optical Model (BOM). This model is based on the Beer–Lambert law, describing the light transport attenuation in the tissue and the non-scattered transmission map, describing the optical transmissivity of the given tissue. Solving this model from a single observed image is an ill-posed problem, hence the scattering component has to be estimated in order to solve this model. At first, the vein image is transformed to its negative version, which is beneficial for scattering illumination estimation. Then the scattering component is estimated by introducing three constraints. Afterwards, the scattering radiation is estimated based on local pixel statistics. Finally, the original finger vein image can be restored (enhanced) by computing a pixel-wise restoration based on the proposed BOM.

Finger Vein Ridge Enhancement (YangShi12)

Yang and Shi [48] suggested another finger vein enhancement scheme, again based on Koschmieder's law and a bank of even-symmetric Gabor filters, like they did in [38]. In contrast to their previous work, they did not use a simple multi-scale multiplication rule to combine the outputs of each individual Gabor filter to the final enhanced vein image, but they only use the single output of a filter per pixel based on the reconstruction rule introduced in [50]. Afterwards, they apply the multi-scale multiplication rule of [38] together with a normalisation rule to arrive at the enhanced vein image. This should help to suppress false vein ridge information.

Intensity Variation Normalisation for Finger Vein Recognition Using Singe Scale Retinex (Retinex)

Inspired by the work of Xie et al. [47] we included a single scale Retinex implementation in our framework. We did not include the guided filter part of the paper though. The Retinex method [28] is based on the assumption that an observed image can be regarded as the multiplication of several illumination and reflectance images. Reflectance changes sharply while illumination changes only smoothly. The Retinex method decomposes the intensity image (input image) in those two images (illumination and reflectance) by trying to estimate the illumination image using a Gaussian filter and subtracting the illumination image from the intensity image in the logarithm domain. The remaining reflectance image, resembling an illumination-normalised output, is the Retinex output.

Contrast Limited Adaptive Histogram Equalisation (CLAHE)

In contrast to global histogram equalisation, Adaptive Histogram Equalisation (AHE) is a local technique, computing several histograms for distinct sections of the image. These histograms are equalised individually and then combined in order to redistribute the lightness values of the image. AHE tends to over amplify the contrast in homogeneous regions of the image as the histogram in these regions is concentrated (only a few distinct grey values occur). Contrast Limited AHE (CLAHE) [55] limits the contrast amplification, in order to reduce the problem of noise amplification. CLAHE has been successfully used as a simple means of enhancing the contrast and quality of vein images. MATLAB's implementation of CLAHE as provided by the `adapthisteq` function is utilisied in our framework.

Speeded Up Adaptive Contrast Enhancement (SUACE)

The contrast enhancement method proposed by Bandara et al. [4] is, especially, tailored to enhance superficial vein images. In contrast to traditional approaches which are based on costly adaptive histogram equalisation methods, SUACE uses a fixed range for enhancing the contrast all over the image, which is shifted according to the calculated illumination at the current pixel position. Therefore, it utilises the response from low-frequency range of the infra-red input image signal, which is calculated by filtering the original image with a Gaussian filter, to adjust the boundaries for the reference dynamic range. This dynamic range is then used in a linear contrast stretching process.

Further Filtering/Image Processing Schemes

In addition to the above-mentioned, vein specific, preprocessing methods, we included several more generic image processing schemes which are able to enhance the vein image quality. These further schemes include image resize, image cropping, image rotation, median filtering, Wiener filtering, unsharp masking and Gaussian high-pass filtering. Most of these methods are based on the image processing functions provided by MATLAB.

4.4.3 Feature Extraction

In the following, the included feature extraction methods are described. These methods are grouped by vein based ones, i.e. outputting a binary vein image, followed by key-point based ones and general purpose ones.

Maximum Curvature (MC)

This feature extraction technique proposed by Miura et al. [32] aims to emphasise only the centre lines of the veins and is therefore insensitive to varying vein widths. The first step is the extraction of the centre positions of the veins by determining the local maximum curvature in cross-sectional profiles obtained in four directions: horizontal, vertical and the two oblique directions. The cross-sectional profile is determined based on the first and second derivates. Then each profile is classified as either being concave or convex, where only the local maxima belonging to a concave profile indicate a vein line. Afterwards, a score according to the width and curvature of the vein region is assigned to each centre position and recorded in a matrix called locus space. Due to noise or other distortions, some pixels may not have been classified correctly at the first step. Thus, the centre positions of the veins are connected using a filtering operation in all four directions taking the 8-neighbourhood of pixels into account. The final binary output image is obtained by thresholding of the locus space using the median as a threshold.

Enhanced Maximum Curvature (EMC)

EMC is an extension of Maximum Curvature by Syarif et al. [41]. In addition to the original MC approach, there is an additional image filtering/enhancement step based on Hessian Vessel filtering in between the extraction of the centre position of the veins and the filtering operation to connect the centre positions in order to extract small vein delineation that is hardly visible in the previously extracted vein patterns. Furthermore, a Histogram of Oriented Gradients (HOG) descriptor is used as feature representation instead of a simple binarisation fo the extracted curvature information as in the original Maximum Curvature. HOG captures edge and gradient structures and thus, the local gradient information of the vein features, more effectively than the simple thresholding based binarisation. In our vein recognition framework, there are two versions of EMC: one that only adds the additional enhancement step, called EMC within the framework and the other one, which is a full implementation of the method as proposed by Syarif et al., called EMC_HOG within the framework.

Wide Line Detector (WLD)

The Wide Line Detector [8] is essentially an adaptive thresholding technique (using isotropic non-linear filtering), i.e. thresholding inside a local neighbourhood region. The difference of the centre pixel to its neighbours inside a circular neighbourhood and the number of pixels inside this neighbourhood with a difference smaller than a predefined threshold are determined. This number is again thresholded to get the final binary output vein image.

Repeated Line Tracking (RLT)

As the veins appear as valleys in the cross-sectional profile of the image, RLT [31] tries to track the veins as dark lines inside the image. The tracking point is repeatedly initialised at random positions and then moved pixel by pixel along the dark line, where the depth of the valley indicates the movement direction. If no "valley" is detected a new tracking operation is started. The number of times a pixel is tracked, is recorded in a matrix. Pixels that are tracked multiple times as belonging to a line statistically have a high likelihood of belonging to a blood vessel. Binarisation using thresholding is applied to this matrix to get the binary output image.

Principal Curvature (PC)

Choi et al. [6] proposed this curvature-based feature extraction method. At first the gradient field of the image is calculated. In order to prevent the unwanted amplification of small noise components, a hard thresholding which filters out small gradients by setting their values to zero is done. Then the gradient at each pixel is normalised to a magnitude of 1 to get a normalised gradient field. This normalised gradient field is smoothed by applying a Gaussian filter. The next step is the actual principal curvature calculation. The curvatures are obtained from the Eigenvalues of the Hessian matrix at each pixel. The two Eigenvectors of the Hessian matrix represent the directions of the maximum and minimum curvature and the corresponding Eigenvalues are the principal curvatures. Only the bigger Eigenvalue which corresponds to the maximum curvature among all directions is used. The last step is a threshold-based binarisation of the principal curvature values to arrive at the binary vein output image.

Gabor Filtering (GF)

Gabor filters are inspired by the human visual system's multichannel processing of visual information and have been widely used in biometrics. A Gabor filter is a Gaussian kernel function modulated by a sinusoidal plane wave. Kumar and Zhou [22] proposed a Gabor filter based finger vein extraction approach. Therefore, a filter bank consisting of several 2D even-symmetric Gabor filters with different orientations (in $\frac{\pi}{k}$ steps where k is the number of orientations) is created. k feature images are extracted by filtering the vein image using the different filter kernels contained in the Gabor filter bank. The final feature image is obtained by summing up all the single feature images from the previous step and thresholding the resulting feature image. This image is then post-processing using morphological operations to remove noise and to get the final binary vein output image.

Anatomy Structure Analysis-Based Vein Extraction (ASAVE)

Yang et al. [51] proposed a new finger vein feature extraction and comparison approach based on incorporating knowledge about the anatomical structure (directionality, continuity, width variability as well as smoothness and solidness) and imaging characteristics of the underlying vein patterns. The vein pattern is extracted by their orientation map-guided curvature based on valley- or half-valley-shaped structures. This curvature is extracted using the Maximum Curvature algorithm [32]. The vein pattern is then further thinned and refined (filling, thinning, denoising and connecting) using morphological operations to make it more reliable. Furthermore, a so-called vein backbone is extracted from the input vein image by thresholding the curvature image, retaining only the most clear and reliable vein branches. This vein backbone is then utilised to align two images during comparison in order to compensate for horizontal as well as vertical displacements. Comparison itself is done using an elastic matching approach, which is able to tolerate small deformations in the two vein patterns. The similarity score is further refined by incorporating the overlap degree of the two vein backbones to arrive at the final output score.

Isotropic Undecimated Wavelet Transform (IUWT)

IUWT [40] is a special type of Wavelet transform which can be implemented in a simple way. At each iteration j, the scaling coefficients c_j are computed by low-pass filtering and the wavelet coefficients w_j by subtraction. The subsequent scaling coefficients of the transform are calculated by a convolution of the jth scale's scaling coefficient with a filter h^j. The subsequent wavelet coefficients are the difference between two adjacent sets of scaling coefficients. Levels 2 and 3 exhibit the best contrast for blood vessels and are thus taken into account for feature extraction. The vein features are extracted by adding the wavelet levels 2 and 3. The final features are obtained by thresholding the resulting Wavelet transform. This binarised image is then post-processed with morphological operations to remove noise.

Deformation Tolerant Feature Point Matching (DTFPM)

This key-point-based technique proposed by Matsuda et al. [27] replaces the conventional SIFT descriptor and key-point detector by vascular pattern tailored ones, taking the curvature and the vein directions into account. This method is robust against irregular shading and vein deformations due to posture changes. At first, the authors apply a technique originally proposed by Yang and Yang [50] for enhancing the vein images. Then a minimum-curvature map is calculated from the enhanced vein images based on Eigenvalue analysis. The feature point locations are determined from this curvature image (smaller Eigenvalue) at any point where the vein shape is non-linear. The feature descriptor takes the vein shape around the key-point location into account and is extracted from the so-called vein pattern map (larger Eigenvalue). The feature vector contains a quantification of the different vein directions inside a variable-sized window around the key-point location. The descriptor is normalised with the help of a finger shape model in a way that the descriptor area becomes smaller the closer the key-point location is to the finger boundaries. The authors employ a deformation tolerant matching strategy by using non-rigid registration. At first, the correspondences between the key-points in the two images for comparison are found. These correspondences are filtered using a local and global histogram technique based on the relative distances between the matched key-points. After this filtering step, the key-point coordinates of one of the involved feature vectors are transformed by applying a non-rigid transformation based on an outlier-robust thin-plate spline model as proposed in [37]. Afterwards, the correspondences between the adjusted key-points are determined again. These updated correspondences are filtered by a comparison of the descriptor distances with fixed thresholds. The final comparison score is determined as the ratio of the matched points and the sum of the number of detected key-points in both images. The authors claim that their proposed method is tolerant against several different types of finger posture changes, e.g. longitudinal finger rotation, translations and bending of the finger.

SIFT with Additional Key-Point Filtering (SIFT)

Key-point based techniques try to use information from the most discriminative points as well as considering the neighbourhood and context information of these points by extracting key-points and assigning a descriptor to each key-point. A SIFT [24]-based technique with additional key-point filtering as described in our previous work [14] is implemented in the vein recognition framework too. The key-point detector and descriptor is the default SIFT one, provided by the vl_feat[12] MATLAB implementation. To suppress the unwanted finger outline information, the key-points located within a certain area around the finger's outline are filtered (removed). The size of this area can be adjusted by a threshold.

SURF with Additional Key-Point Filtering (SURF)

Similar to SIFT, SURF is another general purpose key-point extractor and descriptor proposed by Bay et al. [5]. SURF is designed to be faster than SIFT while maintaining the robustness and description properties of SIFT. Our framework includes an OpenSURF [7] based vein feature extractor implementation with additional key-point filtering as for SIFT (described in [14]).

Finger Vein Recognition based on Deformation Information (Meng18)

The technique proposed by Meng et al. [29] is based on the observation that regular deformations, corresponding to posture changes, can only be present in genuine vein patterns. Thus, they incorporate pixel-based 2D displacements that correspond to these deformations during comparison. These displacements are determined with the help of a DenseSIFT descriptor-based approach. DenseSIFT extracts SIFT [24] descriptors at fixed points, defined by a dense grid. For each pixel, an 128-dimensional feature vector is extracted. Each pixel's feature vector is compared against all feature vectors of the second image to find its nearest neighbour. Afterwards, a displacement matrix recording the pixel-wise displacements of all matched feature vectors is created. The displacement uniformity, calculated from displacement matrix, resembles the final comparison score.

Local Binary Patterns Based (LBP)

LBP has been successfully used in many different kinds of image feature extraction, also in finger vein recognition [23]. It is implemented as another representative of a binarisation-type feature extraction scheme. LBP compares the grey level of a centre pixel to its neighbouring pixels. Each pixel's greyscale value is then represented by

[12]http://www.vlfeat.org/.

the corresponding binary code resulting from the comparison with its neighbourhood. This features can either be used directly during comparison or a histogram-based feature vector is created based on the LBP features. Therefore a histogram of the LBP values per input vein image is created and stored as a feature vector, which is then used during the comparison.

Phase Only Correlation (POC)

As the name suggests, POC [25] uses only the phase information in the frequency domain to compare two images. At first, the 2D Discrete Fourier Transform of both images which are to compare is calculated. Each of the coefficients can be represented by amplitude and phase. Then the cross-phase spectrum of the two images is determined. The POC function is defined as the 2D inverse Discrete Fourier Transform of the cross-phase spectrum. To suppress non-meaningful high-frequency components, a band-limited version of the cross-phase spectrum is calculated, by only including coefficients within a given window, which is centred at the correlation peak. The window size can be defined by two thresholds, a window width and window height, corresponding to the frequency band to be included. This variant is denoted as BLPOC (band-limited phase only correlation).

Morphological Post-Processing Options

Several morphological operations can be optionally applied after the feature extraction to enhance the feature images and remove noise. These operations include Skeletonisation, Thinning, Bridging, Fill, Shrink, Spur, Clean, Area Open, Inverse Area Open, Dilation, Erosion, Top Hat, Bottom Hat, Open and Close. Most of these operations require at least one additional parameter. Their implementation is based on the morphological image processing operations provided by MATLAB.

4.4.4 Comparison

This subsection lists the included comparison schemes, starting by two general purpose ones for binary templates and histogram data, followed by feature-type specific ones.

Miura Matcher (Miura)

For comparing the binary vein features we included the approach proposed by Miura et al. in [31, 32]. This approach is basically a simple correlation measure between an input and a reference image. Finger- as well as hand vein images are not registered to each other and only coarsely aligned (rotation is compensated for finger vein images) in general. Thus, the correlation between the input image and trimmed as well as in x- and y-direction shifted versions of the reference image is calculated. The maximum of these correlation values is normalised and then used as the final comparison score. The output score is a similarity score in the range of [0, 0.5] where 0.5 means a perfect match. This comparison scheme is selected by the comparison type `Miura`.

Histogram Comparison (Histogram)

Mainly for the comparison of the LBP histogram-based features, but not restricted to these features, we included several common histogram comparison metrics: histogram intersection distance, Chi-squared distance, Quadratic Form distance, Bhattacharyya distance, Jensen–Shannon divergence, Kolmogorov–Smirnov distance and Kullback–Leibler divergence. All those distance metrics can be selected if the comparison type is set to `Histogram`.

Feature-Type Specific Comparison

Several feature extraction schemes like DTFPM [27], ASAVE [51], POC [25], SIFT [14], Meng et al. [29] and others require a specific comparison scheme that can only be used with this particular kind of feature. Of course, all those feature specific comparison schemes are included as well and they are selected automatically if one of those feature types is set.

4.4.5 Comparison/Evaluation Protocols

In order to calculate the False Match Rate (FMR) and the False Non-Match Rate (FNMR) as defined by the ISO/IEC 19795-1 standard [39] prior to determining further performance numbers like the Equal Error Rate (EER), several different protocols are included. n_{gen} is the number of genuine comparisons, n_{imp} the number of impostor ones, n_i is the number of images/samples per hand/finger, n_{fh} is the number of hands/fingers that are captured per subject and n_s is the number of subjects.

FVC

This protocol is adopted from the fingerprint verification contests (e.g. the FVC2004 [26]). All possible genuine comparison are performed, i.e. each sample is compared against all remaining samples of the same biometric instance, i.e. finger/hand. No symmetric comparisons are performed, i.e. if the comparison [image A–image B] is performed, the comparison [image B–image A] is not performed as most comparison metrics are symmetric and both comparisons would result in the same score value. The number of genuine comparisons is

$$n_{gen} = \frac{n_i \cdot (n_i - 1)}{2} \cdot n_{fh}$$

For the impostor comparisons, only the first sample of each finger/hand is compared against the first sample of all remaining fingers/hands. As with the genuine comparisons, no symmetric comparisons are performed. The number of impostor comparisons is

$$n_{imp} = \frac{n_{fh} \cdot (n_{fh} - 1)}{2}$$

This protocol speeds up the comparison process as the number of impostor comparisons is greatly reduced while still ensuring that at least each finger/hand is compared against each other finger/hand once. The number of fingers/hands refers to the total number of fingers/hands in the dataset and not the number of fingers/hands per subject, e.g. if there are 60 subjects and 6 fingers in the dataset, then the number of fingers is 360. The above-mentioned number of genuine and impostor comparisons refers to the "probe only" comparison mode, i.e. that the gallery and probe directory are the same. In this case, one sample is not compared against itself. If the "gallery mode" comparison is used, i.e. the gallery directory contains different samples than the probe one, each probe sample is compared against the sample with the same subject/finger/sample ID within the gallery samples. Thus, the number of genuine and impostor comparisons is increased. As an example for the FVC protocol and 60 subjects, 6 fingers per subject and 4 images per finger (UTFVP dataset), the number of genuine comparisons is

$$n_{gen} = \frac{n_i \cdot (n_i + 1)}{2} \cdot n_{fh} = \frac{4 \cdot (4 + 1)}{2} \cdot (60 \cdot 6) = 3600$$

and the number of impostor comparisons is

$$n_{imp} = \frac{n_{fh} \cdot (n_{fh} + 1)}{2} = \frac{(60 \cdot 6) \cdot (60 \cdot 6 + 1)}{2} = 64620$$

FVC (short)

An even shorter version of the FVC protocol in terms of the number of comparisons that are performed is included as well. In this version, the same number of genuine comparisons as for the FVC protocol is performed, but the number of impostor comparisons is further reduced. For the impostor comparisons, only the first sample of each finger/hand per subject is compared with the first sample of the finger/hand with the same ID for all other subjects, resulting in:

$$n_{imp} = n_{fh} \cdot \frac{n_s \cdot (n_s - 1)}{2}$$

impostor comparisons.

Full

This protocol simply performs all possible comparisons without doing any symmetric ones, i.e.

$$n_{gen} = \frac{n_i \cdot (n_i - 1)}{2} \cdot n_{fh}$$

genuine comparisons and

$$n_{imp} = \frac{(n_i \cdot n_{fh}) \cdot (n_i \cdot n_{fh} - 1)}{2}$$

impostor comparisons are performed.

Ton

Ton and Veldhuis used a reduced version of the "Full" protocol in their paper about UTFVP finger vein dataset [45]. As they used about 10% of the dataset to tune the parameters of the recognition schemes, they excluded these samples from the subsequent performance evaluation. In order to do so, they skipped the first finger of the first subject, the second finger of the second subject, the first finger of the seventh subject and so on. This protocol is included in our vein recognition framework too, mainly to obtain recognition performance results that can be directly compared to the ones of the original UTFVP paper.

4.4.6 Performance Evaluation Tools

To evaluate the recognition performance of the different schemes on a particular dataset, several performance figures and plots can be generated by the vein recognition framework automatically. All these figures and plots are based on the genuine and impostor comparison scores that have been calculated according to one of the above-mentioned protocols.

EER/FMR100/FMR1000/ZeroFMR Determination

These basic numbers are commonly used to quantify the performance of biometric recognition schemes. The EER, is the point where the FMR and the FNMR are equal. The FMR100 (the lowest FNMR for FMR = 1%), the FMR1000 (the lowest FNMR for FMR = 0.1%) and the ZeroFMR (the lowest FNMR for FMR = 0%) are included as well. Besides these, the FNMR1000 (the lowest FMR for FNMR = 0.1%) and the ZeroFNMR (the lowest FMR for FNMR = 0%) are included too.

FMR Versus FNMR/ROC/DET Plots

Besides the performance numbers, the vein recognition framework does provide the most common used plots to indicate the recognition performance, which is the FMR versus FNMR plot, the ROC and the DET plot. According to the ISO/IEC 19795-1

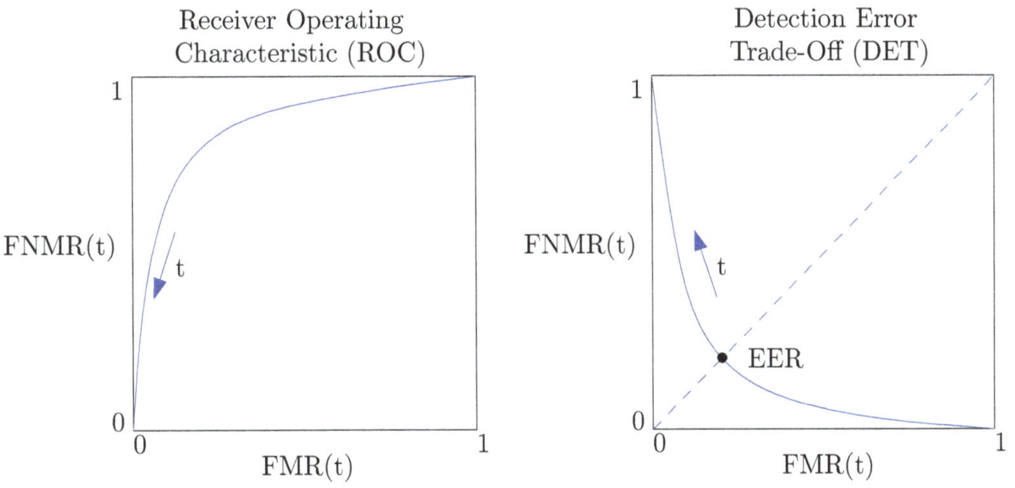

Fig. 4.4 Schematic ISO/IEC 19795-1 compliant ROC (left) and DET plot (right)

standard [39], the ROC is a plot of the rate of false positives (i.e. impostor attempts accepted) on the x-axis against the corresponding rate of true positives (i.e. genuine attempts accepted) on the y-axis plotted parametrically as a function of the decision threshold. The DET plot is a modified ROC curve which plots error rates on both axes (false positives on the x-axis and false negatives on the y-axis). Figure 4.4 shows a schematic ROC and DET plot.

4.4.7 Feature and Score-Level Fusion

The vein recognition framework contains tools and methods to perform feature and score-level fusion. A detailed description of the included feature-level fusion methods can be found in [10]. Regarding score-level fusion, several simple fusion schemes are included. Score normalisation is a vital point for score-level fusion. Consequently, several widely used score nomalisation schemes are included too. Below is a list of the included feature-level and score-level fusion schemes as well as the score normalisation schemes:

- Feature-level fusion
  - Weighted mean and weighted sum
  - Majority vote
  - STAPLE, STAPLER, COLLATE, Spatial STAPLE provided by the MASI Fusion Toolkit [62].
- Score-level fusion
  - Sum, Product, Minimum, Maximum, Mean, Median
  - Weighted versions of the above mentioned.

- Score normalisation
  - Min-Max
  - Z-Score
  - Tanh
  - Median-MAD
  - Double-Sigmoid
  - Adaptive score normalisation for multimodal biometric systems [19].

These fusion and normalisation schemes can easily be extended by providing additional MATLAB implementations of the respective schemes and adding them to the source files of the vein recognition framework.

4.5 Experimental Example

This section gives an experimental baseline example, which should serve as a starting point for our vein recognition framework that is easy to use and reproduce. In the following, the used dataset, vein processing methods and the test protocol are described.

4.5.1 Dataset and Experimental Set-Up

This experimental example is conducted at the University of Twente Finger Vascular Pattern Database (UTFVP) [45]. This database consists of 1440 finger vein images, captured from 60 subjects, with 6 fingers (index, middle and ring finger of both hands) and 4 images per finger. The images are stored in the png format, have a resolution of 672×380 pixels and a density of 126 pixels/cm. The width of the visible blood vessels in the images is between 4 and 20 pixels.

The whole example can be run by using the `runBookChapterExample.m` script which is located inside the `Tests` directory. Only the dataset path in the script file has to be adjusted to point to the location of the UTFVP files.

The employed processing chain consists of the following components:

- Preprocessing: at first the finger is segmented and the background region is masked out by using the LeeRegion [23] method with a filter width of 40 pixels and a filter height of 4 pixels. Afterwards, the finger is normalised using the HuangNormalise [8] approach. Then CLAHE [55] with a clip limit of 0.01 is applied, followed by the enhancement proposed by Zhang et al. [53] with a Gabor filter bandwidth of 1.12 and a Gabor filter Sigma of 3. Finally, the image is resized to half of its original size.
- Feature extraction: two different feature extraction methods are employed. The first one is Miura's Maximum Curvature method (MC) [32] with a Sigma of 2.5.

The second one is Choi's Principal Curvature method (PC) [6] with a Sigma of 2.5 and a Threshold of 1.5 plus an additional morphological post-processing using AreaOpen and InverseAreaOpen with 30 iterations each.
- Comparison: The Miura Matcher [32] with a horizontal shift of 80 pixels, a vertical shift of 30 pixels and a rotational shift of 2° in combination with the FVC evaluation protocol [26] is used during comparison of the extracted vein features. Based on the number of images contained in the UTFVP dataset, this results in 3600 genuine comparisons and 64620 impostor ones.
- Performance evaluation: The recognition performance is evaluated using the EER, the FMR100, the FMR1000 and the ZeroFMR as well as the corresponding DET and ROC plots, which are shown in the following.

4.5.2 *Experimental Results*

Figure 4.5 shows an example image of the UTFVP dataset (first column) and the same image after vein region masking (second column) and after the applied preprocessing (third column). The fourth and rightmost column shows the extracted MC and PC features, correspondingly. The performance evaluation results are listed in Table 4.1 for both, the MC and PC features. MC performed overall better with an EER of 0.37% while PC achieved and EER of 0.92%. The FMR values follow the same trend as the EER ones. The ROC plot is shown in Fig. 4.6 left and the DET plot in Fig. 4.6 right. Note that this example should serve as a starting point and is only for demonstrating the capabilities and basic workflow of the PLUS OpenVein Toolkit. Thus, the performance of the two feature extractors and the whole tool chain is not optimised to achieve the best possible recognition performance.

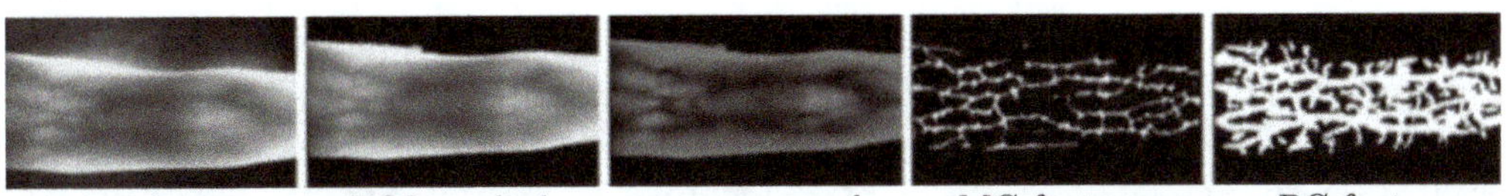

Fig. 4.5 UTFVP example images as processed by the vein recognition toolkit

Table 4.1 Performance evaluation results for MC and PC on the UTFVP dataset

Feature type (%)	EER (%)	FMR100 (%)	FRM1000 (%)	ZeroFMR (%)
MC	0.37	0.28	0.65	1.81
PC	0.92	0.88	1.62	5.56

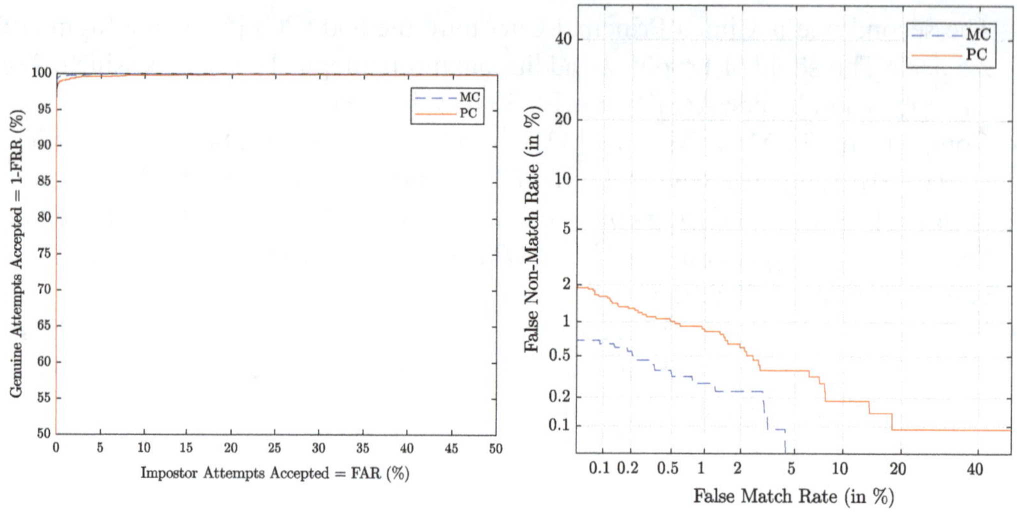

Fig. 4.6 ROC plot (left) and DET plot (right)

4.6 Conclusion and Future Work

In order to conduct research in vein recognition, two important things are necessary: A suitable and available dataset and an implementation of a vein processing tool chain, including preprocessing, feature extraction, comparison and performance evaluation. In this chapter, we presented a new open-source vein recognition framework, called PLUS OpenVein Toolkit, which implements a full vein recognition tool chain. This framework is implemented in MATLAB and contains various preprocessing, feature extraction and comparison methods as well as evaluation protocols and performance evaluation tools. Moreover, it includes feature- and score-level fusion functions. It supports many widely used finger- and hand vein datasets out of the box and it is easy to add support for new datasets. The source code of the framework is available free of charge for research and non-commercial purposes.[13] This chapter explained the basic structure of the framework, described the included vein processing and evaluation schemes and gave an experimental use case example. A more detailed description of all the individual parts is available with the source code. We also established a git repository[14] where every interested researcher is invited to contribute to our vein recognition framework by providing additional vein processing schemes and helping us to improve the code.

The framework is still being extended and improved. We plan to include additional preprocessing and feature extraction schemes as well as to optimise the currently implemented ones for runtime performance. Furthermore, we will include a special version of the FVC protocol, tailored to finger vein recognition, which distinguishes between different fingers (e.g. index vs. pinky one) during the comparisons. This enables an in-depth evaluation of possible differences between fingers of different

[13]Can be downloaded at: http://www.wavelab.at/sources/OpenVein-Toolkit/.

[14]https://gitlab.cosy.sbg.ac.at/ckauba/openvein-toolkit.

size (the pinky finger is much smaller in diameter than the thumb). Finally, we plan to port the whole toolkit to either Python or C++ to get rid of the limitations imposed by MATLAB and to improve the runtime performance.

Acknowledgements This project has received funding from the European Union's Horizon 2020 research and innovation program under grant agreement No. 700259, project PROTECT—Pervasive and UseR Focused BiomeTrics BordEr ProjeCT.

References

1. Anjos A, Günther M, de Freitas Pereira T, Korshunov P, Mohammadi A, Marcel S (2017) Continuously reproducing toolchains in pattern recognition and machine learning experiments. In: International conference on machine learning (ICML). http://publications.idiap.ch/downloads/papers/2017/Anjos_ICML2017-2_2017.pdf
2. Anjos A, Shafey LE, Wallace R, Günther M, McCool C, Marcel S (2012) Bob: a free signal processing and machine learning toolbox for researchers. In: 20th ACM conference on multimedia systems (ACMMM), Nara, Japan (2012). https://publications.idiap.ch/downloads/papers/2012/Anjos_Bob_ACMMM12.pdf
3. Asaari MSM, Suandi SA, Rosdi BA (2014) Fusion of band limited phase only correlation and width centroid contour distance for finger based biometrics. Expert Syst Appl 41(7):3367–3382
4. Bandara AMRR, Rajarata KASHK, Giragama PWGRMPB (2017) Super-efficient spatially adaptive contrast enhancement algorithm for superficial vein imaging. In: 2017 IEEE international conference on industrial and information systems (ICIIS), pp 1–6. https://doi.org/10.1109/ICIINFS.2017.8300427
5. Bay H, Tuytelaars T, Van Gool L (2006) Surf: speeded up robust features. In: European conference on computer vision. Springer, pp 404–417
6. Choi JH, Song W, Kim T, Lee SR, Kim HC (2009) Finger vein extraction using gradient normalization and principal curvature. Proc SPIE 7251:9. https://doi.org/10.1117/12.810458
7. Evans C (2009) Notes on the opensurf library. Technical report CSTR-09-001, University of Bristol
8. Huang B, Dai Y, Li R, Tang D, Li W (2010) Finger-vein authentication based on wide line detector and pattern normalization. In: 2010 20th international conference on pattern recognition (ICPR). IEEE, pp 1269–1272
9. Kauba C (2015) Impact of sensor ageing on finger-image based biometric recognition systems. Master's thesis (2015)
10. Kauba C, Piciucco E, Maiorana E, Campisi P, Uhl A (2016) Advanced variants of feature level fusion for finger vein recognition. In: Proceedings of the international conference of the biometrics special interest group (BIOSIG'16), Darmstadt, Germany, 12 pp
11. Kauba C, Prommegger B, Uhl A (2018) Focussing the beam—a new laser illumination based data set providing insights to finger-vein recognition. In: Proceedings of the IEEE 9th international conference on biometrics: theory, applications, and systems (BTAS2018). Los Angeles, California, USA, 9 pp
12. Kauba C, Prommegger B, Uhl A (2018) The two sides of the finger—an evaluation on the recognition performance of dorsal vs. palmar finger-veins. In: Proceedings of the international conference of the biometrics special interest group (BIOSIG'18), Darmstadt, Germany, 8 pp
13. Kauba C, Prommegger B, Uhl A (2019) PLUS OpenVein—an available fully open-source modular multi-purpose finger-vein scanner. In: Uhl A, Busch C, Marcel S, Veldhuis R (eds) Handbook of vascular biometrics. Springer Science+Business Media, Boston, MA, USA, pp 77–112

14. Kauba C, Reissig J, Uhl A (2014) Pre-processing cascades and fusion in finger vein recognition. In: Proceedings of the international conference of the biometrics special interest group (BIOSIG'14). Darmstadt, Germany, 12 pp
15. Kauba C, Uhl A (2015) Robustness evaluation of hand vein recognition systems
16. Kauba C, Uhl A (2015) Sensor ageing impact on finger-vein recognition
17. Kauba C, Uhl A (2018) Robustness of finger-vein recognition
18. Kauba C, Uhl A (2018) Shedding light on the veins—reflected light or transillumination in hand-vein recognition
19. Khalifa AB, Gazzah S, BenAmara NE (2013) Adaptive score normalization: a novel approach for multimodal biometric systems. World Acad Sci Eng Technol Int J Comput Sci Eng 7(3):882–890
20. Kirchgasser S, Kauba C, Uhl A (2019) Towards understanding acquisition conditions influencing finger-vein recognition
21. Kono M (2000) A new method for the identification of individuals by using of vein pattern matching of a finger. In: Proceedings of the fifth symposium on pattern measurement, Yamaguchi, Japan, 2000, pp 9–12
22. Kumar A, Zhou Y (2012) Human identification using finger images. IEEE Trans Image Process 21(4):2228–2244
23. Lee EC, Lee HC, Park KR (2009) Finger vein recognition using minutia-based alignment and local binary pattern-based feature extraction. Int J Imaging Syst Technol 19(3):179–186
24. Lowe DG (1999) Object recognition from local scale-invariant features. In: Proceedings of the seventh IEEE international conference on computer vision (CVPR'99), vol 2. IEEE, pp 1150–1157
25. Mahri N, Suandi SAS, Rosdi BA (2010) Finger vein recognition algorithm using phase only correlation. In: 2010 International workshop on emerging techniques and challenges for hand-based biometrics (ETCHB). IEEE, pp 1–6
26. Maio D, Maltoni D, Cappelli R, Wayman JL, Jain AK (2004) FVC2004: third fingerprint verification competition. In: ICBA, LNCS, vol 3072. Springer, pp 1–7
27. Matsuda Y, Miura N, Nagasaka A, Kiyomizu H, Miyatake T (2016) Finger-vein authentication based on deformation-tolerant feature-point matching. Mach Vis Appl 27(2):237–250
28. McCann J (1999) Lessons learned from mondrians applied to real images and color gamuts. In: Color and imaging conference, vol 1999. Society for Imaging Science and Technology, pp 1–8
29. Meng X, Xi X, Yang G, Yin Y (2018) Finger vein recognition based on deformation information. Sci China Inf Sci 61(5)
30. Mirmohamadsadeghi L, Drygajlo A (2014) Palm vein recognition with local texture patterns. Iet Biom 3(4):198–206
31. Miura N, Nagasaka A, Miyatake T (2004) Feature extraction of finger-vein patterns based on repeated line tracking and its application to personal identification. Mach Vis Appl 15(4):194–203
32. Miura N, Nagasaka A, Miyatake T (2007) Extraction of finger-vein patterns using maximum curvature points in image profiles. IEICE Trans Inf Syst 90(8):1185–1194
33. Prommegger B, Kauba C, Uhl A (2018) Longitudinal finger rotation—problems and effects in finger-vein recognition
34. Prommegger B, Kauba C, Uhl A (2018) Multi-perspective finger-vein biometrics
35. Prommegger B, Kauba C, Uhl A (2019) A different view on the finger—multi-perspective score level fusion in finger-vein recognition. In: Uhl A, Busch C, Marcel S, Veldhuis R (eds) Handbook of vascular biometrics. Springer Science+Business Media, Boston, MA, USA, pp 395–434
36. Raghavendra R, Venkatesh S, Raja K, Busch C (2018) A low-cost multi-fingervein verification system. In: Proceedings of international conference on imaging systems and techniques (IST 2018), Karkow, Poland
37. Rohr K, Fornefett M, Stiehl HS (1999) Approximating thin-plate splines for elastic registration: integration of landmark errors and orientation attributes. In: biennial international conference on information processing in medical imaging. Springer, pp 252–265

38. Shi Y, Yang J, Yang J (2012) A new algorithm for finger-vein image enhancement and segmentation. Inf Sci Ind Appl 4(22):139–144
39. For Standardization, I.O. (2006) Iso/iec is 19795-1. Information technology—biometric performance testing and reporting—Part 1: Principles and framework
40. Starck JL, Fadili J, Murtagh F (2007) The undecimated wavelet decomposition and its reconstruction. IEEE Trans Image Process 16(2):297–309
41. Syarif MA, Ong TS, Teoh AB, Tee C (2017) Enhanced maximum curvature descriptors for finger vein verification. Multimedia Tools Appl 76(5):6859–6887
42. Tome P, Marcel S (2015) On the vulnerability of palm vein recognition to spoofing attacks. In: The 8th IAPR international conference on biometrics (ICB). http://publications.idiap.ch/index.php/publications/show/3096
43. Tome P, Vanoni M, Marcel S (2014) On the vulnerability of finger vein recognition to spoofing. In: IEEE international conference of the biometrics special interest group (BIOSIG). http://publications.idiap.ch/index.php/publications/show/2910
44. Ton B (2012) Vascular pattern of the finger: biometric of the future? sensor design, data collection and performance verification. Master's thesis, University of Twente
45. Ton B, Veldhuis R (2013) A high quality finger vascular pattern dataset collected using a custom designed capturing device. In: International conference on biometrics, ICB 2013. IEEE. http://doc.utwente.nl/87790/
46. University of Reading: PROTECT Multimodal DB Dataset (2017). http://projectprotect.eu/dataset/
47. Xie SJ, Lu Y, Yoon S, Yang J, Park DS (2015) Intensity variation normalization for finger vein recognition using guided filter based singe scale retinex. Sensors 15(7):17089–17105
48. Yang J, Shi Y (2012) Finger-vein roi localization and vein ridge enhancement. Pattern Recogn Lett 33(12):1569–1579
49. Yang J, Shi Y, Yang J (2012) Finger-vein image restoration based on a biological optical model. In: New trends and developments in biometrics. InTech
50. Yang J, Yang J (2009) Multi-channel gabor filter design for finger-vein image enhancement. In: Fifth international conference on image and graphics, 2009. ICIG'09. IEEE, pp 87–91
51. Yang L, Yang G, Yin Y, Xi X (2017) Finger vein recognition with anatomy structure analysis. IEEE Trans Circuits Syst Video Technol
52. Yin Y, Liu L, Sun X (2011) Sdumla-hmt: a multimodal biometric database. Biomet Recogn 260–268
53. Zhang J, Yang J (2009) Finger-vein image enhancement based on combination of gray-level grouping and circular gabor filter. In: ICIECS 2009 international conference on information engineering and computer science, 2009. IEEE, pp 1–4
54. Zhao J, Tian H, Xu W, Li X (2009) A new approach to hand vein image enhancement. In: Second international conference on intelligent computation technology and automation, 2009. ICICTA'09, vol 1. IEEE, pp 499–501
55. Zuiderveld K (1994) Contrast limited adaptive histogram equalization. In: Heckbert PS (ed) Graphics gems IV. Morgan Kaufmann, pp 474–485

Online Resources

56. Bandara R, Kulathilake H, Giragama MP (2019) Speeded up adaptive contrast enhancement (SUACE). https://github.com/ravimalb/suace/. Accessed 23 Jan 2019
57. Bankhead P, Scholfield CN, McGeown JG, Curtis TM (2019) ARIA—Automated Retinal Image Analyzer. http://petebankhead.github.io/ARIA/. Accessed 23 Jan 2019
58. Cermelj P (2019) INIFILE—INI file reading and writing. https://de.mathworks.com/matlabcentral/fileexchange/2976-inifile. Accessed 23 Jan 2019

59. Funt B, Ciurea F, McCann J (2019) Retinex in Matlab. http://www.cs.sfu.ca/~colour/publications/IST-2000/. Accessed 23 Jan 2019
60. van der Heijden F (2019) Image edge enhancing coherence filter toolbox. https://de.mathworks.com/matlabcentral/fileexchange/25449-image-edge-enhancing-coherence-filter-toolbox. Accessed 23 Jan 2019
61. Mayoue A (2019) BioSecure tool—performance evaluation of a biometric verification system. http://svnext.it-sudparis.eu/svnview2-eph/ref_syst/Tools/PerformanceEvaluation/. Accessed 23 Jan 2019
62. Medical Image Analysis and Statistical Interpretation (MASI) group at Vanderbilt University (2019) MASI label fusion. https://www.nitrc.org/projects/masi-fusion/. Accessed 23 Jan 2019
63. Schauerte B (2019) Histogram distances https://de.mathworks.com/matlabcentral/fileexchange/39275-histogram-distances. Accessed 23 Jan 2019
64. Ton B (2019) Finger region localisation. https://de.mathworks.com/matlabcentral/fileexchange/35752-finger-region-localisation. Accessed 23 Jan 2019
65. Ton B (2019) Miura et al vein extraction methods. https://de.mathworks.com/matlabcentral/fileexchange/35716-miura-et-al-vein-extraction-methods. Accessed 23 Jan 2019
66. Ton B (2019) Simple finger normalisation. https://de.mathworks.com/matlabcentral/fileexchange/35826-simple-finger-normalisation. Accessed 23 Jan 2019
67. Ton B (2019) Wide line detector. https://de.mathworks.com/matlabcentral/fileexchange/35754-wide-line-detector. Accessed 23 Jan 2019
68. Vedaldi A, Fulkerson B (2019) VLFeat—VisionLab features library. http://www.vlfeat.org/. Accessed 23 Jan 2019
69. Xiong G (2019) Local adaptive thresholding. http://de.mathworks.com/matlabcentral/fileexchange/8647-local-adaptive-thresholding. Accessed 23 Jan 2019

Part II
Hand and Finger Vein Biometrics

Chapter 5
Use Case of Palm Vein Authentication

Takashi Shinzaki

Abstract Palm vein authentication is a vein feature authentication technology that uses palm veins as the biometric feature. Palm vein patterns are normally captured using near-infrared light via either the reflection or the transmission methods. In the reflection method, near-infrared rays are emitted towards the palm to be identified and the reflected light is captured for authentication. Because veins are beneath human skin, it is difficult for someone else to copy or steal them, so the palm vein is more secure compared to some other biometric features. Moreover, because palm vein patterns are diverse and complex, they give sufficient information to identify one individual among a large population. As a result, palm vein authentication is secure and highly accurate. As a contactless type of biometric identification, it is suitable for use in applications that require a high level of hygiene or for use in public applications. Several banks in Japan have been using palm vein authentication for ATM security since July 2004. In addition, palm veins have been used in a variety of applications such as door security systems, login management systems for PCs, financial services, payment services and patient identification systems in hospitals. This chapter introduces the technical outline of palm vein authentication and its use cases.

Keywords Palm vein authentication · Vein authentication · Palm vein · Palm vein sensor · Use case · ATM · Payment systems · Airport security · Entry control · Financial services · Flapper gate · Government and municipal · Healthcare · Laptop PC · Login · Tablet · Palm · Vein · Vascular · Near-infrared light

5.1 Introduction

Palm vein authentication is a vein pattern authentication technology that uses palm veins as the biometric feature. Because palm vein patterns exist beneath human skin, it is very difficult to copy or steal someone's palm vein pattern. This means that forgery is very difficult under normal conditions.

T. Shinzaki (✉)
Digital Innovation Core Unit, Fujitsu Laboratories Ltd., 1-1 Kamikodanaka 4-chome, Nakahara-ku, Kawasaki 211-8588, Japan
e-mail: shinzaki@fujitsu.com

A. Uhl et al. (eds.), *Handbook of Vascular Biometrics*, Advances in Computer Vision and Pattern Recognition, https://doi.org/10.1007/978-3-030-27731-4_5

Fujitsu Lab started to develop Palm Vein Authentication as Contactless Hand Biometrics in 2000. At the time, we didn't know which accuracy to expect from hand features, so we evaluated hand features by experimental cameras and illumination. We set up four different cameras to capture different parts of the hand. By using these cameras, we collected about 1,400 hands vein images (palm, finger, back of hand and wrist) from 700 persons. As a result of authentication performance evaluation using these images, we chose palm vein for our product. Because a person's palm vein patterns have web-like complex patterns (Fig. 5.1), they give sufficient information to identify one individual from a large population of people. Compared to the back of the hand or the back of a finger, the palm is a good area for authentication because it does not have any hair which can obscure the vein capture process.

Palm vein patterns are believed to be unique to each individual as with fingerprints or other biometrics. To confirm this, we collected 140,000 palm vein images by 70,000 persons for verification in 2005 [1]. Experiments based on large-scale data show that palm vein patterns have the advantages of consistency and accuracy as a method of personal identification. It has also been shown that palm vein patterns are stable for a sufficiently long time period for the purpose of personal identification.

A patent for hand vein authentication was filed in 1985 by Joseph Rice in the United States [2]. The first device for palm vein authentication was presented by Advanced Biometrics, Inc. in the United States in 1997. In 2003, a novel contactless device was released by Fujitsu in Japan. In 2004, Japanese financial institutions, the Bank of Tokyo-Mitsubishi first adopted Fujitsu's technology for confirming the identity of their customers. This was the first major application in Japan in which a private enterprise adopted vein authentication in a service for the general public. Fujitsu's concept and implementation of a contactless sensor was awarded the Wall

Fig. 5.1 Palm vein image captured by experiment device

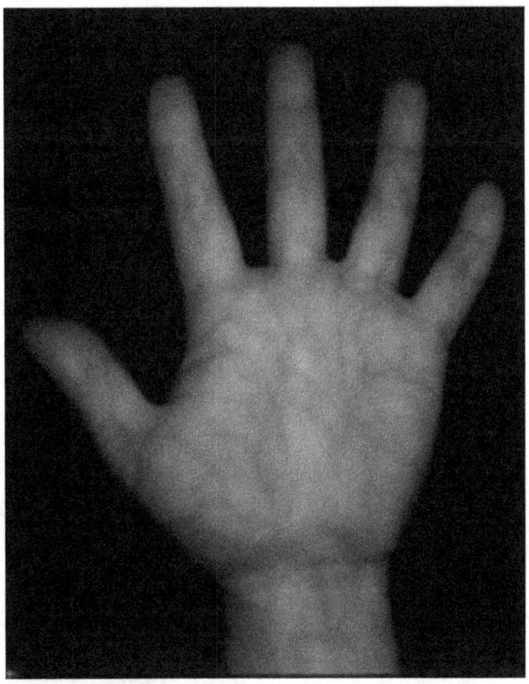

Street Journal's 2005 Technology Innovation Award for Security in Networks [3]. This chapter will provide a broad use case of contactless palm vein authentication.

5.2 Palm Vein Sensing

Vein patterns sit within the subcutaneous tissue of a person's palm and are captured using near-infrared rays. This technology is called near-infrared spectroscopy (NIRS) and imaging. This field of research has been investigated as a technology of in vivo "within the living" measurement for over 10 years [4].

Palm vein images can be captured using two different methods: the reflection method and the transmission method. In the reflection method, the palm is illuminated from the front side and the image is captured on the same side. In the transmission method, the palm is illuminated from the backside of the hand and the image is captured from the front side. In the transmission method, the illumination device and the capture device are separated, facing each other across a palm. While in the reflection method, the illumination device and the capture device can be integrated together to create a more compact device because the direction of the illumination is the same as the direction of image capturing.

5.3 Sensor Products with Reflection Method

We commercialised reflective type of palm vein sensors (Fig. 5.2). Users don't need to touch the sensor; they only have to show their palms to the sensor. To obtain a high-quality palm vein image, the imaging process should be adequately controlled due to the movement or position of the hand. In addition, the illumination should be controlled depending on the environmental light conditions around the sensor.

The contactless method eliminates user concerns about hygiene as users don't have to have direct contact with publicly used devices. The method is also suitable for identification in environments where high hygiene standards are required such as in medical facilities or food factories.

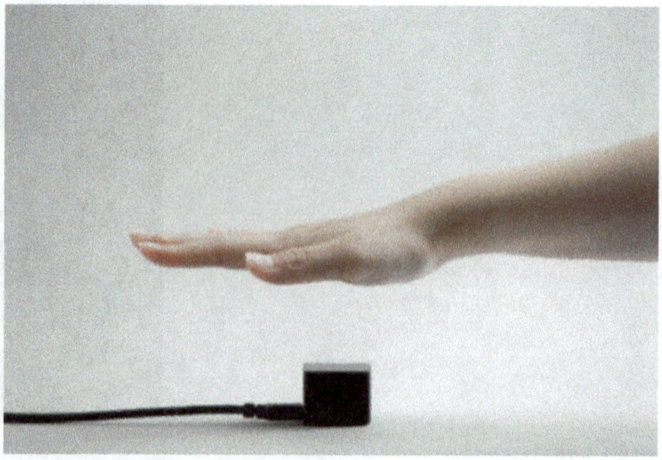

Fig. 5.2 Palm vein sensor product with reflection method

The intensity of the near-infrared rays emitted from the sensor is deemed safe as it is less than the intensity specified in the "Light and Near-Infrared Radiation" guidelines of the American Conference of Governmental Industrial Hygienists (ACGIH) [5].

The first palm vein authentication systems were introduced in ATM services in 2004. To expand the application of palm vein authentication, miniaturisation of the palm vein sensor is continually being promoted. The lighting component was designed to provide a wide radiation range and very bright luminosity, despite its compact implementation, by carefully positioning the LED and optimising the shape of the waveguide. The authentication algorithm was also upgraded to better match the properties of images captured by the miniature sensor.

For security reasons, the sensor should encrypt the palm image prior to transmission to the host PC; templates should also be encrypted for storage or transmission. These functions protect the palm vein image from any unauthorised access or fraud.

In Fujitsu's implementation [6–8], a palm vein authentication sensor is made in the shape of a small box, 25 mm deep × 25 mm wide × 6.0 mm high (Fig. 5.3). Capturing is executed in a contactless manner. With the advancement of sensor miniaturisation, it became possible to incorporate the sensors into laptop PCs and tablets.

As a result, Fujitsu launched a laptop PC with the world's first built-in vein sensor in 2011. In 2014, a tablet with a built-in palm vein authentication sensor was commercialised.

Fig. 5.3 Compact size palm vein sensor

5.4 Matching Performance

At the first stage of palm vein authentication, the palm vein pattern is extracted from the near-infrared image taken by the palm vein sensor. As palm veins exist under human skin, the vein pattern is generally not as clear as other biometric features like fingerprints, so the extraction method is one of the key technological components of palm vein authentication.

The similarity between the captured palm vein to be authenticated and the registered template stored in the database is then calculated. The similarity can be calculated using various methods.

In the verification process (one-to-one matching), the user is authenticated if the similarity score is greater than or equal to the predetermined threshold. In the identification process (one-to-many matching), similarity scores are calculated between the input palm vein image and all of the registered templates in the database. The user's identity is determined to be the user that shows the highest score among these calculated scores and whose score is greater than or equal to the predetermined threshold.

Our latest matching algorithm achieves a false rejection rate of 0.01% (including one retry) and false acceptance rate of 0.00001% or less. This algorithm enables 1:N authentication of up to 10,000 hands (5,000 with both hands registration). Palm vein images of 16,000 hands were collected from 8,000 people for this verification. This authentication performance was calculated based on the ISO/IEC 19795 series.

5.5 Use Cases of Palm Vein Authentication

5.5.1 Usage Situation

Palm vein authentication is used worldwide. Commercial palm vein sensors are shipped in over 1 million units. And in our survey, 86 million people have registered their palm veins. Because palm vein authentication has many public uses, it tends to have more registrants than sensors. This chapter introduces some use cases.

5.5.2 Login Authentication

Palm vein sensors can be embedded in a PC mouse. Using a mouse as a palm vein authentication sensor offers convenience and space-saving advantages. Most companies and government agencies have internal information systems which handle sensitive personal data. Using a mouse with an integrated palm vein authentication sensor enables advanced, high-level security for system logins with the high accuracy and reliability of palm vein authentication in comparison with the conventional combination of ID and password.

With these laptop PCs equipped with palm vein authentication (Fig. 5.4) [9], it is possible to perform pre-boot authentication at BIOS start-up. Furthermore, tablets with built-in palm vein authentication have been put to practical use (Fig. 5.5) [8]. These are mainly used in PC login and second factor authentication solutions. Hundreds of thousands of employees and staff are using this in technology large companies and governments.

Palm vein authentication is also applied to logins for virtual desktops. In Fujitsu, approximately 40,000 employees access their thin-client terminal by using palm vein authentication [10].

Fig. 5.4 Laptop with built-in palm vein authentication

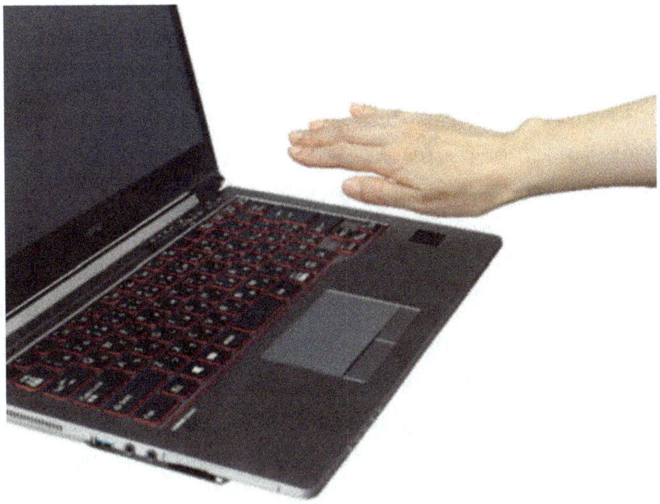

Fig. 5.5 Tablet with built-in palm vein authentication

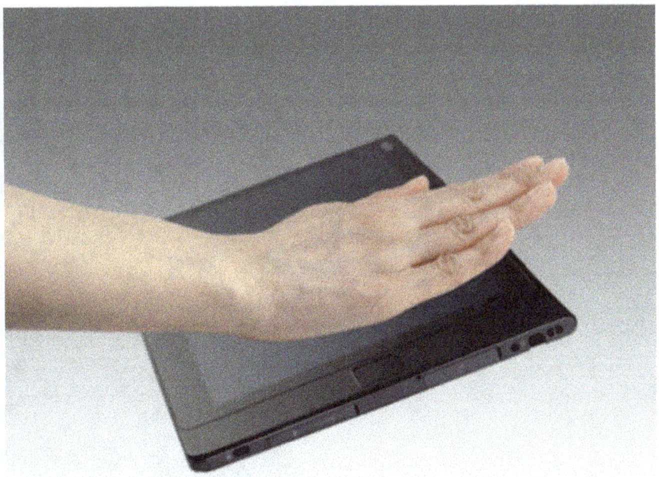

5.5.3 Physical Access Control Systems

Palm vein authentication sensors have been installed in many access control systems (Fig. 5.6). They are used to control entry and exit for rooms or buildings. Palm vein authentication is well suited to access control systems because of the following reasons:

- Palm vein authentication works in a contactless manner; this is an optimal feature for public usage.
- It is simple and easy to use; users only have to show their palms to the device.
- Palm vein patterns are difficult to counterfeit.

Because of the Personal Information Protection Act that went into full effect in Japan on April 2005, the Department of Planning, Information and Management of the University of Tokyo Hospital began using palm vein authentication in a new security system to control room access. The security levels of the system were divided into three access levels: access to the administrative room, the development room and the server room. An access control unit that uses palm vein authentication has been installed at the entrance to each room. The system has been able to restrict an individual's entry in stages.

Additionally, the smart-card-based authentication installed at the entrances to two offices in Japan (Fujitsu Solution Square and the Tokai Branch Office) will make the switch over to palm vein authentication, and a field trial covering some 5,200 employees working at these locations will take place over the course of approximately 1 year. In both cases, identity authentication and integrated operations and management will be performed on a cloud-based platform. Users can pass the gate by waving their hand over the sensor (Fig. 5.7).

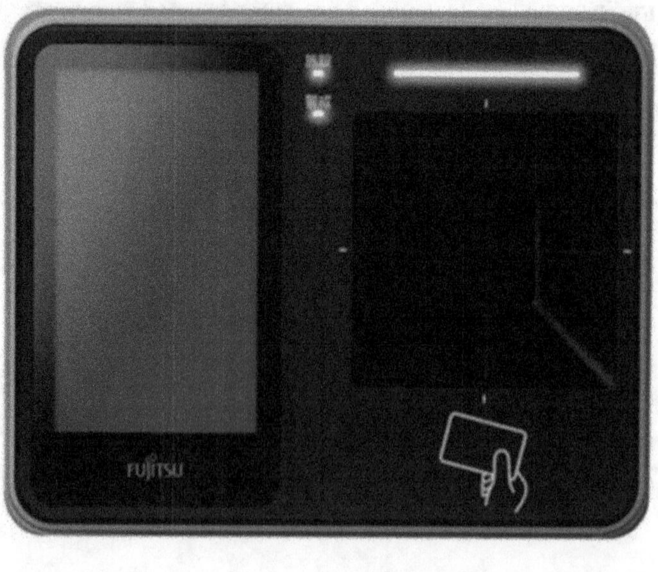

Fig. 5.6 Entry control device

Fig. 5.7 Trial at flapper gate

5.5.4 *Payment Systems*

A payment system using palm vein authentication called "Hand Pay Service" has been introduced by the major Korean credit card company Lotte Card Co., Ltd. Making full use of the palm vein authentication technology proudly provided by Fujitsu, Lotte Card started the first bio-pay service in Korea on May 2016, which allows Lotte Card customers to make lump-sum credit card payments even when they are not carrying their cards, by just using biometrics and phone numbers to authenticate who they are. The encrypted data are divided and stored in the Bio-Information Distributed Data Management Center of the Korea Financial Telecommunications & Clearing Institute (KFTC) and the system environment of Lotte Card, to strengthen security even further. Moreover, it was Fujitsu Korea that established the system that works with the Biometric Information Distributed Data Management Center of the KFTC to which the Lotte Card "Hand Pay Service" is linked (Fig. 5.8).

AEON Credit Service and Fujitsu will begin a field trial of a cardless payment system using Fujitsu's palm vein biometric authentication technology. Starting in September 2018, the trial will take place in selected Ministop convenience stores. Customers use this service by registering in advance, then adding their palm vein pattern to their AEON card information. When paying at a register, customers can pay with their registered AEON card by inputting their date of birth and then scanning the palm of their hand over the reader. Customers can use their AEON card with greater convenience, without the bother of taking the card out of their wallet or purse. AEON Credit Service and Fujitsu will be conducting a field trial for AEON Group employees at a number of Ministop locations beginning in September 2018. Based on the results of the field trial, the companies plan to roll out the technology for use in store locations for the various AEON Group companies.

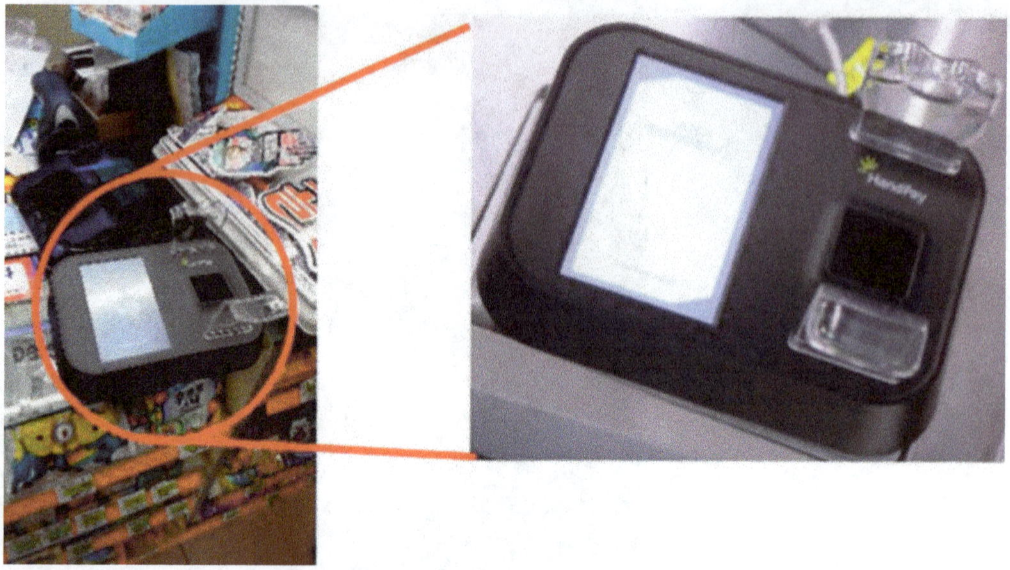

Fig. 5.8 Payment system by using palm vein

5.5.5 *Financial Services*

In 2003, Japan saw a rapid increase in financial damage, caused by fraudulent withdrawals from bank accounts through spoofing with fake bank cards that were made from stolen or skimmed cards. It was a significant social problem. This caused a sharp increase in the number of lawsuits brought forward by victims against financial institutions for their failure to control information used for personal identification. The "Act for the Protection of Personal Information" came into effect on May 2005, and in response, financial institutions in Japan have been focusing on biometric authentication methods together with smart cards, as a way to reinforce the security of personal identification. Palm vein authentication is the form of biometric authentication that was most quickly introduced for customer confirmation at banking facilities; it was first introduced in July 2004, before the act came into effect.

Palm vein authentication in financial services is applied as follows. A user's palm vein pattern is registered at a bank counter and stored on a smart card. This has the advantage of allowing users to carry their own palm vein pattern with them. In the verification process for ATM transactions, the palm vein pattern of the user is captured by a palm vein authentication sensor on the ATM (Fig. 5.9). The captured palm vein pattern is transferred to the user's smart card and compared to the template stored in the smart card. Finally, a matching result score is transmitted back from the smart card, keeping the palm vein template within the smart card.

In addition to Japan, Brazil has also adopted palm vein authentication to identify users in ATM banking transactions. Banco Bradesco S.A., the largest private bank in Latin America, has tested palm vein authentication with various other biometric technologies. Bradesco chose palm vein authentication because of its outstanding

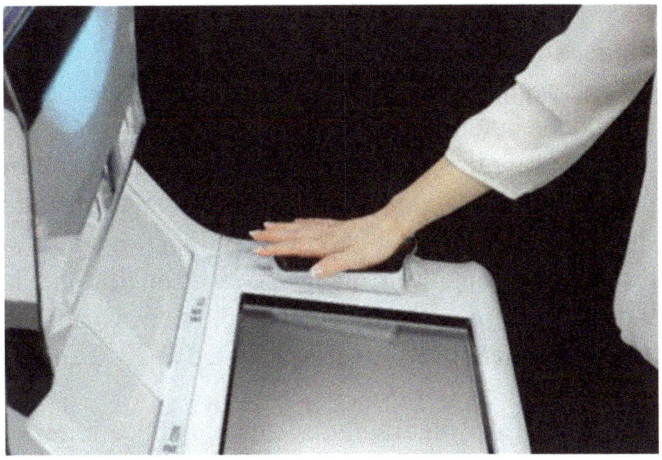

Fig. 5.9 ATM using palm vein authentication

features, such as its high level of verification accuracy and the fact that it is non-invasive and hygienic, making it more easily accepted by customers of the bank.

In 2012, Ogaki Kyoritsu Bank Ltd. in Japan started a new cardless biometric ATM system service applying palm vein authentication. With this system, customers are able to use ATM services for withdrawals, deposits and balance inquiries without passbooks or ATM cards. By combining their date of birth, palm vein authentication and PIN, customers have access to financial services that combines both security and convenience. In a huge disaster situation such as an earthquake, people would evacuate their houses immediately, so they wouldn't have any identifying documents like ATM cards or driver's licenses. Even in a situation like this, the new ATM system will provide financial services to customers by applying the high accuracy rate of palm vein authentication [11].

5.5.6 Health Care

Palm vein authentication is being deployed throughout the Carolinas HealthCare System (CHS) in the United States as part of a solution to effectively register patient information and ensure that the proper medical care is given to the right person, while protecting their medical record and privacy from identity theft and insurance fraud. For this system, the CHS team developed a unique hand guide for the sensor. This hand guide is adapted for a hospital environment, since it incorporates a paediatric plate that adapts the guide so it can be used with young children, accommodating all CHS patients.

The Sapporo Hospital of the Keiyu Association in Japan also adopted palm vein authentication for patient authentication in their electronic medical records system. Patients who are to undergo an operation register their palm vein patterns before the operation. On the day of the operation the registered palm vein pattern and the palm vein pattern scanned from the patient are compared, confirming that the patient to be operated on is the correct person. This avoids the wrong patient being operated on, which might occur if two patients have the same name, for example. Other applications for health care, such as secure access to patient medical records, can also be achieved due to the contactless nature of palm vein authentication and its excellence in terms of hygiene.

In Turkey, the Ministry of Health decided to introduce a nationwide biometric patient authentication system with palm vein authentication for the SSI (Social Security Institution) in order to prevent billing fraud in hospitals and pharmacies. In order to apply for insurance from the government through MEDULA, medical institutions (hospitals, clinics, family doctors, pharmacies and opticians) must implement palm vein authentication. The service started in 2012 and more than 10,000 units are being used.

(MEDULA: the social security application system for customers' medical expenses at all medical institutions.)

5.5.7 Airport Security

In South Korea, the Korea Airports Corporation (KAC) has deployed palm vein authentication system at all 14 domestic airports under its jurisdiction, to ameliorate congestion by identifying boarding passengers with biometric authentication (Fig. 5.10). The domestic airports under KAC's jurisdiction are currently used by about 32 million people per year. Korean citizens, over the age of 14, travelling on domestic flights must have their identity checked before passing through boarding security, and this had previously been done on-site by showing a citizen ID card to security personnel. Because visually confirming a passenger's identity takes time, this process could lead to congestion in the airports, and it had become an issue for KAC.

Fig. 5.10 Palm vein authentication for airport security

In addition, passengers who had not brought their citizen ID cards were not able to board their flights, which compromised the quality of customer service.

KAC has given attention to the high identification accuracy and convenience of palm vein authentication, and therefore decided to deploy a personal identification system using palm vein authentication.

Users can register in advance at registration devices installed in airports, linking their palm vein pattern with their citizen ID number, name and phone number. Then, after scanning a barcode on their ticket, users can confirm their identity by holding out their hand at the newly installed identity confirmation gates before security checkpoints. Users will not have to constantly carry their citizen ID cards, and the system will slash waiting times and enable smoother processing at airports.

This system began operation on 28 December 2018, and it has been used over 1 million times, with 160,000 individuals who have already registered their palm vein patterns.

5.5.8 *Government and Municipal*

The Japan Agency for Local Authority Information Systems introduced palm vein authentication for user authentication of the Resident Registry Network (JUKI-net), implemented for all local government offices. All municipalities, prefectures and governmental agencies use this system to protect the private information of residents. Operational costs such as issuing ID cards and reissuing forgotten or lost IDs or passwords have been reduced. More than 10,700 terminals are connected to this system. The operator can easily understand that he/she has been identified, which will act as a psychological barrier to the intentional leaking of information.

Naka city in Ibaraki prefecture, Japan, introduced a system utilising palm vein authentication technology for the city's new public library in October 2006. The library system is the first of its kind in the world. Users can check out books from the library by using palm vein authentication. Users of the Naka City Public Library will be given a choice between using an ID card with an embedded IC chip or using the palm vein authentication system for identity verification. Users who select palm vein authentication will be able to check out library materials or use its audiovisual section without using ID cards. First, users input their date of birth, then they simply suspend their hand above the authentication device and their palm vein pattern is compared to their pre-registered pattern for verification.

Now, more than 90% of the 20,000 users choose to use palm vein authentication for convenience (Fig. 5.11).

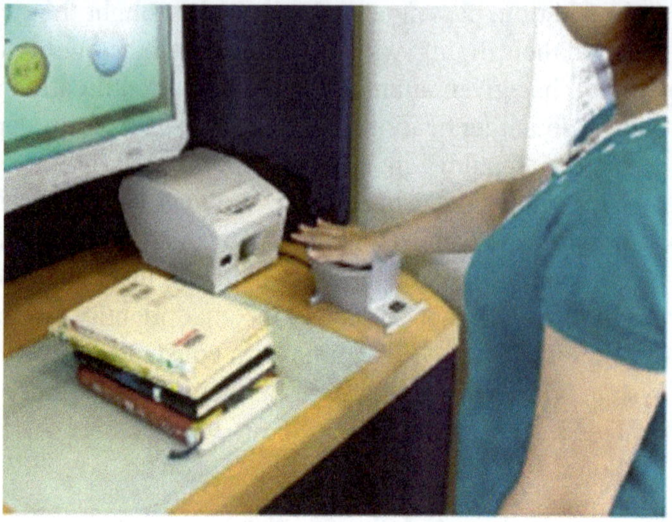

Fig. 5.11 Book lending system

5.6 Conclusion

Palm vein authentication has been used in a variety of applications such as door security systems, login management systems for PCs, financial services, payment services and patient identification systems in hospitals. The vein pattern of the palm has a two-dimensional complexity, and because the image exists under the skin, the acquired image is very stable. Based on these advantages, we believe that palm vein authentication will become more widespread.

References

1. Sasaki S, Kawai H, Wakabayashi A (2005) Business expansion of palm vein pattern authentication technology. Fujitsu 56(4):346–351
2. Rice J (1985) Apparatus for the identification of individuals. US Patent 4,699,149
3. Totty M (2005) A better idea. Wall St J
4. Kim JG, Xia M, Liu H (2005) Extinction coefficients of hemoglobin for near-infrared spectroscopy of tissue. IEEE Eng Med Biol Mag 24:118–121
5. Light and near-infrared radiation: TLV physical agents 7th edition documentation. ACGIH
6. Watanabe M, Endoh T, Shiohara M, Sasaki S (2005) Palm vein authentication technology and its applications. In: Proceedings of biometrics symposium. pp 37–38
7. Iwasaki S, Higashiura Y, Komura K, Nakamura A, Suzuki T, Iwaguchi I (2013) World's smallest and slimmest palm vein biometric authentication sensor. Fujitsu 6(4):350–354
8. Yokozawa H, Morihara T (2013) Palm vein authentication technology embedded in laptop. Fujitsu 64(3):287–292
9. Yokozawa H, Shinzaki T, Yonenaga A, Wada A (2016) Biometric authentication technologies of client terminals in pursuit of security and convenience. Fujitsu Sci Tech J 52(3):23–27
10. Y Suzuki, A Niigata, M Hamada (2016) In-house practice of cloud-based authentication platform service focusing on palm vein authentication. Fujitsu Sci Tech J 52(3):8–14
11. Hattori Y (2015) Realizing new ATM service using palm vein authentication technology Fujitsu 66(3):2–7

Chapter 6
Evolution of Finger Vein Biometric Devices in Terms of Usability

Mitsutoshi Himaga and Hisao Ogata

Abstract In this chapter, the usability of finger vein biometric devices is reviewed and discussed from various viewpoints. Since the usability requirements vary on both the applications and the situations in which the device is used, the requirements need to be carefully reviewed in light of each viewpoint and reflected to the product design.

Keywords Usability · Anti-vandalism · Compactness · Compliance · Durability · High throughput · Mobility · Portability · Universal design · Universality

6.1 Introduction

The term usability is defined as follows:

> the fact of something being easy to use, or the degree to which it is easy to use [1]

Obviously, most industrial products are designed in light of usability in order to meet users' various requirements. These requirements are characterised by factors such as use cases, user profiles, security requirements or local regulations. Since all of these requirements cannot be satisfied by a single device, a variety of devices has been developed and provided to the users who can choose the product's usability features to fit their needs.

M. Himaga
Hitachi, Ltd., Hitachi Omori 2nd Bldg., 27-18, Minami-Oi 6-Chome, Shinagawa-ku, Tokyo 140-8572, Japan
e-mail: mitsutoshi.himaga.jv@hitachi.com

H. Ogata (✉)
Hitachi-Omron Terminal Solutions, Corp., 1 Ikegami, Haruoka-cho, Aichi-ken, Owariasahi-shi 488-8501, Japan
e-mail: hisao_ogata@hitachi-omron-ts.com

A. Uhl et al. (eds.), *Handbook of Vascular Biometrics*, Advances in Computer Vision and Pattern Recognition, https://doi.org/10.1007/978-3-030-27731-4_6

The usability factors of biometric devices include the following:

- Compliance with regulations,
- Compactness,
- Portability and mobility,
- Universal design,
- Durability and anti-vandalism,
- High throughput and
- Universality.

In the following sections, the first experimental implementation of the finger vein biometric technology with a very primitive user interface is introduced. The details of each usability factor considered at the time of industrialisation of the technology are then reviewed and discussed by illustrating use cases in the real world. The key factors how the usability requirements were achieved in the product design are also discussed later in this chapter.

6.1.1 Early Implementation

The basic principle of the finger vein biometrics was discovered in a research on vascular pattern visualisation for medical purposes [2]. Since the primary purpose of the research was to obtain high contrast images that can be used for medical diagnostics, the researchers focused on the image quality rather than the usability of the device in the early stage of the development. As a consequence, the prototype device was large and heavy, and thus not suitable for general public use. One of the first implementations of such experimental equipment is shown in Fig. 6.1.

Fig. 6.1 Prototype finger vein reader

6.1.2 Commercialisation

In order to utilise the technology originally developed for medical equipment for commercial biometric devices, there were a lot of factors to consider. The following three minimal usability features were particularly focused at the time of development.

- Intuitive operation

One of the major issues was the ease of use. As biometric devices are sometimes used as a modality alternative to existing rather complicated authentication procedures (e.g. long passwords which are frequently asked to change, or USB tokens that users are required to type the challenge and response codes every time), the operation of the device is expected to be simple and intuitive. To achieve this goal, the appearance of the device needed to be designed carefully so that users can present their fingers properly without any effort or training.

- Compact design

The device dimension is another factor to consider. Many biometric devices are used in an office environment where the desktop spaces are limited and thus the size of the biometric device needs to be as small as possible.

- Universal design

As a commercial product, it is important to design the device so that it is accepted by various types of users. This means that the size and shape of the image scanning platen need to be designed to be suitable for the majority of fingers. The length and the thickness of fingers of the target users are collected, and the device is designed so that it can accept more than 90% of the user population.

One of the most successful finger vein devices was developed and released by Hitachi, Ltd. in 2006. The device was designed to be used on desktop computers and connected to a PC via USB cable. The vein images were captured by the infrared camera embedded in the bottom part of the device and the comparison process was executed on the connected PC [3]. Its compact body and the intuitive design were widely accepted and employed for many use cases such as logical access control, physical access control or time and attendance systems. This model became a benchmark for other finger vein devices developed later as well as the origin of the following usability evolutions.

6.1.3 Evolutions of the Finger Vein Biometric Devices

The H-1 finger vein device was designed bearing the above-mentioned basic usability requirements in mind and successfully accepted in the market (Fig. 6.2). In the course of the worldwide deployment of the biometric devices, some users pointed out the possibility of further optimisation in terms of usability in order to meet various requirements specific to the use case [4]. In the following sections, the usability

Fig. 6.2 Hitachi finger vein reader H-1

requirements are summarised, and the optimisations applied to the finger vein biometric devices are described.

6.2 Compliance with Regulations

6.2.1 Use Case/Background

In some use cases, the authentication/transaction process needs to be compliant with Public Key Infrastructure (PKI) by law or by regulation. Especially in the banking sector, PKI transactions are widely adopted for both corporate and retail online banking and it is necessary to incorporate PKI functionality into the device.

6.2.2 Usability Requirement Details

In the PKI scheme, every user needs to keep a private key in a secure storage. Typically, private keys are stored in a tamper-proof smart card, in which the key is activated by a PIN number. This scheme is widely employed by credit card transactions and sometimes referred to as "chip-and-pin" scheme. In order to apply biometric authentication in this scheme, the following requirements needed to be satisfied:

- A smart card reader must be equipped in a single body.
- Communications between the biometric reader and the card reader must be secured.
- The "Challenge-Response" protocol must be supported.
- The RSA signing functionality is required.

6.2.3 Challenges

The layout of the smart card reader was the most significant challenge for this implementation. In order to protect the communication between the biometric device and the smart card reader, it was necessary to integrate both components in a single tamper-proof enclosure. Attaching a smart card reader on the hood of the scanner was the easiest option; however, this idea was not employed because the increased height and the weight of the upper part of the device reduced the physical stability.

6.2.4 Implementation

For a stable use on the desktop and consistent user experience with the precedent finger vein devices, a small micro-SIM card reader is embedded under the finger scanning platen. The internal structures around the bottom part of the device were drastically reviewed and redesigned so that the card reader could be embedded without changing the height of the finger presentation. The card slot is accessible from the front of the device so users can visually confirm that the card is properly set. The card can be inserted or removed just by a simple "push-push" action for convenience, which is effective especially when the device is shared by other users. The PKI-enabled finger vein reader B-1 is shown in Fig. 6.3.

6.3 Compactness

6.3.1 Use Case/Background

One of the most common feedbacks from the users concerns the dimension of the device. Although the H-1 device was made compact, some users find the upper hood relatively bulky especially when compared with fingerprint readers.

6.3.2 *Usability Requirement Details*

The height of the finger vein reader needed to be reduced. The footprint (the area occupied on the desktop) also needed to be as small as possible. The requirements to satisfy are as the following:

- A small and flat form factor with a minimum footprint is needed.
- Practical authentication accuracy must be achieved without the hood.

6.3.3 *Challenges*

Since the scanning platen is exposed to the outside, the lighting conditions cannot be controlled. The image contrast is largely influenced by the ambient light and the captured finger vein images can be easily saturated under a strong light such as direct sunlight.

Due to the small form factor, the area available for the scanning platen is very limited. On the other hand, the physical finger area to scan needs to be larger than a certain size in order to achieve practical authentication accuracy.

Fig. 6.3 PKI-enabled finger vein reader B-1

6.3.4 Implementation

In order to suppress the influence of the uncontrollable ambient light, the enclosure is carefully designed. The finger rest is made narrow so that the entire platen is covered with the presented finger. The enclosure is painted in matt black to avoid any undesirable light reflected on its surface. These measures prevent the ambient light from getting into the camera, which largely contributes to the stable image capturing.

The scanning platen was made smaller than the H-1 device by reducing the marginal area of the captured image. This reduces the tolerance of the finger positioning, which affects the usability; however, the narrow finger rest and the newly designed fingertip stop help users to present fingers in a consistent manner. A couple of notches are added to both sides of the front part so that users can place their index finger and ring finger for better stability.

The small factor finger vein reader S-1 is shown in Fig. 6.4.

Fig. 6.4 Finger vein reader S-1

6.4 Portability and Mobility

6.4.1 Use Case/Background

One of the most preferred features is the portability of the device. It is not difficult to imagine a situation where users need to authorise transaction requests when they are out of office and do not have any office environment.

6.4.2 Usability Requirement Details

In the mobile computing scene, the size of the device is an important factor. Especially when users need to authenticate transactions immediately wherever they are, the authentication device needs to be compact enough to bring with. Also, it is inconvenient to work with hardware that requires cable connections. It is quite often the case that no mains are available when working outside the office. Although there are some technologies to reduce the number of wired connections such as PoE (Power over Ethernet) or USB bus power, the user experience is not satisfactory for the mobile use. Taking these factors into account, the following requirements are preferred:

- The dimension must be compact enough to fit in a pocket.
- The device must be powered without a lead.
- Cable connections are not appropriate.

6.4.3 Challenges

In order to reduce the height of the first-generation device H-1, the hood needed to be removed. Since the infrared light source is embedded under the hood, the optical system layout has to be changed. After a careful technical consideration, two infrared LED arrays are placed on both sides of the scanning platen.

6.4.4 Implementation

In order to produce the illumination powerful enough to penetrate the presented finger, a large-capacity lithium–ion rechargeable battery is employed. For the wireless connectivity with small power consumption, the Bluetooth® Low Energy technology was employed.

The mobile finger vein reader B-2 is shown in Fig. 6.5.

Fig. 6.5 Mobile finger vein reader

6.5 Universal Design

6.5.1 Use Case/Background

Unauthorised cash withdrawals from ATMs with counterfeit cards, stolen cards and stolen PINs became a serious social issue about 15 years ago in Japan. Many account holders used a vulnerable PIN such as a birthday, a phone number and a car registration number and financial institutions were expected to introduce countermeasures to reduce the fraud risk promptly. In response to this movement, many financial institutes in Japan decided to introduce finger vein biometrics for ATM transactions [5].

6.5.2 Usability Requirement Details

Since ATM users are general public, it is not realistic to expect all users have received sufficient training before using biometric devices. Therefore, an external design that implies intuitive operations is very important. Biometric ATMs should also be highly accessible for physically challenged people. Thus, the following usability requirements are needed:

- Users need to be able to present their fingers intuitively and straightforwardly without a special training.
- Fingers must be always visible through the authentication process.
- The shape of the enclosure must be friendly for visually impaired users.

6.5.3 Challenges

Since the infrared light source was embedded under the hood of the device in the H-1 device, users could not see their fingers whilst having them scanned. In the course of the proof-of-concept study, some users found it uncomfortable or even scary to insert their fingers into the tunnel under the hood. In order to reduce this psychological stress, the hood needed to be removed and the layout of the light source had to be changed to enhance the usability.

The height of the device should be as low as possible so that users on a wheelchair can easily access the bank card reader and the cash outlet over the biometric device. The device shape itself needs to give an intuitive guide to visually impaired users so that they can understand the proper finger positioning only by touching the device.

6.5.4 Implementation

The hoodless "open-type" finger vein device was developed by introducing a pair of infrared LED arrays embedded on both sides of the scanning platen (Fig. 6.6). An inverted U-shaped fingertip guide was employed to enhance the usability for visually impaired users. The accessibility of the biometric device and other ATM components such as a card reader is carefully checked with a help of handicapped users (Fig. 6.7). The open-type finger vein devices and an implementation example on an ATM are shown in Figs. 6.8 and 6.9, respectively.

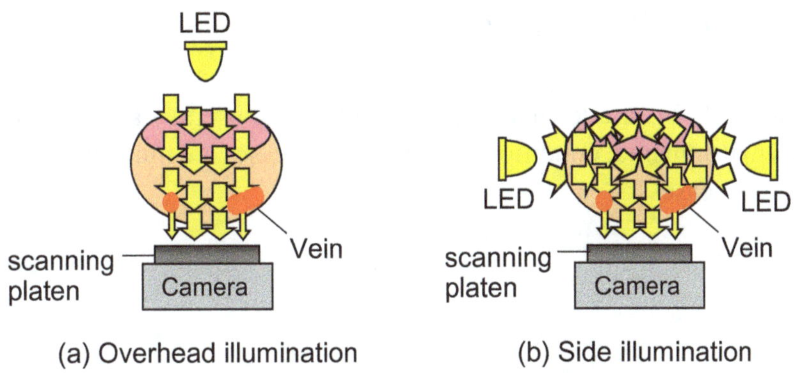

Fig. 6.6 Comparison of finger illumination

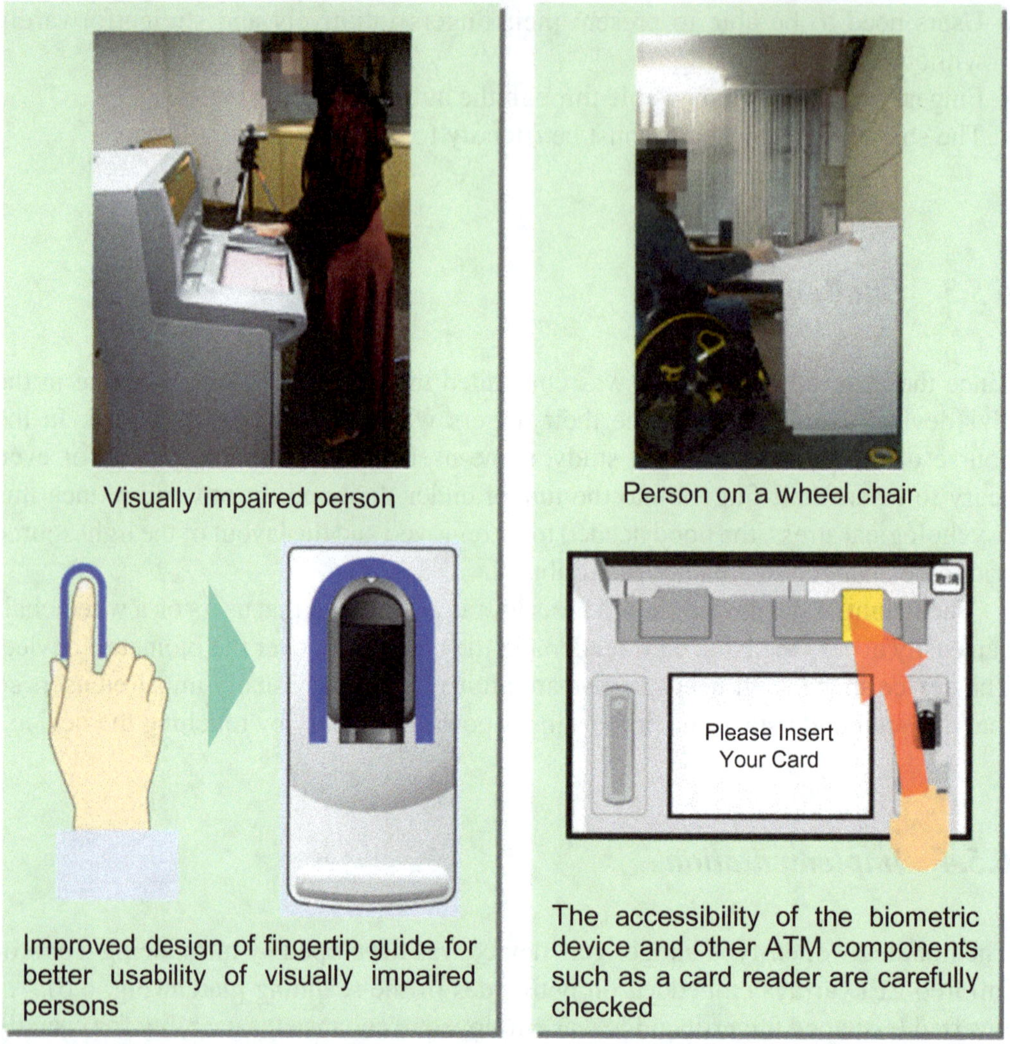

Fig. 6.7 Accessibility tests at the user experience

6.6 Durability and Anti-vandalism

6.6.1 Use Case/Background

In many cases, ATMs are located outdoors to provide users with 24/7 financial services. The environmental conditions of outdoor use cases are much more challenging than indoor use cases.

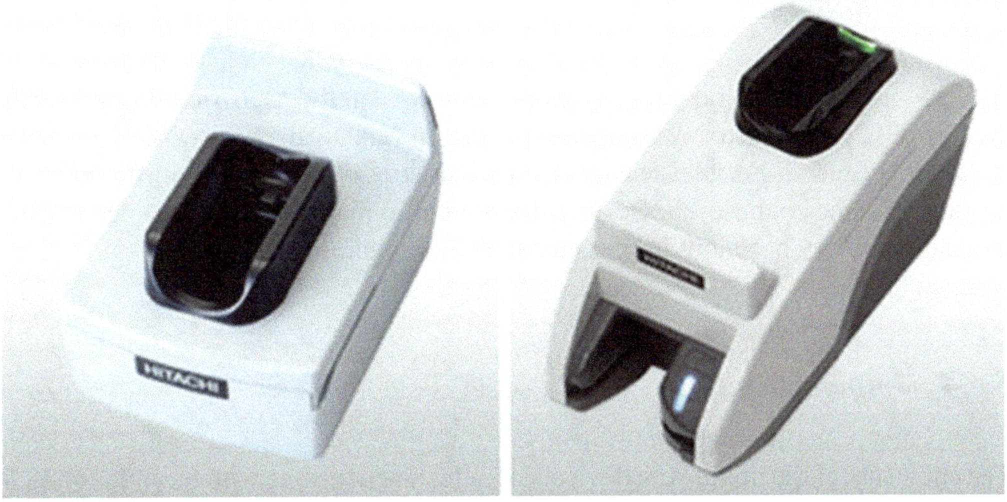

(a) Desktop device (b) Enrolment device

Fig. 6.8 Open-type finger vein reader

Fig. 6.9 Finger vein device installed on ATM

6.6.2 Usability Requirement Details

In order to embed the device on outdoor ATMs, the device needed to be robust against rough ambient conditions. The following requirements needed to be satisfied:

- The device needs to be operable under severe weather such as rain, snow or direct sunlight.
- The enclosure of the device must withstand vandalism.

6.6.3 Challenges

As ATM users are general public, the balance between the user-friendliness and the durability is a key factor. The open-type finger vein readers are widely accepted in Japan because users feel less psychological stress as described in the previous chapter. In some countries, however, there are not so many users to feel such stresses and the durability has more importance than the psychological factor.

6.6.4 Implementation

The enclosure of the finger vein device was redesigned to cope with the outdoor ATM use case scenarios. A hood to protect the scanning platen was added to increase the durability. The round ABS enclosure shown in Fig. 6.10 is designed to withstand vandalism and can hold a weight of an adult male. In the case where the see-through materials are preferred rather than the durable reinforced plastic (see Sect. 6.5.3), the hood can be replaced with the one made of tinted clear plastic as shown in Fig. 6.11. The curvature of the hood is carefully designed to reduce unwanted infrared light reflection inside the tunnel. The hood also acts as a platen protector from dirt, which is effective to maintain the performance and to reduce the number of cleaning visits.

Fig. 6.10 Finger vein enclosure for outdoor ATMs (prototype)

Fig. 6.11 Outdoor ATM finger vein reader installed on an ATM

6.7 High Throughput

6.7.1 Use Case/Background

For physical access, control use cases such as entry to an office building or a ticket barrier in a station, the authentication processing time is a critical factor. Instead of holding a proximity ID card to touch in, it is obviously more convenient if users just need to present their fingers on a reader installed at the entrance. This means that the comparison process needs to be done in the identification mode, or also known as one-to-many authentication.

6.7.2 Usability Requirement Details

In the case of office building scenario, the entrance gate is heavily used typically at the time of open and close of business. The access to the building needs to be granted within the time the existing entrance system (e.g. proximity cards) requires. Otherwise, a long queue will develop at the busiest time.

The following features are needed for this application:

- The authentication must be fast enough to accommodate a large number of visitors.
- One-to-many authentication functionality is required.
- Fingers presented in various manner need to be accepted.

6.7.3 Challenges

In order to maximise the throughput, i.e. the number of successful entry permissions per unit time, it is necessary to design a physical access control system that does not require users to stop at the gate. This means that finger rests employed for other models to encourage users to position their fingers correctly cannot be used and thus the presented fingers cannot be completely stationary.

6.7.4 Implementation

The presented fingers are automatically located in the camera's field of view so that users do not need to place their fingers always in the same position [6]. The distance between the camera and the presented fingers is measured by a range finder so that the captured images have sufficient image resolutions for the following comparison process. The optical system layout of the walk-through finger vein technology and its prototype implementation used in a proof-of-concept are shown in Figs. 6.12 and 6.13, respectively.

6.8 Universality/Availability

6.8.1 Use Case/Background

Biometric authentication is becoming very common in our daily life. One of the most familiar use cases is the logical access control for mobile devices such as smartphones. Biometric modalities such as fingerprint, facial or iris recognitions are

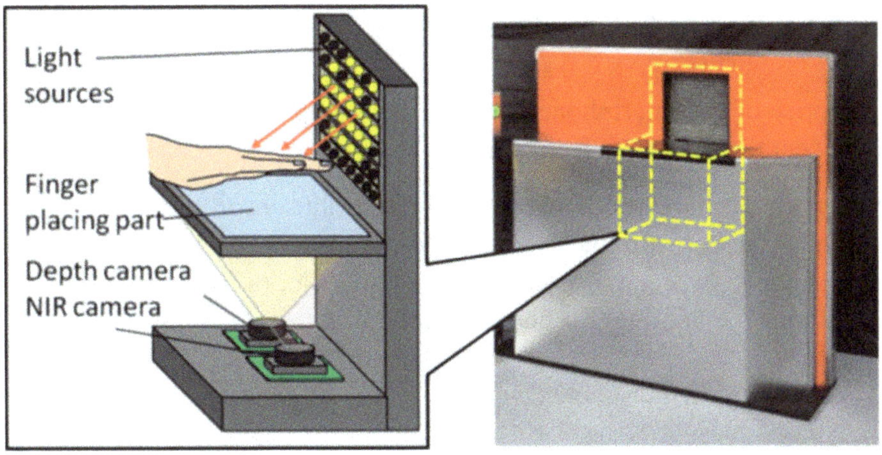

Fig. 6.12 Optical system layout of the walk-through finger vein technology

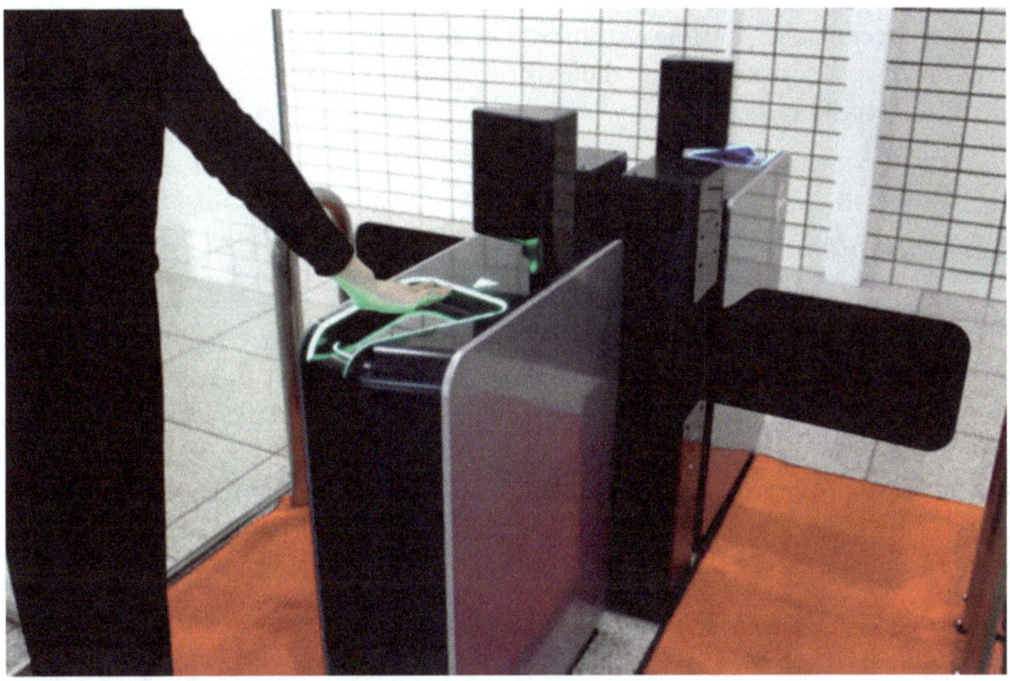

Fig. 6.13 Walk-through finger vein entrance gate used in a proof-of-concept

widely used; however, these technologies typically require a dedicated sensor, which is a hurdle for smartphone manufacturers in terms of cost.

6.8.2 Usability Requirement Details

Since majority of the smartphone users are general public, it is almost obvious for them to expect the following features:

- The form factor must be comparable to fingerprint sensor modules.
- The weight must be minimal for better portability.
- The authentication process should not consume a lot of battery power.
- The cost must be minimal for general public use.

6.8.3 Challenges

Miniaturisation has been a long-awaited evolution for finger vein devices. Although it may be technically possible to achieve the form factor, it is hard to be competitive in terms of cost comparing with the existing biometric readers such as capacitive or swipe fingerprint readers.

6.8.4 Implementation

In order to meet the above-mentioned requirements, the finger vein device was fully implemented by software [7]. The authentication algorithm uses the camera and the System on Chip (SoC) on the smartphone to authenticate the user. The vascular pattern extraction process is drastically re-engineered so that it can locate the internal structure even from images captured by an ordinary visible light camera embedded on the mobile device. The Android™[1] implementation of the finger vein software is shown in Fig. 6.14.

[1] Android is a trademark of Google LLC.

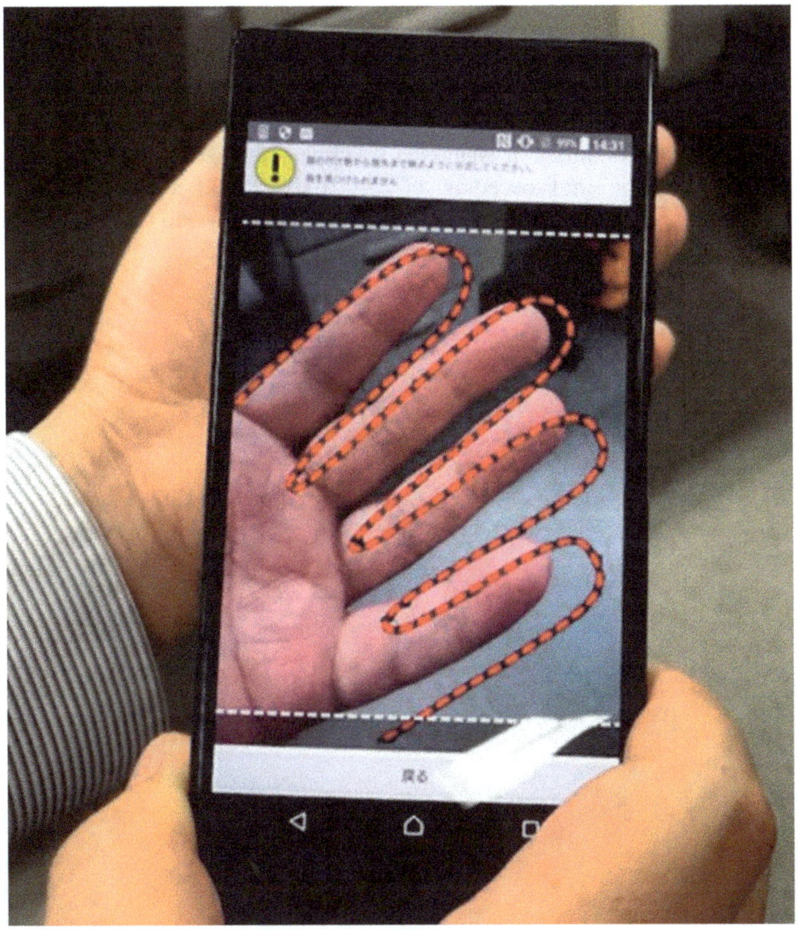

Fig. 6.14 Finger vein software working on Android smartphone (prototype)

6.9 Summary

In this chapter, the user requirements expected for finger vein biometric devices are summarised and reviewed in terms of usability. The backgrounds of the usability requirements are illustrated by quoting real use cases and the product design approaches to satisfy such requirements are discussed. The usability requirements vary over time or by region together with ever-evolving technologies and need to be reviewed time to time in order to satisfy the needs of the mass-market.

References

1. Cambridge business English dictionary
2. Kono M, Ueki H, Umemura S (2002) Near-infrared finger vein patterns for personal identification. Appl Opt 41(35):7429–7436
3. Li Stan Z, Jain Anil (2009) Encyclopedia of biometric recognition. Springer, US

4. Murakami S, Yamaguchi Y, Himaga M, Inoue T (2018) Finger vein authentication applications in the field of physical security. Hitachi Rev 67(5). http://www.hitachi.com/rev/archive/2018/r2018_05/05b04/index.html
5. Ratha NK, Govindaraju V (eds) (2008) Advances in biometrics. Springer-Verlag, London
6. Matsuda Y, Miura N, Nonomura Y, Nagasaka A, Miyatake T (2017) Walkthrough-style multi-finger vein authentication. In: Proceedings of 2017 ICCE, 8–10 Jan 2017
7. Miura N, Nakazaki K, Fujio M, Takahashi K (2018) Technology and future prospects for finger vein authentication using visible-light cameras. Hitachi Rev 67(5). http://www.hitachi.com/rev/archive/2018/r2018_05/05a05/index.html

Chapter 7
Towards Understanding Acquisition Conditions Influencing Finger Vein Recognition

Simon Kirchgasser, Christof Kauba and Andreas Uhl

Abstract Finger vein biometrics are of growing influence in daily life high-security applications like financial transactions. Several application areas of finger vein recognition systems exhibit different environmental and non-environmental conditions, e.g. changes in temperature, illumination, humidity and misplacement of the finger. Experience in the application of various biometrics (e.g. fingerprints, iris, face) shows that acquisition condition changes may affect the recognition process. No systematic analysis on the impact of those condition changes influencing the performance of finger vein recognition systems has been conducted so far. In this chapter, 17 possible acquisition conditions are identified, described and a first proper investigation regarding their influence on the recognition process is performed. This investigation is done based on several well-established finger vein recognition schemes and a score distribution analysis. The insights gained in this chapter might help to improve finger vein recognition systems in the future. The first results reveal several acquisition conditions that significantly decrease the recognition performance. Especially external illumination condition changes and finger tissue temperature variation shows a severe impact. On the other hand, slight misplacement of the finger and sport activities (in particular cycling) has hardly any influence on the recognition performance.

Keywords Finger vein recognition · Biometric data acquisition conditions · Biometric performance evaluation · External influences · Subject-related influences

---

S. Kirchgasser (✉) · C. Kauba · A. Uhl
Department of Computer Sciences, University of Salzburg, Jakob-Haringer-Str. 2, 5020 Salzburg, Austria
e-mail: skirch@cs.sbg.ac.at

C. Kauba
e-mail: ckauba@cs.sbg.ac.at

A. Uhl
e-mail: uhl@cs.sbg.ac.at

A. Uhl et al. (eds.), *Handbook of Vascular Biometrics*, Advances in Computer Vision and Pattern Recognition, https://doi.org/10.1007/978-3-030-27731-4_7

7.1 Introduction

In various biometric applications, e.g. iris or fingerprint recognition, studies have been performed to describe and quantify varying acquisition conditions. Concerning challenging aspects in iris biometrics, an overview is given in [6]. In fingerprint applications, various studies exist too. Some important ones related to the current study can be found in [23, 25, 27]. In [25], the authors, Simon-Zorita et al., evaluated an automatic minutiae-based fingerprint verification system on the MCYT Fingerprint Database [19], which includes several variabilities of factors that occur in a typical daily acquisition process. The effects of a controlled image acquisition (done under ideal environmental, subject and internal conditions) on fingerprint matching results have been investigated in [23] using various methods to enhance the quality of imprints acquired under challenging conditions (including changes in ambient temperature and humidity). Finally, in [27], Stewart et al. took rugged environmental conditions, especially cold weather, into account during tests regarding the performance of fingerprint recognition technology. The experimental results show no critical deficiencies in the recognition performance regarding the considered challenging environmental conditions. Unfortunately, the authors only reported the results for the false rejection rate (FRR), which indicated no relationship between the recognition results and the cold weather condition.

According to the investigations done in other biometric fields, it is necessary to identify, describe and quantify environmental- and non-environmental-based conditions which could influence finger vein (FV) recognition systems. This consideration might have some impact on the performance evaluation, improvement and more frequent employment of FV recognition systems in daily life. Prior to this, several conditions have to be selected and suitable data needs to be acquired. Some considered environmental condition changes will include variations in the skin humidity or in the finger temperature, placing a light source in front of the scanner or putting the finger into a water bath to soften the skin. Subject-related condition changes might exhibit finger misplacement (e.g. finger is not covering the scanner light source entirely), usage of hand or sun lotion and sport activities. A detailed description of all investigated variations is given in Sect. 7.4.

The rest of this chapter is organised as follows: In Sect. 7.2, a detailed review on related work and research results is given. Then the scanner devices used during the data acquisition and the considered conditions are described in Sect. 7.3 and 7.4, respectively. Section 7.5 illustrates the experimental setup. The performance evaluation together with a discussion of the results are presented in Sect. 7.6. Finally, Sect. 7.7 concludes this chapter along with an outlook on future work.

7.2 Varying Acquisition Conditions—A Challenging Aspect in Research and Practical Applications

Varying environmental- or subject-related variations in acquisition conditions should not influence the security and reliability of biometric authentication solutions. This is vital for FV recognition systems as well because they are used in high-security applications, such as financial services, automated teller machines (ATMs) and for securing online banking transactions. Especially FV scanners deployed in ATMs can be influenced by varying environmental conditions easily as those machines are often located outside and thus prone to changes in illumination, temperature and humidity (note: in Japan they are usually inside the bank building). A user might be enrolled inside the bank building but the ATM at which the authentication is performed might be located outside the building and not inside. Thus, there might be direct sunlight shining on the FV scanner device situated at the ATM where the user wants to withdraw money after the authentication. Furthermore, it is possible that the user presents his/her finger in a slightly different way as he/she did during the enrolment. These varying acquisition conditions can cause severe problems in real-life applications because the accuracy and reliability of biometric recognition systems, in particular, of FV-based systems, are undermined.

As motivated in the introduction, several factors can affect the recognition accuracy of vascular pattern based authentication systems. First of all, inherent biological factors may influence the FV recognition process. According to Kumar et al. [12], the quality of finger vein images can vary across the population for different users. This statement was postulated only and was not proven by empirical experiments. These quality variations might be caused by factors like gender (e.g women usually have thinner fingers than men), daily physiological composition [28], medical conditions (e.g. thickness of persons' tissue layers may change due to fat [28]), anaemia, hypotension, hypothermia and various other aspects as discussed in [5, 24].

Another major impact is related to the optical component used in the applied scanner devices. The NIR light, used to render the vein structure visible in the captured images, is absorbed, reflected and scattered during the penetration of the humans' tissue. Light scattering imposes the most severe impact of these three aspects. In biomedical imaging research, these factors have been extensively investigated. Dhawan et al. [9] reviewed several models enabling the propagation of visible and NIR light photons in biological tissue for biomedical and clinical application. This study included (among others) the usage of transillumination NIR light in clinical practice. The results of using NIR transillumination have shown a significant potential in diagnostic applications but there are still difficulties due to scattering of the NIR light in the biological tissue. A more specific application area was discussed by Bashkatov et al. [4]. The authors focused on the description of optical properties of human skin, subcutaneous and mucous tissues using light exhibiting different wavelengths. They reported specific light scattering and absorption coefficients for each of the considered tissues. These coefficients vary highly among the investigated modalities. Consequently, it is not possible to neglect the aspect of biological influences in FV applications but they are usually considered as a given constant factor, which has to be covered by various image preprocessing, restoration and enhancement techniques [29]. Further results regarding optical influences are reported by Baranoski et al. [3]. They simulated light interaction effects within the human skin by the application of computer graphics techniques. The authors only investigated effects introduced by the first layer of the finger tissue. Furthermore, a discussion regarding light scattering influences on the FV recognition performance was not given. Another study by Cheong et al. [7], neglecting real-life recognition aspects, used mathematical models with respect to optical coefficients describing various human tissue layers. The authors described and discussed optical properties of blood vessels (in particular the aorta), liver and muscle tissue. There are several other non-biological factors which might have an impact on the recognition performance of FV-based systems as well. These non-biological factors can be grouped into internal factors and external factors.

At first, we focus on various internal factors. The most important ones are those which are introduced by the biometric scanner device itself. The equipped illumination source might be too bright or too dark either due to a wrong specification of the illumination source, due to problems with the brightness control module or due to fingers being too thick or too thin. Furthermore, the equipped camera module might be sensitive to ambient light changes as sunlight contains NIR light. Another influencing factor is a high sensitivity to dust which affects the camera as well. Both of these image sensor specific internal factors lead to a decrease in the FV image quality. Fortunately, it is possible to cope with these problems by changing the scanner setup or adding additional components. To reduce the sensitivity to ambient light, a daylight blocking filter or a housing around the scanner can be mounted additionally. Moreover, it is possible to use thermal FV imaging as well. Thermal vein pattern images are insensitive to ambient light changes under a wide range of lighting conditions as reported in [15]. However, this adds the necessity to cope with other difficulties like problems with varying ambient temperature or changes in the human body temperature as discussed by the authors of [13].

A recent study of Kauba et al. [11] investigated the impact of several internal factors. The authors considered sensor noise, sensor ageing related defects as well as other image distortions which are potentially present in real-life hand- and FV-pattern acquisition conditions. Moreover, they considered different levels of artificial distortions. Such artificial distortions might be present in practical hand vein applications but fortunately the authors reported that the evaluated hand vein recognition schemes show a high robustness against the investigated influences. In our present study, we ensure that the scanner setup is optimal in order to reduce the number of distorting aspects due to internal factors to a minimum.

The class of external factors can be separated into two independent categories: environmental aspects and subject-related (non-environmental) aspects. These two classes of external influencing factors are the main scope of the current work. Non-environmental-related factors include finger movement during the image acquisition and misplacement of the finger on the scanner device, including tilt, bending and rotation of the finger along its longitudinal axis. Matsuda et al. [17] and Yang et al. [30] investigated the aforementioned finger tilt and non-planar finger rotation. In both works, the authors introduced recognition schemes which are able to deal with non-planar finger rotation up to a certain degree. Matsuda et al. stated that their deformation-tolerant feature point matching scheme is able to cope with non-planar finger rotation up to $\pm 30°$. Yang et al. did experiments with their proposed recognition scheme regarding finger rotation as well but they did not state to what extent of rotation their scheme is robust against. Furthermore, both authors claim that their proposed schemes show a high level of robustness against elastic deformations of the acquired vein patterns. In a more recent study by Prommegger et al. [20], the effects of longitudinal rotation within FV datasets have been investigated. The authors prove experimentally that longitudinal finger rotation poses a severe problem in FV recognition as the resulting vein image may represent entirely different patterns due to the perspective projection. This variation in the perspective projection results in a severe performance decrease using simple recognition schemes if more than $\pm 10°$ rotation is contained in the images. More sophisticated FV recognition schemes are able to handle up to $\pm 30°$ without leading to a performance decrease.

Apart from finger movement related investigations, there are several studies showing that various environmental factors have a crucial impact on FV recognition. The most important aspects are varying ambient light conditions [26], light scattering effects [29] as well as ambient temperature changes as discussed in [18]. Miura et al. [18], Song et al. [26] and Yang et al. [29] discuss these distortions only briefly without any further performance experiments targetting the influence of these variations. However, in [18], an analysis was done in order to quantify the influence of ambient temperature changes while a more robust matching scheme was introduced. The authors proposed a scheme that calculates local maximum curvatures in cross-sectional profiles of an FV image. Thus, fluctuations regarding vein width and brightness, introduced by, e.g. ambient temperature changes and physical activities involving the fingers/hands, are reduced during the feature extraction. The following studies introduce different aspects of complicating factors in FV recognition: In [14], bifurcations and ridge endings (originally fingerprint minutiae types) are selected for image alignment followed by a unique FV code extraction, which is based on local binary patterns. The minutia points' extraction can easily be influenced by distortions introduced during the acquisition of the FV pattern. However, the authors only mention that the number and the positions of minutia points may vary among the acquired data due to possible changes in finger location, different posture and varying lighting conditions. Hashimoto [10] mentions that variations within the FV data need to be controlled. Body metabolism changes, brightness fluctuations due to individual variations in finger size or lighting conditions are discussed as major influencing factors without considering these aspects in the performance evaluation of the recognition process. A recent study by Qin et al. [21] states that a proposed convolutional neural network (CNN) on the one hand makes the recovery of missing vein patterns possible and on the other hand is able to suppress noise resulting from segmentation in case a low-quality image is processed. The detection of such low-quality images is mandatory in the first place and can be done by the application of several available FV quality measures [22, 28].

The main aspects of these studies have in common are (a) challenging aspects are only seen as a given problem and therefore no further investigation is dedicated to them and (b) there are only very few studies available which try to describe the influence on the recognition performance. One recent investigation focusing on the impact of different meteorological aspects like temperature, humidity, atmospheric pressure and wind was performed by Zheng et al. [33]. Based on the experimental results the authors concluded that ambient temperature is the most significant factor. They further proposed two methods, dynamic template selection and a so-called threshold adjustment, to reduce the impact of ambient temperature changes during the recognition process.

For the further development of FV recognition systems, it would be of great value to understand which acquisition variations are causing which amount of degradation in the FV recognition process. This work is dedicated to this important aspect.

7.3 Deployed Scanner Devices

It is possible to categorise the various types of FV scanners into several classes: contactless/full contact scanners and LED/laser light devices are the most important ones. All available COTS FV scanners are full contact and based on transillumination using LEDs. According to the fact that almost all COTS FV scanners do not enable direct access to the raw vein images they acquire, they would be only of little use during this study as we need to conduct a recognition toolchain on the raw vein images to evaluate the used algorithm performance on the dataset containing influenced FV images. This evaluation is mandatory to improve the algorithm's robustness against varying acquisition conditions and could not be done by using COTS FV scanners.

Two different types of illumination can be distinguished. Their classification is based on the relative positioning of the camera module, the finger and the equipped light source. The first method is called light transmission or transillumination and the second one is called reflected light. NIR LEDs as well as NIR laser modules can be deployed for both illumination setups.

In the transillumination concept, the light source and the image sensor are placed on opposite sides of the finger that is acquired. The emitted NIR light passes through the finger, where it is absorbed by the blood vessels and is captured by the imaging module on the opposite side. The veins, or to be more precise the blood vessels, appear as dark lines in the images. We decided to deploy only the transillumination concept as the FV image quality is better compared to the quality of images acquired using reflected light.

Two self-designed FV scanner devices were used to acquire the FV images and are similar to the scanners discussed in Chap. 3. The main difference is that the deployed devices are not able to capture FV images of three fingers at the same time. Only one finger after the other can be processed to acquire the blood vessel pattern. However, one scanner is equipped with a NIR laser illumination module and one with an LED illumination module, both are arranged in a strip placed underneath

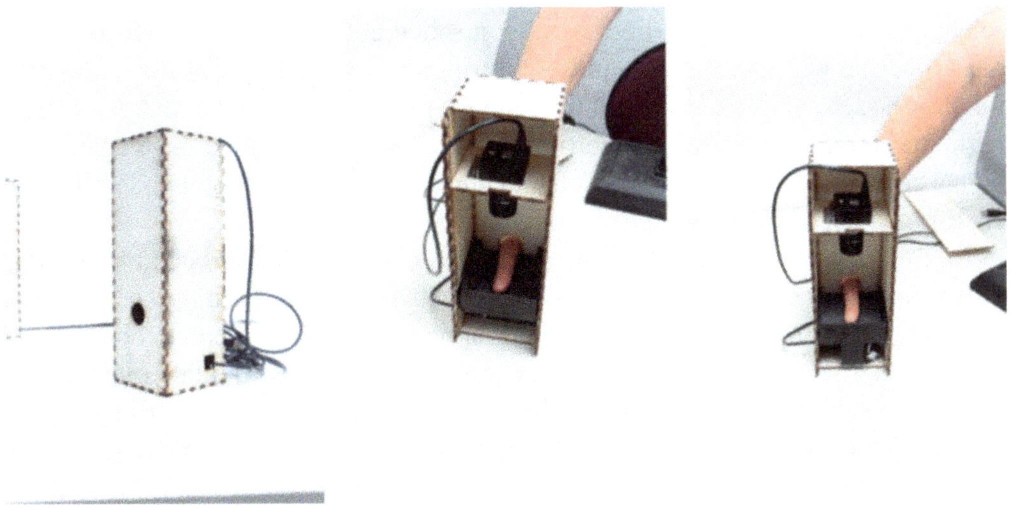

Fig. 7.1 NIR LED and laser-based finger vein scanner (camera on top and finger at bottom)

the finger support. Both scanners are designed in the same way and are based on the transillumination principle. The NIR LEDs have a peak wavelength of 860 nm, while the laser modules have a peak wavelength of 808 nm. The captured FV images have a resolution of 1280×1024 pixels and are stored as 8-bit greyscale images. Furthermore, an additional NIR pass-through filter is mounted to reduce the influence of ambient light and to improve the quality of the acquired images. The used image sensor is an industrial NIR-enhanced camera, IDS Imaging UI-1240ML-NIR [2], equipped with a Fujifilm HF9HA-1B 9 mm wide-angle lens [1]. The scanners are depicted in Fig. 7.1.

A wooden box (left image) surrounds all parts of the device, including the camera module, the NIR light strip and the finger support, in order to reduce the amount of ambient light to a minimum. The middle and right images of Fig. 7.1 reveal the light transmission concept. The camera is placed on top, the finger can be seen in the middle placed on the finger support, and the illumination module is located at the bottom of the wooden box. In the middle image, the LED-based version of the scanner is shown, while the right image represents the laser-based one. Compared to other FV scanners this positioning concept is different and results in the visualisation of the blood vessel patterns which are located at the upper side of the finger.

7.4 Finger Vein Acquisition Conditions Dataset

Currently, there is no publicly available dataset FV that exhibits various environmental and non-environmental acquisition conditions. Thus, we established our own subset, including different environmental and subject-related acquisition variations.

In general, every biometric authentication system consists of an enrolment and a verification stage. During the mandatory enrolment stage, the considered biometric pattern of the user is acquired under controlled and supervised conditions. This ideal situation will likely not be present during the second stage of the authentication process, the verification. Each time the user wants to authenticate him-/herself, he/she has to present his/her biometric trait which is then acquired once again. This biometric data acquisition during authentication might be performed under different environmental conditions.

To simulate a more realistic enrolment and authentication procedure, the data acquisition was performed under a controlled environment. At first, the enrolment was done under optimal and stable environmental conditions and a correct subject's scanner handling was ensured. The authentication was simulated in a second acquisition session, on the same day by manually introducing one specific condition change (environmental or subject related) at a time. This controlled acquisition environment ensured the capturing of data acquired under exactly one varying aspect (disregarding other, additional influences).

The first subset included in our database "reflects" this enrolment subset. This first subset is exhibiting no distorting aspect which is important as a reference and for the baseline recognition evaluation.

Besides the enrolment subset we acquired a total of 17 subsets exhibiting acquisition variations. Seven of these subsets have been acquired under varying environmental conditions and 10 subsets exhibit subject-related condition changes. We aimed to include the most promising aspects relating to acquisition conditions present in real-life deployments of FV recognition systems.

The entire data acquisition was done indoors with indirect illumination (fluorescent lamps at the ceiling) only. The humidity and temperature in the room have been kept stable during the entire process at a level of 23 °C and approximately 75% humidity. Each of the investigated acquisition conditions are introduced intentionally and manually during the acquisition of the specific subset independent from the others. If the humidity of the fingers was changed or sports activity was performed before the acquisition process, the necessary alternations were introduced in a different room or outside (sports) to preserve stable acquisition conditions in the room, where the FV device was placed. This reduces the influence of other conditions than the desired acquisition condition changes. In the following, each of the considered acquisition conditions is described in detail and example images are displayed in Figs. 7.2 and 7.3 for the laser scanner and the LED scanner, respectively. The top-left image in both figures corresponds to the enrolment stage (subset *base*). The other images, all captured from the same finger, are exhibiting one acquisition condition variation each:

base: baseline (no distortion included)

Environmental Condition Changes :

humid: increasing the humidity by putting the fingers next to a humidifier placed in a neighbouring room to prevent humidity changes in the acquisition room.

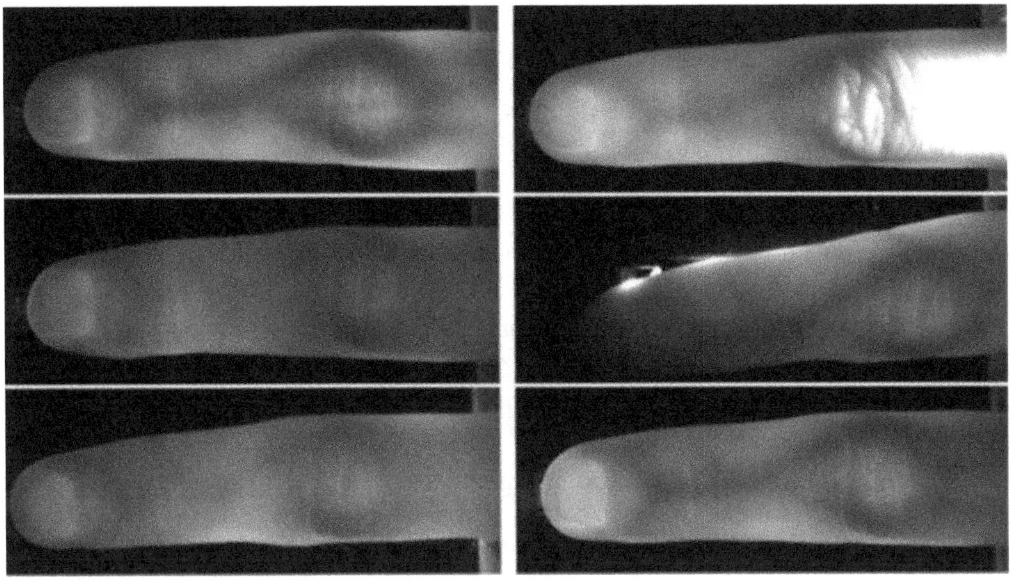

Fig. 7.2 Laser FV scanner images (same finger) of all subsets–1. row: *base* (left), *light* (right)–2. row: $temp - 5$ (left), *badpl* (right)–3. row: *sunlot* (left), *cycle* (right)

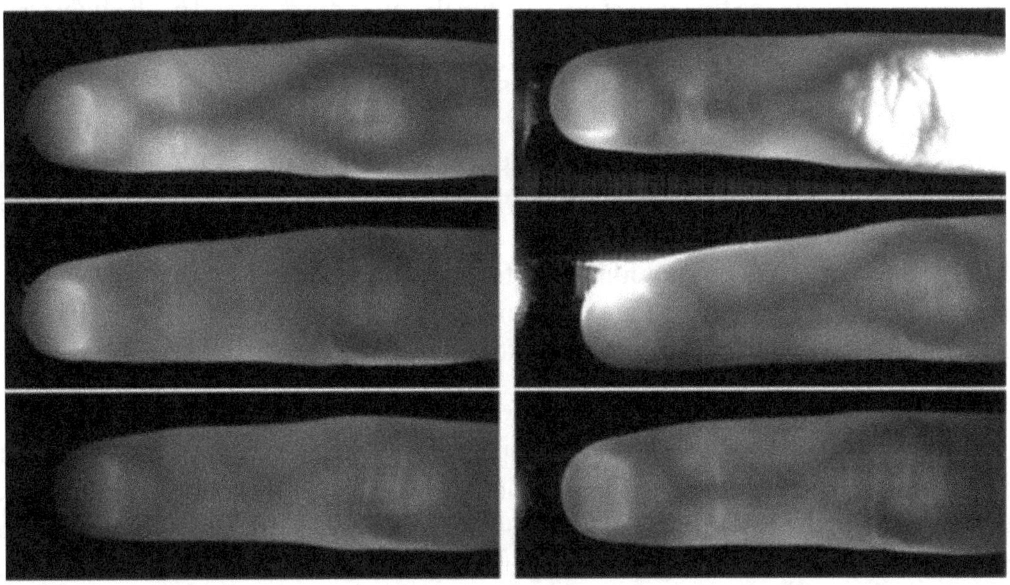

Fig. 7.3 LED FV scanner images (same finger) of all subsets–1. row: *base* (left), *light* (right)–2. row: $temp - 5$ (left), *badpl* (right)–3. row: *sunlot* (left), *cycle* (right)

light: placing a battery torch with a low light emission intensity in front of the scanner

dark: shutting off the room light.

$temp - 5$: lowering the finger's temperature, introduced by an ice water bath where the finger was put in for 5 min.

$temp + 5$: increasing the finger's temperature introduced by a hot water bath where the finger was put in for 5 min.

$skin10$: putting the fingers in a body temperature water bath for 10 min (this does not alter the temperature of the finger, but the skin structure is influenced—besides, the fingers are dried afterwards to avoid influences by the wet fingers).

$skin25$: putting the finger in a body temperature water bath for 25 min.

$\underline{Subject\ Related\ Condition\ Changes}$:

$up5$: putting both arms straight upside to the vertical position and hold this position for 5 min.

$up10$: putting both arms straight upside to the vertical position and hold this position for 10 min.

$tremb$: imitating that the finger placed inside the scanner is trembling.

$badpl$: placing the finger inside the scanner in a way that the light source is not covered entirely.

$bend$: bending the finger inside the scanner.

tip: tilting the finger forward, so only the fingertip is placed on the light strip (the tilting angle is about 10 degrees, and hence most of the illumination goes through the finger's tissue).

$trunk$: tilting the finger backwards, so the fingertip is not touching the light strip but the trunk touches the scanner surface (the tilting angle is about 10 degrees, and hence most of the illumination goes through the finger's tissue).

$handlot$: applying hand lotion to the finger's surface.

$sunlot$: applying sun lotion to the finger's surface.

$cycle$: cycling for about 20 min before the image acquisition.

The subsets represented by the given example images have been selected because they are likely to exhibit severe impact in practical applications. From a visual point of view, it can be concluded that variations as displayed by the middle and last image located in the left column and the first two images in the right column could cause some problems during the recognition process. The visibility of the blood vessel patterns in each of these four images is clearly suppressed by the variation as compared to the top-left baseline image. During the experimental discussion, we will come back to these subsets.

There is currently no detailed knowledge of which variation introduces the most severe impact in terms of recognition accuracy degradation. This study is the first of its kind focusing on environmental- and non-environmental (subject)-related acquisition conditions in the scope of FV recognition. It can serve as a basis for further investigations on this topic. Only two subjects have been acquired due to the very time-consuming process of acquiring the images. This leads to a total of 60 images per condition (six fingers per subject—index, middle and ring finger, each finger was acquired five times). Although the number of images per finger is limited, there is still sufficient data available to quantify the impact of the various distortions.

7.5 Finger Vein Recognition Toolchain and Evaluation Protocol

The first part of the FV recognition toolchain is the FV preprocessing to enhance the vein pattern quality. This process consists of Region-of-Interest (ROI) extraction, image filtering and enhancement. At first, the ROI is extracted from the input images using edge detection. Afterwards, the vein pattern's visibility is enhanced by the application of various techniques: **High Frequency Emphasis Filtering** (HFE) [32], **Circular Gabor Filter** (CGF) [31] and **CLAHE** (local histogram equalisation) [34]. The second part of the FV recognition toolchain includes feature extraction and feature comparison resulting in a list of comparison scores. We selected two well-established binarisation-type feature-extraction methods, **Maximum Curvature** (MC) [18] and **Principal Curvature** (PC) [8], as well as one key point (SIFT) [16] based method with additional key point filtering for the feature extraction. The binarisation-type methods aim to extract the vein pattern from the background resulting in a binary output image, which represents the extracted features. After the feature extraction is completed, it is followed by a comparison of these binary images as proposed by [18].

To obtain the comparison scores, all possible genuine and impostor comparisons are performed. This is done by comparing each image against all remaining ones which finally results in 120 genuine and 1650 impostor comparisons per subset. The comparison scores can be downloaded from: http://www.wavelab.at/sources/Kirchgasser19a/. We utilised the PLUS-OpenVein SDK which was presented in Chap. 4 of this book. A publicly available implementation of the complete processing toolchain can be downloaded from: http://www.wavelab.at/sources/OpenVein-Toolkit/.

We have selected several well-established measures to quantify and categorise the different acquisition conditions. Thus, the average genuine score values (avGen) as well as the average impostor score values (avImp) have been calculated first. The tendency of the avGen and avImp values gives a first hint which acquisition condition might have the most severe impact on the recognition process. The avGen and avImp are listed in the result Tables 7.1 till 7.5 in the second and third columns. Additionally, we have selected the equal error rate (EER), the lowest FNMR for FMR less or equal to 1% (FMR_{100}), the lowest FNMR for FMR less or equal to 1% (FMR_{1000}), Zero Match Rate (zFMR) and Zero Non-Match Rate (zFNMR) as performance measures. These values will be listed in the result tables in columns four till eight given in percentage.

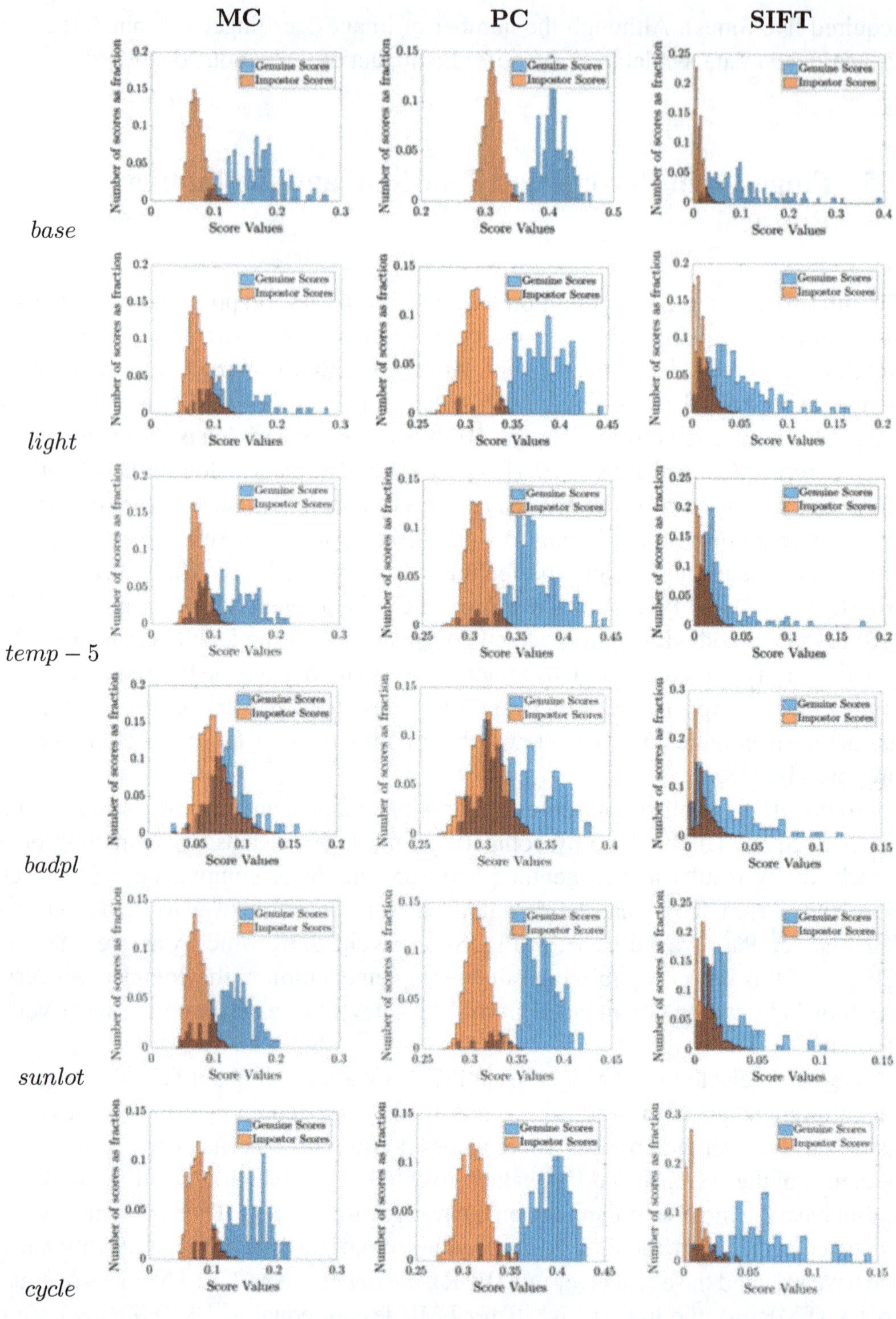

Fig. 7.4 Laser subsets matching score distributions MC (left column), PC (middle column) and SIFT (right column): 1. row: *base*–2. row: *light*–3. row: *temp* − 5–4. row: *badpl*–5. row: *sunlot* and 6. row: *cycle*

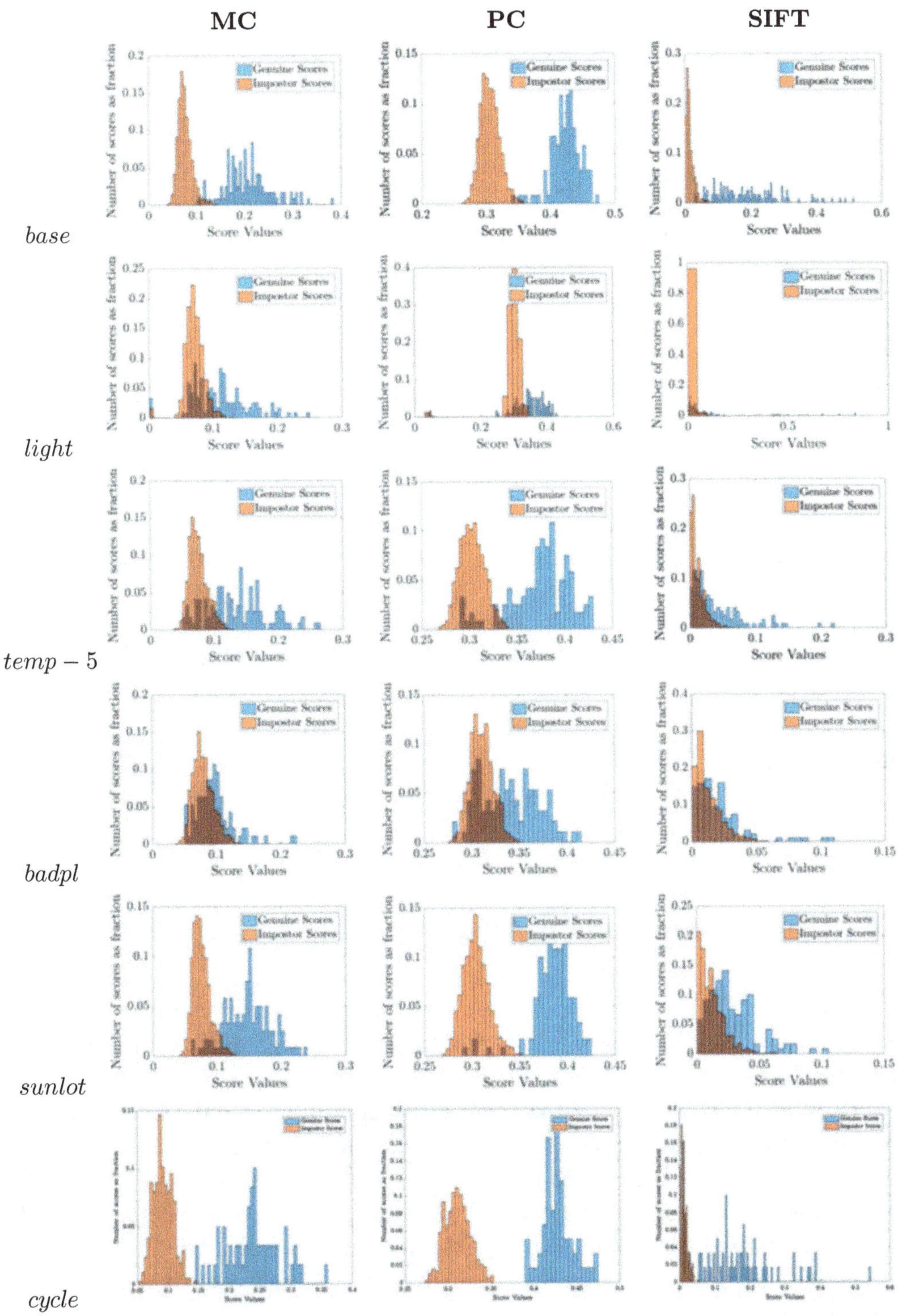

Fig. 7.5 LED subsets matching score distributions MC (left column), PC (middle column) and SIFT (right column): 1. row: base–2. row: *light*–3. row: *temp* − 5–4. row: *badpl*–5. row: *sunlot* and 6. row: *cycle*

Table 7.1 Performance evaluation results for MC using the laser scanner data

Name	avGen	avImp	EER	FMR_{100}	FMR_{1000}	zFMR	zFNMR
Baseline							
base	0.17	0.07	4.15	10.3	16.4	18.9	12.41
External condition changes							
humid	0.14	0.07	10.82	25.8	32.5	48.3	88.7
light	0.12	0.07	12.48	33.3	50.8	61.66	85.7
dark	0.13	0.07	13.29	33.0	47.5	47.5	97.2
$temp - 5$	0.12	0.07	18.34	39.2	51.7	54.2	96.9
$temp + 5$	0.13	0.07	11.45	30.8	43.3	44.2	73.7
*skin*10	0.12	0.07	11.66	34.2	53.3	55.8	92.3
*skin*25	0.13	0.07	8.39	25.8	43.3	43.3	93.3
Subject-related condition changes							
*up*5	0.13	0.07	45.64	7.5	16.6	19.3	99.8
*up*10	0.12	0.07	43.44	6.9	15.5	18.1	98.3
tremb	0.11	0.07	18.65	54.4	79.4	86.6	93.0
badpl	0.09	0.07	22.51	93.5	97.4	97.4	99.9
bend	0.1	0.07	12.14	20.6	33.6	45.6	97.2
tip	0.13	0.07	9.40	61.3	88.0	96.5	62.0
trunk	0.1	0.07	20.85	82.5	98.3	98.3	89.7
handlot	0.14	0.07	15.81	30.8	40.8	43.3	86.4
ID*sunlot*	0.12	0.07	11.66	28.3	36.6	45.8	98.2
cycle	0.16	0.07	8.60	12.5	30.3	30.3	67.4

7.6 Experimental Results Analysis

In the following, all results are discussed in detail together with the general trend of the different acquisition conditions highlighted by the worst and best results which have been achieved.

Figures 7.4 and 7.5 display the score distribution plots for the laser-based and the LED-based scanner, respectively. Each column of both figures corresponds to a single recognition scheme: the left column shows the values for MC, the middle column displays the results obtained using PC and the right column depicts the SIFT results. Each row is dedicated to one subset that has been described before. These subsets have been selected because they are likely to exhibit severe impact in practical applications.

The calculation of the baseline results is a special case: they are calculated by comparing subset *base* with itself, while for other results the comparison is always done between subset *base* as gallery and one of the probe subsets *humid* till *cycle*. This setup is in regards with the usual enrolment/authentication scenario in real-life applications. However, it must be mentioned that the number of performed comparisons is lower for the baseline experiments. As comparisons with the same images

Table 7.2 Performance evaluation results for PC using the laser scanner data

Name	avGen	avImp	EER	FMR_{100}	FMR_{1000}	zFMR	zFNMR
Baseline							
base	0.4	0.31	0.86	0.9	2.6	2.6	1.2
External condition changes							
humid	0.38	0.31	3.52	4.2	5.0	5.8	61.1
light	0.38	0.31	3.33	5.0	5.8	9.2	91.8
dark	0.37	0.31	0.01	10.8	11.7	11.7	91.8
$temp - 5$	0.37	0.3	6.67	8.3	14.2	15.8	96.8
$temp + 5$	0.38	0.31	2.49	2.5	3.3	5.8	92.9
*skin*10	0.37	0.31	4.99	9.2	10.8	15.8	68.3
*skin*25	0.37	0.31	2.49	2.5	5.8	5.8	73.8
Subject-related condition changes							
*up*5	0.38	0.31	40.01	7.1	15.9	18.9	97.3
*up*10	0.36	0.31	40.56	6.7	15.1	17.3	96.6
tremb	0.37	0.31	12.51	13.4	21.4	24.1	95.1
badpl	0.34	0.3	19.85	57.1	70.1	70.1	95.2
bend	0.34	0.31	12.92	17.2	18.9	21.5	99.7
tip	0.38	0.31	5.97	67.6	77.6	77.9	87.6
trunk	0.35	0.31	16.55	55.0	70.8	88.3	99.9
handlot	0.38	0.31	4.99	8.3	12.5	13.3	71.7
sunlot	0.37	0.31	4.99	6.7	7.5	12.5	96.7
cycle	0.4	0.31	3.64	5.3	5.3	5.3	35.1

are excluded the number of impostor scores using subset *base* is reduced. The reader must be aware of this fact while the performance measures of subset *base* and the other subsets are discussed.

The score distribution plots in Figs. 7.4 and 7.5 visually reveal that MC and PC achieve a better performance on the individual subsets as reported for the key point based method SIFT. The high overlap of genuine (coloured blue) and impostor (coloured red) score distribution is not only valid for the presented examples but also for all other considered subsets. The observations are in-line with the subsequent metric based quantification analysis of the results. Except for subset *cycle* a significant increase in the score distributions overlap for all acquisition condition changes can be clearly seen. The distribution plots of subset *base* (first row) and *cycle* show well-separated genuine and impostor comparison scores, only a small intersection area is present for all recognition schemes. This is proven by the performance measures EER, FMR_{100}, FMR_{1000}, zFMR and zFNMR as shown in Tables 7.1, 7.2, 7.3, 7.4 and 7.5, respectively. All the other subsets exhibit a much higher overlap between the score distributions, which again is proven by the other performance measures, in particular, described by an EER increase reporting a recognition performance decrease. For almost all other subsets and feature-extraction methods, the

Table 7.3 Performance evaluation results for SIFT using the laser scanner data

Name	avGen	avImp	EER	FMR_{100}	FMR_{1000}	zFMR	zFNMR
Baseline							
base	0.11	0.02	5.28	19.8	34.5	34.5	43.6
External condition changes							
humid	0.04	0.01	20.62	52.5	65.8	74.2	78.5
light	0.04	0.01	19.09	49.2	62.5	62.5	99.9
dark	0.03	0.01	23.18	62.5	85.8	91.7	99.9
$temp - 5$	0.04	0.01	28.20	73.3	83.3	86.7	99.9
$temp + 5$	0.04	0.01	16.93	53.3	71.7	72.5	99.9
*skin*10	0.03	0.01	16.35	55.0	65.0	82.5	99.9
*skin*25	0.04	0.01	24.99	61.6	83.3	87.5	99.9
Subject-related condition changes							
*up*5	0.03	0.01	44.54	48.5	63.2	67.1	99.9
*up*10	0.04	0.01	43.01	46.5	59.4	63.8	99.9
tremb	0.02	0.01	26.72	67.8	72.3	75.0	99.9
badpl	0.02	0.01	29.23	93.5	99.9	99.9	99.9
bend	0.04	0.01	18.94	51.7	68.1	68.9	99.9
tip	0.06	0.01	8.47	19.6	78.6	88.8	99.9
trunk	0.03	0.01	17.33	70.0	80.8	83.3	99.9
handlot	0.04	0.01	20.75	56.6	67.5	73.3	99.9
sunlot	0.02	0.01	28.08	78.3	87.5	89.1	99.9
cycle	0.06	0.01	25.00	10.6	35.7	35.7	68.0

genuine scores are shifted to the left as the number of low-valued genuine scores is higher compared to those of subset *base* or *cycle*. In these subsets, EER, FMR_{100}, FMR_{1000}, zFMR and zFNMR values are higher as well. When comparing the laser and the LED scanner's score distribution plots (comparing Figs. 7.4 and 7.5) it can further be observed that there is hardly any difference in the detected overall trend of both scanners detectable. This suggests that the selected illumination module does not have an impact on the recognition process for the considered subsets and thus for the evaluated conditions.

The avGen and avImp scores do not show significant differences among the subsets. Furthermore, their values do not exhibit differences within each of the three recognition schemes, so it is not possible to distinguish between the different subsets. Thus, they do not provide any additional information regarding the impact of the various acquisition conditions. It is not possible to distinguish between the single subsets because the values belonging to one of the recognition schemes (MC, PC or SIFT) are nearly identical. This can be seen in column 2 and 3 of each of Tables 7.1, 7.2 and 7.3. Considering subsets *humid* till *sunlot*, the avGen values for MC, PC and SIFT are lower compared to the results of subset *base* and *cycle*. Further details upon the performance metrics for the data acquired by the laser scanner are displayed in Tables 7.1 (for MC), 7.2 (for PC) and 7.3 (for SIFT), respectively.

Table 7.4 Performance evaluation results for MC using the LED scanner data

Name	avGen	avImp	EER	FMR_{100}	FMR_{1000}	zFMR	zFNMR
Baseline							
base	0.21	0.08	1.77	5	6.7	6.7	4.5
External condition changes							
humid	0.16	0.08	10.03	17.5	27.5	31.7	84.8
light	0.12	0.07	25.58	49.2	60.8	70.8	100.0
dark	0.16	0.08	7.50	15.8	25.0	25.0	96.1
$temp - 5$	0.13	0.08	18.34	37.5	43.33	48.33	96.9
$temp + 5$	0.16	0.08	11.80	21.7	26.7	32.5	99.9
$skin10$	0.16	0.08	7.69	9.4	17.0	18.8	96.5
$skin25$	0.16	0.08	7.50	15.0	30.0	36.7	98.3
Subject-related condition changes							
$up5$	0.14	0.08	42.49	98.3	99.2	99.2	99.9
$up10$	0.16	0.08	40.00	99.2	99.9	99.9	99.6
tremb	0.15	0.08	10.91	29.4	41.2	42.9	94.8
badpl	0.12	0.08	34.06	84.0	89.4	89.4	97.2
bend	0.12	0.08	16.66	43.3	58.3	64.2	99.9
tip	0.15	0.08	13.33	23.3	55.0	55.9	99.9
trunk	0.11	0.08	6.66	16.7	21.7	23.3	58.9
handlot	0.15	0.08	17.41	21.7	29.2	29.2	96.8
sunlot	0.15	0.08	8.34	20.0	28.3	31.2	87.7
cycle	0.17	0.08	2.05	1.5	3.0	3.5	4.0

The performance measures for the LED setup are listed in Tables 7.4 and 7.5. The corresponding values of SIFT will not be displayed separately due to the low recognition performance of SIFT. The SIFT results are quite similar to the results of the laser lights scanner, which are presented in Table 7.3. To summarise the results it can be said that there is no difference regarding the overall trend between laser and LED concerning avGen and avImp. However, there are some differences regarding the considered performance metrics. First, the performance on the LED data is better compared to the laser subsets, especially for PC in the most cases. Second, the results exhibit bigger differences among the acquisition conditions. In particular, subset *light*, $temp - 5$ and $temp + 5$ are showing the highest number of FMR_{100}, FMR_{1000}, zFMR and zFNMR values related to environmental condition changes, while the EER is worst for $temp - 5$. If non-environmental acquisition variations are taken into account, $up5$, $up10$ and *badpl* are the most influencing conditions. They exhibit much higher error measures as detected in the baseline results which indicates a much worse overall performance of these subsets.

Based on the EER, FMR_{100}, FMR_{1000}, zFMR and zFNMR results it can be summarised that the impact of varying acquisition conditions on the recognition performance seems to be influenced by (a) certain acquisition conditions and (b) the applied

Table 7.5 Performance evaluation results for PC using the LED scanner data

Name	avGen	avImp	EER	FMR_{100}	FMR_{1000}	zFMR	zFNMR
Baseline							
base	0.42	0.31	0.84	0.8	1.7	1.7	1.3
External condition changes							
humid	0.4	0.31	2.49	2.5	2.5	3.3	91.6
light	0.35	0.30	21.53	33.3	35.8	40.8	99.9
dark	0.39	0.31	0.84	0.8	0.8	1.7	44.7
$temp-5$	0.37	0.30	7.50	10.8	11.7	14.2	79.7
$temp+5$	0.39	0.30	10.00	11.7	14.2	15.0	99.9
$skin10$	0.4	0.30	0.85	0.0	0.9	0.9	0.9
$skin25$	0.39	0.30	0.84	0.8	1.7	1.7	75.3
Subject-related condition changes							
$up5$	0.38	0.3	49.15	98.3	99.9	99.9	97.2
$up10$	0.39	0.31	43.33	99.9	99.9	99.9	98.8
tremb	0.39	0.31	3.35	3.4	10.0	11.0	48.5
badpl	0.34	0.3	27.64	51.1	57.4	61.7	99.8
bend	0.38	0.3	9.15	11.7	13.3	17.5	99.6
tip	0.35	0.31	6.66	7.5	13.3	15.0	93.7
trunk	0.38	0.3	5.79	5.8	11.6	11.7	79.0
handlot	0.38	0.31	9.18	12.5	12.5	12.5	98.5
sunlot	0.38	0.3	3.33	4.2	4.2	5.0	74.5
cycle	0.4	0.31	1.24	0.6	1.2	1.3	1.1

recognition system. The recognition accuracy across all performed experiments is influenced by acquisition condition changes. Some display a high amount of performance degradation, while others hardly show any influence. Furthermore, it is not clear how the impact of the different acquisition variations will change if the number of available distorted FV images is increased. These first results—showing an impact on the recognition process using images acquired under varying conditions—may not necessarily be observed in a large database to the same extent. Nevertheless, we are quite sure that based on the first results, several of the considered acquisition conditions have a high impact on the FV recognition process. These especially include changes in ambient light and temperature as well as misplacement of the finger inside the scanner. In order to get a deeper insight in the particular influence of these conditions, we plan to extend the database in terms of subjects and acquired FV images to perform a more reliable analysis with respect to the influence of varying acquisition conditions on FV recognition systems in practical application scenarios.

7.7 Conclusion

In this chapter, the influence of varying environmental and non-environmental acquisition conditions in FV recognition was evaluated. The main purpose was the quantification and selection of the most influencing factors in terms of recognition accuracy. It is known from other studies that many biometric recognition schemes are influenced by environmental and subject-related factors. However, this aspect has not been investigated comprehensively for FV recognition so far. We selected several promising environmental and non-environmental acquisition condition changes which are likely to influence the acquired vascular pattern images acquired under different acquisition conditions. The current investigation was designed to get some first results in order to identify the potentially most challenging condition changes. For this purpose, we established a first FV image database containing 18 different conditions in total. 60 images per condition have been acquired from 12 individual fingers. Although that only 12 fingers from 2 subjects have been acquired, the results are showing a clear trend. The evaluation, focusing on the quantification of false accepted and rejected comparisons, confirmed that several of the considered conditions have a severe influence on the recognition performance. The recognition performance is decreased for FV images acquired under varying conditions compared against images acquired under optimal conditions, which corresponds to practical applications of FV recognition systems including enrolment and authentication phase.

We identified several severe influencing conditions regarding the recognition performance. The highest influence is observable in subset $up5$ using LED lights and PC. Subsets $badpl$, $light$ and $temp - 5$ were detected as most challenging conditions regardless of the type of the considered FV scanner devices. Thus, variations in environmental and non-environmental acquisition conditions can both result in severe FV recognition performance problems.

Based on these promising first results we plan to extend the acquired subset. It is mandatory to increase the number of subjects in order to gain a better insight into the issues with varying conditions during the application of FV recognition systems in daily life. We are confident that this will contribute to the development of FV recognition systems that are more robust against the influence of typical acquisition conditions present in practical deployments and lead to a more widespread use of FV biometrics in various everyday applications.

References

1. Fujifilm lens description. http://www.fujifilmusa.com/products/optical_devices/machine-vision/2-3-15/hf9ha-1b/index.html. Accessed 16 July 2018
2. IDS camera description. https://de.ids-imaging.com/IDS/datasheet_pdf.php?sku=AB00184. Accessed 16 July 2018

3. Baranoski Gladimir VG, Krishnaswamy Aravind (2004) An introduction to light interaction with human skin. Rev Inform Teor E Apl 11(1):33–62
4. Bashkatov AN, Genina EA, Kochubey VI, Tuchin VV (2005) Optical properties of human skin, subcutaneous and mucous tissues in the wavelength range from 400 to 2000 nm. J Phys D Appl Phy 38(15):2543
5. Bickler PE, Feiner JR, Severinghaus JW (2005) Effects of skin pigmentation on pulse oximeter accuracy at low saturation. Anesthesiol J Am Soc Anesthesiol 102(4):715–719
6. Bowyer KW, Hollingsworth K, Flynn PJ (2008) Image understanding for iris biometrics: a survey. Comput Vis Image Underst 110(2):281–307
7. Cheong W-F, Prahl SA, Welch AJ (1990) A review of the optical properties of biological tissues. IEEE J Q Electron 26(12):2166–2185
8. Choi JH, Song W, Kim T, Lee S-R, Kim HC (2009) Finger vein extraction using gradient normalization and principal curvature. Proc SPIE 7251:9
9. Dhawan AP, D'Alessandro B, Fu X (2010) Optical imaging modalities for biomedical applications. IEEE Rev Biomed Eng 3:69–92
10. Hashimoto J (2006) Finger vein authentication technology and its future. In: 2006 symposium on VLSI circuits, 2006. Digest of Technical Papers. IEEE, pp 5–8
11. Kauba C, Uhl A (2015) Robustness evaluation of hand vein recognition systems. In: Proceedings of the international conference of the biometrics special interest group (BIOSIG'15). Darmstadt, Germany, pp 1–8
12. Kumar Ajay, Zhou Yingbo (2012) Human identification using finger images. IEEE Trans Image Proc 21(4):2228–2244
13. Kumar A, Hanmandlu M, Madasu VK, Lovell BC (2009) Biometric authentication based on infrared thermal hand vein patterns. In: 2009 digital image computing: techniques and applications. IEEE, pp 331–338
14. Lee EC, Lee HC, Park KR (2009) Finger vein recognition using minutia-based alignment and local binary pattern-based feature extraction. Int J Imaging Syst Technol 19(3):179–186
15. Lin Chih-Lung, Fan Kuo-Chin (2004) Biometric verification using thermal images of palm-dorsa vein patterns. IEEE Trans Circuits Syst Video Technol 14(2):199–213
16. Lowe DG (1999) Object recognition from local scale-invariant features. In: Proceedings of the seventh IEEE international conference on computer vision (CVPR'99), vol 2. IEEE, pp 1150 – 1157
17. Matsuda Yusuke, Miura Naoto, Nagasaka Akio, Kiyomizu Harumi, Miyatake Takafumi (2016) Finger-vein authentication based on deformation-tolerant feature-point matching. Mach Vis Appl 27(2):237–250
18. Miura Naoto, Nagasaka Akio, Miyatake Takafumi (2007) Extraction of finger-vein patterns using maximum curvature points in image profiles. IEICE Trans Inf Syst 90(8):1185–1194
19. Ortega-Garcia J, Fierrez-Aguilar J, Simon D, Gonzalez J, Faundez-Zanuy M, Espinosa V, Satue A, Hernaez I, Igarza J-J, Vivaracho C et al (2003) MCYT baseline corpus: a bimodal biometric database. IEEE Proc Vis Image Signal Proc 150(6):395–401
20. Prommegger B, Kauba C, Uhl A (2018) Longitudinal finger rotation—problems and effects in finger-vein recognition. In: Proceedings of the international conference of the biometrics special interest group (BIOSIG'18). Darmstadt, Germany, pp 1–11
21. Qin H, El-Yacoubi MA (2017) Deep representation-based feature extraction and recovering for finger-vein verification. IEEE Trans Inf Forensics Secur 12(8):1816–1829
22. Qin H, Li S, Kot AC, Qin L (2012) Quality assessment of finger-vein image. In: 2012 Asia-Pacific Signal and information processing association annual summit and conference (APSIPA ASC). IEEE, pp 1–4
23. Ratha NK, Bolle RM (1998) Effect of controlled image acquisition on fingerprint matching. In: Proceedings of Fourteenth international conference on Pattern recognition, 1998, vol 2. IEEE, pp 1659–1661
24. Severinghaus JW, Koh SO (1990) Effect of anemia on pulse oximeter accuracy at low saturation. J Clin Monitor 6(2):85–88

25. Simon-Zorita D, Ortega-Garcia J, Fierrez-Aguilar J, Gonzalez-Rodriguez J (2003) Image quality and position variability assessment in minutiae-based fingerprint verification. IEEE Proc Vis Image Signal Proc 150(6):402–408
26. Song W, Kim T, Kim HC, Choi JH, Kong H-J, Lee S-R (2011) A finger-vein verification system using mean curvature. Pattern Recognit Lett 32(11):1541–1547
27. Stewart RF, Estevao M, Adler A (2009) Fingerprint recognition performance in rugged outdoors and cold weather conditions. In: IEEE 3rd international conference on biometrics: theory, applications, and systems, 2009. BTAS'09. IEEE, pp 1–6
28. Xu J, Cui J, Xue D, Feng P (2011) Near infrared vein image acquisition system based on image quality assessment. In: 2011 international conference on electronics, communications and control (ICECC). IEEE, pp 922–925
29. Yang Jinfeng, Shi Yihua (2014) Towards finger-vein image restoration and enhancement for finger-vein recognition. Inf Sci 268:33–52
30. Lu Y, Yang G, Yin Y, Xi X (2017) Finger vein recognition with anatomy structure analysis. IEEE Trans Circuits Syst Video Technol
31. Zhang J, Yang J (2009) Finger-vein image enhancement based on combination of gray-level grouping and circular gabor filter. In: International conference on information engineering and computer science, 2009. ICIECS 2009. IEEE, pp 1–4
32. Zhao J, Tian H, Xu W, Li X (2009) A new approach to hand vein image enhancement. In: Second international conference on intelligent computation technology and automation, 2009. ICICTA'09, vol 1. IEEE, pp 499–501
33. Zheng H, Xu Q, Ye Y, Li W (2017) Effects of meteorological factors on finger vein recognition. In: IEEE international conference on identity, security and behavior analysis, ISBA 2017, New Delhi, India, February 22–24, 2017. pp 1–8
34. Zuiderveld K (1994) Contrast limited adaptive histogram equalization. In: Heckbert PS (ed) Graphics Gems IV. Morgan Kaufmann, pp 474–485

Chapter 8
Improved CNN-Segmentation-Based Finger Vein Recognition Using Automatically Generated and Fused Training Labels

Ehsaneddin Jalilian and Andreas Uhl

Abstract We utilise segmentation-oriented CNNs to extract vein patterns from near-infrared finger imagery and use them as the actual vein features in biometric finger vein recognition. As the process to manually generate ground-truth labels required to train the networks is extremely time-consuming and error prone, we propose several models to automatically generate training data, eliminating the needs for manually annotated labels. Furthermore, we investigate label fusion between such labels and manually generated labels. Based on our experiments, the proposed methods are also able to improve the recognition performance of CNN-network-based feature extraction up to different extents.

Keywords Finger-Vein recognition · Finger-Vein segmentation · Convolutional neutral networks · Fused label training · Automated label training

8.1 Introduction

Finger vein recognition is a biometric method in which a person's finger vein patterns, captured under tissue-penetrating near-infrared (NIR) illumination, are used as a basis for biometric recognition. This process is considered to offer significant advantages compared to classical biometric modalities (e.g. fingerprint, iris and face recognition). For example, finger vein patterns can be captured in a touchless and non-invasive manner, are not influenced by finger surface conditions, can only be captured when the subject is alive and cannot easily get forged.

While many finger vein recognition techniques have been proposed in recent years and commercial products are readily available (and are even used to authenticate

E. Jalilian (✉) · A. Uhl
Department of Computer Sciences, University of Salzburg,
Jakob Haringer Str. 2, 5020 Salzburg, Austria
e-mail: ejalilian@cs.sbg.ac.at

A. Uhl
e-mail: uhl@cs.sbg.ac.at

A. Uhl et al. (eds.), *Handbook of Vascular Biometrics*, Advances in Computer Vision and Pattern Recognition, https://doi.org/10.1007/978-3-030-27731-4_8

financial transactions in ATMs or home banking), yet extracting accurate vein patterns from NIR finger vein images remains far from being trivial. This is mainly due to the often poor quality of the acquired imagery. Poorly designed scanner devices, close distance between finger and the camera (causing optical blurring), poor NIR lighting, varying thickness of fingers, ambient external illumination [34], varying environmental temperature [25] and light scattering [16] represent different aspects which can degrade the finger vein images' quality and cause the images to contain low contrast areas and thus ambiguous regions between vein and non-vein areas. The intensity distributions in these areas can hardly be described by a mathematical model. Therefore, proposing a comprehensive algorithmic solution to extract the actual vein patterns from the NIR finger images is not easy. Nevertheless, even the manual annotation of actual vein patterns in such ambiguous areas (required as ground truth for learning-based methods (i.e. segmentation CNN networks) is extremely difficult and time-consuming and therefore an error-prone process.

In this chapter, we employ three different CNN architectures designed for segmentation to extract finger vein patterns from NIR finger imagery and use the extracted features for the recognition process. Furthermore, with the aim of eliminating the need for manually annotated labels and eventually also improving the networks' feature-extraction capability, we investigate several automatic label generating techniques, as well as label fusion methods, to generate more precise labels to train the networks. After training the networks with these labels and the generation of corresponding vein patterns, we evaluate the recognition performance in terms of receiver operating characteristics and relate the results to those obtained by classical finger vein feature-extraction techniques.

The chapter is structured as follows: Sect. 8.2 describes related works and the state of the art in finger vein recognition and Sect. 8.3 describes vein pattern extraction using three different segmentation CNN architectures as used in this work. In Sect. 8.4, we explain different training label generation, and also fusion techniques used in this work. In Sect. 8.5, we describe the experimental framework used in experimentation. Section 8.6 presents the results, while Sect. 8.7 discusses the obtained results, and finally Sect. 8.8 concludes the chapter.

8.2 Related Works

For a general overview of finger vein recognition techniques, please refer to, e.g. [23] and also the book's introduction chapter. In the first subsection of this section, we briefly describe three state-of-the-art schemes also used in experimentation as reference recognition techniques and used to automatically generate labels required for CNN training. The second subsection reviews the previous employment of CNNs in finger vein recognition, while the third subsection discusses works done in other fields to automatically generate data for CNN training.

8.2.1 Classical Finger Vein Recognition Techniques

Classical finger vein recognition techniques generally fall into two main categories: Profile-based methods and feature-based methods. Feature-based methods assume that in the clear contour of finger vein images, the pixels located in the vein regions have lower values than those in the background. "Repeated Line Tracking" (RLT [24], being of feature-based type) tracks the veins as dark lines in the finger vein image. A tracking point is repeatedly initialized at random positions, and then moved along the dark lines pixel by pixel, where the depth of valley at each position indicates the tracking direction. If no line is detected, a new tracking trail is started. The number of times a pixel is traversed is recorded in a matrix. Pixels that are tracked multiple times have a high likelihood of belonging to a vein. The matrix is then binarised using a threshold.

Profile-based approaches consider the cross-sectional contour of a vein pattern which shows a valley shape. "Maximum Curvature" (MC [25], being of profile-based type) traces only the centre lines of the veins and is insensitive to varying vein width. To extract the centre positions, first the local maximum curvature in the cross-sectional profiles of vein images is determined, using the first and second derivatives. Next, each profile is segmented as being concave or convex, where only local maxima in concave profiles are specified as valid centre positions. Then according to width and curvature of the vein region, a score is assigned to each centre position, and recorded in a matrix called locus space. The centre positions of the veins are connected using a filtering operation subsequently. Eventually, the matrix is binarised using the median of the locus space.

Another profile-based method, exploiting the line-like shape of veins in a pre-defined neighbourhood region is termed "Gabor Filter" (GF [19]). A filter bank consisting of several 2D even symmetric Gabor filters with different orientations is created. Several feature images are extracted using different filters from the filter bank. The final feature image is constructed by fusing all the single images obtained in the previous step, and then morphological operations are used to clear the noise from the image.

Of course, there are many other techniques which often apply classical feature-extraction techniques to the finger vein pattern generation task such as Local binary pattern (LBP [8]), Region Growth [12] and Principal Component Analysis (PCA [15]). However, also other techniques specifically tailored to the problem have been suggested like using vessel-crossings in a minutiae-type manner [3] or the Principal Curvature [17] approach.

8.2.2 CNN-Based Finger Vein Recognition

Recent techniques in deep learning, and especially CNNs, are gaining increasing interest within the biometric community. However, in finger vein recognition prior art is relatively sparse and the extent of sophistication is quite different. The simplest approach is to extract features from certain layers of pre-trained classification networks and feed those features into a classifier to determine similarity to result in a recognition scheme. This approach is suggested by Li et al. [39] who apply VGG-16 and AlexNet feature-extraction and KNN classification for recognition. Extracting vein features as such rather than the binary masks, hinders the application of more advanced training techniques such as label fusion, as used in this work.

Another approach to apply classical classification networks is to train the network with the available enrollment data of certain classes (i.e. subjects). Radzi et al. used a model of reduced-complexity (a four-layered CNN) classifier, with fused convolutional-subsampling architecture for finger vein recognition [35]. Itqan et al. performed finger vein recognition using a CNN classifier of similar structure [29], and Das et al. [5] correspondingly proposed a CNN classifier for finger vein identification. This approach, however, has significant drawbacks in case new users have to be enrolled as the networks have to be retrained, which is not practical.

Hong et al. [13] used a more sensible approach, employing fine-tuned pre-trained models of VGG-16, VGG-19 and VGG-face classifiers, which are based on determining whether a pair of input finger vein images belongs to the same class (i.e. subject) or not. Likewise, Xie and Kumar [40] used several known CCN models (namely, light CNN (LCNN) [38], LCNN with triplet similarity loss function [33], and a modified version of VGG-16) to learn useful feature representations and compare the similarity between finger vein images. Doing so, they eliminated the need for training in case of new enrolled users. However, utilising raw images, the system possesses a potential security threat.

Qin and El-Yacoubi [11] applied a two-step procedure to extract the finger vein patterns from NIR finger images. As the first step, they used a CNN classifier to compute the probability of patch centre pixels to belong to vein patterns, one by one, and labelled them according to the winning class (based on a probability threshold of 0.5). In the next step, in order to reduce finger vein mismatches (as they had the problem of missing vein pixels), they further used a very shallow Fully Convolutional Neural Network (FCN) to recover those missing vein pixels. The approach used in the first network is rather simplistic and computationally demanding compared to the state-of-the-art segmentation networks as used in this work. Moreover, using a further network (the FCN network) to recover the missing pixels, additional processing time is added to the feature-extraction process.

8.2.3 Automated Generation of CNN Training Data

Large amounts of high-quality annotated samples, or ground-truth data, are typically required for CNN training. However, data labelling is an expensive and time-consuming task, especially due to the significant human effort involved. The problem even gets more tedious in case the annotators have to deal with ambiguous images, where clear separation between target regions and the background data is very difficult, as it is the case in many biomedical applications. Given these facts together with the difficulty to persuade medical experts to annotate the required data volumes, it is not surprising that generating ground-truth labels automatically to train CNNs has been suggested for some CNN-based segmentation tasks in medical imaging. In [32], classical techniques were used to segment cells stained with fluorescent markers. The resulting segmentation masks were used as ground-truth labels together with the corresponding bright-field image data to train a CNN. In [14], Canny edge detection was applied to ultrasound images to generate the ground-truth labels required to train a CNN for segmentation of musculo-skeletal ultrasound images. In [9], a part of the ground-truth labels required to train a CNN for brain tumour segmentation was generated by a voted average of segmentation results of top performing classical segmentation algorithms in this field. In [31], a fully convolutional neural network is pre-trained on a large dataset containing ground-truth labels created by existing segmentation tools for brain segmentation, and subsequently fine-tuned with a small dataset containing human expert annotations. In [11], authors used several algorithms to generate a set of finger vein masks and then applied a probabilistic algorithm to each pixel (within the masks) to assign it as being vein or not. However, to the best of the authors' knowledge, this approach (i) has not yet been investigated systematically, and (ii) has not been used jointly or in fusion with manual labels in network training process.

8.3 Finger Vein Pattern Extraction Using CNNs

The first computer vision tasks for which initial CNN architectures were developed include classification [18], bounding box object detection [20] and key point prediction [2]. More recently, CNN architectures have been developed enabling semantic segmentation, in which each pixel is labelled separately with the class of its enclosing object or region. The first techniques, classifying the centre pixel of an entire image patch required immense time and computation resources, especially when used for large-scale (whole image) segmentation. Fully convolutional neural networks are a rich class of architectures, which extend simple CNN classifiers to efficient semantic segmentation engines. Improving the classical CNN design with multi-resolution layer combinations, the resulting architectures are proven to be much better performing than their counterparts consisting of fully connected (FC) layers [22]. As the key distinction, typically the FC layer is replaced in FCN with a decoding mechanism, which uses the down-sampling information to up-sample the low-resolution output maps to the full resolution of the input volumes in a single step, reducing computational cost and improving segmentation accuracy.

There have been already attempts to use FCNs to extract vessel patterns from different human organs. For example, in [6], an FCN is used for segmentation of retinal blood vessels in fundus imagery, or in [26] an FCN is used for vessel segmentation in cerebral DSA series. However, there are significant differences as compared to this work. First, the networks have been trained with manually annotated labels provided by human experts only, second the quality of images is by far better than the NIR finger vein images, and third evaluation has been done with respect to segmentation accuracy relative to the ground-truth labels while in our context segmentation results are indirectly evaluated by assessing recognition performance using the generated vein patterns.

In this work, we use three different FCN architectures to extract the finger vein patterns from NIR finger images. We selected the networks based on diffrent architectural functionalities built in each network, so that we can evaluate endurance of such functionalties in case of finger vein segmentation. The first network architecture used is the U-net by Ronneberger et al. [30]. The network consists of an encoding part, and a corresponding decoding part. The encoding architecture consists of units of two convolution layers, each followed by a rectification layer (ReLU) and a 2×2 down-sampling (Pooling) layer with stride 2. At each down-sampling step, feature channels are doubled. The corresponding decoding architecture consists of units of 2×2 up-convolution layers (up-sampling), which halve the number of feature channels, a concatenation operator with the cropped feature map from the corresponding encoding unit, and two 3×3 convolutions, each followed by a ReLU. At the final layer, a 1×1 convolution is used to map the component feature vectors to the desired number of segmentations. The energy function is computed by a soft-max over the final feature map, combined with the cross-entropy loss function. The cross-entropy then penalises, at each position, the deviation of soft-max ($M_{\lambda(x)}(x)$) from one (1.00) as follows:

$$\varepsilon = \sum_{k'=1} \log(M_{\lambda(x)}(x)), \tag{8.1}$$

where $\lambda : \Omega \rightarrow \{1, \dots, K\}$ is the true label of each pixel, at the position $x \in \Omega$, with $\Omega \subset \mathbb{Z}^2$. The networks soft-max layer generates the final segmentation as a probability map, whose pixel values reflect the probability of a particular pixel to belong to a vein or not. The network has a large number of feature channels, which allow it to propagate context information to higher resolution layers, and offers end-to-end training with limited number of training samples. The network implementation[1] was realised in the TensorFlow framework using the Keras library.

The second network architecture we used to extract the finger vein patterns is RefineNet [21]. RefineNet is a multi-path refinement network, which employs a four-cascaded architecture with four RefineNet units, each of which directly connects to the output of one Residual net [10] block, as well as to the preceding RefineNet block in the cascade. Each RefineNet unit consists of two residual convolution units (RCU), whose outputs are fused into a high-resolution feature map, and then fed into a chained residual Pooling block. The network has multi-path refinement architecture that explicitly exploits all the information available along the down-sampling process to enable high-resolution prediction using long-range residual connections. In this way, the deeper layers that capture high-level semantic features can be directly refined using fine-grained features from earlier convolutions. The network also uses

[1]https://github.com/orobix/retina-unet.

Table 8.1 Networks' training parameters

Network	U-net	RefineNet	SegNet
Optimizer	Stochastic gradient descent	Adam	Stochastic gradient descent
Learning rate	0.08	0.0001	0.003
Momentum	0.9	–	0.01
Weight decay	0.0005	0.1	0.000001
Iteration	300	40,000	30,000

a chained residual pooling mechanism to capture rich background context in an efficient manner. The implementation[2] of this network was also realised in the TensorFlow framework using the Keras library.

The third network architecture we used in our work is identical to the "Basic" fully convolutional encoder–decoder network proposed by Kendall et al. [1], named SegNet. However, we redesigned the softmax layer to segment only the vein pattern. The whole network architecture is formed by an encoder network, and the corresponding decoder network. The network's encoder architecture is organised in four stocks, containing a set of blocks. Each block comprises a convolutional layer, a batch normalisation layer, a ReLU layer and a Pooling layer with kernel size of 2×2 and stride 2. The corresponding decoder architecture, likewise, is organised in four stocks of blocks, whose layers are similar to those of the encoder blocks, except that here each block includes an up-sampling layer. In order to provide a wide context for smooth labelling, in this network, the convolutional kernel size is set to 7×7. A key functionality used in this network is "indices pooling". While several layers of max-pooling and sub-sampling can achieve more translation invariance for robust classification correspondingly there is a loss of spatial resolution of the feature maps. Therefore, it is necessary to capture and store boundary information in the encoder feature maps before sub-sampling is performed. The network utilises a memory-efficient technique for this purpose, storing only the max-pooling indices, i.e. the locations of the maximum feature value in each pooling window is memorised for each encoder feature map. The decoder network up-samples the input feature map(s) using the memorised max-pooling indices from the corresponding encoder feature map(s). The decoder network ends up to a softmax layer which generates the final segmentation map. The network implementation[3] was realised in the Caffe deep learning framework.

Table 8.1 summarises the training parameters (which turned out to deliver best results) we used to train each network in our experiments.

---

[2] https://github.com/eragonruan/refinenet-image-segmentation.

[3] http://mi.eng.cam.ac.uk/projects/segnet/tutorial.html.

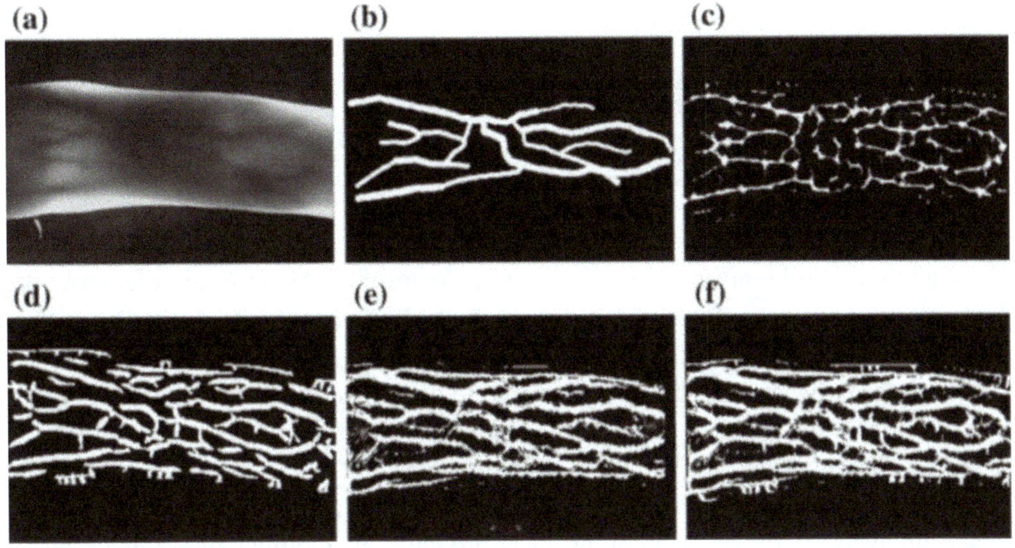

Fig. 8.1 A sample finger vein image (**a**), and its corresponding manual (**b**), MC (**c**), GF (**d**), RLT (**e**), and fused (MC-GF-RLT) (**f**) labels respectively

8.4 Training Label Generation and Setups

From the total samples available in our database (check Sect. 8.5 for database details), we have 388 NIR finger images (covering all subjects in the database) manually annotated (i.e. vein versus non-vein pixels, see Fig. 8.1b for an example) available for training the CNNs. To enable a fair comparison, we generated the same number of corresponding automated labels (also using the identical images), utilising each of the following classical binary vein-pattern extraction algorithms: Maximum Curvature (MC), Gabor Filter (GF) and Repeated Line Tracking (RLT). The technical details of these algorithms are already discussed in Sect. 8.2. For MC and RLT, we utilised the MATLAB implementation of B. T. Ton,[4] and for GF we used a custom implementation as used in [28][5] (see Fig. 8.1c, d and e for corresponding example using each algorithm).

As one of the main objectives of this work, we investigated several training label scenarios, aiming to improve the networks' feature-extraction capabilities, and also eventually eliminating the need for the manually annotated labels. In this way, first we used automatically generated labels adding only 40 pcs of corresponding manual labels to train the networks in each training session. We termed this approach as "automated" training. Next we considered to train the network using automatically generated labels jointly with equivalent number of (i) corresponding manual labels, and also (ii) other (corresponding) automatically generated labels to train the networks. We termed this approach as "joint" training. In particular, in this approach, in each training session, instead of using just one type of label (i.e. manual, MC, GF or

[4]Available on MATLAB Central.

[5]Available at: http://www.wavelab.at/sources/Kauba16e.

Table 8.2 Runtime per input volume for each network

Network	U-net	RefineNet	SegNet
Input volume size	584 × 565	584 × 565	360 × 480
Processing time (s)	3.164	0.138	0.0398

RLT) we used combinations of two or more types of the labels to train the networks. We kept the input data shuffling on during the training process to preserve uniform distribution of training samples.

In an alternative approach, we considered to fuse in between different types of the labels available, to generate single training labels. For this purpose, we utilised the "STAPLE" (Simultaneous Truth And Performance Level Estimation [37]) algorithm to fuse between the binary labels. STAPLE is an algorithm developed for performance analysis of image segmentation approaches in medical imaging based on expectation–maximisation. It takes in a collection of labels and computes a probabilistic estimate of the true labels and a measure of the performance level represented by each label. In our work, we applied STAPLE to fuse between (i) automatically generated labels, (corresponding) manual labels and also (ii) different types of automatically generated labels (see Fig. 8.1f for an example). We termed this approach as "fusion" training.

8.5 Experimental Framework

Database: We used the UTFVP database [36],[6] acquired by the University of Twente with a custom sensor, in our experiments. The UTFVP database contains 1440 finger vein images (with resolution of 672 × 380 pixels), collected from 60 volunteers. The images were captured in two identical sessions with an average time lapse of 15 days. For each volunteer, the vein pattern of the index, ring and middle finger of both hands has been collected twice at each session (each individual finger has been captured four times in total). The percentage of male volunteers was 73% and the percentage of right-handed volunteers was 87%. The width of the visible veins ranges from 4 to 20 pixels which corresponds to vein widths of approximately 0.3–1.6 mm. These vein widths are approximate numbers because the pixel density was determined assuming a flat surface. We resized the images to the corresponding networks' input volume, using bicubic interpolation method, as specified in Table 8.2 (see Fig. 8.1a for a sample of finger vein images in the database).

Network training and finger vein recognition evaluations: We trained each network with different label groups (manual, automated, fused and joint) using a cross-fold training method with disjoint training and testing sets. For this purpose, first we

[6]Available at:https://scs.ewi.utwente.nl/downloads/.

partitioned the whole training set (388 labels) for each label group into two parts (194 labels each). Next, we trained the networks with the first training part, and tested the networks on the remaining samples in the database (1246 samples). Then we did the training with the second part this time, and tested the networks on the remaining samples in the database. Doing so, we tested the networks on all samples in the database without overlapping training and testing sets.

As we wanted the comparison to concentrate on the quality of the pure training labels, we deliberately did not apply any data augmentation technique. Also, while a different number of training samples were used by the network developers (e.g. 35, 376, 1449 samples for U-Net, SegNet and RefineNet, respectively), we selected this number of training samples (194 samples) based on our experimental trials and also the availability of labels. Moreover, as the NIR finger images are acquired under standardised conditions in the sensor, no additional normalisation techniques have been applied. The RefineNet and the SegNet already generate their final outputs as binarized maps, but as the final output of the U-net is in form of probability maps, we binarised these maps using a grey-level threshold function based on the Otsu's algorithm [27]. The algorithm chooses the best threshold to minimise the intra-class variance of the black and white pixels while maximising inter-class scatter. Table 8.2 shows the segmentation runtime per input volume for each network, using TITAN-X (Pascal) GPUs. It is interesting to note that U-net is relatively much slower than the other two networks, which is primarily due to the overlapping-tile strategy, and also the large number of feature channels used in this network.

Finger vein Recognition Evaluations: To quantify the recognition performance of the networks (using their vein pattern outputs), as well as the classically generated vein patterns in comparison, receiver operator characteristic behaviour is evaluated. In particular, the equal error rate EER as well as the FMR1000 (FMR) and the ZeroFMR (ZFMR) are used. For their respective calculation, we followed the test protocol of the FVC2004 [4]. All possible genuine comparisons are performed, i.e. each sample is compared against all remaining samples of the same finger/hand while no symmetric comparisons are performed. So, in total 2160 genuine comparisons are carried out. For the impostor comparisons, only the first sample of each finger/hand is compared against the first sample of all remaining fingers/hands, while no symmetric comparison is performed, resulting in total 64520 impostor comparisons. For matching the binary output features, we adopted the approach by Miura et al. [25], which is essentially the calculation of the correlation between an input and reference image. As the input maps are not registered to each other and only coarsely aligned, using LeeRegion [7] background removal, the correlation between the input image $I(x, y)$ and the reference one is calculated several times while shifting the reference image $R(x, y)$, whose upper-left position is $R(c_w, c_h)$ and lower-right position is $R(w - c_w, h - c_h)$, in x- and y-direction.

$$N_m(s, t) = \sum_{y=0}^{h-2c_h-1} \sum_{x=0}^{w-2c_w-1} I(s + x, t + y) R(c_w + x, c_h + y), \tag{8.2}$$

where $N_m(s, t)$ is the correlation. The maximum value of the correlation is then normalised and used as matching score:

$$score = \frac{N_{m_{max}}}{\sum_{y=t_0}^{t_0+h-2c_h-1} \sum_{x=s_0}^{s_0+w-2c_w-1} I(x, y) + \sum_{y=c_h}^{h-2c_h-1} \sum_{x=c_w}^{w-2c_w-1} R(x, y)}, \tag{8.3}$$

where s_0 and t_o are the indexes of $N_{m_{max}}$ in the correlation matrix $N_m(s, t)$. The score values are in the range $0 \leq score \leq 0.5$.

8.6 Results

Table 8.3 and Fig. 8.2 display the results for training the networks using the manual, automated and joint training methods, providing EER, FMR and ZFMR as well as DET (Detection Error Trade-off) plots, respectively. The baseline result for each network is given using only manually annotated labels ("CNN-Manual"). We observe that the baseline is already quite different for the three networks, i.e. U-Net is superior to RefineNet, while SegNet clearly is worst among the three.

Next we look into results for training networks with the automatically generated labels adding just 40 pcs of corresponding manual labels (automated training). The overall impression is that (i) this approach can improve the results significantly in many cases and (ii) results again differ depending on the network considered. As it can be seen in the table, recognition performance gets considerably improved

Table 8.3 Networks performance, trained with manual, automated and joint labels

Network	U-net			RefineNet			SegNet		
Measures	EER (%)	FMR (%)	ZFMR (%)	EER (%)	FMR (%)	ZFMR (%)	EER (%)	FMR (%)	ZFMR (%)
CNN-Manual	0.877	1.851	5.185	2.735	5.833	11.851	2.917	6.759	12.638
CNN-MC	0.322	0.601	0.925	0.280	0.370	1.574	1.433	2.453	5.648
CNN-GF	0.793	2.731	3.796	2.133	5.046	8.750	1.204	2.685	5.555
CNN-RLT	2.091	11.620	24.861	1.101	2.824	3.750	1.279	3.009	7.592
CNN-Manual-MC	0.924	3.055	3.379	0.933	2.361	17.870	1.531	2.500	3.240
CNN-Manual-GF	0.648	0.925	2.916	2.039	3.564	5.416	2.595	4.675	8.750
CNN-Manual-RLT	1.433	8.518	17.500	1.703	4.027	5.878	1.433	2.361	3.194
CNN-MC-GF-RLT	1.713	15.046	23.750	0.877	2.037	3.055	0.929	1.805	4.027

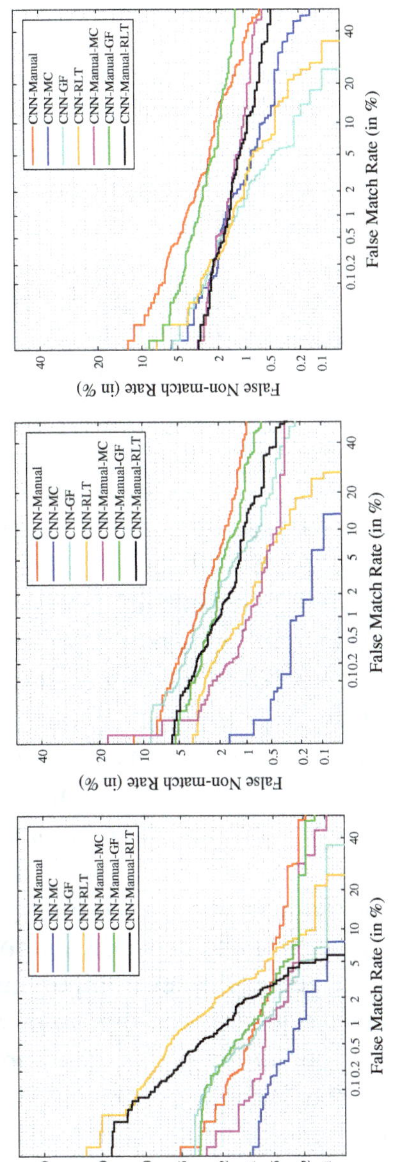

Fig. 8.2 DET curves for the: U-net (left), RefineNet (middle), and SegNet (right)

Table 8.4 Classical algorithms performance

Method	Maximum curvature			Gabor filter			Repeated line tracking		
Measures	EER (%)	FMR (%)	ZFMR (%)	EER (%)	FMR (%)	ZFMR (%)	EER (%)	FMR (%)	ZFMR (%)
Scores	0.4155	0.555	1.296	1.111	2.453	4.120	2.175	5.879	9.351

when training networks with labels generated by the MC algorithm for all networks (compared to training networks with manual labels). As well, labels generated by the GF algorithm improve the networks' performance (especially SegNet's), but in a fewer degree. When trained with the labels generated by the RLT algorithm, SegNet and especially RefineNet recognition results are also clearly improved, while U-net results are significantly deteriorated. Obviously, the different network architectures react very differently when trained with labels of different origin. It is also interesting to directly consider the recognition accuracy of the vein patterns generated by the classical algorithms (recognition results shown in Table 8.4): The very clear ranking is that MC is best, GF is ranked second while RLT exhibits the worst recognition performance. This ranking is not consistently reflected by the vein patterns generated by the networks when trained with these classical algorithms' labels. For the U-net, the ranking is MC, GF, RLT (thus reflecting the "original" ranking), while for the RefineNet the ranking is MC, RLT, GF, and the SegNet's ranking is GF, RLT and MC. Training networks jointly with manual labels and equivalent number of labels generated by the classical algorithms (joint approach) again result in different performance behaviours. As compared to training with manual labels only, results are improved in all cases for SegNet, while for RefineNet and U-net we observe both result improvements as well as degradations, respectively. As compared to the automated training method, we observe both result improvements and degradations for all CNNs. There is a tendency that for those automatically generated labels, which perform well when used just with 40 pcs of manual label in training, we typically do not observe improvements when used jointly with equivalent number of manual labels. Considering training the networks jointly with MC, GF and RLT labels at once (joint method), we get results never improving the best result obtained when training with a single technique (results shown only in Table 8.3) for U-net. However, using such a training configuration, we can improve the performance of SegNet and RefineNet even further than the best result obtained when training with a single technique. Thus, this training configuration can be recommended only for this network.

In order to assess the recognition performance of the vein patterns generated by the different network training approaches presented in Table 8.3, we compare the corresponding recognition performance to that of the vein patterns as generated with classical algorithms directly in terms of DET as presented in Figs. 8.3, 8.4 and 8.5. We conduct this comparison for different CNNs and the automated label generation techniques separately to facilitate a clear comparison. For MC labels (left graphs), we observe that CNN-generated vein patterns considerably enhance the recognition

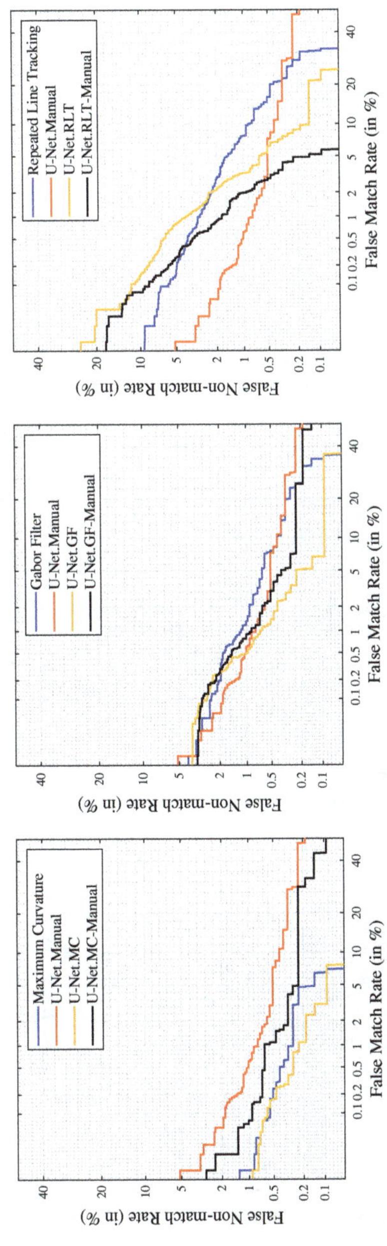

Fig. 8.3 DET curves for the U-net trained with labels generated by: MC (left), GF (middle) and RLT (right)

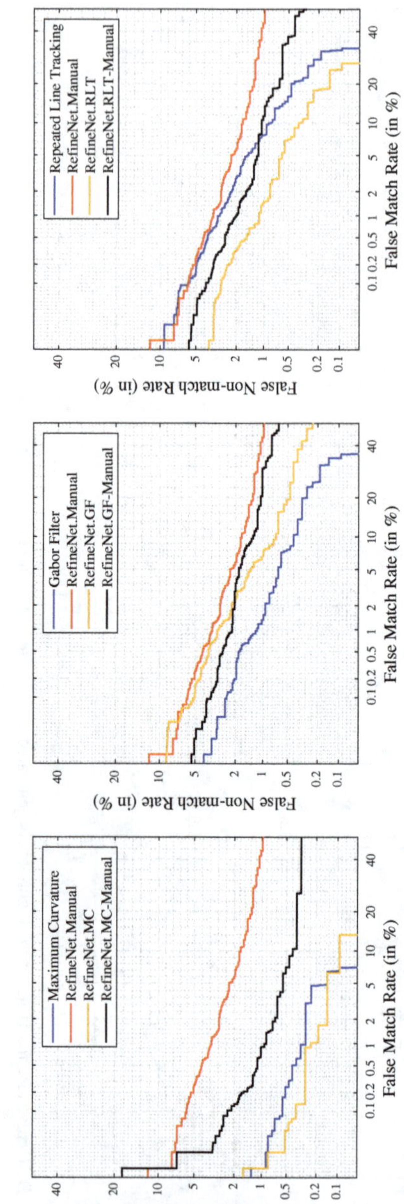

Fig. 8.4 DET curves for the RefineNet trained with labels generated by: MC (left), GF (middle) and RLT (right)

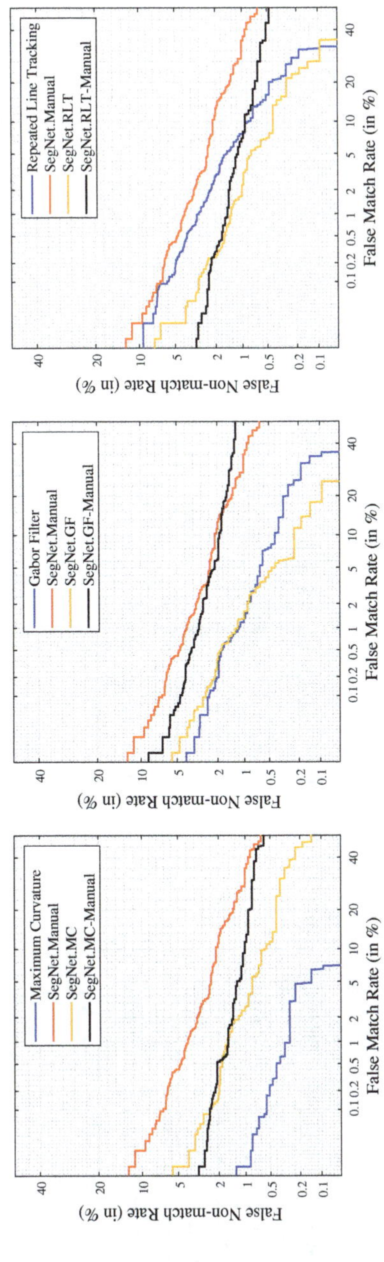

Fig. 8.5 DET curves for the SegNet trained with labels generated by: MC (left), GF (middle) and RLT (right)

Table 8.5 Networks performance, trained with fused labels

Network	U-net			RefineNet			SegNet		
Measures	EER(%)	FMR(%)	ZFMR(%)	EER(%)	FMR(%)	ZFMR(%)	EER(%)	FMR(%)	ZFMR(%)
CNN-Manual&MC	0.462	0.787	1.388	2.128	3.564	4.444	1.573	2.500	3.564
CNN-Manual&GF	0.602	1.342	1.990	2.544	3.796	5.138	0.686	1.388	2.916
CNN-Manual&RLT	3.235	21.620	36.666	1.437	2.870	5.185	2.035	8.611	27.175
CNN-MC&GF&RLT	5.639	45.601	69.722	1.666	5.462	9.120	1.624	5.879	13.703

performance of RefineNet and U-net, respectively, as compared to the classically generated patterns. The most interesting results here are obtained by RefineNet, which clearly outperforms the best classical algorithms results (obtained by MC algorithm) in all terms.

For GF labels (middle graphs), we see improvements using automated and also joint training method for the U-net, while for the SegNet and RefineNet no specific improvement is visible. Finally, for the RLT labels (right graphs), all the CNN-based vein patterns outperform the classical ones, whether using automated or joint training method.

As a further training configuration, we trained the networks considering several training label fusion scenarios. Table 8.5 demonstrates the results for this experiment. Comparing the results to the corresponding results obtained using the joint training method, interestingly we can see that training the networks with the labels generated by fusing all types of automatically generated labels (last line of the table) not only doesn't improve the networks' performance but also undermines them severely (especially in case of U-net). Furthermore, training the networks with labels which are result of fusion between the manual and automatically generated labels by MC or GF algorithms improves the performance of RefineNet, U-net and rather SegNet. We also observe that while training the networks with the labels generated by fusing manual and automatically generated labels by RLT algorithm improves the results obtained by RefineNet, yet this training label configuration degrades the corresponding results for U-net and SegNet.

8.7 Discussion

When analysing our results, the poor performance of the networks trained with manual labels is surprising. Thus, the first issue to be discussed is the quality/accuracy of our manual labels (see Fig. 8.6a for an example). Human annotators have been instructed to only annotate vein pixels without any ambiguity in order to avoid false-positive annotations. When looking at the example, it is obvious that manual labels are restricted to rather large-scale vessels, while fine-grained vasculature is entirely missed/avoided. The correspondingly segmented vein patterns (i.e. the outputs of CNNs trained with the manual labels, 8.6e, i and m in the example figures) are rather sparse and it may be conjectured that these patterns simply do not contain sufficiently high entropy to facilitate high-accuracy recognition. In contrast, MC labels and their corresponding outputs of CNNs trained with these labels (8.6f, j and n in the figures) exhibit much more fine-grained vasculature details, reflected in much better recognition accuracy. RLT vein patterns, on the other hand, tend to over-segment and obviously also contain many false-positive vein pixels (e.g. at the border between finger texture and background, 8.6d in the figures). Consequently, this also applies to outputs of CNNs trained with RLT labels (see 8.6h, l and p in the figures).

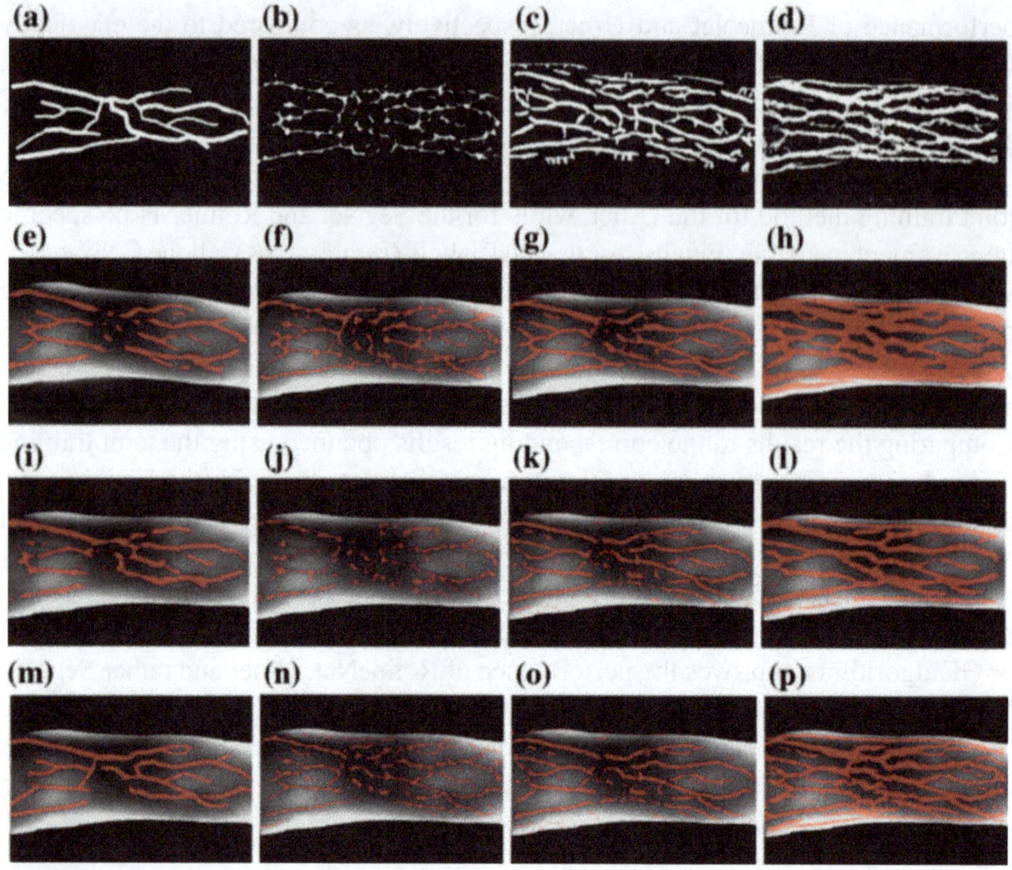

Fig. 8.6 A sample of manual (**a**), MC (**b**), GF (**c**), RLT (**d**) labels, and thier corresponding segmentation results when used to train: U-net (**e**, **f**, **g**, **h**), SegNet (**i**, **j**, **k**, **l**) and RefineNet (**m**, **n**, **o**, **p**), respectively

We have observed that in many configurations, utilising automatically generated labels is beneficial for the recognition performance of the vein patterns generated by CNN-based segmentation (i.e. training U-net and RefineNet with labels automatically generated by MC algorithm). However, there is significant interplay of the nature of the used labels (in particular, their accuracy with respect to the relation between false-positive and false-negative vein pixels) and the network architecture. Interestingly, it is not the case that training with the vein patterns generated by the classical algorithm exhibiting the best recognition performance (i.e. MC) does lead to the best performing CNN segmentations for all networks. As observed before, the ranking among the schemes is not maintained after network training, which indicates a distinct capability of the networks to cope with false positives (highly present in RLT labels for example) and false negatives (obviously highly present in manual labels).

For example, while the performance of SegNet and especially RefineNet improve when trained with labels generated by the RLT algorithm, the U-net's performance clearly degrades when trained with identical labels. In general, the RefineNet exhibits comparably better segmentation capabilities, especially when trained with MC labels.

Basically, this network has a multi-path refinement architecture, which exploits the information available along the down-sampling process to enable high-resolution prediction, emphasising on preservation of edges and boundaries. Consequently, introducing further vein pixels to the network by automatically generated or fused labels seems to improve the actual network vein pattern extraction capabilities significantly (compared to the other two networks).

The network architecture of the U-net has been proven to excel in many biomedical applications, and when trained with precise vein labels, it is able to deal well with the ambiguous boundary issue between vein and non-vein regions in finger vein images. This capability is mainly due to the large number of feature channels built in the network architecture, which allow for propagating key context information to higher resolution layers. However, due to the high sensitivity of the network, imprecise labels can equally degrade the network's performance seriously. A simple comparison of the network's performance when trained with labels generated by the MC algorithm (more precise labels, some false negatives) with when trained with labels generated by the RLT algorithm (less precise labels with more false positives) underpins this behaviour, as also reflected in Fig. 8.6.

The SegNet network is unable to extract vein patterns from the NIR finger images well when trained with manual labels. However, the network's performance consistently improves by introducing further vein pixel labels using automatically generated or fused labels. This network shows good ability to exclude the incorrectly labelled vein pixels (i.e. false positives) during the training process, as imprecise labels (i.e. those generated by RLT algorithm) do not degrade the network's performance significantly. This ability of the network is mainly owed to the up-sampling mechanism used in this network, which uses max-pooling indicts from the corresponding encoder feature maps to generate the up-sampled feature maps without learning.

Considering the applied training approaches (fusion versus joint), as the results show, in majority of cases (i.e. training networks jointly with labels automatically generated by all classical algorithms), the latter approach (joint) performs superior to the fusion technique, and results more in improvement of networks' performance rather than degradation. However, the extent of such improvement/degradation again is subject to the interplay of the nature of the used labels and the network architecture. Conflicting results obtained by Unet and RefineNet when trained jointly with manual and automatically generated labels by MC or GF algorithms indicates this fact clearly. Therefore, we can conclude that selection of the proper network training approach is highly subject to these two key factors (nature of the used labels and the network architecture).

8.8 Conclusion

In this work, we proposed a new model for finger vein recognition using fully convolutional neural networks (FCN), focusing on direct extraction of actual finger vein patterns from the finger images by segmentation, and using them as the actual finger vein features for the recognition process. In this context, we trained three different FCN architectures, utilising different combinations of manual and automatically generated labels, and evaluated the respective recognition performance of the generated vein patterns in each case. We showed that automatically generated labels (whether used solely or fused with manual labels) can improve the network's performance in terms of achieved recognition accuracy. It also turned out that these improvements are highly dependent on the interplay between properties of the used labels and the network architecture. In any case, we have demonstrated that utilising automatically generated labels to train the networks eliminates the need for manual labels, whose generation is an extremely cumbersome, difficult and error-prone process.

In future works, we will change the way how to employ and combine additionally available label data. In particular, we will assess the strategy to pre-train with manual labels (as they do not contain false-positive vein pixels) and refine networks with automatically generated ones (as these do contain more fine-grained vascular details). Also, an evaluation of cross-database (using training data from a different vein sensor) and cross-vessel type (using training data of different vessel types, e.g. retinal vasculature) training will be conducted. Finally, we will look into augmentation techniques specifically tailored to the observed problem with the manual labels, i.e. scaling the data to model also more detailed and finer vessel structures.

Acknowledgements This project received funding from the European Union's Horizon 2020 research and innovation program under the grant agreement no. 700259

References

1. Badrinarayanan V, Kendall A, Cipolla R (2017) Segnet: a deep convolutional encoder-decoder architecture for image segmentation. IEEE Trans Pattern Anal Mach Intell 39(12):2481–2495
2. Ce L, Jenny Y, Antonio T (2011) Sift flow: dense correspondence across scenes and its applications. IEEE Trans Pattern Anal Mach Intell 33(5):978–994
3. Cheng-Bo Y, Hua-Feng Q, Yan-Zhe C, Xiao-Qian H (2009) Finger-vein image recognition combining modified hausdorff distance with minutiae feature matching. Interdiscip Sci Comput Life Sci 1(4):280–289
4. Dario M, Davide M, Raffaele C, Jim W, Anil J Fvc (2004) Third fingerprint verification competition. In: Lecture notes in biometric authentication. Springer, pp 1–7
5. Das R, Piciucco E, Maiorana E, Campisi P (2018) Convolutional neural network for finger-vein-based biometric identification. IEEE Tran Inf Forensics Secur 1–1
6. Dasgupta A, Singh S (2017) A fully convolutional neural network based structured prediction approach towards the retinal vessel segmentation. In: Proceedings of 14th international symposium on biomedical imaging (ISBI 2017). IEEE, pp 248–251
7. Eui-Chul L, Hyeon-Chang L, Kang-Ryoung P (2009) Finger vein recognition using minutia-based alignment and local binary pattern-based feature extraction. Int J Imaging Syst Technol 19(3):179–186
8. Eui-Chul L, Hyunwoo J, Daeyeoul K (2011) New finger biometric method using near infrared imaging. Sensors 11(3):2319–2333
9. Havaei M, Davy A, Warde-Farley D, Biard A, C-Courville A, Bengio Y, Pal C, Marc-Jodoin P, Larochelle H (2017) Brain tumor segmentation with deep neural networks. Med Image Anal 35: 18–31

10. He K, Zhang X, Ren S, Sun J (2015) Deep residual learning for image recognition. arXiv:1512.03385
11. Huafeng Q, El-Yacoubi M (2017) Deep representation-based feature extraction and recovering for finger-vein verification. IEEE Trans Inf Forensics Secur 12(8):1816–1829
12. Huafeng Q, Lan Q, Chengbo Y (2011) Region growth-based feature extraction method for finger-vein recognition. Opt Eng 50(5):1–9
13. Hong H-G, Lee M-B, Park K-R (2017) Convolutional neural network-based finger-vein recognition using nir image sensors. Sensors 17(6):1–21
14. Jabbar SI, Day CR, Nicholas H, Chadwick EK (2016) Using convolutional neural network for edge detection in musculoskeletal ultrasound images. In: Proceedings of international joint conference on neural networks (IJCNN). IEEE, pp 4619–4626
15. Jian-Da W, Chiung-Tsiung L (2011) Finger-vein pattern identification using principal component analysis and the neural network technique. Expert Syst Appl 38(5):5423–5427
16. Jinfeng Y, Yihua S (2014) Towards finger-vein image restoration and enhancement for finger-vein recognition. Inf Sci 268:33–52
17. Joon-Hwan C, Wonseok S, Taejeong K, Seung-Rae L, Hee-Chan K (2009) Finger vein extraction using gradient normalization and principal curvature. In: Proceeding of SPIE, image processing: machine vision applications II, vol 7251. International Society for Optics and Photonics, pp 1–9
18. Krizhevsky A, Sutskever I, Hinton GE (2012) Imagenet classification with deep convolutional neural networks. In: Proceedings of the 25th international conference on neural information processing systems, vol 1 of NIPS 12, pp 1097–1105
19. Kumar A, Zhou Y (2012) Human identification using finger images. IEEE Trans Image Process 21(4):2228–2244
20. LeCun Y, Boser B, Denker JS, Henderson D, Howard RE, Hubbard W, Jackel LD (1989) Backpropagation applied to handwritten zip code recognition. Neural Comput 1(4): 541–551
21. Lin G, Anton M, Chunhua S, Reid I (2017) Refinenet: multi-path refinement networks for high-resolution semantic segmentation. In: Proceedings of IEEE conference on computer vision and pattern recognition (CVPR), pp 5168–5177
22. Long J, Shelhamer E, Darrell T (2015) Fully convolutional networks for semantic segmentation. In: Proceedings of the IEEE conference on computer vision and pattern recognition, pp 3431–3440
23. Lu Y, Gongping Y, Yilong Y, Lizhen Z (2014) A survey of finger vein recognition. In: Zhenan S, Shiguang S, Haifeng S, Jie Z, Yunhong W, Weiqi Y (eds) Lecture notes in Chinese conference on biometric recognition. Springer International Publishing, pp 234–243
24. Naoto M, Akio N, Takafumi M (2004) Feature extraction of finger-vein patterns based on repeated line tracking and its application to personal identification. Mach Vis Appl 15(4):194–203
25. Miura N, Nagasaka A, Miyatake T (2007) Extraction of finger-vein patterns using maximum curvature points in image profiles. IEICE Trans Inf Syst 90(8):1185–1194
26. Neumann C, Tnnies K-D, Pohle-Frhlich R (2018) Angiounet—a convolutional neural network for vessel segmentation in cerebral dsa series. In: Proceedings of the 13th international joint conference on computer vision, imaging and computer graphics theory and applications—volume 4: VISAPP. INSTICC, SciTePress, pp 331–338
27. Otsu N (1979) A threshold selection method from gray-level histograms. IEEE Trans Syst Man Cybern 9(1):62–66
28. Piciucco E, Maiorana E, Kauba C, Uhl A, Campisi P (2016) Cancelable biometrics for finger vein recognition. In: Proceedings of the 1st workshop on sensing, processing and learning for intelligent machines (SPLINE 2016), Aalborg, Denmark, pp 1–6
29. Radzi F, Khalid S-I, Gong F, Mustafa N, Chiew-Wong Y, Mat-ibrahim M (2016) User identification system based on finger-vein patterns using convolutional neural network. ARPN J Eng Appl Sci 11(5):3316–3319
30. Ronneberger O, Fischer P, Brox T (2015) U-net: convolutional networks for biomedical image segmentation. In: Lecture notes in international conference on medical image computing and computer-assisted intervention. Springer, pp 234–241

31. Roy-Abhijit G, Conjeti S, Navab N, Wachinger C (2018) Fast MRI whole brain segmentation with fully convolutional neural networks. In: Bildverarbeitung für die Medizin 2018. Springer, pp 42–42
32. Sadanandan-Sajith K, Ranefall P, Le-Guyader S, Whlby C (2017) Automated training of deep convolutional neural networks for cell segmentation. Sci Rep (Nature Publisher Group) 7:1–1
33. Schroff F, Kalenichenko D, Philbin J (2015) Facenet: a unified embedding for face recognition and clustering. arXiv:1503.03832
34. Song W, Kim T, Chan-Kim H, Hwan-Choi J, Joong-Kong H, Rae-Lee S (2011) A finger-vein verification system using mean curvature. Pattern Recogn Lett 32(11):1541–1547
35. Syafeeza-Ahmad R, Mohamed-Khalil H, Rabia B (2016) Finger-vein biometric identification using convolutional neural network. Turkish J Electr Eng Comput Sci 24(3):1863–1878
36. Ton BT, Veldhuis RNJ (2013) A high quality finger vascular pattern dataset collected using a custom designed capturing device. In: Lecture notes in 2013 international conference on biometrics (ICB), pp 1–5
37. Warfield S, Zou K, Wells W (2004) Simultaneous truth and performance level estimation (staple): an algorithm for the validation of image segmentation. IEEE Trans Med Imag 23(7):903–921
38. Wu X, He R, Sun Z, Tan T (2018) A light CNN for deep face representation with noisy labels. IEEE Trans Inf Forensics Secur 13(11): 2884–2896
39. Li X, Huang D, Wang Y (2016) Comparative study of deep learning methods on dorsal hand vein recognition. In: Lecture notes in Chinese conference on biometric recognition. Springer, pp 296–306
40. Xie C, Kumar A (2018) Finger vein identification using convolutional neural network and supervised discrete hashing. Pattern Recogn Lett

Chapter 9
Efficient Identification in Large-Scale Vein Recognition Systems Using Spectral Minutiae Representations

Benedikt-Alexander Mokroß, Pawel Drozdowski, Christian Rathgeb and Christoph Busch

Abstract Large biometric systems, e.g. the Indian AADHAAR project, regularly perform millions of identification and/or de-duplication queries every day, thus yielding an immense computational workload. Dealing with this challenge by merely upscaling the hardware resources is often insufficient, as it quickly reaches limits in terms of purchase and operational costs. Therefore, it is additionally important for the underlying systems software to implement lookup strategies with efficient algorithms and data structures. Due to certain properties of biometric data (i.e. fuzziness), the typical workload reduction methods, such as traditional indexing, are unsuitable; consequently, new and specifically tailored approaches must be developed for biometric systems. While this is a somewhat mature research field for several biometric characteristics (e.g. fingerprint and iris), much fewer works exist for vascular characteristics. In this chapter, a survey of the current state of the art in vascular identification is presented, followed by introducing a vein indexing method based on proven concepts adapted from other biometric characteristics (specifically spectral minutiae representation and Bloom filter-based indexing). Subsequently, a benchmark in an open-set identification scenario is performed and evaluated. The discussion focuses on biometric performance, computational workload, and facilitating parallel, SIMD and GPU computation.

B.-A. Mokroß (✉)
ICOGNIZE GmbH, Dietzenbach, Germany
e-mail: benedikt-alexander.mokross@icognize.de

P. Drozdowski · C. Rathgeb · C. Busch
da/sec – Biometrics and Internet Security Research Group, Hochschule Darmstadt, Germany
e-mail: pawel.drozdowski@h-da.de

C. Rathgeb
e-mail: christian.rathgeb@h-da.de

C. Busch
e-mail: christoph.busch@h-da.de

P. Drozdowski
Norwegian Biometrics Laboratory, NTNU, Gjøvik, Norway

A. Uhl et al. (eds.), *Handbook of Vascular Biometrics*, Advances in Computer Vision and Pattern Recognition, https://doi.org/10.1007/978-3-030-27731-4_9

Keywords Spectral Minutiae Representation (SMR) · Bloom filter · Identification · Biometric identification · Efficient Identification · Binary search tree · Column Principal Component Analysis (CPCA) · CPCA-Tree · Maximum curvature · Indexing

9.1 Introduction

One of many catalysts for the rapid market value increase of biometrics is government-driven, large-scale biometric deployments. Most prominent examples include the Indian AADHAAR project [20], which aims to enrol the entire Indian population of 1.3 billion individuals and—at the time of writing—has already enrolled over 1.2 billion subjects, as well as several immigration programmes like the UAE or the European VIS- and EES-based border control. The operation of such large-scale deployments yields immense computational load in or duplicate enrolment checks, where—in the worst case—the whole database has to be searched to make a decision. Upscaling the hardware in terms of computing power quickly reaches certain limits in terms of, e.g. hardware costs, power consumption or simply practicability. Therefore, the underlying system's software needs to implement efficient strategies to reduce its computational load. Traditional indexing or classification solutions (e.g. [21, 37]) are ill-suited: the fuzziness of the biometric data does not allow for naïvehashing or equality comparison methods. A good read for further understanding the problem with traditional approaches is found in [17]. This matter is the key motivation and the main focus of this chapter.

One emerging biometric characteristic that steadily increases its market share[1] and popularity is the vascular (blood vessels) pattern in several human body parts. The wrist, back of hand and finger vessels hold the most interest since they are intuitive to capture for users and feature several advantageous properties, whereby back of hand and wrist vessels are less prone to displacement due to stretching or bending the hand. Many accurate (in terms of biometric performance) approaches and algorithms for vascular pattern recognition have emerged over time (i.e. [7, 23, 39]). However, most of them employ slow and complex algorithms, inefficient comparison methods and store their templates in an incompatible format for most template protection schemes. In other words, they generate a very high computational workload for the system's hardware. While several biometric characteristics such as fingerprint [9] and iris [15] are already covered by workload reduction research, it is only a nascent field of research for the vascular characteristics. This chapter addresses the palm vein characteristic with a focus on the biometric identification scenario and methods for reducing the associated computational workload.

[1] 2014 [30], 2016 [11], 2017 [29].

9.1.1 Organisation

This chapter is organised as follows:

- Section 9.1.3 outlines requirements and considerations for the selection of the algorithms used later in this chapter.
- Section 9.2 outlines four key computational workload reduction concepts with an algorithm proposal for each concept.
- In Sect. 9.3, an overview of the conducted experiments using the presented concepts and algorithms is provided.
- Subsequently, Sect. 9.4 lists and discusses the results obtained from the experiments.
- Finally, Sect. 9.5 concludes this chapter with a summary.

9.1.2 Workload Reduction in Vein Identification Systems

While computational cost is not a pressing issue for biometric systems in verification mode (one-to-one comparisons), high computational costs generate several concerns in large-scale biometric systems operated in identification (one-to-many search and comparison) mode. Aside from the naïveapproach of exhaustively searching the whole database for a mated template resulting in high response times and therefore lowering usability, frustrating users and administrators, and thus lowering acceptance, another issue is presented by Daugman [12]. Accordingly, it is demonstrated that the probability of having at least one False-Positive Identification (FPI)—the False-Positive Identification Rate (FPIR)—in an identification scenario to be computed using the following formula[2]: $\text{FPIR} = (1 - (1 - \text{FMR})^N)$. Even for systems with very low *FMR*, this relationship is extremely demanding as the number of enrolled subjects (N) increases. Without a reduction of the penetration rate (number of template comparisons during retrieval), large biometric systems quickly reach a point where they will not behave like expected: the system could fail to identify the correct user or—even worse—allow access to an unauthorised individual. While this is less of an issue for very small biometric systems, larger systems need to reduce the number of template comparisons in an identification or Duplicate Enrolment Check (DEC) scenario to tackle the computational workload and false-positive occurrences.

Therefore, it is strongly recommended to employ a strategy to reduce the number of necessary template comparisons (computational workload reduction) for all, not only vein, modalities. As already mentioned in Sect. 9.1, computational workload reduction for vein modalities remains an insufficiently researched topic and— at the time of writing—no workload reduction approaches directly target vascular biometric systems. However, certain feature representations used in fingerprint-based biometric systems may also be applicable to vein-based systems, and hence facilitating the usage of existing concepts for computational workload reduction, as well

[2] This equation ignores other error sources like failure-to-acquire (FTA).

as development of new methods. Since the vascular pattern can also be presented by minutiae (further called vein minutiae) which show almost identical characteristics compared to fingerprint minutiae, several workload reduction methods targeting minutiae-based fingerprint approaches might be usable after adaption to the more fuzzy vein minutiae.

9.1.3 Concept Focus

To utilise the maximum potential of the system's hardware, all of the methods and algorithms presented in this chapter are carefully selected by the authors upon the following requirements:

1. The lookup process has to be implementable in a multi-threaded manner, without creating much computational overheads (in order to manage the threads and their communication).
2. The comparison algorithm has to be computable in parallel without stalling processing cores during computation.

For requirement 1, the lookup algorithm has to be separable into multiple instances, each working on a different distinct subset of the enrolment database.

In order to understand requirement 2, a brief excurse in parallel computing is needed (for a more comprehensive overview, the reader is referred to [8]). Parallel computation (in the sense of SIMD: Single Instruction, Multiple Data) is not as trivial as multi-threading where one process spawns multiple threads that are run on one or multiple CPU cores. There are multiple requirements for an algorithm to be computable in parallel, of which the two most important are as follows:

1. No race conditions must occur between multiple cores.
2. Multiple cores need to have the same instructions at the same time in their pipeline.

Therefore, the comparison algorithm should not rely on if-branches or jumps and the shared memory (if any) must be read-only. This results in another requirement: the feature vectors should be fixed length across all queries and templates to avoid waiting for processing templates of different sizes. However, while fixed-length template comparisons are not automatically more efficient to compute, they offer various other benefits. For example, comparisons in systems utilising fixed-length templates can usually be better optimised and implemented as simple and fast binary operations (e.g. XOR, see, for example, [16]). Furthermore, most binarisation and template protection approaches also rely on fixed-length vectors (e.g. see [22]).

Fulfilling these requirements allows for an efficient usage of SIMD instructions on modern CPUs and general-purpose GPUs (GPGPUs), hence utilising the maximum potential of the system's hardware.

Therefore, the Spectral Minutia Representation (SMR) [35] was chosen as data representation in this chapter. Compared to shape- or graph-based approaches—like the Vascular Biometric Graph Comparison earlier introduced in this book—it fulfils all requirements: the templates using this floating-point based and fixed-length data representation can be compared by a simple image-correlation method, merely using multiplications, divisions and additions. Further, the SMR is very robust towards translations and rotations can be compensated fast. The SMR can further be binarised, which replaces the image-correlation comparison method with a simple XOR operation comparison method and thus fully allows for utilising the maximum potential of the system's hardware. Thus, it is also compatible with various template protection approaches which rely on fixed-length binary representations. The computational efficiency of the binary SMR comparison is the main reason for the selection of the SMR as data representation. Other methods like the maximum curvature (see [24]) or Gabor filters (e.g. [38]) offer binary representations too and are less expensive in terms of computational costs while extracting the biometric features in the designated data representation. However, both the maximum curvature and the Gabor filter template comparisons are—benchmarked against the binary SMR template comparison—rather complex and expensive in terms of computational cost. Facing the high number of template comparisons needed for an identification or a duplicate enrolment check in large-scale biometric databases, the computational cost of a single SMR feature extraction is negligible with respect to the aggregate computational costs of the template comparisons. Therefore, in large-scale identification scenarios, it is more feasible to employ a computationally expensive feature-extraction algorithm with a computationally efficient comparator. Furthermore, the SMR is applicable to other modalities that can be represented by minutiae. This includes most vascular biometrics, fingerprints and palm prints. Therefore, the same method can be used for those modalities and facilitate feature-level information fusion. In particular, in this chapter, the presented system was also applied successfully for the fingerprint modality.

9.2 Workload Reduction Concepts

Section 9.1.2 covered the motivation behind the reduction of template comparisons in a biometric system. The same section also covered the motivation to reduce the complexity of template comparisons, namely, to achieve shorter template comparison times, thus additionally reducing the computational workload and shorten transaction times. The following sections propose components to reduce the number of necessary template comparisons and reduce the complexity of a single template comparison for a highly efficient biometric identification system. Later in the chapter, the proposed system is comprehensively evaluated.

9.2.1 Efficient Data Representation

Key for rapid comparisons are data representations that allow for non-complex template comparisons. Comparison subsystems and data storage subsystems can use raw minutiae (location) vectors or the vascular pattern skeletal representation as biometric templates. However, this introduces several problems, starting with privacy concerns in terms of storing the raw biometric features and ending with computational drawbacks (at least in parallel computing and the usage of CPU intrinsics) due to variable-sized feature vector sizes, whereby even probes of the same subject differ in their number of features (minutiae points). A post-processing stage can convert the raw feature vector to a fixed feature size representation that should not be reversible to the raw representation.

Inspired by the Fourier–Mellin transform [10] used to obtain a translation, rotation and scaling-invariant descriptor of an image, the SMR [18, 33] transforms a variable-sized minutiae feature vector in a fixed-length translation, and implicit rotation- and scaling-invariant spectral domain. In order to prevent the resampling and interpolation introduced by the Fourier transform and the polar-logarithmic mapping, the authors introduce a so-called *analytical* representation of the minutiae set and a so-called *analytical* expression of a continuous Fourier transform, which can be evaluated on polar-logarithmic coordinates. According to the authors, the SMR meets the requirements for template protection and allows faster biometric comparisons.

9.2.1.1 Spectral Minutiae Representation

In order to represent a minutiae in its analytical form, it has to be converted into a Dirac pulse to the spatial domain. Each Dirac pulse is described by the function $m_i(x, y) = \omega(x - x_i, y - y_i), i = 1, \ldots, Z$ where (x_i, y_i) represents the location of the i-th minutiae in the palm vein image. Now the Fourier transform of the i-th minutiae $(m_i(x, y))$ located at (x, y) is given by

$$\mathscr{F}\{m_i(x, y)\} = exp(-\mathrm{j}(w_x x_i + w_y y_i)), \tag{9.1}$$

with a sampling vector w_x for the angular direction and sampling vector w_y for the radial direction. Based on this analytical representation, the authors introduced several types of spectral representations and improvements for their initial approach. This chapter focuses on one of the initial representations, called the Spectral Minutia Location Representation (SML), since it achieved the best stability and thus the best biometric performance in previous experiments in [25]. It only uses the minutiae location information for the spectral representation:

$$\mathscr{M}(w_x, w_y) = \left| \sum_{i=1}^{Z} exp(-\mathrm{j}(w_x x_i + w_y y_i)) \right|. \tag{9.2}$$

In order to compensate small errors in the minutiae location, a Gaussian low-pass filter is introduced by the authors. Thus, the magnitude of the smoothed SML with a fixed σ is defined as follows:

$$\mathscr{M}(w_x, w_y; \sigma^2) = \left| exp\left(-\frac{w_x^2 + w_y^2}{2\sigma^{-2}}\right) \sum_{i=1}^{Z} exp(-\mathrm{j}(w_x x_i + w_y y_i)) \right| \tag{9.3}$$

in its analytical representation. By taking the magnitude—further denoted as absolute-valued representation—the translation-invariant spectrum is received (Fig. 9.1b).

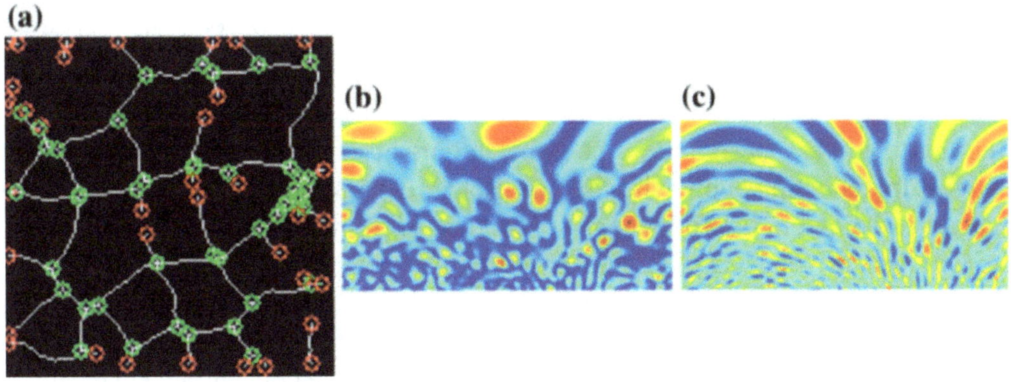

Fig. 9.1 Illustration of the spectral minutiae approach: **a** visualisation of input minutiae of an extracted vein pattern (red = endpoints, green = bifurcations); **b** complex-modulus SML Fourier spectrum sampled on a polar-logarithmic grid; **c** real-valued SML Fourier spectrum sampled on a polar-logarithmic grid

When sampling the SML on a polar-logarithmic grid, the rotation of the minutiae becomes horizontal circular shifts. For this purpose, sampling of the continuous spectra (Eq. 9.3) is proposed by Xu and Veldhuis [33] using $Xy = 128$ (M in [33]) in the radial direction, with λ logarithmically distributed between $\lambda_{min} = 0.1$ and $\lambda_{max} = 0.6$. The angular direction β for SML is proposed between $\beta = 0$ and $\beta = \pi$ in $Xx = 256$ (N in [33]) uniformly distributed samples. A sampling between $\beta = 0$ and $\beta = \pi$ is sufficient due to the symmetry of the Fourier transform for real-valued functions.

Since the SML yields spectra with different energies, depending on the number of minutiae per sample, each spectrum has to be normalised to reach zero mean and unit energy:

$$X = \frac{\mathcal{M} - \overline{\mathcal{M}}}{\sigma(\mathcal{M})^2}. \tag{9.4}$$

Throughout this chapter, statements that only apply for the Spectral Minutiae Location Representation will explicitly mention the abbreviation SML, while statements that are applicable to the Spectral Minutiae Representation in general will explicitly mention the abbreviation SMR.

9.2.1.2 Spectral Minutiae Representation—Feature Reduction

Sampling the spectra on a $Xx = 256$ and $Xy = 128$ grid yields a $Xx \times Xy = 32,768$ decimal-unit-sized feature vector. This large-scale feature vector introduces two drawbacks as given below:

Storage Considering $Xx \times Xy = 32{,}768$ double-precision float (64 bit) values, each template would take $2{,}097{,}152$ bit = 256 kB RAM or data storage.

Comparison Complexity Processing a $Xx \times Xy = 32{,}768$ sized feature vector is a large computational task and limits comparison speeds, especially with large-scale databases in biometric identification scenarios.

In order to address these issues, the same authors of the SMR approach introduced two feature reduction approaches in [36]. Both are based on well-known algorithms and are explained in the following subsections. In this chapter, the Column Principal Component Analysis (CPCA)—based on the idea of the well-known Principal Component Analysis (PCA) originally presented in [26]—is used. In summary, to receive the SMR reduced with the CPCA feature reduction (SMR-CPCA), the PCA only is applied to the columns of the SMR. The features are concentrated in the upper rows after applying the CPCA, and thus the lower rows can be removed, resulting in a $Xx \times Xy_{CPCA}$ sized feature vector. According to [36], the achieved feature reduction is up to 80% by employing the SML reduced with the CPCA feature reduction (SML-CPCA) approach while maintaining the biometric performance of the original SML.

Since $\sum_{i=1}^{Z} exp(-j(w_x x_i + w_y y_i)) \in \mathbb{C}$, thus $\mathscr{M}(w_x, w_y) \in \mathbb{R}$, every element in X is defined as a 32 bit or 64 bit floating-point real-valued number. Comparisons or calculations (especially divisions) with single- or double-precision floating points are a relatively complex task compared to integer or binary operations. In order to address this computational complexity and comply with other template protection or indexing approaches where a binary feature vector is required, the SML (e.g. Fig. 9.2a, d) as well as the other SMR can be converted to a binary feature vector as presented in [32]. The binarisation approach yields two binary vectors: a so-called *sign-bit* vector and a so-called *mask-bit* vector:

sign bit The sign-bit vector (Fig. 9.2b, e) contains the actual features of the SMR in a binary representation. Each bit is set according to one of the two binarisation approaches.

mask bit Since binary representations suffer from bit flips on edges in fuzzy environments, a second vector (Fig. 9.2c, f) is introduced. This vector marks the likely-to-be-stable—called reliable—sign bits and is generated by applying a threshold (MT) to the spectrum.

The mask contained in the mask-bit vector is not applied to the sign bit; instead, it is kept as auxiliary data and applied during the comparison step. This approach equals the masking procedure in iris recognition (see [13, 14]).

9.2.1.3 Spectral Minutiae Representation—Comparison

The most proven performance in SMR comparison is reached with the so-called direct comparison.[3] It yields the most reliable comparison scores, while keeping a minimal computational complexity.

[3] In [35], the comparison method is named *direct matching*, where *matching* is used as a non-ISO compliant synonym for the term *comparison*.

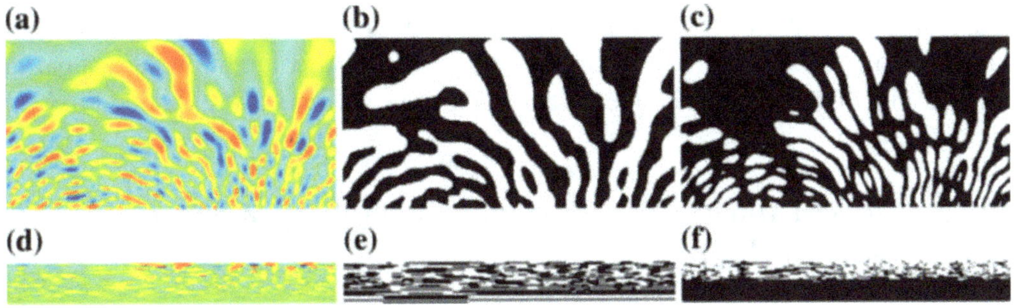

Fig. 9.2 Input and result of the SML binarisation for SML and SML-CPCA: **a** real-valued SML input; **d** real-valued SML-CPCA input; **b** the spectral sign bit obtained from (**a**); **e** the spectral sign bit obtained from (**d**); **c** the spectral mask bit obtained from (**a**); **f** the spectral mask bit obtained from (**d**)

Let $R(m, n)$ be the spectrum of the reference template and $P(m, n)$ the spectrum of the probe template, both sampled on the polar-logarithmic grid and normalised. Then, the similarity-score $E_{DM}^{(R,P)}$ is defined as

$$E_{DM}^{(R,P)} = \frac{1}{MN} \sum R(m, n)P(m, n). \tag{9.5}$$

The score is thus defined by correlation, which is a common approach in image processing.

For comparing two binary SMRs or SMR-CPCAs, a different approach is introduced in [32], which is also used in the iris modality [13, 14].

After converting $R(m, n)$ and $P(m, n)$ into their individual mask bit and sign bit (see previous Sect. 9.2.1.2), yielding $\{maskR, signR\}$ and $\{maskP, signP\}$, the Fractional Hamming Distance (FHD) can be applied on those binary representations.

$$FHD^{(R,P)} = \frac{\|(signR \otimes signP) \cap maskR \cap maskP\|}{\|maskR \cap maskP\|}. \tag{9.6}$$

The inclusion of masks in the Hamming Distance masks out any fragile (likely-to-flip) bits and only compares the parts of the sign-bit vector where the mask-bit vectors overlap. Therefore, only the reliable areas are compared. This typically improves the recognition performance.

9.2.1.4 Spectral Minutiae Representation—Template Protection Properties

It is not possible to revert the spectral minutiae representation back to their initial minutiae input [33], so the irreversibility requirement of the ISO/IEC 24745 [28] standard is fulfilled. However, the spectral minutiae representation itself does not fulfil the unlinkability and renewability requirements. This issue can be tackled, e.g. with permutations of columns with application-specific keys. Depending on which templates are used in the training set of the CPCA feature reduction, a partial renewability and unlinkability (see [28]) can also be achieved, as explained in [25].

9.2.1.5 Spectral Minutiae Representation—Embedding Minutiae Reliability Data

It is possible that a feature-extraction pipeline may generate falsely extracted minutiae (a.k.a a spurious minutiae). Some pipelines are able to determine a genuine certainty for each minutiae, which describes the certainty that the extracted reference point is a genuine minutiae and not a spurious minutiae. When this minutiae reliability (q_M, ranging 1–100%[4]) is known, the Dirac pulse (Eq. 9.1) of each minutiae can be weighted linearly (w_i, ranging 0.01–1.0, corresponding to q_M) to its reliability:

$$\mathscr{M}(w_x, w_y; \sigma^2) = \left| exp\left(-\frac{w_x^2 + w_y^2}{2\sigma^{-2}}\right) \sum_{i=1}^{Z} w_i \, exp(-\mathrm{j}(w_x x_i + w_y y_i)) \right|. \tag{9.7}$$

Stronger reliability corresponds with a higher weight w_i for minutiae $m_i(x, y, q_M)$. This approach is further called Quality Data-Enhanced Spectral Minutia Location Representation (QSML) throughout this chapter.

9.2.1.6 Spectral Minutiae Representation—Conclusions

The SML is a promising, flexible and highly efficient data representation that allows for fast comparisons using simple floating-point arithmetic in its real- or absolute-valued form. Even faster comparisons are achieved using only bit comparisons in its binary form with apparently no impairment in biometric performance. It is also possible to embed quality information. Furthermore, the SML is adaptable to template protection method which is a requirement of the ISO/IEC 24745 standard. This fixed-length representation can be compressed up to $Xx = 256$ and $Xy_{CPCA} \approx 24$ bits, whereby every template is sized only 0.75 kB resulting in a 750 MB database with 1,000,000 enrolled templates.

9.2.2 *Serial Combination of SMR*

In the previous section, the SMR variant SML was introduced. As already mentioned, the SML can be represented as a real- or absolute-valued vector of its complex feature vector. Experiments in previous work (see [25]) have shown that both representations

[4]A reliability of 0% should not be possible since no minutiae would have been detected in the first place.

show different results in terms of comparison scores when applied on fuzzy vein minutiae. We found that for the

absolute-valued SML, the corresponding template is less often the template with the highest score. However, on the other hand, we observed a much lower pre-selection error for rank 10 shortlists when using the absolute-valued representation compared to the

real-valued SML, which more often fails to return a high score for the corresponding template among many templates. However, among just a few templates, the real-valued SML finds the correct template more reliably with a better score distribution than the absolute-valued SML.

The discussion of this behaviour is beyond scope of this chapter. However, this behaviour can effectively be used as an advantage by the proposed biometric system. Instead of using either absolute- or real-valued SML, both variants are incorporated: the absolute-valued representation is used during the identification lookup process to find a rank-1 to rank-10 shortlist, whereas the real-valued representation is then used to verify the rank-1 shortlist or find the correct reference template among the rank-n shortlist.

The usage of both representations does not increase the computational workload when creating the templates over the level of working with the absolute-valued representation alone since the real-valued representation is a by-product of calculating the absolute-valued representation. However, the storage requirements are doubled. Furthermore, in the shortlist, the comparison costs of the real-valued representation are also added.

9.2.3 Indexing Methods

In Sect. 9.2.1, an efficient data representation to effectively reduce the computational costs and time spent for template comparisons is presented. Despite the efficient data representation, the system is still subject to the challenges introduced in Sect. 9.1.2. In this section, two methods necessary to reduce the number of template comparisons are presented.

9.2.3.1 Bloom Filter

Following the conversion of the SML templates into their binary representation, the enrolled templates are organised into tree-based search structures by adapting the methods of [27] and [15].

1. The binary SML templates are evenly split into J equally sized blocks of adjustable height and width ($H \times W$). Subsequently, a simple transformation function is applied to the blocks column-wise, whereby each column $(c_1, \ldots, c_W)$ is mapped to its corresponding decimal integer value.

2. For each block, an empty (i.e. all bits set to 0) Bloom filter ($\mathbf{b}$) of length 2^H is created and the indices corresponding to the decimal column values are set to 1 (i.e. $\mathbf{b}\left[\text{int}(c_j)\right] = 1$).
3. Hence, the resulting template ($\mathbf{B}$) is a sequence of J such Bloom filters—$[\mathbf{b}_1, \ldots, \mathbf{b}_J]$.
4. The dissimilarity (DS) between two Bloom filter-based templates (denoted $\mathbf{B}$ and $\mathbf{B}'$) can be efficiently computed, as shown in Eq. 9.8, where $|\cdot|$ represents the population count, i.e. Hamming weight. Implementations of Eq. 9.8 can utilise intrinsic CPU operations and are trivially parallelisable, thus fulfilling the requirements stated in Sect. 9.1.3.

$$DS(\mathbf{B}, \mathbf{B}') = \frac{1}{J} \sum_{j=0}^{J} \frac{|\mathbf{b}_j \oplus \mathbf{b}'_j|}{|\mathbf{b}_j| + |\mathbf{b}'_j|}. \tag{9.8}$$

The Bloom filter-based templates are—to a certain degree—rotation invariant. This is because H columns are contained within a block and hence mapped to the same Bloom filter in the sequence, which means that contrary to the raw SML, no fine alignment compensation (normally achieved via circular shifts of the template along the horizontal axis) is needed during the template comparison stage. Furthermore, the data representation is sparse, which is a crucial property for the indexing steps described below:

1. The list of N enrolled templates is (approximately evenly) split and assigned to T trees. This step is needed (for any sizeable N values) to maintain the sparseness of the data representation.
2. Each node of a tree (containing $I = {}^{N}\!/_{T}$ templates) is constructed through a union of templates, which corresponds to the binary OR applied to the individual Bloom filters in the sequence. The tree root is constructed from all templates assigned to the respective trees (i.e. $\bigcup_{i=1}^{I} B_i$), while the children at subsequent levels are created each from half of the templates of their parent node (e.g. at first level—the children of the root node—$\bigcup_{i=1}^{I/2} B_i$ and $\bigcup_{i=\frac{I}{2}+1}^{I} B_i$).
3. The templates ($\mathbf{B}_1, \ldots, \mathbf{B}_i$) are inserted as tree leaves.

After constructing the trees, the retrieval can be performed as shown below:

1. A small number of the most promising trees (t) out of T constructed trees can be pre-selected (denoted $\frac{t}{T}$) based on comparison scores between the probe and root nodes.
2. The chosen trees are successively checked until the first candidate identity is found or all the pre-selected trees have been visited. Note that for the genuine transactions, thanks to the pre-selection step, the trees most likely to contain the sought identity are visited first. A tree is traversed by—at each level—computing the comparison score between its nodes and the probe, and choosing the path with the best score. Once a leaf is reached, a final comparison and check against a decision threshold takes place. The tree traversal idea is based on the representation sparseness: as long as—at each level—the relation $DS_{genuine} \ll DS_{impostor}$

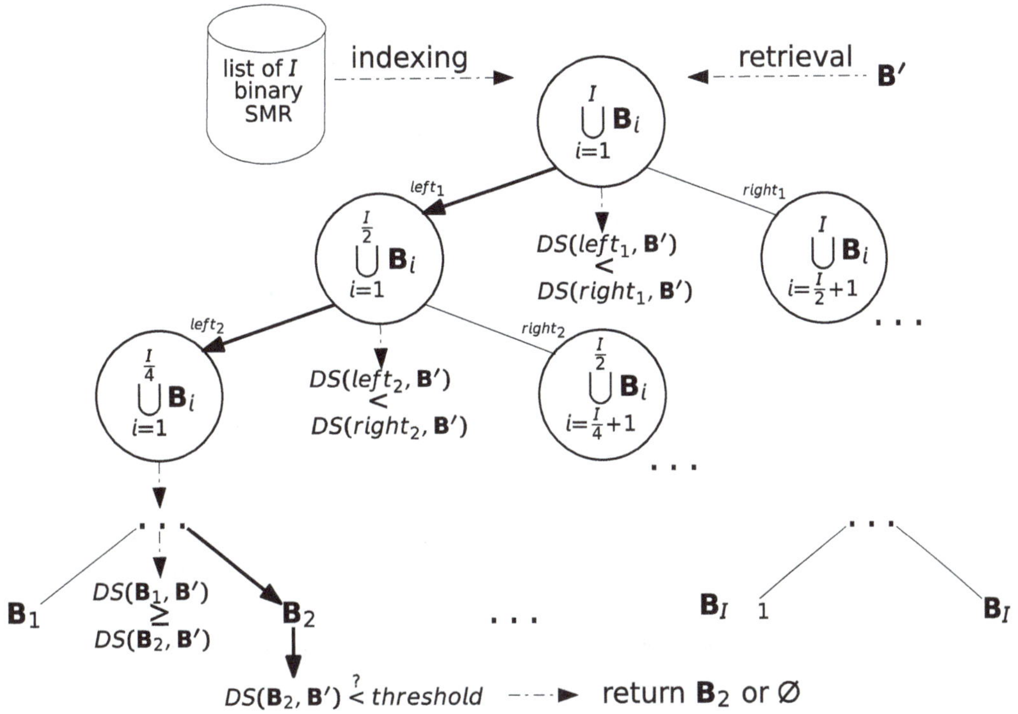

Fig. 9.3 Indexing and retrieval in the Bloom filter-based system. In this case, the retrieval follows the bold arrow path down to a leaf, where the final decision is made

generally holds true, the genuine probes will be able to traverse the tree using the correct path to reach a matching leaf template.

The complexity of a single lookup is $O\,(T + t * (2 * log_2 I))$. As it is sufficient to pre-select only a small fraction of the constructed trees, i.e. $t \ll T$, the lookup workload remains low, while arbitrarily many enrollees can be accommodated by constructing additional trees. For reference, Fig. 9.3 shows the indexing and retrieval in a single tree. If multiple trees are constructed, the search is trivially parallelisable by simultaneously traversing many trees at once.

9.2.3.2 CPCA-Tree

The second approach—called an SMR-CPCA binary search tree (CPCA-Tree)—follows the same tree construction and traversal strategy as the Bloom filter-Tree introduced in the previous section. However, instead of using a Bloom filter or another template transformation approach, the CPCA-Tree stores binary SML-CPCA templates directly. The CPCA-Tree approach has shown an advantage in terms of biometric performance over the Bloom filter-Tree in previous experiments (see [25]) when benchmarking both indexing methods with heavily degraded (i.e. very fuzzy) data since the comparison of CPCA templates does not strongly rely on stable columns like the Bloom filter. However, while the CPCA-Tree is more robust in fuzzy environments, it is to be expected that one single CPCA-Tree cannot store as many templates as one single Bloom filter-Tree: the binary SMR-CPCA features a high inter-class variance, whereby all set bits in the binary SMR-CPCA matrices are differently distributed and there are few unanimous bits. Therefore, the bits set in a binary SMR-CPCA have few bit collisions with SMR-CPCA from other subjects, respectively, from other biometric instances and when merging SMR-CPCA, the population count rises quickly, thus diminishing the descriptive value. In other words, the sparsity of upper level nodes quickly decreases to a point—typically around more than 65% of the bits set—where no correct traversal direction decisions are possible.

There are at least three approaches to store the binary SMR-CPCA templates.

SMR-CPCA Components (SMR-CPCA-C) The spectral binarisation method by Xu and Veldhuis [32] yields two binary matrices: a sign bit and a mask bit. These two matrices represent the two components of the SMR-CPCA-C representation.

SMR-CPCA Applied (SMR-CPCA-A) Instead of keeping both binary components, the mask bit is applied to the sign bit, yielding the applied bit. The applied bit matrix represents the single-component representation of SMR-CPCA-A.

SMR-CPCA Mixed (SMR-CPCA-M) Fusing both concepts by keeping the mask bit but replacing the sing bit with the applied bit.

In the experiments, the SMR-CPCA-M is used since it achieved the best biometric performance of these three representations in previous work [25]. Thus, it is required to extend the binary tree to store the applied bit and the mask bit, since both are required for the SMR-CPCA-M approach, which is commonly referred to as an auxiliary data scheme. In terms of tree construction, the applied bits are merged and the mask bits are merged upon fusing two leaves to one node.

9.2.4 Hardware Acceleration

Strictly speaking, the usage of hardware acceleration in the sense of multi-threaded systems, parallel systems or distinct hardware like FPGA processors is no workload reduction per se, as it does not reduce the number of template comparisons needed or reduce the size of the data. However, it is an important step to achieve an optimum efficiency of the system's hardware and is therefore also in scope of this chapter. As already accentuated in Sect. 9.1.3, the selected approaches should be implementable in congruency with the requirements of parallel and multi-threaded systems. Our system combines two approaches (SML and indexing with binary search trees) that are evaluated for these requirements.

Implementing the binary search tree in a parallel manner is not feasible. Search trees might not be balanced or when using multiple trees, the trees differ in size. However, they are well suited for multi-threaded computation. When multiple trees were built (as would be the case in any sizeable system), each tree can be searched in one of a pool of threads. However, the SMR is perfectly suited for real parallel processing. Each element of its fixed-length feature vector can be calculated equally without any jumps or conditions. Furthermore, the calculation of one single element can be broken down to very few instructions and basic arithmetic. For example, in SSE-SIMD environments, up to four 32 bit vector elements can be calculated at a time [2] and in modern AVX-512-SIMD up to 16 32 bit vector elements at a time [1] for the real- or absolute-valued SMR. The whole calculation is also easily implementable in languages like OpenCL, which enables parallel computation on GPGPUs and other parallel systems. Next, the comparison process is also free of jumps or conditions and can also be processed in a paralleled environment where the previous statements[5] also apply.

9.2.5 Fusion of Concepts

The previous sections introduced several workload reduction concepts. In fact, these concepts can be combined. This section describes the process visualised in Fig. 9.4, where all concepts are joined to one biometric system.

In terms of data processing, both the enrolment and query process are equal: after extracting the minutiae from the biometric sample, the absolute- and real-valued representations of the SML are calculated and the binary form of the absolute-valued SML is derived as introduced in Sect. 9.2.1. For the enrolment process, a binary representation ($\mathbf{X}^b$) of an SML template ($\mathbf{X}$) is now enrolled in the indexing trees and the floating-point representation ($\mathbf{X}^f$) is kept for each enrolled template.

Upon receiving a biometric probe that has to be identified, the binary representation is used to find a shortlist (rank-1 or rank-n) by traversing the built trees. Choosing $n > T$, respective $n > t$ is not feasible since every tree will always return the same enrolled template for the same query. Figure 9.4 is simplified to the case where $t = n$. Subsequently, the floating-point representation of the SML query will then be compared to the real-valued SML reference templates found in the shortlist by the comparison and decision subsystem.

Accordingly, all previous concepts are fused: the binary representation—regardless of whether it is extracted from the real- or absolute-valued representation—is used to efficiently look up a small shortlist and the floating-point representation— again independent of whether it is the real or absolute valued—is used to receive a more distinct comparison score distribution. There are multiple combination possibilities, e.g. real-valued binary for enrolment and real-valued floating point for the shortlist comparison or absolute-valued binary for enrolment and real-valued floating point for the shortlist comparison. It is expected that the former yields the best biometric performance since similar experiments in [25] already revealed competitive results and it is unclear, whether the binary representation of the absolute-valued SML retains the same properties (see Sect. 9.2.2) as the floating-point SML.

[5]It has to be noted, that for the binary SMR, up to two rows can be processed with one AVX-512-SIMD instruction.

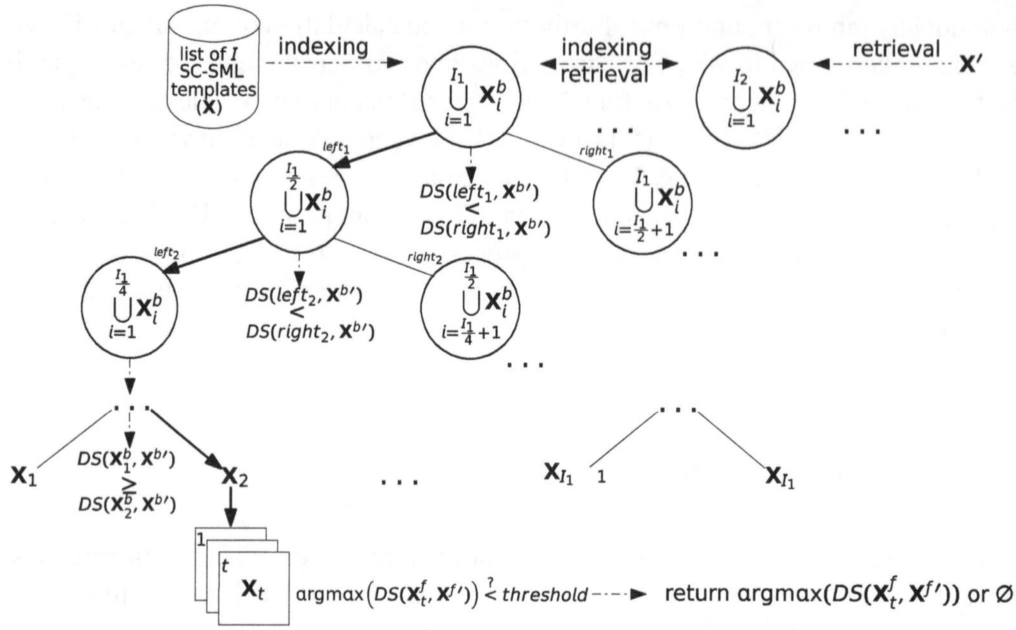

Fig. 9.4 Indexing and retrieval in the Bloom filter or CPCA-Tree-based system. In this case, the retrieval follows the bold arrow path down to a leaf, where the final decision is made

9.3 Experiments

The following sections describe the vein data used for experiments, its preparation and a description of how the experiments to evaluate the proposed methods were conducted. This chapter merely focuses on open-set scenarios, whereby verification experiments are beyond the scope.

9.3.1 Experimental Setup

9.3.1.1 Dataset

At the time of writing, the PolyU multispectral palm-print database (PolyU) [3] is the largest publicly available vascular dataset containing Near-Infrared (NIR) palm-print images usable for (palm) vein recognition known to the authors. It comprises images of 250 subjects with 6 images per hand. The images have a predefined and stable Region of Interest (ROI). All images have a very low-quality variance and are all equally illuminated. It is not possible to link the left- and the right-hand instance of one subject by their labels and vascular pattern; therefore, every instance is treated as a single enrolment subject identifier (in short "subject") as listed in Table 9.1. Since the PolyU dataset aims for palm-print recognition, it features a high amount of skin texture, which interferes with the vein detection and makes it a challenging

Table 9.1 Dataset overview

Instances	Images	Resolution	ROI
500	3000	128 × 128 px	128 × 128 px

dataset for the feature-extraction pipeline, which comprises the maximum curvature [24] approach with some prepended image optimisation like noise removal.

9.3.2 Performance Evaluation

Comparison scores are obtained in an open-set identification as follows:

1. One reference template is enrolled for each subject.
2. All remaining probe templates are compared against the enrolled references.
3. The scores are then categorised as

false-positive identification identification transactions by data subject not enrolled in the system, where an identifier is returned.

false-negative identification identification transactions by users enrolled in the system in which the user's correct identifier is not among those returned.

The dataset has been split into four groups: enrolled, genuine, impostor and training (for the CPCA feature reduction). An overview of the relevant numbers is listed in Table 9.2. In order to ease the indexing experiments, an enrolment set of 2^n is preferred.

With a limited number of subjects (500), 256 enrollees offer the best compromise between largest 2^n-enrolment and the number of impostor queries.

The results of the experiments are reported as a Detection Error Trade-off Curve (DET). To report the computational workload required by the different approaches, the workload metric

$$W = N * p * C \tag{9.9}$$

where N represents the number of enrolled subjects, p represents the penetration rate and C represents the costs of one single one-to-one template comparison (i.e. number of bits that are compared), and the fraction

$$F = \frac{W_{proposed}}{W_{baseline}} \tag{9.10}$$

introduced by Drozdowski et al. [15] will be used.

In tables and text, the biometric performance is reported with the Equal Error Rate (EER). However, when evaluating the *best biometric performance*, the results are first ordered by the False-Negative Identification Rate (FNIR) at FPIR = 0.1%,

Table 9.2 Dataset partitioning overview and resulting number of comparison trials in a naïve system, samples in parentheses

Enrolled templates (N)	Genuine comparison trials	Impostor comparison trials	Training samples
256	327,680 (1280)	350,208 (1368)	96

then ordered by the EER. This is due to the nature of the EER, whereby it does not describe the biometric performance at important low FPIR, i.e. an experiment with EER = 5% can feature an FNIR at FPIR = 0.1% of 20% while an experiment with EER = 5.5% can feature an FNIR at FPIR = 0.1% of 13%. In real-world scenarios, the latter example result is more relevant than the former.

9.3.3 Experiments Overview

The following enumeration serves as an overview of the experiments conducted in this chapter:

Spectral Minutiae Representation The basic implementation, comparing vein probes based on minutiae with the SML in both absolute- and real-valued representation. In an identification scenario, the database is searched exhaustively, e.g. every query template (probe) is compared with every enrolled template (reference). *These experiments represent the biometric performance and workload baseline for the workload reduction approaches in the following experiments.*

CPCA Feature Reduction Repetition of the above identification experiments, but with CPCA feature reduction for both binary and floating-point SML—further called SML-CPCA—to evaluate whether the biometric performance suffers from the feature reduction.

Binary Spectral Minutiae Representation The same experiments (for both SML representations) as above are repeated with the binary representations of the SML to evaluate whether the biometric performance is degraded by this binarisation process.

Serial Combination of SML With the baseline for all representations of the SML,[6] these experiments are used to validate the assumption that the observed advantages of both SML representations can be used to increase the biometric performance.

Indexing Methods The binary representations of both absolute- and real-valued SML are indexed with the presented Bloom filter-Trees and CPCA-Trees approaches to evaluate whether the biometric performance is degraded by these indexing schemes.

[6] Real-valued, absolute-valued, real-valued SML-CPCA, absolute-valued SML-CPCA, binary real-valued SML-CPCA and binary absolute-valued SML-CPCA.

Fusion of Concepts Both indexing and serial combination of SML will be combined as presented in Sect. 9.2.5. This experiment evaluates whether both concepts can be combined to achieve a higher biometric performance due to the serial combination, combined with a low computational workload due to the indexing scheme.

9.4 Results

This section reports and comments on the results achieved by the experiments presented in the previous section.

9.4.1 Spectral Minutiae Representation

The SML experiments are split in multiple stages to approximate its ideal settings and tuning for fuzzy vascular data.

9.4.1.1 Baseline

In order to assess the results of the main experiments (indexing approaches), a baseline is needed. Figure 9.5a shows the DET curves of the introduced SML and QSML in both real- and absolute-valued sampling. It is clearly visible that the real-valued representation is much more accurate than the absolute-valued representation. Furthermore, Fig. 9.5b contains plots of the real-valued SML, QSML and Spectral Minutia Location Representation with minutiae pre-selection (PSML) thresholds of *0.1, 0.2 and 0.3.

While the authors of [31, 34] recorded good results using the absolute-valued sampling for their verification purposes, it falls far behind the real-valued sampling in identification experiments.

The selected dataset introduces some difficulties for the feature-extraction pipeline used. Recall that the PolyU dataset is a palm-print and not palm vein dataset, and therefore it includes the fuzzy skin surface, which would not be included in a designated vascular dataset. It is mainly selected because due to its size rather than quality. Various optimisation experiments were run and are reported in the following section to increase the recognition performance. Implementing a robust feature extractor is beyond the scope of this chapter.

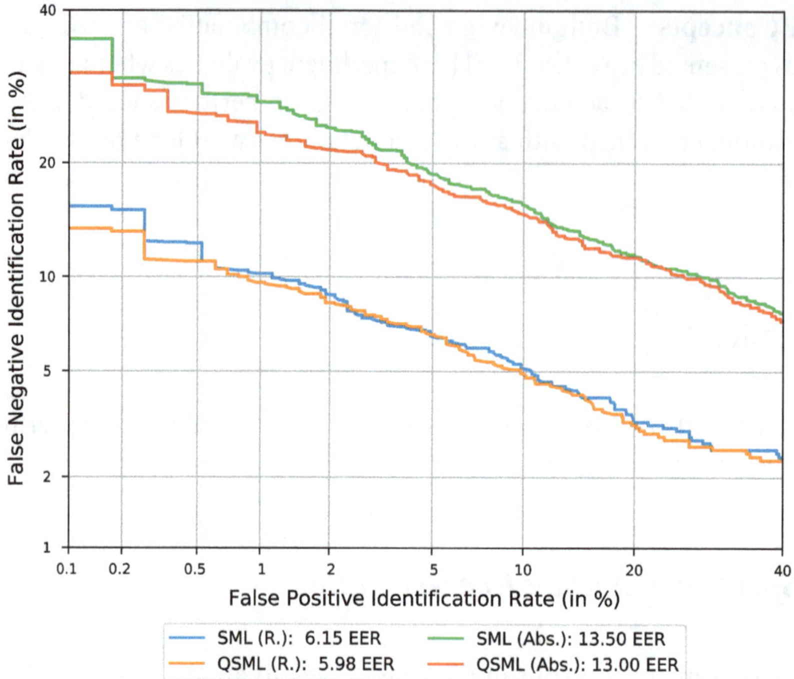

(a) Real/Absolute

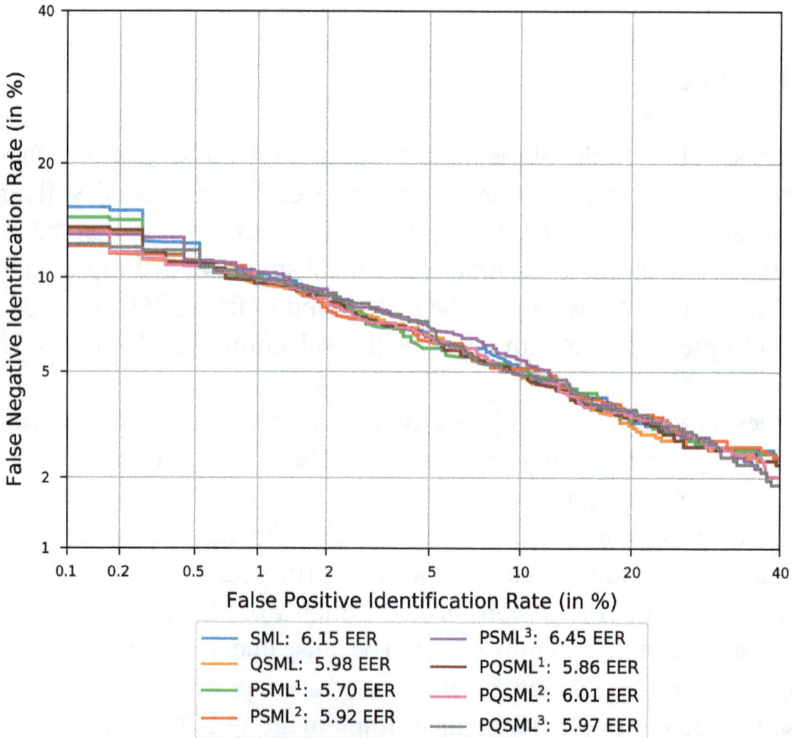

(b) Minutiae pre-selection

Fig. 9.5 DET curve's benchmark of the SML and QSML. Used q_M: ${}^1q_M \geq 0.1$, ${}^2q_M \geq 0.2$ and ${}^3q_M \geq 0.3$

9.4.1.2 Optimisation

The feature extractor (maximum curvature [24]) used is able to report quality (reliability; q_M) data in the limits of (0, 1]—where 1 represents a 100% minutiae reliability and 0 no minutiae at all—about the extracted pattern; therefore, the QSML can be used. Using this data to remove unreliable minutiae in terms of defining a q_M threshold (i.e. a minutiae reliability of at least 20%), the recognition performance can be increased as shown in Fig. 9.5b. Using $q_M \geq 0.2$ as a threshold for the so-called PSML and quality data-enhanced Spectral Minutia Location Representation with minutiae pre-selection (PQSML) achieved the best results in the experiments.

Additionally, it is possible to reduce the SML and QSML samplings λ_{max} to fade out higher (*more accurate*) frequencies, which increases the significance of the lower, more stable (*but less distinct*) frequencies. Experiments showed that using $\lambda_{max} \approx 0.45$ instead of the original $\lambda_{max} \approx 0.6$ resulted in the best compromise between low and high frequencies. This optimisation process is further referred to as tuning.

9.4.1.3 CPCA

In order to investigate the impact of the CPCA compression on the recognition performance, the same procedure as for the SML and QSML is repeated using the CPCA compression.

Applying CPCA to the tuned SML and QSML results in no noticeable performance drop, as shown in Fig. 9.6. Again, using $\lambda_{max} \approx 0.45$ instead of the original $\lambda_{max} \approx 0.6$ resulted in the best compromise between low and high frequencies. One mentionable result of these experiments is that the tuned QSML-CPCA performs slightly better than the full-featured and tuned QSML.

9.4.1.4 Summary

In summary, even with a moderately reliable feature-extraction pipeline, the SML achieved acceptable results. Employing quality data in terms of minutiae reliability improved the biometric performance and an additional λ_{max}-tuning also improved the biometric performance (as shown in Fig. 9.7). For the following experiments, the tuned QSML-CPCA with minutiae pre-selection of $q_M \geq 0.2$ will be used as a biometric performance baseline and will further be called PQSML-CPCA. The corresponding workload for the SML[7] is $W \approx 2.52 \times 10^7$.

[7] $N = 256, p = 1, C = 256 \times 128 \times 3$; Measurements on the machine running the experiments resulted in three times slower floating-point SML comparisons than binary SML bit comparisons.

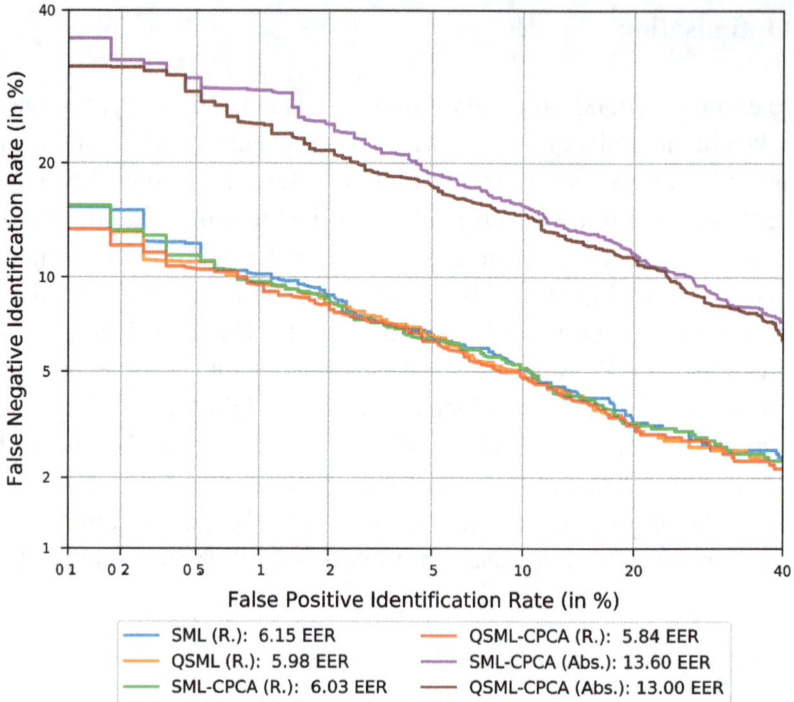

(a) Real/Absolute

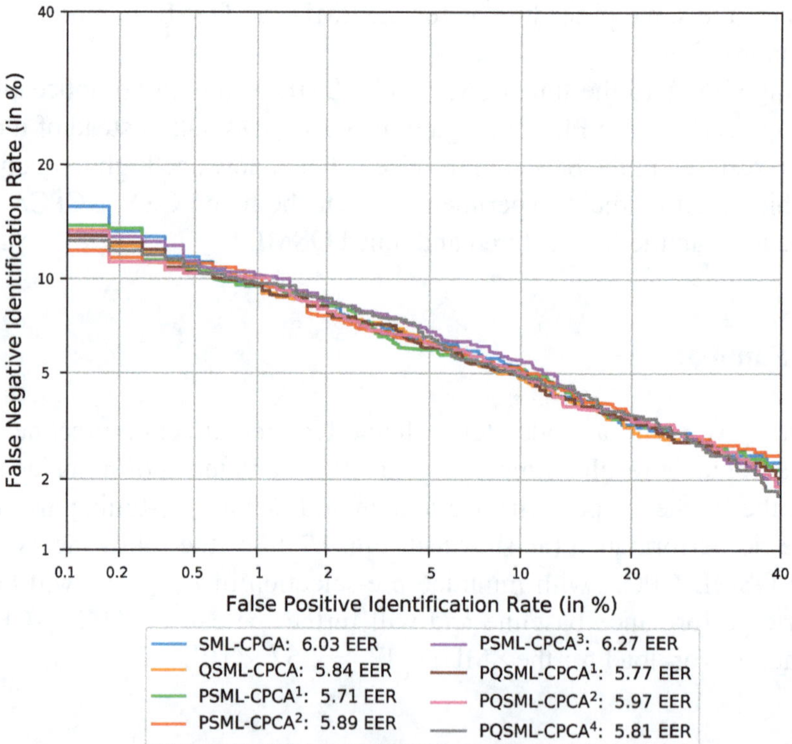

(b) Minutiae pre-selection

Fig. 9.6 DET curves benchmark of the SML-CPCA and QSML reduced with the CPCA feature reduction (QSML-CPCA). Used q_M: $^1q_M \geq 0.1$, $^2q_M \geq 0.2$ and $^3q_M \geq 0.3$

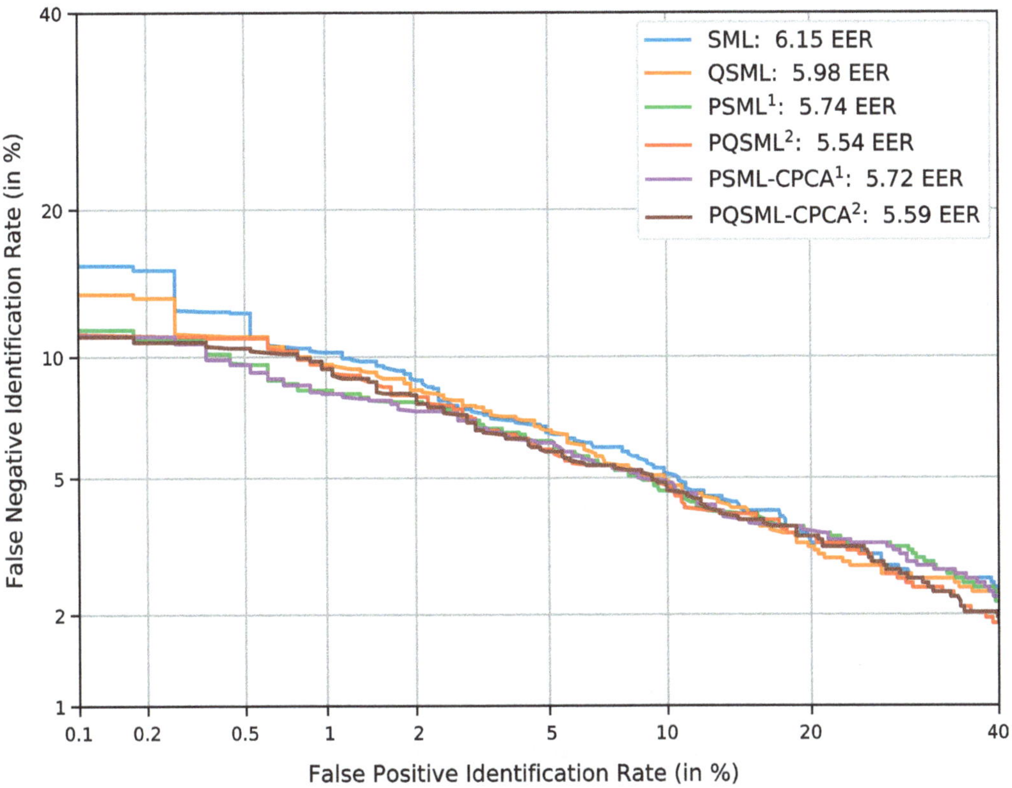

Fig. 9.7 DET curves comparison of the best performing configurations of each approach. Used parameters: $^1q_M \geq 0.2$, $\lambda_{max} = 0.45$ and $^2q_M \geq 0.2$, $\lambda_{max} = 0.44$

9.4.2 Binary Spectral Minutiae Representation

The next SML optimisation step is to binarise the SML floating-point vector. This step shrinks the feature vector by a factor of 32 and enables the usage of highly efficient binary and intrinsic CPU operations for template comparisons. Intrinsic CPU operations are also available for floating-point values. However, the binary intrinsics are favourable since they are more efficient and allow for a higher number of feature vector element comparisons with a single instruction. Practically, it is possible to binarise the full-featured SML, as well as the more compact SML-CPCA. However, it holds special interest to achieve a high biometric performance with the binarised (P)SML-CPCA or (P)QSML-CPCA to receive the smallest possible feature vector. Interestingly, the binary CPCA-reduced variants perform better than their larger counterpart, as is visible in the DET plots of Fig. 9.8. Moreover, the binary QSML-CPCA outperforms its minutiae-pre-selection counterparts. By analysing the other binary QSML-CPCA results, this result could be a coincidence. At this point, the 256×128 floats sized (PQ)SML got shrunk to a 256×20-bit sized (PQ)SML-CPCA without exhibiting a deterioration of the biometric performance. The workload for

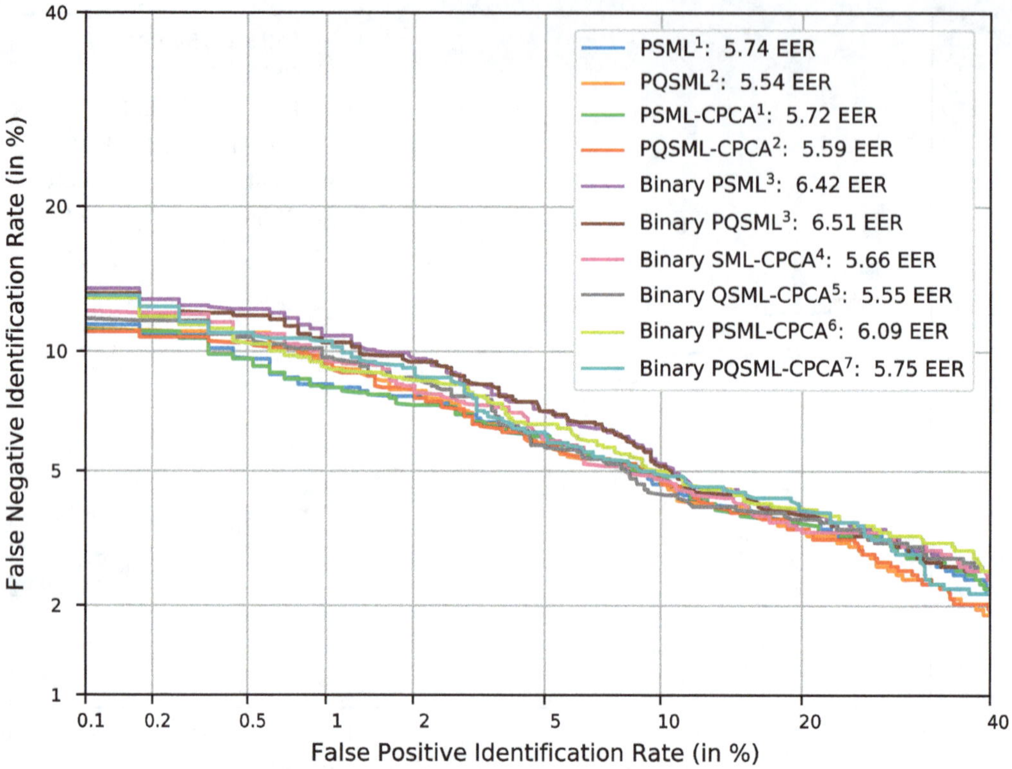

$^{1}\lambda_{max} = 0.45, q_M \geq 0.2$	$^{2}\lambda_{max} = 0.44, q_M \geq 0.2$
$^{3}\lambda_{max} = 0.43, q_M \geq 0.2, MT = 0.54$	
$^{4}\lambda_{max} = 0.41, MT = 0.89$	$^{5}\lambda_{max} = 0.41, MT = 0.84$
$^{6}\lambda_{max} = 0.41, q_M \geq 0.2, MT = 0.81$	$^{7}\lambda_{max} = 0.40, q_M \geq 0.2$

Fig. 9.8 DET curves benchmark for the binary SML and QSML

the binary (PQ)SML-CPCA[8] is only at $W \approx 1.31 \times 10^6$. This results in $F \approx 5\%$ for the binary (PQ)SML-CPCA compared to the full-featured (PQ)SML.

9.4.3 Serial Combination of SMR

The serial combination of PQSML experiments was run with different settings ranging from rank-1 to rank-25. Only the PQSML was experimented with since it mostly performed better than the other representations. Using a rank-10 to rank-15 (~5%) pre-selection with the absolute-valued PQSML then comparing the real-valued PQSML templates of the generated shortlist achieved the best results as shown in Fig. 9.9. Both were sampled with the same settings, whereby only one SMR sampling is needed; recall that, the real-valued SMR is a by-product when calculating the absolute-valued SMR. However, it is questionable whether the EER decrease

[8] $N = 256, p = 1, C = 256 \times 20$.

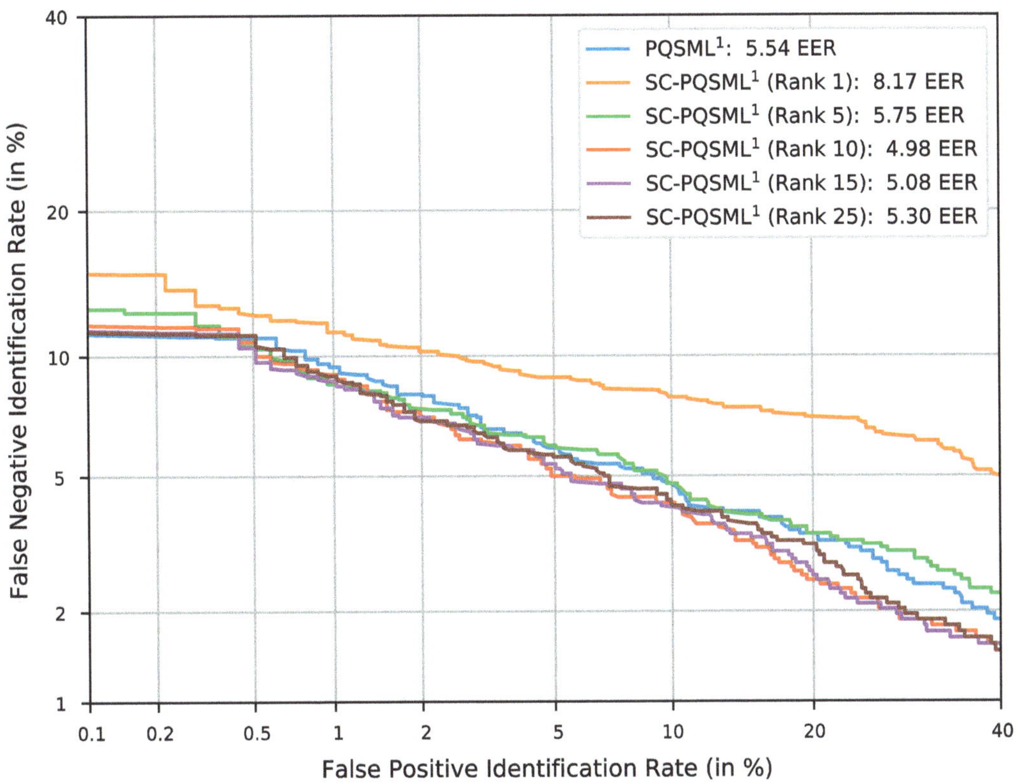

Fig. 9.9 DET curves benchmark for different Serial Combination of QSML settings. Used parameters: ${}^{1}q_M \geq 0.2$, $\lambda_{max} = 0.44$

achieved justifies the introduced online workload $W \approx 2.64 \times 10^7$ ($\digamma \approx 105\%$), compared to the $W \approx 2.52 \times 10^7$ calculated for the (PQ)SML, yielded by this method if the shortlist is not generated using the efficient, binary representation.

9.4.4 *Indexing Methods*

The previous experiments demonstrated that it is possible to reduce the workload drastically without a major impairment of the biometric performance by compressing and subsequently binarising the PQSML. However, it is still necessary to exhaustively search the whole database. In this section, the results of the indexing experiments conducted to reduce the number of necessary template comparisons are reported.

9.4.4.1 Bloom Filter

First experiments showed a severely impaired biometric performance loss of about 15% points (Fig. 9.10) compared to the results reported in Sect. 9.4.2 when employing Bloom filter indexing. The origin of the poor performance of the applied to binary

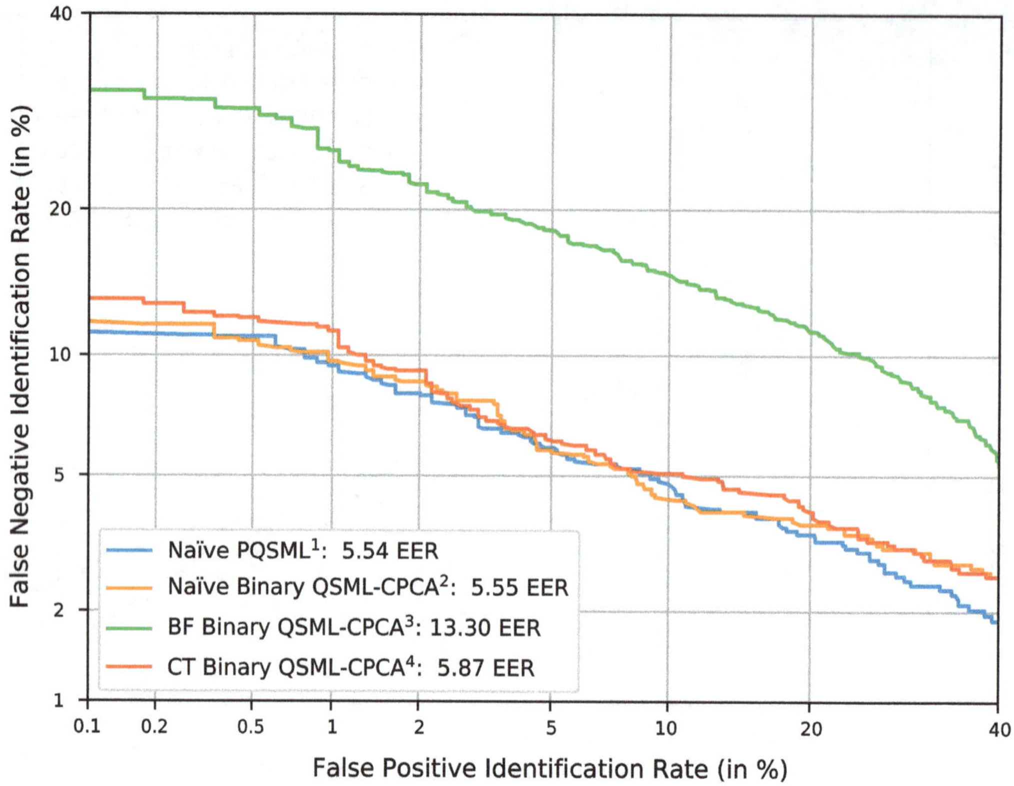

$^{1}\lambda_{max} = 0.44, q_M \geq 0.2 | ^{2}\lambda_{max} = 0.41, MT = 0.84$
$^{3}\lambda_{max} = 0.41, MT = 0.80, T = 64, t = 31, W = 5, H = 4$
$^{4}\lambda_{max} = 0.44, MT = 0.54, T = 64, t = 17$

Fig. 9.10 DET curves benchmark for the Bloom filter and CPCA-Tree indexing approach using binary PQSML-CPCA (BF → Bloom filter; CT → CPCA-Tree)

PSML-CPCA templates is the high number of bit errors when comparing two mated binary PSML-CPCA. This Bloom filter implementation strongly relies on stable columns in the J blocks of the binary vector across their height H to offer a high biometric performance. The iris naturally yields comparatively stable columns when aligned and unrolled and therefore the Bloom filter performs exemplary. However, due to the nature of the SMR— which includes various frequencies—this stability is not ensured: smaller feature-extraction inconsistencies yield much more noise in the upper frequencies of the SMR, which then result in more Bloom filter errors, mostly along the columns. A more in-depth discussion of this behaviour is given in Sect. 9.4.2 of [25]. Even at a very high MT of 0.9, the average bit error rate is 13% with an error in more than 50% of the columns, which is excessive for a reliable Bloom filter transformation that needs stable column bits.

While analysing the issue in further depth, it was found that the Bloom filter reliably looked up correct templates for genuine queries but failed to achieve a separable score distribution. Therefore, the Bloom filter indexing might not be feasible if used on its own, although it performs well in a serial combination approach. The best biometric performance was recorded at $t/T = 31/64$ resulting in a workload[9] of $W \approx 7.7 \times 10^5$, achieving $\mathcal{F} \approx 3.1\%$.

9.4.4.2 CPCA-Tree

In its basic implementation, the CPCA-Tree surpasses the basic Bloom filter indexing in both the FNIR-to-FPIR ratio, as well as EER. It achieves a similar EER to the naïve binary QSML-CPCA and naïve QSML-CPCA. Thus, the CPCA-Tree indexing approach reaches a similar biometric performance as the naïve approaches, albeit with a much lower workload[10] of $W \approx 6.8 \times 10^5$, which results in $\mathcal{F} = 1.7\%$.

Therefore, if a serial combination approach is not desired because due to its complexity, the CPCA-Tree is a good compromise between complexity, workload and biometric performance.

9.4.5 Fusion of Concepts

As already mentioned in the experiment's description, the fusion of concepts combines the serial combination of (PQ)SML and the indexing schemes following the scheme presented in Sect. 9.2.5. In the first run of the experiment, $\mathbf{X}^b$ was extracted from the real-valued QSML and $\mathbf{X}^f$ is the real-valued QSML, and out of t selected trees only one (rank-1) template was selected for the shortlist. While this did not affect the biometric performance of the CPCA-Tree indexing, the Bloom filter indexing transcends the biometric performance of the CPCA-Tree indexing approach for lower FPIR with the rank-1 serial combination scheme. However, the Bloom filter indexing could not catch up at higher FPIR rates. Using a higher pre-selection rank for the Bloom filter indexing scheme did not result in a higher biometric performance.

In these experiments, the pre-selection rank is set equal to the number of searched trees t. Upon first glance, the results of the higher pre-selection rank experiments for the CPCA-Tree indexing do not deviate much compared to the rank-1 experiments, whereby only the EER is slightly lower. Note the number of searched trees t, with a higher rank, a comparable biometric performance is achieved by traversing lesser trees. This is an important property for scaling in large-scale databases. For medium-scale databases, the overhead introduced by the additional floating-point comparisons when comparing the query with the templates in the shortlist would void the workload reduction achieved by the reduction of traversed trees. Furthermore, the experiments using a real-valued pre-selection/real-valued decision achieved a higher biometric performance than the absolute-valued pre-selection/real-valued decision

---

[9] $N = 256, Xy_{CPCA} = 20, W = 5, H = 4, C = (2^H * \frac{Xy_{CPCA}}{H}) * \frac{Xx}{W} = 4096, p = \frac{T + t * (2 * log_2(\frac{N}{T}))}{N} \approx 0.73.$

[10] $N = 256, Xy_{CPCA} = 20, C = Xx * Xy_{CPCA}, p = \frac{T + t * (2 * log_2(\frac{N}{T}))}{N} \approx 0.51.$

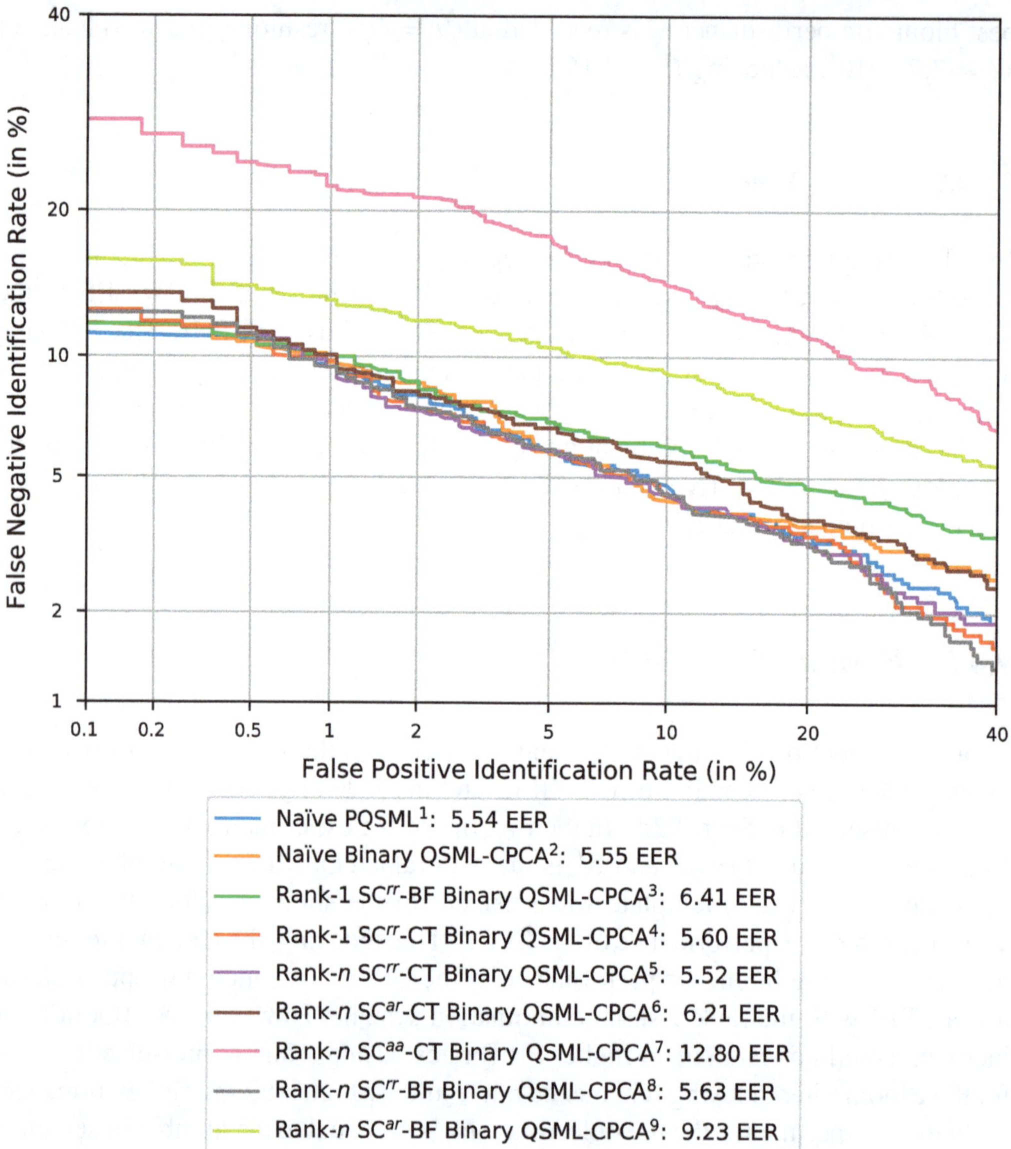

$^{1}\lambda_{max} = 0.44, q_M \geq 0.2$ | $^{2}\lambda_{max} = 0.41, MT = 0.84$
$^{3}\lambda_{max} = 0.41, MT = 0.11, T = 64, t = 25, W = 5, H = 4$
$^{4}\lambda_{max} = 0.43, MT = 0.61, T = 64, t = 26$ | $^{5}\lambda_{max} = 0.46, MT = 0.72, T = 64, n = t = 18$
$^{6}\lambda_{max} = 0.45, MT = 0.69, T = 64, t = 29$ | $^{7}\lambda_{max} = 0.59, MT = 0.68, T = 64, n = t = 30$
$^{8}\lambda_{max} = 0.41, MT = 0.54, T = 64, n = t = 24, W = 4, H = 4$
$^{9}\lambda_{max} = 0.41, MT = 0.45, T = 64, n = t = 31, W = 4, H = 4$
BF $\rightarrow$ Bloom filter; CT $\rightarrow$ CPCA-Tree; SC $\rightarrow$ Serial Combination
$^{rr} \rightarrow$ real-v. pre-selection, real-v. decision; $^{ar} \rightarrow$ absolute-v. pre-selection, real-v. decision
$^{aa} \rightarrow$ absolute-v. pre-selection, absolute-v. decision

Fig. 9.11 DET curves benchmark for the Bloom filter and CPCA-Tree indexing approach using binary PQSML-CPCA

Table 9.3 Workload for the best performing indexing scheme of each approach

	Rank-1 SC^{rr}-BF^3	Rank-1 SC^{rr}-CT^4	Rank-n SC^{rr}-BF^8	Rank-n SC^{rr}-CT^5
W	6.9×10^5	8.8×10^5	9.7×10^5	1.2×10^6
F (%)	2.7	3.5	3.9	4.7
EER (%)	6.4	5.6	5.6	5.5

and the absolute-valued pre-selection/absolute-valued decision. Therefore, the statement of Sect. 9.2.2 that the absolute-valued SML is better suited for lookup but the real-valued SML yields more distinctive comparison scores does not apply on the binary representation of the absolute-valued (PQ)SML. The recorded workloads in this experiment are consolidated in Table 9.3 and the DET curves are shown in Fig. 9.11.

9.4.6 *Discussion*

Most results have already been discussed in previous sections. Finally, at least three properties for a new biometric deployment have to be considered when choosing one of the presented approaches: scalability, complexity and biometric performance. If a system simple to implement is desired, the CPCA-Tree indexing is recommended, given that it is easy to implement and it achieved biometric performance comparable with the contestants. Conversely, if the implementation complexity is less an issue, scalability and biometric performance have to be considered. In terms of scalability, the rank-n serial combination is the recommended approach, whereby it achieved a biometric performance comparable with that of the other approaches at the smallest number of traversed trees (smallest computational workload). Regarding the biometric performance, the rank-1 serial combination real/real indexing scheme achieved the best results. Table 9.4 summarises the rating for all best performing configurations of each approach from best (++) to worst (−−) with gradations of good (+), neutral (o) and bad (−).

To deterministically benchmark the different indexing methods and configurations, the Euclidean distance between the baseline operation point ($B_{EER} = 5.5\%$, $B_F = 1\%$) and the best performing configuration of each approach—as shown in Eq. 9.11—can be used.

$$\Delta(EER, F) = \sqrt{(EER - B_{EER})^2 + (F - B_F)^2} \tag{9.11}$$

The smaller the $\Delta(TP, F)$ for an approach, the closer that its point of operation is to the baseline operation point, whereby smaller is more preferable. Choosing the baseline operation point ($F = 1\%$, $EER = 5.5\%$) instead of the optimal operation

Table 9.4 Qualitative rating of each indexing scheme from best (++) to worst (−−) with gradations of good (+), neutral (o) and bad (−)

Approach	Complexity	Biometric performance	Workload
Naïve PQSML	++	++	−−
Bloom filter	+	−−	+
CPCA-Tree	++	+	++
Rank-1 SC^{rr}-BF	o	+	+
Rank-1 SC^{rr}-CT	+	+	+
Rank-*n* SC^{rr}-BF	−−	+	o
Rank-*n* SC^{rr}-CT	−	+	o

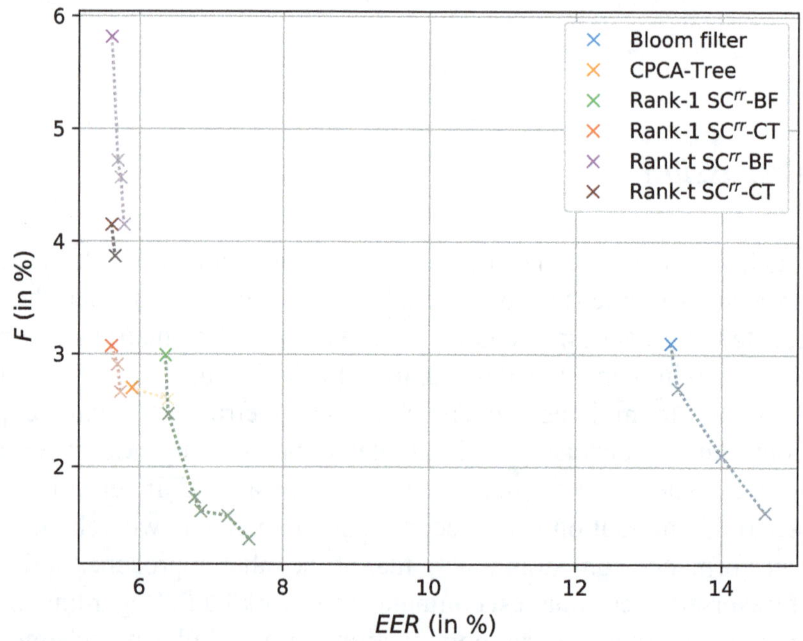

Fig. 9.12 Scatterplot of Table 9.5

point ($EER = 0\%$, $F \approx 0\%$) moves the emphasis of the distance to the performance of the indexing schemes rather than to the performance of the baseline system.

The data of Table 9.5 is visualised as scatterplot in Fig. 9.12. Note that the naïvePQSML system is not plotted since $F = 100\%$ would render the y-axis scaling of the plot impractical.

Table 9.5 Rating by Euclidean distance ($\Delta(EER, F)$) to baseline operation point ($F = 1\%, EER = 5.5\%$)

Approach	W	F (%)	EER (%)	$\Delta(EER, F)$
CPCA-Tree	6.8×10^5	2.7	5.9	1.7
Rank-1 SC^{rr}-BF	6.9×10^5	2.7	6.4	2.0
Rank-1 SC^{rr}-CT	8.8×10^5	3.5	5.6	2.5
Rank-n SC^{rr}-BF	9.7×10^5	3.9	5.6	2.9
Rank-n SC^{rr}-CT	1.2×10^6	4.7	5.5	3.7
Bloom filter	7.7×10^5	3.1	13.3	8.1
Naïve PQSML	2.5×10^7	100.0	5.5	99.0

9.5 Summary

Vascular patterns are an emerging biometric modality with active research and promising avenues for further research topics. With the rising acceptance of biometric systems, increasingly large-scale biometric deployments are put into operation. The operation of such large deployments yields immense computational load. In order to maintain a good biometric performance and acceptable response times—to avoid frustrating their users—computational workload reduction methods have to be employed. While there are many recognition algorithms for vascular patterns, most of them rely on inefficient comparison methods and hardly any computational workload reduction approaches for vein data can be found.

A recently published biometric indexing approach based on Bloom filters and binary search trees for large-scale iris databases was adopted for vascular patterns. In order to further develop this indexing approach, the vascular pattern skeletal representation of the raw palm vein images was extracted and the minutiae—the endpoints and bifurcations—of the extracted vascular pattern were then transformed using a Fourier transformation based approach originally presented for the fingerprint characteristic. When transforming the floating-point representation yielded by the Fourier transformation to a binary form, it is possible to apply the Bloom filter indexing. It has been demonstrated that the Bloom filter indexing system is capable of achieving a biometric performance close to the naïvebaseline, while reducing the necessary workload by an additional $\approx$37% on top of the workload reduction achieved with the CPCA compression and binarisation. Some of the approaches used by the Bloom filter in [15] were not feasible and the fuzziness of the vascular pattern prevented a higher workload reduction without losing too much biometric performance. However, the most important approaches have been successfully applied, and thus the system appears to be scalable in terms of workload reduction, biometric performance and enrollees.

An additional, less complex, biometric indexing approach merely using a reduced form of the binary Fourier transformation representation and binary search trees has been presented. It adopts most workload reduction strategies that are used for the

Bloom filter indexing approach and achieved a better biometric performance with only a slightly lower computational workload reduction (compared to a naïveimplementation using the reduced binary Fourier representation) of $\approx 36\%$. Since the presented approach follows the same theory and implementations as the binary search trees of the Bloom filter indexing, it also appears to be scalable in terms of workload reduction, biometric performance and enrollees.

The respective advantages and disadvantages of the two indexing methods were outlined based on the results from the previous sections. It has been shown that the CPCA-Tree achieves good performance with less stable templates than the Bloom filter. However, it is to be expected that the Bloom filter will outperform the CPCA-Tree approach with more stable templates. Furthermore, the potential for computational workload reduction is much higher using the Bloom filter based method.

The overall workload is reduced to an average of 3% compared to the baseline of the naïveimplementation using the Fourier representation in both systems. All approaches used are perfectly implementable in either multi-threaded or parallel environments. The presented indexing approaches are well suited to run in multiple threads yielding hardly any overhead. Furthermore, the data representation used can efficiently be computed and compared with SIMD introduction and intrinsics, whereby both computation and comparison do not rely on jumps or conditions. Therefore, it is perfectly suited for highly parallel computation on GPGPUs or manycore CPUs, hence utilising the maximum potential of the system's hardware.

The workload reduction approaches achieved very promising results, which were doubtless limited by the biometric performance of the base system. It is to be expected that with a higher biometric baseline performance, a higher workload reduction can be achieved: with more stable templates, a more robust indexing can be achieved, thus further reducing the workload. Several early experiments and approaches in [25] already achieved a significant biometric baseline performance gain ($EER < 0.3\%$), which will be used in future work. Since the base system achieved a very high biometric performance for fingerprints, the workload reduction approaches can be adopted to the fingerprint modalities and is subject to future work.

Finally, it should be noted that there is a lack of publicly available large (palm-) vein datasets (with more than 500 palms) suitable for indexing experiments. Most datasets comprise only 50–100 subjects (100–200 palms). In order to fairly and comprehensively assess the computational workload reduction and scalability of indexing methods, large-scale data is absolutely essential. As such, entities (academic, commercial and governmental alike) that possess or are capable of collecting the requisite quantities of data could share their datasets with the academic community, thereby facilitating such evaluations. Another viable option is an independent benchmark (such as, e.g. FVC Indexing [6], IREX one-to-many [4] and FRVT 1:N [5] for fingerprint, iris and face, respectively), which could also generate additional interest (and hence research) in this field from both the academic and the commercial perspective. Lastly, the generation of synthetic data (e.g. finger veins [19]) is also a possibility, albeit on its own, it cannot be used as a substitute for real large-scale data.

Acknowledgements This work was partially supported by the German Federal Ministry of Education and Research (BMBF), by the Hessen State Ministry for Higher Education, Research and the Arts (HMWK) within the Center for Research in Security and Privacy (CRISP), and the LOEWE-3 BioBiDa Project (594/18-17).

References

1. Intel intrinsics guide: _mm_mul512_ps. https://software.intel.com/sites/landingpage/IntrinsicsGuide/#expand=3675,3675,3681&techs=AVX_512&text=_mm512_mul_ps
2. Intel intrinsics guide: _mm_mul_ps. https://software.intel.com/sites/landingpage/IntrinsicsGuide/#expand=3675,3675&techs=SSE&text=_mm_mul_ps
3. Polyu multispectral palmprint database. http://www.comp.polyu.edu.hk/~biometrics/MultispectralPalmprint/MSP.htm
4. Iris exchange (irex) (2017). https://www.nist.gov/programs-projects/iris-exchange-irex-overview
5. Face recognition vendor test (frvt) 1:n 2018 evaluation (2018). https://www.nist.gov/programs-projects/frvt-1n-identification
6. Fvc-ongoing indexing (2019). https://biolab.csr.unibo.it/fvcongoing/UI/Form/BenchmarkAreas/BenchmarkAreaFIDX.aspx
7. Abbas A, George LE (2014) Palm vein recognition and verification system using local average of vein direction. Int J Sci Eng Res 5(4):1026–1033
8. Baxter S (2011) Modern GPU—introduction to GPGPU—GPU performance. http://web.archive.org/web/20111007211333/, http://www.moderngpu.com/intro/performance.html
9. Cappelli R, Ferrara M, Maltoni D (2011) Fingerprint indexing based on minutia cylinder-code. IEEE Trans Pattern Anal Mach Intell 33(5):1051–1057
10. Casasent D, Psaltis D (1976) Position, rotation, and scale invariant optical correlation. Appl Opt 15(7):1795–1799
11. Credence Research: Biometrics technology market by technology (face recognition, hand geometry, voice recognition, signature recognition, iris recognition, afis, non-afis & others), end use vertical (government, military and defense, healthcare, banking and finance, consumer electronics, residential and commercial security, transportation and immigration & others)—growth, share, opportunities & competitive analysis, 2015–2022 (2016). http://www.credenceresearch.com/report/biometrics-technology-market
12. Daugman J (2000) Biometric decision landscapes. University of Cambridge, Computer Laboratory, Tech. rep
13. Daugman J (2003) The importance of being random: statistical principles of iris recognition. Pattern Recogn 36(2):279–291
14. Daugman J (2004) How iris recognition works. IEEE Trans Circ Syst Video Technol 14(1):21–30
15. Drozdowski P, Rathgeb C, Busch C (2017) Bloom filter-based search structures for indexing and retrieving iris-codes. IET Biom
16. Drozdowski P, Struck F, Rathgeb C, Busch C (2018) Benchmarking binarisation schemes for deep face templates. In: 2018 25th IEEE international conference on image processing (ICIP). IEEE, pp 191–195
17. Hao F, Daugman J, Zielinski P (2008) A fast search algorithm for a large fuzzy database. IEEE Trans Inf Forensics Secur 3(2):203–212
18. Hartung D, Olsen MA, Xu H, Busch C (2011) Spectral minutiae for vein pattern recognition. In: 2011 international joint conference on biometrics (IJCB). IEEE, pp 1–7
19. Hillerstrom F, Kumar A, Veldhuis R (2014) Generating and analyzing synthetic finger vein images. In: 2014 international conference of the biometrics special interest group (BIOSIG). IEEE, pp 1–9

20. India: Aadhaar issued summary. https://portal.uidai.gov.in/uidwebportal/dashboard.do
21. Indyk P, Motwani R (1998) Approximate nearest neighbors: towards removing the curse of dimensionality. In: Proceedings of the thirtieth annual ACM symposium on theory of computing. ACM, pp 604–613
22. Lim M, Teoh ABJ, Kim J (2015) Biometric feature-type transformation: making templates compatible for secret protection. IEEE Sig Process Mag 32(5):77–87
23. Lin S, Tai Y (2015) A combination recognition method of palmprint and palm vein based on gray surface matching. In: 2015 8th international congress on image and signal processing (CISP). IEEE, pp 567–571
24. Miura N, Nagasaka A, Miyatake T (2007) Extraction of finger-vein patterns using maximum curvature points in image profiles. IEICE Trans 90-D(8):1185–1194. http://dblp.uni-trier.de/db/journals/ieicet/ieicet90d.html#MiuraNM07
25. Mokroß BA (2017) Efficient biometric identification in large-scale palm vein databases. Master's thesis, Hochschule Darmstadt. https://dasec.h-da.de/wp-content/uploads/2017/12/Thesis-mokross-vein_indexing.pdf
26. Pearson K (1901) On lines and planes of closest fit to systems of points in space. Lond Edinb Dublin Philos Mag J Sci 2(11):559–572
27. Rathgeb C, Baier H, Busch C, Breitinger F (2015) Towards bloom filter-based indexing of iris biometric data. In: ICB. IEEE, pp 422–429. http://dblp.uni-trier.de/db/conf/icb/icb2015.html#RathgebBBB15
28. Rathgeb C, Busch C (2012) Multi-biometric template protection: Issues and challenges. In: New trends and developments in biometrics. IntechOpen
29. Tractica LLC: Biometrics market forecasts: Global unit shipments and revenue by biometric modality, technology, use case, industry segment, and world region: 2016–2025 (2017). https://www.tractica.com/research/biometrics-market-forecasts/
30. Transparency Market Research: Biometrics technology (face, hand geometry, voice, signature, iris, afis, non-afis and others) market—global industry analysis size share growth trends and forecast 2013–2019 (2014). https://www.transparencymarketresearch.com/biometrics-technology-market.html
31. Xu H, Veldhuis RN (2009) Spectral minutiae representations of fingerprints enhanced by quality data. In: IEEE 3rd international conference on biometrics: theory, applications, and systems, 2009. BTAS'09. IEEE, pp 1–5
32. Xu H, Veldhuis RN (2010) Binary representations of fingerprint spectral minutiae features. In: 2010 20th international conference on pattern recognition (ICPR). IEEE, pp 1212–1216
33. Xu H, Veldhuis RN (2010) Spectral minutiae representations for fingerprint recognition. In: 2010 Sixth international conference on intelligent information hiding and multimedia signal processing (IIH-MSP). IEEE, pp 341–345
34. Xu H, Veldhuis RN, Bazen AM, Kevenaar TA, Akkermans TA, Gokberk B (2009) Fingerprint verification using spectral minutiae representations. IEEE Trans Inf Forensics Secur 4(3):397–409
35. Xu H, Veldhuis RN, Kevenaar TA, Akkermans AH, Bazen AM (2008) Spectral minutiae: a fixed-length representation of a minutiae set. In: IEEE computer society conference on computer vision and pattern recognition workshops, 2008. CVPRW'08. IEEE, pp 1–6
36. Xu H, Veldhuis RN, Kevenaar TA, Akkermans TA (2009) A fast minutiae-based fingerprint recognition system. IEEE Syst J 3(4):418–427
37. Zezula P, Amato G, Dohnal V, Batko M (2006) Similarity search: the metric space approach, vol 32. Springer Science & Business Media
38. Zhang H, Liu Z, Zhao Q, Zhang C, Fan D (2013) Finger vein recognition based on gabor filter. In: Sun C, Fang F, Zhou ZH, Yang W, Liu ZY (eds) Intelligence science and big data engineering. Springer, Berlin, Heidelberg, pp 827–834
39. Zhou Y, Kumar A (2011) Human identification using palm-vein images. IEEE Trans Inf Forensics Secur 6(4):1259–1274

Chapter 10
Different Views on the Finger—Score-Level Fusion in Multi-Perspective Finger Vein Recognition

Bernhard Prommegger, Christof Kauba and Andreas Uhl

Abstract In finger vein recognition, the palmar view of the finger is used almost exclusively, with some exceptions where the dorsal view is utilised. Only little attention has been paid to all other views around the finger's longitudinal axis. We established a multi-perspective finger vein dataset comprising of views all around the finger's longitudinal axis, captured using our self-developed rotating multi-perspective finger vein capture device. The performance of the single views is evaluated using common finger vein recognition algorithms. Based on these single view scores, several score-level fusion experiments involving different fusion strategies are carried out in order to determine the best performing set of views and feature extraction methods to be fused in terms of recognition accuracy while minimising the number of views involved. Our experimental results show that the recognition performance can be significantly improved over the best performing single view one with as few as two views and two-feature extraction methods involved.

Keywords Finger vein recognition · Multi-perspective fusion · Biometric fusion · Score-level fusion · Multi-algorithm fusion · Multi-perspective finger vein capture device · Finger vein dataset

---

B. Prommegger (✉) · C. Kauba · A. Uhl
Department of Computer Sciences, University of Salzburg,
Jakob-Haringer-Str. 2, 5020 Salzburg, Austria
e-mail: bprommeg@cs.sbg.ac.at

C. Kauba
e-mail: ckauba@cs.sbg.ac.at

A. Uhl
e-mail: uhl@cs.sbg.ac.at

A. Uhl et al. (eds.), *Handbook of Vascular Biometrics*, Advances in Computer Vision and Pattern Recognition, https://doi.org/10.1007/978-3-030-27731-4_10

10.1 Introduction

Finger vein recognition as one representative of vascular pattern biometrics deals with the vascular pattern inside the fingers of a human. Since one of the first mentions of finger veins as a biometric trait in academia by Kono [1] in 2000, they have received much attention not only from academia but also from industry. Commercial off-the-shelf (COTS) finger vein capture devices, as well as most research papers solely, use the palmar (front side of the finger) view in combination with light transmission (the light source and the image sensor are placed on opposite sides of the finger) as illumination source. Multi-perspective finger vein recognition deals with two or more arbitrary perspectives around the finger's longitudinal axis. Despite the advantages of multi-perspective finger vein biometrics over single view ones, these additional perspectives have not got much attention so far. Moreover, there is no publicly available multi-perspective finger vein dataset yet.

This chapter is based on our previous work [2] where we designed a novel, multi-perspective finger vein capture device in order to establish the first multi-perspective finger vein data set. This dataset comprises of images captured all around the finger's longitudinal axis in 1° steps. Based on this dataset, each of the different views has been evaluated individually and some simple fusion experiments have been conducted. The main focus of this chapter is on the fusion of multiple perspectives and feature extraction methods in order to determine the best performing combination in terms of recognition accuracy by employing a more advanced multi-sample score-level fusion scheme as well as by applying further fusion strategies in terms of view and feature combinations. We analyse all possible pairs and triples of perspectives and all possible combinations of the used feature extraction methods. In addition, we combine the best results of our multi-perspective and multi-algorithm fusion experiments to one single combined fusion. Our main goal is to minimise the number of views and feature extraction methods involved, while maximising the recognition accuracy. A typical multi-perspective finger vein capture device contains one image sensor and one light source situated at the right position per desired view. The more views are to be captured, the more camera and illumination modules have to be equipped, thus increasing the production costs, the complexity and the overall size of the finger vein capture device. If the number of desired perspectives is further increased, the construction of a suitable capture device is no longer feasible without the need of rotating parts. Our current multi-perspective finger vein capture device is such a rotating device, making it more susceptible to malfunctions and external influences than a capture device containing no rotating parts. Moreover, the capturing time is increased as the capture device has to rotate all around the finger. Hence, it is beneficial to reduce the number of different views to be captured to a minimum in order to reduce the complexity and production costs of the biometric capture device and to avoid the need for a rotating device while still preserving the advantages of a multi-perspective capture device.

The rest of this chapter is structured as follows: Sect. 10.2 starts with a description of multi-perspective finger vein biometrics including related work regarding other views than the palmar and dorsal one in finger vein recognition. Our multi-perspective finger vein capture device design is described in Sect. 10.3. Section 10.4 introduces our multi-perspective finger vein dataset captured with the aforementioned device. Section 10.5 gives an overview of biometric fusion in general followed by related work on biometric fusion in finger vein recognition. Section 10.6 explains our experimental set-up, including the finger vein recognition tool chain as well as the fusion framework we utilised and lists the experimental results, followed by a results discussion. Section 10.7 concludes this paper an gives and outlook on future work.

10.2 Multi-perspective Finger Vein Biometrics

The majority of the available finger vein recognition schemes as well as all available COTS finger vein capture devices deal with the palmar (also called ventral) view of the finger. There are only some exceptions where the dorsal view is used. Raghavendra and Busch [3] proposed the first dorsal finger vein acquisition and a complete recognition tool chain including several different feature extraction schemes. In the scope of the PROTECT project (http://www.projectprotect.eu), we acquired the first publicly available dorsal finger vein dataset [4] using the predecessor of our open-source finger vein capture device. In [5], we established a larger dorsal finger vein dataset captured using both of our proposed open-source finger vein capture devices, which design is decribed in Chap. 3 of this book [6].

There are more views around the finger than the palmar and dorsal one that can be captured. A single finger is an elliptical cylinder-shaped object, hence, there are all possible views around its longitudinal axis (360° of rotation) available. Multi-perspective finger vein recognition describes the use of two or more of these perspectives around the finger's longitudinal axis. Multi-perspective finger vein recognition has several advantages over the single perspective one: The vein patterns of the palmar and dorsal view as well as of the perpendicular views are independent from each other [7]. By fusing more than one perspective that is independent enough from each other (i.e. the rotation angle between the single perspectives has to differ enough for the perspectives to be independent of each other), the overall recognition performance can be increased easily. Tome et al. [8, 9] showed that finger vein and hand vein recognition systems are susceptible to a simple type of presentation attack. By using a paper printout of the vein pattern, they were able to successfully spoof several finger vein capture devices. This paper printout is a flat, 2D representation of the vein pattern. If a biometric capture device takes finger vein images from different perspectives, such simple 2D printout attack finger vein presentation will not be identified as bona fide finger vein presentation. Thus, a multi-perspective finger vein capture device is successfully able to prevent this kind of presentation attack. However, multi-perspective finger vein recognition bears some disadvantages too: The biometric capture devices get more complex, either more than one camera and illumination module are needed, or the capture device has to be build in a rotating manner. This leads to higher production costs of multi-perspective capture devices and especially rotating capture devices are more error prone due to the moving parts. Another disadvantage is the bigger size of a multi-perspective capture device compared to single perspective ones. The multiple image sensors/illuminator modules or the rotating parts need more space than just a single image sensor in combination with one illumination module.

Lu et al. [10] proposed a multi-perspective finger vein recognition system using two cameras. The cameras are placed at an angle of 60° next to each other, each camera is located 30° apart from the palmar view. They applied feature—as well as score-level fusion using the two views captured simultaneously by the two cameras and were able to improve the recognition performance of the single view ones. Zhang et al. [11] employed a binocular stereoscopic vision device to do 3D point cloud matching of hand veins and knuckle shape. Their capture device set-up consist of two cameras, placed in a relative position of about 45° next to each other, each one equipped with an NIR-pass filter. There is only a single light transmission illuminator placed underneath the palm of the hand. The 3D point clouds are generated by extracting information from the edges of the hand veins and knuckle shapes and then compared utilising a kernel correlation method, especially designed for unstructured 3D point clouds. The authors claim that their proposed method is faster and more accurate compared to 2D vein recognition schemes. In [12] the authors propose a 3D hand vein capturing system based on a rotating platform and a fixed NIR camera. The camera is located above the hand, the hand is put on a handle with an integrated light transmission illuminator. This handle is mounted on a rotating plate. Then the plate rotates around the z-axis. However, the degree of rotation is limited due to the limited movement of the hand in this position. A 3D point cloud is generated from the single view images and matched using kernel correlation. This should help to overcome hand registration and posture change problems present in hand vein recognition if only 2D vein patterns/images are available.

Nevertheless, true multi-perspective finger vein recognition (evaluating more than two different views around the finger) has not been investigated so far, except for our previous work [2]. One reason herefore might be the lack of available multi-perspective finger vein datasets. In order to acquire such a dataset a suitable biometric capture device, able to capture the different views to be acquired, is essential. Capturing these additional perspectives could be done by utilising either a COTS capture device or one of the capture devices proposed in other works by simply turning the finger around its longitudinal axis. However, it is difficult to position the finger in the correct rotational angle. Thus, rotating the finger itself implies the disadvantage of an inaccurate rotation angle and deviations in the rotation angle across different iterations, leading to a low repeatability and a low quality dataset. In order to acquire a suitable multi-perspective finger vein dataset comprising of images captured in several, defined perspectives, either a biometric capture device comprising of several cameras and illumination modules, able to capture more than one view simultaneously, or a rotating biometric capture device able to capture these views consecutively, is necessary. If only a limited number of perspectives are involved, a suitable biometric capture device can be built without any rotating parts, just by equipping an individual image sensor and an associated illumination module per desired

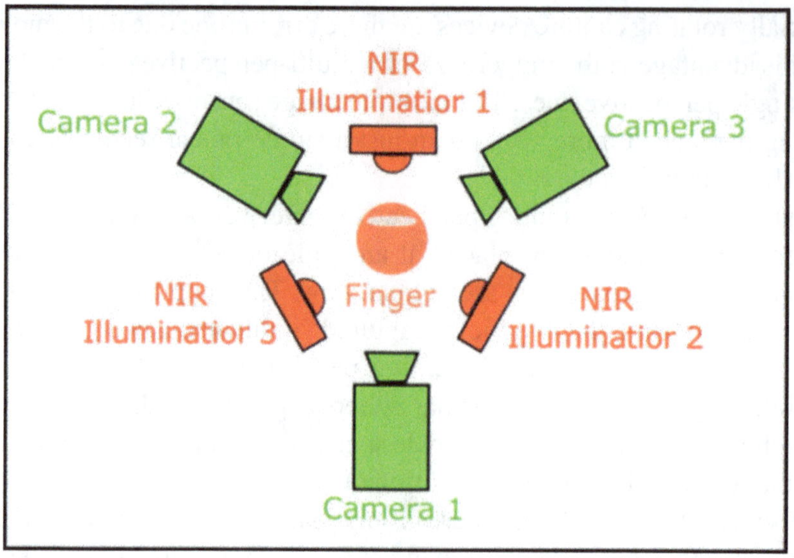

Fig. 10.1 Multi-perspective finger vein set-up exhibiting three different perspectives based on three image sensors and three illuminator modules

view (an example with three different views is shown in Fig. 10.1). The illumination intensity has to be adjusted per view as the path to penetrate the finger is different for each individual view, requiring a stronger or weaker illumination depending on the distance. If more perspectives are desired, rotating the capture device around the finger while the finger remains in a fixed position during the acquisition process is the only feasible option.

The design and construction of a practicable biometric capture device is a complex task. Furthermore, the actual data acquisition is a tedious and time-consuming work. In our previous paper [2], we proposed a rotating multi-perspective finger vein capture device that is able to capture the finger all around its longitudinal axis (360°). We established a multi-perspective finger vein dataset consisting of 252 individual fingers. Based on this dataset, we evaluated the different views around the finger in 5° steps and concluded that the palmar followed by the dorsal one achieve the best single view recognition performance. Moreover, we applied a simple score-level fusion strategy and showed that the recognition performance can be improved by fusing more than one view. This chapter is an extension of our previous work. Based on our proposed multi-perspective finger vein capture device, we refine and extend our previous results by the following:

- Improving the recognition tool chain to improve the single view results, especially the ROI extraction and by including a new recognition scheme proposed by Matsuda et al. [13].
- Employing an advanced score-level fusion framework (BOSARIS [14]).
- Exploring different fusion strategies in terms of which views to include in the fusion.
- Evaluating multi-algorithm fusion per view (fusion is done at score level).

- Combining multi-perspective and multi-algorithm fusion.

The purpose of our evaluations is to maximise the recognition performance while minimising the number of single views involved. If only a limited number of views is involved, the capture device can be built without the need for any rotating parts just by equipping an individual image sensors and an illumination modules per desired view. A biometric capture device which relies on rotating parts is more error prone and more susceptible to external influences, the rotation speed can vary due to increased friction or it can be completely blocked if the finger is not properly inserted. The rotating parts exhibit a higher wear than non-moving parts and are thus more prone to failures. Moreover, the acquisition time of a rotating capture device is higher compared to a non-rotating one as the device needs to rotate around the finger in order to capture the different views. Furthermore, a capturing device exhibiting a closed box design, where the capture subject has to put his finger into a "black hole" poses psychological disadvantages and leads to discomfort. Hence, in practical applications of multi-perspective finger vein biometrics only a capture device built in a non-rotating and open manner is feasible. Consequently, we aim to identify the best combination of two or three views to include in the fusion in order to build such a multi-perspective finger vein capture device based on fixed, non-moving parts only. Figure 10.1 shows the schematic principle of such a capture device for three perspectives: it consists of three independent image capturing pairs, each consisting of its own NIR illumination module and NIR camera.

10.3 Multi-perspective Finger Vein Capture Device

In order to acquire a multi-perspective finger vein dataset, we designed a custom finger vein capture device tailored to this purpose. For more details on the general principle of a finger vein scanner and the vascular pattern recognition basics, the interested reader is referred to our open finger vein scanner chapter [6] and the introductory chapter [15] of this book, respectively. Our multi-perspective finger vein capture device is able to capture images from all around the finger's longitudinal axis (360°). An illustration of the unwrapped finger vein capture device with all its parts labelled can be seen in Fig. 10.2. Its outside dimensions (of the aluminium frame including the rotating part) are 258 × 325 × 455 mm (width × height × depth). The rotating part (rotator) has a diameter of 380 mm. The device consists of an aluminium frame, where the rotation motor and the control board are located and a rotator, which rotates around the finger. The rotating part is connected to a stepping motor by two cogwheels. These cogwheels have a gear ratio of 1:5/3 (motor to rotor). The stepping motor (SY42STH47-1684A [16]) which drives the rotator has 200 steps per full rotation (1.8° per single step). We use a micro-stepping of $1/16$, thus one step corresponds to 0.0675°. Hence, it is possible to capture a maximum of 5333 different perspectives of the finger. Located on the right side of the device is the image sensor, an IDS Imaging UI-1240ML-NIR industrial NIR-enhanced camera

[17]. It has a max. resolution of 1280 × 1024 pixels, a max. frame rate of 25 fps and is equipped with a Fujiflim HF9HA-1b 9 mm 2/3" wide-angle lens [18]. To reduce the influence of ambient light, an additional NIR long-pass filter (MIDOPT LP780 [19], with a cut-off wavelength of about 750 nm and a useful range of 780–1000 nm) is mounted on top of the camera lens. The illumination module is located on the opposite side of the image sensor (the left side in Fig. 10.2). Our multi-perspective finger vein capture device is based on the light transmission principle. Instead of typical NIR LEDs the illumination module consists of five NIR laser modules with a peak emission wavelength of 808 nm placed in a strip. Laser diodes have several advantages over LEDs, especially, if the finger is not placed directly on top of the illumination module as mentioned in Chapter [6]. Due to the rotating principle of the biometric capture device, it is not possible for the finger to touch the illumination module, which prevents the use of LEDs without impacting the image quality. Each laser module consists of a NIR laser diode, a control PCB for the laser diode and a housing with a focus-adjustable lens. The plane of focus of the laser modules is set at the axis of rotation where the finger is placed, leading to the highest possible amount of illumination at the position of the finger. Each of the laser modules can be brightness controlled separately (by adjusting the operating current) and independently, enabling a uniform illumination along the whole finger. The finger is put into the capture device at its axis of rotation (in the centre of the image in Fig. 10.2). A fingertip stabiliser (a custom 3D printed part which inside is shaped like the outside of a fingertip) is located at the inside bottom of the rotating part and a height-adjustable finger trunk stabiliser, which is basically a wooden plate with a hole in the middle is located above the rotating part. These finger stabilisers help to reduce finger movements during one acquisition run to a minimum. The finger is put into the capture device so that its tip is inside the fingertip stabiliser, pushing the height-adjustable plate down. Afterwards, this individual finger height is fixed using four screws on the top of the scanner and remains fixed until a new finger is to be captured. All parts except the stepping motor, the camera including the lens and NIR long-pass filter) are self-designed and manufactured by ourselves, including several 3D printed parts, the wooden housing of the rotating part, the housing of the control board, the control board itself and the aluminium frame.

The acquisition process is semi-automated. At first, the subject has to put the finger into the device. Then the height of the finger trunk stabiliser plate has to be adjusted and the operator initiates one capturing run (360° around the finger's longitudinal axis), starting the automated part of the acquisition process.

During this automated data acquisition part, the illumination for each laser module is set automatically by the help of an automated brightness control algorithm. This algorithm tries to achieve a sufficient and uniform illumination along the finger in order to obtain an optimal image contrast. It evaluates the average grey level of the image area around the centre of each laser module i ($GL^i_{current}$) and compares this value to a predefined target grey level (GL^i_{target}). If there is a deviation between these two values, the operating current of the corresponding laser module is adjusted: $I^i_{corr} = \frac{GL^i_{target} - GL^i_{current}}{GL_{\max}} \cdot \frac{I_{\max}}{2 \cdot n}$, where $GL_{\max}$ is the maximum grey value (255 for 8 bit

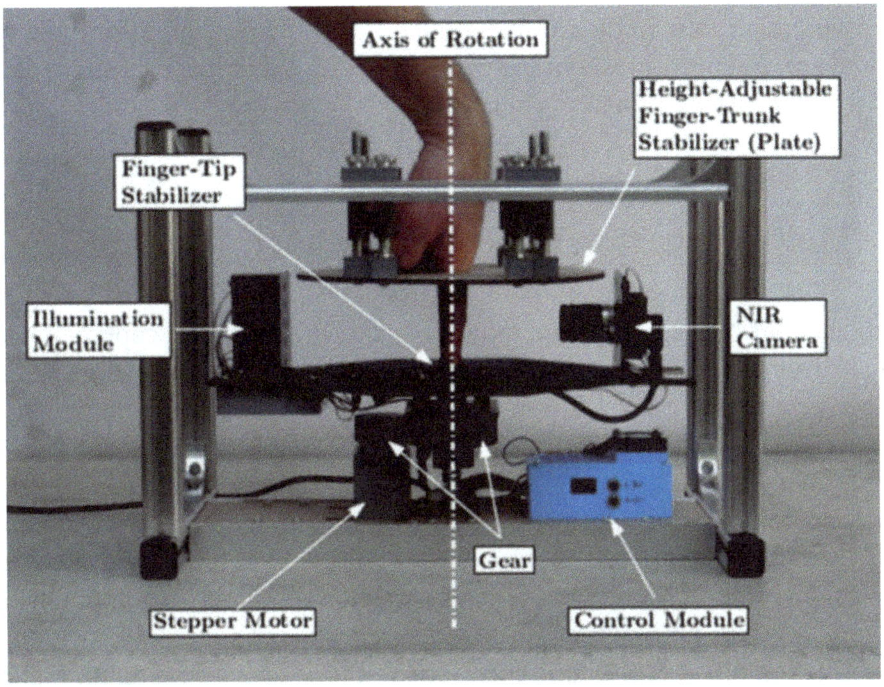

Fig. 10.2 Self-designed multi-perspective finger vein capture device (image originally published in [2], ©2018 IEEE)

images) and n is the number of the current iteration. Initially, all laser modules are set to half of their maximum operating current I_{max} (corresponding to its maximum intensity). The algorithm finishes in at most $\log_2(I_{max})$ steps.

After the optimal intensity level for each laser module is set, the video sequence recording is started. The rotator starts to rotate around the finger and an indicator LED is turned on to synchronise the video stream. The rotation is stopped when the rotator reaches its start position again and at this point the indicator LED is turned off. A few frames later the video sequence recording is stopped too. The videos are recorded in the MP4 container format using the MJPG video codec with a frame rate of 15 fps and YUV colour space. The speed of the rotation and the video frame rate are synchronised such that a defined resolution (in degree) of images per full rotation (video frames) is met and the desired degree steps can later be extracted from single, individual frames without the need for temporal interpolation. The set illumination intensity remains the same for the whole capturing run until all perspectives are captured. This ensures the compatibility and comparability of the single, individual perspectives to each other. The different projections in 1° steps corresponding to single video frames are then extracted out of the video sequence. The capture device's indicator LED is utilised to synchronise the video frames with the beginning and the end of the rotation. In theory, there should be 361 images per full rotation run (0° and 360° is captured separately). Due to slight variations in the rotation speed and the video frame rate, there are between 357 and 362 frames instead of 361. Thus, it became necessary to map the frame with the minimum deviation from the desired rotational angle to the corresponding perspective, resulting in a maximum deviation of 0.5° from the desired rotation angle.

10.4 Multi-perspective Finger Vein Dataset

With the help of our self-designed multi-perspective finger vein capture device, we established a multi-perspective finger vein dataset in order to be able to conduct our multi-perspective score-level fusion experiments. This dataset currently consists of 63 subjects, 4 fingers per subject (index and middle finger of the left and right hand) and 5 runs per finger. The thumb and the pinky finger were not included as they are too short compared to the index and middle. The ring finger was skipped as well as it turned out to be too uncomfortable for the subjects to put it in the capture device for the whole capturing process. The finger was removed and inserted in the device again after each run. During each run, a video sequence of a full 360° rotation with a target resolution of 1° (each frame corresponds to a 1° step) is captured. Figure 10.3 shows the capture device during the data acquisition process. The acquisition process takes approximately 45 s per capture attempt, hence it takes about 15 min to capture a single subject, including all four fingers, 5 runs per finger. The whole dataset consists of $63 \times 4 \times 5 \times 361 = 454{,}860$ images in total. The extracted video frames have a resolution of 1024×1280 pixels and are 8-bit greyscale images stored in png format.

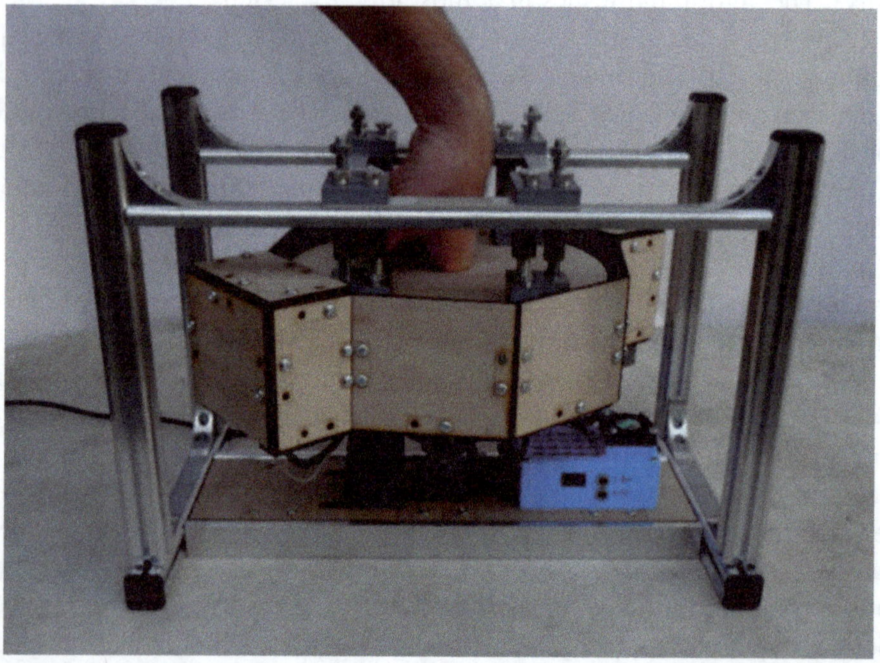

Fig. 10.3 Data acquisition with the multi-perspective finger vein capture device (image originally published in [2], ©2018 IEEE)

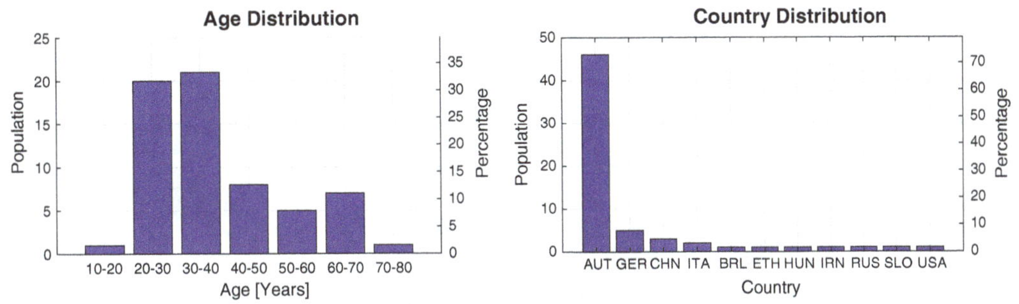

Fig. 10.4 Age (left, image originally published in [2], ©2018 IEEE) and country of origin distribution (right) for the multi-perspective finger vein dataset

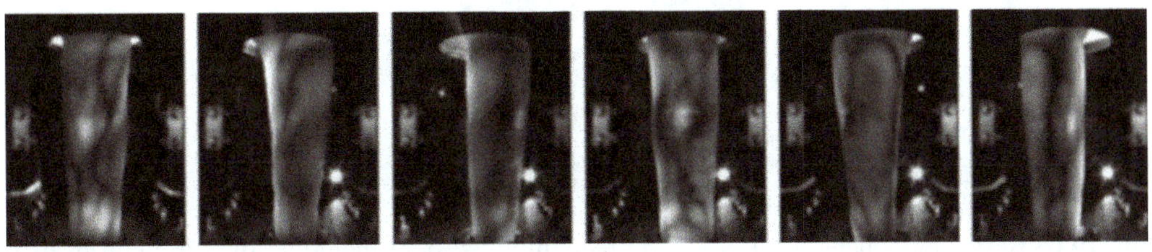

Fig. 10.5 Multi-perspective finger vein dataset example images, from left to right: 0°, 60°, 120°, 180°, 240°, 300° (image originally published in [2], ©2018 IEEE)

The finger is always located in the centre area of the image, thus the images are then cropped to 650×1280 pixels to retain the usable finger area only. Figure 10.5 shows some example images in different perspectives from 0° to 300°. It can be clearly seen that the visible vein lines vary among the different perspectives. The black part at the centre top area in the images results from the finger trunk stabilisation plate, which is pushed in further or less depending on the length of the finger.

The gender distribution of the 63 subjects is almost balanced with 27 (42.7%) female and 36 (57.3%) male subjects. The subjects represent a good cross section among all different age groups, as the age distribution, depicted in Fig. 10.4 left, shows. There is only a slight overhang among the 20–40 year old subjects. The youngest subject was 18 and the oldest one 79 years old. The subjects are from 11 different countries (Austria, Brazil, China, Ethiopia, Hungary, Iran, Italy, Russia, Slovenia, USA) while the majority of subjects are white Europeans (73%). The origin country distribution is depicted in Fig. 10.4 right. The dataset is available for research purposes and can be downloaded at http://wavelab.at/sources/PLUSVein-FR/.

10.5 Biometric Fusion

Like every typical biometric recognition system, a finger vein recognition system consists of five steps/modules: image acquisition, preprocessing, feature extraction, comparison and the final decision. This recognition tool chain is depicted in Fig. 10.6.

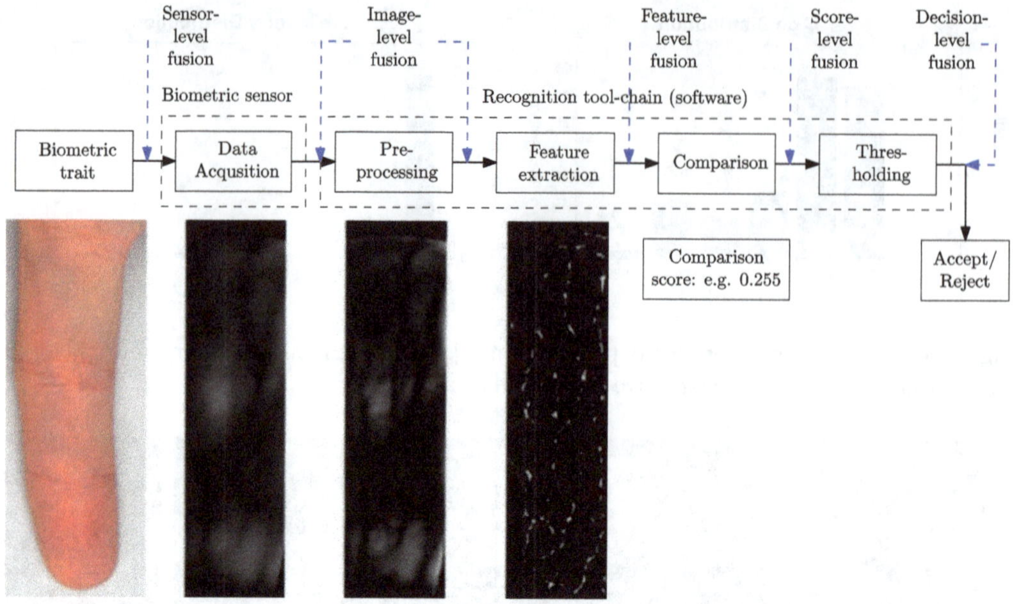

Fig. 10.6 Basic components of a biometric recognition system including the different levels of fusion by taking the example of finger veins (second row)

There are two modes, enrolment and authentication. Authentication includes both, verification as well as identification. During enrolment one or several finger vein images are captured and the extracted biometric templates are stored in a database. During authentication a new template is extracted from a newly captured image and compared against one or more templates stored in the database. The result is a comparison score. Finally the decision module outputs for the capture subject an "accept" or "reject" depending on the evaluation of the comparison score against a threshold.

According to the ISO/IEC TR 24722:2015 standard [20], biometric fusion can be regarded as a combination of information from multiple sources, i.e. sensors, characteristic types, algorithms, instances or presentations in order to improve the overall system's performance and to increase the systems robustness.[1] Biometric fusion can be categorised according to the level of fusion and the origin of input data. The different levels of fusion correspond to the components of a biometric recognition system:

- Sensor-level fusion: is also called multisensorial fusion and describes using multiple sensors for capturing samples of one biometric instance [20]. This can either be done by the sensor itself or during the biometric processing chain. An example of sensor-level fusion are finger vein images that have been captured using different wavelength of near-infrared light and fused by merging the different wavelength bands to obtain one single output image. This can be done by a single biomet-

[1]Recognition performance is just one aspect. PAD performance (robustness against presentation attacks) is another aspect to keep in mind.

ric capture device. Another example is the acquisition and fusion of fingerprint images captured using optical, electrostatic and acoustic sensors.
- Image-level fusion: during data acquisition, the biometric capture device itself might be able to capture multiple samples of the same biometric trait and combine those samples to a single output sample. Image-level fusion corresponds to fusing several images captured from the same biometric trait but not necessarily within the sensor device. Image-level fusion can also be applied after preprocessing so the input to the fusion module is the preprocessed images. One example of image-level fusion is a finger vein capture device that captures more than one finger simultaneously and combines the images from the individual fingers into a single output image, which is also called multi-instance.
- Feature-level fusion: during template creation, several meaningful features, describing the biometric trait's properties, are extracted from the preprocessed images and stored in a feature vector, commonly denoted as biometric template. Feature-level fusion combines several such feature vectors to form a new, higher dimensional feature vector which should represent a subject's biometric traits in a different and more discriminant way. Dimensionality reduction methods are beneficial in combination with feature-level fusion to extract the most significant and discriminative features and to save storage space.
- Score-level fusion: during the comparison step, two templates are compared against each other and a similarity or dissimilarity score is calculated. Score-level fusion combines two or more of those scores into a new, single score. The input scores can originate from different comparison modules. They should either be compatible with each other (e.g. all are similarity scores exhibiting the same range of possible values) or else a score normalisation technique has to be applied during the fusion.
- Decision-level fusion: the output of the decision module is a binary one, which can be interpreted as match/non-match or accept/reject. Decision-level fusion combines two or more of these binary output decisions to a single output one. Usually, majority of voting schemes are employed at decision-level fusion. Note that at the decision level, the least information is available (only a binary decision), compared to the other levels of fusion.

Regarding the origin of the input data, biometric fusion can be categorised into:

- Multi-modal fusion: multiple different types of biometric traits from the same subject is fused together. A popular example is the fusion of information from fingerprints and finger veins or iris and periocular.
- Multi-instance fusion: multiple instances of the same type of biometric trait are fused together. For example, several finger vein images from different fingers of the same subject or information from both irises of one subject are fused together.
- Multi-presentation fusion: multiple samples of the same instance of biometric trait is captured and fused, e.g. several finger veins of the same finger is captured and fused together.

- Multi-algorithmic fusion: multiple feature representations are generated using the same input data, e.g. several different finger vein features are extracted with different algorithms from the same input image and fused together.

There is no direct dependency between the origin of the input data and the level of fusion that is employed.

10.5.1 Fusion in Finger Vein Recognition

This subsection provides an overview of related work in biometric fusion involving finger veins. The first subsection discusses several single modality fusion approaches. The second subsection lists multi-modality fusion approaches which include finger veins among other biometric traits.

10.5.1.1 Single Modality (Finger Vein Only) Fusion

Table 10.1 gives an overview of related work on single modality fusion in finger vein recognition, i.e. only data from finger veins is utilised during fusion at different levels. The table lists the level of fusion applied, the origin of the input data to the fusion, the number of images and subjects contained in the used dataset, the reported biometric performance (EER if not stated otherwise) and the year of publication, sorted according to fusion level and year of publication. All the related works listed in Table 10.1 are described in the following.

Yang and Jia [21] presented a multispectral finger vein fusion approach by fusing enhanced finger vein images captured in different wavelengths. They applied an image denoising method followed by image registration and a brightness adjustment prior to the image-level fusion of images captured in six different wavelength bands. Their image-level fusion strategy operates pixel-wise and is based on an improved regional energy integration method in the spatial domain. The comparison scores are obtained by phase-only correlation. They achieved a minimum EER of 11.02% by fusing all six bands.

Guan et al. [22] applied feature-level fusion to Wavelet transform based vein image features. The high- and low-frequency Wavelet features are obtained independently and then fused by a simple nearest-neighbour rule. They did several experiments using different training set sizes and arrived at a maximum recognition rate of 94.35%. Yang and Zhang [23] proposed a feature-level scheme using global and local features. The local features are extracted using a Gabor filter framework and the global ones using 2D invariant moments. The fusion itself is performed by a weighted fusion strategy based on canonical correlation analysis. They reported a lowest FAR of 1.15% and a FRR of 2.47% for their fused features. Gupta and Gupta [24] proposed a feature-level fusion approach of two distinct binary vein features (the features are binary vein images). The first type of features is extracted using repeated

Table 10.1 Related work in single modality finger vein fusion, ordered according to fusion level and year of publication

Reference	Fusion level	Origin	Images/subjects	Performance (EER)	Year
[21]	Image	Multi-sample	5760/60	11.02%	2012
[22]	Feature	Single-sample	2044/292 (fingers)	Recognition rate: 94.35%	2009
[23]		Single-sample	640/64	FAR: 1.15%, FRR: 2.47%	2010
[24]		Single-sample	3132/156	2.98%	2015
[26]		Single-sample	1440/60	0.19%	2016
[27]	Score	Single-sample	1200/100	0.28%	2010
[28]		Multi-instance	1440/80	0.83% (fusion of 3 fingers)	2012
[29]		Single-sample	4000/50	0.011%	2012
[30]		Single-sample	4080/30	1.56%	2013
[31]		Single-sample	4260/71 (680/85)	2.63%/0.78%	2013
[32]		Single-sample	3804/634 (fingers)	2.84%	2013
[33]		Single-sample	1440/60	0.27%	2014
[2]		Multi-sample	454860/63	0.04%	2018
[35]	Decision	Single-sample	1620/54	FAR: 0.0086% at 1% FRR	2009

line tracking [25]. The second type of features is obtained by multi-scale matched filtering. A variational approach is proposed to fuse both feature extraction methods. The score calculation is conducted by first aligning the two input images with the help of an affine transformation. The affine transformation matrix is found using a gradient descent optimisation based on a sum of squared differences cost function. The authors report a minimum EER of 2.98%. Kauba et al. [26] used different binary vein feature extraction schemes and applied several advanced feature-level fusion schemes (COLLATE, STAPLE, STAPLER), which were originally proposed for segmentation of magnetic resonance imaging (MRI) brain images together with simple average and majority voting based fusion in the finger vein domain. They conducted two different sets of experiments exhibiting two different fusion strategies. In the first one, only a single feature extraction scheme was used with a set of several different feature extraction parameters per input image. The output features obtained for the individual parameters where then fused together. In the second set, different feature extraction schemes were applied per input image and their outputs were fused. The authors showed that both strategies (single feature extractor as well as multiple feature extractors) lead to an improvement in the recognition accuracy. The best EER achieved for the first strategy was 0.29% and for the second one 0.19% compared to the best EER for the single features of 0.47%.

Zhou and Kumar [27] proposed a score-level fusion scheme for palm vein recognition based on multiple representations. They extracted four different kinds of features, two based on their proposed representations. The first ones are using Hessian phase information from the vein images, the second ones using localised Radon transform to generate a kind of orientation encoding. The other two ones are based on Ordinal Code and a Laplacian representation, respectively. These four feature representations are compared individually to get the output scores which are then fused by applying a heuristic fusion rule. The authors arrived at a minimum EER of 0.28%. Yang et al. [28] did a score-level fusion of extracted features from multiple fingers of the same subject. They used LBP based features and a Hamming distance based comparison module to generate the scores. These scores are then fused using a simple sum rule in combination with triangular norm. Their best reported EER of 0.83% was achieved by fusion ring, middle and index finger using Frank's t-norm. In [29] Kang Park used local as well as global vein features in combination with score-level fusion. The local features are extracted by the help of LBP and compared using the Hamming distance. The global ones are Wavelet transform based features which are compared using the Euclidean distance. The comparison scores are then fused with the help of a radial basis function based support vector machine. Park reported a best achieved EER of 0.0011%. Liu et al. [30] proposed a score-level fusion scheme including pixel as well as super-pixel based finger vein features. LBP, vein pattern structure based and vein minutiae based features form the pixel based features. The super-pixel based image segmentation is done using the SLIC method. Histogram, gradient and entropy features extracted from the super-pixel based segmentation are then combined and form the super-pixel based features. An Euclidean distance based comparison of both individual features is performed to calculate the comparison scores. These scores are normalised and fused by using the weighted average fusion strategy. The weights are tuned to achieve an optimal EER. They reported a minimum EER of 1.56%. Qin et al. [31] applied score-level fusion to multiple representations of the same finger vein pattern. The vein pattern is represented by three different types of features: finger vein shape based, finger vein orientation based and SIFT feature point based features. The former two are subregion partitioned and subregion compared with the help of the SIFT based features, which are treated individually, leading to three comparison scores. The scores are normalised using the Z-score normalisation and then fused by applying a weighted-sum rule based fusion as well as a support vector machine based fusion. They achieved minimum EERs of 2.63 and 0.78%. Lu et al. [32] proposed a score-level fusion scheme based on Gabor features. Usually, the individual filter responses obtained from the Gabor filter bank are weighted and/or directly combined into a single output feature. Instead, the authors extract and compare the output of each single Gabor filter channel separately.

The corresponding comparison scores are then fused using a simple weighted-sum rule. The authors were able to get an EER of 2.84% using their proposed method. Kauba et al. [33] tested different preprocessing cascades in order to improve the individual performance of the single finger vein feature extraction schemes. Binary and SIFT/SURF based features were compared individually to obtain the output scores. These scores were normalised using Min-Max normalisation and then fused using weighted sum/product/average/minimum/maximum fusion rule. The best fusion rule in terms of lowest EER was chosen accordingly. They were able to achieve a minimum EER of 0.27% with the help of score-level fusion compared to a minimum EER of 0.47% for the single features. In our previous work [2], we performed a multi-sample score-level fusion of several different perspectives around the finger. Therefore, we established a multi-perspective finger vein dataset with the help of our self-designed multi-perspective finger vein capture device, described in Sects. 10.4 and 10.3, respectively. Several different perspectives starting from 2 up to 72 were fused at score-level for 4 different kinds of extracted features using a simple sum-rule based fusion. We achieved a best overall EER of 0.039% for the fusion of 18 different views and Maximum Curvature [34] features.

Yang et al. [35] proposed a decision-level fusion approach based on three different finger vein feature representations. They extracted a topological feature, a local moment based feature and a vein shape based feature. These features were compared individually by means of a nearest cosine classifier outputting the class which the input feature belongs to. These output decisions were then fused by the help of the Dempster–Shafer algorithm. The authors reported a lowest FAR of 0.0086% at a FRR of 1%.

10.5.1.2 Multi-modality Fusion Including Finger Veins

In addition to the single modality fusion approaches, several multi-modality fusion approaches including finger veins as one of the involved biometric traits were proposed. Table 10.2 gives an overview of these approaches, including the reference to the original publication, the fusion level, the involved biometric traits, the number of subjects in the dataset used, the reported performance (EER if not stated otherwise) and the year of publication. Most approaches fuse finger-related biometrics, including fingerprint, finger texture, finger shape, finger knuckle and finger veins. There are only two approaches involving other biometrics than finger-related ones. Razzak et al. [36] fused face and finger veins and He et al. [37] fused face, fingerprints and finger veins. Both applied score-level fusion. The number of involved traits varies between at least two and at most four. Fingerprint is the most prominent one [37–46] besides finger veins that is included in the fusion followed by finger texture [38, 43, 45, 47–49] as the second most prominent one and finger shape [42, 43, 50–52] as the third one. The majority of the approaches is based on feature-level and score-level fusion, there are only two decision-level fusion approaches compared to eight

Table 10.2 Related work in finger vein fusion, multi-modality fusion involving finger veins, ordered according to fusion level and year of publication

References	Fusion level	Involved traits	Subjects	Performance (EER)	Year
[40]	Feature	Fingerprint, finger veins	40	1.85% FRR and 0.97% FAR	2011
[44]		Fingerprint, finger veins	64	1.35% FAR at 0% FRR	2012
[46]		Fingerprint, finger veins	40	1.485%	2012
[48]		Finger texture, finger veins	220	0.45%	2012
[49]		Finger texture, finger veins	220	0.435%	2014
[43]		Finger texture, finger shape, fingerprint, finger veins	100	0.00796%	2015
[45]		Finger texture, fingerprint, finger veins	300	0.415%	2016
[51]	Score	Finger shape, finger veins	816	0.075%	2010
[37]		Face, fingerprint, finger veins	510	99.8% GAR at 0.01% FAR	2010
[36]		Face, finger veins	35	5% FAR and 92.4% GAR	2010
[47]		Finger texture, finger veins	312	0.08%	2012
[52]		Finger shape, finger veins	120	4%	2013
[50]		Finger shape, finger veins	492	1.78%	2014
[42]		Finger shape, fingerprint, finger knuckle, finger veins	100	0.0319%	2014
[38]		Finger texture, fingerprint, finger veins	378	0.109%	2015
[41]	Decision	Fingerprint, finger veins	33	1.86%	2011
[39]	Feature/decision	Fingerprint, finger knuckle, finger veins	165	0.04%	2016

feature-level and eight score-level ones. All proposed fusion approaches showed a significant improvement in the recognition accuracy of the fusion compared to using finger veins only.

10.6 Experimental Analysis

This section describes the experimental part of this chapter. At first, the used subset of the dataset introduced in Sect. 10.4 is explained. Afterwards, the finger vein recognition tool chain which is employed during the experimental analysis is described. This is followed by a presentation of the fusion strategy and the applied score-level fusion framework. Afterwards, the experimental protocol to determine the FAR and FRR and consequently the recognition performance in terms of EER/FMR1000/ZeroFMR is explained. Then the results of the individual fusion strategies are given and discussed. Finally, this section is concluded with an overall results discussion.

10.6.1 Finger Vein Dataset

To reduce the amount of data during the fusion, we used a subset of the multi-perspective finger vein dataset [2] only. Not all 360 different perspectives are evaluated, but only each fifth one is considered. Thus, there is a total of 73 different perspectives ($\frac{360^\circ}{5^\circ/step} = 72$ plus the last one which is $360^\circ = 0^\circ$ again results in 73). All 63 capture subjects, 4 fingers per subject and 5 images per view and finger are considered. This results in a total of $73 \times 63 \times 4 \times 5 = 91{,}980$ images instead of 454,860 for the total dataset.

10.6.2 Finger Vein Recognition Tool chain

The finger vein recognition tool chain includes all steps of a biometric recognition system starting with the extraction of the Region of Interest (ROI) to preprocessing, feature extraction and comparison. The input data are the images of the different individual perspectives acquired from the 3D capture device, the output is a comparison score that can be used to determine whether the provided finger belongs to a certain (enrolled) data subject or not.

ROI Extraction

Prior to the ROI extraction, the finger is aligned and normalised. The alignment should place the finger always in the same position in the image, independent of the relative position of the finger during the acquisition. To achieve this, the finger lines (edge between finger and the background of the image) are detected and the centre

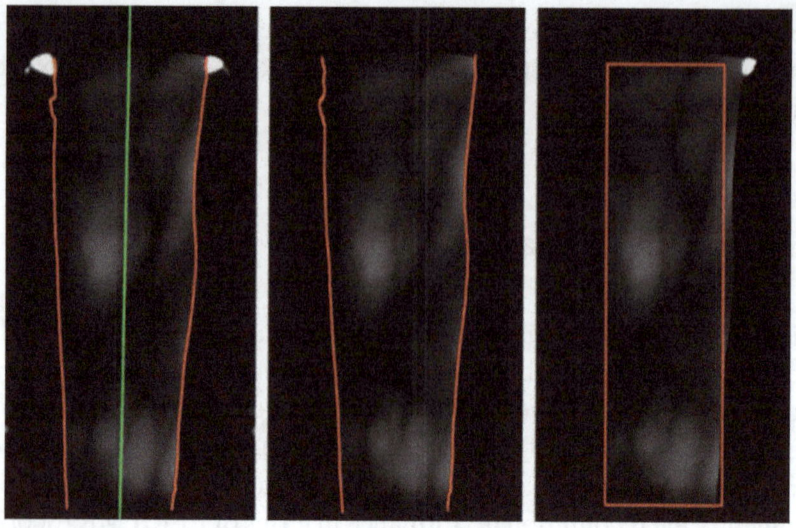

Fig. 10.7 ROI extraction process (images originally published in [2], ©2018 IEEE)

line (in the middle of the two finger lines) is determined. Afterwards, the centre line of the finger is rotated and translated in a way that it is placed in the middle of the image and the image region outside of the finger is masked by setting the pixels to black. The final step is to extract a rectangular ROI of a fixed size (1100×300 pixel) from a fixed position. The three steps are visualised in Fig. 10.7. The implementation used is based on the method proposed in [53].

Preprocessing

Preprocessing tries to enhance the low contrast and improve the image quality. In the following the preprocessing methods, we employed in our finger vein recognition tool chain are explained.

Simple **CLAHE** [54] or other local histogram equalisation techniques are most prevalent according to the literature for this purpose. A localised contrast enhancement technique like CLAHE is a suitable baseline tool to enhance the vein images as they exhibit unevenly distributed contrast. CLAHE has an integrated contrast limitation (clip limit) which should avoid the amplification of noise.

High-Frequency Emphasis Filtering (**HFEF**) [55], originally proposed for hand vein image enhancement tries to enhance the vein images in the frequency domain. At first, the discrete Fourier transform of the image is computed, followed by the application of a Butterworth high-pass filter of order n. The authors originally proposed to use a global histogram equalisation but we decided to apply CLAHE instead.

Circular Gabor Filter (**CGF**) as proposed by Zhang and Yang [56] is another finger vein image enhancement technique which is rotation invariant and achieves an optimal joint localisation in both, the spatial and the frequency domain. The authors originally suggested to use grey level grouping for contrast enhancement but we again apply CLAHE instead.

Furthermore, the images were resized to half of their original size, which not only speeded up the comparison process but also improved the results. For more details on the preprocessing methods, the interested reader is referred to the authors' original publications.

Feature Extraction

We used five different feature extraction methods. The first three techniques discussed aim to extract the vein pattern from the background resulting in a binary image (vein pattern based methods) followed by a comparison of these binary images using a correlation measure. All algorithms are well-established finger vein recognition algorithms. We used the publicly available implementations published in [5].

Maximum Curvature (MC [34]) aims to emphasise only the centre lines of the veins and is therefore insensitive to varying vein widths. The first step is the extraction of the centre positions of the veins by determining the local maximum curvature in cross-sectional profiles obtained in four directions: horizontal, vertical and the two oblique directions. The cross-sectional profile is determined based on the first and second derivates. Then each profile is classified as either being concave or convex, where only the local maxima belonging to a concave profile indicate a vein line. Afterwards, a score according to the width and curvature of the vein region is assigned to each centre position and recorded in a matrix called locus space. Due to noise or other distortions, some pixels may not have been classified correctly at the first step, thus the centre positions of the veins are connected using a filtering operation in all four directions taking the 8-neighbourhood of pixels into account. The final binary output image is obtained by thresholding of the locus space using the median as a threshold.

Principal Curvature (PC [57]): At first the gradient field of the image is calculated. In order to prevent the unwanted amplification of small noise components, a hard thresholding which filters out small gradients by setting their values to zero is done. Then the gradient at each pixel is normalised to a magnitude of 1 to get a normalised gradient field. This normalised gradient field is smoothed by applying a Gaussian filter. The next step is the actual principal curvature calculation. The curvatures are obtained from the Eigenvalues of the Hessian matrix at each pixel. The two Eigenvectors of the Hessian matrix represent the directions of the maximum and minimum curvature and the corresponding Eigenvalues are the principal curvatures. Only the bigger Eigenvalue which corresponds to the maximum curvature among all directions is used. The last step is a threshold based binarisation of the principal curvature values to arrive at the binary vein output image.

Gabor Filter (GF [47]): Gabor filters are inspired by the human visual system's multichannel processing of visual information and have been widely used in biometrics. A Gabor filter is a Gaussian kernel function modulated by a sinusoidal plane wave. Kumar and Zhou [47] proposed a Gabor filter based finger vein extraction approach. Therefore, a filter bank consisting of several 2D even symmetric Gabor filters with different orientations (in $\frac{\pi}{k}$ steps where k is the number of orientations) is created. k feature images are extracted by filtering the vein image using the different filter kernels contained in the Gabor filter bank. The final feature image is obtained by summing all the single feature images from the previous step and thresholding the resulting feature image. This image is then post-processed using morphological operations to remove noise to get the final binary vein output image.

In contrast to the vein pattern based techniques described above, two key-point based techniques were used. Key-point based techniques try to use information from the most discriminative points as well as considering the neighbourhood and context information around these points by extracting key-point locations and assigning a descriptor to each detected key-point location.

The first one is a **Scale-Invariant Feature Transform** (SIFT [58]) based technique with additional key-point filtering along the finger boundaries to suppress information originating from the finger shape instead of the vascular pattern. This technique was originally proposed by Kauba et al. [33].

Deformation-Tolerant Feature Point Matching (DTFPM [13]): The second key-point based technique replaces the conventional SIFT descriptor and key-point detector by vascular pattern tailored ones. This method is robust against irregular shading and vein deformations due to posture changes. At first, the authors apply a technique originally proposed by Yang and Yang [59] for enhancing the vein images. Then a minimum-curvature map is calculated from the enhanced vein images based on Eigenvalue analysis. The feature point locations are determined from this curvature image (smaller Eigenvalue) at any point where the vein shape is non-linear. The feature descriptor takes the vein shape around the key-point location into account and is extracted from the so-called vein pattern map (larger Eigenvalue). The feature vector contains a quantification of the different vein directions inside a variable-sized window around the key-point location. The descriptor is normalised with the help of a finger shape model in a way that the descriptor area becomes smaller the closer the key-point location is to the finger boundaries. The authors claim that their proposed method is tolerant against several different types of finger posture changes, e.g. longitudinal finger rotation, translations and bending of the finger.

Comparison

For the comparison of the binary feature images we extended the approach in [25] and [34]. As the input images are neither registered to each other nor aligned, the correlation between the input image and in x- and y-direction shifted versions of the reference image is calculated. The maximum of these correlation values is normalised and then used as the final comparison score.

The SIFT features are compared by finding their nearest neighbours/best correspondences and calculating a score based on the distances between the corresponding key-points.

DTFPM employs a deformation tolerant comparison strategy by using non-rigid registration. At first, the correspondences between the key-points in the two images for comparison are found. These correspondences are filtered using a local and global histogram technique based on the relative distances between the corresponding key-points. After this filtering step, the key-point coordinates of one of the involved feature vectors are transformed by applying a non-rigid transformation based on an outlier-robust thin-plate spline model as proposed in [60]. Afterwards, the correspondences between the adjusted key-points are determined again. These updated correspondences are filtered by a comparison of the descriptor distances with fixed thresholds. The final comparison score is determined as the ratio of the matched points and the sum of the number of detected key-points in both images.

10.6.3 Score-Level Fusion Strategy and Toolkit

We applied three different fusion strategies. The first strategy involves the fusion of all possible combinations of pairs of distinct views (which are $\binom{N}{k} = \binom{73}{2} = 2628$ combinations, 73 different views are considered) as well as all possible three tuples of distinct views (which are $\binom{73}{3} = 62196$ combinations) for each of the five-feature extraction methods. As motivated in the introduction, it is beneficial if the number of involved views is as little as possible to reduce the complexity and the production costs of the biometric capture device and to be able to build such a device without any moving parts. Thus, only pairs and three tuples are considered here. The second strategy employs the fusion of all possible combinations of feature extraction methods per view. There are $\binom{5}{2} + \binom{5}{3} + \binom{5}{4} + \binom{5}{5} = 26$ combinations per perspective, resulting in a total of 10,830 different fusion combinations. Here, our aim is to identify the best combination of features for each individual view which does not necessarily have to be the same across all the different views. The third strategy is a combination (fusion) of the best results obtained during the first and second one.

All three fusion strategies are applied at score-level. The second strategy could be applied at feature-level too, but not for all the involved feature extraction types as they are not compatible with each other. The feature-level fusion of MC, PC and GF is possible while the fusion of DTFPM and SIFT with any of the other feature extraction types is not possible. Feature-level fusion is not possible for the first strategy at all, as there is no meaningful way to combine the features of different perspectives, e.g. by merging the extracted vein lines or using majority voting as the visible vein lines differ for each view. Score-level fusion usually performs better than decision-level fusion, as there is more information available at the score level and there are more variants to fuse the individual scores. Hence, we decided to apply score-level fusion in all three fusion strategies.

In our previous work [2], a simple sum based fusion rule, without any weights for the input scores, was applied. In this work, a more advanced score-level fusion approach, namely the BOSARIS toolkit [14] is utilised. BOSARIS provides a MATLAB based framework for calibrating, fusing and evaluating scores from binary classifiers and has originally been developed for automatic speaker recognition. It can be applied to any biometric trait where two alternate classes are distinguished (genuine/impostor). The toolkit provides several functionalities, e.g. a normalised Bayes error rate plot, ROC and DET plots, including efficient algorithms to generate these plots for large score files, logistic regression solutions for the fusion of several subsystems, solutions for calibration (mapping scores to likelihood ratios), a logistic regression optimiser and an efficient binary score file format. During this work, we only harness the fusion capabilities of BOSARIS though. BOSARIS needs a supervised training phase where combination weights are trained based on logistic regression in order to fuse multiple input systems into a single output one providing well-calibrated log-likelihood-ratios. This is achieved by employing a general purpose, unconstrained convex optimisation algorithm, which is used to train the logistic regression fusion and calibration methods. Hence, BOSARIS needs a training set of data to find the optimal combination of weights for the actual fusion in order to minimise the classification error and thus to maximise the recognition performance based on the fused output scores. BOSARIS has the option to set a target prior according to the costs of a miss and a false alarm for the training phase of the fusion. We set this target prior to 0.5 assuming that the costs of a miss and a false alarm are both weighted equally.

10.6.4 Evaluation Protocol

The experiments are split into four parts: in the first part, we analyse the recognition performance of all single perspectives. Every perspective is considered as a separate dataset. Here, we do not perform any cross-projection comparison. The images are processed as described in Sect. 10.6.2 and 73 projections all around the finger in 5° steps are extracted. The recognition performance is quantified in terms of the EER as well as the FMR1000 (the lowest FNMR for FMR = 0.1%) and the ZeroFMR (the lowest FNMR for FMR = 0%). The performance values are calculated for each single perspective. For the parameter optimisation, the data set is divided into two roughly equal-sized subsets. The division is based on the contained subjects, i.e. all fingers of the same person are in one subset. Each subset is used to determine the parameters which are then applied to the other subset. This ensures a 100% separation of the data used for determining the optimal parameters and the actual test set. The necessary comparison scores for the FAR/FRR calculation, which is the basis for the EER/FMR1000/ZeroFMR calculation, are determined according to the test protocol of the FVC2004 [61]: to compute the genuine scores, all possible genuine comparisons are done. Instead of computing all possible impostor scores only the first image of a finger is compared against the first image of all other fingers. The final results are evaluated based on the combined scores (genuine and impostor) of both test runs. The parameter optimisation is executed only for the palmar dataset. The same parameter settings are also applied for the experiments on the other perspectives. The resulting number of comparisons for both subsets are listed in Table 10.3. All performance-related result values are given in percentage terms, e.g. 0.04 means 0.04%.

In the second part of our experiments, we fuse different features originating from the same feature extraction method but extracted from different perspectives as described in Sect. 10.6.3. The third part of the experiments is dedicated to a multi-algorithm fusion. We fuse all possible combinations of the five employed feature extraction methods at score level based on the scores obtained during the first part of the experiments, resulting in 2-, 3-, 4- and 5-tuples. In the last part, we com-

Table 10.3 Number of comparisons for each subset

Name	Subjects	Genuine	Impostor	Total
Subset 1	32	1280	8128	9408
Subset 2	31	1240	7626	8866
Total	63	2520	15,754	18,274

bine the two strategies of multi-perspective and multi-algorithm fusion. Based on the results from the two individual fusion strategies we determine the best possible combinations/fusion of perspectives and feature extraction methods. All four parts are evaluated using the same protocol to determine the performance figures. For all fusion experiments, the input data are the comparison scores generated during the single perspective experiments. We apply a fivefold cross-validations procedure, where we use every fold once for the training of the fusion module. The determined fusion parameters are applied to the test data consisting of the four remaining folds. The final results are evaluated based on the combined scores (genuine and impostor) of all five test runs.

We provide the scores files for each individual perspective and feature extraction methods as well as a script to run BOSARIS and generate all the fused scores files and performance figures we used during our experiments. These files and the scripts can be downloaded at http://www.wavelab.at/sources/Prommegger19b/.

10.6.5 Single Perspective Performance Results

The single perspective analysis for MC, PC, GF and SIFT have already been carried out in our previous work [2]. We added DTFPM as an additional key-point based recognition scheme. We had to change our ROI extraction to make the ROIs compatible with DTFPM. Our previous ROI approach selected a fixed size rectangle placed at the centre of the finger, independent of the finger's width. DTFPM is sensitive to parts of the finger outline and background areas that are contained in the input images and expects the finger width normalised to the ROI height. Thus, we updated our ROI extraction scheme as described in Sect. 10.6.2 and recalculated the results for the already evaluated algorithms based on the new ROIs. Note that due to the new ROIs these updated results are different from our previous work. Figure 10.8 top shows the results in terms of EER. There are two lines for every method: the thin line shows the actual EER value, the thicker line is a smoothed version calculated based on the EER using a moving average filter of size 5, which should highlight the trend of the recognition performance. The images captured of neighbouring views contain quite a similar vein structures (note that our step-width is 5°), thus the recognition performance is similar too. The best results are obtained around the palmar (0°, 360°) and dorsal (180°) region. The results of the perspectives in-between are inferior. This

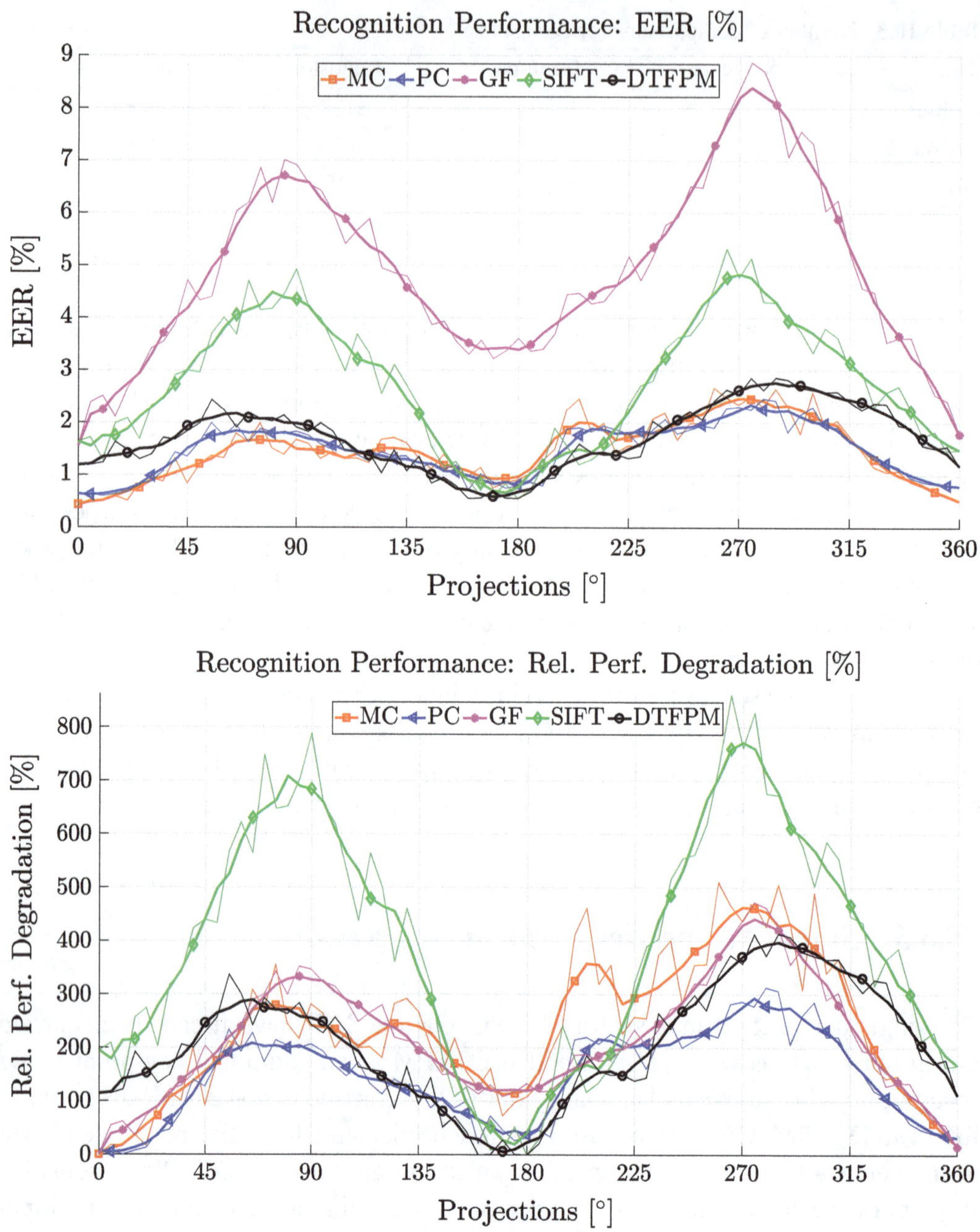

Fig. 10.8 Recognition performance for different projections: EER (top) and relative performance degradation in relation to the best performing view (bottom)

is due to the fact, that they contain fewer visible vein lines and thus fewer vein information than the palmar and dorsal view. Figure 10.9 shows the original ROI, the ROI after preprocessing and the extracted features (using MC) for the views 0°, 90°, 180° and 270°. It reveals that the 90° and 270° views contain less vein information than the palmar and dorsal view. Moreover, the vein extraction algorithms include some features related with the texture of the finger. This is especially visible at 180° where

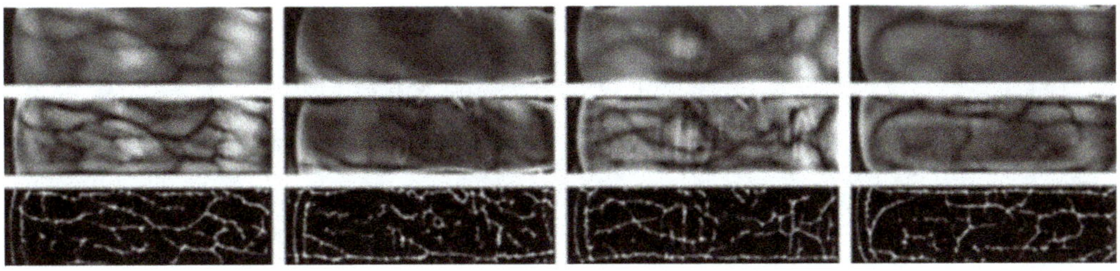

Fig. 10.9 ROI (first row), enhanced images (second row) and extracted MC features (third row) for different projections (originally published in [2], ©2018 IEEE). Note that there are less vein lines visible for 90° and 270° compared to 0° and 180°

some of the features are related with the finger knuckles instead of veins. These features are visible as horizontal lines in the feature image.

For the key-point based algorithms, especially SIFT, the palmar region exhibits a better performance than the other perspectives as well, but the best performance is achieved around the dorsal region. For SIFT this can be explained based on the employed preprocessing: only image (vein) enhancement and no vein extraction (binarisation) ahead of the SIFT key-point calculation is applied. Hence, the non-vein finger texture information is not suppressed in the input images of SIFT. Especially, the structure of finger knuckles seem to contain a lot of additional information which SIFT is able to exploit during feature extraction. Finger knuckles have been introduced by Zhang et al. [62] as an independent biometric characteristic. Yang et al. [63] experienced a similar behaviour. They fused the finger texture of the dorsal view with the vein structure of the palmar view which leads to an improvement in the recognition performance. Consequently, the additional information originating from the finger knuckles and the finger texture present at the dorsal view leads to the superior performance of SIFT for the dorsal view compared to the palmar one.

Table 10.4 lists the information regarding the best and worst perspective for each feature extraction method. MC, PC and GF perform best around the palmar view (note that 360° = 0°), while SIFT and DTFPM perform best around the dorsal view. The overall best result was achieved for MC at 0° with an EER of 0.44% (±0.15) where the number in brackets is the confidence interval. For all feature extraction methods, the worst results can be reported around 270°. The Relative Performance Degradation (RPD) of the different perspectives is visualised in Fig. 10.8 bottom. The RPD, stated in Eq. (10.1), is calculated with respect to the minimum EER ($EER^{FT}_{\min}$) reached for a certain feature extraction method, where $EER^{FT}_{perspective}$ is the EER of the current perspective. The maximum performance degradation across the different algorithms is between 200 and 800%.

$$RPD^{FT}_{perspective} = \frac{EER^{FT}_{perspective} - EER^{FT}_{\min}}{EER^{FT}_{\min}} \tag{10.1}$$

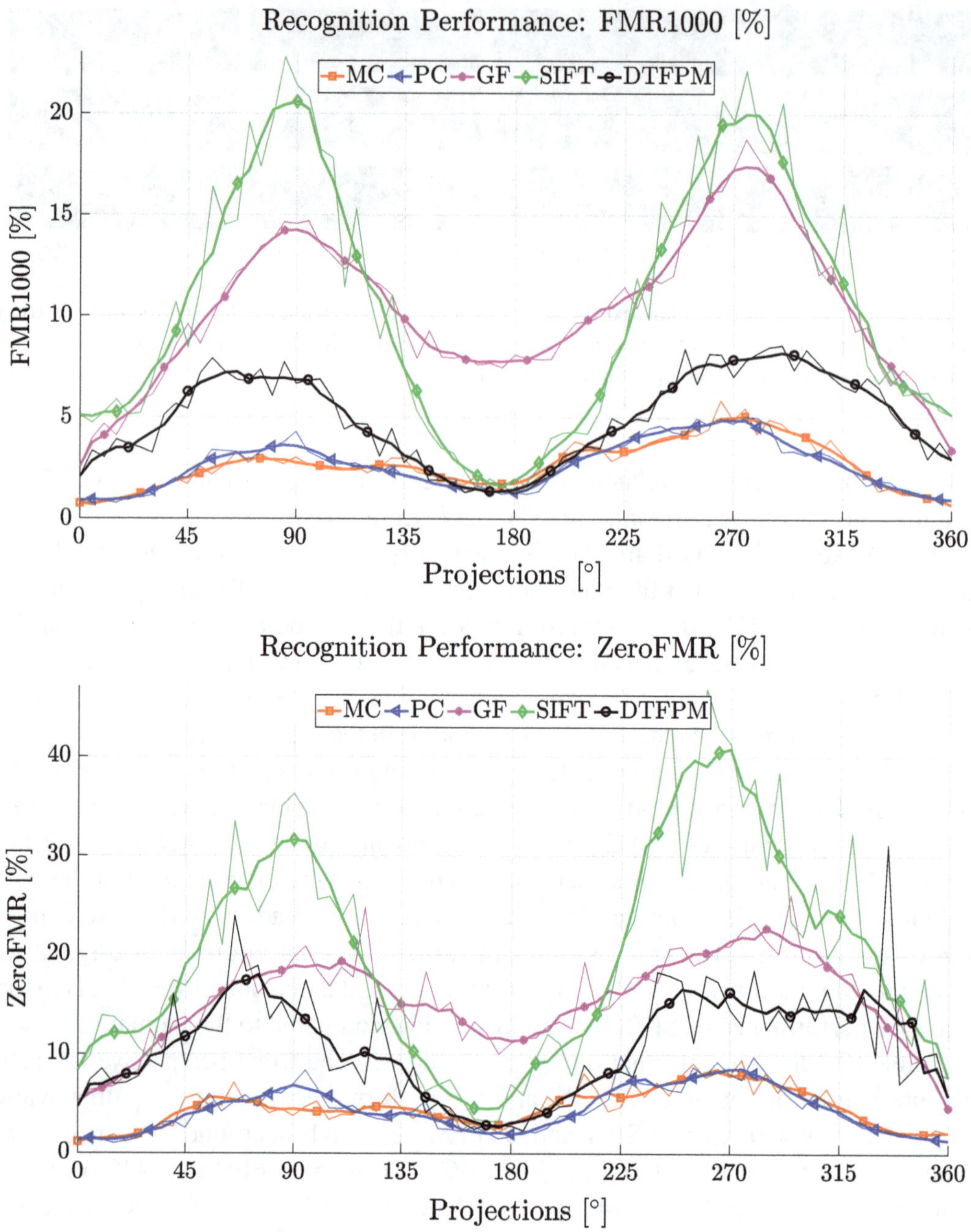

Fig. 10.10 Recognition performance among the different projections: FMR1000 (top), ZeroFMR (bottom)

The FMR1000 and ZeroFMR are visualised in Fig. 10.10 top and bottom, respectively. They follow the same trend as the EER: a good performance around the palmar and dorsal region and an inferior one for the views in between.

Table 10.4 Best/worst single perspective results per feature extraction method and single perspective

Feature type	Best perspective				Worst perspective			
	View	EER	FMR1000	ZeroFMR	View	EER	FMR1000	ZeroFMR
MC	0°	**0.44 (±0.15)**	0.76	1.15	260°	2.67 (±0.37)	4.46	7.69
PC	10°	0.60 (±0.18)	0.87	1.35	280°	2.47 (±0.36)	5.02	9.79
GF	0°	1.55 (±0.28)	2.54	5.13	275°	8.87 (±0.65)	18.76	22.54
SIFT	180°	0.55 (±0.17)	1.35	6.98	265°	5.33 (±0.53)	20.67	42.98
DTFPM	160°	0.56 (±0.17)	1.31	3.13	285°	2.87 (±0.38)	8.51	12.56

10.6.6 Multi-perspective Fusion Results

In the second part of our experiments, we analyse the impact of fusing the extracted features of the same feature extraction method from multiple perspectives (MPF). In detail, we evaluate the fusion of all possible pairs and three tuples.

The first part of this section deals with the fusion of all possible pairs. Figure 10.11 shows heat maps of the EER for all combinations per feature extraction method (top row: MC, PC, bottom row: GF, SIFT and DTFPM). The perspectives involved in the fusion are plotted on x- and y-axis, whereas the performance in terms of EER is visualised using a colour scheme from light/white which corresponds to a low EER (good performance) to dark/red which corresponds to a high EER (bad performance). The actual logarithmic scale is given in the colour bar on the right side of the plots. Note that the results are symmetric with regard to the main diagonal (45°). This diagonal corresponds to the single perspective performance results and is visible as dark line (high EER) in all five plots.

According to the performance analysis of the single perspectives (Sect. 10.6.5), the palmar and dorsal region perform best. Although, there are slight variations among the different feature extraction methods, the results obtained from the single perspectives are confirmed by the two-perspective fusion: a combination of two perspectives including the palmar (close to 0°, 360°) or dorsal (close to 180°) region always results in a good recognition performance. A fusion of two views in-between those two regions result in an inferior performance. For MC, PC and GF the EER for all fusion combinations including the palmar (area along the outer edges of the plot) and dorsal view (cross lines in the centre) perform better (light, white to yellow colours) than fusion combinations without these views (dark, orange to red colours), achieving the best results when both regions are fused (light, white colour).

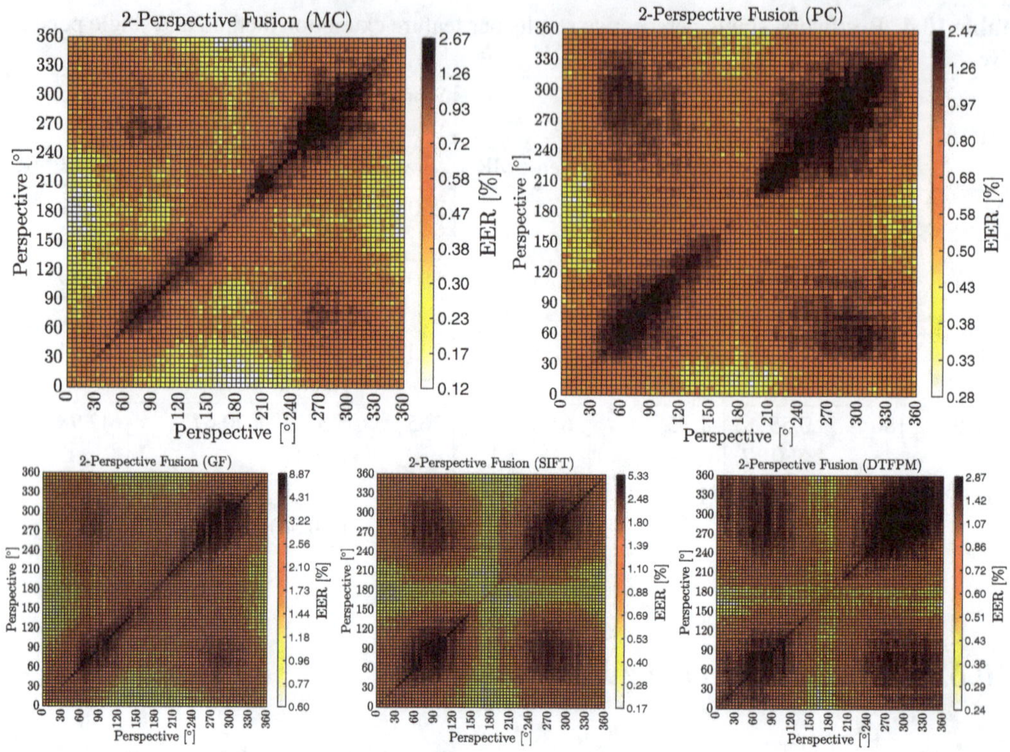

Fig. 10.11 Recognition performance for two-view fusion. Top row: MC (left), PC (right), bottom row: GF (left), SIFT (middle) and DTFPM (right)

Both key-point based methods show a different behaviour. The fusion of the palmar and dorsal region is still superior to all other fusion combinations, but SIFT and DTFPM perform well if the dorsal perspective is included in the fusion in general. This can also be seen in the plots as the 180° cross shows light, white to yellow colours which indicates a good performance. For SIFT, this is even more pronounced than for DTFPM.

Table 10.5 lists the best results in terms of EER, FMR1000 and ZeroFMR for each feature extraction method in detail. MC when fusing 0° and 180° achieves the overall best performance with an EER of 0.12%. For the evaluation of the results, the single perspective baseline EER and the relative performance increase (RPI) with respect to the baseline EER, as calculated in Eq. (10.2), are stated. The performance increase compared to the best single view result is between 110% (PC) and 270% (MC), which corresponds to a 2–3.5 times lower EER than the single perspective performance, respectively.

$$RPI = \frac{EER_{Baseline} - EER_{Fusion}}{EER_{Fusion}} \tag{10.2}$$

In addition to all pairs, all possible triples are evaluated. Table 10.6 shows the five best performing combinations per feature extraction method. Again the single perspective baseline EER and the relative performance increase is included. The highest

Table 10.5 Best two-perspective fusion results per feature extraction method. Best result is highlighted **bold font**. For comparability also the single perspective baseline EER and the relative performance improvement (based on the single perspective performance) is included

Feature type	2 Perspective fusion					Single perspective		Rel. Perf.
	View 1	View 2	EER	FMR1000	ZeroFMR	View	EER	Incr. [%]
MC	0°	180°	**0.12 (±0.08)**	0.12	0.16	0°	0.44	**264.90**
PC	10°	190°	0.28 (±0.12)	0.36	0.56	10°	0.60	113.14
GF	140°	360°	0.60 (±0.18)	0.80	1.56	0°	1.55	156.48
SIFT	165°	205°	0.17 (±0.09)	0.36	1.63	180°	0.55	229.72
DTFPM	0°	160°	0.24 (±0.11)	0.32	1.55	160°	0.56	132.27

recognition performance improvement is between 150% for PC and 1100% for MC which is in any case better than the best two-perspective fusion (see Table 10.5). The overall best result with an EER of 0.036% is achieved using MC when fusing the 5°, 170° and 235° view.

Table 10.6 also includes the perspectives of interest. It is striking, that once again a lot of combinations include perspectives close to the palmar (0°, 360°) and dorsal (180°) regions. Thus, we additionally analysed the occurrence of the palmar and dorsal view in the top 25 results for each feature extraction method. All angles within a certain range around 0° and 180° are mapped to the palmar and dorsal region, respectively. Three different mapping ranges are evaluated: ±15° (345° – 15°, 165° – 195°), ± 20° (340°–20°, 160° –200°) and ± 25° (335°–25°, 155° –205°). The results are presented in Table 10.7. It turns out that the best performing individual region (palmar for MC, PC, GF and dorsal for SIFT and DTFPM) is present in most of the top 25 fusion combinations. At a mapping range of ±25° it is even included in at least 96% of the top 25 results. For this mapping range also the opposite region is part of at least 80% of the combinations, except for GF (only 24%). For GF, this can be explained by the big performance difference of palmar (~1.5%) and dorsal region (~3.6%).

In order to be able to decide whether a three-perspective fusion is beneficial compared to a two-perspective approach, one way is to calculate the significance of the recognition performance improvement. We use the method proposed in [64] to calculate a boundary for the significance from the achieved EERs. Table 10.8 lists the χ^2 values in detail. The following translations of χ^2 values into p_v values can be used to interpret the values stated in the table: $\chi^2 = 6.6$ corresponds to $p_v = 0.01 (\equiv 1\%)$, $\chi^2 = 7.9$ to $p_v = 0.005 (\equiv 0.5\%)$ and $\chi^2 = 10.8$ to $p_v = 0.001 (\equiv 0.1\%)$. Thus, all performance improvements exhibiting $\chi^2 > 6.6$ are regarded as significant. The resulting χ^2 values indicate that a fusion of two and three perspectives lead to

Table 10.6 Recognition performance for three-view fusion: five best results per feature extraction method. Best result per feature extraction method is highlighted **bold font**. For comparability also the single perspective baseline EER and the relative performance improvement (based on the single perspective performance) is included

Feature type	3 Perspective fusion						Single perspective		Rel. Perf.
	View 1	View 2	View 3	EER	FMR1000	ZeroFMR	View	EER	Impr. [%]
MC	5°	170°	235°	**0.036 (±0.04)**	0.040	0.240	0°	0.44	**1111.78**
	0°	210°	235°	0.036 (±0.04)	0.040	0.120			1107.27
	10°	165°	215°	0.039 (±0.05)	0.040	0.159			1019.25
	20°	160°	235°	0.039 (±0.05)	0.040	0.040			1014.94
	165°	235°	355°	0.039 (±0.05)	0.040	0.159			1014.94
PC	10°	175°	200°	**0.238 (±0.11)**	0.401	0.602	10°	0.60	**150.21**
	20°	205°	235°	0.239 (±0.11)	0.319	0.638			149.65
	175°	235°	360°	0.239 (±0.11)	0.399	0.518			149.65
	140°	190°	360°	0.239 (±0.11)	0.282	0.524			149.59
	155°	210°	360°	0.239 (±0.11)	0.399	0.839			149.45
GF	125°	225°	360°	**0.284 (±0.12)**	0.401	1.325	0°	1.55	**446.48**
	90°	205°	360°	0.313 (±0.13)	0.638	1.794			394.98
	75°	140°	360°	0.321 (±0.13)	0.442	1.165			383.32
	120°	220°	355°	0.321 (±0.13)	0.758	1.475			383.09
	120°	200°	360°	0.321 (±0.13)	0.481	0.882			382.82
SIFT	165°	205°	350°	**0.058 (±0.05)**	0.040	0.635	180°	0.55	**857.58**
	20°	170°	210°	0.075 (±0.06)	0.040	0.714			643.62
	170°	205°	350°	0.081 (±0.06)	0.079	0.476			585.30
	170°	205°	335°	0.081 (±0.06)	0.079	0.635			585.30
	140°	205°	350°	0.081 (±0.06)	0.079	0.714			585.30

(continued)

Table 10.6 (continued)

Feature type	3 Perspective fusion						Single perspective		Rel. Perf.
	View 1	View 2	View 3	EER	FMR1000	ZeroFMR	View	EER	Impr. [%]
DTFPM	5°	160°	280°	**0.159 (±0.09)**	0.559	1.837	160°	0.56	**249.88**
	0°	180°	295°	0.162 (±0.09)	0.439	1.276			243.31
	15°	160°	295°	0.162 (±0.09)	0.439	1.637			243.04
	0°	180°	185°	0.165 (±0.09)	0.437	1.033			237.24
	0°	180°	245°	0.169 (±0.09)	0.439	2.396			228.78

Table 10.7 Analysis of the occurrence of palmar and dorsal views per feature extraction method in the 25 best three-perspective fusions. Both means that palmar and dorsal are present at the same combination.

Feature type (%)	Max distance ±15°			Max distance ±20°			Max distance ±25°		
	Palmar	Dorsal	Both	Palmar	Dorsal	Both	Palmar	Dorsal	Both
MC	84.0	52.0	40.0	92.0	76.0	68.0	**100.0**	84.0	84.0
PC	92.0	68.0	68.0	**100.0**	68.0	68.0	**100.0**	80.0	80.0
GF	**100.0**	8.0	8.0	**100.0**	16.0	16.0	**100.0**	24.0	24.0
SIFT	80.0	88.0	68.0	84.0	88.0	72.0	92.0	96.0	88.0
DTFPM	92.0	60.0	56.0	**100.0**	**100.0**	**100.0**	**100.0**	**100.0**	**100.0**

a significant improvement compared to the single view performance, whereas the improvement for a three perspective fusion compared to fusing two views is lower but still significant for MC, GF and SIFT.

10.6.7 Multi-algorithm Fusion Results

This time different feature extraction methods per perspective are fused (MAF) instead of perspectives per feature extraction method. We evaluate all possible pairs, triples, quadruples and the combination of all five- feature extraction methods, resulting in 26 different combinations per perspective. Figure 10.12 shows the best fusion result per number of fused feature extraction methods. The best result, for example, two-feature extraction methods included in the fusion at 0° means that the best performing pair of features in terms of EER of all pairs calculated at 0° is depicted. It

Table 10.8 Estimated χ^2 from the EER for multi-perspective fusion. Best results per number of involved views is highlighted **bold font**

Feature extraction method	Best EER for [n] involved views			Significance $n_1 \rightarrow n_2$ (χ^2 value)		
	n = 1	n = 2	n = 3	n = 1→n = 2	n = 1→n = 3	n = 2→n = 3
MC	**0.44 (±0.15)**	**0.12 (±0.08)**	**0.036 (±0.04)**	33.415	62.660	8.265
PC	0.60 (±0.18)	0.28 (±0.12)	0.238 (±0.11)	21.264	28.576	0.622
GF	1.55 (±0.28)	0.60 (±0.18)	0.284 (±0.12)	**76.708**	**159.698**	**20.642**
SIFT	0.55 (±0.17)	0.17 (±0.09)	0.058 (±0.05)	36.650	72.755	10.054
DTFPM	0.56 (±0.17)	0.24 (±0.11)	0.159 (±0.09)	23.391	140.869	3.005

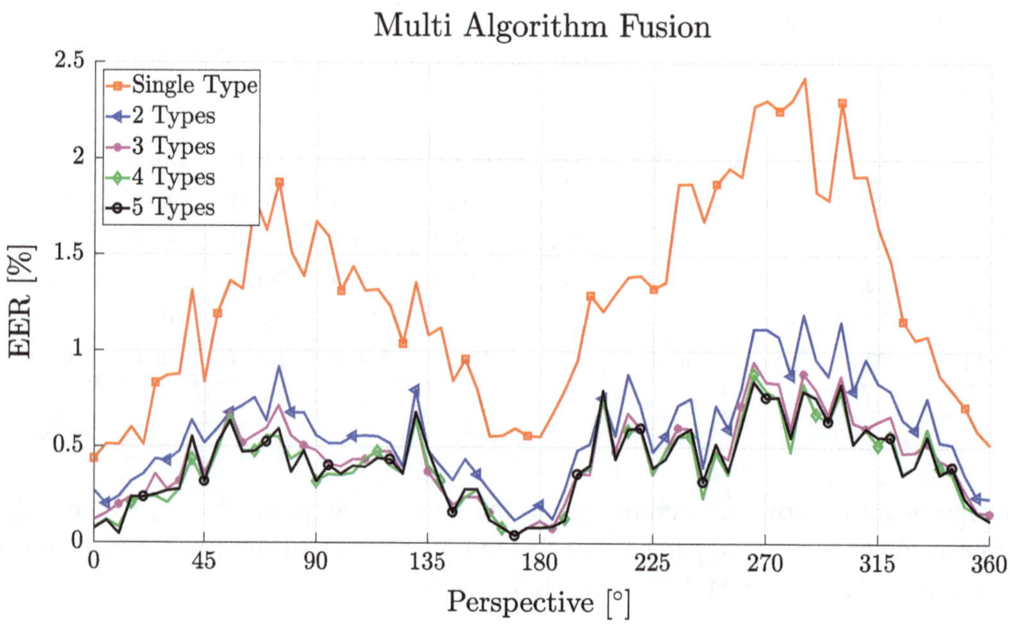

Fig. 10.12 Recognition performance for multi-algorithm fusion: best result in terms of EER per number of feature extraction methods fused is depicted for each perspective

can be seen that even the fusion of two-feature extraction methods increases the performance remarkably. Adding the third feature extraction method further improves the result, whereas fusing four- or five-feature extraction methods does not further improve the recognition performance significantly.

Table 10.9 lists the results of the MAF in more detail. The column occurrence states how often in terms of perspectives a feature extraction method combination performs superior to all other combinations of the same number of included feature

Table 10.9 Multi-algorithm fusion results per number of included features. Occurrence indicates the numbers of perspectives for which the specified combination achieves the best score, the given EER values are calculated over all perspectives. The two view columns state at which view the best and worst performance has been achieved. The best result per number of included feature extraction methods is highlighted **bold face**

# Features included	Feature types	Occurrences	Best		Avg	Worst	
			EER	View	EER	EER	View
1	MC	34 (46.58%)	**0.44 (±0.15)**	0°	1.46	2.67 (±0.37)	260°
	PC	19 (26.03%)	0.60 (±0.18)	10°	1.47	2.47 (±0.36)	280°
	DTFPM	16 (21.92%)	0.56 (±0.17)	160°	1.71	2.87 (±0.38)	285°
	SIFT	4 (5.48%)	0.55 (±0.17)	180°	2.75	5.33 (±0.53)	265°
	GF	–	1.55 (±0.28)	0°	4.89	8.87 (±0.65)	275°
2	PC, DTFPM	31 (42.47%)	0.20 (±0.10)	180°	0.66	1.32 (±0.26)	205°
	MC, DTFPM	22 (30.14%)	0.13 (±0.08)	185°	0.68	1.47 (±0.28)	285°
	MC, SIFT	11 (15.07%)	**0.12 (±0.08)**	170°	0.78	1.83 (±0.31)	265°
	SIFT, DTFPM	8 (10.96%)	0.16 (±0.09)	175°	1.04	2.08 (±0.33)	265°
	MC, PC	1 (1.37%)	0.32 (±0.13)	10°	0.95	1.95 (±0.32)	285°
	PC, SIFT	–	0.24 (±0.11)	180°	0.92	1.88 (±0.31)	265°
	GF, DTFPM	–	0.32 (±0.13)	180°	1.17	2.32 (±0.35)	265°
	GF, SIFT	–	0.40 (±0.14)	170°	1.63	3.56 (±0.43)	265°
	MC, GF	–	0.44 (±0.15)	0°	1.39	2.54 (±0.36)	300°
	PC, GF	–	0.51 (±0.16)	360°	1.28	2.32 (±0.35)	265°

(continued)

Table 10.9 (continued)

# Features included	Feature types	Occurrences	Best		Avg	Worst	
			EER	View	EER	EER	View
3	MC, SIFT, DTFPM	33 (45.21%)	**0.04 (±0.05)**	170°	0.50	0.99 (±0.23)	285°
	MC, PC, DTFPM	23 (31.51%)	0.12 (±0.08)	185°	0.52	1.23 (±0.25)	205°
	PC, SIFT, DTFPM	11 (15.07%)	0.12 (±0.08)	165°	0.53	0.96 (±0.22)	270°
	PC, GF, DTFPM	3 (4.11%)	0.23 (±0.11)	245°	0.62	1.31 (±0.26)	205°
	MC, GF, DTFPM	2 (2.74%)	0.16 (±0.09)	185°	0.66	1.47 (±0.28)	285°
	MC, PC, SIFT	1 (1.37%)	0.12 (±0.08)	170°	0.64	1.31 (±0.26)	265°
	MC, GF, SIFT	–	0.12 (±0.08)	170°	0.77	1.76 (±0.30)	265°
	GF, SIFT, DTFPM	–	0.12 (±0.08)	175°	0.82	1.68 (±0.30)	265°
	PC, GF, SIFT	–	0.25 (±0.11)	170°	0.82	1.71 (±0.30)	265°
	MC, PC, GF	–	0.32 (±0.13)	0°	0.94	1.91 (±0.31)	285°
4	MC, PC, SIFT, DTFPM	51 (69.86%)	**0.04 (±0.05)**	170°	0.42	0.88 (±0.21)	265°
	MC, PC, GF, DTFPM	10 (13.70%)	0.12 (±0.08)	185°	0.51	1.23 (±0.25)	205°
	MC, GF, SIFT, DTFPM	9 (12.33%)	0.04 (±0.05)	170°	0.50	1.07 (±0.24)	275°
	PC, GF, SIFT, DTFPM	3 (4.11%)	0.11 (±0.08)	185°	0.50	1.00 (±0.23)	265°
	MC, PC, GF, SIFT	–	0.09 (±0.07)	170°	0.63	1.32 (±0.26)	265°
5	MC, PC, GF, SIFT, DTFPM	73 (100.00%)	**0.04 (±0.05)**	170°	0.41	0.84 (±0.21)	265°

extraction methods. The minimum, average and maximum EER are determined based on the results for all perspectives of the given feature extraction method combination. Considering single feature extraction methods, MC or PC are included in more than 70% of the best results. GF is not included in any combination that performs best for any perspective. The results of fusing feature extraction method pairs clearly show that it is beneficial to fuse a vein pattern based algorithm (MC, PC, GF) to a key-point based one (SIFT, DTFPM). The combinations of either MC/PC and SIFT/DTFPM are leading to 98% of the best results in two-feature extraction methods fusion.

Table 10.10 Estimated χ^2 from the EER for multi-algorithm fusion

Nr of features EER	n = 1 0.44 (±0.15)	n = 2 0.12 (±0.08)	n = 3 0.04 (±0.05)	n = 4 0.04 (±0.05)	n = 5 0.04 (±0.05)
n = 1 0.44 (±0.15)	–	33.42	60.91	60.91	60.91
n = 2 0.12 (±0.08)	33.42	–	7.31	7.31	7.31
n = 3 0.04 (±0.05)	60.91	7.31	–	0	0
n = 4 0.04 (±0.05)	60.91	7.31	0	–	0
n = 5 0.04 (±0.05)	60.91	7.31	0	0	–

DTFPM (83%) is involved more often than SIFT (26%). Again, GF is not present in any of the best combinations. The overall best result with an EER of 0.04% is achieved when fusing MC, PC, SIFT and DTFPM. Once again, the analysis of the perspective, at which the best result is achieved, confirms, that views from the palmar (0°, 360°) and dorsal (180°) region perform best.

Same as for the two-perspective fusion, we also check the performance increase of three-perspective fusion on its significance. Table 10.10 lists the results in detail. The resulting χ^2 values indicate, that a fusion of two or more feature extraction methods is always beneficial compared to a single feature extraction method. The same holds true when comparing a two-feature extraction method fusion to a three, four or five one. However, applying a four or five feature-type fusion instead of a three feature-type one leads to no significant improvements anymore.

10.6.8 Combined Multi-perspective and Multi-algorithm Fusion

In this section, we combine multiple perspectives and multiple feature extraction methods into one combined fusion method (CMPMAF). For the selection of the relevant perspectives and feature extraction methods we considered the results for multi-perspective fusion (Sect. 10.6.6) and feature extraction method fusion (Sect. 10.6.7). Although the χ^2 values for the multi-perspective fusion in Table 10.8 are only boundaries, they still indicate that the performance increase from two to three perspectives is significant for MC, GF and SIFT. The drawback of adding additional perspectives is the added cost/complexity to the system (additional camera and illumination module, higher computational costs). Therefore, we decided that the significance of the improvement is not high enough to justify the extra effort. As

Table 10.11 Performance results: Fusion of vein pattern based with key-point based features for both, palmar and dorsal view. The best result is highlighted **bold face**

Feature types	Perspectives	EER	FMR1000	ZeroFMR
MC, SIFT	0°, 180°	**0.04 (±0.05)**	0.04	0.64
MC, DTFPM	0°, 180°	0.08 (±0.07)	0.08	0.12
PC, SIFT	0°, 180°	0.16 (±0.09)	0.16	0.32
PC, DTFPM	0°, 180°	0.16 (±0.09)	0.16	0.24
GF, SIFT	0°, 180°	0.20 (±0.10)	0.20	0.60
GF, DTFPM	0°, 180°	0.20 (±0.10)	0.20	0.28

a result of this, we only consider the two perspective fusion. The results presented in Fig. 10.11 and Table 10.5 show that the best results are achieved when fusing palmar and dorsal view. This behaviour can be confirmed when analysing the occurrence of certain perspectives of the three-perspective fusion: Table 10.7 states that the palmar and dorsal region is part of most of the top 25 results. Therefore, we selected 0° and 180° for our combined fusion.

For MAF, the significance analysis (see Table 10.10) indicates that the performance increase from a two to a three feature extraction method fusion is significant but would lead to additional computational costs (for score-level fusion, every feature extraction method needs to be processed by the whole processing chain up to the comparison). Thus, we decided to include the two-feature extraction method MAF into our combined fusion strategy only. Furthermore, the results listed in 10.9 state that 88% of the best two-feature extraction method fusion combinations include one vein pattern based (MC, PC, GF) and one key-point based (SIFT, DTFPM) feature. Therefore, we analysed all possible combinations of those feature extraction methods using both, palmar and dorsal view. Table 10.11 lists the results of the CMPMAF. We evaluated all six possible combinations and arrived at a best EER of 0.04% with a confidence interval of 0.05% for the combined fusion of MC and SIFT for palmar and dorsal view. This result is 11 times better than the best single perspective result (MC at 0° with an EER of 0.44%). All other combinations also perform well. The worst result with an EER of 0.20% is achieved when fusing GF with either SIFT or DTFPM. This is still more than two times better than the best single perspective result. For the sake of completeness, we also calculated the results of the best 3-, 4- and 5-MAF combinations with the palmar and dorsal view. These results, listed in Table 10.12, show that the EER can be further improved. The best result with an EER of 0 is achieved when fusing the scores of all five feature types.

Table 10.13 compares the performance of the best combined two-perspective two-algorithm fusion with the best results of all other fusion strategies. One can see that the calculated χ^2 indicates a significant performance improvement with respect to the single perspective, the 2-MPF and the 2-MAF strategy. All other fusion strategies achieved about the same EER.

Table 10.12 Performance results: Fusion of vein pattern based with key-point based features for both, palmar and dorsal view. The best result is highlighted **bold face**

Feature types	Perspectives	EER	FMR1000	ZeroFMR
MC, SIFT, DTFPM	000°, 180°	0.04 (±0.04)	0.00	0.36
MC, PC, SIFT, DTFPM	000°, 180°	0.01 (±0.01)	0.00	0.12
MC, PC, GF, SIFT, DTFPM	000°, 180°	**0.00 (±0.00)**	0.00	0.00

Table 10.13 Comparison of the best two-perspective two-algorithm fusion combination to the best result of the other fusion strategies including the relative performance improvement, the factor, by which the EER decreased and the boundary χ^2 for significance

Fusion strategy	EER	EER CMPMAF	Rel. Perf. Impr. [%]	Factor	χ^2
Single perspective	0.44 (±0.15)	0.04 (±0.05)	1000	11	60.91
2-MPF	0.12 (±0.08)		200	3	7.31
3-MPF	0.04 (±0.04)		0	1	0.00
2-MAF	0.12 (±0.08)		200	3	7.31
3-MAF	0.04 (±0.05)		0	1	0.00
4-MAF	0.04 (±0.05)		0	1	0.00
5-MAF	0.04 (±0.05)		0	1	0.00

10.6.9 Results Discussion

The evaluation of the independent recognition performances for different projections revealed, that indeed the widely used palmar perspective performed best, followed by the dorsal one performing second best. The views in-between exhibit a slightly worse performance, which is still acceptable. Our results indicate that the presence of finger texture and finger knuckles has a positive influence on the recognition performance. Figure 10.9 shows, that the well-established feature extraction algorithms not only extract features resulting from the finger veins but also from the skin texture of the finger and therefore inherently fuse texture and vein structure. The best single view result was achieved using MC features at the palmar view with an EER of 0.44%.

However, the main objective of this work was to find a suitable trade-off between the number of involved views and feature extraction methods and the recognition performance. In order to arrive at a design decision for a multi-perspective finger vein capture device, several aspects have to be considered: first of all, the gain in recognition accuracy, followed by the production costs and complexity of the biometric capture device which is directly related to the number of involved views and finally the computational complexity of the finger vein recognition system including the capturing time, i.e. the total processing time, which is related to both, the number of different views and the number of different feature extraction methods involved. Adding more perspectives or feature extraction methods increases the complexity of the finger vein sensor and the recognition tool chain. For every feature extraction method, all steps of the recognition tool chain from preprocessing to comparison need to be executed. Adding further perspectives additionally increases the cost and complexity of the capture device's hardware by the need of either adding more camera/illumination modules (one per perspective) or a rotator that moves camera and illumination module into position. Ideally, the number of perspectives and feature extraction methods are kept to a minimum. Furthermore, additional aspects like an improved resistance against presentation attacks and an increased robustness against environmental influences should be included too. Therefore, the decision on how many perspectives and feature extraction methods are used has to be a trade-off between added cost/complexity and improvement of the recognition performance. Our proposed design is based on the findings during the fusion evaluations.

The multi-perspective fusion results showed that by fusing two independent views, in particular, the palmar and dorsal view, a significant performance gain can be achieved. Adding a second perspective improved the recognition performance between a factor 2–3.5, depending on the feature extraction method. The best result with an EER of 0.12% was achieved using MC features fusing the palmar and dorsal view. Adding a third view still improves the performance compared to two perspectives, but not to the same extent (significance) as from a single perspective to the 2-MPF. In this case, the best result of 0.036% EER was achieved using MC when fusing 5°, 170° and 235°. A biometric capture device able to capture the palmar and the dorsal view simultaneously can be built without any moving parts. Two cameras and two illumination modules are sufficient. Each additional view poses noticeable extra costs in terms of hardware (camera and illumination modules) and complexity of the capture device construction. Therefore, one must decide whether the improvement in accuracy justifies the extra effort. As our results show, the performance improvement from a 2-MPF to a 3-MPF is not as significant as from a single perspective to a 2-MPF, a two-perspective capture device, capturing the vein structure from the palmar and dorsal region is the best choice.

For MAF, a single perspective capturing device is sufficient. Such a biometric capture device can be built in a more compact and less expensive manner than a multi-perspective one. Moreover, existing finger vein capture devices acquiring images of the palmar view, can be utilised to apply multi-algorithm fusion too. However, adding an additional feature type to the MAF increases the computational cost. The MAF results showed, that the fusion of different feature extraction methods per single view improves the overall performance remarkably as well. The best results were obtained when fusing vein pattern based algorithms (especially MC and PC) with key-point based methods (SIFT, DTFPM). The best MAF result with an EER of 0.04% was achieved when fusing MC, SIFT and DTFPM in the dorsal region. Including more feature types does not improve the performance compared to the 3-MAF. As the computational complexity for the calculation and comparison of DTFPM features are higher than for the other features types, and the performance increase compared to the best 2-MAF utilising MC and SIFT (EER = 0.12%) features is not as significant as from a single perspective to the 2-MAF, the best MAF option is a 2-MAF including MC and SIFT features.

In a third step, we combined MPF and MAF. By using the best performing perspectives of the two-perspective approach (palmar and dorsal) and combining them with a vein pattern based (MC, PC or GF) and a key-point based method (SIFT or DTFPM), we were able to achieve an EER of 0.04% utilising MC and SIFT. This corresponds to an improvement by a factor of 11 compared to the best single perspective performance, while achieving similar results as for the best MPF and MAF strategies. Adding more feature types to the combined fusion strategy further improved the result. Combining palmar and dorsal view together with all five feature types resulted in a perfect result with EER, FMR1000 and ZeroFMR of 0%.

A multi-perspective finger vein capture device is more resistant against presentation attacks, especially against simple paper printout based attacks. Depending on the actual construction of the multi-perspective capture device, it might also be more robust against contamination (e.g. dust and dirt, sun protection lotion or hand cream on the finger surface) of the finger due to the fact that more than one perspective is captured. Hence, the two-perspective capture device is the preferred option over the single perspective, multi-algorithm fusion one regarding these additional aspects.

Taking all the above-mentioned considerations into account, especially the additional advantages provided by a multi-perspective capture device in terms of resistance against presentation attack and robustness against external influences, the most preferable option is to design a two-perspective capture device capturing the palmar and the dorsal view applying a two-algorithm fusion including MC and SIFT features, whereas by including only one view the advantages of multi-perspective recognition can not be retained. The second feature extraction method can be included without involving additional hardware costs just by extending the recognition tool chain and putting up with the extended processing time, which makes the two-feature version beneficial in any case. This proposed finger vein capture device set-up arrives at an EER of 0.04%, which is a performance gain by a factor of 11 compared to the best single-view, single feature performance. Hence, this option provides an optimal trade-off between recognition accuracy, construction costs and processing time.

10.7 Conclusion and Future Work

In this chapter, we introduced multi-perspective finger vein recognition. For most work reported in the literature, only the palmar view is used in finger vein recognition. However, as the finger is an elliptically shaped cylinder, there are several other views available all around the finger's longitudinal axis. In order to be able to exploit these additional views, a suitable biometric capture device able to capture these different views is necessary. This chapter is based on our previous work [2], where we constructed a rotating, multi-perspective finger vein capture device which was then utilised to capture a multi-perspective finger vein data set. Based on this dataset, the recognition performance of each view was evaluated individually. Then we applied three different score-level fusion strategies, the first one fusing all possible pairs and triples of distinct views, the second one fusing all different feature combinations per each single view and the third one combining the first two approaches. The first strategy was employed to find out the best performing pairs and three tuples of views in terms of recognition performance. The more views are desired to be captured, the higher the complexity and production costs of a suitable biometric capture device. At some point (a certain number of desired views), only a rotating device is able to capture the desired views. A rotating capture device bears several disadvantages, e.g. it is more prone to failures and has an increased capturing time. If only a limited number of views is involved, the production costs and the complexity of the biometric capture device are kept low. The second strategy was applied to investigate the best feature extraction method combination per view. The third strategy, which combines the first two approaches, was applied to find out if the recognition results can be further improved.

The single view evaluation results confirmed that the widely used palmar perspective, followed by the dorsal one (not taking views which are only a few degrees off from the palmar and dorsal view into account), achieves the best performance in finger vein recognition. All the perspectives in-between the palmar and dorsal one exhibit an inferior recognition performance to the palmar and dorsal one. Regarding the multi-perspective score-level fusion it turned out that a fusion of only two perspectives increases the recognition performance significantly, where a fusion of the palmar and the dorsal view performed best. Adding a third perspective still improves the results over the two perspective ones, but not to the same extent as the two perspective ones. The multi-algorithm fusion achieves similar results to the multi-perspective one, arriving at an EER of 0.04% for the combination of three-feature extraction methods. A pure multi-algorithm fusion is preferable in terms of hardware costs and capture device's complexity but does not exhibit the advantages of a multi-perspective recognition in regards to resistance against presentation attacks and increased robustness against external influences. By applying both fusion approaches at the same time for the best performing two perspectives (palmar and dorsal) and the best performing two distinct feature extraction methods (MC, a vein pattern based one and SIFT, a key-point based one), we were able to improve the recognition performance by a factor of 11 compared to the best single view result, achieving an EER of 0.04%.

Regarding recognition performance, hardware costs, processing time and robustness against presentation attacks and external influences the overall best option is to go for the combined multi-perspective and multi-algorithm fusion. In particular, a finger vein capture device capturing the palmar and the dorsal view including MC and SIFT features in a combined fusion provides the best trade-off between the above mentioned considerations and is, therefore, our preferred design decision.

Future Work

The first step will be the construction of a combined multi-perspective and multi-algorithm type fusion finger vein capture device to prove its applicability in real-life applications of finger vein recognition. We plan to do extended tests with this device, regarding presentation attacks, robustness against external influences like changing ambient conditions as well as subject-related influences.

Besides the capture device construction, our future work will include further analysis using our multi-perspective finger vein dataset. There are several other aspects besides the single perspective performance and the fusion of multiple perspectives which can be evaluated based on this dataset. One example is the robustness evaluation of different finger vein recognition algorithms against longitudinal finger rotation, which we already performed in a separate work [65]. We showed that this kind of rotation poses a severe problem for most algorithms. Since for our dataset the longitudinal rotation angle is known, we will test different techniques to compensate the finger rotation, either by estimating the rotation angle based on the captured images only or by using the known rotation angle and then applying a rotation compensating transform.

Another interesting question is if the best performing view is consistent across different subjects/fingers. To perform this analysis we will extend our dataset to contain at least 100+ subjects and then conduct a subject/finger based analysis to find out if the palmar perspective is the best one for all or at least a majority of the subjects/fingers or if there are significant differences.

Another field of interest is finger vein recognition in the 3D space. Therefore, we want to reconstruct a 3D model of the finger vein structure based on multiple images captured in different perspectives and apply different feature extraction and comparison strategies.

Acknowledgements This project has received funding from the European Union's Horizon 2020 research and innovation programme under grant agreement No. 700259, project PROTECT—Pervasive and UseR Focused BiomeTrics BordEr ProjeCT.

References

1. Kono M (2000) A new method for the identification of individuals by using of vein pattern matching of a finger. In: Proceedings of fifth symposium on pattern measurement, Yamaguchi, Japan, pp 9–12
2. Prommegger B, Kauba C, Uhl A (2018) Multi-perspective finger-vein biometrics. In: Proceedings of the IEEE 9th international conference on biometrics: theory, applications, and systems (BTAS2018), Los Angeles, California, USA, pp 1–9
3. Raghavendra R, Busch C (2015) Exploring dorsal finger vein pattern for robust person recognition. In: 2015 international conference on biometrics (ICB), pp 341–348
4. University of Reading. PROTECT multimodal DB dataset, June 2017. http://projectprotect.eu/dataset/
5. Kauba C, Prommegger B, Uhl A (2018) Focussing the beam—a new laser illumination based data set providing insights to finger-vein recognition. In: Proceedings of the IEEE 9th international conference on biometrics: theory, applications, and systems (BTAS2018), Los Angeles, California, USA, pp 1–9

6. Kauba C, Prommegger B, Uhl A (2019) Openvein—an open-source modular multi-purpose finger-vein scanner design. In: Uhl A, Busch C, Marcel S, Veldhuis R (eds) Handbook of vascular biometrics. Springer Science+Business Media, Boston, MA, USA, pp 77–112
7. Gray H, Goss CM (1974) Anatomy of the human body. Am J Phys Med Rehabil 53(6):293
8. Tome P, Marcel S (2015) On the vulnerability of palm vein recognition to spoofing attacks. In: The 8th IAPR international conference on biometrics (ICB)
9. Tome P, Vanoni M, Marcel S (2014) On the vulnerability of finger vein recognition to spoofing
10. Lu Y, Yoon S, Park DS (2014) Finger vein identification system using two cameras. Electron Lett 50(22):1591–1593
11. Zhang Q, Zhou Y, Wang D, Hu X (2013) Personal authentication using hand vein and knuckle shape point cloud matching. In: 2013 IEEE Sixth international conference on biometrics: theory, applications and systems (BTAS). IEEE, pp 1–6
12. Qi Y, Zhou Y, Zhou C, Hu X, Hu X (2016) Vein point cloud registration algorithm for multi-pose hand vein authentication. In: 2016 IEEE international conference on identity, security and behavior analysis (ISBA). IEEE, pp 1–6
13. Matsuda Y, Miura N, Nagasaka A, Kiyomizu H, Miyatake T (2016) Finger-vein authentication based on deformation-tolerant feature-point matching. Mach Vis Appl 27(2):237–250
14. Brümmer N, De Villiers E (2013) The bosaris toolkit: theory, algorithms and code for surviving the new dcf.arXiv:1304.2865
15. Uhl A (2019) State-of-the-art in vascular biometrics. In: Uhl A, Busch C, Marcel S, Veldhuis R (eds). In: Handbook of vascular biometrics. Springer Science+Business Media, Boston, MA, USA, 3–62
16. Changzhou Songyang Machinery & Electronics New Technic Institute (2018) SY42STH47-1684A high torque hybrid stepping motor data sheet. https://www.pololu.com/file/0J714/SY42STH38-1684A.pdf. Accessed 20 June 2018
17. IDS Imaging Development Systems GmbH (2018) UI-ML1240-NIR NIR-enhanced industrial camera data sheet. https://de.ids-imaging.com/IDS/datasheet_pdf.php?sku=AB00184. Accessed 20 June 2018
18. Fujifilm Corporation (2018) Fujifilm HF9HA-1B product page. http://www.fujifilmusa.com/products/optical_devices/machine-vision/2-3-15/hf9ha-1b/index.html. Accessed 20 June 2018
19. Midopt Corporation (2018) MIDOPT LP780 NIR pass-through filter product page. http://midopt.com/filters/lp780/. Accessed 20 June 2018
20. International Electrotechnical Commission et al (2015) Multimodal and other multibiometric fusion. ISO/IEC TR 24722
21. Yang J, Jia Y (2012) A method of multispectral finger-vein image fusion. In: 2012 IEEE 11th international conference on signal processing (ICSP), vol 1. IEEE, pp 753–756
22. Guan F, Wang K, Mo H, Ma H, Liu J (2009) Research of finger vein recognition based on fusion of wavelet moment and horizontal and vertical 2dpca. In: 2nd international congress on image and signal processing, 2009 CISP'09. IEEE, pp 1–5
23. Yang J, Zhang X (2010) Feature-level fusion of global and local features for finger-vein recognition. In: 2010 IEEE 10th international conference on signal processing (ICSP). IEEE, pp 1702–1705
24. Gupta P, Gupta P (2015) An accurate finger vein based verification system. Digital Signal Process 38:43–52
25. Miura N, Nagasaka A, Miyatake T (2004) Feature extraction of finger-vein patterns based on repeated line tracking and its application to personal identification. Mach Vis Appl 15(4):194–203
26. Kauba C, Piciucco E, Maiorana E, Campisi P, Uhl A (2016) Advanced variants of feature level fusion for finger vein recognition. In: Proceedings of the international conference of the biometrics special interest group (BIOSIG'16), Darmstadt, Germany, pp 1–12
27. Zhou Y, Kumar A (2010) Contactless palm vein identification using multiple representations. In: 2010 fourth IEEE international conference on biometrics: theory applications and systems (BTAS). IEEE, pp 1–6

28. Yang Y, Yang G, Wang S (2012) Finger vein recognition based on multi-instance. Int J Digital Content Technol Appl 6(11)
29. Park KR (2012) Finger vein recognition by combining global and local features based on svm. Comput Inf 30(2):295–309
30. Liu F, Yang G, Yin Y, Xi X (2013) Finger-vein recognition based on fusion of pixel level feature and super-pixel level feature. In: Biometric recognition. Springer, pp 274–281
31. Qin H, Qin L, Xue L, He X, Chengbo Y, Liang X (2013) Finger-vein verification based on multi-features fusion. Sensors 13(11):15048–15067
32. Lu Y, Yoon S, Park DS (2013) Finger vein recognition based on matching score-level fusion of gabor features. J Korean Inst Commun Inf Sci 38(2):174–182
33. Kauba C, Reissig J, Uhl A (2014) Pre-processing cascades and fusion in finger vein recognition. In: Proceedings of the international conference of the biometrics special interest group (BIOSIG'14), Darmstadt, Germany, Sept 2014
34. Miura N, Nagasaka A, Miyatake T (2007) Extraction of finger-vein patterns using maximum curvature points in image profiles. IEICE Trans Inf Syst 90(8):1185–1194
35. Yang J, Shi Y, Yang J, Jiang L (2009) A novel finger-vein recognition method with feature combination. In: 2009 16th IEEE international conference on image processing (ICIP). IEEE, pp 2709–2712
36. Razzak MI, Yusof R, Khalid M (2010) Multimodal face and finger veins biometric authentication. Sci Res Essays 5(17):2529–2534
37. He M, Horng SJ, Fan P, Run RS, Chen RJ, Lai JL, Khan MK, Sentosa KO (2010) Performance evaluation of score level fusion in multimodal biometric systems. Pattern Recogn 43(5):1789–1800
38. Kang W, Chen X, Qiuxia W (2015) The biometric recognition on contactless multi-spectrum finger images. Infrared Phys Technol 68:19–27
39. Khellat-Kihel S, Abrishambaf R, Monteiro JL, Benyettou M (2016) Multimodal fusion of the finger vein, fingerprint and the finger-knuckle-print using kernel fisher analysis. Appl Soft Comput 42:439–447
40. Lin K, Han F, Yang Y, Zhang Z (2011) Feature level fusion of fingerprint and finger vein biometrics. In: International conference in swarm intelligence. Springer, pp 348–355
41. Park YH, Tien DN, Lee HC, Park KR, Lee EC, Kim SM, Kim HC (2011) A multimodal biometric recognition of touched fingerprint and finger-vein. In: 2011 international conference on multimedia and signal processing (CMSP), vol 1. IEEE, pp 247–250
42. Peng J, El-Latif AAA, Li Q, Niu X (2014) Multimodal biometric authentication based on score level fusion of finger biometrics. Optik-Int J Light Electron Opt 125(23):6891–6897
43. Peng J, Li Q, El-Latif AAA, Niu X (2015) Linear discriminant multi-set canonical correlations analysis (ldmcca): an efficient approach for feature fusion of finger biometrics. Multimed Tools Appl 74(13):4469–4486
44. Yang J, Zhang X (2012) Feature-level fusion of fingerprint and finger-vein for personal identification. Pattern Recogn Lett 33(5):623–628
45. Yang J, Zhong Z, Jia G, Li Y (2016) Spatial circular granulation method based on multimodal finger feature. J Electr Comput Eng
46. Yang Y, Lin K, Han F, Zhang Z (2012) Dynamic weighting for effective fusion of fingerprint and finger vein. PICA: Prog Intell Comput Appl 1(1):50–61
47. Kumar A, Zhou Y (2012) Human identification using finger images. IEEE Trans Image Proc 21(4):2228–2244
48. Yang W, Huang X, Liao Q (2012) Fusion of finger vein and finger dorsal texture for personal identification based on comparative competitive coding. In: 2012 19th IEEE international conference on image processing (ICIP). IEEE, pp 1141–1144
49. Yang W, Huang X, Zhou F, Liao Q (2014) Comparative competitive coding for personal identification by using finger vein and finger dorsal texture fusion. Inf Sci 268:20–32
50. Asaari MAM, Suandi SA, Rosdi BA (2014) Fusion of band limited phase only correlation and width centroid contour distance for finger based biometrics. Expert Syst Appl 41(7):3367–3382

51. Kang BJ, Park KR (2010) Multimodal biometric method based on vein and geometry of a single finger. IET Comput Vis 4(3):209–217
52. Xiaoming X, Yilong Y, Gongping Y, Xianjing M (2013) Personalized fusion method based on finger vein and finger contour. J Comput Res Dev 9:015
53. Lu Y, Xie SJ, Yoon S, Yang J, Park DS (2013) Robust finger vein ROI localization based on flexible segmentation. Sensors 13(11):14339–14366
54. Zuiderveld K (1994) Contrast limited adaptive histogram equalization. In: Heckbert PS (ed) Graphics gems IV. Morgan Kaufmann, pp 474–485
55. Zhao J, Tian H, Xu W, Li X (2009) A new approach to hand vein image enhancement. In: Second international conference on intelligent computation technology and automation, 2009. ICICTA'09, vol 1. IEEE, pp 499–501
56. Zhang J, Yang J (2009) Finger-vein image enhancement based on combination of gray-level grouping and circular gabor filter. In: International conference on information engineering and computer science, 2009. ICIECS. IEEE, pp 1–4
57. Choi JH, Song W, Kim T, Lee SR, Kim HC (2009) Finger vein extraction using gradient normalization and principal curvature. Proc SPIE 7251:1–9
58. Lowe DG (1999) Object recognition from local scale-invariant features. In: Proceedings of the seventh IEEE international conference on computer vision (CVPR'99), vol 2. IEEE, pp 1150–1157
59. Yang J, Yang J (2009) Multi-channel gabor filter design for finger-vein image enhancement. In: Fifth international conference on image and graphics, 2009. ICIG'09. IEEE, pp 87–91
60. Rohr K, Fornefett M, Stiehl HS (1999) Approximating thin-plate splines for elastic registration: Integration of landmark errors and orientation attributes. In: Biennial international conference on information processing in medical imaging. Springer, pp 252–265
61. Maio D, Maltoni D, Cappelli R, Wayman JL, Jain AK (2004) FVC2004: third fingerprint verification competition. In: ICBA, vol 3072. Springer, pp 1–7
62. Zhang L, Zhang L, Zhang D (2009) Finger-knuckle-print: a new biometric identifier. In: 2009 16th IEEE international conference on image processing (ICIP). IEEE, pp 1981–1984
63. Yang W, Yu X, Liao Q (2009) Personal authentication using finger vein pattern and finger-dorsa texture fusion. In: Proceedings of the 17th ACM international conference on multimedia. ACM, pp 905–908
64. Hofbauer H, Uhl A (2016) Calculating a boundary for the significance from the equal-error rate. In: Proceedings of the 9th IAPR/IEEE international conference on biometrics (ICB'16), pp 1–4
65. Prommegger B, Kauba C, Uhl A (2018) Longitudinal finger rotation—problems and effects in finger-vein recognition. In: Proceedings of the international conference of the biometrics special interest group (BIOSIG'18), Darmstadt, Germany

Part III
Sclera and Retina Biometrics

Chapter 11
Retinal Vascular Characteristics

Lukáš Semerád and Martin Drahanský

Abstract This chapter begins with a description of eye anatomy followed by the anatomy of retinas as well as the acquisition methods for obtaining retinal images. Our own device for capturing the vascular pattern of the retina is introduced in the following text. This chapter presents our aim to estimate the information present in human retina images. The next section describes the search for diseases found in retinal images, and the last section is devoted to our method for generating synthetic retinal images.

Keywords Synthetic retinal images · Vascular bed · Diabetic retinopathy · Hard exudates · Age-related macular degeneration · Druses · Exudates · Bloodstream mask · Information amounts · Bifurcations and crossings · Neural network · Human eye · Retina · Fundus camera · Slit lamp · Blind spot · Fovea · Device EYRINA · Retina recognition

11.1 Introduction

Just like several other biometric characteristics, our eyes are completely unique and, thus, can be used for biometric purposes. There are two core parts in our eyes that even show high biometric entropy. The first is the *iris* and the second is the *retina*, which is located at the backside of the eyeball and not observable by the naked eye. Recognition based on these two biometric characteristics is a relatively new method and little effort has been invested by industries.

The iris and the retina as elements inside the eye are very well protected against damage. The iris and retina patterns are unique to every individual (this also applies to monozygotic twins) and the structure is as follows (see Fig. 11.1) [1, 2]. The *cornea* is located at the front of the eye. It is a transparent connective tissue that, along with

L. Semerád (✉) · M. Drahanský
Faculty of Information Technology, Centre of Excellence IT4Innovations,
Brno University of Technology, Brno, Czechia
e-mail: isemerad@fit.vutbr.cz

M. Drahanský
e-mail: drahan@fit.vutbr.cz

A. Uhl et al. (eds.), *Handbook of Vascular Biometrics*, Advances in Computer Vision and Pattern Recognition, https://doi.org/10.1007/978-3-030-27731-4_11

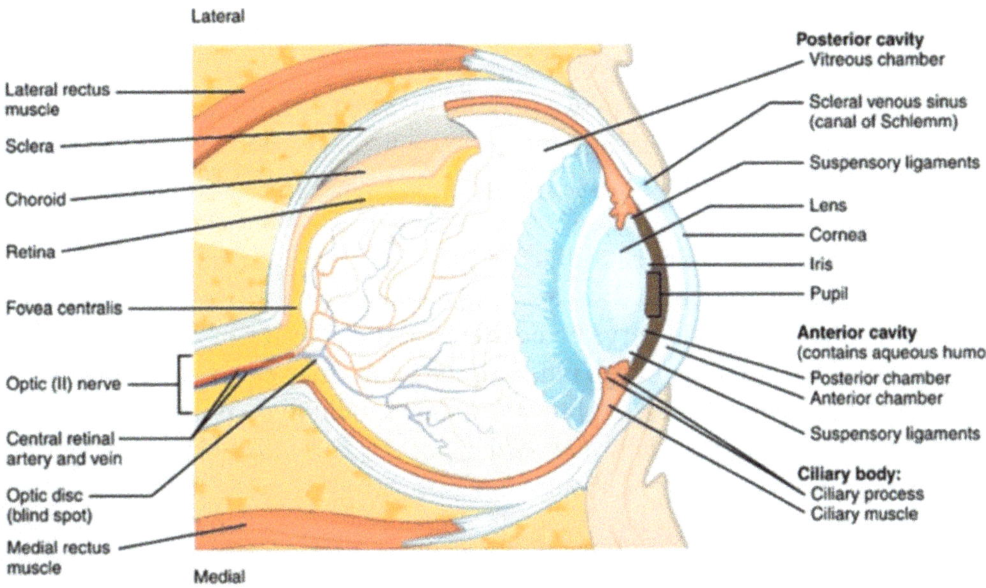

Fig. 11.1 Anatomy of the human eye [42]

the lens, allows the light to break into the eye. The *iris* has the shape of an annulus; it is a circularly arranged musculature that narrows/enlarges the pupil. The *pupil* is an opening in the middle of the iris, regulating the amount of light coming into the eye. The *sclera* is a white visible layer covering the entire eyeball, which passes into the cornea in the front. The retina is the inner part containing cells sensitive to light. It shows the image, much like a camera. The *optic nerve* carries many nerve fibres that enter the central nervous system.

There are two scientific disciplines that deal with eye characteristics—those are ophthalmology and biometrics. *Ophthalmology* is a medical discipline aimed at analysing and treating the health of the eye and its associated areas. In the field of *biometrics* (recognising an individual based on the unique biometric characteristics of the human body), the unique properties of the eye are not subject to change in time, and they are also so unique that it is possible to unequivocally identify two distinct individuals apart from each other in order to verify the identity of that person.

11.1.1 Anatomy of the Retina

The retina is considered to be a part of the *Central Nervous System* (CNS) [1, 2]. This is the only part of the CNS that can be observed noninvasively. It is a light-sensitive layer of cells located in the back of the eye with a thickness of 0.2–0.4 mm. It is responsible for sensing the light rays that hit it through the pupil, and a lens that turns and inverts the image. The only neurons that react directly to light are *photoreceptors*. These are divided into two main types: *cones* and *rods*. For adults, the retina covers approximately 72% of the inner eye. The entire surface of the retina contains about 7 million cones and 75–150 million rods. This would compare the eye to a 157-megapixel camera. Rods are used to detect light and are capable of responding to the impact of one to two photons by providing black-and-white vision. Cones are used to detect colours and are divided into three types depending on which base colour they are sensitive to (red, green, blue), but these are less sensitive to light intensity [1, 2].

We can observe the two most distinctive points on an eye's retina—see Fig. 11.2. It is a *blind spot* (or an optical disc) and a *macula* (*yellow spot*) [1, 2]. A blind spot is the point where the optic nerve enters the eye; it has a size of about 3 mm^2 and lacks all receptors. So if the image falls into the blind spot, it will not be visible to a person. The brain often "guesses" how the image should look in order to fill in this place. On the other hand, the *macula* (*yellow spot*) [1, 2] is referred to as the sharpest vision area; it has a diameter of about 5 mm and the cones predominate it (it is less sensitive to light). This area has the highest concentration of light-sensitive cells, whose density decreases towards the edges. The centre of the macula is *fovea*, which is the term describing receptor concentration and visual acuity. Our direct view is reflected in this area. Interestingly enough, the macula (yellow spot) is not really yellow, but slightly redder than the surrounding area. This attribute, however, was given by the fact that yellow appears after the death of an individual.

The retina vessel's apparatus is similar to the brain, where the structure and venous tangle remain unchanged throughout life. The retina has two main sources of blood: the *retinal artery* and the *vessels*. Larger blood flow to the retina is through the blood vessel that nourishes its outer layer with photoreceptors. Another blood supply is provided by the retinal artery, which primarily nourishes the inside of the retina. This artery usually has four major branches.

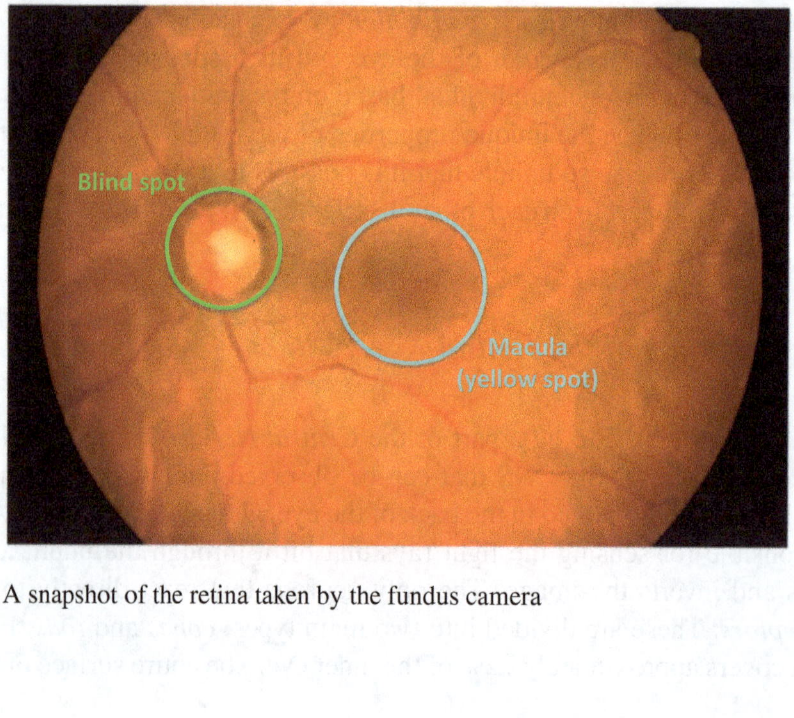

Fig. 11.2 A snapshot of the retina taken by the fundus camera

The retina located inside the eye is well protected from external influences. During life, the vessel pattern does not change and is therefore suitable for biometric purposes.

The retina acquires an image similar to how a camera does. The beam passing through the pupil appears in the focus of the lens on the retina, much like the film. In the medical field, specialised optical devices are used for the visual examination of the retina.

The iris is beyond the scope of this chapter, however, some interesting works include [3–5].

11.1.2 History of Retinal Recognition

In 1935, ophthalmologists *Carleton Simon* and *Isidore Goldstein* discovered eye diseases where the image of the bloodstream in two individuals in the retina was unique for each individual. Subsequently, they published a journal article on the use of vein imaging in the retina as a unique pattern for identification [6]. Their research was supported by Dr. Paul Tower, who in 1955 published an article on studying monozygotic twins [7]. He discovered that retinal vessel patterns show the least resemblance to all the other patterns examined. At that time, the identification of the vessel's retina was a timeless thought.

With the concept of a simple, fully automated device capable of retrieving a snapshot of the retina and verifying the identity of the user, Robert Hill, who established EyeDentify in 1975, devoted almost all of his time and effort to this development. However, functional devices did not appear on the market for several years after [8, 9].

Several other companies attempted to use the available fundus cameras and modify them to retrieve the image of the retina for identification purposes. However, these fundus cameras had several significant disadvantages, such as the relatively complicated alignment of the optical axis, visible light spectra, making the identification quite uncomfortable for the users, and last but not least, the cost of these cameras was very high.

Further experiments led to the use of Infrared (IR) illumination, as these beams are almost transparent to the choroid that reflect this radiation to create an image of the eye's blood vessels. IR illumination is invisible to humans, so there is also no reduction in the pupil diameter when the eye is irradiated.

The first working prototype of the device was built in 1981. The device with an eye-optic camera used to illuminate the IR radiation was connected to an ordinary personal computer for image capture analysis. After extensive testing, a simple correlation comparison algorithm was chosen to be the most appropriate.

After another four years of hard work, EyeDentify Inc. launched *EyeDentification System 7.5*, where verification is performed based on the retina image and the PIN entered by the user with the data is stored in the database [8, 9].

The last known retinal scanning device to be manufactured by EyeDentify Inc. was the *ICAM 2001*. This device might be able to store up to 3,000 subjects, having a storage capacity of up to 3,300 history transactions [8]. Regrettably, this product was withdrawn from the market because of user acceptance and its high price. Some other companies like Retica Systems Inc. were working on a prototype of retinal acquisition devices for biometric purposes that might be much easier to implement into commercial applications and might be much more user friendly. However, even this was a failure and the device did not succeed in the market.

11.1.3 Medical and Biometric Examination and Acquisition Tools

First of all, we will start with the description of existing medical devices for retinal examination and acquisition, followed by biometric devices. The medical devices provide high-quality scans of the retina, however, the two major disadvantages are predetermining these devices to fail within the biometric market—first, because of their very high price, which ranges from the thousands (used devices) to the tens of thousands of EUR; second, because of their manual or semi-automatic mode, where medical staff is required. So far, there is no device on the market that can scan the retina without user intervention, i.e. something that is fully automatic. We are working on this automatic device, but its price is not yet acceptable for the biometric market.

11.1.3.1 Medical Devices

The most commonly used device for examining the retina is a *direct ophthalmoscope*. When using an ophthalmoscope, the patient's eye is examined from a distance of several centimetres through the pupil. Several types of ophthalmoscopes are currently known, but the principle is essentially the same: the eye of the investigated data subject and the investigator is in one axis, and the retina is illuminated by a light source from a semipermeable mirror, or a mirror with a hole located in the observation axis at an angle of 45° [10]. The disadvantage of a direct ophthalmoscope is a relatively small area of investigation, the need for skill when handling, and patient cooperation.

For a more thorough examination of the eye background, the so-called *fundus camera* is used (as shown in Fig. 11.3), which is currently most likely to have the greatest importance in retina examinations. It allows colour photography to capture almost the entire surface of the retina, as can be seen in Fig. 11.2. The optical principle of this device is based on so-called indirect ophthalmoscopy [10]. Fundus cameras are equipped with a white light source (i.e. a laser) to illuminate the retina and then scan it with a CCD sensor. Some types can also find the centre of the retina and automatically focus it, using a frequency analysis of the scanned image.

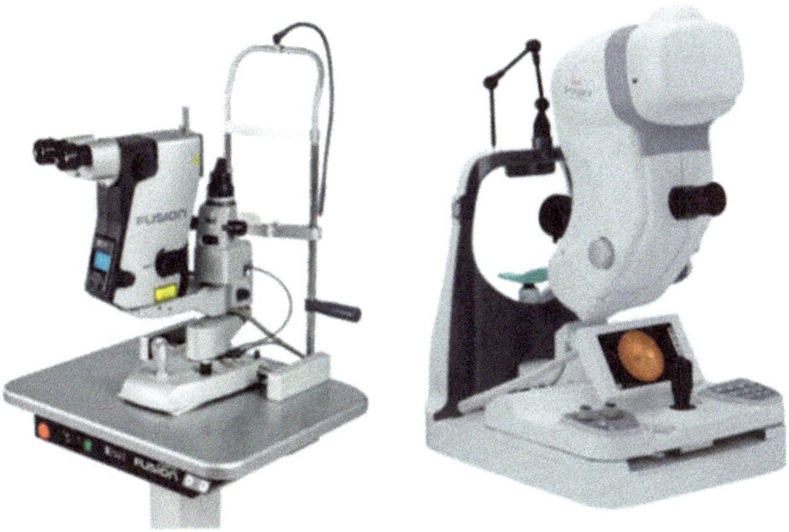

Fig. 11.3 (Left) Slit lamp example [43]; (right) example of a non-mydriatic fundus camera [44]

The main ophthalmoscopic examination methods of the anterior and posterior parts of the eye include direct and indirect ophthalmoscopy as well as the most widely used examination, a *slit lamp* (see Fig. 11.3 on the left), which makes it possible to examine the anterior segment of the eye using so-called *biomicroscopy*. A *fundus camera*, sometimes referred to as a *retinal camera*, is a special device for displaying the posterior segment of the optic nerve, the yellow spots and the peripheral part of the retina (see Fig. 11.3 on the right). It works on the principle of indirect ophthalmoscopy where a source of primary white light is built inside the instrument. The light can be modified by different types of filters, and the optical system is focused on the data subject's eye, where it is reflected from the retina and points back to the fundus camera lens. There are mydriatic and non-mydriatic types that differ in whether or not the subject's eye must be taken into mydriasis. The purpose of mydriasis is to extend the human eye's pupil so that the "inlet opening" is larger, allowing one to be able to read a larger portion of the retina. Of course, non-mydriatic fundus cameras are preferred because the data subject can immediately leave after the examination and can drive a motor vehicle, which is not possible in the case of mydriasis. However, mydriasis is necessary for some subjects. The price of these medical devices is in the order of tens of thousands of EUR, which is determined only by medically specialised workplaces.

The mechanical construction of the optical device is a rather complex matter. It is clear that the scanning device operates on the principle of medical eye-optic devices. These so-called retinoscopes, or fundus cameras, are relatively complicated devices and the price for them is quite high as well.

The principle is still the same as it is for a retinoscope, where a beam of light is focused on the retina and the CCD camera scans the reflected light. The beam of light from the retinoscope is adjusted so that the eye lens focuses on the surface of the retina. This reflects a portion of the transmitted light beam back to the ophthalmic

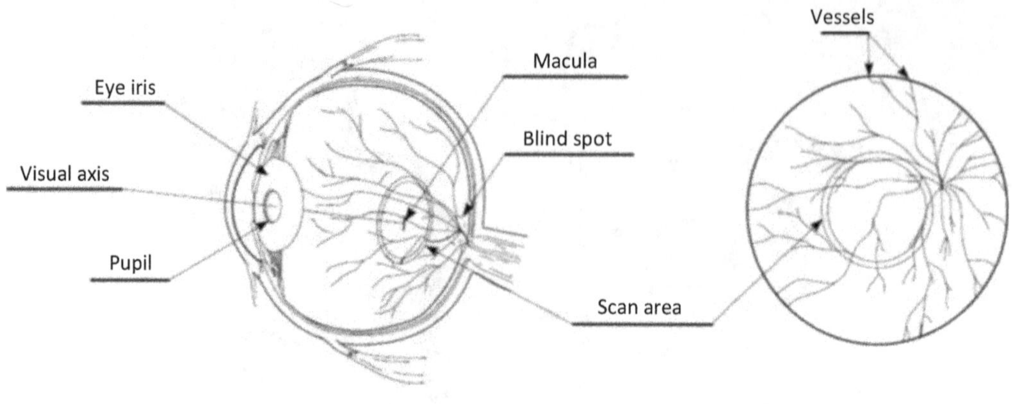

Fig. 11.4 The functional principle for obtaining a retinal image of the eye background

lens that then readjusts it, the beam leaving the eye at the same angle below which the eye enters (return reflection). In this way, an image of the surface of the eye can be obtained at about 10° around the visual axis, as shown in Fig. 11.4. The device performed a circular snapshot of the retina, mainly due to the reflection of light from the cornea, which would be unusable during raster scanning.

11.1.3.2 Biometric Devices

The first products from EyeDentify Inc. used a relatively complicated optical system with rotating mirrors to cover the area of the retina—this system is described in U.S. Pat. No. 4,620,318 [11]. To align the scan axis and the visual axis, the so-called UV-IR cut filters (*Hot Mirrors*—reflect infrared light and passes through the visible light) are used in the design. A schematic drawing of the patent is in Fig. 11.5. The distance between the eye and the lens was about 2–3 cm from the camera. The alignment system on the optical axis of the instrument is an important issue, and it is described in more detail in U.S. Pat. No. 4,923,297 [12].

Newer optical systems from EyeDentify Inc. were much easier and had the benefits of repairing optical axes with less user effort than the previous systems. The key part

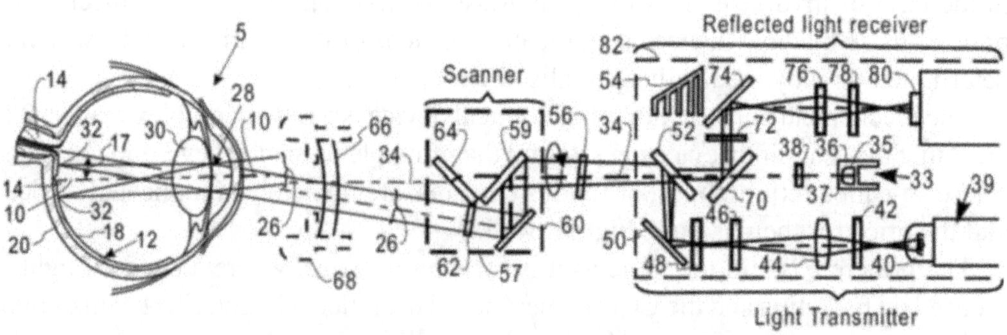

Fig. 11.5 The first version of the EyeDentification System 7.5 optical system [12]

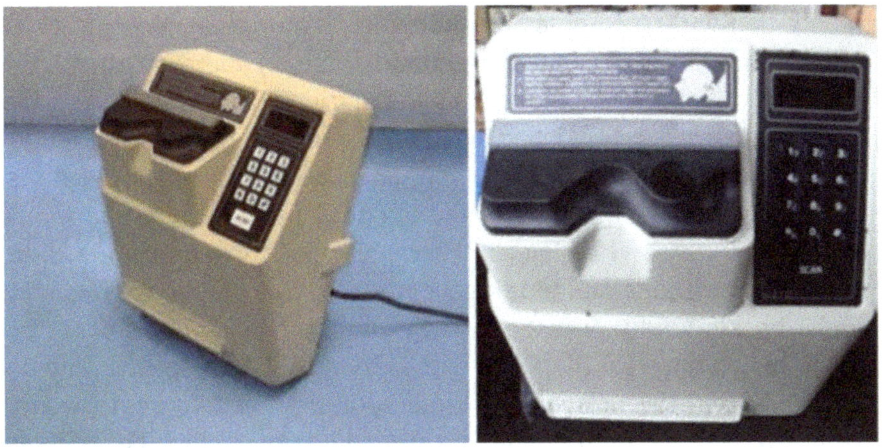

Fig. 11.6 (Left) EyeDentify [9]; (right) EyeDentificationSystem [45]

was a rotating scanning disc that carried multifocal Fresnel lenses. This construction is described in U.S. Pat. No. 5,532,771 [13].

A pioneer in developing these identification systems is primarily EyeDentify Inc., who designed and manufactured the EyeDentification System 7.5 (see Fig. 11.6) and its latest ICAM 2001 model, which was designed in 2001. Other companies are Retinal Technologies, known since 2004 as Retica Systems, but details of their system are not known. The company TPI (Trans Pacific Int.) has recently offered an ICAM 2001-like sensor, but there is no longer any information about it available.

11.1.3.3 Device EYRINA

At the end of this subsection, we will devote our attention to our own construction of an interesting and nonexistent device that can be used in both the field of biometric systems and in the field of ophthalmology—we call it EYRINA. This device is a fully automatic non-mydriatic fundus camera. Many years ago, we started with a simple device (see Fig. 11.7 on the left), but over time, we came to the third generation of the device (see Fig. 11.7 on the right). We are now working on the fourth generation

Fig. 11.7 A non-mydriatic fundus camera—first generation left, second generation middle and third generation right

of this device that will be completely automatic. The original concept was focused only on the retina (a direct view in the optical axis of the eye), then we arrived (second generation) to retrieve the retina and the iris of the eye in one device, while the third and fourth generation is again focused solely on the retina of the eye. The third generation can already find the eye in the camera, move the optical system to the centre of the image (alignment of the optical axis of the eye and the camera) and take pictures of the eye retina (in the visible spectrum) to shoot a short video (in the infrared spectrum). The fourth generation will be able to capture almost the entire ocular background (not just a direct view in the optical axis of the eye) and combine the image into one file. This will, of course, be associated with software that can already find the macula and blind spot, arteries and vessels, detect and extract bifurcations and crossings and find areas with potential pathological findings while we can detect exudates/druses and haemorrhages, including the calculation of their overall area. In the future, we will focus on the reliability and accuracy of detectors and extractors, including other types of illnesses that will be in the interest of ophthalmologists.

The central part of the third generation built two tubes with optics that can compensate the diopter distortion approx. ± 10 D. The left tube is connected to the motion screw and the NEMA motor, i.e. we were able to move the frontal (left) tube. The eye is very close to the eyebrow holder. Between these two tubes, we have a semipermeable mirror. Under this mirror is an LED for making the look of the patient to be fixed on a concrete position. The illumination unit is placed behind the mirror on the covering unit. Behind the background (right) tube is a high-resolution camera. The mainboard and PCBs are placed in the back of the fundus camera, where the connectors and cables are placed as well. The connection is done using a USB cable to the computer.

The image of a real eye from the second version of EYRINA could be found in Fig. 11.8. Now, we just used an ophthalmologic eye phantom for version 3.

Version 3 was able to automatically capture a direct view to the eye, i.e. pupil detection, focusing and taking pictures automatically; however, it is not possible to

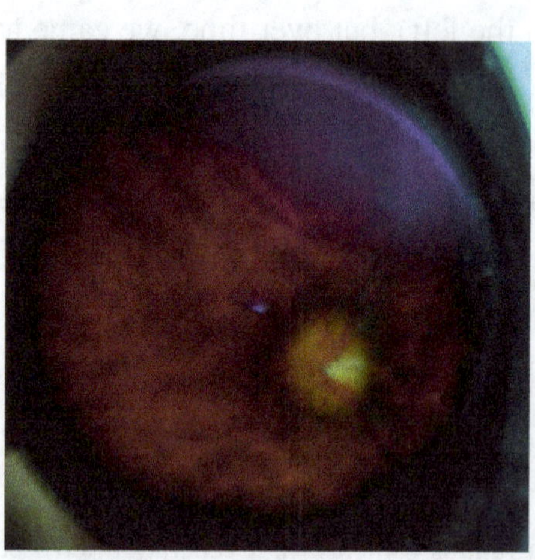

Fig. 11.8 Retinal image of a real retina from the second version of EYRINA

Fig. 11.9 Model of the construction of a fourth-generation device

capture images for retinal images stitching, and if the user has not centred the optical axis of his/her eye with the optical axis of the camera system, the view to the eye is not correct. The new version 4 has a 5-axes manipulator, which is able to find the centred position of both optical axes (eye and camera) automatically. The other new parts are the compensation of diopter distortion ±12 D (with additional rings for up to ±30 D), automatic composition of scanned images, automatic recognition of the optic disc, macula and selected pathologies, and a Wi-Fi/USB connection. The model of the fourth version of this fundus camera is visible in Fig. 11.9. This camera should be ready for laboratory installation in Autumn 2019.

11.1.4 Recognition Schemes

In the introductory chapter is an overview about the existing work on retina recognition. There are several schemes that could be used for the recognition of retinal images. For example, there are different approaches for retina image biometric recognition. Farzin [8] and Hill [9] segment the blood vessels, from which it generates features and stores up to 256 12-bit samples reduced to a reference record of 40 bytes for each eye. Contrast information is stored in the time domain. Fuhrmann and Uhl [14] extract vessels, from which the retina code is obtained. This is a binary code that describes the vessels around the optical disc.

The first idea for recognition (described in Chap. 3.1) is based on the work of Arakala et al. [15], where the biometric entropy of retina and recognition based on area around the optical disc is calculated. We have extended this area and started using it for identification. Our idea of localisation points to the retinal vascular bed and is based on the similarity of the structure with the papillary lines in the fingerprints. There, bifurcation, termination, position and direction of the minutiae are detected. In retinas, blood vessels are not as severely terminated as in fingerprints, gradually diminishing until lost. Therefore, we do not detect termination. On the contrary, the bifurcation here is terminated. In addition, the complicated structure of the several layers of blood vessels over one another is virtually crossing the vessels in the image. It is not easy to know what is crossing and what is bifurcation, so we detect these features together. We then base biometric recognition on these points.

We are also looking for the centre of the blind spot and the fovea. We created a coordinate system with the centre in the middle of abscissa between the centre of the blind spot and the centre of the fovea. The individual points are then represented by the angle and distance in these units, i.e. the results are a set of vectors showing the concrete place in the retinal image. Thus, we are invariant to the different way of acquiring the retina, since the optical axes of the eye and the sensing device may not always be unified.

In the retina, the situation is relatively simple because the algorithms are searching the image for *bifurcations* and *crossings* of the retinal vascular system, whose positions clearly define the biometric instance (i.e. the retina pattern). An example is shown in Fig. 11.10. Recognition becomes problematic when a stronger pathological phenomenon (e.g. a haemorrhage) occurs in the retina that affects the detection and extraction of bifurcations and crossings. For biometric systems, it should be noted that their use also includes the disclosure of information about their own health status since, as mentioned above, a relatively large amount of information on human health can be read from the image of an iris, and that is, especially, the case for a retina as well. It is therefore up to each of us in regard to how much we will protect this private information and whether or not we will use the systems. However, if the manufacturer guarantees that the health information does not get stored, and only the unique features are stored (not the image), then the system may be used based on data protection legislation (e.g. GDPR).

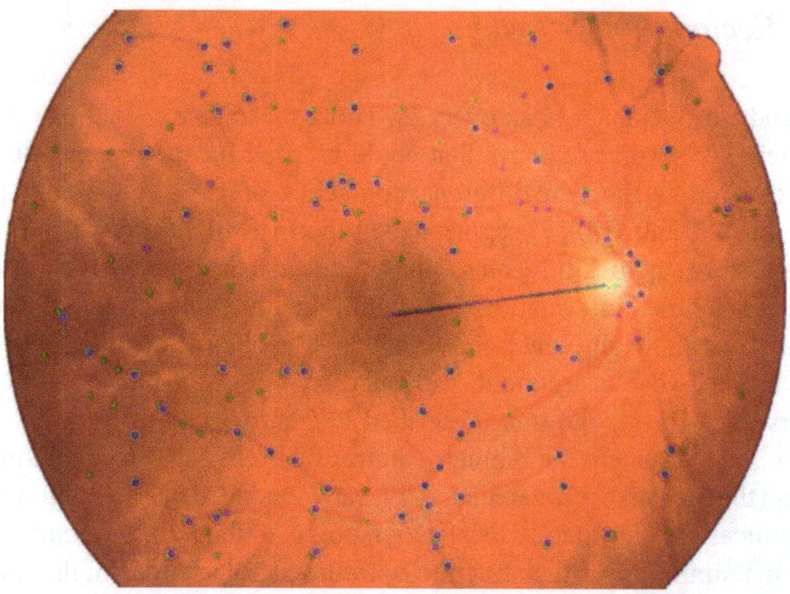

Fig. 11.10 Extracted features (bifurcations and crossings, incl. the connection of macula and blind spot) in the retina [37]

11.1.5 Achieved Results Using Our Scheme

The aim of this work was to compare manually marked and automatically found bifurcations/crossings using our application, *RetinaFeatureExtractor*, and find out the success of the automatic search. First, we created a Python *extract_features.py* script that reads retina images from the selected folder and uses *RetinaFeatureExtractor* to find bifurcations/crossings for each image and save them into text files in the same hierarchy as the source images. After obtaining a set of automatically found bifurcations/crossings, we designed an algorithm for comparing them to manually selected bifurcations/crossings (ground truth). We then created a Python *comparison.py* script that compares the found bifurcations.

The algorithm automatically finds bifurcations/crossings that are paired with the manually found bifurcations/crossings. The algorithm works as follows:

- Converts the found bifurcations/crossings to the same coordinate system.
- For each manually found bifurcation/crossing, it locates around the size t candidates for pairing and remembers their distance.
- If the number of manually found bifurcations/crossings and candidates for pairing is not the same, the smaller of the sets is completed with placeholders.
- Builds a complete bipartite graph where one disjunctive set of vertices is created by the manually found bifurcations/crossings, and the second by the candidates. It also set the price of edges between the manually found bifurcations/crossings and their corresponding candidates and computes the distance. For other edges, it sets the value from the interval $<t+1, \infty)$.
- Finds the minimum matching in the bipartite graph.
- From paired pairs, it removes those where one of the bifurcations/crossings is a placeholder, or those pairs of them where the distance is greater than t.
- Calculates the percentage of the manually marked points that have been paired.

In both sets, the positions of the blind and yellow spot are given. It is in files with manually marked bifurcations/crossings and the blind spot is marked with a rectangle, and in automatically found bifurcations/crossings it is a circle. The yellow spot is in both file types marked with a circle. Bifurcations/crossings are expressed by r and ψ. The r is the distance from centre of the blind spot, but it is recalculated so that the distance from the centre of blind spot to the centre of the yellow spot is 1. The ψ stands for the angle from the blind spot with zero value to the centre of yellow spot.

We decided to convert the found bifurcations/crossings into a Cartesian coordinate system. We needed to calculate the distance between the centre of the blind spot (hereafter C_{BS}) and yellow spot (hereafter C_{YS}). In the file with manually marked bifurcations/crossings, only the centre of the rectangle indicating the blind spot had to be calculated; in the expression of the circles, their centre was already contained. We then calculated their Euclidean distance (hereinafter d). Afterwards, we calculated the angle between the centres of both spots (hereafter α) according to Eq. (1.1).

$$\alpha = arctg2((y.C_{YS} - y.C_{BS}), (x.C_{YS} - x.C_{BS})). \tag{1.1}$$

Using Eq. (1.2), we calculated the bifurcation/crossing distance from the blind spot:

$$v = r \cdot d \tag{1.2}$$

Then, using Eqs. (1.3) and (1.4), we calculated the coordinates dx and dy:

$$dx = d \cdot \cos(\psi + \alpha), \tag{1.3}$$

$$dy = d \cdot \sin(\psi + \alpha). \tag{1.4}$$

The resulting point of bifurcation/crossing in the Cartesian system is obtained as $[dx + x.C_{BS}; dy + y.C_{BS}]$.

We saved the converted points to the list and used their position in the list that we could use as ID to compile disjunctive sets. We assigned a placeholder ID with a value of -1. To calculate the minimum pairing we used the fact that this problem can be converted to the problem of integer programming [16]. After the calculation, we obtained the edges between the individual vertices of the graphs and we could calculate how many manually found bifurcations/crossings were paired. The resulting image for the comparison is shown in Fig. 11.11.

We used three publicly available databases: Drions [17], Messidor [18] and HRF (High-Resolution Fundus Image Database) [19].

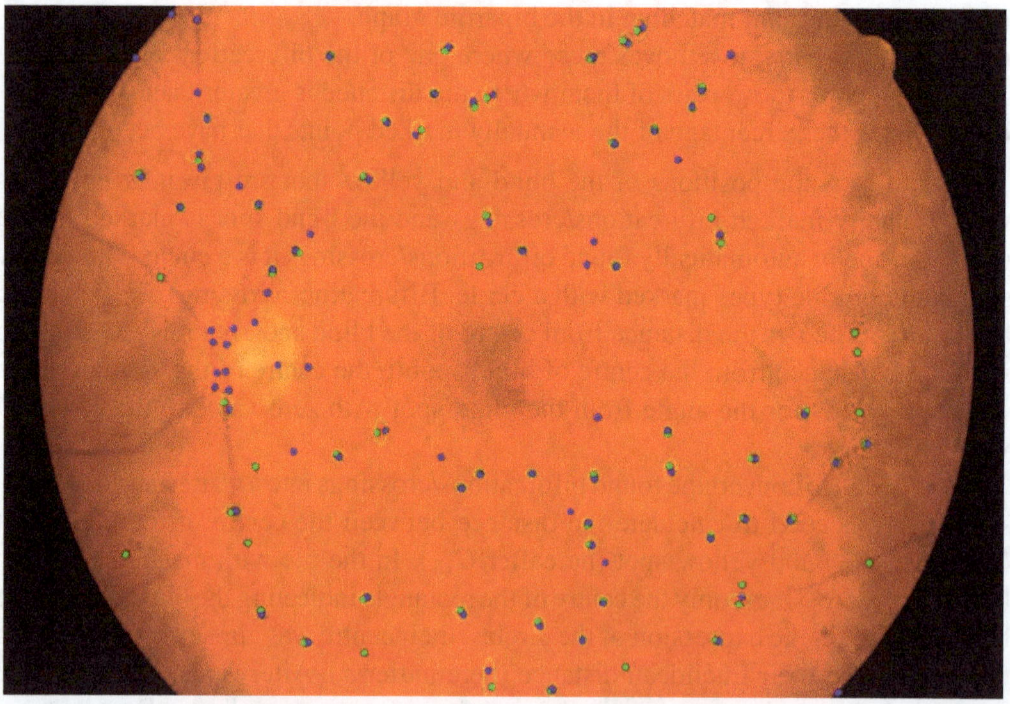

Fig. 11.11 The resulting image for the comparison of manually and automatically found bifurcations/crossings

Table 11.1 The summarised results for manual and automatic bifurcation/crossing detection

Database	Average success rate [%]	Average marking error [%]	Average point spacing [px]
Drions images	62	47	5.25
HRF	66	31	4.55
Messidor (Base12)	74	65	4.25
Messidor (Base13)	79	63	5.01
Messidor (Base22)	61	45	4.65
Messidor (Base3)	82	72	4.95
Average	70.67	53.83	4.78

The *Drions* database consists of 110 colourised digital retinal images from the Ophthalmology Service at Miguel Servet Hospital, Saragossa (Spain). Images are in RGB JPG format, and the resolution is 600 × 400 with 8 bits/pixel [17]. The *Messidor* database originally contains 1,200 eye fundus colour numerical images of the posterior pole. Images were acquired by 3 ophthalmologic departments. The images were captured using 8 bits per colour plane at 440 × 960, 240 × 488 or 304 × 536 pixels. The *HRF* database contains 15 images of healthy patients, 15 images of patients with diabetic retinopathy and 15 images of glaucomatous patients.

We used images from these databases to compare our manually selected and automatically marked bifurcations and crossings in them.

The results are summarised in Table 11.1.

At the same time, we have modified and improved our algorithm that we tested on the VARIA database [20], which contains 233 images from 139 individuals. We conducted a classic comparison of found bifurcations/crossings that correspond to the fingerprint method. The DET curve is shown in Fig. 11.12.

ALG-1 is an elementary algorithm that only shrinks images to one-fifth, smoothes them, and equalises the histogram.

ALG-3 processes images as follows: after processing ALG-1, it detects an optical disc and fovea and then aligns the images to a uniform plane. Next, it highlights the vessels in the image and crops the compared area around the optical disc.

ALG-2 compared to ALG-3 does not cut the image, only on the optical disc area. Moreover, the resulting image is applied to edge detection.

Source code of algorithms is available on [21].

11.1.6 Limitations

There are some limitations in retinal biometrics that discourage greater use in biometric systems. There is currently no system that can remove these shortcomings to a greater extent [9]:

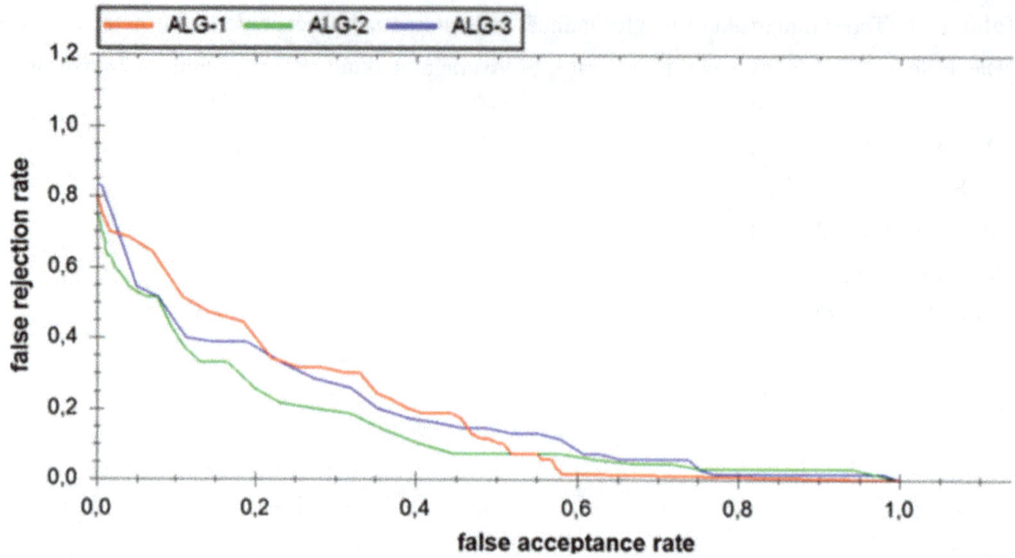

Fig. 11.12 The DET curve for our three versions of the algorithm *RetinaFeatureExtractor*

- *Fear of eye damage*—The low level of infrared illumination used in this type of device is completely harmless to the eye, but there is a myth among the lay public that these devices can damage the retina. All users need to be familiar with the system in order to gain confidence in it.
- *Outdoor and indoor use*—Small pupils can increase the false rejection rate. Since the light has to pass through the pupil twice (once in the eye, then outward), the return beam can be significantly weakened if the user's pupil is too small.
- *Ergonomics*—The need to come close to the sensor may reduce the comfort of using the device.
- *Severe astigmatism*—Data subjects with visual impairments (astigmatism) are unable to focus the eye onto the point (a function comparable to measuring the focusing ability of the eye for an ophthalmologist), thus avoiding the correct generation of the template.
- *High price*—It can be assumed that the price of the device, especially the retroviral optical device itself, will always be greater than, for example, the price of fingerprint or voice recognition capture devices.

The use of retinal recognition is appropriate in areas with *high-security requirements,* such as nuclear development, arms development, as well as manufacturing, government and military facilities and other critical infrastructure.

11.2 Eye Diseases

The main focus of this chapter is on ophthalmology in regard to examining the retina of the eye, taking into account, of course, the overall health of the eye (e.g. cataracts or increased intraocular pressure). Within the retina is a relatively large line of diseases and damages that interest medical doctors, but they are detailed in an encyclopaedia of ophthalmology consisting of hundreds of pages (e.g. [22] (1,638 pages) or [23] (2,731 pages)). The largest group is diabetes and Age-related Macular Degeneration (ARMD). Occasionally exudates/druses or haemorrhages (bleeding or blood clots) appear in the retina; however, as mentioned above, potential damage (e.g. perforation or retinal detachment) or retinal disease is such a matter.

In comparison with other biometric characteristics (e.g. fingerprints, the vascular patterns of the hand or finger), the role of diseases connected to a concrete biometric information career (e.g. finger, hand) plays a very important role. It is not only the *ageing* factor, which can bring some changes into the retinal image sample, but the pathologies on the retina can disable the subject, making them unable to use the biometric system. The most common disease manifestations are related to diabetes mellitus and ARMD, whereas these pathologies (e.g. haemorrhages and aneurisms) can change the quality of the image so much that the vascular pattern is partially covered or completely invisible. Therefore, a short description of the most important and the most widespread retinal diseases are mentioned and shortly described to get the feeling of how much they can decrease the biometric performance of the recognition algorithms. These diseases are expected to influence recognition scheme described in the Sect. 11.1.4. The impact on biometric recognition is based on our observations and has no empirical evidence.

Diabetes mellitus (DM, diabetes) [24] is a disease characterised by elevated blood glucose (hyperglycemia) due to the relative or absolute lack of insulin. Chronic hyperglycemia is associated with long-lasting damage, dysfunction and failure of various organs in the human body—especially, the eyes, kidneys, heart and blood vessels. Most types of diabetes [24] fall into two broader categories: type 1 and type 2.

While diabetes mellitus (diabetes) has been described in ancient times, *diabetic retinopathy* [25, 26] is a disease discovered relatively late. Diabetic Retinopathy (DR) is the most common vascular disease of the retina. It is a very common late complication of diabetes and usually occurs after more than 10 years of having diabetes.

Diabetic retinopathy occurs in several stages. The first stage can only be detected by fluorophotometry. The next stage is called *simple*, *incipient* or *Non-proliferative Diabetic Retinopathy* (NPDR). This is characterised by the formation of small *micro-aneurysms* (vessel bulging), which often crack and result in another typical symptom—the formation of small *intrarethral* or *pre-renal haemorrhages*. Because the micro-aneurysms and haemorrhages include blood, their colour is very similar to the vessel pattern colour, i.e. if larger areas in the eye are affected by these diseases, it is expected to the biometric recognition performance drops down, because the recognition of retinal images is based on the comparison of vessel structures for both images. Microinfarcts have a white colour, a fibrous structure, and are referred to as "cotton stains". If the capillary obliteration is repeated at the same site, heavy exudates arise. These are a sign of chronic oxygen deficiency. They are yellow, sharply bounded, and formed by fat-filled cells. This stage is called *Proliferative Diabetic Retinopathy* (PDR) [25, 26].

Micro-aneurysms (MA) [25, 26] are considered to be basic manifestations of diabetic retinopathy. Although micro-aneurysms are characteristic of diabetic retinopathy, they cannot be considered a pathologic finding for this disease. They can, however, manifest in many other diseases. MAs are the first lesions of the DR that are proven by biomicroscopic examination. The flowing MA leads to the formation of edema and annularly deposited exudates. Their size is between 12 μm and 100 μm. These are round dark red dots, which are very difficult to distinguish from a micro-haemorrhage. Unlike these, they should have more bordered edges. If their size is greater than 125 μm, it must be taken into account that they may be micro-haemorrhages. As mentioned above, their colour is similar to the vascular pattern and it is expected that they influence biometric recognition performance.

Depending on the location within the retina, we can distinguish *haemorrhage* intraretinally and sub-retinally [25, 26]. Haemorrhages occur secondarily as a result of the rupture of micro-aneurysms, veins and capillaries. Spotted haemorrhages are tiny, round red dots kept at the level of capillaries and only exceptionally deeper (see Fig. 11.13 right). Their shape is dependent on their location, but also on the origin of the bleeding. Spontaneous haemorrhages have the characteristic appearance of stains and their colour is light red to dark. As mentioned above, their colour is similar to a vascular pattern and it is expected that they influence the biometric recognition performance.

Hard exudates (Fig. 11.13 left) [25, 26] are not only characteristic of diabetic retinopathy. They are also found in many other diseases. Hard-dotted exudates are round, clear yellow dots. They create different clusters with a pronounced tendency to migrate. Stubborn hard exudates are predominantly surface-shaped and have the shape of a hump. The colour of this pathology is different from the vascular structure, so it does not affect biometric recognition performance, but it can affect the ability of preprocessing algorithms to prepare the image for venous structure extraction.

Soft exudates (Fig. 11.13 left) [25, 26] are considered to be a typical manifestation of diabetic retinopathy, but it can also be found in other diseases. They result from

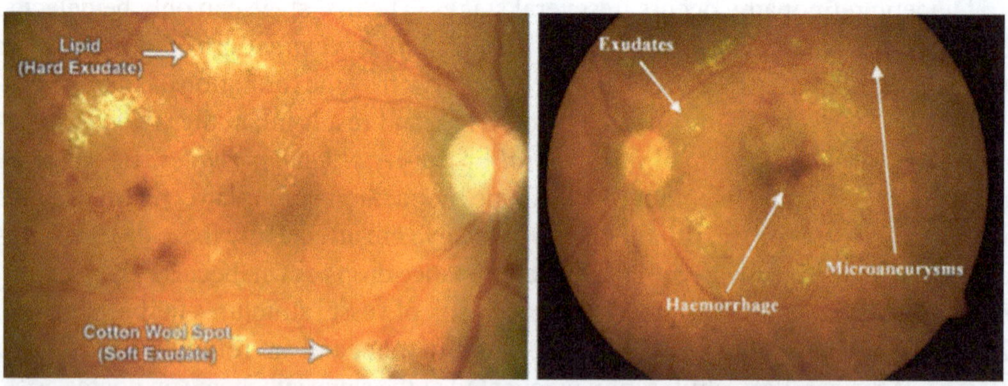

Fig. 11.13 (Left) Hard and soft exudates [46] and (right) haemorrhage and micro-aneurysms [47]

arteriolar occlusions (closures) in the nervous retinal layer. They are often accompanied by a plague-like haemorrhage. There are often extended capillaries along the edges. The colour of this pathology is different from the venous structure, so it does not affect biometric recognition performance, but it can affect the ability of preprocessing algorithms to prepare the image for venous structure extraction.

Age-related Macular Degeneration (ARMD) [27–29] is a multifactorial disease. The only reliably proven cause of ARMD development is age. ARMD is characterised by a group of lesions, among which we classically include the accumulation of deposits in the depth of the retina—drunia, neovascularisation, fluid bleeding, fluid accumulation and geographic atrophy.

Based on clinical manifestations, we can distinguish between dry (atrophic, non-exudative) and wet (exudative, neovascular) disease [27–29]. The dry form affects less than 90% of patients and is about 10% moist.

Dry form—This is caused by the extinction of the capillaries. Clinical findings found that in the dry form of ARMD druses, there are changes in pigmentation and some degree of atrophy. The terminal stage is called *geographic atrophy*. The *druses* are directly visible yellowish deposits at the depth of the retina, corresponding to the accumulation of pathological material in the inner retinal layers. The druses vary in size, shape, appearance. Depending on the type, we can distinguish between soft and hard druses. Soft druses are larger and have a "soft look". They also have a distinct thickness and a tendency to collapse. Druses that are less than half the diameter of the vein at the edge of the target, and they are referred to as small (up to 63 μm) and respond to hard druses. Druses $\geq$125 μm are large and respond to soft druses. Hard druses are not ophthalmoscopically trapped up to 30–50 μm [30]. *Geographic atrophy* is the final stage of the dry, atrophic form of ARMD—see Figs. 11.14 and 11.15. It appears as a sharp, borderline oval or a circular hypopigmentation to depigmentation or direct absence of retinal pigment epithelium. Initially, the atrophy is only light, localised, and gradually spreading often in the horseshoe shape around the fovea. The development of atrophy is related to the presence of druses and, in particular, their collapse or disappearance [27–29].

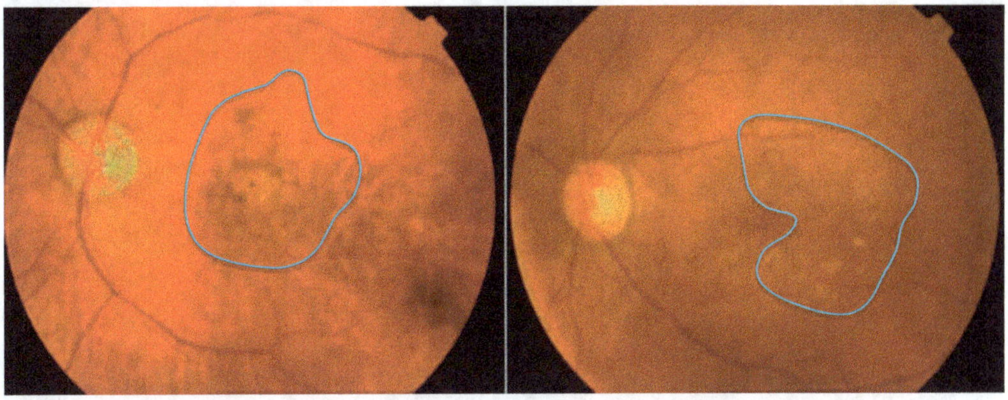

Fig. 11.14 (Left) ARMD—soft druses [48]; (right) ARMD—hard druses [28]

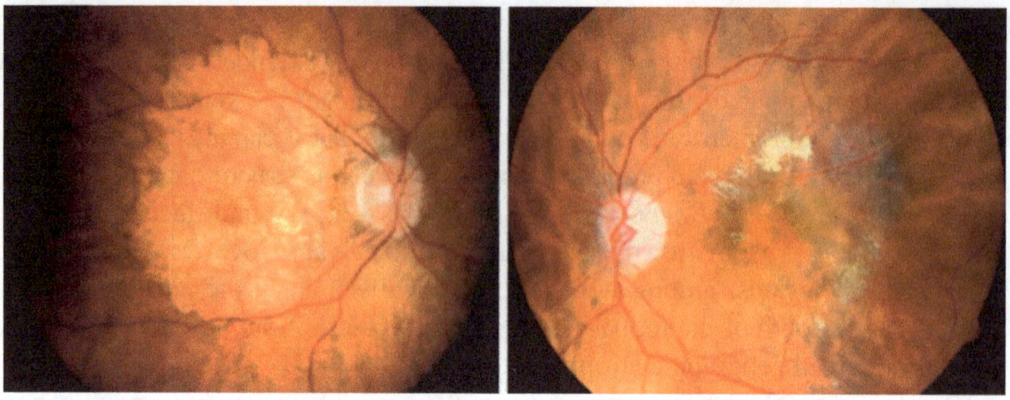

Fig. 11.15 (Left) Geographic atrophy [28]; (right) wet form with edema [49]

Moist form—This is caused by the growth of newly formed vessels from the vasculature that spread below the Bruch membrane. Within the Bruch membrane, cracks are created by which the newly created vessels penetrate under the pigment tissue and later under the retina. The newly created vessels are fragile and often bleed into the sub-retinal space [27–29].

In this case, soft and hard druses are not comparable in colour and shape with the vascular pattern in retinal images; however, they can influence the image pre-processing algorithms, which are preparing the image for extraction of the vascular pattern. Herewith the biometric recognition performance can dropdown. However, this is not a big change. All of the algorithms for retinal image preprocessing should be adopted to treat such diseases to be able to reliably extract the vascular pattern.

The *retinal detachment* (see Fig. 11.16 left) of the eye occurs when a variety of cracks appear in the retina, causing the vitreous fluid to get under the retina and lift it up. Oftentimes, this detachment occurs at the edge of the retina, but from there it slowly moves to the centre of vision when untreated. The ageng process can result in small deposits within the retina, which can create a new connection between the

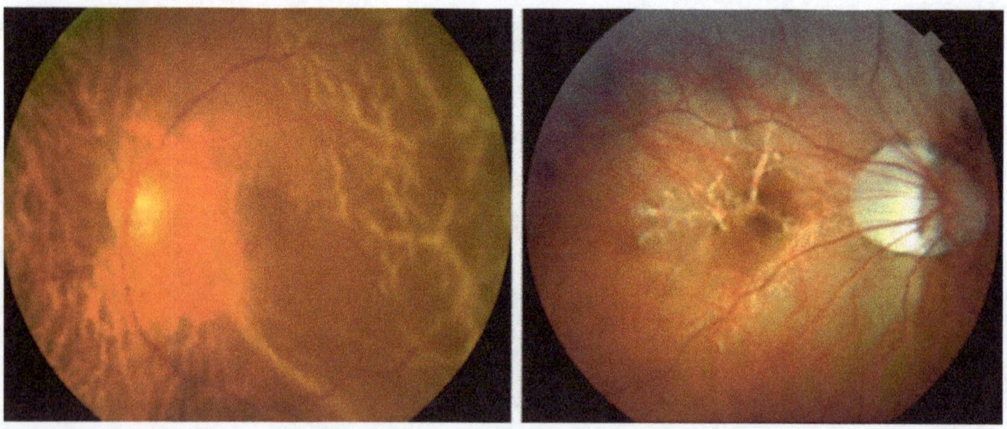

Fig. 11.16 (Left) Retinal detachment [48]; (right) retinal (lacquer) crack [50]

vitreous and the retina [29, 31]. This disease completely destroys the concrete (up the complete) parts of the retina, whereas the vascular pattern is lifted and moved in space, i.e. the original structure before and after this disease is so different that the subject is not be recognised when using a biometric system based on retinal images.

The *retina* can *crack* (see Fig. 11.16 right) in the eye of a person for various reasons. This may be due to the complications of another eye disease, a degenerative form of eye disease, or it can also occur when eye or brain injury occurs. This cracking usually occurs if the retina is not properly perfused for a long time [29, 31]. This means that the venous system beneath the top layer of the retina begins to intermingle, i.e. a new venous structure appears in the retinal image that is difficult to distinguish from the top layer, disabling recognition from the originally stored biometric template. However, it is possible to create a new biometric template in the actual status of the disease that is adapted to the current status after every successful biometric verification.

Retinal inflammation is also known as *retinitis*. Inflammation of the retina of the eye can cause viruses and parasites, but the most common cause is bacteria. In many cases, inflammation of the retina is not isolated and is accompanied by the inflammation of the blood vessel, which holds the retina with blood [29, 31]. Retinitis creates new and distinctive patterns, mostly dark in colour, which greatly complicate the extraction of the venous structure. It is expected to thus have a very strong influence on biometric recognition performance.

Swelling of the *retina*, or diabetic macular edema, affects diabetics as the name suggests. This swelling occurs after leakage of the macula by the fluid. This swelling may occur for data subjects who suffer from long-term diabetes, or if they have too high glucose levels during treatment. Swelling is caused by damage to the retina and its surroundings. These catheters then release the fluid into the retina, where it accumulates, causing swelling [29, 31]. The influence to biometric recognition performance is comparable with the manifestation of retinal detachment—the structure is changed within the space, thus having an impact on the position of vascular system in the retinal layer.

Relatively frequent diseases of the retina are circulatory disorders, where the retinal vessel closes. These closures arise mostly as a result of arteriosclerosis, which is a degenerative vascular disease where it is narrowing and a lower blood supply to tissues [29, 31].

Central vision artery occlusion causes a sudden deterioration in vision. On the ocular background there is a narrowed artery, retinal dyspnea and swelling. Drugs for vascular enlargement, thrombus dissolving medicines and blood clotting drugs are applied [29, 31].

The *closure of the central retinal vein* is manifested by the rapid deterioration of vision; the thrombus causes vein overpressure, vein enlargement is irregular and retinal bleeding occurs. Drugs are used to enlarge the blood vessels and after a time, the thrombi are absorbed, or the circulatory conditions in the retina are improved via laser [29, 31].

Circulatory disorders always have a very significant effect on the colour of the cardiovascular system, making the veins and arteries very difficult to detect, especially when the vessel is combined with its haemorrhage. In this case, it is not possible to reliably detect and extract the venous system, thereby dramatically reducing biometric recognition performance. Even image preprocessing algorithms will not cope with this problem.

11.2.1 Automatic Detection of Druses and Exudates

The disease occurring in the retina may occasionally prevent the proper evaluation of biometric features. Retinal disease can significantly affect the quality and performance of the recognition. The subject can be warned that the quality of his/her retina is changing and artefacts (warn to go to an ophthalmologist) appear, i.e. they are making recognition difficult. Large areas of the retina image impacted by disease or any disorder will lower the recognition performance, and thus retina image quality counts by rating the concepts of ISO/IEC 29794-1. At the present time, we are focusing on detecting and delimiting the exudates/druses and haemorrhages in the image, automatically detecting the position of the macula and blind spot. These are the reference points by which we determine the location of pathological findings. We associate the centre of gravity of the blind spot with the centre of gravity of the macula (yellow spot). Afterwards, we locate the centre of a given point on this abscissa, which is the reference point for comparing and positioning not only the biometric features in the image, but also the diseases and disorders. The greatest negative consequence of vision is spread to the part called the fovea centralis, where the sharpest vision is located. Once this area is damaged, it has a very significant impact on sight. It is also relevant to detect the quality of blood flow within the retina. There is still a lot to do in all areas of imaging and video processing for medical purposes, as input data is very different.

Due to the lack of images with ARMD in the creation of this work, the images with exudates will be used as well. Druses arising from ARMD are very similar to those exudates that occur in diabetic retinopathy. For this reason, it is possible to detect these findings with the same algorithm. In both cases, there are fatty substances deposited in the retina, which have a high-intensity yellow colour (see Fig. 11.20). Their number, shape, size and position on the retina differ from patient to patient.

The detection of droplets and exudates works with the green channel of the default image (Fig. 11.17 left). A normalised blur with a mask of 7×7 pixels is used. This is due to the exclusion of small, unmarked areas that are sometimes difficult to classify by an experienced ophthalmologist. This Gaussian adaptive threshold is then superimposed on this fuzzy image, which is very effective in defining suspicious areas. The threshold for Gauss's adaptive threshold is calculated individually for each pixel where this calculation is obtained by the weighted sum of the adjacent pixels of a given pixel from which a certain constant is subtracted. In this case, the surrounding area is 5 pixels, and the reading constant is 0, so nothing is deducted. The result of this threshold can be seen in Fig. 11.17 middle. Only now a mask containing the areas of the bloodstream and optical disc that have already been detected earlier

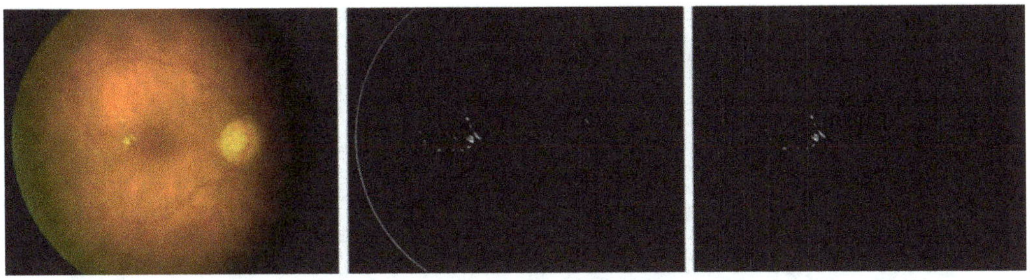

Fig. 11.17 (Left) Original image; (middle) thresholding; (right) obtained suspicious areas

can be applied. If this mask was used at the beginning, it would adversely affect this threshold because it would create too much contrast in the image between the excluded areas and the rest of the retina. This would cause the contours of the blood vessels and the optical disc to be included in suspicious areas, which is undesirable. After the mask is applied, the image is then subjected to a median smoothing with a 5×5 matrix size to remove the noise. The resulting suspicious areas are captured in Fig. 11.17 right.

Retinal images, whose bloodstream contrasts very well with the retina, cause the contours of these vessels to be included in suspicious areas. To prevent this, it is necessary to adjust the bloodstream mask before it is used. Editing is a dilation of this mask in order to enlarge the blood vessels. The difference between the original and the dilated mask is shown in Fig. 11.18 left and right. As soon as this mask is applied, unwanted contours are excluded from the image being processed. A comparison between suspicious areas using an untreated and modified mask can be seen in Fig. 11.19 left and right.

The final step is to determine which of the suspected areas are druses or exudates and which not. For this purpose, the HSV colour model is used, to which the input image is converted. The HSV colour model consists of three components: hue, saturation and value, or the amount of white light in the image.

First, the contours of the suspicious areas are determined in order to calculate their contents. If the content of a given area is greater than 3 pixels, the corresponding

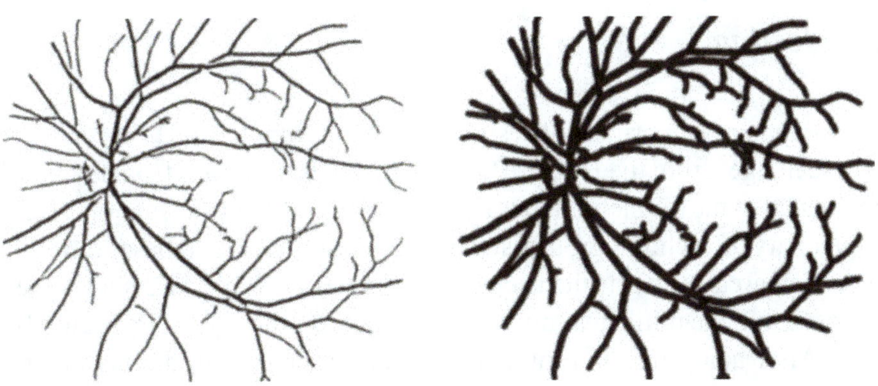

Fig. 11.18 (Left) Original mask; (right) mask after dilatation

Fig. 11.19 (Left) Suspicious areas with untreated mask; (right) suspicious areas with a modified mask

Table 11.2 Overview of HSVs for classification of suspicious areas

Value	Limit 1	Limit 2	Limit 3
H	30–12	30–15	30–19
S	255–170	255–120	255–187
V	255–120	255–84	255–75

area in the HSV image is located. From this, the average colour tone, saturation and brightness of this area can be calculated. Experimenting on the different images set out the limits set out in Table 11.2. If one of the areas falls within one of these limits, it is a druse or exudate.

Once a region has been classified as a finding, its centre of gravity is calculated using the mathematical moments, which represents the centre from which a circle is created to indicate the finding. Labelling is first performed on a blank image, from which external contours are selected after checking all areas. These are plotted in the resulting image so that individual circles do not overlap the detected findings. The result of the detection can be seen in Fig. 11.20 (see Fig. 11.21).

11.2.2 Testing

The algorithm has been primarily designed to detect findings in Diaret databases, but we also use images from the HRFIDB, DRIVE, and four frames from the bottom of a camera located in the biometric laboratory at the Faculty of Information Technology, Brno University of Technology, to test the robustness. These databases differ in image quality, which greatly affects the accuracy of detection. Table 11.3 shows their basic characteristics. In the initial testing of other databases, the algorithm seemed entirely unusable. After analysng the problem of incorrect detection, the parameters were modified and the algorithm achieved better results.

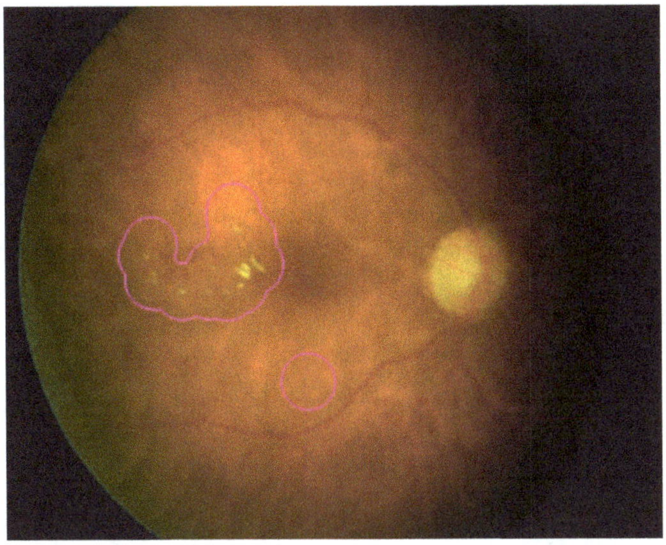

Fig. 11.20 Detection result

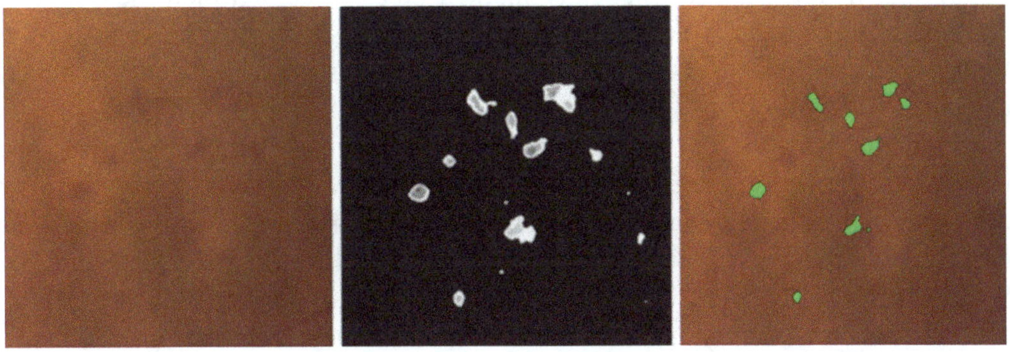

Fig. 11.21 Haemorrhage (left), detection of suspected areas (centre) and haemorrhage (right)

Table 11.3 Database characteristics

Database	Number of frames	Format	Size	Camera	FOV
DIARETDB 0	89	PNG	1,500 × 1,152	–	50°
DIARETDB 1	130	PNG	1,500 × 1,152	–	50°
HRFIDB	16	JPG	3,504 × 2,336	Canon CR-1	45°
DRIVE	20	TIF	565 × 584	Canon CR5	45°
BUT retinal database	4	PNG	3,888 × 2,592	Canon CR-1	–

To evaluate the success of detecting the background mask, optical disc and fovea, an ophthalmologist is not required. These parts of the retina may also be determined by a layman after initial training on the basic anatomy of the retina. However, to evaluate the accuracy of detection, it is necessary to compare these results with the actual results, where detection was performed by a manual physician, optimally an ophthalmologist. These findings are relatively difficult to identify and detection requires practice. Evaluating images is also time consuming. Determination of the findings was carried out manually on the basis of a test program in the presence of a student at the Faculty of Medicine at the Masaryk University in Brno. In addition, the DIARETBD0 and DIARETDB1 databases are attached to *diaretdb0_groundtruths* and *diaretdb1_groundtruths*, where there is information about what symptoms are found in the image (red small dots, haemorrhages, hard exudates, soft exudates, neovascularisation).

In order to detect micro-aneurysms, haemorrhages, exudates and druses, a test program has been developed to speed up and automatically evaluate this process. The test program will display two windows to the user. The first window will display an original image with automatically marked holes through which the matrix is placed. On this matrix, you can click through the cursor to pixels (30×30) that we want to mark as finds. In the second window there is an original image from the database—see Fig. 11.22.

The output from the test program provides four types of data: true positive, false positive, true negative, false negative. We obtain these values by comparing ground truth and automatically evaluated areas for each frame. The resulting values are averaged from all images in order to determine overall sensitivity and specificity. Sensitivity for us, in this case, represents the percentage of the actually affected parts of the retina classified by automatic detection as affected. The true positive rate is obtained using the formula:

$$TPR = \frac{TP}{TP + FN}. \tag{2.1}$$

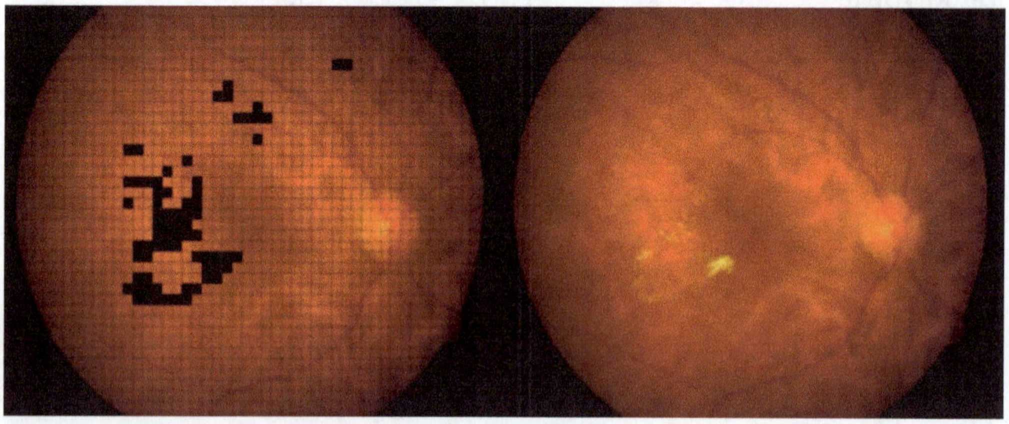

Fig. 11.22 Making ground truths of diseases

Specificity, or true negative rate in our case, means the percentage of healthy parts classified by automatic detection as a healthy retina. We will calculate it according to this relationship:

$$TNR = \frac{TN}{TN + FP}. \tag{2.2}$$

As we can see in Table 11.4, the optical disc was misidentified in eight cases. Incorrect optical disc detection is caused by poor image quality; these shots contain shadows or light reflections from the bottom of the camera. In one case, incorrect detection causes an exudate of the same size and intensity as the optical disc.

The following two tables show the results of individual flaw detection tests (Tables 11.5 and 11.6).

To test the possibility of using the algorithm for other fundus cameras, we use images from the HRFIDB [19] and DRIVE [32] databases, along with four frames from the BUT retinal database. In the first test, the algorithm over these databases showed zero usability. This result causes a different image quality. Table 11.7 shows the success of optical disc detection. The best results were obtained over the HRFIDB database and on the pictures from the BUT database. These pictures are of good quality and do not contain significant disease manifestations.

The following tables show the success of detecting findings: exudates, druses, micro-aneurysms, haemorrhages (Tables 11.8 and 11.9).

There were no signs in the pictures taken from the school camera (Table 11.10).

Table 11.4 Optical disc

Database	True positive	False positive	Success rate [%]
DIARETDB0	85	4	95.29
DIARETDB1	126	4	96.82

Table 11.5 Results of DIARETDB0

Diaretdb0	Sensitivity [%]	Specificity [%]	Success rate [%]
Exudates and druses	94.26	99.41	99.65
Microanalysis and haemorrhage	92.66	99.24	99.24

Table 11.6 Results of DIARETDB1

Diaretdb1	Sensitivity [%]	Specificity [%]	Success rate [%]
Exudates and druses	90.28	99.32	99.65
Microanalysis and haemorrhage	91.46	99.35	99.42

Table 11.7 Results of OD detection

Database	True positive	False positive	Success rate [%]
HRFIDB	16	0	100.00
DRIVE	19	1	94.73
BUT retinal database	4	0	100.00

Table 11.8 Results of HRFIDB

HRFIDB	Sensitivity [%]	Specificity [%]	Success rate [%]
Exudates and druses	69.81	98.76	98.36
Micro-aneurysm and haemorrhage	18.30	99.87	99.51

Table 11.9 Results—DRIVE

Drive	Sensitivity [%]	Specificity [%]	Success rate [%]
Exudates and druses	63.63	99.70	99.70
Micro-aneurysm and haemorrhage	NA	98.63	98.53

Table 11.10 Results—BUT retinal database

BUT retinal database	Sensitivity [%]	Specificity [%]	Success rate [%]
Exudates and druses	NA	99.93	99.93
Micro-aneurysm and haemorrhage	NA	99.97	99.95

11.3 Biometric Information Amounts in the Retina

The third part of this chapter summarises our research in computing the amount of information in retinal images. We analysed the available databases on the Internet and on our own, we computed the amount of bifurcations and crossings there are, and made a first model of the occurrence of these points in the retina. Based on this result we are working on computing a theoretical model for estimating the amount of information (the maximum amount of embedded information in the retina). The grid with occurrence probability distribution is shown in the figures as the end of this section.

In the future, we want to start determining entropy in retina images. Entropy is sometimes also referred to as a system disorder. It is one of the basic concepts in many scientific fields. Information entropy is also called Shannon entropy. In the following lines, the entropy term will always mean information entropy. We will count entropy as a combination of possible variants. For example, fingerprinting methods can be used to calculate retinal biometric entropy. The entropy counting of the biological properties of the eye itself is limited by the sensing device. The resulting entropy is then related to the available resolution. The reason why we want to estimate the maximum, average and minimal entropy is to get the idea of how precise the recognition could be and how many people we can use this technology for. It is believed that the retinal biometric entropy is corresponding to 10 times more then our population has, however, this has not been proven until today.

Estimations for eye biometric entropy were done by several researchers. Daugman [33] analysed binary iris features, on which the Hamming distance is used for comparing all subjects of a database to each other. He related the score distribution to a Bernoulli Experiment having $N = \frac{\mu(1-\mu)}{\sigma^2}$ degrees of freedom, where μ is the observed Hamming distance mean value and σ^2 is the variance, respectively.

Adler et al. [34] referred to the biometric information as biometric uniqueness measurement. The approaches are based on a brute force estimate of collision, estimating the number of independent bits on binarised feature vectors and the relative entropy between genuine and impostor subspaces.

Nauch et al. [35] analysed the entropy of *i*-vector feature spaces in speaker recognition. They compared the duration-variable p subspaces (Gaussian distribution $p(x) \sim \mathrm{N}(\overrightarrow{\mu_p}, \Sigma_p))$ with the full-duration q spaces (Gaussian distribution $q(x) \sim \mathrm{N}(\overrightarrow{\mu_q}, \Sigma_q))$, simulating the automatic recognition case for the analytic purposes of estimating the biometric information of state-of-the-art speaker recognition in a duration-sensitive manner.

Arakala et al. [15] used an enrollment scheme based on individual vessels around the blind spot. Each vein line is represented by a triple position thickness angle, where the position is the angle in degrees to the centre of the blind spot, the thickness of the vessel is again in degrees and the angle is the slope of the vessel against the thought line passing through the centre of the blind spot. It was found that the position attribute corresponds to a uniform distribution of probability, the distribution of the angles corresponded to a normal distribution with a centre at 90° and a mean deviation of 7.5°. Two peaks appeared in thickness, so the description of the probability distribution was divided into peak and normal distributions. The study resulted in an approximate entropy value of 17 bits.

11.3.1 Theoretical Determination of Biometric Information in Retina

Based on the previously mentioned work [15], we try to count biometric entropy in a wider area around the blind spot. First, we mark the ring area with a radius of distance between the blind spot and fovea and cut off the blind spot. Then we mark crossings and bifurcations. The resulting region we unfold from polar coordinates to Cartesian ones. The resulting rectangle is then used for easier indexing of the place.

Using this principle, we expect deployment at any point of area. Then, using the combinatorial Eq. (3.1), we calculate the maximum (theoretical) number of feature points. We simulate all combinations of points in area. In this equation, we are particularly interested in the position of the points, then the angle at which the

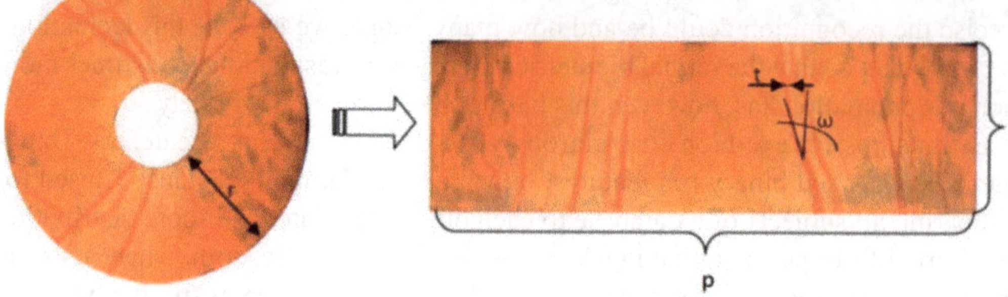

Fig. 11.23 Unfolding interest area

individual vessels are at the centre of the blind spot, and finally their thickness.

$$\Psi = \binom{p \cdot r}{n} \cdot \binom{\omega + 2}{3} \cdot \binom{t + 1}{2}, \tag{3.1}$$

where r is the width of the ring in pixels, p is the width in pixels of the expanded ring around the blind spot, n is the average number of features (crossings and bifurcations) in the image, ω is the number of possible angles that the vessels enclose with each other and t (in the Fig. 11.23) is the maximum vessel thickness. The first part of the formula expresses the possible location of features. It is a combination without repetition—two features cannot occur in the same place. The angles ω usually have a value of about 120°, as their sum will always be 360°. Angles can be repeated, so a repeat combination is used in the formula. Likewise for the last part. The vessel thicknesses of two out of three will be used for their resolution. The third thickness is usually the same as one of the two previous ones.

When adding derived parameters from several retina samples, we can approximately calculate how many combinations of all parameters are within their limits.

$$\Psi = \binom{p \cdot r}{n} \cdot \binom{\omega + 2}{3} \cdot \binom{t + 1}{2} = \binom{360 \cdot 120}{20} \cdot \binom{60 + 2}{3} \cdot \binom{12 + 1}{2} = 6.2 \times 10^{80}. \tag{3.2}$$

11.3.2 Used Databases and Applications

For the purpose described at the beginning of this section, we used three publicly available databases: Messidor [18], e-ophtha [36] and High-Resolution Fundus (HRF) [19]. The *Messidor* database contains 1,200 eye fundus colour numerical images of the posterior pole. Images were acquired by three ophthalmologic departments using a colour video 3CCD camera on a Topcon TRC NW6 non-mydriatic retinograph with a 45° field of view. The images were captured using 8 bits per colour plane, at 440 × 960, 240 × 488 or 304 × 536 pixels. 800 images were captured with pupil dilation (one drop of Tropicamide at 0.5%) and 400 without dilation. The *e-ophtha* database contains 47 images with exudates and 35 images with no lesions. The *HRF* database contains 15 images of healthy patients, 15 images of patients with diabetic retinopathy and 15 images of glaucomatous patients. Binary gold standard vessel segmentation images are available for each image. Additionally, the masks determining Field of View (FOV) are provided for particular datasets. The gold standard data is generated by a group of experts working in the field of retinal image analysis and medical staff from the cooperating ophthalmology clinics.

We randomly selected 460 images from Messidor, 160 images from e-ophtha and 50 images from HRF. In the selected retinal images, both left and right eye images were available. Images were reduced to a resolution of about 1 Mpx in order to fit images on screen.

We developed three application software modules (marked as SW_1, SW_2 and SW_3). SW_1 was developed for manually marking blind spots, yellow spots and features as well as determining their polar coordinates. We marked all retinal images via SW_1 one by one. At first, we marked the boundary of the blind spot and then the centre of the yellow spot. SW_1 considered the blind spot as the pole and the line between the blind spot to the yellow spot as the polar axis. Therefore, the angle between the two spots was 0°. SW_1 considered the distance between two spots as the unit distance. Usually, the distance in pixels was not equal for two different retinal images. However, SW_1 considered distance as one unit for each image. Therefore, the position of the yellow spot in every image was $(1, 0°)$ in polar coordinates. After marking two spots, we marked each feature by a single click. SW_1 estimated the polar coordinates of each feature by increasing clockwise and scaling distance.

SW_2 was developed to conduct the marking process automatically and to compare its detection accuracy with the manually marked-up results. The details of this software were summarised in one master thesis [37].

SW_3 was developed to estimate the number of features in different regions as shown in Fig. 11.23. SW_3 loaded all marked retinal images one by one and mapped the polar coordinates of features to Cartesian coordinates. After that, SW_3 presented the intensity of occurring features in the area of 5×5 pixels by a range of varying shades of grey. The darker shade represented the higher occurrence of features, whereas the lighter shade represented a lower occurrence. Then SW_3 drew two circles in order to show the boundary of the location of features, where the inner circle covered a 90% area of the outer circle. Two circles were split up into four sectors by a horizontal line and a vertical line. Radiuses were drawn every 18°, which split each sector into five regions. The percentage of the occurrence of features in each region was written outside of the outer circle. SW_3 also drew two ellipses, E_{blind} and E_{yellow}, in order to show the region surrounding the blind spot and the yellow spot, respectively. The sizes of the ellipses were dependent on a threshold value δ_1. That means the size of a single ellipse was increased until the number of features inside that ellipse did not cross the δ_1 value. SW_3 also drew an arc along the *x*-axis. The width of the arc was decided by a threshold value of δ_2. We set δ_1 to 10 and δ_2 to 500, based on the number of labelled points in all retinae.

11.3.3 Results

On average, we found 48 features on each image. The success rates of locating blind spots and the yellow spot automatically were 92.97% and 94.05%, respectively. The wrong localisation of spots was caused primarily because of spots that were too bright or too dark. The average deviation of a feature marked by SW_1 and SW_2 was about 5 pixels [37]. E_{blind} occupied 2.040% of the retina area, whereas E_{yellow} occupied 2.728% of the retina area, as shown in Fig. 11.24. The number of features is very low inside E_{blind} and E_{yellow}, especially inside E_{yellow}. Therefore, E_{yellow} was bigger than E_{blind}. On the real retinal image, near the yellow spot, the branches were so small and the blood vessels were so thin that they were not captured by the fundus camera. Therefore, a wide empty space can be seen near E_{yellow} in Fig. 11.24. We also noticed that the major blood vessels often directed to four main directions from the blind spot.

By creating a bifurcation and crossings scheme, we can now start generating formulas for calculating the biometric entropy of retinal images using our biometric recognition method. In the Fig. 11.24, there are areas around the blind spot and the fovea where almost no markers are present. The area between the maximum edge (grey in the picture) of the points and the (green) inner circle is eliminated from the calculation. It's a part that did not have to be seen in most of the pictures.

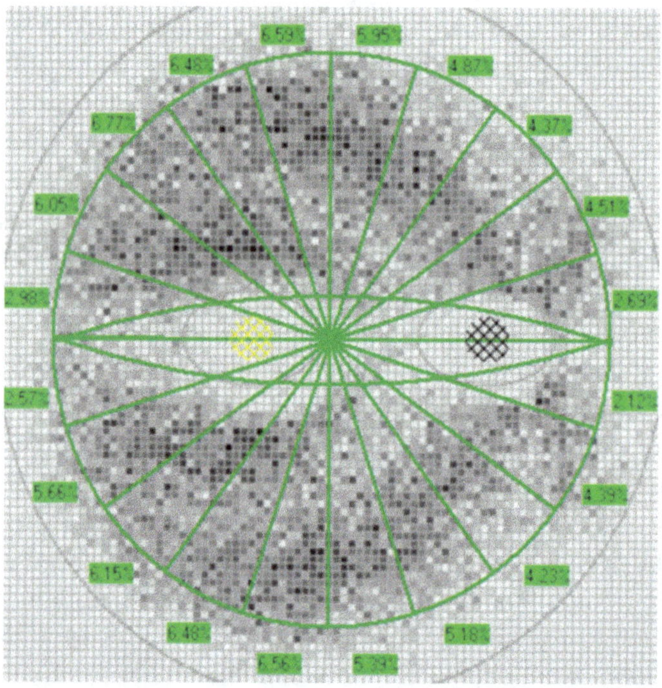

Fig. 11.24 Merged all bifurcations and crossings from the marked images

11.4 Synthetic Retinal Images

The last section of this chapter will be devoted to our generator of synthetic retinal images. We are able to generate a synthetic retinal image, including the blind spot, macula and vascular patterns with randomly generated or predefined features (crossings and bifurcations). Now we are working on the additional features that will decrease the quality of such images, e.g. reflections, diseases. We are also working on supplementing that with something that will generate diseases and damage on the image of retina, so we can create a unique database for deep learning.

The main reason for a such generator is that it is very difficult to get a large-scale database(s) with thousands of retinal images. To collect retinal images from subjects, you need the appropriate equipment (minimally digital ophthalmoscope or even better a fundus camera) and you need to find the volunteers who will be willing to let their retinas get acquired. The best way, comparably with fingerprint areas in biometric systems (synthetic image generators SFinGe, Anguli and SyFDaS), is to use a generator of synthetic images. With that it is possible to generate any large-scale database, where you can predefine (in a configuration file) the setting, i.e. how many images with which background, distortions and features should be generated. Therefore, this part is very important for biometric systems, because with this way the training and testing of algorithms for biometric retinal recognition could be done on large-scale databases. It is important that the quality of the images correspond to the real images, i.e. some work is still ahead of us.

First, a basic idea of how the generator will work and how its main parts are identified is described. Furthermore, the designs of the individual parts of the generator are described in greater detail and are intended to create partial sections of the resulting image. The aim is to design the generator so that it generates images as close as possible to real images of the retina. Real images often have a very different look in terms of colour distribution or detail. One of the test options which we compare the reality of created images is using the bifurcation and crossing searching described in Sect. 11.1.4.

The generator is able to create the desired number of randomly generated synthetic retinal images at the selected resolution and the selected general properties, such as the image angle or the zoom rate according to the specified parameters.

The generator can then generate a large number of images of the retina, where it is possible to train and test various algorithms. If we add a disease creation module to the generator, we can also test algorithms for further detection.

11.4.1 Vascular Bed Layer

The retinal vasculature of the retina consists of the arterial and venous channels. Both of these beds can be divided into upper and lower branches, which are further divided into nasal and temporal branches.

When generating the texture of this layer, the generator uses pre-generated branching positions for the arterial and vein branches. The method for generating these positions is described in Sect. 11.4.4. Generally, the generator first creates separate textures of the arterial and venous channels, which then merge into one final texture (see Fig. 11.25). This division is necessary due to the way the vascular bed is rendered. It counts that blood vessels do not cross each other.

Partial textures are merged so that when the artery and vein are in the same position, a new value of the colour and transparency of the texture is calculated at that position. In this calculation, both original colours are used with respect to transparency, with the unified textured vein being drawn above the artery. If only the artery or vein is at the given position, it will be redrawn into the resulting texture unchanged. If there is no vessel in the position, this position remains transparent on the resulting texture.

Partial textures then arise through the gradual plotting of the individual branches of the arterial or venous passages.

In order for a natural resulting vessel shape, it is necessary that the connectors between the individual branches of the branch take the form of a curve without significant sharp breaks at the branching points. Because the curve is the link between the sequences of points, it cannot be divided into several parts at one point. Therefore, the branched tree of the given branch is plotted sequentially, as shown in Fig. 11.26. A description of this plotting is given in Chap. 4.4.

Gradual rendering takes place by gradually forming a curve from the initial point of the branch of the vascular stream, which passes through the following branches of branching, where it continues with a wider vessel at any one of the endpoints of the vascular bed. As soon as the vessel is drawn from the beginning to the end, a

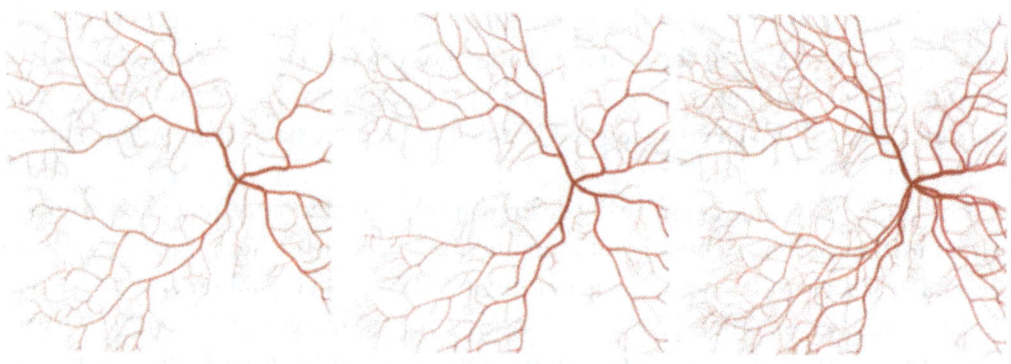

Fig. 11.25 (Left) Arterial fluid texture; (middle) vein texture; (right) resulting vascular fluid texture

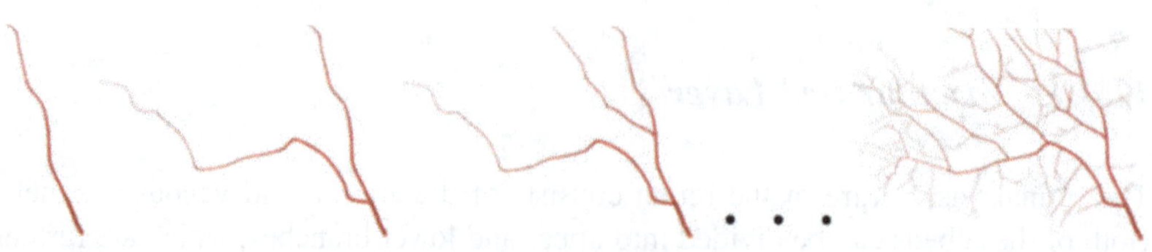

Fig. 11.26 Gradual rendering of the upper temporal branch

Fig. 11.27 Connecting the new vessel to the already depicted vessel at the branch point

new starting point is chosen as one of the already drawn branch points, in which the beginning has the widest still unrefined vessel. The vessel with this starting point will be drawn in the same way as the first vessel. This procedure is repeated until all the blood vessels of the branch are drawn. To plot the vessel the cubic Bézier curve is used: see [38].

The vessel is plotted sequentially from the starting point to the endpoint following the pair of branching points running consecutively. For each point's pair and the relevant control points that affect the shape of the curve between them, the partial points of the curve are then calculated.

Calculated Bézier curve points are then linked by lines whose points are calculated using the Bresenham algorithm. A texture of the blood vessel is drawn around this curve, consisting of partial segments. For each point of the curve, a semicircle is drawn in the direction of the line below which the point belongs. The Bresenham algorithm is also used to draw this semicircle, with the radius of the circle (line length) equal to half the width of the vessel at that point. In this rendering process, all points belonging to the texture of the vessel are rendered, but for one point its colour is calculated several times with different parameters. The resulting colour is selected as the colour whose individual components have the highest value. The lightest and least transparent colour corresponds to the smallest distance from the centre of the vessel.

This method of selecting the resulting point colour is the reason why arteries and veins have to be plotted separately and then combined into one texture in another way. However, it is used when plotting a new vessel to connect this vessel to the already drawn vessel at the branch point: see Fig. 11.27.

The basic RGB colour of the texture is in the artery (160, 15, 15) and in the vein (150, 5, 15). The individual colour components are adjusted for each frame by multiplying by *rand* (0.99, 1.01).

11.4.2 Layers

When looking at the real images of retinas, it is possible to easily identify four different parts of the image that can be generated separately and then be combined into a final image. These subparts are represented as image layers in the generator, where the lowermost layer contains the background texture of the retina. Here, the layer containing the texture of the optic nerve target overlaps. Both of these layers are covered by another layer containing the texture of the vascular bed. All layers then overlay the textured frame layer. Figure 11.28 shows the plot of the individual layers in the given order.

The layer has the shape of a square surface on which the texture is applied. The side size of this area is equal to the shorter side of the rendering window, which is multiplied by two scaling parameters. The centre of the layer is aligned to the centre of the rendering window, with only the parts of the generated text within the rendering window being included in the resulting image.

Because of the layer size and texture variable applied to it, the generator uses a custom coordinate system to create textures, where it then maps the individual pixels of the texture.

Scaling, shifting and rotating the layer and the texture are designed to be independent of texture generation. While scaling modifies the layer size and does not manipulate the coordinate system, rotation and displacement do not change the position of the layer but are applied to the coordinate system.

As can be seen in the real frames shown in the earlier sections of this work, the images of the retina do not always occupy the whole area of the image, or sometimes they are partially cut-off. Therefore, we resize the layer so that the size of the rendering window does not change, as well as the resolution of the resulting image.

As with the first case, but this time without changing the frame texture layer size, it is possible to choose how much of the retina is presented in the image, so be sure to choose the pixel size of the fundus camera that would capture such a frame. Different settings for this parameter are shown in Fig. 11.29.

Real motion capture is not always ideal. The image is more or less rotated and possibly slightly shifted. The displacement may also be deliberate if another part of the retina is being captured. For this reason, these transformations also allow the proposed generator. Both transformations are applied to the coordinate system, not to the layer itself. First, a shift is made followed by rotation. For each layer, it is possible to set the own rotation and displacement size with both layers transforming over layers. Thus, when the background is rotated and shifted, the target of the optic nerve and the vascular bed is shifted. Further transformation at the optic nerve target layer can then change its position relative to the background. Likewise, the position of the vascular bed can be changed to the lower two layers. Since these transformations

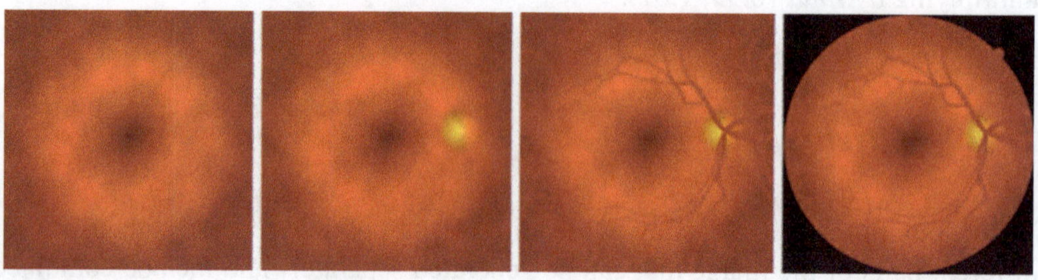

Fig. 11.28 A gradual render of layers. (left) Background layer; (left middle) adding a layer of the optic nerve target; (right middle) adding a vascular bed layer; (right) adding a layer of frame

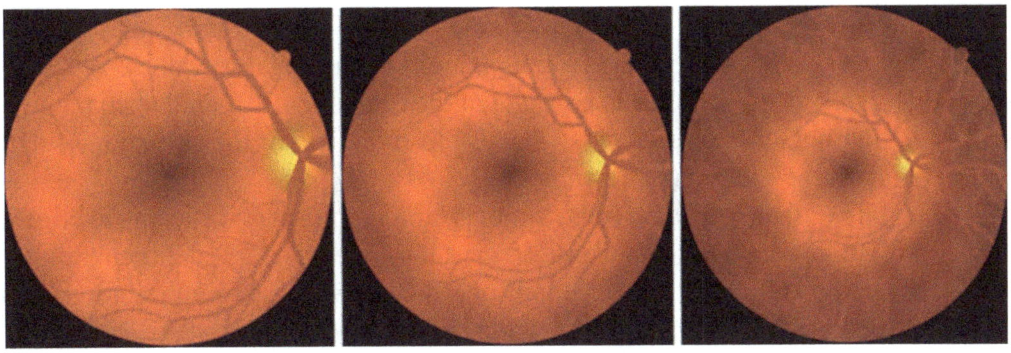

Fig. 11.29 The different sizes of the retrieved part of the retina: (left) maximal zoom; (middle) central zoom; (right) no zoom

are intended to simulate a different eye position when capturing the retina, they are not applied to the frame layer.

11.4.3 Background Layers

The retina background is mostly reddish; the fovea and ex-macular periphery are darker. The area between the fovea and the border of the macular area is then lighter. In a more detailed view, smaller objects of different colours and intensities are visible throughout the area, creating a dense vascular network of the cavity.

The generated background texture is opaque to basic RGB colour (200, 60, 40). Figure 11.30 shows the resulting background texture.

This function describes the randomness of the background texture and is generated by the shadowing choroid. It uses Perlin noise, which has three octaves, frequency and amplitude set to 1, and returning values from interval <−1;1>. Perlin noise is also initialised by a random number, making it different for each frame.

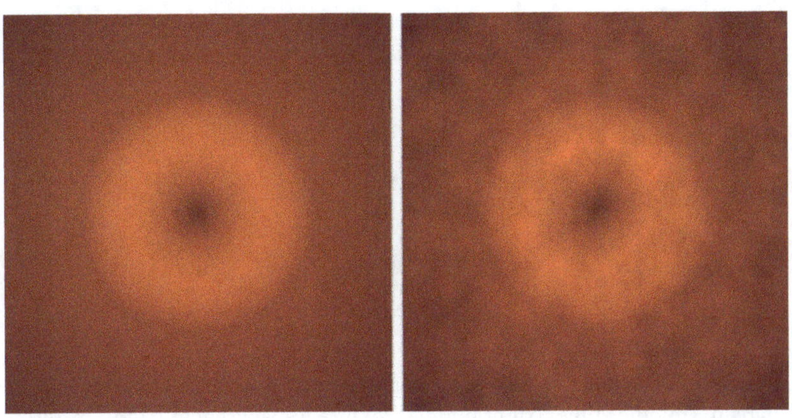

Fig. 11.30 (Left) The resulting background texture without a noise function; (right) with a noise function

Graphically, the function is depicted in Fig. 11.31 where the dark areas indicate the positive values of the noise and the light areas of the negative values. When the dark area is getting lighter, the closer value of the function is to 1 and when the light area is getting lighter, the function's value is closer to -1. At the transition of dark and light areas, the function has a value of 0.

The texture of the Optic Disc (OD) target is largely transparent except the ellipse-shaped area that contains the texture of the OD target itself. When generating a texture inside this ellipse, the base colour of the RGB value is again returned (250, 250, 150). Each folder is multiplied by the function *rand* (0.98, 1.02), as well as background textures to ensure the variability of the base colour for different images.

Figure 11.32 shows the resultant texture of the OD target (cut from the overall layer texture) together with the individual colour components from which it was composed. However, the colour of the texture still changes in the final rendering, and because of its partial transparency, its colour also affects the colour of the background texture beneath it.

For each image, the final position of the OD is slightly different due to accidental slight rotation and displacement. When the left-eye image is generated, the rotation is 180°.

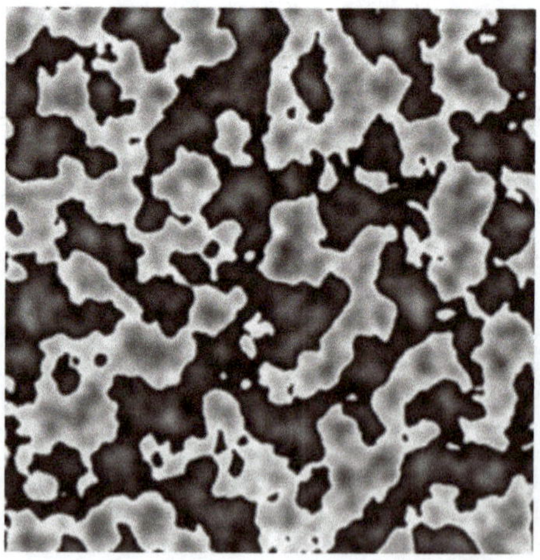

Fig. 11.31 Noise function

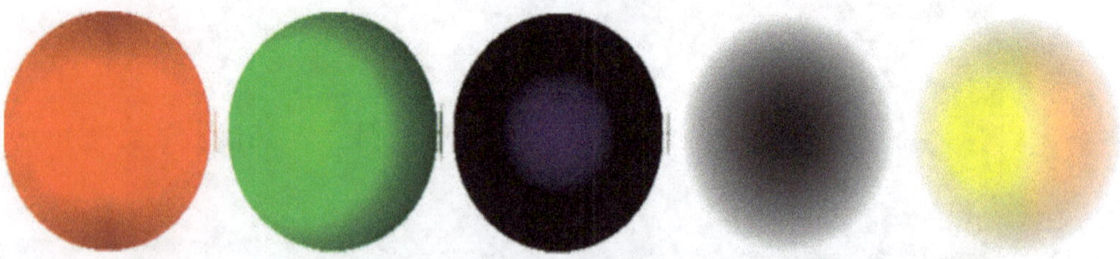

Fig. 11.32 The texture of the optic nerve target and its parts: (left) red texture colour component; (left middle) green; (middle) blue; (right middle) texture transparency; (right) resulting texture

11.4.4 Generating a Vascular Bed

Before drawing a vascular bed, it is first necessary to generate the branch positions of the blood vessels and properties of these points needed for plotting. These points are generated separately for each of the major branches of the artery and vein. Branching points are generated for all branches by the same algorithm with different values of some parameters. Their generation is divided into two parts. First, a tree of branch points is generated, and then the positions of individual points are gradually calculated with respect to the already calculated positions of the other points in the tree.

Each branch point has several properties that need to be generated:

- **Point position** (counted later),
- **Distance from previous point**—length of line between these two points,
- **Vessel width**—value from interval <0;1> , where 1 has a vessel at the starting point of a given branch, and a value of 0 has the endpoints of a given branch.
- Point type
  - Y-branching—the vessel is divided into two approximately equally wide vessels,
  - T-branching—the vessel is divided into a wide and narrow vessel,
  - no branching—the vessel is not split, just passing through the point,
  - end of vessel.
- **Types of vessel** (see Fig. 11.33)

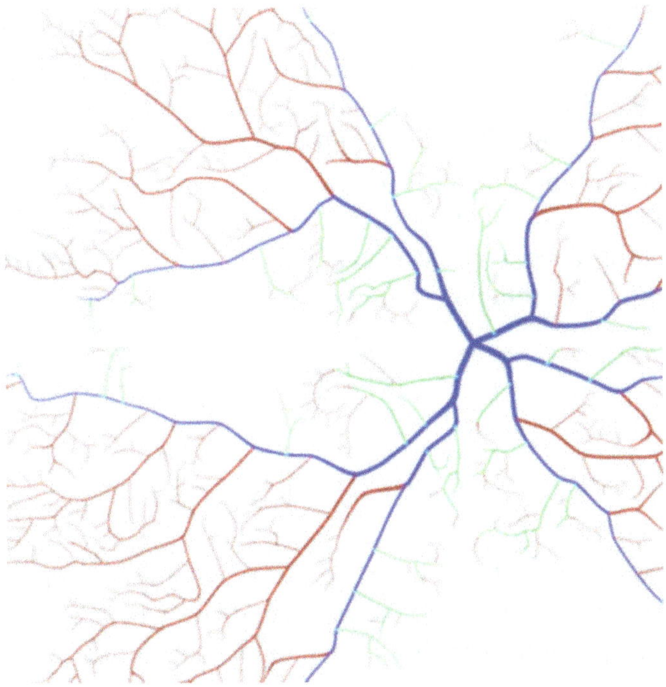

Fig. 11.33 Colour illustration of different types of vessels

- left and right strong blood vessels (blue),
- left/right wider weak blood vessel emerging from the left/right strong blood vessel (green),
- other blood vessels (red).

The root of the branch tree is the point located at the centre of the optic nerve target. It creates one of the following branching points, and then generates the tree recursively so that each new branching point generates the following two branch points. Generation ends when the vessel's width at the newly created point is ≤ 0. The properties of the following branch points are also calculated, and the design of the method of calculating some of them was based on the information published in [39].

The distance from the previous point d is calculated for the following two points according to the vessel width w_a at the current point as follows:

$$d = \begin{cases} rand(0.15,\ 0.05)\ \text{for}\ w_a > 0.15 \\ rand(0.05,\ 0.02)\ \ \text{else} \end{cases}. \tag{4.1}$$

This has the consequence of the narrow blood vessels having more branches.

First, depending on the type of branch of the current point, the ratio is calculated to which the right and left successor are divided. If it is the current point Y-branch, the ratio of right and left successors is calculated as r: $(1 - r)$, where $r = rand$ (0.45, 0.55). In case of T-branching, it is 50% probability $r = rand$ (0.95, 0.99), otherwise $r = rand$ (0.01, 0.05).

If the current point is a part of the leftmost or rightmost strong blood vessel, this probability is altered in the T-branch, such that the weaker T-branch branches are generated towards the boundary of the quadrant. In the beginning, there is a 70% probability that the weaker vessel is generated towards the boundary of the quadrant. If this happens, this probability will decrease by 10% for the type of vessel (left or right); if not, the probability will increase by 10%.

The value of the vessel's width is then calculated for both of the following branch points using their distance from the actual point, the vessel width at the current point, and the division ratio as follows:

$$w_r = \left(w_a \times \sqrt{r}\right) - \left(w_a \times \frac{d_r}{10}\right) - \frac{d_r}{20}, \tag{4.2}$$

$$w_l = \left(w_a \times \sqrt{1-r}\right) - \left(w_a \times \frac{d_l}{10}\right) - \frac{d_l}{20}. \tag{4.3}$$

If the width of the calculated vessel at the next point is not positive, this point is marked as the vessel endpoint. If the calculated width is negative, the distance of that point from the previous point is adjusted to the width of the vessel, which at that point is equal to zero.

In other cases, it is decided whether the following point will be a Y-branch or a T-branch. One of the auxiliary features of a point is the probability of selecting the

Y-Branch for its following branching points, that is, at the starting point, set to 20%. If the selected branch type of the next branch is the Y-branch, then this probability is set to 0% at this next point. If the T-branch is selected and the next point is the weaker T-branch of the current point, the probability for this next point is set to 40%. Otherwise, the probability is increased by 25%.

First, the position of the leftmost and rightmost points of thick blood vessels (type 1) is calculated, then it points the position of the left/right wider weak blood vessels resulting from vascular type 1 (type 2) and finally, the position of the other vessel (type 3). Within these types of vessels, the order of points in the calculation of the positions is given by the width of the vessel at a given point, with the positions of the wider vessels being counted first. Point positions are counted in this order because not all tree branch points generated will eventually be used.

When calculating the position of a particular branch point, the set of positions on which this point may be located is first determined. From the beginning, these are the positions around the previous branch point at the distance that this particular point has generated as a property. Then, depending on the direction of the vessel at the previous point, this set is limited by the interval of angles in which the position of the point may be. For each of the remaining positions, the weight of the position is calculated based on the deviation from the centre of the interval.

On the real images, the observed part of the retina is circular and the rest of square image is black. A majority of the right-hand portion of the image tends to see a smaller part of the retina in the shape of a semicircle or rectangle. This is to know where the picture is; for example, if it is not turned.

The generator allows you to choose which quadrant the mark will be in, and also whether the mark will have the shape of a semicircle or rectangle. The generated texture has a black colour and, depending on the coordinates, only the transparency of the texture changes.

11.4.5 Testing

We are now comparing the created synthetic retinal images with our ground truth. We use manually marked, real retinal images to create a density map, where there are the most bifurcation and crossing points. Using the same procedure, we want to automatically create a density map for synthetic retinal images and compare both results.

We developed the applications SW_1 and SW_2 (see Sect. 11.3.2). SW_1 was developed for manually marking blind spots, yellow spots and features, as well as determining their polar coordinates. We marked all retinal images via SW_1 one by one.

SW_2 was developed to estimate the number of feature points in different regions. SW_2 loaded all marked retinal images one by one and mapped polar coordinates of feature points to Cartesian coordinates. After that, SW_2 presented the intensity of occurring features in 5×5 pixels by a range of shades of grey. The darker shade

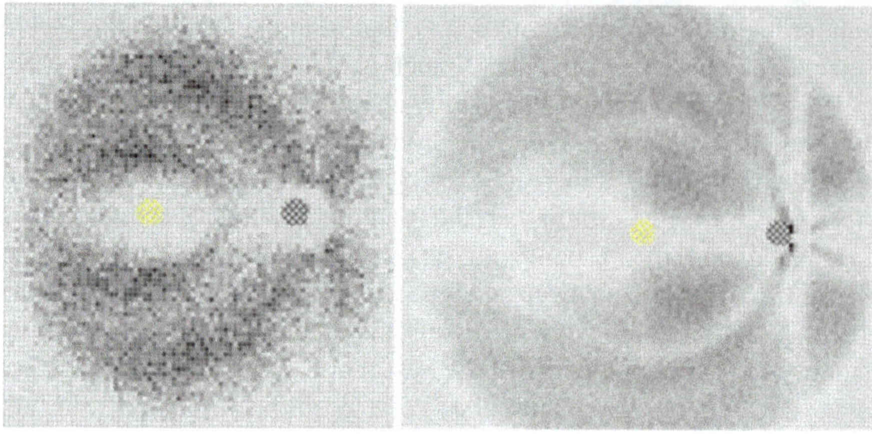

Fig. 11.34 (Left) Density occurrence of summarised real retinas; (right) density in synthetically generated retinas

represented higher occurrence of features, whereas the lighter shade represented lower occurrence.

Using the application described in the previous chapters, 1,000 images were generated in which the crossover and bifurcation were found. The occurrence frequencies were merged with the SW_2 described in Sect. 11.2.2 and graphically represented result seen in Fig. 11.34 left.

It was then possible to visually compare the results of synthetic and real retinal images. In Fig. 11.34 right, there are visible features on the blind spot. It's a side effect. On real retinas, there were no marked features inside the blind spot.

Figure 11.34 shows the summarised occurrences of crosses and bifurcations for real (left) and synthetic (right) retinal images. Picture (left) is marked manually and picture (right) is marked automatically. Both pictures are made up of about a thousand retinas. The shades' range of the right picture is expanded because automated search for markers included features inside the blind spot. Features inside the blind spot in the left image were removed during manual labelling. Although the application generates blood vessels in the synthetic retina symmetrically, some similarities with the summation from the real retina can be traced.

The application is composed only of basic algorithms. As a result, there could be regular shapes seen in Fig. 11.34 right. We assume that, based on real retinas research, we can better specify the distribution of crossings and bifurcations in the model.

11.4.6 Generating Synthetic Images Via Neural Network

In another application, we first generate healthy images, where we can train algorithms for detection and extraction of the optical disc and fovea. Furthermore, we generate diseased retinal images with manifestations of ARMD and diabetes, e.g.

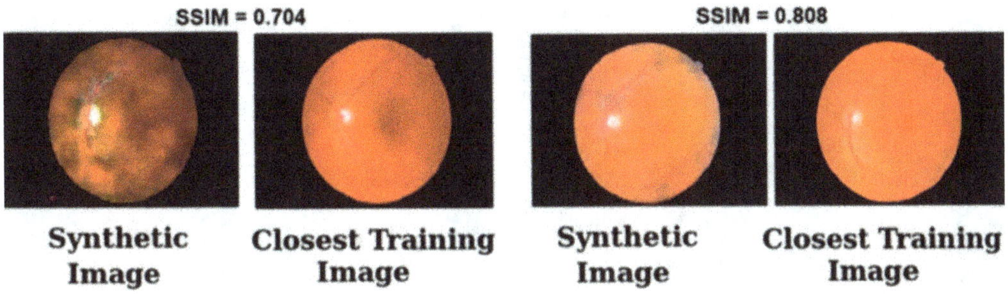

Fig. 11.35 Comparison of synthetic image and the closest training image from the database

haemorrhages, exudates. The neural network learns such images, which we have in the training set. At the moment, we only have images only for ARMD and diabetes; however, new images are stored in the database, i.e. it is possible to add new features representing new ophthalmologic diseases.

In biometric systems, it is often the case that a damaged image does not pass through the recognition. However, there is often not enough training data for detecting algorithms. Therefore, it is advisable to create large databases of synthetic meshes damaged by disease.

We have trained Generative Adversarial Networks (GANs) [40] to generate synthesised retinal images. A GANs-based retinal image synthesiser consists of two neural networks: a Generator (G) and a Discriminator (D). We have not used any extra information (such as blood vessel trees) to generate retinal images using GANs. However, we have emphasised maintaining a balance between the two competitors (i.e. G) and (D) during training. We have found that if this balance is not kept, G may end up generating only blurry retina images without high-level structures, such as blood vessel trees, optic discs, macula, etc.

Algorithm of GANs-based Retinal Synthesiser is as follows:

- For k times
  - Prepare a mini-batch of retinal images $\left\{(x, \hat{x})_{i=1}^{m}\right\}^{kn}$ where m is the mini-batch size.
  - Update D using $\left\{(x, \hat{x})_{i=1}^{m}\right\}^{kn}$.
- For r times
  - Prepare a mini-batch of noise vectors, $\left\{(z)_{i=1}^{m}\right\}^{rn}$.
  - Update G using $\left\{(z)_{i=1}^{m}\right\}^{rn}$.

We have used 1,200 images from the public database *Messidor* [18]. These images were acquired by three ophthalmologic departments using a colour video 3CCD camera on a Topcon TRC NW6 non-mydriatic retinograph with a 45-degree field of view. The images were captured using 8 bits per colour plane. Among these 1,200 images, 588 images were 960 × 1440, 400 images were 1488 × 2240 and 212 images were 1536 × 2304. In our experiments, we resized all of the images to the same size (i.e. 256 × 256) by bicubic interpolation.

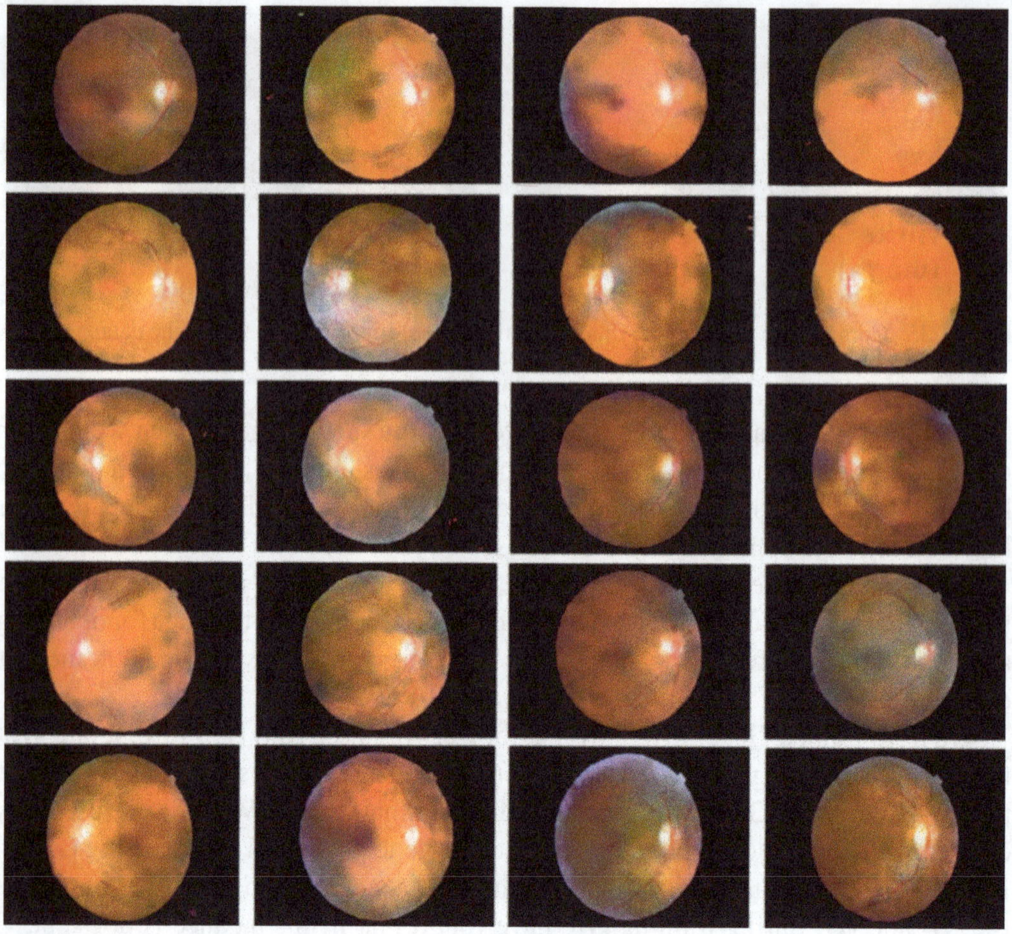

Fig. 11.36 Examples of generated synthetic retinal images

We have followed the deep convolutional neural network-based architecture suggested in [41] with minor modifications. Table 2 shows the model architecture for 256 × 256-sized images. The mini-batch size was set to 32 (i.e. m = 32). Noise vectors were drawn from the uniform distribution. As a loss function, binary cross-entropy was used. As an optimiser, RMSProp with a learning rate of 0:0001 and a decay of $3e^{-8}$ was used. The dropout value was set to 0:5. For batch normalisation, momentum was set to 0:5 instead of default value 0:99. For LeakyReLU, it was set to 0.2 instead of the default value of 0:3. For all convolutional and transposed convolutional layers, stride = 2, kernel size = 5 and padding = same was used. l2 regularisation was applied only for weights and biases of the transposed convolutional layers. For all other settings, the default values of Tensor Flow's Keras API were used.

After training, the generator is used to generate synthesised retinal images from noise vectors. The Structural SIMilarity (SSIM) measure shows how similar the synthesised images are to the training data. SSM = 0 means there is no similarity and SSIM = 1 means that two images are the same. You can see some achieved results from this GAN generator of synthetic retinal images in Figs. 11.35 and 11.36.

A sample database of generated images is available at https://strade.fit.vutbr.cz/databases/synthetic_retina.

The database is separated into two parts: healthy images and disease-affected images, which is especially diabetes and ARMD.

Acknowledgements This work was supported by The Ministry of Education, Youth and Sports of the Czech Republic from the National Programme of Sustainability (NPU II); project "*IT4Innovations excellence in science—LQ1602*" and the BUT project "*Secure and Reliable Computer Systems*", FIT-S-17-4014.

References

1. Barajas H (2015) Atlas of the human eye: anatomy and biometrics. Palibrio, p 74. ISBN 978-1506510330
2. Snell RS, Lemp MA (2013) Clinical anatomy of the eye, 2nd edn. Wiley-Blackwell. ISBN 978-0632043446
3. Bergmüller T, Christopoulos E, Schnöll M, Uhl A (2015) Recompression effects in iris segmentation. In: Proceedings of the 8th IAPR/IEEE international conference on biometrics (ICB'15). Phuket, Thailand, pp 1–8
4. Nguyen K et al (2018) Iris recognition with off-the-shelf CNN features: a deep learning perspective. IEEE Access 6:18848–18855
5. Trokielewicz M, Czajka A, Maciejewicz P (2019) Iris recognition after death. IEEE Trans Inf Forensics Secur 14(6):1501–1514
6. Goldstein I, Simon C (1935) A new scientific method of identification. N Y State J Med 35
7. Tower P (1955) The fundus oculi in monozygotic twins: report of six pairs of identical twins. AMA Arch Ophthalmol 54:225–239
8. Farzin H, Abrishami-Moghaddam H, Moin MS (2008) A novel retinal identification system. EURASIP J Adv Signal Process Hindawi 2008:10. https://doi.org/10.1155/2008/280635
9. Hill RB (1996) Retina identification. In: Biometrics: personal identification in networked society. Springer, New York, pp 123–141
10. Timberlake GT, Kennedy M (2005) The direct ophthalmoscope—how it works and how to use it. University of Kansas, p 39. Available online on http://web.media.mit.edu/~raskar/Eye/TheDirectOphthalmoscope.pdf
11. Hill RB (1986) U.S. Patent 4,620,318. http://www.freepatentsonline.com/4620318.pdf
12. Arndt JH (1990) U.S. Patent 4,923,297. http://www.freepatentsonline.com/4923297.pdf
13. Johnson JC, Hill RB U.S. Patent 5,532,771. http://www.freepatentsonline.com/5532771.pdf
14. Fuhrmann T, Hämmerle-Uhl J, Uhl A (2009) Usefulness of retina codes in biometrics. In: Advances in image and video technology, 3rd Pacific Rim symposium, Japan, Springer LNCS 5414. ISSN 0302-9743
15. Arakala A, Culpepper JS, Jeffers J, Turpin A, Boztas S, Horadami KJ, McKendrick AM Entropy of the retina template. RMIT University, Melbourne, Australia
16. Shih HP 2008 Two algorithms for maximum and minimum weighted bipartite matching. Department of Computer Science and Information Engineering National Taiwan University
17. Carmona E, Rincón M, García-Feijoo J, Martínez-de-la Casa J (2008) Identification of the optic nerve head with genetic algorithms. Artif Intell Med 43:243–259
18. Decencière E, Zhang X, Cazuguel G, Lay B, Cochener B, Trone C, Gain P, Ordonez R, Massin P, Erginay A, Charton B, Klein JC (2014) Feedback on a publicly distributed database: the messidor database. Image Anal Stereol 33(3):231–234
19. Kohler T, Budai A, Kraus M, Odstrčilík J, Michelson G, Hornegger J (2013) Automatic no-reference quality assessment for retinal fundus images using vessel segmentation. In: 26th IEEE international symposium on computer-based medical systems. pp 95–100

20. Ortega M, Penedo MG, Rouco J, Barreira N, Carreira MJ (2009) Retinal verification using a feature points based biometric pattern. EURASIP J Adv Signal Proc 2009. Article ID 235746:13 pp
21. https://github.com/Lukass2/RetinaFeatureVectorExtractor.git
22. Albert DM, Miller JW et al (2008) Principles and practice of ophthalmology, 3rd edn. ISBN 978-1-4160-0016-7
23. Ryan SJ (2006) Retina. Elsevier Mosby. ISBN 0323043232
24. Diagnosis and classification of diabetes mellitus. Diabetes Care, American Diabetes Association, Issue 33, 2010, pp 62–69. https://doi.org/10.2337/dc10-s062
25. Scanlon PH, Wilkinson CP, Aldington SJ, Matthews DR (2009) A practical manual of diabetic retinopathy management. Wiley-Blackwell. ISBN 978-1-405-17035-2
26. Sosna T (2016) Diabetická retinopatie (Diabetic retinopathy), 2nd edn. Prague, Axonite CZ. ISBN 9788088046059
27. Cavallotti CAP, Cerulli L (2008) Age-related changes of the human eye. Humana Press, p 400
28. Kolář P (2008) Věkem podmíněná makulární degenerace (Aged-related macular degeneration), 1st edn. Prague, Grada. ISBN 9788024726052
29. Kanski JJ (2007) Clinical ophthalmology—a systematic approach, 6th edn. Elsevier, p. 942. ISBN 978-0-08-044969-2
30. Ernest J. *Makulární degenerace* (*Macular degeneration*). Prague, Mladá fronta, 1st Edition, 2010, ISBN 9788020423634
31. Pašta J (2017) Základy očního lékařství (Basics of ophthalmology). Charles University, Karolinum, Prague. ISBN 978-80-246-2460-0
32. Staal J, Abramoff M, Niemeijer M (2004) Ridge based vessel segmentation in color images of the retina. IEEE Trans Med Imaging 23(4):501–509
33. Daugman J (2006) Probing the uniqueness and randomness of iriscodes: results from 200 billion iris pair comparisons. Proc IEEE 94(11):1927–1935
34. Adler A, Youmaran R, Loyka S (2006) Towards a measure of biometric information. In: Canadian conference on electrical and computer engineering, (CCECE'06). pp 210–213
35. Nautsch A, Rathgeb C, Saeidi R, Busch C (2015) Entropy analysis of I-vector feature spaces in duration-sensitive speaker recognition. In: 40th IEEE ICASSP conference, 19–24 April 2015. Brisbane, Australia
36. Decencière E, Cazuguel G, Zhang X, Thibault G, Klein JC, Meyer F, Marcotegui B, Quellec G, Lamard M, Danno R, Elie D, Massin P, Viktor Z, Erginay A, La B, Chabouis A (2013) Teleophta: machine learning and image processing methods for teleophthalmology. IRBM, Elsevier Masson 34(2):196–203
37. Pres M (2016) Bifurcation localization in retina images. MSc thesis, supervised by: Lukas Semerad, Brno University of Technology, Faculty of Information Technology, Czech Republic
38. Mortenson ME (1999) Mathematics for computer graphics applications. Industrial Press Inc., p 264. ISBN 9780831131111
39. Zamir M, Medeiros JA, Cunningham TK (1979) Arterial bifurcations in the human retina. J Gen Physiol 74(4):537–548
40. Goodfellow IJ, Pouget-Abadie J, Mirza M, Xu B, Warde-Farley D, Ozair S, Courville AC, Bengio Y (2014) Generative adversarial networks. CoRR, abs/1406.2661
41. Radford A, Metz L, Chintala S (2015) Unsupervised representation learning with deep convolutional generative adversarial networks. CoRR, abs/1511.06434
42. Anatomy and physiology, Connexions Web site. http://cnx.org/content/col11496/1.6/
43. Optimis Fusion. http://www.askin.cz/prednesegmentove/. Accessed 6 June 2018
44. Kowa VX-20. http://dfv.com.au/products/diagnostic/diagnostic-imaging/kowa-vx-20-mydriatic-non-mydriatic-integrated-fundus-camera/. Accessed 6 June 2018
45. https://cryptologicfoundation.org/visit/museum/acquisitions/acquisitionarchivessection/individualequipmentitems/rfsignalgenerator.html. Accessed 11 June 2018
46. http://retinagallery.com/displayimage.php?album=228&pid=2596#top_display_media
47. Nugroho HA et al (2015) Automated microaneurysms (MAs) detection in digital colour fundus images using matched filter. In: 2015 international conference on computer, control, informatics and its applications (IC3INA). pp 104–108

48. Dalton M (2012) Evaluating the risks of retinal detachment in cataract patients. Eyeworld. https://www.eyeworld.org/article-evaluating-the-risks-of-retinal
49. Vlhká forma s edémem (Wet form with edema). Prague, Mladá frona. https://img.mf.cz/062/617/c.jpg. Accessed 25 June 2018
50. Retina Image Bank®. https://imagebank.asrs.org/file/1428/lacquer-cracks

Chapter 12
Vascular Biometric Graph Comparison: Theory and Performance

Arathi Arakala, Stephen Davis and K. J. Horadam

Abstract Vascular biometric templates are gaining increasing popularity due to simple and contact free capture and resilience to presentation attacks. We present the state of the art in Biometric Graph Comparison, a technique to register and compare vascular biometric templates by representing them as formal graphs. Such graphs consist of a set of vertices, representing the branch, termination and crossover points in the vascular pattern, and a set of edges. An edge represents the relationship between a pair of feature points that are directly connected by a vessel segment in a vascular biometric image. We summarise how this information has been successfully used over the past 8 years to improve registration and recognition performance for the vasculature under the palm, wrist, hand and retina. The structural properties of biometric graphs from these modalities differ, with retina graphs having the largest number of vertices on average and the most complex structure, and hand graphs having the smallest number of vertices on average and being the least connected. All vascular graphs have similarities to trees, with the ratio of edges to vertices being close to 1. We describe our most recent algorithms for biometric graph registration and comparison, and our performance results. We are interested in the possibility of using biometric graphs in a template protection scheme based on the paradigm of dissimilarity vectors. As a first step, we wish to improve registration. Certain modalities like retina have an intrinsic reference frame that makes registration more straightforward. Other modalities may not have an intrinsic reference frame. To overcome this, we introduce the notion of anchors—subgraphs of a biometric graph, having between 5 and 10 vertices, that occur consistently in samples from the same individual—that would enable the dissimilarity vector scheme to be applied to any vascular modality. Experiments on palm and wrist databases show that all individuals had at least some sets of 6 captures which could be used to identify an anchor,

A. Arakala (✉) · S. Davis · K. J. Horadam
Discipline of Mathematical Sciences, School of Science, RMIT University, Melbourne, Australia
e-mail: arathi.arakala@rmit.edu.au

S. Davis
e-mail: stephen.davis@rmit.edu.au

K. J. Horadam
e-mail: kathy.horadam@rmit.edu.au

A. Uhl et al. (eds.), *Handbook of Vascular Biometrics*, Advances in Computer Vision and Pattern Recognition, https://doi.org/10.1007/978-3-030-27731-4_12

and anchors were identified in 94% and 88% for the palm and wrist databases, respectively.

Keywords Biometric graphs · Graph comparison · Dissimilarity vector representation · Vascular graphs

12.1 Introduction

The purpose of this Chapter is to provide a single resource for biometric researchers to learn and use the current state of the art in Biometric Graph Comparison[1] for vascular modalities.

Vascular biometric recognition is the process of identifying and verifying an individual using the intricate vascular pattern in the body. Sources of vascular patterns for personal identification and verification are the palm, dorsal hand, wrist, retina, finger and face. Traditionally, vascular patterns have been compared using feature-based or image-based templates. Here we work with feature-based templates only. The basic feature points in a vascular network are vessel terminations (where the vessels leave the image frame of reference or become too fine to be captured in the image), vessel bifurcations (where one vessel splits into two) or (in two-dimensional images) vessel crossovers, where two vessels appear to intersect.

Biometric Graph Comparison (BGC) is a feature-based process, which enhances and improves on traditional point pattern matching methods for many vascular modalities. Its key idea is the replacement of a feature point based representation of a biometric image by a spatial graph based representation, where the graph edges provide a formal and concise representation of the vessel segments between feature points, thus incorporating connectivity of feature points into the biometric template. This added dimension makes the concepts and techniques of graph theory newly available to vascular biometric identification and verification.

In particular, the comparison process is treated as a noisy graph comparison problem, involving local minimisation of a graph editing algorithm. From this, we can extract a Maximum Common Subgraph (MCS), the noisily matched part found to be common to the two graphs being compared. Part of the fascination and value of working with BGC has been to investigate the topology of the MCS: MCSs from two vascular images from the same biometric instance usually look very different from those from different instances.

Over the years since its introduction, BGC has been shown by ourselves and colleagues to improve recognition accuracy, and if more of the topology of the MCS is used to discriminate between genuine and impostor comparisons, this improvement can be quite dramatic. It is also possible to exploit specific graphical characteristics of different modalities to speed up the recognition process.

[1]Previously we used the non-standard term Biometric Graph Matching (BGM).

The Chapter is organised as follows. In Sect. 12.2, we define the vascular Biometric Graph and explain its background and context. A very brief description is given of its extraction from a vascular image. Section 12.3 outlines the formal description of the two components, registration and comparison, of BGC, with some history of its development from its earliest form in [7] to its newest form presented here. (Pseudocode for our Algorithms appears in the Appendix.) In Sect. 12.4, we summarise the body of results in [6–8, 20, 21]. We compare the graph topology of the public retina, hand, palm and wrist databases we use, and describe the topological features of MCSs we have identified from which to derive comparison scores. We provide the supporting evidence for our view that the Biometric Graph representation increases the speed and accuracy of registration, accuracy of comparison, and that using multiple graph structures in the MCS can improve comparison scores over single structures.

Section 12.5 presents one stage of an application of BGC to the problem of privacy protection of vascular templates. The key idea is a feature transformation using a dissimilarity vector approach. Preliminary investigation of the comparison performance of this approach has given encouraging results for retina databases, where an intrinsic alignment exists in the images [5]. A new problem is faced if no such alignment exists. Here we present our first results on a potential solution to this problem, where we look for small but characteristic structures we call "anchors", which appear in sufficiently many of an individual's samples to be used for registration.

12.2 The Biometric Graph

This section presents the Biometric Graph we use for application to vascular biometric modalities. We describe our motivation for using a spatial graph representation over more traditional feature point based templates. We provide a formal definition of a vascular Biometric Graph and give a brief overview of the extraction process.

12.2.1 The Biometric Graph

Biometric Graphs, as we define them, were first introduced in 2011 [17] for the fingerprint modality. Extraction of ridge bifurcations and terminations as feature points is a fundamental technique in a ridge-based modality, and usually, ridge skeletons are also extracted from images. The novelty of the Biometric Graph concept lies in constructing a formal spatial graph from these extracted feature points only. Each feature point is represented as a vertex (also called a node). An edge (also called a link) is a straight line drawn between adjacent pairs of feature points on the skeleton. The edge preserves, in summary form, the connectivity relationship between feature points typically found by tracing along the ridge skeleton. (This differs from the earlier ISO/IEC 19794–8:2006 standard, in which additional "virtual minutiae" and "continuation minutiae" are inserted along the skeleton, to facilitate piecewise-linear representation of the connecting ridgeline.) A disadvantage of our representation is that more detailed information held by a ridgeline curving between feature points is lost, particularly in regions of high curvature where an edge forms a shortcut between feature points. Figure 12.9 in Appendix 1 demonstrates this. An advantage of our spatial graph representation which can outweigh this loss of information is computational efficiency. An edge can be represented in code concisely by its two end vertices. Furthermore, the full repertoire of graph theoretical techniques is available for data analysis.

12.2.1.1 Vascular Graphs

Direct observation of two-dimensional images of vessel-based modalities shows the physical branching and crossing network of vessels strongly resembles a formal spatial graph drawn in the plane. For example, there is some visible similarity between the pattern of the principal retinal vessels and a rooted tree (with the root vertex in the optic disc), and some visible similarity between the pattern of the principal wrist vessels and a ladder graph or lattice. These similarities to spatial graphs are more pronounced to the naked eye for vascular modalities than in the ridge-based modalities for which we first studied Biometric Graphs. Fundamentally, this is because blood vessels do not often exhibit high curvature, so in most cases the vessel segment between adjacent feature points is quite well represented by a straight line. This was our motivation in [7] for introducing Biometric Graphs and Biometric Graph Comparison into vascular biometric modalities.

The idea of a vascular graph has arisen independently (and at approximately the same time) in the biomedical literature. Drechsler and Laura [13], working with three-dimensional hepatic vessel CT (computed tomography) images of the liver, extract a three-dimensional vascular graph from the vessel skeleton (using voxels not pixels—crossovers do not occur). They classify voxels into three classes: regular, end (terminations) and branch (bifurcations). Branch and end voxels are represented by vertices in the graph, while regular voxels are grouped and represented by edges. The vascular graph provides data for further image recognition, registration and surgical planning. Deng et al. [12] extract a vascular graph (which they term a vascular structure graph model) from the skeleton of the vessel tree in two-dimensional retinal fundus images, to register the images for clinical diagnosis and treatment of retina diseases.

Definition 12.1 A *vascular graph* extracted from a vascular image is a spatial graph with the vessel features of terminations and bifurcations (and crossovers if the image is two-dimensional) forming the graph vertices. A pair of vertices will have an edge between them if and only if we can trace along a vessel from one feature to another, without encountering any other feature in between. More formally, if I is a vascular image then its vascular graph is $g = (V, E, \mu, \nu, A)$, where V is a set of vertices representing the feature points extracted from I, E is a set of edges between those pairs of vertices representing feature points which are adjacent in I, μ is the vertex labelling function, ν is the edge labelling function and A is the attribute set (which may be empty) comprising a set of vascular attributes that apply to feature points or to the vessel segments connecting them. The *order* of g is the number of vertices $|V|$ and the *size* of g is the number of edges $|E|$. If the vascular image I is of a biometric modality then g is a *(vascular) Biometric Graph (BG)*.

For the BGs in our research, μ associates each vertex with its unique two-dimensional spatial coordinates (x, y) while ν associates each edge with its two-dimensional Euclidean length ℓ and slope θ.

12.2.2 Biometric Graph Extraction

To construct the Biometric Graph from a two-dimensional biometric image, the vessel skeleton is extracted from the image and the feature points are found. The feature points are labelled to form the vertex set, and their coordinates are recorded. The existence of an edge between vertices is determined by tracing the skeleton from each feature point until another is encountered. The length and slope of each edge is calculated and recorded. Other feature point and vessel segment attributes can be calculated at the same time.

Differences in image capture device and lighting source require different image processing techniques for different modalities to reduce noise. There are some common image processing steps in skeleton extraction for any vascular modality, including grayscale conversion, Region-of-Interest (ROI) selection, noise reduction, binarisation and skeleton thinning. Those we employed for palm, dorsal hand, wrist and retina images are described in [6, 8, 20, 21] and the references therein, and will not be further detailed here. For skeleton extraction from finger images, see [23].

A specific problem encountered with extracted skeletons has been the existence of genuine short spurs due to tiny vessels and spurious short spurs due to noise [6, 8, 13, 23]. This is overcome in post-processing by pruning the skeleton of branches shorter than a heuristically selected threshold such as 5, 10 or 15 pixels. For palm vessels, an additional complication has been the inclusion of short to medium length spurs in the skeleton which correspond to skin ridges or flexion creases. Palm principal ridges and creases can be considered as part of the biometric pattern and are difficult to remove completely. However, our experiments have shown that removing the short to medium spurs after the detection of vertices and edges improves the process of registration and comparison. See [8] for details. Wrist vessel skeletons often have segments running perpendicular to the main direction of the vessels, some of which are due to flexion creases, but as some are vessels, these segments are not removed [6].

Feature points are extracted from the 1-pixel-wide skeleton by counting neighbouring pixels in a standard 3×3 pixel window moving across the skeleton. One neighbour indicates a termination pixel, two neighbours indicate a vessel pixel, three neighbours indicate a bifurcation pixel and four or more neighbours indicate a crossover pixel. As a consequence of image noise, neighbouring pixels in the same 3×3 pixel region may be labelled as bifurcation points. To handle this, if a central pixel is a bifurcation point and there are two or more neighbours which are bifurcation points on different sides of the central pixel, then only the central pixel is listed as the bifurcation point.

A much faster method of extracting feature points from the vessel skeleton, which may be preferable to the above, is the use of convolutional kernels as in [1].

The vertex and edge labels form the basic biometric template. Additional attributes can be extracted from the skeleton to create richer templates. Vertex attributes can include type (termination, branching or crossover). Edge attributes can include the length (as a pixel count) of the skeleton segment between two feature points and the vessel segment average width (or calibre) which can be measured before thinning the skeleton.

Figure 12.1 shows typical vascular pattern images from the databases of each of the four modalities we have investigated and their corresponding Biometric Graphs, extracted as above.

Biometric Graphs have been similarly extracted from skeletons of finger vessels by Nibbelke [23] and from skeletons of face vessels by Gouru [16]. Whilst skeleton tracing is probably the best technique in current use for identifying adjacent feature points in the image skeleton, it is possible that alternatives may prove useful. Khakzar and Pourghassem [19], working with retina images, determine for each pair of feature points whether they are adjacent or not by deleting the two points from the skeleton and checking if the remaining connected components of the skeleton all contain feature points. Existence of a component without feature points means the two points are connected in the skeleton, otherwise they are not. Connectivity is recorded in (the upper half of) an adjacency matrix. However, edge attributes aren't extracted in this approach, and since the adjacency matrix can be found immediately from the edges found by skeleton tracing, it is not clear if the approach has advantages over skeleton tracing.

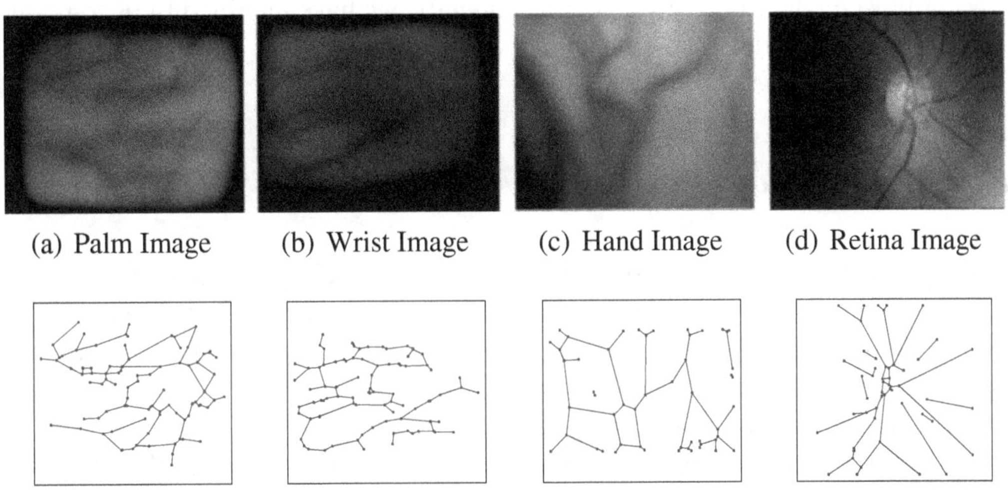

(a) Palm Image (b) Wrist Image (c) Hand Image (d) Retina Image

(e) Palm Graph (f) Wrist Graph (g) Hand Graph (h) Retina Graph

Fig. 12.1 Vascular patterns from four modalities **a** Palm **b** Wrist **c** Hand and **d** Retina vessels and their corresponding spatial graphs in (**e**–**h**)

12.3 The Biometric Graph Comparison Algorithm

In this section, we present a formal description of the Biometric Graph Comparison Algorithm. The algorithm has two parts: BGR (Registration) which requires 4 steps; and BGC (Comparison), in which the 3 steps are finding the graph edit distance, identifying the Maximum Common Subgraph (MCS) and scoring comparisons using graph-based difference measures.

In our opinion, graph registration is the key component of the algorithm, and is more critical than the graph comparison component. Although it can often be assumed that the capture mechanism enforces an approximate alignment of biometric images in the first place, experience tells us that alignment is seldom ideal, and large differences can occur between captures from the same person, particularly as the time between captures increases. Unless two extracted BGs from the same biometric instance can be aligned well, comparison cannot be effective. Essentially this is because we need a good similarity score for a genuine match, in order to minimise the number of false non-matches. The variance of genuine similarity scores across a population tends to be higher than the variance of impostor similarity scores, which have a distribution of low scores that is roughly independent of registration.

Alignment on a point pattern, such as the set of vertices in a BG, is a standard matching technique. Commonly used methods are the Iterative Closest Point (ICP) algorithm and the Modified Hausdorff Distance (MHD) algorithm. Registration using point pattern alignment algorithms has been previously studied for hand and palm vasculature. In 2009, Chen et al. [10] showed that ICP provided better alignment and consequently superior recognition results than either MHD or point-to-point comparison for palm veins.

In 2014, we showed [21] that for hand veins, registering on edges of BGs using our Biometric Graph Registration (BGR) algorithm gives as good or better recognition performance than either ICP or MHD applied to the point patterns of vertices, especially when the BGs are small. Subsequently, we have modified BGR to permit registration on structures larger than single edges.

12.3.1 BGR-Biometric Graph Registration

Our registration algorithm, in essence, a greedy RANSAC algorithm, looks for structural similarities in a pair of graphs on which to align them, so that the two graphs are in the same spatial frame, free from the effects of translation and rotation of their images during capture.

There is no restriction on what type of structure (i.e. subgraph) can be used for alignment within a particular modality and database. For instance, the algorithm could be tested on a database for different choices of alignment structure, so that the structure giving the best performance could be identified. Or, the frequency of occurrence of different types of structure within the database could be used to select a preferred structure. Or, if a particular structure was found to be characteristic of a database, appearing more frequently than might be expected in a random spatial graph with comparable numbers of vertices and edges such a "motif" structure could be identified and chosen to align on. Or, it is possible that for a particular modality, each biometric instance exhibits a characteristic structure in most of its images, and such an "anchor" structure could be used for registration.

If the modality possesses an intrinsic coordinate system which can be identified in each database image, registration by the structure might not be required.

To take advantage of the additional structural information in a BG, we align on an edge, or a more complex subgraph such as a *claw*[2] (a degree 3 vertex plus its 3 adjacent edges and 3 neighbouring vertices), a pair of claws joined by a common edge (which we call a *two-claw*), or we could choose a cycle of length 3 or 4. In theory there is no restriction to the type of subgraph chosen for alignment, but computational limits, time constraints and the smaller number of more complex structures present in a BG usually dictate that simpler structures are preferable.

The BGR algorithm is described in more detail in Appendix 2. The algorithm is flexible so that any structure could be used for alignment. It has four steps which are outlined in the following subsection. The four design parameters in the BGR algorithm are a *structure* S, a *similarity score function* f depending on the structure selected, a structure pair *shortlist length* L and a vertex comparison *tolerance* ε. The structures S we have used are: *Edges (E), Claws (C)* and *Two-claws (T)*. If we need to specify the parameters we denote the algorithm by BGR (S, f, L, ε).

Our initial implementation of BGR in 2011 was for BGR (E, f, L, ε) [7]. This has undergone some modification in the intervening years, so that in 2015 we introduced an improved shortlisting mechanism [8] for edge pairs in Step 3 of BGR rather than simply selecting the L highest scoring pairs. We discovered that most edge pairs (in palm BGs) were short and often scored a high rank compared to longer pairs. This prevented longer pairs that gave a better registration from appearing in the top L shortlist. To overcome this, for BGR (E, f, L, ε) we split the set of edge pairs into long and short edge pairs. The mean of the medians of the edge lengths in the two graphs is selected as the threshold. If both edges of an edge pair are longer than this threshold, the edge pair is categorised as long. All other edge pairs are labelled as short. The shortlist consists of the $L/2$ top scoring long edge pairs and the $L/2$ top scoring short edge pairs. This modification ensures that long edge pairs that potentially give better alignment can be included in the shortlist to get a better registration of the graphs. This modification implies that lines 13–19 in the general algorithm in Appendix 2 are run twice, once each for the $L/2$ long and $L/2$ short edges.

In our earlier work [5–8, 20, 21] we assumed that the images in a database are roughly pre-aligned. Here, to provide the most generally applicable registration algorithm, we have modified the similarity scoring of edge pairs in Step 2 of BGR to remove any dependence on pre-alignment. This modification means that in lines

[2]Previously we called this a star, inaccurately, as it is formally a 3-star: an n-star is a vertex of degree $n \geq 1$, plus its adjacent edges and neighbouring vertices.

29–31 of the algorithm in Appendix 2, only the edge lengths are used and edge slopes are not.

12.3.1.1 BGR Algorithm Outline

Step 1: Initialisation Select S, f, L and ε. The two graphs g and g' to be registered are inputs to the algorithm. The registration process begins by identifying and listing all the structures of the selected type S in each graph.

Step 2: Similarity scoring structure pairs Each structure in the first graph g and structure in the second graph g' is compared using f to obtain a similarity score. The similarity function chosen depends on the structure. For example, when edge pairs are compared they are scored based on the similarity of their lengths only (if no pre-alignment is assumed) or of their lengths and slopes (if some pre-alignment is assumed). When claw pairs are compared they are scored based on the similarity of the lengths of their three edges and two included angles. When two-claw pairs are compared, the similarity of the corresponding claw structures and connecting edges determines the score.

Step 3: Shortlisting structure pairs and aligning on them The structure pairs are ordered based on decreasing order of similarity score. The top L high scoring structure pairs (for $S = C$ or $S = T$) or the top $L/2$ short and top $L/2$ long edges (for $S = E$) are shortlisted for further processing. For every shortlisted structure pair, the two graphs are translated and rotated so that a specific part of the structure becomes the origin of the reference frame. For example, if edges are used, the vertex with smaller x coordinate becomes the centre of the coordinate system and the other vertex defines the direction of the positive x-axis. If claws are used, the centre of the claw becomes the origin while the longest edge defines the direction of the positive x-axis. If two-claws are used, the connecting edge defines the coordinate system, again taking the vertex with smaller x coordinate as the origin of the reference frame.

Step 4: Pair alignment scoring and graph registration With both graphs in the same coordinate system, aligned on a shortlisted pair, each vertex in the first graph g is matched to a vertex in the second graph g' by finding the first vertex in g' that is within ε pixels from it. If a vertex in g does not find a corresponding vertex in g' within ε pixels of it, it will not be matched. The total number of matched vertices is normalized by the geometric mean of the number of vertices in the two graphs to provide a rough measure of alignment we call *QuickScore* (QS). That is, if g has n vertices, g' has n' vertices and the aligned graphs have c matched vertices within tolerance ε, the distance between g and g' is calculated to be

$$QS(g, g') = 1 - \frac{c}{\sqrt{n \times n'}}. \tag{12.1}$$

The pair of structures that gives the smallest score is chosen to register g and g'. The resulting registered graphs are denoted g_a and g'_a.

12.3.1.2 Other Approaches to Registration of BGs

Deng et al. [12] in 2010, working with retina BGs, used a two-stage process for registration, also based on edge-to-edge correspondence. Their first (global) registration stage is also a RANSAC variant, where a vertex plus its neighbours in g is compared in g'. In practice, they restrict to degree 2 and 3 vertices, which corresponds to us choosing 2-stars and claws, respectively, as the structure (Their second stage registers vessel shape so is not in the scope of BGR). Using the BG vertex set, they compare the registration performance of several spatial topological graph structures commonly used in computer vision and graph-matching research: the Delaunay triangulation graph (DT), the minimum spanning tree of the DT graph, the k-nearest neighbour graph (KNN) and the minimum spanning tree of the KNN graph. They show that the BG technique substantially outperforms these other topological graph structures in graph registration, and state this is because BG characterises anatomical properties of the retinal vessels while the others do not.

Lupascu et al. [22], working with manually extracted retina BGs and $S = E$, enlarge the feature vector describing each edge from 2 to 9 dimensions by adding further spatial information relating to end vertices and midpoint of the edge, and vary f to be the Euclidean distance in 9-dimensional space. They set $L = 30$ to test g against g' and also test g' against g, choosing only the edge pairs which appear in both lists. Then they use a quadric model to estimate the global transformation between the images using the endpoints of the matched edges.

Nibbelke [23], works with the earlier version of BGR (E, f, L, ε) for finger vessel BGs. He systematically tests alternatives to steps 2 and 3 of the algorithm. First, he tries to improve the rough pre-orientation of images provided by the capture system by testing if the midline of the finger provides an intrinsic reference frame, but finds this not to be robust, leading to worse recognition performance than BGR in several experiments. Orienting all edges in the same direction before comparison does improve performance, as does sorting edge pairs using only their 1-dimensional difference in slope (i.e. using $f = \Delta\theta$ and ignoring their difference in length). He also varies f to include weighting the difference in slope, to overcome the same problem of not finding the best edges for registration in the top L. His best results are found for $f = \Delta\theta$.

If an intrinsic reference frame does exist for pre-alignment in a particular vascular modality, it can be used to register the BGs. We have used this approach effectively with retina BGs in [5] (see Sect. 12.5) taking the centre of the optic disc as the centre of the graph coordinate system while the frame orientation is kept the same.

If no intrinsic reference frame exists for pre-alignment in a particular vascular modality, and we cannot even assume rough pre-alignment by virtue of the capture mechanism, then the BG may provide topological information we can use instead. We investigate this approach in our search for "anchors" in Sect. 12.5.

12.3.2 BGC-Biometric Graph Comparison

The second part of our algorithm is *noisy graph comparison*, to quantify the similarity between a pair g_a and g'_a of registered BGs. If we take advantage of the topology of the BGs in both the registration and noisy graph comparison algorithms, the speed and accuracy of graph comparison can be greatly enhanced.

The algorithm we use is based on using edges as structures as in [20], which is generalised in [6], and further generalised here. The BGC algorithm is flexible, so that any structure can be used. It has three steps: determination of the *minimum graph edit path* between g_a and g'_a, construction of the *Maximum Common Subgraph* (MCS) of g_a and g'_a, and finally, measurement of the difference between g_a and g'_a using the MCS.

We have previously demonstrated that the topology of MCSs generated from pairs of graphs from the same biometric instance (mated comparison) is different from that of MCSs generated from graphs from different instances (non-mathed comparison) [6, 21].

The four design parameters in the BGC algorithm are: a *structure* S, cost matrix *weights* α_1 and α_2 used in the edit distance computation and *measure* d for scoring the distinctiveness or difference of g_a and g'_a. The structures S we have used are *Vertices (V), Edges (E), Claws (C)* and *Two-claws (T)*. If we need to specify the parameters, we denote the algorithm by BGC$(S, \alpha_1, \alpha_2, d)$.

12.3.2.1 BGC Algorithm Outline

Step 1: Graph Edit Distance The comparison process assumes that we have identified and listed all the structures of the selected type S in each registered graph. The registered graphs are compared using an inexact graph matching technique that computes the minimum cost *graph edit path* that converts g_a to g'_a. To do this, we use the Hungarian algorithm based method proposed by Riesen and Bunke [26]. One graph can be converted to another by 3 types of edit operations—insertions, deletions and substitutions. Each edit operation will incur a cost and the *graph edit distance* is the sum of the edit costs.

Selection of the right costs for these operations is critical to getting a meaningful measure of edit distance. The form of cost matrix we use is

$$\mathbf{C} = \begin{bmatrix} \mathbf{C}_1 & \mathbf{C}_2 \\ \mathbf{C}_3 & \mathbf{C}_4 \end{bmatrix} \tag{12.2}$$

and depends on the choice of S. If the number of structures in g_a is m and in g'_a is m', $\mathbf{C}$ is a $(m + m') \times (m' + m)$ square matrix, $\mathbf{C}_1 = [c_{ij} | 1 \le i \le m, 1 \le j \le m']$ and c_{ij} represents the the cost of substituting structure u_i of g_a with structure v_j of g'_a. The sub-matrices $\mathbf{C}_2$ and $\mathbf{C}_3$ are square $m \times m$ and $m' \times m'$ matrices, respectively, with all elements outside the main diagonal equal to ∞. The diagonal elements, $c_{i\delta}$ of $\mathbf{C_2}$ and $c_{\delta j}$ of $\mathbf{C_3}$ indicate the cost of deleting structure i from g_a and inserting structure j into g'_a, respectively. $\mathbf{C_4}$ is an all zero matrix.

Cost matrix $\mathbf{C}$ is fed into the suboptimal optimisation algorithm, which finds a local minimum edit cost. Output will be this lowest cost of converting g_a to g'_a and the list of edit operations that achieve it. The larger the number of structures in each pair of graphs, the bigger the matrices will be and the longer it will take the Hungarian algorithm to compute the optimum result.

The cost matrix entries we use depend on structure S and two weights α_1 and α_2. The case $S = V$ appears below as Example 12.1. Cost matrices for other structures are defined on similar lines (see Appendix 3) , where α_2 will be weighted by the sum of the degrees of all the vertices in the structures.

Example 12.1 (Vertex-based cost matrix, i.e. $m = |V|, m' = |V'|$.) Denote the degree of a vertex by $D(.)$ and the Euclidean distance between two vertex labels (spatial coordinates) by $||.||$. The cost of substituting a vertex v_i of g_a with a vertex v'_j of g'_a is given by

$$c_{ij} = ||v_i, v'_j|| + \varpi_{ij}. \tag{12.3}$$

where ϖ_{ij} is the cheapest cost obtained as output when applying the Hungarian algorithm on a cost matrix for subgraphs g_{v_i} and $g'_{v'_j}$ (see [7] for details). These subgraphs are constructed from the vertices v_i and v'_j and their first-hop neighbourhoods, respectively. The total cost of deleting a vertex will be the sum of the cost of deleting the vertex itself (α_1) and the cost of deleting its neighbourhood vertices (α_2 for each neighbouring vertex),

$$c_{i\delta} = \alpha_1 + (\alpha_2 \times D(v_i)). \tag{12.4}$$

Similarly, the cost of inserting a vertex is

$$c_{\delta j} = \alpha_1 + (\alpha_2 \times D(v'_j)). \tag{12.5}$$

Step 2: Maximum Common Subgraph We use the locally optimal edit path output by the Hungarian algorithm to define a subgraph of g'_a. It includes all those structures of g'_a that are included in the list of substitutions. The structures deleted from g_a and the structures inserted into g'_a are excluded, but any additional corresponding edges are included. This subgraph is called the Maximum Common Subgraph (MCS) of g_a and g'_a as it represents all those structures in g'_a that are "matched" to structures in g_a. We also call it an S-*induced subgraph* of g'_a as the subgraph is induced by the substituted structures in g'_a (Note that defining the MCS as a subgraph of g_a is equivalent.).

Definition 12.2 Assume BGC($S, \alpha_1, \alpha_2, -$) has been applied to registered graphs g_a and g'_a in Step 1 above. Their (S-induced) *Maximum Common Subgraph (MCS)* is the subgraph of g'_a consisting of all structures in g'_a that are included in the list of

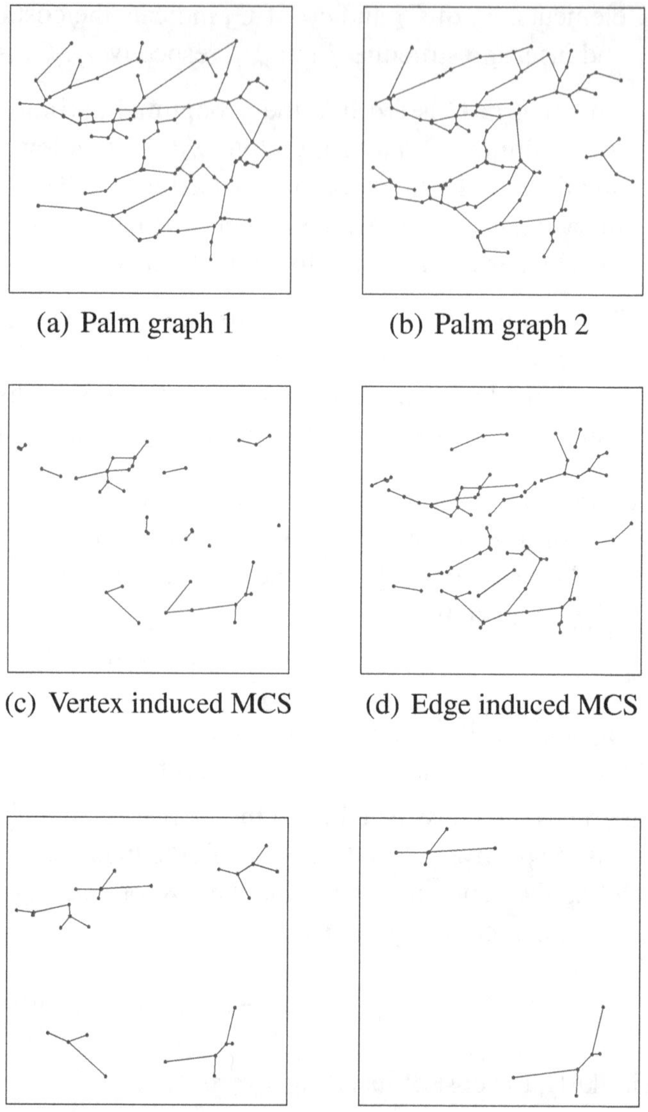

(a) Palm graph 1 (b) Palm graph 2 (c) Vertex induced MCS (d) Edge induced MCS (e) Claw induced MCS (f) Two-claw induced MCS

Fig. 12.2 This figure shows the Maximum Common Subgraph between the palm vessel graphs in **a** and **b** resulting from applying BGC with the structure S to be **c** vertices, **d** edges, **e** claws and **f** two-claws. Vertex- and edge-induced MCSs are bigger than claw- and two-claw-induced MCSs as the conditions for the structures to match in the former cases are not as strict as in the latter

substitutions, *together with* any edges that exist between these substituted structures in g'_a, for which a corresponding edge exists in g_a.

Depending on the structure used, the MCS can be vertex induced, edge induced, claw induced or two-claw induced. Figure 12.2 shows each type of MCS for a typical pair of palm BGs from the same biometric instance. The edge induced MCS is the most connected with the richest structure of the four. As S gets more complex than E, the corresponding MCS will be sparser, but the nodes and edges that form part of the MCS will be more reliable. In our experience, the node-induced subgraph tends to miss out on some of the structure that is present in the edge-induced subgraph. Therefore, overall for the biometric graphs in the databases we studied, we prefer S to be edges.

Table 12.1 Difference measures between g_1 and g_2, determined by counts of structures in their MCS

d	d_v	d_e	d_t	$d_{c_1c_2}$	ρ_{c_1}
M	$\|V_m\|$	$\|E_m\|$	$\|T_m\|$	$\|V_{c_1}\| + \|V_{c_2}\|$	$\|E_{c_1}\|$
N_i or N	$\|V_i\|$	$\|E_i\|$	$\|T_i\|$	$\|V_i\|$	$\|V_{c_1}\|$

Step 3: Difference Measures The MCS topology is used to define difference measures between g_a and g'_a. There are many potential score functions to separate genuine and impostor comparisons. We have tested 20 which are described in Sect. 12.4.3. A selection of 5, that have proved the most effective, is presented in Table 12.1. One of them, the Bunke–Shearer metric d_v , is already known [9]. Call the two aligned graphs being compared $g_1 = (V_1, E_1)$ and $g_2 = (V_2, E_2)$, with $g_m = (V_m, E_m)$ as their MCS. All sets from g_i, $i \in \{1, 2, m\}$, are subscripted with i. Corresponding sets used to define the measures are the vertex set V_i, the edge set E_i and the set of two-claws T_i. We are also interested in $c_i = (V_{c_i}, E_{c_i})$, $i = 1, 2$, the first and second largest connected components of g_m. The measures have two forms, a distance

$$d = 1 - \frac{M}{\sqrt{N_1 \times N_2}} \tag{12.6}$$

or density

$$\rho = M/N \tag{12.7}$$

as detailed in Table 12.1.

The previous Sections have dealt with the formal aspects of vascular Biometric Graph Comparison. In the next Section, we summarise the performance and practical advantages and disadvantages already discovered using BGC.

12.4 Results

This section will describe the public vascular databases used for BGC so far and compare key BG statistics across them. We summarise experimental results we have obtained by applying BGC to BGs from databases of the four modalities we have studied. The important outcomes from this work are

- that using graph structure in the registration algorithm can increase the speed and accuracy of registration;
- that graph structure in the MCS can be exploited to increase recognition accuracy; and
- that using multiple graph structures can improve similarity scores over single structures.

12.4.1 Vascular Databases

To our knowledge, the BGC algorithm has been tested on five vascular modalities: *Palm* vessels representing the vascular pattern under the palm of the hand; *Wrist* vessels representing the vascular pattern on the inside of the wrists; *Hand* vessels representing the vascular pattern under the skin on the back (dorsal surface) of the hand; *Retina* vessels representing the vascular pattern supplying blood to the retina; and *Finger* vessels representing the vascular pattern under the skin of the finger. We have tested the first four modalities. Finger vessel has been tested by Nibbelke [23], who found that in this case BGC was not competitive with standard point pattern comparison techniques. Gouru [16] in his work on *Face* vessels representing the vascular pattern under the skin of the face, uses a database collected by the University of Houston and extracts BGs. He claims to test BGC but no details are given in [16].

Details of the databases used are summarised in Table 12.2. All are either available for download or on request from the researchers who collected them. The palm and wrist image databases are obtainable from the Poznan University of Technology (PUT) [18] and can be downloaded at http://biometrics.put.poznan.pl/vein-dataset. The hand image databases are from Singapore's Nanyang Technical University [27] with images captured in the near-infrared (SNIR) and far-infrared (SFIR) wavelengths over three sessions each separated by a week. This database exemplifies the kind of variation that can be expected in captures taken across sessions. This is typical of a biometric scenario, where translation and rotation of the images occur between captures due to human factors. Access to this database was obtained by emailing the authors of [27]. Retina images are from the publicly available VARIA database [24] accessible at http://www.varpa.es/research/biometrics.html. In Sect. 12.5 we also refer to the ESRID retina database collected by RMIT University (c.f. [2]). This database can be accessed by emailing the second author of [2]. The finger image database used by Nibbelke [23] is from the University of Twente (UT) and can be accessed by emailing the lead author of [23].

12.4.2 Comparison of Graph Topology Across Databases

In principle, there is no restriction on the structure used by the BG registration and comparison algorithms. In practice, there are restrictions imposed by both the physical form of the vasculature and by the limitations of image resolution and image processing. How do we know what range of options is available?

We have already noted the visible similarity of vascular graphs to trees or ladders. This results from the way the vasculature forms physically. Its purpose is to deliver blood to and from tissues, with the capillaries forming the very fine vessels connecting the arterial system to the venous system. Capillaries are so fine that this interconnection is lost in many images, and vessels appear to terminate rather than

Table 12.2 Vessel image databases used for BGC

Database	Subjects × instances	No. of sessions	Samples/session	Total samples
PUT palm	50 × 2 (left, right)	3	4	600
PUT wrist	50 × 2 (left, right)	3	4	600
SFIR hand[a]	34	1	≥2	173
SNIR hand[a]	123	1	≥2	732
VARIA retina[a]	37	1	≥2	97
ESRID retina	46	1	9	414
UT finger	60 × 6 (different fingers)	2	2	1440

[a]Subset obtained after removal of subjects who had only 1 sample present

rejoin. Typically, vessels do not branch into more than two sub-branches at the same point. As well, while distinct principal veins and arteries might enter the biometric ROI at separate points, all of the vasculature derived from each such vessel will be connected. No sub-branches will actually be disconnected from a parent vessel.

Consequently, in a BG that is perfectly extracted from a high-quality two-dimensional vascular image, there will be relatively few cycles, which will mostly result from vessel crossovers. Vertices will have a low degree (most likely ≤ 4 with maximum degree 4 occurring at crossovers). There will be no isolated vertices (i.e. minimum degree will be 1) and the ratio of edges to vertices (the *density* of the BG) will be similar to that of a tree and so, close to 1. The BG will be connected.

In practice, the image quality will affect the connectivity of the BG, as the image processing algorithm will be unable to extract features from poor quality regions of the image. The more complex the structure of interest, the greater the chance that an occurrence of it will not be extracted in the BG from a particular image, because a component vertex or edge is missing as a result of noise in the image, or suboptimal sensing or image processing. For this reason we are also interested in the largest connected component C_1 of the BG. The size of the largest component is an indication of the amount of noise in the image that has not been compensated for by the image processing.

12.4.2.1 BG Statistics

A very basic question is how much the underlying BG statistics vary for different databases for the same modality, as well as how much they vary for different modalities. In Table 12.3, we record fundamental statistics for different BG databases: numbers of vertices, edges, claws and two-claws, density and number of vertices in the largest connected component C_1 of the BG.

Table 12.3 Mean (standard deviation) of BG topologies for each database. All data except for the last row appear in [6]. Here V is the vertex set, E the edge set, C the claw set, VC_1 the vertex set of the largest connected component C_1, and T the two-claw set

Database	$\|V\|$	$\|E\|$	$\|E\|/\|V\|$	$\|VC_1\|$	$\|C\|$	$\|T\|$
Palm Left	103 (27.9)	109.9 (19.47)	1.05 (0.03)	93.7 (21.68)	37.6 (7.97)	28.21 (8.39)
Palm Right	98.5 (18.8)	104.1 (20.75)	1.05 (0.03)	89.5 (21.35)	35.4 (8.3)	26.39 (8.53)
Wrist Left	83.07 (16.66)	86.2 (18.61)	1.03 (0.04)	72.1 (19.76)	27.01 (7.85)	19.18 (8.14)
Wrist Right	81.4 (16.11)	83.9 (17.82)	1.02 (0.04)	70.5 (19.43)	25.6 (7.31)	17.66 (7.54)
Hand SFIR	51.7 (9.38)	48.8 (9.6)	0.94 (0.06)	34.6 (12.94)	21.6 (5.35)	19.94 (6.59)
Hand SNIR	39.4 (13.07)	37.6 (13.1)	0.95 (0.03)	27.9 (11.76)	17.3 (6.38)	15.36 (6.47)
Ret. VARIA	70.3 (27.9)	67.1 (29.23)	0.94 (0.07)	48.6 (20.98)	28.9 (13.7)	29.65 (15.28)
Ret. ESRID	146.2 (86.7)	152.6 (92.7)	1.03 (0.04)	109 (68.9)	73.3 (45.1)	75.4 (48.7)

Table 12.3 shows some interesting differences and similarities between the different vascular graphs. All the graphs have density quite close to 1, reflecting their similarity to trees, as expected. The maximum degree of a vertex for each BG was also determined but not recorded here as for every database the mode of the maximum degrees is 3. Between 30 and 40% of vertices in the BGs on average in every database form claws. This indicates that bifurcations are commonplace in our vascular modalities while crossovers are not as commonly seen.

Within modalities, the far-infrared images (SFIR) for hand vessels are superior to the near-infrared (SNIR) as far as being able to extract BGs with usable structure is concerned. With retina, the ESRID graphs are much larger and more connected than VARIA graphs. There is also a large variation across the sizes of the graphs in ESRID when compared to VARIA. The probability of finding a two-claw structure in a retina BG is higher on average than for the other modalities.

The hand BGs are, nonetheless, the smallest and least structured of all modalities, with lower connectivity evidenced by only 70% of their vertices belonging to the largest component. The palm BGs are the second largest (after retina BGs) and most structured, with a higher connectivity than the other graphs demonstrated both by density and the fact that over 90% of the vertices belong to the largest component.

12.4.2.2 Proximity Graphs

Another topological measure we use to characterise the different BG modalities is the distance a BG is from a *proximity graph* on the same vertex set. Proximity graphs were defined by Davis et al. [11]. A proximity graph p_ε on spatial vertex set V is one where a pair of vertices in V have an edge between them if and only if they are less than ε units apart. That is, for a proximity graph, the edges are completely defined by the spatial arrangement of its vertices. The closer a graph is to a proximity graph, the more predictable its edges are.

Table 12.4 [6] The mean (standard deviation) distance of a BG to its nearest proximity graph

Database	Proximity graph distance
Palm	0.017 (0.004)
Wrist	0.022 (0.006)
Hand SFIR	0.032 (0.007)
Hand SNIR	0.046 (0.018)
Retina VARIA	0.031 (0.010)

Thus, if $g = (V, E, \mu, \nu, A)$ is a BG there is a family of proximity graphs $\{p_\varepsilon, \varepsilon \geq 0\}$ defined by V. For each ε, a normalised distance between g and p_ε can be determined from their adjacency matrices, using formulas described in [11]. The value of the proximity graph distance varies from 0 to 1, where zero implies that the graph is a proximity graph. The minimum of these distances over the available range of ε decides the specific value of the bound ε and the closest proximity graph p_ε to g. Table 12.4 shows the average and standard deviation of this distance from a BG to its nearest proximity graph, for each of the databases.

The BGs from palm and wrist vessels have the lowest average distances to a proximity graph, implying that their edges are more predictable than the other BG modalities. Edges are more likely to occur between nearby vertices in palm and wrist BGs than for other modalities, which suggests that the relational information in the graph representation is less surprising (has lower entropy). In principle, the higher the distance, the more promising the vascular pattern is as a biometric modality.

12.4.3 Comparison of MCS Topology in BGC

In previous work [6–8, 20, 21], we have investigated many potential structures and graph statistics in MCSs for their usefulness in BGC for finding information that will satisfactorily separate genuine MCSs from impostor MCSs. Genuine MCSs usually look quite different from impostor MCSs, the latter appearing fragmented and broken as seen in Fig. 12.3. We have attempted in numerous ways to find measures that capture this visually striking difference.

Here, we summarise our findings and discuss reasons for restricting to the structures and corresponding similarity score measures we now use.

Our initial application of BGC [7] was to the retina modality, which has been repeatedly shown (on very small databases) to have high accuracy, with complete separation of genuine and impostor scores typically being demonstrated for vertex comparison approaches. In [7], with manually extracted BGs from the VARIA retina database, we introduced the original BGC (with $S = V$ in the comparison step). We tested 8 measures based on the MCSs for both genuine and impostor comparisons. The 6 normalised quantities were d_v, d_e and the differences $n2$, $n3$, $p2$, $p3$ using Eq. (12.6) corresponding to numbers of vertices of degree ≥ 2, vertices of degree

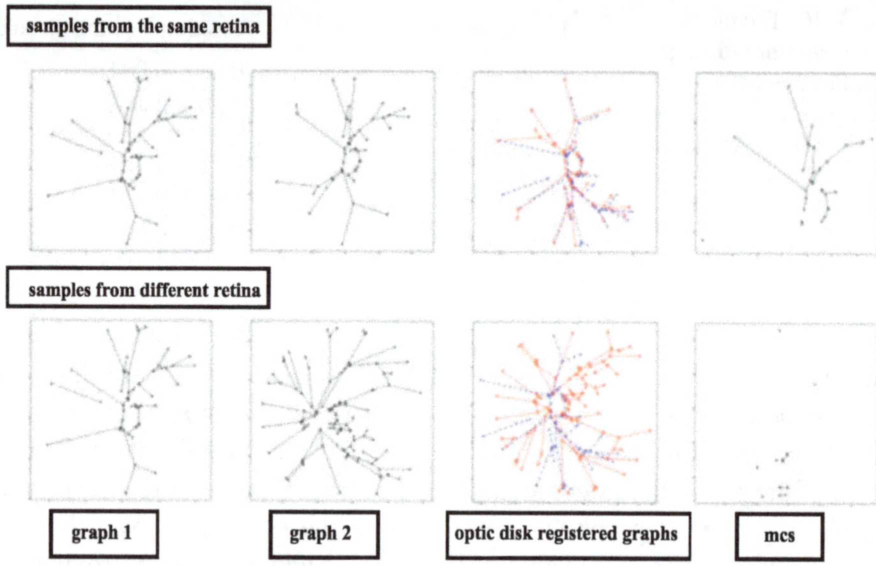

Fig. 12.3 This is an example of the BGC algorithm when two samples from the same retina instance are compared (genuine comparison) versus when two samples from different retina instances are compared (impostor comparison). Note the MCSs are visually different, with the genuine MCS having more vertices and a more complex structure than the impostor MCS

≥ 3, paths of length 2 and paths of length 3 in g_1, g_2 and g_m, respectively. The 2 unnormalised quantities were the density $\rho_m = |E_m|/|V_m|$ of g_m and the variance σ_D^2 of the degree distribution of g_m. Of these, the score distances for genuine comparisons using vertices of degree ≥ 3 and paths of length 3 were too high to warrant further use. Vertices of degree ≥ 2 and paths of length 2 were also not further considered, as they correlated too highly with either d_v or d_e.

Score fusion using d_v and d_e gave better, but not significantly better, performance than either single measure, probably because these measures are highly correlated. In fact the least correlated measures are d_v, ρ_m and σ_D^2. These measures completely separated scores in two or three dimensions, an improvement on separation in one dimension which is expected to become significant in larger retina databases.

In [20], we developed the first full BGC system to automatically extract retina BGs and compare them, again using the VARIA database. Our intention was to see if the results of [7] could be improved using automatic extraction of BGs. We retained the measure d_v, introduced $d_{c_1c_2}$ based on the two largest connected components of g_m, and replaced σ_D^2 by the maximum degree D_{max} of a vertex in g_m (another unnormalised quantity). Again we showed that using d_v alone gave complete separation in the training set. Using two or all three measures in a combination of an SVM classifier and KDE curves [20] or surfaces gave dramatic improvements in False Match rate (FMR) (up to several orders of magnitude), when False Non-Match Rate (FNMR) was very low.

For hand vessel BGs using the SNIR and SFIR databases in [21], we tested the 7 measures d_v, d_e, $|V_{c_1}|$, $|V_{c_1}| + |V_{c_2}|$, σ_D^2, D_{max} and, for the first time, the average degree μ_D of the vertices in the MCS. The best-separating individual measures were d_v, d_e and $|V_{c_1}| + |V_{c_2}|$, but as d_v and d_e are highly correlated, the relatively uncorrelated measures d_v, $|V_{c_1}| + |V_{c_2}|$ and σ_D^2 were tested to see if multidimensional scoring would improve performance over individual measures. In contrast to the case for retina, we found little advantage in increasing the number of measures used. We attribute this to the fact that hand BGs are appreciably smaller and more fragmented than retina BGs (see Table 12.3 and [21, Fig. 3]) and will have correspondingly less available topology in their MCSs to exploit.

As a consequence of these experiments, the measures we focussed on were d_v, d_e, $d_{c_1c_2}$, ρ_m; and d_{c_1} and d_{c_2}, the measures using Eq. (12.6) corresponding to the number of vertices in c_1 and c_2, respectively.

For the larger palm vessel BGs, in [8] we test these 6 measures[3] and a further 4: ρ_{c_1}; the ratio of the number of isolated vertices I to the number of connected vertices; the normalised total length d_ℓ of the edges in c_1; and the ratio $n4$ of the number of vertices with degree ≥ 4 in g_m, to $|V_m|$. Equal Error rates using single measures were competitive (under 5%) for within session comparisons for the measures d_v, d_e, d_{c_1}, $d_{c_1c_2}$, ρ and d_ℓ, with three of these, d_v, d_e and $d_{c_1c_2}$, having competitive EERs across sessions as well. The measure d_e outperformed all others. Testing score pairs showed that pairing d_e with any of d_{c_1}, $d_{c_1c_2}$ and d_ℓ improved performance over the single score d_e, with (d_e, d_ℓ) having the maximum gain.

In [6], we tested our ideas on all four modalities using a uniform approach. Our results are outlined in the Sect. 12.4.4, which explains the selection of difference measures in Table 12.1.

- Our attempts to quantify our observation that higher degree vertices occur more frequently in genuine MCSs than in impostor MCSs $(n2, n3, \mu_D, \sigma_D^2, n4)$ coalesced in the single measure d_C of claws (i.e. of degree 3 vertices).
- Our efforts to quantify our observation that connected components are larger in genuine MCSs than in impostor MCSs led to the measures d_{c_1}, d_{c_2}, $d_{c_1c_2}$, d_I.
- Our wish to capture some spatial information rather than counts alone resulted in d_ℓ and a new measure d_a found using Eq. (12.6) from the area of the smallest rectangle containing the entire graph.
- Our efforts to quantify our observation that genuine MCSs have higher complexity than impostor MCSs led us to use ρ_m, ρ_{c_1}, D_{max} and a new measure d_t using Eq. (12.6) for the number of two-claws.

For convenience this subsection is summarised in Table 12.5. Measures that we have only tested once before 2017 $(p2, p3, \mu_D, n4)$ are not included. Plainly this topic is by no means exhausted.

12.4.4 Comparison of BGC Performance Across Databases

In this subsection, we outline the results and conclusions of our paper [6], in which we evaluated the performance of BGC for the databases of Sect. 12.4.1. The individuals

[3] In fact the corresponding similarity measure $1 - d$ was used for the normalised measures.

Table 12.5 Difference measures used in BGC

Year	Mode	d_v	d_e	d_C	$d_{c_1c_2}$	d_{c_1}	d_{c_2}	ρ_m	ρ_{c_1}	σ_D^2	D_{max}	d_I	d_ℓ	d_a	d_t
2011 [7]	Retina	✓	✓	✓[a]				✓		✓					
2013 [20]	Retina	✓			✓						✓				
2014 [21]	Hand	✓	✓		✓[b]	✓[b]				✓	✓				
2015 [8]	Palm	✓	✓		✓	✓	✓	✓	✓			✓[c]	✓		
2017 [6]	All[d]	✓	✓	✓	✓	✓	✓	✓	✓		✓	✓	✓	✓	✓

[a] $n2$ and $n3$ count the degree ≥ 2 and ≥ 3 vertices. d_C counts the degree 3 vertices (or claws)
[b] Un-normalised counts used
[c] Ratio of I to number of connected vertices, rather than normalised using Eq. (12.6)
[d] Retina, hand, palm, wrist

in each of the five databases (2 for hand) were divided in two, with BGs for one half used for training and the other for testing, to maintain independence. For full details of the experiments, see [6].

The first training experiment was to tune for BGR: to identify the best structure $S \in \{E, C, T\}$ for graph registration for each database, the optimal pair shortlist length L and the tolerance ε. This list was selected based on observation. For each S, L was varied by steps of 40 through the range [20, 220]. Because accurate registration is crucial to the performance of BGC, we selected the L leading to highest registration accuracy. There is a consequent trade-off in speed versus accuracy, as Table 12.6 demonstrates.

The second training experiment was to tune the parameters of BGC: the structure $S \in \{V, E, C, T\}$ and parameters α_1, α_2 for the graph edit computations and the difference measure d for scoring MCSs. The parameters were each stepped by 2 in the range [3, 9]. For each database, a subset of 1000 genuine and 1000 impostor comparisons was selected at random and their MCSs computed and scored with the 13 graph measures (see Table 12.5) to find the values giving optimal separation. To check if any combination of measures would improve separation, we combined all 13 measures and used LDA to check this, but found no significant improvement over single measures. For all databases, selecting V for the cost matrix structure and d_v

Table 12.6 [6] The chosen registration structures S and shortlist values L for each database and the average registration times

Database	S	L	Time (s)
Palm	E	220	20
Wrist	E	60	7
Hand SFIR	T	60	0.8
Hand SNIR	E	60	1.9
Retina VARIA	T	100	1.8

Table 12.7 [6] The graph matching parameters chosen based on best performance on the training set

Database	α_1	α_2	Best d	2nd best d	3rd best d
Palm	5	3	d_e	d_v	ρ_{c_1}
Wrist	3	7	d_e	d_v	ρ_{c_1}
SFIR Hand	3	7	d_v	d_e	d_t
SNIR Hand	3	5	d_v	d_e	ρ_{c_1}
Retina VARIA	3	9	d_v	d_e	$d_{c_1c_2}$

Table 12.8 [6] Comparison performance using BGC on the test set at 2 specific thresholds obtained from the *training set experiments*—FMR100 and FMR1000

Threshold	Palm	Wrist	Hand—SFIR	Hand—SNIR	Retina
	FNMR %	FNMR %	FNMR %	FNMR %	FNMR %
FMR100	3.63	26.9	4.39	0.54	0.07
FMR1000	6.242	44.06	8.79	99.72	0.86

or d_e gave the best separation. Table 12.7 summarises the results. The five graph measures on the MCS that we found to be the best difference measures, are d_v, d_e, ρ_{c_1}, $d_{c_1c_2}$ and d_t.

After tuning, we tested BGC on the remaining half of the individuals and determined FMR and FNMR of comparisons at three distance thresholds chosen from the training experiments—EER, FMR100 and FMR1000. ROCs for the SNIR Handvein database training set do not appear in [6] and are given in Appendix 4. All databases other than the wrist, gave error rates under 5% at the EER threshold. Those for palm, hand and retina were comparable with our previous results or the literature. Table 12.8 records our results.

We have already shown for hand vessels [21] that including edge information in BGC improves recognition performance over point pattern comparison. Our final experiment was to apply ICP to register graph pairs, then apply Step 4 of BGR to count matched vertices in the two graphs, again scoring using QuickScore (Eq. (12.1)) for consistency. In all cases, BGC outperformed point pattern comparison using ICP registration. See Table 6 of [6] for exact values.

12.5 Anchors for a BGC Approach to Template Protection

The purpose of biometric authentication is to link a subject unequivocally to the authentication token. The biometric template used to form the token comprises personal and sensitive information and is often encrypted when stored. However, as biometric data is noisy, comparison with an incoming biometric sample cannot be done in the encrypted domain using cryptographic hash functions as these require exactness of data. Consequently, most authentication systems decrypt the stored biometric data, compare the unencrypted templates and make an authentication decision. This makes the biometric template vulnerable during comparison.

Thus, finding a template protection scheme which permits direct comparison of protected templates is desirable. In any such scheme, performance degradation over unprotected comparison must be marginal. Further, the ISO/IEC 24745:2011 standard [25] states the following two criteria to protect biometric information: (a) *Irreversibility* where the biometric raw data cannot be retrieved from the template or token, and (b) *Unlinkability* where multiple independent instances of a subject cannot be linked to identify the subject.

We are interested in the possibility of using biometric graphs in a template protection scheme based on a dissimilarity vector model.

12.5.1 Dissimilarity Vector Templates for Biometric Graphs

We want to investigate the feasibility of protecting a BG template by representing it as a vector of dissimilarities from a fixed set of reference BGs extracted from a separate, external set of instances. Such reference graphs are termed "cohorts". The reason that cohort-based dissimilarity vectors may be a solution to having template-protected biometric comparison for automatic identity authentication is that the biometric sample data need not be stored. Only the cohort graphs and the dissimilarity vector are required for authentication. On the face of it, neither of these reveal any direct information about the biometric sample data of enrolled individuals.

In preliminary work [5], we use retina as an example to conduct the first step of this investigation: to test if the comparison performance of the dissimilarity vector templates is similar to that of unprotected template comparison.

Cohorts are typically not used in existing dissimilarity vector implementations because of the expectation that graphs which are not a member of any class will be dissimilar to all classes and hence not useful for classification. Contrary to this, we found that when retina graphs are registered on the optic disc then graphs extracted from images of the same retina are surprisingly and consistently dissimilar, or similar, to other retina graphs external to the classification set, when the dissimilarity is defined by the BGC algorithm with slack graph comparison parameters.

Figure 12.4 shows an example of a dissimilarity vector for a retina graph.

We have shown that the dissimilarity vector approach is accurately able to compare and verify samples with only a small loss in performance over direct comparison using BGC. Once performance is established, the next step would be to establish rigorous security bounds on irreversability and unlinkability as conducted by Gomez-Barrero et al. [14, 15]. This is an area of future work.

12.5.2 Anchors for Registration

Amongst the modalities presented here, retinae have an intrinsic reference frame defined by the location of optic disk and fovea. Palm vein patterns have a reference

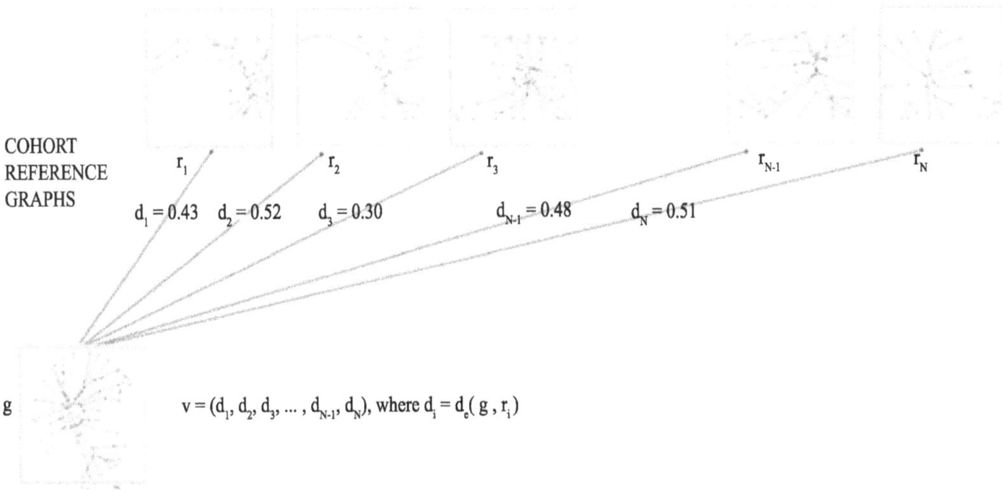

Fig. 12.4 An example of a dissimilarity vector for a retina graph g in ESRID from a set of cohort graphs in VARIA. The dissimilarity vector $v = (d_1, d_2, \cdots, d_N)$ is the vector of dissimilarities from the ordered set of cohort graphs $(r_1, r_2, \cdots, r_N)$. Each $d_i\ \forall 1 \leq i \leq N$ is calculated as $d_i = d_e(g, r_i)$, where d_e is some measure of dissimilarity between graphs g and r_i

frame defined by the hand contour. For other vascular patterns, an intrinsic reference frame has not been identified (for finger graphs, the midline of the finger was found by Nibbelke [23] not to be robust), and because of the noise associated with presentation of a biometric sample and graph extraction, graphs extracted from images from the same individual do not consistently register with reference graphs in the same way when using BGR and are not consistently dissimilar. The retina graphs in both the ESRID and VARIA databases are roughly pre-aligned because the presentation of the retina is always with the head upright, and so a common reference frame for a pair of retina graphs extracted from these images can be found by centring each graph on the centre of the optic disk (also extracted from the associated retina image).

Hence, a barrier to generalising the dissimilarity vector approach to template protection to other vascular graphs is the ability to register presentations of a vascular pattern from the same individual in the same way so that their dissimilarity from a set of reference graphs has the possibility to be consistent. The alternative, which is to use BGR, gives a set of scores that are essentially drawn from a distribution of impostor comparison scores and are different from one sample to the next.

In an attempt to achieve consistent registration, we consider identifying subgraphs of a smaller size that are consistently extracted in multiple presentations of a subject's biometric data despite the noise in the image presentation and extraction process. We term this small subgraph, should it exist, the *anchor* for a set of biometric graphs from an individual.

Definition 12.3 A BG *anchor* for an individual is a small connected subgraph that appears consistently in BGs extracted from multiple good samples from the individual and that does not by itself reveal identifying information about the individual.

Whether such an anchor exists for every enrolled subject is the first question, which we attempt to answer here for two of the databases we have studied. Whether registration on such an anchor then leads to dissimilarity vectors that can be used for accurate classification is a separate question and is future work.

12.5.3 The Search for Anchors

The BGC algorithm can be used recursively to find anchors. Let $g_1, g_2, \dots, g_n$ be the BGs of the n samples of a subject for which we need to find an anchor.

The first step is to use the BGC algorithm to find the MCS between a pair of graphs. Let m_{12} be the MCS of the graphs g_1 and g_2. BGC is then used to find the MCS between m_{12} and the third graph in the list g_3. Let this be denoted by m_{123}. This is the common graph between g_1, g_2 and g_3. If we continue this process, the common graph between the n graphs $g_1, g_2, \dots, g_n$ is the MCS between $m_{123\cdots n-1}$ and g_n and is denoted by $m_{123\dots n}$. This graph represents the graph structure that is common to the n samples from a subject. If the graph samples are of high quality, we often find this common graph to be large with significant amount of structure. Therefore, the entire common graph would be inappropriate to use as an anchor associated with a template protection scheme. On the basis of observation and experimentation, we have isolated two criteria to derive an anchor from $m_{123\dots n}$:

- It is the largest connected component of $m_{123\cdots n}$ that has a minimum of at least 5 vertices and maximum of 10 vertices. This criteria ensures that the anchor is not so large as to reveal significant structure of a subject's BG.
- This connected component must have at least one claw. In cases where there was an absence of a claw (i.e. the component was a path) we observed that the anchor was not uniquely found.

One way to satisfy the above two criteria is to vary the weights α_1 and α_2 in the cost matrix $\mathbf{C}$ of the BGC algorithm used when finding anchors. When α_1 and α_2 are small, the MCS returned will be very small and sparse. As we want to have recursively generated MCSes to have a bit more structure, we found it beneficial to recursively slacken α_2 until we find a common graph of the n graphs that will give an anchor that satisfies the above two conditions.

To study the possibility of finding anchors and the various factors that impact this for a database, we need a database that has multiple samples of the same subject. The PUT datasets of palm and wrist vessels had 12 samples per subject across 3 sessions and were satisfactory for our experiments.

For both databases we chose n, the number of graphs of a subject used to find an anchor, as $n = 6$. We used the remaining 6 samples as test samples to determine if an anchor can be found in a new incoming sample. We set $\alpha_1 = 1$ in the cost matrix $\mathbf{C}$ and recursively increased α_2 from 4 to 16 in steps of 2 in the anchor-finding algorithm.

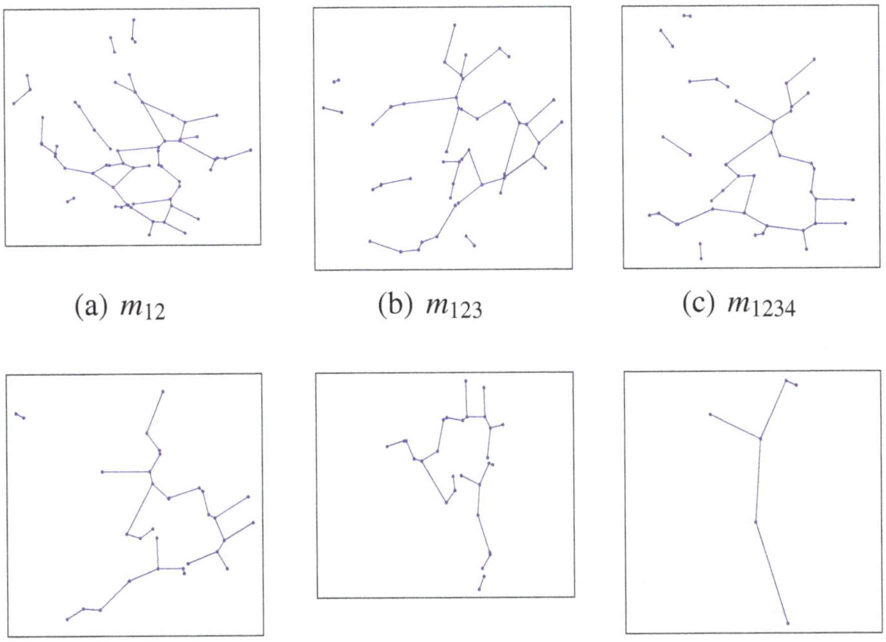

(a) m_{12} (b) m_{123} (c) m_{1234}

(d) m_{12345} (e) m_{123456} (f) Anchor

Fig. 12.5 This figure shows the common graphs and the final anchor obtained when BGC is used recursively, pairwise on a set of BGs from an individual in the PUT palm database to create the anchor for that individual. Observe that as expected, the size of the common graph as we increase the number of BGs gets smaller. **f** shows the extracted anchor (Graphs are not on the same scale)

Figure 12.5a–e shows the process of recursively applying the BGC algorithm to obtain a common graph among 6 BGs of a subject in the PUT Palm database. We observe that as the number of samples used increases, the common graph tends to get smaller and sparser compared to previous common graphs. For a graph to become part of the common graph it must exist in all the BGs used to form it. The criteria get harder to satisfy as the number of BGs increase. Figure 12.5f and shows the anchor, a subgraph of m_{123456} in Fig. 12.5e, which is the largest connected component of maximum order 10 with at least one claw.

12.5.4 Queries and Discoveries for Anchors

To understand if the use of anchors is practical for registering BGs, we used the palm and wrist databases to investigate the following questions:

1. How likely is it that an anchor cannot be found for a subject in the database and what are the possible reasons for failure to find an anchor?
2. If an anchor is generated using a few samples of a subject, how do we determine if it exists in a new probe sample of the same subject. How reliable is this anchor?

3. How often will an anchor fail to be found in a new probe sample of an enrolled subject? If this happens, what are the causes?

For both databases, we chose 6 BGs from the 12 BGs of each subject in 4 ways giving 4 different attempts at finding an anchor. As the PUT database had 50 subjects, we had 200 trials to find an anchor and we noted the number of trials that failed to find an anchor (first column of Table 12.9).

Once an anchor is found, it needs to be reliably found in a new sample of the same subject. The existence of an anchor in a larger graph can be determined using the BGR algorithm described in Sect. 12.3.1.1. The BGR algorithm will attempt to find an aligning edge between the anchor and a BG of an individual. *Anchor overlap* is defined as the fraction of vertices in the anchor that found a comparison vertex in the BG. 100% overlap indicates the anchor has been exactly found in the BG and can be reliably used to establish a coordinate frame of registration. Figure 12.6 shows an anchor and its overlap in a new probe sample for the palm and wrist BGs. Figure 12.6b, d show an example where the anchor overlap is less than 50%. These are both situations when the anchor has not been found as the anchor just did not exist in the BG. The mean and standard deviation anchor overlap for the palm and wrist databases is shown in column 2 of Table 12.9.

Based on the distribution of anchor overlap in a database, it is possible to choose a minimum value O_t for the anchor overlap to consider an anchor to be reliable. Choosing a specific O_t for each database, we measure for each individual, the number of times in the 6 BGs where the anchor is reliably found. This result is shown in column 3 of Table 12.9.

The distributions of anchor overlap and success rates of finding an anchor reliably for both databases is shown in Fig. 12.8. The source code for the anchor-finding algorithms are available at [3].

12.5.5 Results

Column 1 of Table 12.9 shows that BGs of an individual in the palm database had a greater chance of generating an anchor than BGs of an individual in the wrist database. Anchors are not generated when the BGs from the samples of the individual fail to find a common subgraph among all of them. This happens if even one BG does not have enough common area of capture amongst the six. Figure 12.7a shows an example where 6 BGs from the wrist vein graph could not generate an anchor. Figure 12.7b shows the BGC applied recursively to get a common graph that did not satisfy the two conditions for an anchor, i.e. there was no component of size between 5 and 10 that had at least one claw.

We next wanted to test, if for every failure in getting an anchor, when the selection of BGs changed, would we be able to get an anchor for the individual? We found that out of the 10 individuals whose trials failed to give an anchor in the palm database, only 2 of the individuals failed again when the selection of BGs changed. For the

Table 12.9 Results from experiments on finding anchors in the PUT palm and wrist databases

Database PUT	Trials that failed to generate anchors (%)	Anchor overlap across the database (%)	Number of reliable anchor registrations per person
Palm	6	75.17 (16.94)	3.68 (1.96)
Wrist	14	76.6 (14.6)	3.96 (1.64)

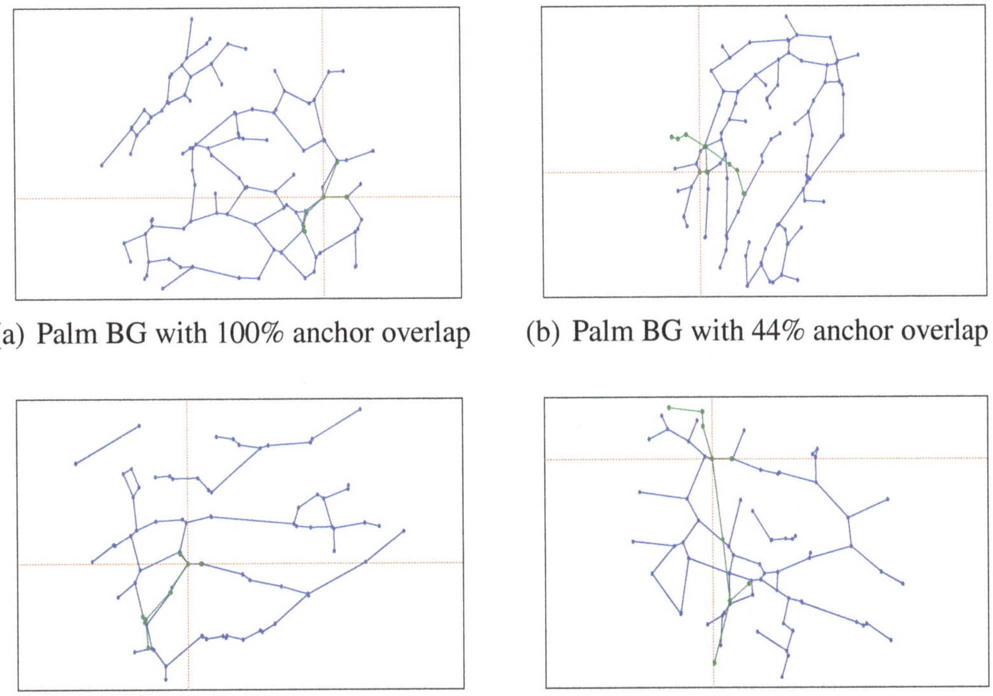

(a) Palm BG with 100% anchor overlap (b) Palm BG with 44% anchor overlap

(c) Wrist BG with 100% anchor overlap (d) Wrist BG with 44% anchor overlap

Fig. 12.6 This figure shows examples of Palm and Wrist BGs where the overlap is 100% **(a)** and **(c)**, and where the overlap is less than 50% **(b)** and **(d)**. The anchors are in green and the BGs are in blue

wrist database, 21 individuals failed in a trial to get an anchor, out of them only 3 failed again when the BGs selected were changed. This shows that in practice, if an anchor is not found in a set of samples, it is possible to get an individual to re-enrol until their set of enrolled BGs can give an anchor.

Figure 12.8a, c show the distribution of the anchor overlap measure in the palm and wrist databases. Table 12.9 shows that the mean value of the overlap is over 75% for both. Based on this distribution, we choose O_t to be 70% and measure the number of times we could reliably find an anchor among the remaining 6 BGs that were not used to get the anchor. Figure 12.8b, d show the distribution of number of times the anchor is found reliably in the remaining samples of an individual in the palm and wrist databases, when O_t is set to be 70%. Table 12.9 shows that while the palm BGs were more successful overall in finding anchors, once anchors were found, the

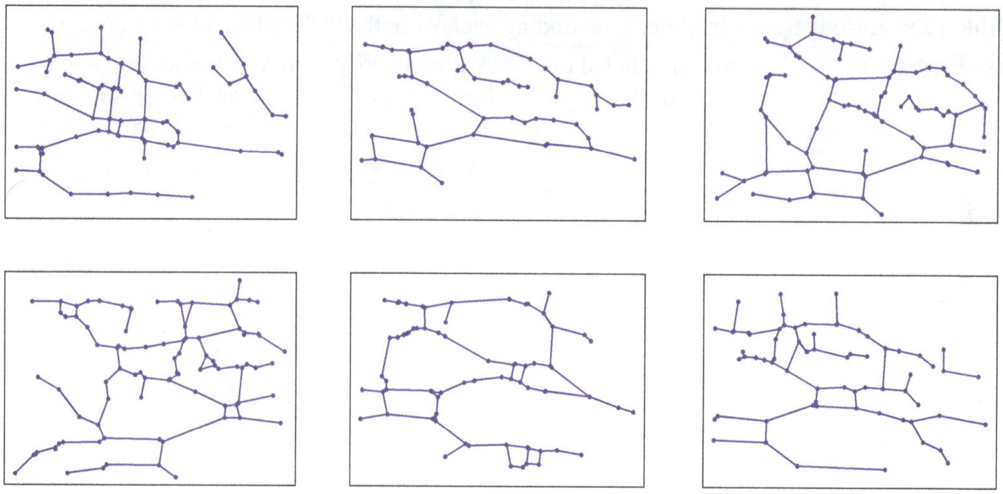

(a) Set of 6 wrist BGs that failed to give an anchor

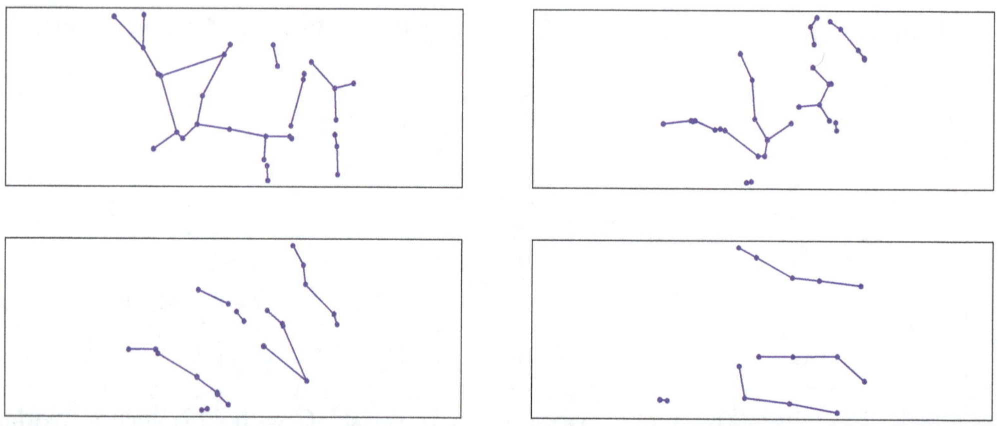

(b) BGC recursively applied to get common graphs

Fig. 12.7 This figure illustrates how 6 wrist BGs can fail to give an anchor. The final common graph did not have a component of maximum size 10 with at least one claw

wrist BGs had a greater chance of finding the anchor in the remaining BGs from the individual. In practice, it would be possible to request resubmission of the biometric sample if the previously identified anchor wasn't found.

12.5.6 Conclusion

This chapter has explained the basic foundations of representing vascular biometric samples as formal graphs. It has generalised the graph registration and comparison algorithms, BGR and BGC, respectively, and summarised our findings from testing the efficiency and effectiveness of BGR and BGC on 4 different modalities–

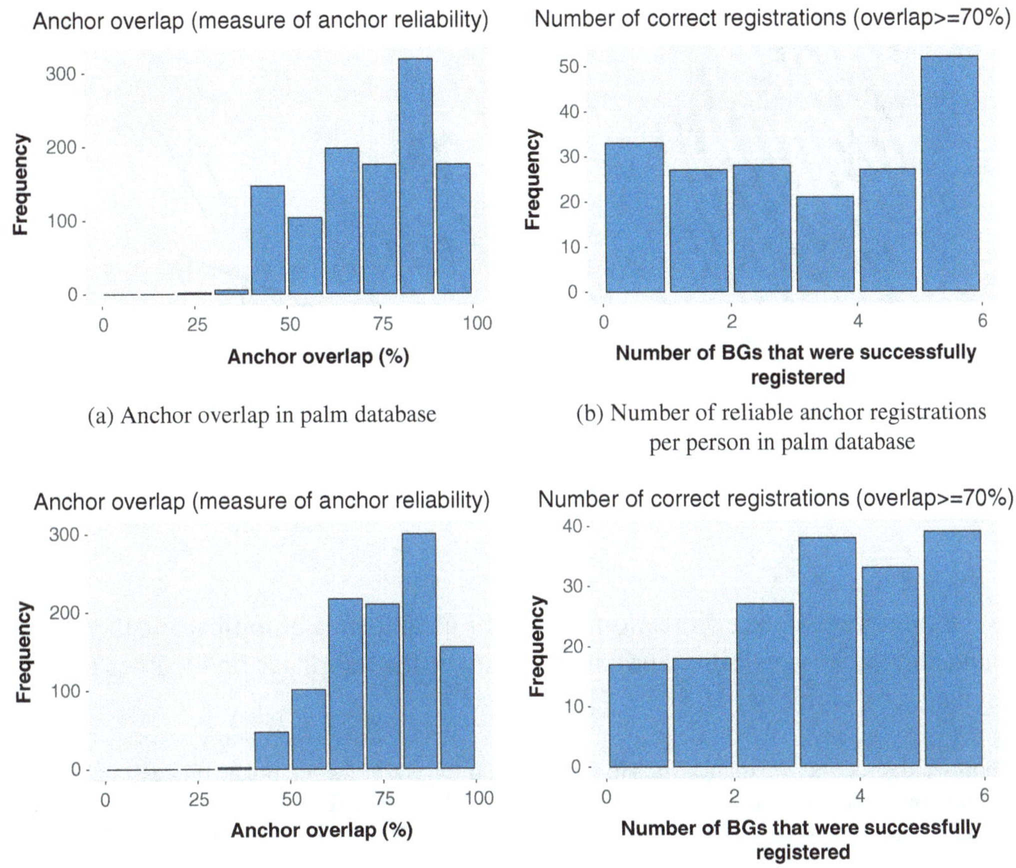

(a) Anchor overlap in palm database

(b) Number of reliable anchor registrations per person in palm database

(c) Anchor overlap in wrist database

(d) Number of reliable anchor registrations per person in wrist database

Fig. 12.8 This figure shows the histograms of the anchor overlap in the palm and wrist databases. Once an anchor is found, the number of reliable registrations of the anchor per subject, when $O_t = 70\%$ is also shown for both databases. Here test set denotes those 6 BGs not used to get the anchor

palm, wrist, hand and retina. The results show that the relational information in BGs provides better recognition accuracy compared to point pattern approaches. We introduced a modification of BGC with the potential to create a template protection scheme using dissimilarity vectors. We also introduced the concept of anchors, a method to register a BG with a consistent reference frame when, unlike retina, there is no intrinsic reference frame. The choice of anchor and structural restrictions are necessary for them to be used to implement biometric template protection using the dissimilarity vector paradigm. We tested the ease of finding anchors and the likelihood for one to be found reliably in BGs that were not used to identify the anchor. The results show us that with proper selection of BGs, we can always find an anchor for an individual.

In the future we want to apply the concept of anchors to test the accuracy of the dissimilarity vector representation for other modalities like palm vein and hand vein. We also plan to conduct a thorough security analysis of the dissimilarity vector rep-

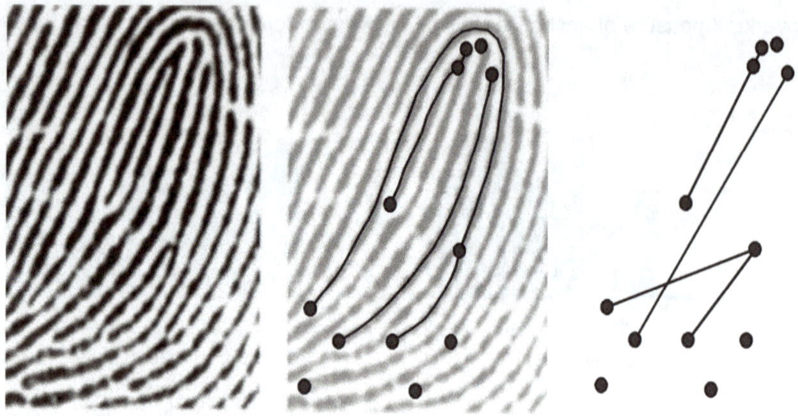

Fig. 12.9 The extraction of a Biometric Graph from a section of fingerprint image. Note that the BG edges represent the ridgeline connectivity relationships between pairs of minutiae, not the ridgeline itself

resentation as a template protection scheme by establishing empirical and theoretical bounds on the irreversibility and unlinkability of the templates on the lines of work conducted by Gomez et al. [14, 15].

Acknowledgements We thank Drs. Hao, Jeffers and Lajervadi for the image processing involved in extracting Biometric Graphs. We thank Dr. Aliahmad and Prof. Kumar for providing the ESRID database. The work has been partly funded by the Australian Research Council grant DP120101188.

Appendix 1

Here is an example of the original Biometric Graph, as introduced in [17] (Fig. 12.9).

Appendix 2

This section gives the pseudocode for the BGR algorithm described in Sect. 12.3.1. It is a corrected and updated version of the algorithm in [6]. The source code for the BGR and BGC algorithms is available at [4].

Require: Graphs g and g' with vertex sets $\mathbf{V} = \{v_1, v_2, \cdots, v_m\}$ and $\mathbf{V}' = \{v'_1, v'_2, \cdots, v'_{m'}\}$ and vertex sets $\mathbf{E} = \{e_1, e_2, \cdots, e_n\}$ and $\mathbf{E}' = \{e'_1, e'_2, \cdots, e'_{n'}\}$, respectively. Let L be the number of structure pairs to shortlist and let ε be the tolerance to match vertex pairs.

Ensure: Aligned graphs g_a and g'_a having same edge links as g and g' but with new spatial coordinates.

$g_a \leftarrow \varnothing$ and $g'_a \leftarrow \varnothing$. ▷ Initialise the registered graphs that will be returned at the end of the algorithm

S $= \{ s_1, s_2, \cdots, s_n \}$ is the list of structures in g.
S' $= \{ s'_1, s'_2, \cdots, s'_{n'} \}$ is the list of structures in g'.
$M_{dist} \leftarrow 0$ ▷ Initialise a matrix of size $n \times n'$ with zeros.
for $a = 1$ to n **do**
    for $b = 1$ to n' **do**
        $d_{ab} =$ STRUCTDIST(s_a, s_b, F) ▷ This function returns the distance between the two structures. The flag F indicates if the structure is an edge, claw or two-claw.
        $M_{dist}[a, b] \leftarrow d_{ab}$
    end for
end for

Sort the contents of M_{dist} in increasing order.
$M_{shortlist}$ is a matrix with 3 columns.
Every row m_i stores the 3-tuple (d_{abi}, a_i, b_i).
d_{abi} is taken from the sorted M_{dist} with the first row of $M_{shortlist}$, m_1 having d_{ab1}, the smallest distance.
a_i and b_i indicate the corresponding row and column of d_{abi} in M_{dist}.

$d_{struct} \leftarrow (0, 0, \cdots, 0)_{1 \times L}$ ▷ A vector to store the distances between graphs when aligned on each of the shortlisted structure pairs
for $i = 1$ to L **do**
    $a = a_i, b = b_i$ where $m_i \in M_{shortlist}$
    $g_o =$ TRANSROT(g, e_a). ▷ Translate and rotate g with respect to the specific edge in the shortlisted structure
    $g'_o =$ TRANSROT(g', e'_b).
    $d_{struct}[i] =$ QUICKSCORE(g_o, g'_o, ε) ▷ Compute a distance based on vertex correspondence between the translated and rotated graphs
end for

$d_{min} =$ MIN (d_{struct}).
a_{min} and b_{min} are the row and column in $M_{shortlist}$ corresponding to d_{min}.
$g_a =$ TRANSROT($g, e_{a_{min}}$).
$g'_o =$ TRANSROT($g', e'_{b_{min}}$).
return g_a, g'_a and d_{min}.

function EUCDIST($A = (a_1, a_2, \cdots, a_z)$, $B = (b_1, b_2, \cdots, b_z)$)
    $d = \sqrt{(a_1 - b_1)^2 + (a_2 - b_2)^2 + ...(a_z - b_z)^2}$ **return** d
end function

function STRUCTDIST(s_a, s_b, F) $d_{structPair} \leftarrow \varnothing$
    if F ==“edge” **then** ▷

$E_a \leftarrow (l_a, \theta_a)$ ▷ The length and slope of the edge
$E_b \leftarrow (l'_b, \theta'_b)$
$d_{struct\,Pair} = \frac{1}{0.5(l_a + l'_b)}$EUCDIST$(E_a, E_b)$ ▷ The Euclidean distance between the lengths l and l' and slopes θ and θ' of the vertex pair.
end if
if F =="claw" **then**
$L_a \leftarrow (l_{1a}, l_{2a}, l_{3a})$ ▷ The three edges of the claw in decreasing order of edge length
$\Theta_a \leftarrow (\theta_{12a}, \theta_{23a})$ ▷ The angles between first and second vertex and the second and third vertex.
$L'_b \leftarrow (l'_{1b}, l'_{2b}, l'_{3b})$
$\Theta_b \leftarrow (\theta'_{12b}, \theta'_{23b})$
$l_\delta \leftarrow$ EUCDIST(L_a, L'_b)
$a_\delta \leftarrow$ EUCDIST(Θ_a, Θ'_b)
$d = l_\delta + a_\delta$
$d_{struct\,Pair} = d$
end if
if F =="two-claw" **then** ▷ A two-claw has two-claw structures connected by a common edge
$L_a \leftarrow (l_{1a}, l_{2a}, l_{3a}, l_{4a}, l_{5a}, l_{6a})$
▷ l_1 and l_4 are the longest edges of the first and second claw structures. The other two edges follow the longest edge in decreasing order of length.
$\Theta_a \leftarrow (\theta_{12a}, \theta_{23a}, \theta_{45a}, \theta_{56a})$ ▷ The four internal angles, two each from each of the two-claws.
l_{*a} is the length of the connecting edge between the two-claws in structure a where $* \in \{1, 2, 3, 4, 5, 6\}$.
$L'_b \leftarrow (l'_{1b}, l'_{2b}, l'_{3b}, l'_{4b}, l'_{5b}, l'_{6b})$
$\Theta'_b \leftarrow (\theta'_{12b}, \theta'_{23b}, \theta'_{45b}, \theta'_{56b})$
l'_{*b} is the length of the connecting edge between the two-claws in structure b where $* \in \{1, 2, 3, 4, 5, 6\}$.
$d_1 =$ EUCDIST$(L_a[1:3], L'_b[1:3])$ + EUCDIST$(\Theta_a[1:3], \Theta'_b[1:3])$
$d_2 =$ EUCDIST$(L_a[4:6], L'_b[4:6])$ + EUCDIST$(\Theta_a[4:6], \Theta'_b[4:6])$
$d_3 =$ EUCDIST(l_{*a}, l'_{*b}).
$d_{struct\,Pair} = d_1 + d_2 + d_3$
end if
return $d_{struct\,Pair}$
end function

function TRANSROT(g, e)
$g_o \leftarrow g$
The vertex of e with the smaller x coordinate will be the origin of the coordinate system.
The edge e will be define the positive direction of the x-axis.

Recalculate all the vertex attributes of g_o in the new coordinate system. **return** g_o.
end function

function QUICKSCORE(g, g', ε)
Label all vertices of g and g' as unmatched.
$C = 0$ ▷ Counter for number of vertex pair matches between g and g'
for $i = 1$ to m **do**
for $j = 1$ to m' **do**
if v_i is labelled unmatched and v'_j is labelled unmatched and EUCDIST(q_i, q'_j) $\leq \varepsilon$ **then**
$C = C + 1$. ▷ v_i matches with v'_j.
Label v_i and v'_j as matched. ▷ $q_i = (q_{1i}, q_{2i})$ is the vertex attribute of v_i and q'_i is the vertex attribute of v'_i .
end if
end for
end for
$d = 1 - \frac{C}{\sqrt{m \times m'}}$. **return** d.
end function

Appendix 3

This section presents details of the cost matrices that use complex structures like edges (E), claws (C) and two-claws (T) as structures, as described in Sect. 12.3.2.

Edge-based cost matrix:

Let u_i, v_i be the start and end vertices of e_i in g and u'_i, v'_i be the start and end vertices of e'_j in g'. The cost of substituting e_i with e'_j given by

$$c_{ij} = ||u_i, u'_j|| + ||v_i, v'_j|| \tag{12.8}$$

where $||.||$ denotes Euclidean distance between the spatial coordinates of the vertices. The cost of deleting e_i is

$$c_{i\delta} = \alpha_1 + (\alpha_2 \times (D(u_i) + D(v_i))) \tag{12.9}$$

The cost of inserting e'_j is

$$c_{\delta j} = \alpha_1 + (\alpha_2 \times (D(u'_i) + D(v'_i))) \tag{12.10}$$

where $D()$ denotes vertex degree. α_1 denotes the cost for deleting or inserting an vertex. α_2 denotes the cost for deleting or inserting the vertices neighbouring the start and end vertices of the vertex. The cost matrix will have size $|E| \times |E'|$, where $|.|$ denotes cardinality of the set.

Claw-based cost matrix:

Let c_i and c'_j be the centres of the claws s_i and s'_j in g and g'. Let u_i, v_i, w_i and u'_j, v'_j, w'_j be the end vertices of the three vertices ordered in decreasing order of length for each of the claw structures.

The cost of substituting s_i with s'_j given by

$$c_{ij} = ||c_i, c'_j|| + ||u_i, u'_j|| + ||v_i, v'_j|| + ||w_i, w'_j|| \tag{12.11}$$

where $||.||$ denotes Euclidean distance between the spatial coordinates of the vertices. The cost of deleting s_i is

$$c_{i\delta} = \alpha_1 + (\alpha_2 \times (D(u_i) + D(v_i) + D(w_i))) \tag{12.12}$$

The cost of inserting s'_j is

$$c_{\delta j} = \alpha_1 + (\alpha_2 \times (D(u'_i) + D(v'_i) + D(w'_i))) \tag{12.13}$$

where $D()$ denotes vertex degree. α_1 denotes the cost for deleting or inserting a claw. α_2 denotes the cost for deleting or inserting the vertices neighbouring the end vertices of the claw. The cost matrix will have size $|S| \times |S'|$, where $|.|$ denotes cardinality of the set.

Two-claw-based cost matrix:

Let t_i and t'_j be two-claw structures in g and g'. Each two-claw structures has two-claws connected by a common vertex. Let b_i and c_i be the centre vertices of t_i and $u_i, v_i, w_i, x_i, y_i, z_i$ be the 6 end vertices of two-claw structures ordered on vertex length. u_i and x_i will represent the longest vertices of the claw structures centred on b_i and c_i. Similarly let b'_j and c'_j represent the centres of the claws and $u'_j, v'_j, w'_j, x'_j, y'_j z'_j$ represent the end vertices of the vertices belonging t'_j. The cost of substituting t_i with t'_j given by

$$c_{ij} = ||b_i, b'_j|| + ||c_i, c'_j|| + ||u_i, u'_j|| + ||v_i, v'_j|| + ||w_i, w'_j|| + ||x_i, x'_j|| + ||y_i, y'_j|| + ||z_i, z'_j|| \tag{12.14}$$

where $||.||$ denotes Euclidean distance between the spatial coordinates of the vertices. The cost of deleting t_i is

$$c_{i\delta} = \alpha_1 + (\alpha_2 \times (D(u_i) + D(v_i) + D(y_i) + D(z_i))) \tag{12.15}$$

where the u_i, v_i, y_i, z_i represent the vertices that do not connect the two-claw centres.

The cost of inserting t'_j is

$$c_{\delta j} = \alpha_1 + (\alpha_2 \times (D(u'_i) + D(v'_i) + D(y'_i) + D(z'_i))) \qquad (12.16)$$

where $D()$ denotes vertex degree. u'_j, v'_j, y'_j, z'_j represent the vertices that do not connect b'_j and c'_j. α_1 denotes the cost for deleting or inserting a two-claw. α_2 denotes the cost for deleting or inserting the vertices neighbouring the end vertices of the two-claw vertices. The cost matrix will have size $|T| \times |T'|$, where $|.|$ denotes cardinality of the set.

Appendix 4

In [6] we compared the performance of BGC with standard point pattern based comparison algorithms. Each vascular database was divided into a training and

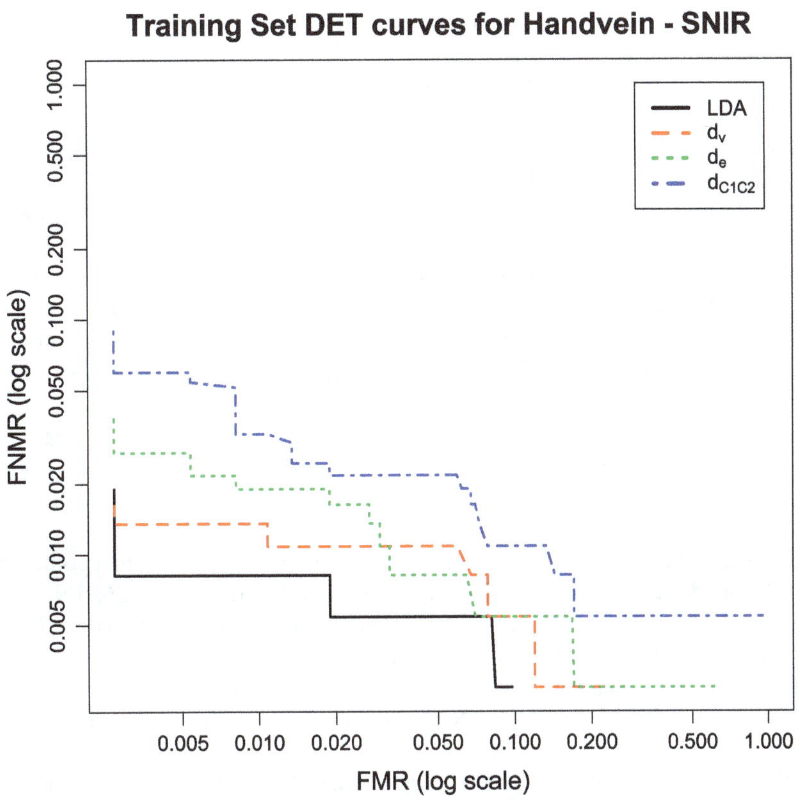

Fig. 12.10 DET curve for the top 3 best performing distance measures in the SNIR handvein training dataset. The performance of each distance measure is compared to that obtained when combining the 3 features using an LDA classifier. Results showed that combining the features did not cause a significant improvement in performance over the best performing measure d_v

testing set. The training set was used to determine the best structure for registration, parameters for the graph comparison algorithm and the best distance measure. Once these parameters were picked they were used to test the performance on the testing database at three thresholds corresponding to three specific points from the training database Detection Error Tradeoff (DET) curves—EER, FMR100 and FMR1000. Figure 12.10 shows the DET curves from the SNIR Handvein training dataset. This was not published in [6]. The DETs for all other modalities are available in Fig. 7 in [6].

References

1. Aastrup Olsen M, Hartung D, Busch C, Larsen R (2011) Convolution approach for feature detection in topological skeletons obtained from vascular patterns. In: 2011 IEEE workshop on computational intelligence in biometrics and identity management (CIBIM), pp 163–167 (2011)
2. Aliahmad B, Kumar DK, Hao H, Kawasaki R (2013) Does fractal properties of retinal vasculature vary with cardiac cycle? In: 2013 ISSNIP biosignals and biorobotics conference: biosignals and robotics for better and safer living (BRC), pp 1–4 (2013). https://doi.org/10.1109/BRC.2013.6487480
3. Arakala A. Source code for anchors for graph registration. https://github.com/ArathiArakalaRMIT/anchor_dissimilarityVector
4. Arakala A. Source code for biometric graph matching for vascular biometrics. https://github.com/ArathiArakalaRMIT/BGM_for_vascular_graphs
5. Arakala A, Davis SA, Hao H, Aliahmad B, Kumar DK, Horadam KJ (2019) Template protected biometrics using dissimilarity vectors (preprint 2019)
6. Arakala A, Davis SA, Hao H, Horadam KJ (2017) Value of graph topology in vascular biometrics. IET Biom 6(2):117–125. https://doi.org/10.1049/iet-bmt.2016.0073
7. Arakala A, Davis SA, Horadam KJ (2011) Retina features based on vessel graph substructures. In: 2011 international joint conference on biometrics (IJCB), pp 1–6 (2011). https://doi.org/10.1109/IJCB.2011.6117506
8. Arakala A, Hao H, Davis S, Horadam K (2015) The palm vein graph-feature extraction and matching. In: Proceedings of the first international conference on information systems security and privacy (ICISSP), pp 56–64. Loire Valley, France. https://doi.org/10.5220/0005239102950303
9. Bunke H, Shearer K (1998) A graph distance metric based on the maximal common subgraph. Pattern Recogn Lett 19(3–4):255–259. https://doi.org/10.1016/S0167-8655(97)00179-7
10. Chen H, Lu G, Wang R (2009) A new palm vein matching method based on ICP algorithm. In: Proceedings of the 2nd international conference on interaction sciences: information technology, culture and human, ICIS '09, pp 1207–1211. ACM, New York, NY, USA. https://doi.org/10.1145/1655925.1656145. URL http://doi.acm.org.ezproxy.lib.rmit.edu.au/10.1145/1655925.1656145
11. Davis S, Abbasi B, Shah S, Telfer S, Begon M (2014) Spatial analyses of wildlife contact networks. J R Soc Interface 12(102). https://doi.org/10.1098/rsif.2014.1004. http://rsif.royalsocietypublishing.org/content/12/102/20141004

12. Deng K, Tian J, Zheng J, Zhang X, Dai X, Xu M (2010) Retinal fundus image registration via vascular structure graph matching. J Biomed Imaging 2010(14):1–13. https://doi.org/10.1155/2010/906067
13. Drechsler K, Laura CO (2010) Hierarchical decomposition of vessel skeletons for graph creation and feature extraction. In: 2010 IEEE international conference on bioinformatics and biomedicine (BIBM), pp 456–461. https://doi.org/10.1109/BIBM.2010.5706609
14. Gomez-Barrero M, Galbally J, Rathgeb C, Busch C (2018) General framework to evaluate unlinkability in biometric template protection systems. IEEE Trans Inf Forensics Secur 13(6):1406–1420. https://doi.org/10.1109/tifs.2017.2788000. https://app.dimensions.ai/details/publication/pub.1100133741. https://app.dimensions.ai. Accedded 28 Feb 2019
15. Gomez-Barrero M, Rathgeb C, Galbally J, Busch C, Fierrez J (2016) Unlinkable and irreversible biometric template protection based on bloom filters. Inf Sci 370:18–32. https://doi.org/10.1016/j.ins.2016.06.046. https://app.dimensions.ai/details/publication/pub.1052550524. https://app.dimensions.ai. Accessed 28 Feb 2019
16. Gouru R (2013) A vascular network matching algorithm for physiological face recognition. Master's thesis, Houston, TX, USA
17. Horadam KJ, Davis SA, Arakala A, Jeffers J (2011) Fingerprints as spatial graphs-nodes and edges. In: Proceedings of international conference on digital image computing techniques and applications, DICTA, pp 400–405. Noosa, Australia
18. Kabacinski R, Kowalski M (2011) Vein pattern database and benchmark results. Electron Lett 47(20):1127–1128
19. Khakzar M, Pourghassem H (2017) A retinal image authentication framework based on a graph-based representation algorithm in a two-stage matching structure. Biocybern Biomed Eng 37(4):742–759. https://doi.org/10.1016/j.bbe.2017.09.001
20. Lajevardi S, Arakala A, Davis S, Horadam K (2013) Retina verification system based on biometric graph matching. IEEE Trans Image Process 22(9):3625–3635
21. Lajevardi S, Arakala A, Davis S, Horadam K (2014) Hand vein authentication using biometric graph matching. IET Biom 3(4):302–313. https://doi.org/10.1049/iet-bmt.2013.0086
22. Lupacu CA, Tegolo D, Bellavia F, Valenti C (2013) Semi-automatic registration of retinal images based on line matching approach. In: Proceedings of the 26th IEEE international symposium on computer-based medical systems, pp 453–456. https://doi.org/10.1109/CBMS.2013.6627839
23. Nibbelke V (2017) Vascular pattern recognition for finger veins using biometric graph matching. Master's thesis, Twente, Netherlands
24. Ortega M, Penedo MG, Rouco J, Barreira N, Carreira MJ (2009) Retinal verification using a feature points-based biometric pattern. EURASIP J Adv Signal Process 2009:1–13
25. Rathgeb C, Busch C (2012) Multi-biometric template protection: issues and challenges. In: Yang J, Xie SJ (eds) New trends and developments in biometrics (chap. 8). IntechOpen, Rijeka. https://doi.org/10.5772/52152
26. Riesen K, Bunke H (2010) Graph classification and clustering based on vector space embedding, 1st edn. World Scientific
27. Wang L, Leedham G, Cho SY (2007) Infrared imaging of hand vein patterns for biometric purposes. IET Comput Vis 1(3–4):113–122

Chapter 13
Deep Sclera Segmentation and Recognition

Peter Rot, Matej Vitek, Klemen Grm, Žiga Emeršič, Peter Peer and Vitomir Štruc

Abstract In this chapter, we address the problem of biometric identity recognition from the vasculature of the human sclera. Specifically, we focus on the challenging task of multi-view sclera recognition, where the visible part of the sclera vasculature changes from image to image due to varying gaze (or view) directions. We propose a complete solution for this task built around Convolutional Neural Networks (CNNs) and make several contributions that result in state-of-the-art recognition performance, i.e.: (i) we develop a cascaded CNN assembly that is able to robustly segment the sclera vasculature from the input images regardless of gaze direction, and (ii) we present ScleraNET, a CNN model trained in a multi-task manner (combining losses pertaining to identity and view-direction recognition) that allows for the extraction of discriminative vasculature descriptors that can be used for identity inference. To evaluate the proposed contributions, we also introduce a new dataset of ocular images, called the *Sclera Blood Vessels, Periocular and Iris* (SBVPI) dataset, which represents one of the few publicly available datasets suitable for research in multi-view sclera segmentation and recognition. The datasets come with a rich

P. Rot and M. Vitek are first authors with equal contributions.

P. Rot · M. Vitek (✉) · Ž. Emeršič · P. Peer
Faculty of Computer and Information Science, University of Ljubljana, Večna pot 113, 1000 Ljubljana, Slovenia
e-mail: matej.vitek@fri.uni-lj.si

P. Rot
e-mail: peter.rot93@gmail.com

Ž. Emeršič
e-mail: ziga.emersic@fri.uni-lj.si

P. Peer
e-mail: peter.peer@fri.uni-lj.si

K. Grm · V. Štruc
Faculty of Electrical Engineering, University of Ljubljana, Tržaška cesta 25, 1000 Ljubljana, Slovenia
e-mail: klemen.grm@fe.uni-lj.si

V. Štruc
e-mail: vitomir.struc@fe.uni-lj.si

A. Uhl et al. (eds.), *Handbook of Vascular Biometrics*, Advances in Computer Vision and Pattern Recognition, https://doi.org/10.1007/978-3-030-27731-4_13

set of annotations, such as a per-pixel markup of various eye parts (including the sclera vasculature), identity, gaze-direction and gender labels. We conduct rigorous experiments on SBVPI with competing techniques from the literature and show that the combination of the proposed segmentation and descriptor-computation models results in highly competitive recognition performance.

Keywords Ocular biometrics · Vascular biometrics · Deep learning · Sclera segmentation · Sclera recognition · Dataset · Eye recognition

13.1 Introduction

With the growing need for secure authentication systems, forensic applications and surveillance software, biometric recognition techniques are attracting interest from research groups and private companies trying to improve the current state of the technology and exploit its immense market potential. Among the existing biometric characteristics used in automated recognition systems, ocular traits offer a number of advantages over other modalities such as contactless data acquisition, high recognition accuracy and considerable user acceptance. While iris recognition is the predominant technology in this area, recent research [1, 2] is looking increasingly at additional ocular characteristics that can complement iris-based features and contribute towards more secure and less-spoofable authentication schemes within this branch of biometrics [3].

One trait that presents itself as a particularly viable option in this context is the vasculature of the sclera. The eye's sclera region contains a rich vascular structure that is considered unique for each individual, is relatively stable over time [4] and can hence be exploited for recognition and authentication purposes, as also evidenced by recent research efforts [1, 5]. As suggested in [6], the vascular patterns also exhibit other desirable properties that make them appealing for recognition systems, e.g. the patterns are discernible despite potential eye redness and also in the presence of contact lenses that may adversely affect iris recognition systems. Despite the potential of the sclera vasculature for biometric recognition, research on this particular trait is still in its infancy and several research problems need to be addressed before the technology can be deployed in commercial systems, e.g.:

- The sclera vasculature contains distinct, but also finer blood vessels that need to be segmented from the input ocular images to ensure competitive recognition performance. As emphasised in the introductory chapter of the handbook, these vessels feature very different border types and have a complex texture that is difficult to model, which makes vasculature segmentation highly challenging. To approach this problem, existing solutions typically adopt a two-stage procedure, where the sclera region is first identified in the ocular images and the vasculature structure is then extracted using established (typically unsupervised) algorithms based, for example, on Gabor filters, wavelets, gradient operators and alike [1, 7–9]. While these approaches have shown promise, recent research suggests that supervised techniques result in much better segmentation performance [5, 10], especially if challenging off-angle ocular images need to be segmented reliably. However, next to the difficulty of sclera vasculature segmentation task itself, the lack of dedicated and suitably annotated datasets for developing supervised techniques has so far represented one of the major roadblocks in the design of competitive sclera recognition systems.

- Due to the particularities (and potentially unconstrained nature) of the image acquisition procedure, ocular images are in general not aligned well with respect to a reference position. Additionally, as the gaze direction may vary from image to image, not all parts of the sclera vasculature are necessarily visible in every captured image. To efficiently compare sclera images and facilitate recognition, discriminative features need to be extracted from the segmented vasculature. These features have to be robust with respect to variations in position, scale and rotation and need to allow for comparisons with only parts of the located vascular structure. Existing solutions, therefore, commonly rely on hand-crafted image descriptors, such as Scale-Invariant Feature Transforms (SIFTs), Histograms of Oriented Gradients (HOGs), Local Binary Patterns (LBPs) and related descriptors from the literature [5, 8, 9]. These local descriptor-based approaches have dominated the field for some time, but, as indicated by recent trends in biometrics [11–14], are typically inferior to learned image descriptors based, for example, on Convolutional Neural Networks (CNNs).

In this chapter, we try to address some of the challenges outlined above and present a novel solution to the problem of sclera recognition built around deep learning and Convolutional Neural Networks (CNNs). Specifically, we first present a new technique for segmentation of the vascular structure of the sclera based on a cascaded SegNet [15] assembly. The proposed technique follows the established two-stage approach to sclera vasculature segmentation and first segments the sclera region from the input images using a discriminatively trained SegNet model and then applies a second SegNet to extract the final vascular structure. As we show in the experimental section, the technique allows for accurate segmentation of the sclera vasculature from the input images even under different gaze directions, thus facilitating feature extraction and sclera comparisons in the later stages.

Next, we present a deep-learning-based model, called ScleraNET, that is able to extract discriminative image descriptors from the segmented sclera vasculature. To ensure that a single (learned) image descriptor is extracted for every input image regardless of the gaze direction and amount of visible sclera vasculature, we train ScleraNET within a multi-task learning framework, where view-direction recognition is treated as a side task for identity recognition. Finally, we incorporate the segmentation and descriptor-computation approaches into a coherent sclera recognition pipeline.

To evaluate the proposed segmentation and descriptor-computation approaches, we also introduce a novel dataset of ocular images, called *Sclera Blood Vessels, Periocular and Iris (SBVPI)* and make it publicly available to the research community. The dataset represents one of the few existing datasets suitable for research in (multi-view) sclera segmentation and recognition problems and ships with a rich set of annotations, such as a pixel-level markup of different eye parts (including the sclera vasculature) or identity, gaze-direction and gender labels. Using the SBVPI dataset, we evaluate the proposed segmentation and descriptor-computation techniques in rigorous experiments with competing state-of-the-art models from the literature. Our experimental results show that the cascaded SegNet assembly achieves competitive segmentation performance and that the ScleraNET model generates image descriptors that yield state-of-the-art recognition results.

In summary, we make the following contributions in this chapter:

- We propose a novel model for sclera vasculature segmentation based on a cascaded SegNet assembly. To the best of our knowledge, the model represents the first attempt to perform sclera vasculature segmentation in a supervised manner and is shown to perform well compared to competing solutions from the literature.
- We present ScleraNET, a CNN-based model able to extract descriptive image representations from ocular images with different gaze directions. Different from existing techniques, the model allows for the description of the vascular structure of the sclera using a single high-dimensional image descriptor even if the characteristics (position, scale, translation, visibility, etc.) of the vascular patterns vary from image to image.
- We introduce the *Sclera Blood Vessels, Periocular and Iris* (SBVPI) dataset—a dataset of ocular images with a distinct focus on research into sclera recognition. We make the dataset publicly available: http://sclera.fri.uni-lj.si/.

The rest of the chapter is structured as follows: In Sect. 13.2, we survey the relevant literature and discuss competing methods. In Sect. 13.3, we introduce our sclera recognition pipeline and elaborate on the segmentation procedure and ScleraNET models. We describe the novel dataset and its characteristics in Sect. 13.4. All parts of our pipeline are evaluated and discussed in rigorous experiments in Sect. 13.5. The chapter concludes with a brief summary and directions for future work in Sect. 13.6.

13.2 Related Work

In this section, we survey the existing research work relevant to the proposed segmentation and descriptor-computation approaches. The goal of this section is to provide the necessary context for our contributions and motivate our work. The reader is referred to some of the existing surveys on ocular biometrics for a more complete coverage of the field [8, 16–18].

13.2.1 Ocular Biometrics

Research in ocular biometrics dates back to the pioneering work of Daugman [19–21], who was the first to show that the texture of the human iris can be used for identity recognition. Daugman developed an iris recognition system that used Gabor filters to encode the iris texture and to construct a discriminative template that could be used for recognition. Following the success of Daugman's work, many other hand-crafted feature descriptors were proposed [22–25] to encode the texture of the iris.

With recent research on iris recognition moving towards unconstrained image acquisition settings and away from the Near-Infrared (NIR) spectrum towards visible light (VIS) imaging, more powerful image features are needed that can better model the complex non-linear deformations of the iris typically seen under non-ideal lightning conditions and with off-angle ocular images. Researchers are, therefore, actively trying to solve the problem of iris recognition using deep learning methods, most notably, with Convolution Neural Networks (CNNs). The main advantage of using CNNs for representing the iris texture (compared to the more traditional hand-crafted image descriptors) is that features can be learned automatically from training data typically resulting in much better recognition performance for difficult input samples. Several CNN-based approaches have been described in the literature over the last few years with highly promising results, e.g. [26–30].

Despite the progress in this area and the introduction of powerful (learned) image descriptors, there are still many open research question related mostly to unconstrained image acquisition conditions (e.g. the person is not looking straight into the camera, eyelashes cover the iris, reflections appear in the images, etc.). To improve robustness of ocular biometric systems in such settings, additional ocular traits can be integrated into the recognition process, such as the sclera vasculature [1] or information from the periocular region [31, 32] . These additional modalities have received significant attention from the research community and are at the core of many ongoing research projects—see, for example, [1, 16, 33–40].

The work presented in this chapter adds to the research outlined above and introduces a complete solution to the problem of multi-view sclera recognition with distinct contributions for vasculature segmentation and descriptor computation from the segmented vascular structure.

13.2.2 Sclera Recognition

Recognition systems based on the vasculature of the sclera typically consist of multiple stages, which in the broadest sense can be categorised into a (i) a vasculature segmentation stage that extracts the vascular structure of the sclera from the image, and (ii) a recognition stage, where the vascular structure is represented using suitable image descriptors and the descriptors are then used for comparisons and subsequent identity inference.

The first stage (aimed at vasculature segmentation) is commonly subdivided into two separate steps, where the first step locates the sclera in the image and the second extracts the vasculature needed for recognition . To promote the development of automated segmentation techniques for sclera segmentation (the first step), several competitions were organised in the scope of major biometric conferences [5, 10, 41, 42]. The results of these competitions suggest that supervised segmentation techniques, based on CNN-based models represent the state of the art in this area and significantly outperform competing unsupervised techniques. Particularly successful here are Convolutional Encoder–Decoder (CED) networks (such as Seg-

Net [15]) , which represent the winning techniques from the 2017 and 2018 sclera segmentation competitions—see [5, 10] for details. In this chapter, we build on these results and incorporate multiple CED models into a cascaded assembly that is shown in the experimental section to achieve competitive performance for both sclera and vasculature segmentation.

To extract the vascular structure from the segmented sclera region, image operators capable of emphasising gradients and contrast changes are typically used. Solutions to this problem, therefore, include standard techniques based, for example, on Gabor filters, wavelets, maximum curvature, gradient operators (e.g. Sobel) and others [1, 7–9]. As suggested in the sclera recognition survey in [8], a common aspect of these techniques is that they are unsupervised and heuristic in nature. In contrast to the outlined techniques, our approach uses (typically better performing) supervised segmentation models, which are possible due to the manual markup of the sclera vasculature that comes with the SBVPI dataset (introduced later in this chapter) and, to the best of our knowledge, is not available with any of the existing datasets of ocular images.

For the recognition stage, existing techniques usually use a combination of image enhancement (e.g. histogram equalisation, Contrast-Limited Adaptive Histogram Equalization (CLAHE) or Gabor filtering [1, 43]) and feature extraction techniques, with a distinct preference towards local image descriptors, e.g. SIFT, LBP, HOG, Gray-level Co-occurrence Matrices, wavelet features or other hand-crafted representations [6, 8, 44–46]. Both dense and sparse (keypoint) image descriptors have already been considered in the literature. With ScleraNET, we introduce a model for the computation of the first learned image descriptor for sclera recognition. We also make the model publicly available to facilitate reproducibility and provide the community with a strong baseline for future research in this area.

13.2.3 Existing Datasets

A variety of datasets is currently available for research in ocular biometrics [16] with the majority of existing datasets clearly focusing on the most dominant of the ocular modalities—the iris [5, 9, 47, 48, 48–55]. While these datasets are sometimes used for research into sclera recognition as well, a major problem with the listed datasets is that they are commonly captured in the Near-Infrared (NIR) spectrum, where most of the discriminative information contained in the sclera vasculature is not easily discernible. Furthermore, existing datasets are not captured with research on vascular biometrics in mind and, therefore, often contain images of insufficient resolution or images, where the Region-Of-Interest (ROI) needed for sclera recognition purposes is not well visible. While some datasets with characteristics suitable for sclera recognition research have been introduced recently (e.g. MASD [5]), these are, to the best of our knowledge, not publicly available.

Table 13.1 shows a summary of some of the most popular datasets of ocular images and also lists the main characteristics of the SBVPI dataset introduced in this

Table 13.1 Comparison of the main characteristics of existing datasets for ocular biometrics. Note that most of the datasets have been captured with research in iris recognition in mind, but have also been used for experiments with periocular (PO) and sclera recognition techniques. The dataset introduced in Sect. 13.4 of this chapter is the first publicly available dataset dedicated to sclera recognition research

Dataset	Modality	Public	NIR/VIS	Image size	# Subjects	# Images	SC-M‡	VS-M*	Gaze
CASIA Iris v1 [47]	Iris	Yes	NIR	320 × 280	54	756	No	No	Static
CASIA Iris v2 [47]	Iris	Yes	NIR	640 × 480	60	2400	No	No	Static
CASIA Iris v3 [47]	Iris	Yes	NIR	640 × 480	> 700	22034	No	No	Static
CASIA Iris v4 [47]	Iris	Yes	NIR	640 × 480	> 2800	54601	No	No	Static
ND-IRIS-0405 [49]	Iris	Yes	NIR	640 × 480	356	64980	No	No	Static
UTIRIS [50]	Sclera, iris	Yes	Both	2048 × 1360	79	1540	No	No	Static
UBIRIS v1 [48]	Sclera, iris	Yes	VIS	800 × 600	241	1877	No	No	Static
UBIRIS v2 [52]	Sclera, PO†, iris	Yes	VIS	400 × 300	261	11102	No	No	Variable
IITD [51]	Iris	Yes	NIR	320 × 240	224	1120	No	No	Static
MICHE-I [53]	Sclera, PO, iris	Yes	VIS	2048 × 1536	92	3732	No	No	Static
UBIPr [54]	PO	Yes	VIS	500 × 400	261	10950	No	No	Variable
IMP [55]	PO	Yes	Both	260 × 270	62	930	No	No	Static
IUPUI [9]	Sclera, PO, iris	No	Both	n/a	44	352	No	No	Variable
MASD [5]	Sclera	No	VIS	7500 × 5000	82	2624	Partial	No	Variable
SBVPI (ours)	Sclera, PO, iris	Yes	VIS	3000 × 1700	55	1858	Full	Partial	Variable

†PO—periocular, ‡SC-M—sclera markup, *VS-M—vasculature markup

chapter. While researchers commonly resort to the UBIRISv1 [48], UBIRISv2 [52], UTIRIS [56], or MICHE-I [53] datasets when conducting experiments on sclera recognition, their utility is limited, as virtually no sclera-specific metadata (e.g. sclera markup, vasculature markup, etc.) is available with any of these datasets. SBVPI tries to address this gap and comes with a rich set of annotations that allow for the development of competitive segmentation and descriptor-computation models.

13.3 Methods

In this section, we present our approach to sclera recognition. We start with a high-level overview of our pipeline and then describe all of the individual components.

13.3.1 Overview

A high-level overview of the sclera recognition pipeline proposed in this chapter is presented in Fig. 13.1. The pipeline consist of two main parts: (i) a cascaded SegNet assembly used for Region-Of-Interest (ROI) extraction and (ii) a CNN model (called ScleraNET) for image-representation (or descriptor) computation.

The cascaded SegNet assembly takes an eye image as input and generates a probability map of the vascular structure of the sclera using a two-step segmentation procedure. This two-step procedure first segments the sclera from the input image and then identifies the blood vessels within the sclera region using a second segmentation step.

The CNN model of the second part of the pipeline, ScleraNET, takes a probability map describing the vascular patterns of the sclera as input and produces a discriminative representation that can be used for matching purposes. We describe both parts of our pipeline in detail in the next sections.

13.3.2 Region-Of-Interest (ROI) Extraction

One of the key steps of every biometric system is the extraction of the Region-Of-Interest (ROI). For sclera-based recognition systems, this step amounts to segmenting the vascular structure from the input image. This structure is highly discriminative for every individual and can, hence, be exploited for recognition. As indicated in the previous section, we find the vasculature of the sclera in our approach using a two-step procedure built around a cascaded SegNet assembly. In the remainder of this section, we first describe the main idea behind the two-step segmentation procedure, then briefly review the main characteristics of the SegNet model and finally describe

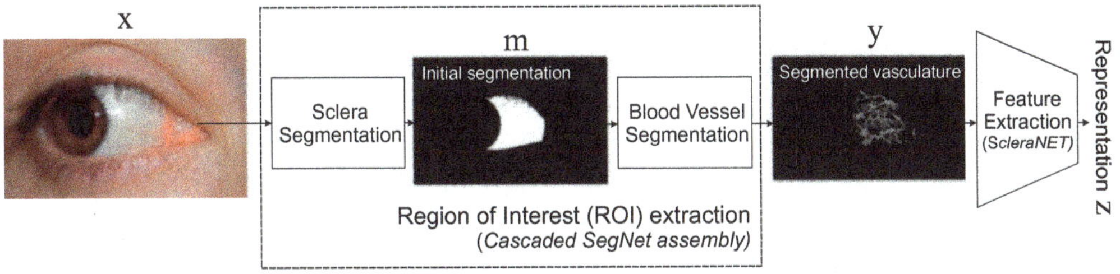

Fig. 13.1 Block diagram of the proposed sclera recognition approach. The vascular structure of the sclera is first segmented from the input image **x** using a two-step procedure. A probability map of the vascular structure **y** is then fed to a CNN model (called ScleraNET) to extract a discriminative feature representation that can be used for sclera comparisons and ultimately recognition. Note that **m** denotes the intermediate sclera region (or masks) generated by the first segmentation step and **z** represent the learned vasculature descriptor extracted by ScleraNET

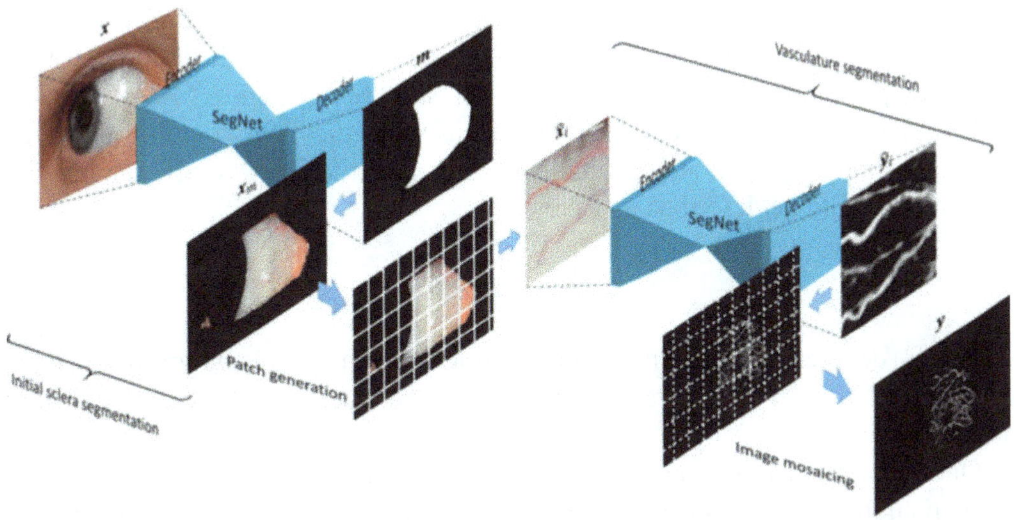

Fig. 13.2 Illustration of the two-step segmentation procedure. In the initial segmentation step, a binary mask of the sclera region is generated by a SegNet model. The mask is used to conceal irrelevant parts of the input image for the second step of the segmentation procedure, where the goal is to identify the vascular structure of the sclera by a second SegNet model. To be able to capture fine details in the vascular structure the second step is implemented in a patch-wise manner followed by image mosaicing. Please refer to the text for an explanation of the symbols used in the image

the training procedure used to learn the parameters of the cascaded segmentation assembly.

13.3.2.1 The Two-Step Segmentation Procedure

The cascaded SegNet assembly used for ROI extraction in our pipeline is illustrated in Fig. 13.2. It consists of two CNN-based segmentation models, where the first tries to generate a binary mask of the sclera region from the input image and the second aims to extract the vascular structure from within the located sclera. The segmentation models for both steps are based on the recently introduced SegNet architecture from [15]. SegNet was chosen as the backbone model for our segmentation assembly, because of its state-of-the-art performance for various segmentation tasks, competitive results achieved in the recent sclera segmentation competitions [5, 10] and the fact that an open- source implementation is publicly available.[1]

Note that our two-step procedure follows existing unsupervised approaches to sclera vasculature segmentation, where an initial sclera segmentation stage is used to simplify the segmentation problem and constrain the segmentation space for the second step, during which the vasculature is extracted. Our segmentation procedure is motivated by the fact that CNN-based processing does not scale well with image size. Thus, to be able to process high-resolution input images, we initially locate the sclera region from down-sampled images in the first segmentation step and then process image patches at the original resolution in the second segmentation step with the goal of capturing the fine-grained information on the vascular structure of the sclera. Note that this information would otherwise get lost if the images were down-sampled to a size manageable for CNN-based segmentation.

If we denote the input RGB ocular image as $\mathbf{x}$ and the binary mask of the sclera region generated by the first SegNet model as $\mathbf{m}$, then the first (initial) segmentation step can formally be described as follows:

$$\mathbf{m} = f_{\theta_1}(\mathbf{x}), \tag{13.1}$$

where f_{θ_1} denotes the mapping from the input $\mathbf{x}$ to the segmentation result $\mathbf{m}$ by the first CNN model and θ_1 stands for the model parameters that need to be learned during training.

Once the sclera is segmented, we mask the input image $\mathbf{x}$ with the generated segmentation output $\mathbf{m}$ and, hence, exclude all image pixels that do not belong to the sclera from further processing, i.e.:

$$\mathbf{x}_m = \mathbf{x} \odot \mathbf{m}, \tag{13.2}$$

where $\odot$ denotes the Hadamard product. The masked input image $\mathbf{x}_m$ is then used as the basis for the second segmentation step.

Because the vasculature of the sclera comprises large, but also smaller (finer) blood vessels, we use a patch-wise approach in the second segmentation step. This patch-wise approach allows us to also locate large blood vessels within the sclera region, but also the finer ones that would get lost (or overseen) within a holistic segmentation approach due to poor contrast and small spatial area these vessels occupy. Towards this end, we split the masked input image $\mathbf{x}_m$ into M non-overlapping patches $\{\hat{\mathbf{x}}_i\}_{i=1}^{M}$ and subject them to a second segmentation model f_{θ_2} that locates the vascular structure $\hat{\mathbf{y}}_i$ within each patch:

$$\hat{\mathbf{y}}_i = f_{\theta_2}\left(\hat{\mathbf{x}}_i\right), \text{ for } i = 1, \ldots, M. \tag{13.3}$$

[1]SegNet on GitHub: https://github.com/alexgkendall/caffe-segnet.

Here, θ_2 denotes the model parameters of the second SegNet model that again need to be learned on some training data.

The final map of the vascular structure $\mathbf{y}$ is generated by re-assembling all generated patches $\hat{\mathbf{y}}_i$ using image mosaicing. Note that different from the first segmentation step, where a binary segmentation mask $\mathbf{m}$ is generated by the segmentation model, $\mathbf{y}$ represents a probability map, which was found to be better suited for recognition purposes than a binary mask of the vasculature (details on possible segmentation outputs are given in Sects. 13.3.2.2 and 13.3.2.3).

To ensure robust segmentation results when looking for the vascular structure of the sclera in the second segmentation step, we use a data augmentation procedure at run-time. Thus, the masked image $\mathbf{x}_m$ is randomly rotated, cropped and shifted to produce multiple versions of the masked sclera. Here, the run-time augmentation procedure selects all image operations with a probability of 0.5 and uses rotations in the range of $\pm 8°$, crops that reduce the image size by up to 1% of the spatial dimensions, and shifts up to ± 20 pixels in the horizontal and up to ± 10 pixels in the vertical direction. Each of the generated images is then split into M patches which are fed independently to the segmentation procedure. The output patches $\hat{\mathbf{y}}_i$ are then reassembled and all generated maps of the vascular structure are averaged to produce the final segmentation result.

As indicated above, the basis for the ROI extraction procedure is the SegNet architecture, which is used in the first, but also the second segmentation step. We, therefore, briefly describe the main SegNet characteristics in the next section.

13.3.2.2 The SegNet Architecture

SegNet [15] represents a recent convolutional encoder–decoder architecture proposed specifically for the task of semantic image segmentation. The architecture consists of two high-level building blocks: an encoder and a decoder. The goal of the encoder is to compress the semantic content of the input and generate a descriptive representation that is fed to the decoder to produce a segmentation output [57, 58].

SegNet's encoder is inspired by the VGG-16 [59] architecture, but unlike VGG-16, the encoder uses only convolutional and no fully connected layers. The encoder consists of 13 convolutional layers (followed by batch normalisation and ReLU activations) and 5 pooling layers. The decoder is another (inverted) VGG-16 model again without fully connected layers, but with a pixel-wise softmax layer at the top. The softmax layer generates a probability distribution for each image location that can be used to classify pixels into one of the predefined semantic target classes. During training, the encoder learns to produce low-resolution semantically meaningful feature maps, whereas the decoder learns filters capable of generating high-resolution segmentation maps from the low-resolution feature maps produced by the encoder [57].

A unique aspect of SegNet are so-called skip-connections that connect the pooling layers of the encoder with the corresponding up-sampling layers of the decoder. These skip-connections propagate spatial information (pooling indices) from one part of the model to the other and help avoid information loss throughout the network.

Consequently, SegNet's output probability maps have the same dimensions (i.e. width and height) as the input images, which allows for relatively precise segmentation. The number of output probability maps is typically equal to the number of semantic target classes—one probability map per semantic class [57]. The reader is referred to [15] for more information on the SegNet model.

13.3.2.3 Model Training and Output Generation

To train the two SegNet models, f_{θ_1} and f_{θ_2}, and learn the model parameters θ_1 and θ_2 needed by our segmentation procedure, we use categorical cross-entropy as our training objective. Once the models are trained, they return a probability distribution over the $C = 2$ target classes (i.e. *sclera vs. non-sclera* for the first SegNet and *blood vessels vs. other* for the second SegNet in the cascaded assembly) for each pixel location. This is, for every location $s = [x, y]^T$ in the input image, the model outputs a distribution $\mathbf{p}_s = [p_{sC_1}, p_{sC_2}]^T \in \mathbb{R}^{C\times 1}$, where p_{sC_i} denotes the probability that the pixel at location s belongs to the ith target class C_i and $\sum_{i=1}^{C} p_{sC_i} = 1$ [57]. In other words, for each input image the model returns two probably maps, which, however are only inverted versions of each other, because $p_{sC_1} = 1 - p_{sC_2}$.

When binary segmentation results are needed, such as in the case of our sclera region $\mathbf{m}$, the generated probability maps are thresholded by comparing them to a predefined segmentation threshold Δ.

13.3.3 ScleraNET for Recognition

For the second part of our pipeline, we rely on a CNN model (called ScleraNET) that serves as a feature extractor for the vasculature probability maps. It needs to be noted that recognition techniques based on the vascular structure of the sclera are sensitive to view (or gaze) direction changes, which affect the amount of visible vasculature and consequently the performance of the final recognition approach. As a consequence, the vasculature is typically encoded using local image descriptors that allow for parts-based comparisons and are to some extent robust towards changes in the appearance of the vascular structure. Our goal with ScleraNET is to learn a single discriminative representation of the sclera that can directly be used for comparison purposes regardless of the given gaze direction. We, therefore, use a Multi-Task Learning (MTL) objective that takes both identity, but also gaze direction into account when learning the model parameters. As suggested in [60], the idea of MTL is to improve learning efficiency and prediction accuracy by considering multiple objectives when learning a shared representation. Because domain information is shared during learning due to the different objectives (pertaining to different tasks), the representations learned by the model offer better generalization ability than representations that rely only on a single objective during training. Since we try to jointly learn to recognise gaze direction and identity from the vascular structure of the sclera with ScleraNET, the intermediate layers of the model need to encode information on both tasks in the generated representations.

In the following sections, we elaborate on ScleraNET and discuss its architecture, training procedure and deployment as a feature (or descriptor) extractor.

13.3.3.1 ScleraNET Architecture

The ScleraNET model architecture builds on the success of recent CNN models for various recognition tasks and incorporates design choices from the AlexNet [61] and VGG models [59]. We design the model as a (relatively) shallow network with a limited number of trainable parameters that can be learned using a modest amount of training data [11], but at the same time aim for a network topology that is able to generate powerful image representations for recognition. Consequently, we built on established architectural design choices that have proven to work well for a variety of computer vision tasks.

As illustrated in Fig. 13.3 and summarised in Table 13.2, the architecture consists of 7 convolutional layers (with ReLU activations) with multiple max-pooling layers in between followed by a global average pooling layer, one dense layer and two softmax classifiers at the top.

The first convolutional layer uses 128 reasonably large 7×7 filters with a stride of 2 to capture sufficient spatial context and reduce the dimensionality of the generated feature maps. The layer is followed by a max-pooling layer that further reduces the size of the feature maps by $2\times$ along each dimension. Next, three blocks consisting of two convolutional and one max-pooling layer are utilised in the ScleraNET model. Due to the max-pooling layers, the spatial dimensions of the feature maps are halved after each block. To ensure a sufficient representational power of the feature maps, we double the number filters in the convolutional layers after each max-pooling operation. The output of the last of the three blocks is fed to a global average pooling layer and subsequently to a 512-dimensional Fully Connected (FC) layer. Finally, the FC layer is connected to two softmax layers, upon which an identity-oriented and a view-direction-oriented loss is defined for the MTL training procedure. The softmax layers are not used during run-time.

13.3.3.2 Learning Objective and Model Training

We define a cross-entropy loss over each of the two softmax classifiers at the top of ScleraNET for training. The first cross-entropy loss L_1 penalises errors when classifying subjects based on the segmented vasculature, and the second L_2 penalises errors when classifying different gaze directions. The overall training loss is a Multi-Task Learning (MTL) objective:

$$L_{total} = L_1 + \lambda L_2. \tag{13.4}$$

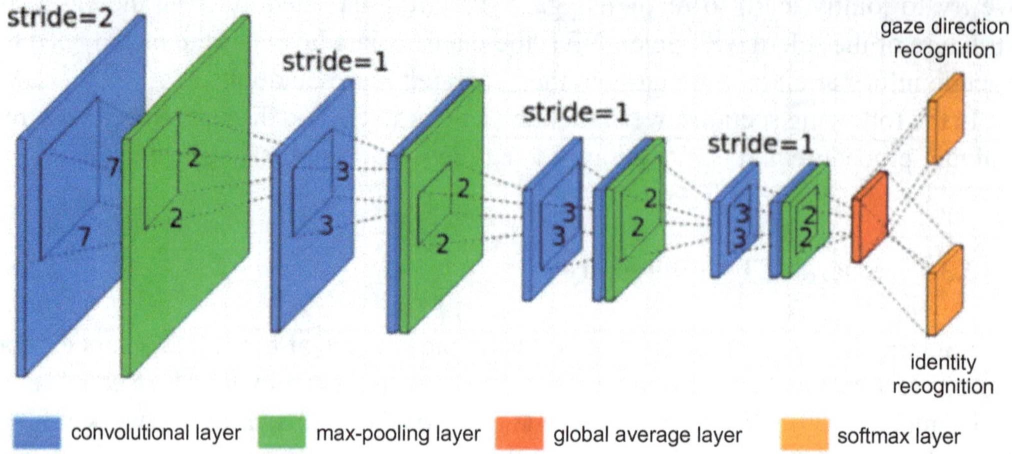

Fig. 13.3 Overview of the ScleraNET model architecture. The model incorporates design choices from the AlexNet [61] and VGG [59] models and relies on a Multi-Task Learning (MTL) objective that combines an identity and gaze-direction-related loss to learn discriminative vasculature representations for recognition

Table 13.2 Summary of the ScleraNET model architecture

No.	Layer type	# Filters	Description
1.	conv	128	7 × 7 (stride of 2)
2.	max-pooling		2 × 2
3.	conv	128	3 × 3 (stride of 1)
4.	conv	128	3 × 3 (stride of 1)
5.	max-pooling		2 × 2
6.	conv	256	3 × 3 (stride of 1)
7.	conv	256	3 × 3 (stride of 1)
8.	max-pooling		2 × 2
9.	conv	512	3 × 3 (stride of 1)
10.	conv	512	3 × 3 (stride of 1)
11.	max-pooling		2 × 2
12.	global average pooling		
13.	dense	512	
14.	softmax (2×)		Multi-task objective

To learn the parameters θ of ScleraNET, we minimise the combined loss over some training data and when doing so give equal weights to both loss terms, i.e. $\lambda = 1$.

As suggested earlier, the intuition behind the MTL objective is to learn feature representations that are useful for both tasks and, thus, contribute to (identity) recognition performance as well as to the accuracy of gaze-direction classification. Alternatively, one can interpret the loss related to gaze-direction classification as a regularizer for the identity recognition process [62]. Hence, the additional term helps to learn (to a certain extent) view-invariant representations of the vasculature, or to put it differently, it contributes towards more discriminative feature representations across different views.

13.3.3.3 Identity Inference with ScleraNET

Once the ScleraNET model is trained, we make it applicable to unseen identities by performing network surgery on the model and removing both softmax layers. We then use the 512-dimensional output from the fully connected layer as the feature representation of the vascular structure fed as input to the model.

If we again denote the probability map of the vascular structure produced by our two-step segmentation procedure as $\mathbf{y}$ then the feature representation calculation procedure implemented by ScleraNET can be described as follows:

$$\mathbf{z} = g_\theta(\mathbf{y}), \tag{13.5}$$

where g_θ again denotes the mapping from the vascular structure $\mathbf{y}$ to the feature representation $\mathbf{z}$ by the ScleraNET model and θ stands for the model's parameters. The feature representation can ultimately be used with standard similarity measures to generate comparison scores for recognition purposes.

13.4 The Sclera Blood Vessels, Periocular and Iris (SBVPI) Dataset

In this section, we describe a novel dataset for research on sclera segmentation and recognition called *Sclera Blood Vessels, Periocular and Iris* (SBVPI) , which we make publicly available for research purposes from http://sclera.fri.uni-lj.si/. While images of the dataset contain complete eyes, including the iris and periocular region, the focus is clearly on the sclera vasculature, which makes SBVPI the first publicly available dataset dedicated specifically to sclera (segmentation and) recognition research. As emphasised in the introductory chapter of the handbook, currently there exists no dataset designed specifically for sclera recognition, thus, SBVPI aims to fill this gap.

In the remainder of this section, we describe the main characteristics of the introduced dataset, discuss the acquisition procedure and finally elaborate on the available annotations.

13.4.1 Dataset Description

The SBVPI (Sclera Blood Vessels, Periocular and Iris) dataset consists of two separate parts. The first part is a dataset of periocular images dedicated to research in periocluar biometrics and the second part is a dataset of sclera images intended for

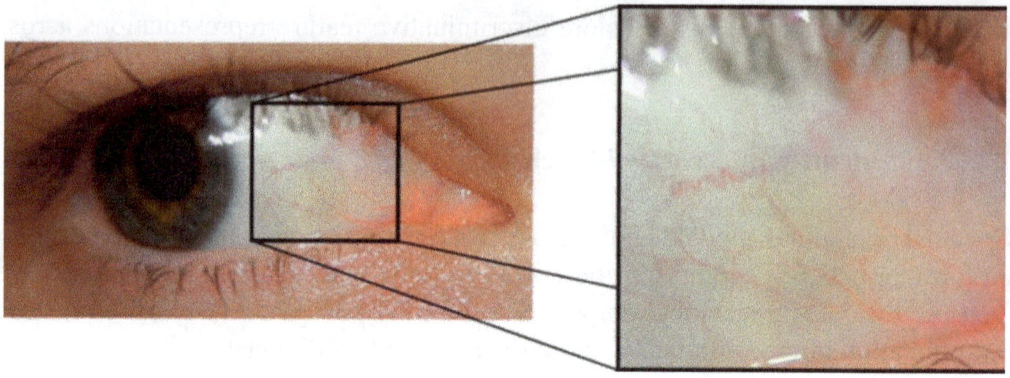

Fig. 13.4 An example image from the SVBPI dataset with a zoomed in region that shows the vascular patterns of the sclera

research into vascular biometrics. We focus in this chapter on the second part only, but a complete description of the data is available from the webpage of SBVPI.

The sclera-related part of SBVPI contains 1858 RGB images of 55 subjects. Images for the dataset were captured during a single recording session using a Digital Single-Lens Reflex camera (DSLR) (Canon EOS 60D) at the highest resolution and quality setting. Macro lenses were also used to capitalise on the quality and details visible in the captured images. The outlined capturing setup was chosen to ensure high-quality images, on which the vascular patterns of the sclera are clearly visible, as shown in Fig. 13.4.

During the image capturing process, the camera was positioned at a variable distance between 20 and 40 centimetres from the subjects. Before acquiring a sclera sample, the camera was always randomly displaced from the previous position by moving it approximately 0–30 cm left/right/up/down. During the camera-position change, the subjects also slightly changed the eyelid position and direction of view. With this acquisition setup, we ensured that the individual samples of the same eye looking at the same direction is always different from all other samples of the same eye looking in the same direction. It is known that the small changes in view direction cause complex non-linear deformations in the appearance of the vascular structure of the sclera [7] and we wanted our database to be suitable for the development of algorithms robust to such kind of changes.

The captured samples sometimes contained unwanted facial parts (e.g. eyebrows, parts of the nose, etc.). We, therefore, manually inspected and cropped (using a fixed aspect ratio) the captured images to ensure that only a relatively narrow periocluar region was included in the final images as shown in the samples in Fig. 13.5. The average size of the extracted Region-Of-Interest (ROI) was around 1700×3000 pixels, which is sufficient to also capture the finer blood vessels of the sclera in addition to the more expressed vasculature. Thus, 1700×3000 px was selected as the target size of the dataset and all samples were rescaled (using bicubic interpolation) to this target size to make the data uniform in size.

The image capturing process was inspired by the MASD dataset [5]. Each subject was asked to look in one of four directions at the time, i.e. straight, left, right and up. For each view direction, one image was captured and stored for the dataset. This

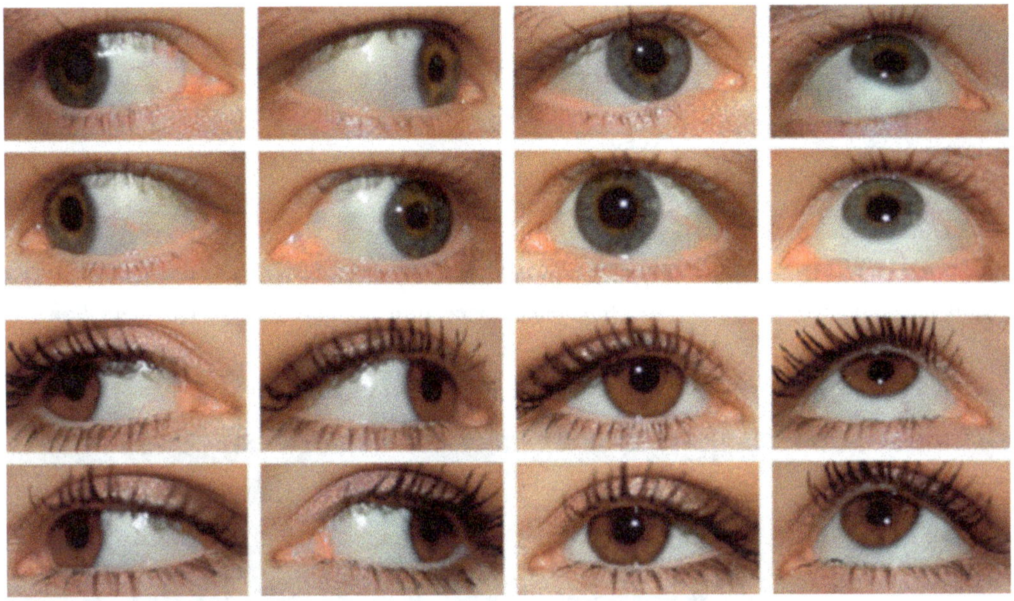

Fig. 13.5 Sample images from the SVBP dataset. The dataset contains high-quality samples with a clearly visible sclera vasculature. Each subject has at least 32 images covering both eyes and 4 view directions, i.e. up, left, right and straight. The top two rows show 8 sample images of a male subject and the bottom two rows show 8 sample images of a female subject from the dataset

process was repeated four times, separately for the left and right eye, and resulted in a minimum of 32 images per subject (i.e. 4 repetitions × 4 view directions × 2 eyes)—some subjects were captured more than four times. The images were manually inspected for blur and focus and images not meeting subjective quality criteria were excluded during the recording sessions. A replacement image was taken if an image was excluded. Subjects with sight problems were asked to remove prescription glasses, while contact lenses, on the other hand, were allowed. Care was also taken that no (or minimal) reflections caused by the camera's flash were visible in the images.

The final dataset is gender balanced and contains images of 29 female and 26 male subjects all of Caucasian origin. The age of the subjects varies from 18 to 80 with the majority of subjects being below 35-year old. SBVP contains eyes of different colours, which represents another source of variability in the dataset. A summary of the main characteristics of SBVP is presented in Table 13.3. For a high-level comparison with other datasets of ocular images, including those used for research in sclera recognition, please refer to Table 13.1.

13.4.2 Available Annotations

The dataset is annotated with identity (one of 55 identities), gender (male or female), eye class (left eye or right eye) and view/gaze-direction labels (straight, left, right, up), which are available for each of the 1858 SVBPI sclera images. Additionally,

Table 13.3 Main characteristics of the SVBP dataset

Characteristic	Description
Acquisition device	DSLR camera, Canon EOS 60D + macro lenses
Number of images	1858
Number of subjects	55
Number of images per subject	32 minimum, but variable
Image size	1700 × 3000 px
Available annotations	Identity, gender, view direction, eye markup (segmentation masks)

Fig. 13.6 Examples of the markups available with the SBVPI dataset. All images contain manually annotated irises and sclera regions and a subset of images has a pixel-level markup of the sclera vasculature. The images show (from left to right): a sample image from SBVPI, the iris markup, the sclera markup and the markup of the vascular structure

ground truth information about the location of certain eye parts is available for images in the dataset. In particular, all 1858 images contain a pixel-level markup of the sclera and iris regions, as illustrated in Fig. 13.6. The vascular structure and pupil area are annotated for a subset of the dataset i.e. 130 images. The segmentation masks were generated manually using the GNU Image Manipulation Program (GIMP) and stored as separate layers for all annotated images. The markups are included in SBVPI in the form of metadata.

The available annotations make our dataset suitable for research work on sclera recognition, but also segmentation techniques, which is not the case with competing datasets. Especially the manual pixel-level markup of the sclera vasculature is a unique aspect of the sclera-related part of SBVPI.

13.5 Experiments and Results

In this section, we evaluate our sclera recognition pipeline. We start the section with a description of the experimental protocol and performance metrics used, then discuss the training procedure for all parts of our pipeline and finally proceed to the presentation of the results and corresponding discussions. To allow for reproducibility of our results, we make all models, data, annotations and experimental scripts publicly available through http://sclera.fri.uni-lj.si/.

13.5.1 Performance Metrics

The overall performance of our recognition pipeline depends on the performance of the segmentation part used to extract the vascular structure from the input images and on the discriminative power of the feature representation extracted from the segmented vasculature. In the experimental section we, therefore, conduct separate experiments for the segmentation and feature extraction parts of our pipeline. Next, we describe the performance metrics used to report results for these two parts.

Performance metrics for the segmentation experiments: We measure the performance of the segmentation models using standard performance metrics, such as *precision*, *recall* and the $F1$-*score*, which are defined as follows [57, 58, 63]:

$$precision = \frac{TP}{TP + FP}, \tag{13.6}$$

$$recall = \frac{TP}{TP + FN}, \tag{13.7}$$

$$F1\text{-}score = 2 \cdot \frac{precision \cdot recall}{precision + recall}, \tag{13.8}$$

where TP denotes the number of true positive pixels, FP stands for the number of false positive pixels and FN represents the number of false negative pixels.

Among the above measures, precision measures the proportion of correctly segmented pixels with respect to the overall number of true pixels of the target class (e.g. the sclera region) and, hence, provides information about how many segmented pixels are in fact relevant. Recall measures the proportion of correctly segmented pixels with respect to the overall number of pixels assigned to the target class and, hence, provides information about how many relevant pixels are found/segmented. Precision and recall values are typically dependent—it is possible to increase one at the expense of the other and vice versa by changing segmentation thresholds. If a simple way to compare two segmentation models is required, it is, therefore, convenient to combine precision and recall into a single metric called F1-score, which is also used as an additional performance metric in this work [57].

Note that when using a fixed segmentation threshold Δ, we obtain fixed precision and recall values for the segmentation outputs, while the complete trade-off between precision and recall can be visualised in the form of precision–recall curves by varying the segmentation threshold Δ over all possible values. This trade-off shows a more complete picture of the performance of the segmentation models and is also used in the experimental section [57].

Performance metrics for the recognition experiments: We measure the performance of the feature extraction (and recognition) part of our pipeline in verification experiments and report performance using standard False Acceptance (FAR) and False Rejection error Rates (FRR). FAR measures the error over the illegitimate verification attempts and FRR measures the error over the legitimate verification attempts. Both error rates, FAR and FRR, depend on the value of a decision threshold (similar to the precision and recall values from the previous section) and selecting a threshold that produces low FAR values contributes towards high FRR scores and vice versa, selecting a threshold that produced low FRR values generates high FAR scores. Both error rates are bounded between 0 and 1. A common practice in biometric research is to report Verification Rates (VER) instead of FRR scores, where VER is defined as 1-FRR [11, 64–66]. We also adopt this practice in our experiments.

Toshow the complete trade-off between FAR and FRR (or VER), we generate Receiver Operating Characteristic (ROC) curves by sweeping over all possible values of the decision threshold. We then report on several operating points from the ROC curve in the experiments, i.e. the verification performance at a false accept rate of 0.1% (VER@0.1FAR), the verification performance at a false accept rate of 1% (VER@1FAR) and the so-called Equal Error Rate (EER), which corresponds to the ROC operating point, where FAR and FRR are equal. Additionally, we provide Area Under the ROC Curve (AUC) scores for all recognition experiments, which is a common measure of the accuracy of binary classification tasks, such as biometric identity verification.

13.5.2 Experimental Protocol and Training Details

We conduct experiments on the SBVPI dataset introduced in Sect. 13.4 and use separate experimental protocols for the segmentation and recognition parts of our pipeline. The protocols and details on the training procedures are presented below.

13.5.2.1 Segmentation Experiments

The segmentation part of our pipeline consists of two components. The first generates an initial segmentation result and locates the sclera region in the input image, whereas the second segments the vasculature from the located sclera.

Sclera segmentation: To train and test the segmentation model for the first component of our pipeline, we split the sclera-related SBVPI data into two (image and subject) disjoint sets:

- *A training set* consisting of 1160 sclera images. These images are further partitioned into two subsets. The first, comprising 985 images, is used to learn the model parameters and the second, comprising 175 images, is employed as the validation set and used to observe the generalization abilities of the model during training and stop the learning stage if the model starts to over-fit.
- *A test set* consisting of 698 sclera images. This set is used to test the final performance of the trained segmentation model and compute performance metrics for the experiments.

To avoid over-fitting, the training data (i.e. 985 images) is augmented by a factor of 40 by left–right flipping, cropping, Gaussian blurring, changing the image brightness and application of affine transformations such as scale changes, rotations (up to $\pm 35°$) and shearing.

Training of the SegNet model for the initial segmentation step (for sclera segmentation) is conducted on a GTX 1080 Ti with 11GB of RAM. We use the Caffe implementation of SegNet made available by the authors[2] for the experiments. The input images are rescaled to fixed size of 360×480 pixels for the training procedure. The model weights are learned using Stochastic Gradient Descent (SGD) and Xavier initialization [67]. The learning rate is set to 0.001, the weight decay to 0.0005, the momentum to 0.9 and the batch size to 4. The model converges after 26, 000 iterations.

Vasculature segmentation: The second component of our pipeline requires a pixel-level markup of the vascular structure of the sclera for both the training and the testing procedure. The SBVP dataset contains a total of 130 such images, which are used to learn the SegNet model for this part and assess its performance. We again partition the data into two (image and subject) disjoint sets:

- *A training set* of 98 images, which we split into patches of manageable size, i.e. 360×480 pixels. We generate a total of 788 patches by sampling from the set of 98 training images and randomly select 630 of these patches for learning the model parameters and use the remaining 158 patches as our validation set during training. To avoid over-fitting, we again augment the training patches 40-fold using random rotations, cropping and colour manipulations.
- *A test set* consisting of 32 images. While the test images are again processed patch-wise, we report results over the complete images and not the intermediate patch representations.

To train the segmentation model for the vascular structure of the sclera, we use the same setup as described above for the sclera segmentation model.

13.5.2.2 Recognition Experiments

The vascular structure of the sclera is an epigenetic biometric characteristic with high discriminative power that is known to differ between the eyes of the same subject. We, therefore, treat the left and right eye of each subject in the SBVPI dataset as a unique identity and conduct recognition experiments with 110 identities. Note that such a methodology is common for epigenetic biometric traits and has been used regularly in the literature, e.g. [68, 69].

For the recognition experiments, we split the dataset into subject disjoint training and test sets, where the term subject now refers to one of the artificially generated 110 identities. The training set that is used for the model learning procedure consists of 1043 images belonging to 60 different identities. These images are divided between

[2] Available from: https://github.com/alexgkendall/caffe-segnet.

the actual training data (needed for the learning model parameters) and the validation data (needed for the early stopping criterion) in a ratio of 70% versus 30%. The remaining 815 images belonging to 50 subjects are used for testing purposes.

For the training procedure, we again use a GTX 1080 Ti GPU. We implement our ScleraNET model in Keras and initialize its weights in accordance with the method from [67]. We use the Adam optimizer with a learning rate of 0.001, beta1 equal to 0.9 and beta2 equal to 0.999 to learn the model parameters. We augment the available training data on the fly to avoid over-fitting and to ensure sufficient training material. We use random shifts (± 20 pixels in each direction) and rotations ($\pm 20^\circ$) for the augmentation procedure. The model reaches stable loss values after 70 epochs. As indicated in Sect. 13.3.3.3, once trained, the model takes 400×400 px images as input and returns a 512-dimensional feature representation at the output (after network surgery). The input images to the model are complete probability maps of the sclera vasculature down-sampled to the target size expected by ScleraNET. Note that because the down-sampling is performed after segmentation of the vasculature, information on the smaller veins is not completely lost when adjusting for the input size of the descriptor-computation model.

13.5.3 Evaluation of Sclera Segmentation Models

We start our experiments with an evaluation of the first component of the sclera recognition pipeline, which produces the initial segmentation of the sclera region. The goal in this series of experiments is to show how the trained SegNet architecture performs for this task and how it compares to competing deep models and existing sclera segmentation techniques. We need to note that while the error from this stage is propagated throughout the entire pipeline to some extent, these errors are not as critical as long as the majority of the sclera region is segmented from the input images. Whether the segmentation is precise (and able to find the exact border between the sclera region and fine details such as the eyelashes, eyelids, etc.) is not of paramount importance at this stage.

To provide a frame of reference for the performance of SegNet, we implement 4 additional segmentation techniques and apply them to our test data. Specifically, we implement 3 state-of-the-art CNN-based segmentation models and one segmentation approach designed specifically for sclera segmentation. Note that these techniques were chosen, because they represent the top performing techniques from the sclera segmentation competitions of 2017 and 2018. Details on the techniques are given below:

- *RefineNet-50* and *RefineNet-101*: RefineNet [70] is recent deep segmentation model built around the concept of residual learning [71]. The main idea of RefineNet is to exploit features from multiple levels (i.e. from different layers) to produce high-resolution semantic feature maps in a coarse-to-fine manner. Depending on the depth of the model, different variants of the model can be trained.

In this work, we use two variants, one with 50 model layers (i.e. RefineNet-50) and one with 101 layers (i.e. RefineNet-101). We train the models on the same data and with the same protocol as SegNet (see Sect. 13.5.2.1) and use a publicly available implementation for the experiments.[3] Note that RefineNet was the top performer of the sclera 2018 segmentation competition held in conjunction with the 2018 International Conference on Biometrics (ICB) [10].

- *UNet*: The UNet [72] model represents a popular CNN architecture particularly suited for data-scarce image translation tasks such as sclera segmentation. Similarly to SegNet, the model uses an encoder–decoder architecture but ensures information flow from the encoder to the decoder by concatenating feature maps from the encoder with the corresponding outputs of the decoder. We train the models on the same data and with the same protocol as SegNet. For the experiments we use our own Keras (with TensorFlow backend) implementation of UNet and make it publicly available to the research community.[4]
- *Unsupervised Sclera Segmentation (USS)* [73]: Different from the models above, USS represents an unsupervised segmentation technique, which does not rely on any prior knowledge. The technique operates on greyscale images and is based on an adaptive histogram normalisation procedure followed by clustering and adaptive thresholding. Details on the method can be found in [73]. The technique was ranked second in the 2017 sclera segmentation competition. Code provided by the author of USS was used for the experiments to ensure a fair comparison with our segmentation models.

Note that the three CNN-based models produce probability maps for the sclera vasculature, whereas the USS approach returns only binary masks. In accordance with these characteristics we report precision, recall and F1-scores for all tested methods (the CNN models are thresholded with a value of Δ that ensures the highest possible F1-score) in Table 13.4 and complete precision–recall curves only for the CNN-based methods in Fig. 13.7. For both the quantitative results and the performance graphs, we also report standard deviations to have a measure of dispersion across the test set.

The results show that the CNN-based models perform very similarly (there is no statistical difference in performance between the models). The unsupervised approach USS, on the other hand, performs somewhat worse, but the results are consistent with the ranking reported in [5]. Overall, the CNN models all achieve near-perfect performance and are able to ensure F1-scores of around 0.95. Note that such high results suggest that performance for this task is saturated and further improvements would likely be a consequence of over-fitting to the dataset and corresponding manual annotations.

The average processing time per image (calculated over a test set of 100 images) is 1.2s for UNet, 0.6s for RefineNet-50, 0.8s for RefineNet-101, 0.15s for SegNet and 0.34s for USS. In our experiments, SegNet is the fastest of the tested models.

We show some examples of the segmentation results produced by the tested segmentation models in Fig. 13.8. Here, the first column shows the original RGB ocular

[3] Available from https://github.com/guosheng/refinenet.

[4] Available from: http://sclera.fri.uni-lj.si/.

Table 13.4 Segmentation results generated based on binary segmentation masks. For the CNN-based models, the masks are produced by thresholding the generated probability maps with a value of Δ that ensures the highest possible F1-score, whereas the USS approach is designed to return a binary mask of the sclera region only. Note that all CNN perform very similarly with no statistical difference in segmentation performance, while the unsupervised USS approach performs somewhat worse. The reported performance scores are shown in the form $\mu \pm \sigma$, computed over all test images

Algorithm	Precision	Recall	F1-score
UNet [72] (ours)	0.936 ± 0.044	0.930 ± 0.037	0.933 ± 0.037
RefineNet-50 [70] (ours)	0.959 ± 0.020	0.959 ± 0.020	0.959 ± 0.018
RefineNet-101 [70] (ours)	0.953 ± 0.025	0.951 ± 0.023	0.952 ± 0.021
SegNet [5, 57] (ours, this chapter)	0.949 ± 0.024	0.949 ± 0.022	0.949 ± 0.021
USS [5, 73]	0.729 ± 0.041	0.718 ± 0.039	0.723 ± 0.036

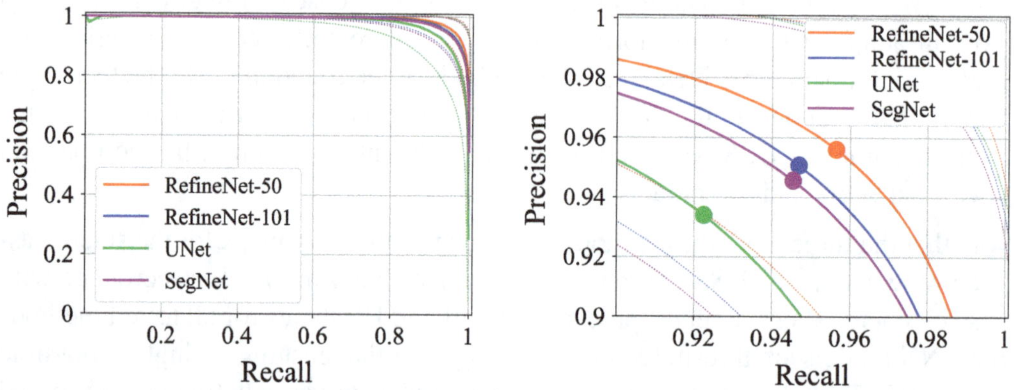

Fig. 13.7 Precision–recall curves for the tested CNN models. USS is not included here, as it returns only binary masks of the sclera region. The left graph shows the complete plot generated by varying the segmentation threshold Δ over all possible values, whereas the right graph shows a zoomed in region to highlight the minute differences between the techniques. The marked points stand for the operating points with the highest F1-Score. The dotted lines show the dispersion (σ) of the precision and recall scores over the test images

images, the second shows the manually annotated ground truth and the remaining columns show results generated by (from left to right): USS, RefineNet-50, RefineNet-101, SegNet and UNet. These results again confirm that all CNN-based models ensure similar segmentation performance. All models segment the sclera region well and differ only in some finer details, such as eyelashes, which are not really important for the second segmentation step, where the vasculature needs to be extracted from the ocular images.

Consequently, any of the tested CNN-based segmentation models could be used in our sclera recognition pipeline for the initial segmentation step, but we favour

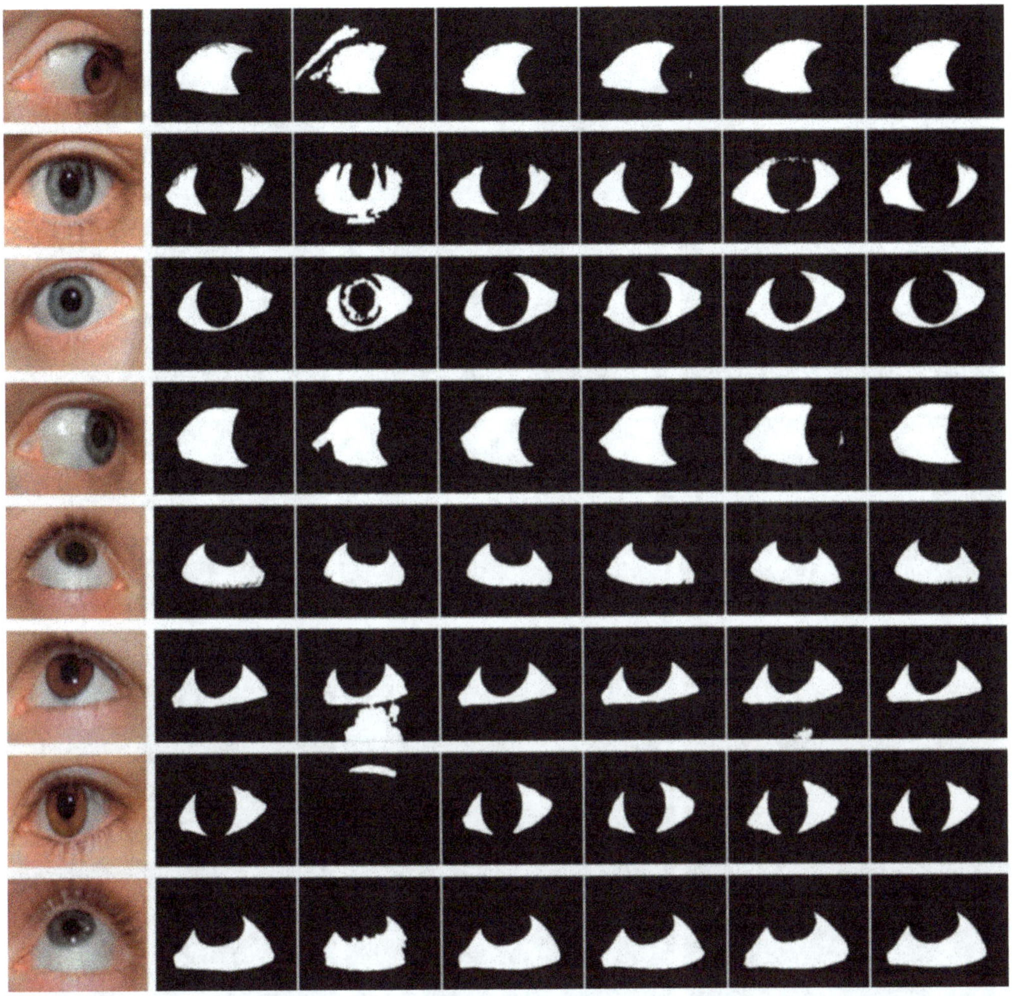

Fig. 13.8 Visual examples of the segmentation results produced by the tested segmentation models. The first column shows the input RGB ocular images, the second the manually annotated ground truth and the remaining columns show the results generated by (from left to right): USS, RefineNet-50, RefineNet-101, SegNet and UNet. Note that the CNN models (last four columns) produce visually similar segmentation results and differ only in certain fine details

SegNet because of the fast prediction time, which is 4 times faster the second fastest CNN model, i.e. RefineNet-50.

13.5.4 Evaluation of Vasculature Segmentation Models

In the next series of experiments, we evaluate the performance of the second segmentation step of our pipeline, which aims to locate and segment the vascular structure of the sclera from the input image. The input to this step is again an RGB ocular image (see Fig. 13.9), but masked with the segmentation output produced by the SegNet model evaluated in the previous section.

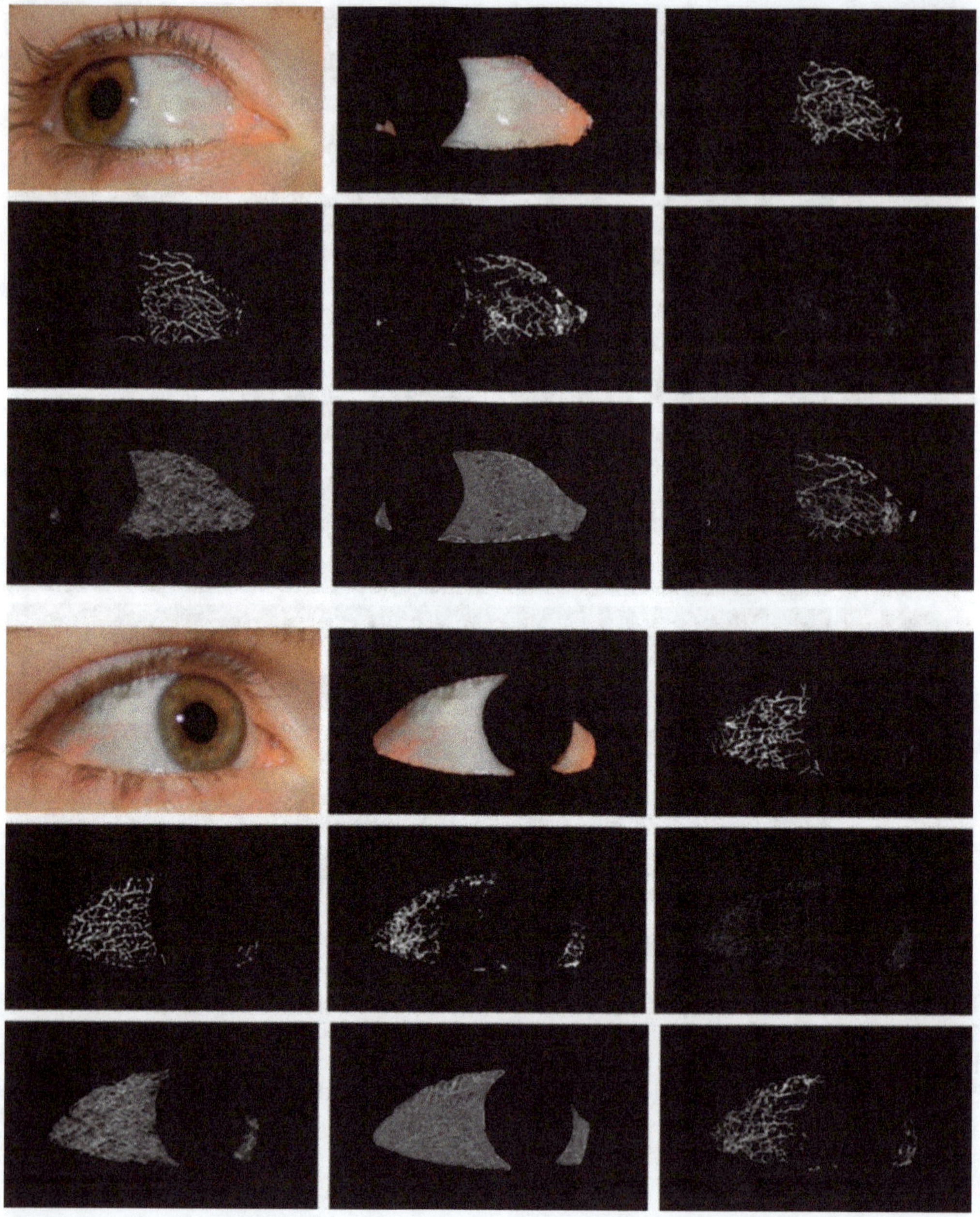

Fig. 13.9 Examples of vasculature segmentation results. Each of the two image blocks shows (from left to right and top to bottom): the input RGB ocular image, the input image masked with the sclera region produced by the initial segmentation step, the ground truth markup, results for the proposed cascaded SegNet assembly, and results for the Adaptive Gaussian Thresholding (AGT), and the NMC, NRLT, Coye and B-COSFIRE approaches. The results show the generated binary masks corresponding to the operating point used in Table 13.5. Note that the proposed approach most convincingly captures the characteristics of the manual vasculature markup. Best viewed electronically and zoomed in

As emphasised earlier, we conduct segmentation with our approach in a patch-wise manner to ensure that information about the finer details of the sclera vasculature is not lost. Because the second SegNet model of the cascaded assembly outputs probability maps, we use adaptive Gaussian thresholding [74] to generate binary masks to compare with the manually annotated ground truth. To assess performance, we compute results over the binary masks and again report fixed precision, recall and F1-score values in this series of experiments. The performance scores are computed for the operating point on the precision–recall curve that corresponds to the maximum possible F1-score. We again report standard deviations in addition to the average scores to have a measure of dispersion for the results of the test data.

For comparison purposes, we implement a number of competing techniques from the literature that are regularly used for vessel segmentation in the field of vascular biometrics, i.e. (i) Adaptive Gaussian Thresholding (AGT) [74], (ii) Normalized Maximum Curvature (NMC) [75], (iii) Normalized Repeated Line Tracking (NRLT) [76], (iv)) Coye filtering [77] and (v) the B-COSFIRE approach from [78, 79]. The NMC and NRLT approaches represent a modified version of the original segmentation techniques and are normalised to return continuous probability maps rather than binarized segmentation results. The hyper-parameters of all baseline techniques (if any) are selected to maximise performance. The techniques are implemented using publicly available source code.[5] We note again that no supervised approach to sclera vasculature segmentation has been presented in the literature so far. We focus, therefore, exclusively on unsupervised segmentation techniques in our comparative assessment.

The results of the experiments are presented in Table 13.5. As can be seen, SegNet ensures the best overall results by a large margin with an average F1-score of 0.727. The B-COSFIRE techniques, regularly used for vasculature segmentation in retina images, is the runner-up with an average F1-score of 0.393, followed closely by AGT thresholding with an F1-score of 0.306. The NMC, NRLT and Coye filter approaches result in worse performance with F1-scores below 0.25. While the performance difference between the SegNet model and the competing techniques is considerable, it is also expected, as SegNet is trained on the manually annotated vasculature, while the remaining approaches rely only on local image characteristics to identify the vascular structure of the sclera. As a result, the vasculature extracted by the unsupervised techniques (NMC, NRLT, Coye filter and B-COSFIRE) does not necessarily correspond to the markup generated by a human annotator. However, the low-performance scores of the unsupervised techniques do not indicate that the extracted vasculature is useless for recognition, but only that there is low correspondence with the manual markup. To investigate the usefulness of the extracted vascular patterns of these

[5]Code for the techniques is available from: AGT from OpenCV: https://opencv.org/, NMC and NRLT from Mathworks: https://www.mathworks.com/matlabcentral/fileexchange/35716-miura-et-al-vein-extraction-methods

Coye filter from Mathworks: https://www.mathworks.com/matlabcentral/fileexchange/50839-novel-retinal-vessel-segmentation-algorithm-fundus-images

B-COSFIRE from Mathworks: https://www.mathworks.com/matlabcentral/fileexchange/49172-trainable-cosfire-filters-for-curvilinear-structure-delineation-in-images.

Table 13.5 Comparison of vasculature segmentation techniques. Results are presented for the proposed cascaded SegNet assembly, as well as for five competing unsupervised segmentation approaches from the literature. The probability maps generated by the techniques have been thresholded to allow for comparisons with the annotated binary vasculature markup. Note that the proposed approach achieves the best overall performance by a large margin

Algorithm	Precision	Recall	F1-score
SegNet [15] + AGT (ours, this chapter)	0.806 ± 0.155	0.675 ± 0.131	0.727 ± 0.120
Adaptive Gaussian thresholding (AGT)	0.308 ± 0.119	0.372 ± 0.201	0.306 ± 0.120
Normalized maximum curvature (NMC)	0.240 ± 0.097	0.247 ± 0.044	0.232 ± 0.062
Normalized repeated line tracking (NRLT)	0.145 ± 0.055	0.314 ± 0.114	0.191 ± 0.066
Coye filter	0.143 ± 0.070	0.376 ± 0.085	0.198 ± 0.078
B-COSFIRE	0.351 ± 0.142	0.480 ± 0.083	0.393 ± 0.116

techniques for recognition, we conduct a series of recognition experiments in the next section.

To put the reported results into perspective and show what the scores mean visually, we present in Fig. 13.9 some qualitative segmentation results. Here, each of the two image blocks shows (from left to right and top to bottom): the input ocular image, the masked sclera region, the ground truth annotation and results for the proposed cascaded SegNet assembly, the Adaptive Gaussian Thresholding (AGT), and the NMC, NRLT, Coye and B-COSFIRE techniques. It is interesting to see what level of detail the SegNet-based model is able to recover from the input image. Despite the relatively poor contrast of some of the finer veins, the model still successfully segments the sclera vasculature from the input images. The B-COSFIRE results are also convincing when examined visually, but as emphasised earlier do not result in high-performance scores when compared to the manual markup. Other competing models are less successful and generate less precise segmentation results. However, as suggested above, the competing models use no supervision to learn to segment the vascular structures and therefore generate segmentation results that do not correspond well to the manual markup.

To further highlight the quality of the segmentation ensured by the SegNet-based model, we show a close up of the vascular structure of an eye and the corresponding segmentation output in Fig. 13.10. We see that the model successfully segments most of the vascular structure, but also picks up on the eyelashes, which very much resemble the vein patterns of the sclera even from a human perspective. In the area where reflections are visible, the model is not able to recover the vascular structure from the input image. Furthermore, despite the patch-wise processing used with the cascaded SegNet segmentation approach, we observe no visible artifacts caused

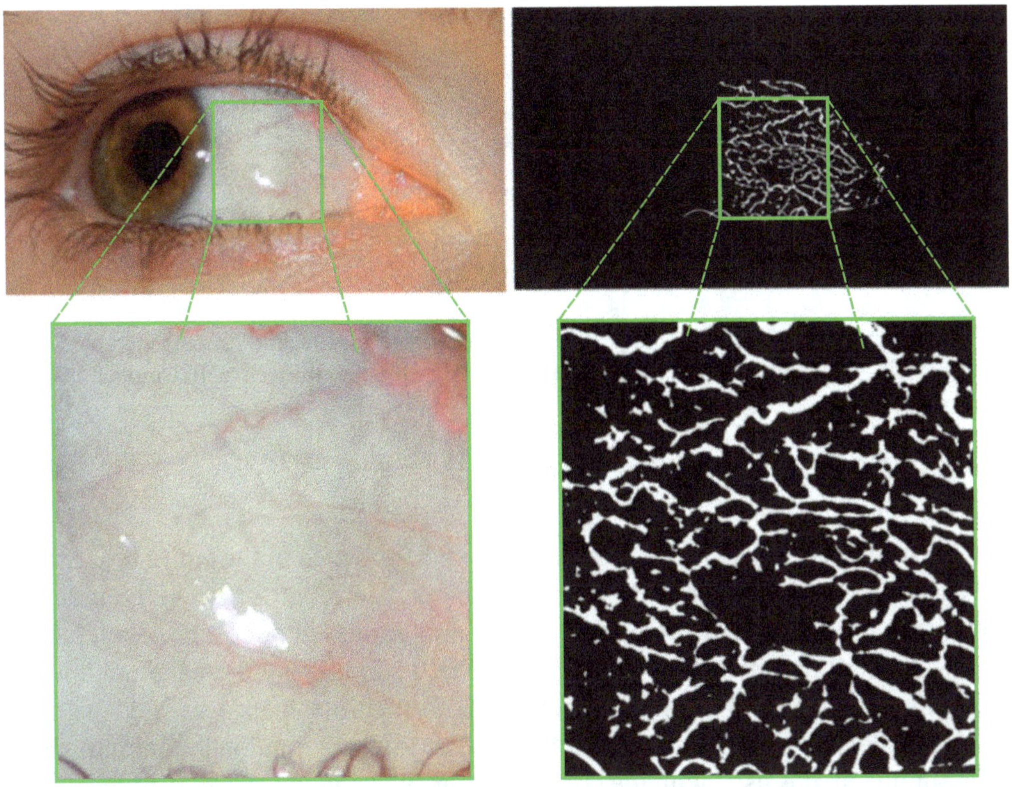

Fig. 13.10 Visualisation of the fine vascular structure recovered by our segmentation model. The image shows a zoomed in region of the vascular structure of the eye (on the left) and the corresponding binarized output of our model (on the right)

by the re-assembly procedure. We assume this is a consequence of the run-time augmentation step that smooths out such artifacts.

Because the segmentation is performed in a patch-wise manner, the average time needed to process one input image with the proposed model in this part is 5.6 seconds when using a single GPU (please note that this step can be parallelised using multiple GPUs, because patch predictions can be calculated independently). For comparison, the average processing time for AGT is 1.2 s, for NMC it is 32.5 s, for NRLT the processing time is 7.9 s, for Coye it is 1.2 s and for the B-COSFIRE the processing time is 13.9 s. However, note that different programming languages were used for the implementation of the segmentation methods, so the processing times need to be interpreted accordingly. For the proposed cascaded SegNet assembly, the entire region-of-interest extraction step (which comprises the initial sclera segmentation and vascular structure segmentation steps), takes around 6 s using a single GPU for one input image on average.

Overall, these results suggest that the trained segmentation model is able to produce good quality segmentation results that can be used for recognition purposes. We evaluate the performance of our recognition approach with the generated segmentation outputs next.

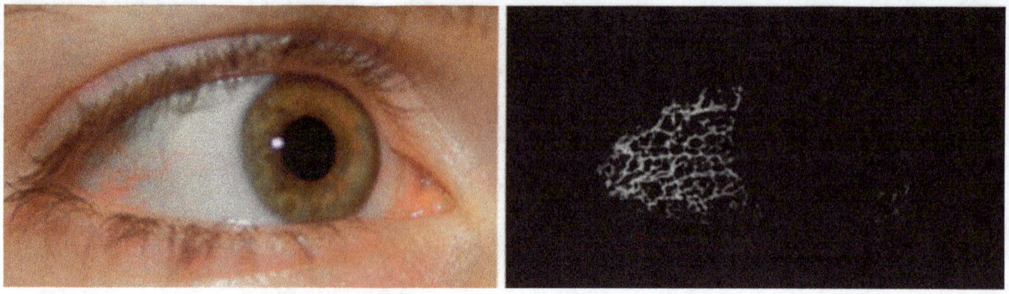

Fig. 13.11 Example of an input image and the corresponding probability map generated by the SegNet model. The probability mask on the left is used as input to the ScleraNET model

13.5.5 Recognition Experiments

In the last series of experiments, we assess the performance of the entire recognition pipeline and feed the segmented sclera vasculature into our ScleraNET model for feature extraction. Note again that we use the probability output of the segmentation models as input to ScleraNET (marked **y** in Fig. 13.2) and not the generated binary masks of the vasculature. An example of the probability map generated with the SegNet model is shown in Fig. 13.11. Once a feature representation is computed from the input image, it is used with the cosine similarity to compute similarity scores and to ultimately conduct identity inference. The feature computation procedure takes 0.1 s per image on average.

To evaluate the recognition performance of ScleraNET, we conduct verification experiments using the following experimental setup:

- We first generate user templates by randomly selecting four images of each subject in the test set. We sample the test set in a way that ensures that each template contains all four gaze directions (i.e. up, down, left and right). Since each subject has at least 4 images of each gaze direction, we are able to generate multiple templates for each subject in the test set.
- Next, we use all images in the test set and compare them to the generated user templates. The comparison is conducted by comparing (using the cosine similarity) the query vasculature descriptor to the descriptors of each image in the template. The highest similarity score is kept as the score for the query-to-template comparison. If the query image is also present in the template, we exclude the score from the evaluation.
- We repeat the entire process 5-times to estimate average performance scores as well as standard deviations. The outlined setup results in a total of 1228 legitimate and 121572 illegitimate verification attempts in each of the 5 repetitions.

Becausethe ocular images are not aligned, we implement multiple descriptor-based approaches for comparison. Specifically, we implement the dense SIFT (dSIFT hereafter) approach from [8] and several keypoint based techniques. For the latter, we compute SIFT [80], SURF [81] and ORB [82] descriptors using their corresponding keypoint detectors. For each image-pair comparison, we use the average Euclidean

Table 13.6 Results of the recognition experiments. The table shows performance scores for five different descriptor-computation strategies and five approaches to vasculature segmentation. For each performance metric, the best overall result is coloured red and the best results for a given segmentation approach is coloured blue. The proposed ScleraNET model ensures competitive performance significantly outperforming the competing models when applied on the segmentation results generated by the proposed cascaded SegNet assembly

Segment.	Algorithm	VER@0.1FAR	VER@1FAR	EER	AUC
C. SegNet (ours)	ScleraNET (ours)	0.181 ± 0.009	0.459 ± 0.009	0.145 ± 0.002	0.933 ± 0.002
	SIFT	0.184 ± 0.076	0.452 ± 0.040	0.176 ± 0.005	0.903 ± 0.005
	SURF	0.023 ± 0.007	0.126 ± 0.010	0.286 ± 0.004	0.782 ± 0.005
	ORB	0.017 ± 0.004	0.080 ± 0.011	0.351 ± 0.003	0.704 ± 0.005
	Dense SIFT	0.326 ± 0.016	0.507 ± 0.010	0.221 ± 0.004	0.865 ± 0.002
NMC	ScleraNET	0.002 ± 0.001	0.023 ± 0.003	0.425 ± 0.004	0.596 ± 0.004
	SIFT	0.000 ± 0.000	0.000 ± 0.000	0.500 ± 0.000	0.500 ± 0.000
	SURF	0.017 ± 0.024	0.031 ± 0.016	0.488 ± 0.013	0.535 ± 0.010
	ORB	0.000 ± 0.000	0.005 ± 0.005	0.504 ± 0.006	0.497 ± 0.006
	Dense SIFT	0.063 ± 0.014	0.184 ± 0.028	0.371 ± 0.012	0.683 ± 0.010
NRLT	ScleraNET	0.112 ± 0.011	0.311 ± 0.006	0.196 ± 0.008	0.888 ± 0.004
	SIFT	0.000 ± 0.000	0.014 ± 0.005	0.500 ± 0.001	0.500 ± 0.002
	SURF	0.000 ± 0.000	0.021 ± 0.013	0.492 ± 0.008	0.509 ± 0.005
	ORB	0.000 ± 0.000	0.021 ± 0.010	0.502 ± 0.005	0.499 ± 0.007
	Dense SIFT	0.047 ± 0.004	0.153 ± 0.010	0.362 ± 0.008	0.701 ± 0.004
Coye	ScleraNET	0.067 ± 0.008	0.215 ± 0.007	0.267 ± 0.006	0.812 ± 0.004
	SIFT	0.000 ± 0.000	0.036 ± 0.014	0.496 ± 0.001	0.507 ± 0.002
	SURF	0.000 ± 0.000	0.000 ± 0.000	0.500 ± 0.005	0.497 ± 0.005
	ORB	0.002 ± 0.001	0.023 ± 0.005	0.451 ± 0.005	0.568 ± 0.006
	Dense SIFT	0.091 ± 0.005	0.234 ± 0.018	0.300 ± 0.004	0.772 ± 0.004
B-COSFIRE	ScleraNET	0.042 ± 0.004	0.140 ± 0.008	0.337 ± 0.005	0.723 ± 0.006
	SIFT	0.000 ± 0.000	0.012 ± 0.005	0.488 ± 0.002	0.522 ± 0.003
	SURF	0.000 ± 0.000	0.000 ± 0.000	0.494 ± 0.005	0.513 ± 0.003
	ORB	0.000 ± 0.000	0.008 ± 0.002	0.467 ± 0.003	0.539 ± 0.004
	Dense SIFT	0.110 ± 0.011	0.242 ± 0.011	0.325 ± 0.006	0.748 ± 0.005

distance between matching descriptors as the similarity score for recognition. Since the descriptor-based approaches are local and rely on keypoint correspondences, they are particularly suitable for problems such as sclera recognition, where (partially visible) unaligned vascular structures under different views need to be matched against each other. We conduct experiments with the vasculature extracted with the proposed cascaded SegNet assembly, so we are able to evaluate our complete processing pipeline, but also with the segmentation results produced by the competing segmentation approaches evaluated in the previous section, i.e. NMC, NRLT, Coye and B-COSFIRE.

From the results in Table 13.6 and Fig. 13.12 (results for ScleraNET in the figures are marked as CNN), we see that the proposed pipeline (cascaded SegNet assembly +

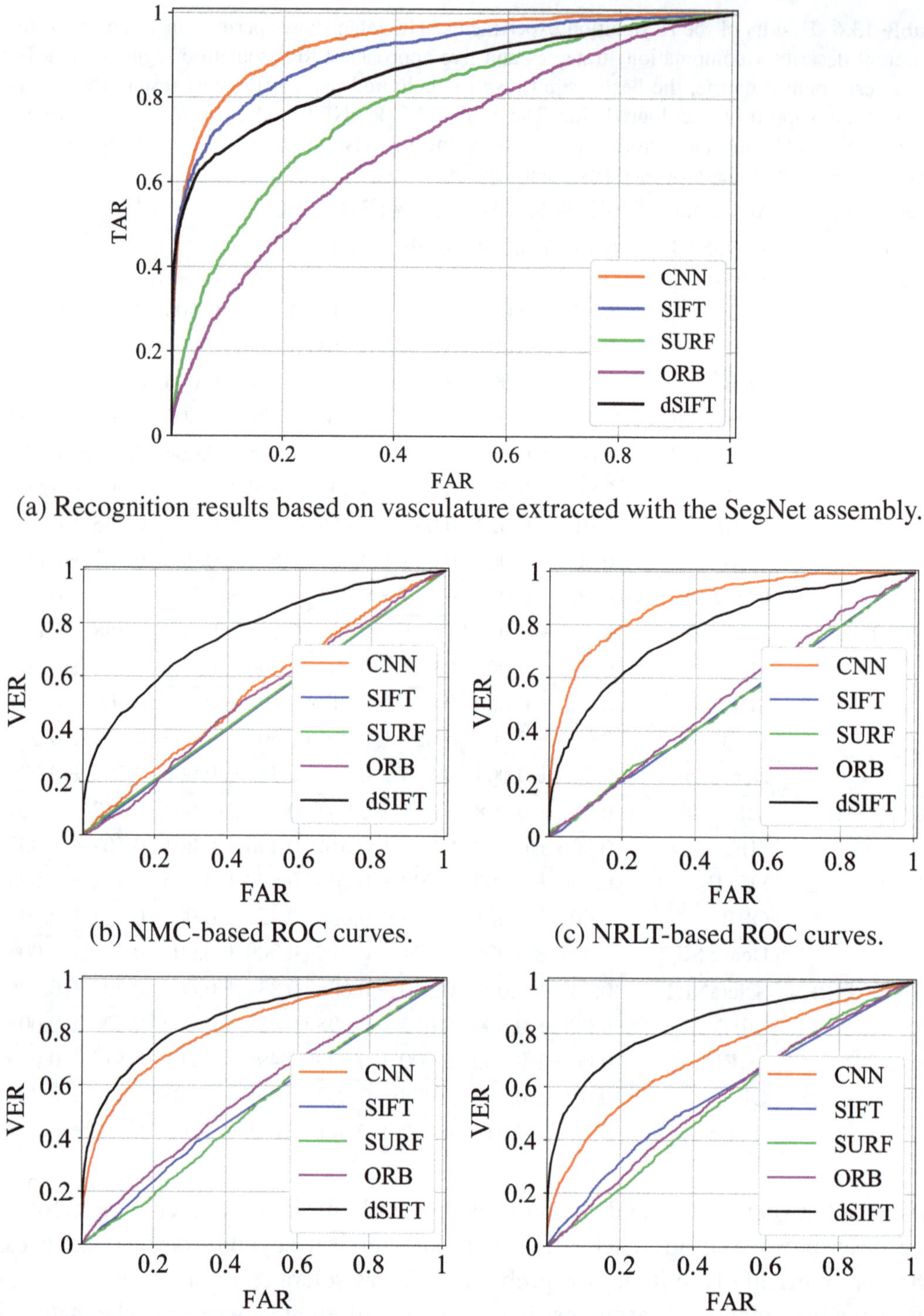

(a) Recognition results based on vasculature extracted with the SegNet assembly.

(b) NMC-based ROC curves.

(c) NRLT-based ROC curves.

(d) Coye-filter-based ROC curves.

(e) B-COSFIRE-based ROC curves.

Fig. 13.12 Results of the verification experiments. The graphs show recognition results for several feature extraction techniques and multiple approaches to vasculature segmentation. The pipeline proposed in this chapter results in the best overall performance

ScleraNET) ensures an average AUC of 0.933 for the verification experiments compared to the average AUC of 0.903 for the runner-up, the SIFT-based approach. Interestingly, the dSIFT approach is very competitive at the lower FAR values, but becomes less competitive at the higher values of FAR—see Fig. 13.12a. This behaviour can likely be ascribed to the dense nature of the descriptor, which makes it difficult to reliably compare images when there is scale and position variability present in the samples. The remaining three descriptors, SIFT, SURF and ORB, are less competitive and result in lower performance scores.

The segmentation results generated by the proposed cascaded SegNet assembly appear to be the most suitable for recognition purposes, as can be seen by comparing the ROC curves from Fig. 13.12b–e, to the results in Fig. 13.12a, or examining the lower part of Table 13.6. While the NMC, NRLT, Coye and B-COSFIRE segmentation results (in the form of probability maps) result in above-random verification performance with the ScleraNET and dSIFT descriptors, the performance is at chance for the keypoint-descriptor-based methods—SIFT, SURF and ORB. The reason for this is the difficulty of finding matching descriptors in the images, which leads to poor performance. The ScleraNET model, on the other hand, seems to generalise reasonably well to segmentation outputs with characteristics different from those produced by the cascaded SegNet assembly. It achieves the best performance with the NRLT and Coye segmentation techniques, it is comparable in performance to dSIFT on B-COSFIRE segmented vasculature and is second only to dSIFT with the NMC approach. This is surprising, as it was not trained on vascular images produced by these methods. Nonetheless, it seems to be able to extract useful descriptors for recognition from these images as well.

Overall, the results achieved with the proposed pipeline are very encouraging and present a good foundation for further research, also in the context of multi-modal biometric systems built around (peri-)ocular information.

13.6 Conclusion

We have presented a novel approach to sclera recognition built around convolutional neural networks. Our approach uses a two-step procedure that first locates the vascular structure of the sclera from the input image and then extracts a discriminative representation from the segmented vasculature that can be used for image comparisons and ultimately recognition. The two-step segmentation procedure is based on cascaded SegNet assembly, the first supervised approach to sclera vasculature segmentation presented in the literature, while the descriptor-computation procedure is based on a novel CNN-based model, called ScleraNET, trained in a multi-task manner. We evaluated our approach on a newly introduced and publicly available dataset of annotated sclera images and presented encouraging comparative results with competing methods. As part of our future work, we plan to integrate the presented pipeline with other ocular traits into a multi-modal recognition system.

Acknowledgements This research was supported in parts by ARRS (Slovenian Research Agency) Research Program P2-0250 (B) Metrology and Biometric Systems, ARRS Research Program P2-0214 (A) Computer Vision, and the RS-MIZŠ and EU-ESRR funded GOSTOP. The GPU used for this research was donated by the NVIDIA Corporation.

References

1. Alkassar S, Woo WL, Dlay SS, Chambers JA (2017) Robust sclera recognition system with novel sclera segmentation and validation techniques. IEEE Trans Syst Man Cybern Syst (TSMC) 47(3):474–486
2. Ali Z, Park U, Nang J, Park JS, Hong T, Park S (2017) Periocular recognition using uMLBP and attribute features. KSII Trans Internet Inf Syst (TIIS) 11(12):6133–6151
3. Jain AK, Ross A, Prabhakar S et al (2004) An introduction to biometric recognition. IEEE Trans Circuits Syst Video Technol 14(1)
4. Patil V, Patil AM (2017) Human identification method: sclera recognition. Int J Comput Sci Netw (IJCSN) 6(1):24–29
5. Das A, Pal U, Ferrer MA, Blumenstein M, Štepec D, Rot P, Emeršič Ž, Peer P, Štruc V, Kumar SA et al (2017) SSERBC 2017: sclera segmentation and eye recognition benchmarking competition. In: International joint conference on biometrics (IJCB), pp 742–747
6. Derakhshani R, Ross A (2007) A texture-based neural network classifier for biometric identification using ocular surface vasculature. In: International joint conference on neural networks 2007 (IJCNN 2007), pp 2982–2987. IEEE
7. Zhou Z, Du EY, Thomas NL, Delp EJ (2012) A new human identification method: sclera recognition. IEEE Trans Syst Man Cybern (TSMC) Part A Syst Hum 42(3):571–583
8. Das A, Pal U, Ferrer Ballester MA, Blumenstein M (2013) Sclera recognition using dense-sift. In: 2013 13th international conference on intelligent systems design and applications (ISDA), pp 74–79. IEEE
9. Zhou Z, Du EY, Thomas NL, Delp EJ (2011) Multi-angle sclera recognition system. In: 2011 IEEE workshop on computational intelligence in biometrics and identity management (CIBIM), pp 103–108. IEEE
10. Das A, Pal U, Ferrer MA, Blumenstein M, Štepec D, Rot P, Peer P, Štruc V (2018) SSBC 2018: sclera segmentation benchmarking competition. In: International conference on biometrics (ICB), pp 303–308
11. Emeršič Ž, Štepec D, Štruc V, Peer P (2017) Training convolutional neural networks with limited training data for ear recognition in the wild. arXiv:1711.09952
12. Emeršič Ž, Meden B, Peer P, Štruc V (2018) Evaluation and analysis of ear recognition models: performance, complexity and resource requirements. Neural computing and applications, pp 1–16
13. Emeršič Ž, Štepec D, Štruc V, Peer P, George A, Ahmad A, Omar E, Boult TE, Safdaii R, Zhou Y et al (2017) The unconstrained ear recognition challenge. In: 2017 IEEE international joint conference on biometrics (IJCB), pp 715–724. IEEE
14. Grm K, Štruc V, Artiges A, Caron M, Ekenel HK (2017) Strengths and weaknesses of deep learning models for face recognition against image degradations. IET Biom 7(1):81–89
15. Badrinarayanan V, Kendall A, Cipolla R (2017) Segnet: a deep convolutional encoder-decoder architecture for image segmentation. IEEE Trans Pattern Anal Mach Intell (TPAMI) 39(12):2481–2495
16. Nigam I, Vatsa M, Singh R (2015) Ocular biometrics: a survey of modalities and fusion approaches. Inf Fusion 26:1–35
17. De Marsico M, Petrosino A, Ricciardi S (2016) Iris recognition through machine learning techniques: a survey. PRL 82:106–115

18. Nguyen K, Fookes C, Jillela R, Sridharan S, Ross A (2017) Long range iris recognition: a survey. PR 72:123–143
19. Daugman J (1993) High confidence visual recognition of persons by a test of statistical independence. IEEE Trans Pattern Anal Mach Intell (TPAMI) 15(11):1148–1161
20. Daugman J (2009) How iris recognition works. In: The essential guide to image processing, pp 715–739. Elsevier
21. Daugman J (2007) New methods in iris recognition. IEEE Trans Syst Man Cybern (TSMC) Part B 37(5):1167–1175
22. Monro DM, Rakshit S, Zhang D (2007) DCT-based iris recognition. IEEE Trans Pattern Anal Mach Intell (TPAMI) 29(4):586–595
23. Miyazawa K, Ito K, Aoki T, Kobayashi K, Nakajima H (2008) An effective approach for iris recognition using phase-based image matching. IEEE Trans Pattern Anal Mach Intell (TPAMI) 30(10):1741–1756
24. Sun Z, Tan T (2009) Ordinal measures for iris recognition. IEEE Trans Pattern Anal Mach Intell (TPAMI) 31(12):2211–2226
25. Sun Z, Zhang H, Tan T, Wang J (2014) Iris image classification based on hierarchical visual codebook. IEEE Trans Pattern Anal Mach Intell (TPAMI) 36(6):1120–1133
26. Gangwar A, Joshi A (2016) Deepirisnet: deep iris representation with applications in iris recognition and cross-sensor iris recognition. In: 2016 IEEE international conference on image processing (ICIP), pp 2301–2305, Sept 2016
27. Liu N, Zhang M, Li H, Sun Z, Tan T (2016) Deepiris: learning pairwise filter bank for heterogeneous iris verification. Pattern Recogn Lett 82:154–161
28. Xingqiang T, Jiangtao X, Peihu L (2017) Deep convolutional features for iris recognition. In: Proceedings of the 12th Chinese conference biometric recognition CCBR 2017, pp 391–400, Cham, 2017. Springer International Publishing
29. Zhao Z, Kumar A (2017) Towards more accurate iris recognition using deeply learned spatially corresponding features. In: International conference on computer vision, ICCV 2017, pp 1–10
30. Nguyen K, Fookes C, Ross A, Sridharan S (2018) Iris recognition with off-the-shelf CNN features: a deep learning perspective. IEEE Access 6:18848–18855
31. Park U, Ross A, Jain AK (2009) Periocular biometrics in the visible spectrum: a feasibility study. In: 2009 IEEE 3rd international conference on biometrics: theory, applications, and systems, pp 1–6. IEEE
32. Uzair M, Mahmood A, Mian A, McDonald C (2013) Periocular biometric recognition using image sets. In: IEEE winter conference on applications of computer vision (WACV), pp 246–251
33. Sequeira A, Chen L, Ferryman J, Wild P, Alonso-Fernandez F, Bigun J, Raja K, Raghavendra R, Busch C, Freitas Pereira T et al (2017) Cross-eyed 2017: cross-spectral iris/periocular recognition database and competition. In: IEEE international joint conference on biometrics (IJCB)
34. Proença H, Neves J (2018) Deep-prwis: periocular recognition without the iris and sclera using deep learning frameworks. IEEE Trans Inf Forensics Secur (TIFS) 13(4):888–896
35. Zhao Z, Kumar A (2017) Accurate periocular recognition under less constrained environment using semantics-assisted convolutional neural network. IEEE Trans Inf Forensics Secur (TIFS) 12(5):1017–1030
36. Alonso-Fernandez F, Bigun J (2015) Near-infrared and visible-light periocular recognition with gabor features using frequency-adaptive automatic eye detection. IET Biom 4(2):74–89
37. Das A, Mondal P, Pal U, Blumenstein M, Ferrer M (2017) Sclera vessel pattern synthesis based on a non-parametric texture synthesis technique. In: Proceedings of computer vision and image processing (CVIP), pp 241–250. Springer
38. Alkassar S, Woo WL, Dlay S, Chambers J (2016) Sclera recognition: on the quality measure and segmentation of degraded images captured under relaxed imaging conditions. IET Biom 6(4):266–275
39. Yadav D, Kohli N, Doyle J, Singh R, Vatsa M, Bowyer K (2014) Unraveling the effect of textured contact lenses on iris recognition. IEEE Trans Inf Forensics Secur (TIFS) 9(5):851–862

40. Raja KB, Raghavendra R, Vemuri VK, Busch C (2015) Smartphone based visible iris recognition using deep sparse filtering. PRL 57:33–42
41. Das A, Pal U, Ferrer MA, Blumenstein M (2015) SSBC 2015: sclera segmentation benchmarking competition. In: International conference on biometrics: theory, applications, and systems (BTAS), pp 1–6
42. Das A, Pal U, Ferrer MA, Blumenstein M (2013) SSRBC 2016: sclera segmentation and recognition benchmarking competition. In: International conference on biometrics (ICB), pp 1–6
43. Maxwell EG, Tripti C (2013) A comparison between contrast limited adaptive histogram equalization and gabor filter sclera blood vessel enhancement techniques. Int J Soft Comput Eng (IJSCE) 3(4):22–5
44. Tankasala SP, Doynov P, Derakhshani RR, Ross A, Crihalmeanu S (2011) Biometric recognition of conjunctival vasculature using GLCM features. In: 2011 international conference on image information processing (ICIIP), pp 1–6, Nov 2011
45. Das A, Pal U, Ferrer Ballester MA, Blumenstein M (2014) Fuzzy logic based selera recognition. In: 2014 IEEE international conference on fuzzy systems, pp 561–568
46. Das A, Pal U, Ferrer Ballester MA, Blumenstein M (2013) A new method for sclera vessel recognition using OLBP. In: Sun Z, Shan S, Yang G, Zhou J, Wang Y, Yin Y (eds) Biometric Recognition. Springer International Publishing, Cham, pp 370–377
47. CASIA Iris Image Database. http://biometrics.idealtest.org/
48. Proença H, Alexandre L (2005) Ubiris: a noisy iris image database. In: International conference on image analysis and processing (ICIAP), pp 970–977. Springer
49. Bowyer KW, Flynn PJ (2016) The ND-IRIS-0405 iris image dataset. Technical report, Notre Dame University
50. Hosseini MS, Araabi BN, Soltanian-Zadeh H (2010) Pigment melanin: pattern for iris recognition. IEEE Trans Instrum Meas 59(4):792–804
51. Kumar A, Passi A (2010) Comparison and combination of iris matchers for reliable personal authentication. Pattern Recogn 43(3):1016–1026
52. Proença H, Filipe S, Santos R, Oliveira J, Alexandre LA (2010) The UBIRIS.v2: a database of visible wavelength iris images captured on-the-move and at-a-distance. IEEE Trans Pattern Anal Mach Intell (TPAMI) 32(8):1529–1535
53. De Marsico M, Nappi M, Riccio D, Wechsler H (2015) Mobile iris challenge evaluation (MICHE)-I, biometric iris dataset and protocols. Pattern Recogn Letters 57:17–23
54. Padole CN, Proenca H (2012) Periocular recognition: analysis of performance degradation factors. In: 5th IAPR international conference on biometrics (ICB), pp 439–445
55. Sharma A, Verma S, Vatsa M, Singh R (2014) On cross spectral periocular recognition. In: IEEE international conference on image processing (ICIP), pp 5007–5011. IEEE
56. Hosseini MS, Araabi BN, Soltanian-Zadeh H (2010) Pigment melanin: pattern for iris recognition. IEEE Trans Instrum Meas (TIM) 59(4):792–804
57. Rot P, Štruc V, Peer P (2018) Deep multi-class eye segmentation for ocular biometrics. In: IEEE international work conference on bioinspired intelligence (IWOBI)
58. Emeršič Ž, Gabriel L, Štruc V, Peer P (2018) Convolutional encoder-decoder networks for pixel-wise ear detection and segmentation. IET Biom 7(3):175–184
59. Simonyan K, Zisserman A (2015) Very deep convolutional networks for large-scale image recognition
60. Kendall A, Gal Y, Cipolla R (2018) Multi-task learning using uncertainty to weigh losses for scene geometry and semantics. In: Proceedings of the IEEE conference on computer vision and pattern recognition, pp 7482–7491
61. Krizhevsky A, Sutskever I, Hinton G (2012) Imagenet classification with deep convolutional neural networks. In: Conference on neural information processing systems (NIPS), pp 1097–1105
62. Yin X, Liu X (2017) Multi-task convolutional neural network for pose-invariant face recognition. IEEE Trans Image Process (TIP)

63. Lozej J, Meden B, Štruc V, Peer P (2018) End-to-end iris segmentation using u-net. In: IEEE international work conference on bioinspired intelligence (IWOBI)
64. Križaj J, Štruc V, Dobrišek S (2013) Combining 3d face representations using region covariance descriptors and statistical models. In: 2013 10th IEEE international conference and workshops on automatic face and gesture recognition (FG), pp 1–7. IEEE
65. Štruc V (2012) The PhD face recognition toolbox: toolbox description and user manual. Faculty of Electrical Engineering Ljubljana
66. Vesnicer B, Žganec Gros J, Pavešić N, Štruc V (2012) Face recognition using simplified probabilistic linear discriminant analysis. Int J Adv Robot Syst (IJARS) 9(5):180
67. Glorot X, Bengio Y (2012) Understanding the difficulty of training deep feedforward neural networks. In: Proceedings of the thirteenth international conference on artificial intelligence and statistics (AISTATS), pp 249–256
68. Štruc V, Pavešić N (2009) Phase congruency features for palm-print verification. IET Signal Process 3(4):258–268
69. Savič T, Pavešić N (2007) Personal recognition based on an image of the palmar surface of the hand. Pattern Recogn 40(11):3152–3163
70. Lin G, Milan A, Shen C, Reid I (2017) Refinenet: multi-path refinement networks for high-resolution semantic segmentation. In: IEEE conference on computer vision and pattern recognition (CVPR)
71. Wang F, Jiang M, Qian C, Yang S, Li C, Zhang H, Wang X, Tang X (2017) Residual attention network for image classification. In: 2017 IEEE conference on computer vision and pattern recognition (CVPR), pp 6450–6458
72. Ronneberger O, Fischer P, Brox T (2015) U-Net: convolutional networks for biomedical image segmentation. In: 18th international conference, proceedings, part III, medical image computing and computer-assisted intervention (MICCAI), pp 234–241. Springer International Publishing, Cham
73. Riccio D, Brancati N, Frucci M, Gragnaniello D (2017) An unsupervised approach for eye sclera segmentation. In: Iberoamerican congress on pattern recognition (CIARP), pp 550–557. Springer
74. Gonzalez RC, Woods RE (2007) Image processing. Digit Image Process 2
75. Miura N, Nagasaka A, Miyatake T (2007) Extraction of finger-vein patterns using maximum curvature points in image profiles. IEICE Trans Inf Syst 90(8):1185–1194
76. Miura N, Nagasaka A, Miyatake T (2004) Feature extraction of finger-vein patterns based on repeated line tracking and its application to personal identification. Mach Vis Appl 15(4):194–203
77. Coye T (2015) A novel retinal blood vessel segmentation algorithm for fundus images. http://www.mathworks.com/matlabcentral/fileexchange/50839. matlab central file exchange. Accessed 4 Mar 2019
78. Azzopardi George, Strisciuglio Nicola, Vento Mario, Petkov Nicolai (2015) Trainable cosfire filters for vessel delineation with application to retinal images. Med Image Anal 19(1):46–57
79. Strisciuglio Nicola, Azzopardi George, Vento Mario, Petkov Nicolai (2016) Supervised vessel delineation in retinal fundus images with the automatic selection of B-COSFIRE filters. Mach Vis Appl 27(8):1137–1149
80. Lowe DG (1999) Object recognition from local scale-invariant features. Int J Comput Vis (ICCV) 2:1150–1157. IEEE
81. Bay H, Tuytelaars T, Van Gool L (2006) Surf: speeded up robust features. In: European conference on computer vision, pp 404–417. Springer
82. Rublee E, Rabaud V, Konolige K, Bradski G (2011) ORB: an efficient alternative to sift or surf

Part IV
Security and Privacy in Vascular Biometrics

Chapter 14
Presentation Attack Detection for Finger Recognition

Jascha Kolberg, Marta Gomez-Barrero, Sushma Venkatesh, Raghavendra Ramachandra and Christoph Busch

Abstract Whereas other biometric characteristics, such as the face, are readily available for an eventual attacker through social media or easy to capture with a conventional smartphone, vein patterns can only be acquired with dedicated sensors. This fact makes them relevant not only for recognition purposes but especially for Presentation Attack Detection (PAD), for instance, in combination with fingerprint recognition. In this chapter, we make use of this combination and present a finger vein-based PAD algorithm to detect presentation attacks targeting fingerprint recognition. The experiments are carried out on a newly collected database, comprising 32 species of Presentation Attack Instruments ranging from printed artefacts to more sophisticated fingerprint overlays. The results show that our method preserves a convenient usage while detecting around 90% of the attacks. However, thin and transparent fingerprint overlays remain very challenging.

Keywords Presentation attack detection · Fingerprint recognition

14.1 Introduction

In spite of the many advantages offered by biometric recognition with respect to other traditional authentication methods (the well-known Lema "forget about PINs or

J. Kolberg (✉) · M. Gomez-Barrero · C. Busch
da/sec - Biometrics and Internet Security Research Group, Hochschule Darmstadt, Darmstadt, Germany
e-mail: jascha.kolberg@h-da.de

M. Gomez-Barrero
e-mail: marta.gomez-barrero@h-da.de

C. Busch
e-mail: christoph.busch@h-da.de

S. Venkatesh · R. Ramachandra
Norwegian Information Security Laboratory, Norwegian University of Science and Technology, NTNU, Gjøvik, Norway
e-mail: sushma.venkatesh@ntnu.no

R. Ramachandra
e-mail: raghavendra.ramachandra@ntnu.no

A. Uhl et al. (eds.), *Handbook of Vascular Biometrics*, Advances in Computer Vision and Pattern Recognition, https://doi.org/10.1007/978-3-030-27731-4_14

passwords, you are your own key"), biometric systems are also vulnerable to external attacks. As a consequence, the security and privacy offered by biometric recognition systems can be undermined. Given its serious implications, the vulnerabilities of biometric systems to different types of attacks have been the subject of numerous studies in the last decades for different characteristics, including fingerprint [9, 18, 64], face [1], iris [23, 26, 27], voice [3] or multimodal systems [2, 10, 28].

Among other possible points of attack [64], the biometric capture device is probably the most exposed one: the attacker does not need to know any details about the inner modules of the biometric system in order to attack the sensor. To fool the biometric system, he can present the capture device with a *Presentation Attack Instrument* (PAI), such as a 3D mask [16], a printed finger vein image [76] or a fingerprint overlay [18]. These attacks are known in the literature as *Presentation Attacks* (PA) [38].

In order to prevent such attacks, *Presentation Attack Detection* (PAD) methods have been recently developed to automatically distinguish between bona fide (i.e. real, live or genuine) presentations and access attempts carried out by means of PAIs [49]. Incorporating such countermeasures in biometric systems are crucial, especially in unattended scenarios. Given the importance of increasing the robustness of biometric systems to these attacks, and hence the systems' security, this area of research has attracted a considerable attention within the biometric community in the last decade. In fact, several international projects like the European Tabula Rasa [70] and BEAT [48], or the more recent US Odin research program [55], deal with these security concerns. In addition, the LivDet liveness detection competition series on iris [79] and fingerprint [80] have been running since 2009. In turn, these initiatives have led to a wide number of publications on PAD methodologies for several biometric characteristics, including iris [19], fingerprint [47, 67], or face [20].

Compared to other biometric characteristics, such as fingerprint or handwritten signature, the use of finger vein for recognition purposes are relatively new: the first commercial applications date back to 2005 by Hitachi Ltd [45]. The first studies on the vulnerability of finger vein recognition systems to presentation attacks were carried out only in 2014 [76]. In this work, Tome et al. showed how a simple print out of a finger vein image could successfully fool the system in up to 86% of the attempts. A similar evaluation was carried out by Tome and Marcel [74] in 2015 for palm vein images, where the success rate of the attacks reached figures as high as 75%. It is hence crucial to protect vein-based systems from these presentation attacks, which, given their simplicity, can be carried out by potentially any individual. This is especially relevant for finger vein, due to the extended use of the corresponding sensors in ATMs (i.e. unsupervised scenario) in countries as diverse as China,[1] Turkey,[2] Taiwan,[3] or Poland.[4]

These facts call for a joint effort within the biometrics community to develop PAD techniques for vein-based systems. In this context, the first approach based on Fourier

[1] https://findbiometrics.com/finger-vein-authentication-atms-china-502087/.

[2] http://www.hitachi.com/New/cnews/120206b.pdf.

[3] http://www.hitachi-omron-ts.com/news/201607-001.html.

[4] http://edition.cnn.com/2010/WORLD/europe/07/05/first.biometric.atm.europe/index.html.

and wavelet transforms was proposed in 2013 by Nguyen et al. [51]. Two years later, the first competition on finger vein PAD was organised [75], where three different teams participated. Since then, different PAD approaches have been presented, based on either a video sequence and motion magnification [60], texture analysis [44, 61, 71], image quality metrics [7], or more recently, neural networks [52, 59, 63] and image decomposition [58].

All the aforementioned works are focused on the detection of printed finger vein images, or, in some cases, of replay attacks carried out with digital displays [61]. In all cases, almost perfect error rates are achieved, thereby indicating that such PAIs can be easily detected with the current techniques. However, the applications of finger vein-based PAD are not limited to finger vein recognition. In fact, the development of multimodal capture devices which are able to acquire both finger vein images or videos, and finger photos, opens new lines of research [62]: biometric recognition can be based on fingerprints extracted from the photos, and PAD techniques can be developed for the finger vein data. This approach is being currently followed in the BATL project [6] within the US Odin research program [55]: among other sensors, finger vein images are used to detect fingerprint presentation attacks. As with the aforementioned finger vein print outs, it has already been shown that fingerprints can be recovered even from the stored ISO templates [18], and then be transformed into a PAI, which is recognised as a fingerprint. However, most fingerprint PAIs do not take into account the blood flow, which is also harder to simulate. On the other hand, the finger vein printed images analysed in the finger vein PAD literature will not be able to fool the fingerprint scanner, as it contains no fingerprint. We can therefore also include a finger vein PAD module in multimodal finger sensors designed for fingerprint recognition, thereby making it harder for an eventual attacker to design a PAI which is able to bypass both sensors.

In this chapter, we will first summarise in Sect. 14.2 the main concepts and evaluation metrics for biometric PAD defined in the recent ISO/IEC 30107 standard [38, 39]. The state of the art in fingervein and fingerprint PAD is subsequently reviewed in Sect. 14.3. We will then describe the multimodal sensor developed in the BATL project and the proposed approach to finger vein-based PAD to detect fingerprint PAIs (Sect. 14.4). The proposed method is evaluated according to the ISO/IEC 30107 standard [39] in Sect. 14.5. The chapter ends with the final discussion and conclusions in Sect. 14.6.

14.2 Presentation Attack Detection

Presentation attacks are defined within the ISO/IEC 30107 standard on biometric presentation attack detection [38] as the "*presentation to the biometric data capture subsystem with the goal of interfering with the operation of the biometric system*". The attacker may aim at impersonating someone else (i.e. impostor) or avoiding being recognised due to black-listing (i.e. identity concealer).

In the following, we include the main definitions presented within the ISO/IEC 30107-3 standard on biometric presentation attack detection—part 3: testing and reporting [39], which will be used throughout the chapter:

- Bona fide presentation: "*interaction of the biometric capture subject and the biometric data capture subsystem in the fashion intended by the policy of the biometric system*". That is, a normal or genuine presentation.
- Attack presentation/presentation attack: "*presentation to the biometric data capture subsystem with the goal of interfering with the operation of the biometric system*". That is, an attack carried out on the capture device to either conceal your identity or impersonate someone else.
- Presentation Attack Instrument (PAI): "*biometric characteristic or object used in a presentation attack*". For instance, a silicone 3D mask or an ecoflex fingerprint overlay.
- PAI species: "*class of presentation attack instruments created using a common production method and based on different biometric characteristics*".

In order to evaluate the vulnerabilities of biometric systems to PAs, the following metrics should be used:

- Impostor Attack Presentation Match Rate (IAPMR): "*proportion of impostor attack presentations using the same PAI species in which the target reference is matched*".
- Attack Presentation Classification Error Rate (APCER): " *proportion of attack presentations using the same PAI species incorrectly classified as bona fide presentations in a specific scenario*".
- Bona Fide Presentation Classification Error Rate (BPCER): " *proportion of bona fide presentations incorrectly classified as presentation attacks in a specific scenario*".

Derived from the aforementioned metrics, a global measure can be computed for an easier benchmark across different systems: the Detection Equal Error Rate (D-EER). It is defined as the error rate at the operating point where APCER = BPCER.

14.3 Related Works

In addition to the initial review of the existing works on finger vein PAD presented in the introductory chapter, we first survey those works in detail, further discussing the PAI species analysed and the detection performance achieved (see Sect. 14.3.1). We subsequently summarise in Sect. 14.3.2 the most relevant works on fingerprint PAD, since our main aim is to detect fingerprint PAIs with finger vein images. For more details and a more extensive survey on fingerprint PAD, the reader is referred to [47, 67].

14.3.1 Finger Vein Presentation Attack Detection

A summary of the most relevant works in finger vein PAD is presented in Table 14.1, classified according to the feature types extracted (handcrafted versus deep learning) and the publication year. In addition, the main performance metrics over the selected database is reported.

As mentioned in Sect. 14.1, research on finger vein recognition is relatively new. As a direct consequence, the pioneering work on finger vein PAD was published as recent as in 2013 [51]. Nguyen et al. proposed the combination of features in both spatial and frequency domains through the Fourier and two different wavelet transforms (i.e. Haar and Daubechies). They achieved a D-EER as low as 1.5% in their experiments on a self-acquired database comprising both bona fides and a single PAI species: printed finger vein images.

One year later, in 2014, Tome et al. analysed in-depth the vulnerabilities of finger vein recognition systems to PAs, revealing an alarming IAPMR up to 86% for simple print outs of vein images [76]. This study motivated Tome et al. to organise the first competition on finger vein PAD in 2015 [75]. In addition to the baseline system developed at Idiap,[5] three teams participated, proposing different approaches to detect the PAs, namely: (i) Binarised Statistical Image Features (BSIF), (ii) a monogenic global descriptor to capture local energy and local orientation at coarse level and (iii) a set of local descriptors including Local Binary Patterns (LBP), Local Phase Quantisation (LPQ), a patch-wise Short-time Fourier transform (STFT) and a Weber Local Descriptor (WLD). In all cases, the final classification was carried out with Support Vector Machines (SVMs), achieving remarkable detection rates with a low complexity. Another byproduct of the competition was the establishment of the Idiap Research Institute VERA Fingervein Database [77] as a benchmark for finger vein PAD (see Table 14.1) with a single PAI species: printed images. This, in turn, motivated the biometrics community to pursue the development of more efficient PAD techniques.

Also in 2015, Raghavendra et al. [60] analysed short video sequences with the aid of Eulerian video magnification [78]. The goal was to amplify the blood flow and thus detect the printed artefacts. They compared the newly proposed method with reimplementations of the algorithms presented in [75] over a self-acquired database: the ACER was reduced 5 to 23 times, thus proving the soundness of the proposed approach. In the same year, Tirunagari et al. proposed the use of Dynamic Mode Decomposition (DMD), which is a mathematical method developed to extract information from non-linear complex fluid flows [71]. They designed a windowed DMD technique in order to extract micro-texture information from a single image, which is decomposed into its maximum variance at column level, and the corresponding residual or noise image. Using SVMs for classification over the VERA DB, they achieved D-EERs outperforming other texture descriptors.

As for other biometric characteristics, texture patterns have been extensively analysed for finger vein PAD. In addition to the approaches presented in [71, 75],

[5] http://www.idiap.ch/en/scientific-research/biometrics-security-and-privacy.

Table 14.1 Summary of the most relevant methodologies for **finger vein** presentation attack detection. For performance evaluation, the metrics are the ones reported in the articles, where "Acc." stands for detection accuracy

Category	Year	References	Description	Performance	Database
Hand-crafted	2013	[51]	FFT, Haar and Daubechies wavelets + Fusion	D-EER $\geq$ 1.5%	Own DB
		[60]	Video analysis with Eulerian Video Magnification (EVM)	APCER = 5.20%	Own DB
				BPCER = 2.00%	
		[61]	Steerable pyramids	APCER = 2.4%	Own DB
				BPCER = 0.4%	
	2015	[75]	BSIF	APCER = 0%	VERA (full)
				BPCER = 8.00%	
			Monogenic scale space based texture descriptors	APCER = 0%	
				BPCER = 0%	
			LBP, LPQ, STFT, WLD	APCER = 0%	
				BPCER = 0%	
		[71]	Windowed DMD as micro-texture descriptor	D-EER = 0.08%	
	2016	[44]	LBP Extensions	Acc $\geq$ 95%	
	2017	[7]	Image Quality Assessment + Fusion	Acc $\approx$ 99.8%	
	2018	[58]	Total Variation Decomposition + LBP	APCER = 0%	
				BPCER = 0%	
Deep learning	2017	[59]	FPNet (ad-hoc CNN)	APCER = 0%	
				BPCER = 0%	
		[52]	D-CNN (AlexNet or VGG-16) + PCA + SVM	APCER = 0%	
				BPCER = 0%	
	2018	[63]	D-CNN (AlexNet) + LDA or SVM	APCER = 1.82% / 0%	Own DB
				BPCER = 0%	

Raghavendra and Busch included a new PAI species in a subsequent work [61]: a smartphone display. In this case, they considered the residual high frequency band extracted from steerable pyramids and a SVM, achieving again ACERs around 3%. The following year, Kocher et al. thoroughly analysed different LBP extensions in [44], to finally conclude that the baseline LBP technique performs as good as its "improvements". Finally, in a combined approach, Qiu et al. used total variation decomposition to divide the finger vein sample into its structural and noise components [58]. Using again LBP descriptors and SVMs, they achieved a perfect detection accuracy with APCER = BPCER = 0% over the VERA DB.

Another approach followed for PAD, in general, is based on the use of image quality assessment [21]. This technique was also analysed by Bhogal et al. in [7] for finger vein. In particular, they considered six different measures and their combinations, achieving a detection accuracy over 99%.

Finally, in the last years, Deep Learning (DL) has become a thriving topic [33], allowing computers to learn from experience and understand the world in terms of a hierarchy of simpler units. This way, DL has enabled significant advances in complex domains such as natural language processing [69], computer vision [81], biometric recognition in general, and finger vein PAD in particular. In this context, in 2017, Qiu et al. designed a new Convolutional Neural Network (CNN) for finger vein PAD, which they named FPNet [59]. This network achieved a perfect detection accuracy over the VERA DB. In the same year, Nguyen et al. used two different pre-trained models (i.e. AlexNet [46] and VGG-16 [66]) for the same task. After extracting the features with these nets, Nguyen et al. reduced their dimensionality with Principal Component Analysis (PCA) and used SVMs for final classification. Again, a perfect detection rate over the VERA DB was reported. In a similar fashion, Raghavendra et al. analysed in [63] the use of AlexNet with Linear Discriminant Analysis (LDA) and SVMs for classification purposes, also achieving perfect error rates over a self-acquired database.

14.3.2 Fingerprint Presentation Attack Detection

The excellent performance of the finger vein PAD methods described above has motivated us to also use finger vein images to detect fingerprint PAIs. However, let us first review the state of the art in fingerprint PAD. Given the vast number of articles studying this problem, we will summarise the most relevant ones for the present study and refer the reader to [47, 67, 72] for more comprehensive reviews.

In general, PAD approaches can be broadly classified into two categories: *software-based* methods perform a deeper analysis of the captured data to distinguish between bona fide and attack presentations, *hardware-based* setups make use of information captured by additional sensors. In contrast to the younger finger vein PAD research field, where only the former have been studied so far, for fingerprint PAD both approaches have been followed. Tables 14.2 and 14.3 provide a summary of the reviewed works, classified into soft- and hardware-based approaches. In addi-

Table 14.2 Summary of the most relevant methodologies for **software-based fingerprint** presentation attack detection. For performance evaluation, the metrics are the ones reported in the articles, where CCR stands for correct classification rate and ACER for average classification error rate

Year	References	Description	Performance	#PAI	Database
2007	[11]	Score fusion of pore spacing, noise, and statistical properties	CCR = 85.2%	1	Own DB
2008	[53]	LBP texture and wavelet energy fusion	CCR = 97.4%	2	Own DB
2011	[17]	Closed sweat pore extraction	APCER = 21.2% BPCER = 8.3%	4	Own DB
	[50]	Active sweat pore localisation	N/A	0	BFBIG-DB1
2014	[22]	25 image quality metrics	APCER < 13% BPCER ≤ 14%	3	LivDet 2009
	[40]	Multiscale LBP	D-EER = 7.52%	7	LivDet 2011
2016	[54]	Pre-trained CNNs (Best: VGG)	ACER = 2.90%	8	LivDet 2009-13
2017	[32]	Bag of Words and SIFT	APCER = 5% BPCER = 4.3%	7	LivDet 2011
2018	[41]	LBP extracted from Gaussian pyramids (PLBP)	ACER = 21.21%	7	LivDet 2013
	[12]	Minutiae-centred CNN several different scenarios	APCER < 7.3% BPCER = 1%	12	LivDet 2011-15, MSU-FPAD, PBSKD
	[13]	Minutiae-centred CNN generalisation	APCER = 4.7% BPCER = 0.2%	12	MSU-FPAD, PBSKD

tion, the number of PAI species and the main performance metrics over the selected databases are reported.

A typical example of software-based approaches is the detection of sweat pores in high-resolution fingerprint images [11, 17, 50]. Sweat pores are not visible in latent fingerprints and, because of their tiny size, it is challenging to include them in artefacts. Therefore, the existence of sweat pores can be utilised as an indicator of a bona fide sample.

Another classical approach, widely applied not only to fingerprint but to other biometric characteristics, is the extraction of textural information. Nikam and Agarwal [53] were among the first ones in 2008 to analyse this kind of approaches. On the one hand, they extracted Local Binary Pattern (LBP) histograms to capture textural details. On the other hand, the ridge frequency and orientation information were characterised using wavelet energy features. Both feature sets were fused and the dimensionality reduced with the Sequential Forward Floating Selection (SFFS) algorithm. For classification, the authors utilised a hybrid classifier, formed by fusing three classifiers: a neural network, SVMs and K-nearest neighbours. Over a self-

Table 14.3 Summary of the most relevant methodologies for **hardware-based fingerprint** presentation attack detection. For performance evaluation, the metrics are the ones reported in the articles

Year	References	Description	Performance	#PAI	Database
2011	[34]	Multi-spectral blanching effect, pulse	APCER = 0%	4	Own DB
			BPCER = 0%		
2013	[15]	Optical methods pulse, pressure, skin reflections	APCER = 10%	N/A	Own DB
			BPCER < 2%		
2018	[29]	SWIR spectral signatures + SVM	APCER = 5.7%	12	Own DB
			BPCER = 0%		
	[73]	SWIR + CNN	APCER = 0%	12	Own DB
			BPCER = 0%		
	[43]	LSCI + SVM	APCER = 15.5%	32	Own DB
		BSIF, LBP, HOG, histogram	BPCER = 0.2%		
	[37]	SWIR, LSCI + patch-based CNN	APCER = 0%	17	Own DB
			BPCER = 0%		
	[30]	Weighted score fusion + SVM SWIR, LSCI, vein	APCER = 6.6%	35	Own DB
			BPCER = 0.2%		
2019	[72]	SWIR + CNN fusion (pre-trained and from scratch)	APCER $\approx$ 7%	35	Own DB
			BPCER = 0.1%		
	[31]	Fusion of: SWIR + CNN and LSCI + hand-crafted features	APCER $\leq$ 3%	35	Own DB
			BPCER $\leq$ 0.1%		

acquired database comprising two different PAI fabrication materials and several mould materials, an overall classification rate up to 97.4% is reported.

In 2009, the LivDet competition series on fingerprint and iris started in a bi-annual basis [25]. The datasets provided quickly became the de facto standard for fingerprint PAD evaluations. For instance, Jia et al. [40] continued the research line based on texture information and proposed the use of two different variants of multi-scale LBP in combination with SVMs. Over the LivDet 2011 dataset, their method achieved a D-EER of 7.52%. More recently, Jiang et al. presented another approach to extract LBP features from multiple scales in [41]. In particular, a Gaussian pyramid was constructed from the input samples and the corresponding LBP histograms, extracted from three different levels, were classified using an SVM. Achieving an

ACER of 21% over the LivDet 2013 dataset, this method outperformed the algorithms presented in the competition.

In a more general approach, Galbally et al. [22] use 25 complementary image quality features to detect presentation attacks for face, iris and fingerprint on legacy data. Regarding fingerprint, they compare their approach with other state-of-the-art methods on the LivDet 2009 fingerprint database, which includes three different PAI species. Their results are competitive for 2014 and even outperform some previously published PAD algorithms on the same dataset. Their main advantage is its independency of the modality, and, additionally, the method is "simple, fast, non-intrusive, user-friendly, and cheap".

All the aforementioned approaches focus on the basic scenario where all PAI species in the test set are also included in the training test. However, a more realistic, and challenging, scenario should include additional "unknown attacks", or PAI species only used for testing purposes. In such a case, the detection performance usually decreases. To tackle this issue, Gonzalez-Soler et al. analysed in [32] the use of the Bag of Words feature encoding approach applied to local keypoint-based descriptors (dense Scale Invariant Feature Transform, SIFT). They compare their detection performance with other existing methods using feature descriptors, with no encoding schemes, and show a relative 25% improvement on the average Average Classification Error Rate (ACER, the performance metric used in the LivDet competitions) over the LivDet 2011 with respect to the state of the art. In addition, they present a fully compliant ISO evaluation in terms of APCER and BPCER for the first time for the LivDet datasets.

In contrast to the handcrafted approaches mentioned above, most of the newest approaches rely on deep learning. One of the first works directly related to fingerprint PAD based on conventional capture devices (i.e. a software-based method), was carried out by Nogueira et al. [54]. In more details, the following three CNNs were tested: (i) the pre-trained VGG [66], (ii) the pre-trained Alexnet [46] and (iii) a CNN with randomly initialised weights and trained from scratch. The authors benchmarked the ACER obtained with the networks over the LivDet 2009, 2011 and 2013 databases to a classical state of the art algorithm based on LBP. The best detection performance is achieved using a VGG pre-trained model and data augmentation (average ACER = 2.9%), with a clear improvement with respect to LBP (average ACER = 9.6%). It should be also noted that the ACER decreased between 25% and 50% (relative decrease) for all three networks tested when data augmentation was used.

More recently, Chugh et al. presented the current state of the art for the LivDet datasets in [12], and they evaluated it on multiple publicly available datasets including three LivDet datasets (2011, 2013, 2015), as well as their own collected and published MSU-FPAD and Precise Biometric Spoof-Kit datasets (PBSKD), which include in total 12 PAI species and more than 20000 samples. The so-called *Fingerprint Spoof Buster* [12] is a convolutional neural network (CNN) based on MobileNet [35], which is applied to minutiae-centred patches. Splitting the CNN input into patches allows them to train the network from scratch without over-fitting. They evaluate several different test scenarios and outperform other state-of-the-art approaches on the LivDet datasets. In a subsequent work [13], the *Fingerprint Spoof Buster's* generalisation capability is analysed by applying a leave-one-out protocol on all 12 PAI species from the MSU-FPAD and PBSKD datasets. They observe that some materials are harder to detect when not included during training and specify an optimised training set comprising six of twelve PAIs. The testing results in an APCER of 4.7% at a BPCER of 0.2%.

Even if the aforementioned works manage to achieve remarkably low error rates, PAD can also benefit from information captured by additional sensors, as any other pattern recognition task. To that end, some hardware-based approaches utilise different illumination techniques or capture the pulse frequencies. Hengfoss et al. [34] analysed in 2011 the reflections for all wavelengths between 400 and 1650 nm on the blanching effect. This effect appears when the finger is pressed against a surface and the blood is squeezed out due to the compression of the tissue. Furthermore, they utilise pulse oximetry but admit that this approach takes more time and thus is less desirable for PAD. They manage to correctly distinguish living fingers, cadaver fingers and three PAIs for both methods, and conclude that those dynamic effects (i.e. blanching and pulse) only occur for living fingers. Two years later, Drahansky et al. [15] proposed new optical handcrafted PAD methods for pulse, colour change under pressure and skin reflection for different wavelengths (470, 550 and 700 nm). These methods are evaluated on a database comprising 150 fingerprints, achieving the best results for the wavelength approach. Additionally, they analyse 11 different skin diseases that could occur on the fingertip. However, the influence on the detection performance was not tested.

Over the last five years, it has been shown that the skin reflection within the Short-wave Infrared (SWIR) spectrum of 900–1700 nm are independent from the skin tone. This fact was first analysed by NIST [14] and later on confirmed by Steiner et al. [68] for face PAD. Building upon the work of [68], Gomez-Barrero et al. [29] apply the spectral signature concept first developed for facial images to fingerprint PAD. Their preliminary experiments, over a rather small database, show that most materials, except for orange play doh, respond different than human skin in the SWIR wavelengths of 1200, 1300, 1450 and 1550 nm. However, with the use of fine-tuned CNNs, also the orange play doh is correctly classified in a subsequent work [73]. In a follow-up study [72], Tolosana et al. benchmark both pre-trained CNN models, and design and train a new residual CNN from scratch for PAD purposes for the same SWIR data. Over a larger dataset including 35 different PAI species and more than 4700 samples, they show that a combination of two different CNNs can achieve a remarkable performance: an APCER around 7% for a BPCER of 0.1%. In addition, the evaluation protocol includes 5 PAI species considered only for testing, thereby proving the soundness of their approach even in the presence of unknown attacks.

Additionally, it has been shown that Laser Speckle Contrast Imaging (LSCI) can be used for PAD purposes [43]. The LSCI technique comes from biomedical applications, where it has been applied to visualise and monitor microvascular blood flow in biological tissues, such as skin and retina [65]. Keilbach et al. capture the blood movement beneath the skin to differentiate living fingers from presentation attacks in [43]. However, the utilised laser also penetrates thin transparent fingerprint overlays, thereby detecting the underlying blood flow and falsely classifying the presentation as a bona fide one. Therefore, for a BPCER of 0.2% (system focused on the user convenience), the APCER increases to 15.5%.

Combining SWIR and LSCI, Hussein et al. [37] use a patch-based CNN to classify multi-spectral samples from both domains. For both techniques, low error rates are reported and a combined fusion achieves a perfect detection performance over a database compromising 551 bona fides and 227 PAs, including 17 different PAI species.

Further research by Gomez-Barrero et al. [30] applies a score-level fusion method based on handcrafted features to benefit from different domains, including SWIR, LSCI and vein images. Their training set comprises only 136 samples in order to evaluate the approach on 4531 samples in the test set containing 35 different PAI species. The weights for the fusion are computed on 64 samples of the development set. An APCER $< 10\%$ for a BPCER $= 0.1\%$ is reported, as well as an APCER of 6.6% for a BPCER $= 0.2\%$, thus yielding secure systems even for very low BPCERs.

Lastly, in a subsequent work by Gomez-Barrero et al. [31], the SWIR CNN approaches proposed in [72] are combined with an enhancement of the handcrafted features extracted from the LSCI data in [43]. This combined approach, tested on the same database comprising 35 different PAI species, shows a clear improvement on the detection capabilities of the proposed method, even if only 2 sets of images are used (i.e. reduced capture device cost): the D-EER is reduced from 2.7 to 0.5%.

14.4 Proposed Finger Vein Presentation Attack Detection

As indicated in Sect. 14.1, we will now focus on the development of PAD techniques based on finger vein data, in order to detect fingerprint PAIs. It should be noted that the PAD algorithm can process data that is captured simultaneously with a single capture device from both the finger vein and the fingerprint. Otherwise, if the capture with both sensors was done sequentially, the attacker might exchange the PAI used for fingerprint verification with his bona fide finger for the PAD capture process. Therefore, in this section, we first describe a multimodal capture device which is able to acquire both fingerprint and finger vein images (Sect. 14.4.1). We subsequently present an efficient PAD method applied to the finger vein data in Sect. 14.4.2. Given that some fingerprint overlays may still reveal part of the vein structure, we will focus on texture analysis to detect PAs in a real-time fashion using a single image.

14.4.1 Multimodal Finger Capture Device

Given the requirement to capture both fingerprint and finger veins, a contact-less multimodal capture device is used to acquire photos of fingerprints as well as finger veins. A diagram of the inner components of the capture device is depicted in Fig. 14.1. As it may be observed, the camera and illumination boards are placed inside a closed

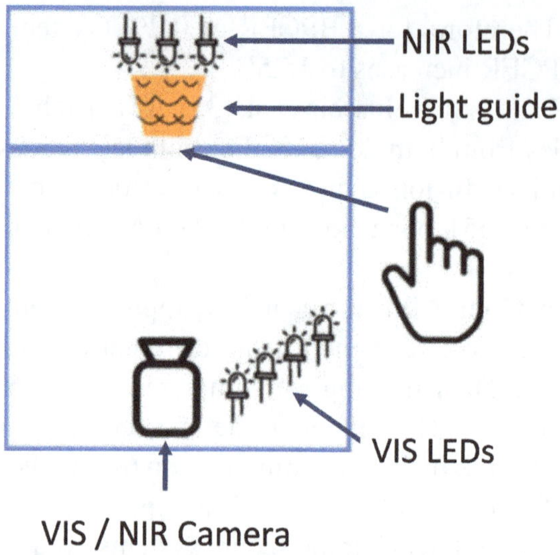

Fig. 14.1 Sensor diagram: a box, with a slot in the middle to place the finger, encloses all the components: a single camera, two sets of LEDs for visible (VIS) and NIR illumination and the light guide necessary for the finger vein capture (more details in Sect. 14.4.1.2)

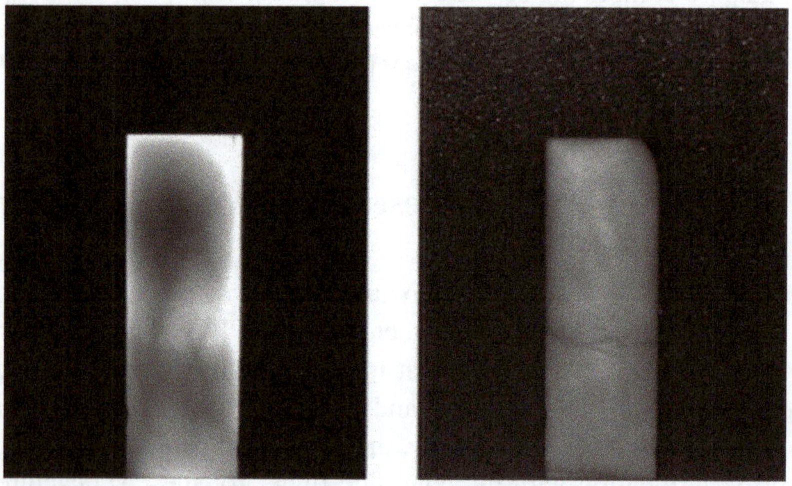

(a) Finger vein (NIR) sample. (b) Finger photo (VIS) sample.

Fig. 14.2 Full bona fide samples as they are captured by the camera

box, which includes an open slot in the middle. When the finger is placed there, all ambient light is blocked and therefore only the desired wavelengths are used for the acquisition of the images. In particular, we have used a Basler acA1300-60gm Near-infrared (NIR) camera, which captures 1280 × 1024 px. images, with an Edmunds Optics 35mm C Series VIS-NIR Lens. This camera is used for both frontal visible (VIS) light images and NIR finger vein samples (see the following subsections for more details on each individual sensor).

An example finger photo as it is captured by the camera is shown in Fig. 14.2, for both the finger vein and the finger photo acquisition. As it can be seen, the

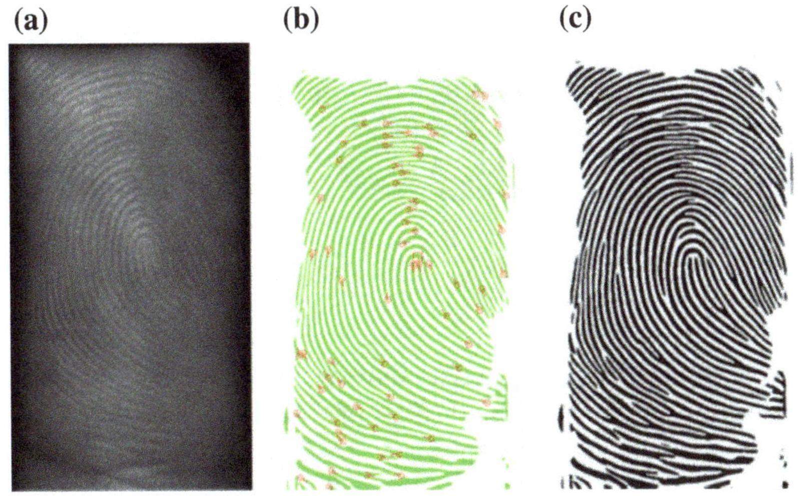

Fig. 14.3 Bona fide finger photos: **a** visible (VIS) light image, **b** minutiae extracted with Verifinger and **c** fingerprint enrolled with Verifinger

central Region of Interest (ROI) corresponding to the open slot where the finger is placed needs to be extracted from the background before the images can be further processed. Given that the finger is always placed over the open slot, and the camera does not move, a simple fixed size cropping can be applied.

14.4.1.1 Finger Photo Sensor

The most important requirement for the design of the finger photo sensor is its compatibility with legacy (optical) sensors. In other words, we need to make sure that fingerprints can be extracted from the finger photos captured within the visible wavelengths and be subsequently used for verification with Commercial off-the-shelf (COTS) systems. In order to fulfil this requirement, the resolution and focus of the selected camera and lens combination need to be high enough to yield fingerprints with at least the equivalence to 500 dpi resolution. We have therefore chosen the aforementioned Basler and Edmunds Optics components.

To illustrate how the finger photos can be used for fingerprint recognition, Fig. 14.3 shows the captured bona fide sample (Fig. 14.3a). Next to it, the minutiae extracted with Neurotechnology VeriFinger SDK[6] (Fig. 14.3b), which has been defined as the standard fingerprint recognition SDK within the Odin program, and the corresponding enrolled fingerprint (Fig, 14.3c) are depicted. As it may be observed, the minutiae are correctly detected within the fingerprint area. It should be noted that, if this system should be used in combination with optical sensors, the finger photo needs to be flipped (left-to-right) before enrolment or comparison.

[6] https://www.neurotechnology.com/verifinger.html.

Fig. 14.4 Bona fide finger vein ROI, of size 830 × 240 px

14.4.1.2 Finger Vein Sensor

The finger vein capture device comprises three main components, namely: (i) a NIR light source behind the finger with 20 LEDs of 940 nm, (ii) the corresponding NIR camera and lens and (iii) an elevated physical structure to obtain the adequate amount of light.

It should be noted that, in order to capture high-quality finger vein samples, it is vital to let only the right amount of light intensity penetrate through the finger. To achieve the correct amount of light transmission, a physical structure with elevation is placed to concentrate the light intensity to the specified area, referred to in Fig. 14.1 as "light guide". The subject interacts with the sensor by placing a finger on the small gap provided between the NIR light source and the camera. The NIR spectral light is placed facing the camera in a unique way, so that the light emitting from the NIR spectrum penetrates through the finger. Since the haemoglobin blocks the NIR illumination, the veins appear as darker areas in the captured image. A sample image is depicted in Fig. 14.4, where the veins are clearly visible even before preprocessing the sample.

14.4.2 Presentation Attack Detection Algorithm

As mentioned at the beginning of this Section, we will focus on texture analysis of the finger vein samples in order to discriminate bona fide samples from presentation attacks. To that end, we have chosen a combination of Gaussian pyramids and Local Binary Patterns (LBP), referred to as PLBP, which was proposed in [57] as a general descriptor. The main advantage of this texture descriptor lies on the fact that, by extracting the LBP features from the hierarchical spatial pyramids, texture information at different resolution levels can be considered. In fact, the PLBP approach was used in [41] for fingerprint PAD over the LivDet 2013 DB [24], achieving results within the state of the art for only three pyramid levels. In order to analyse the influence of the different pyramid levels, we compare the results using up to 16 pyramid levels.

The flowchart of the proposed method is shown in Fig. 14.5. First, the Gaussian pyramids are computed from the original cropped image or ROI (see Fig. 14.4). Subsequently, LBP images are generated for every pyramid level, resulting in the PLBP images. Then, histograms are computed from the PLBP images and classified

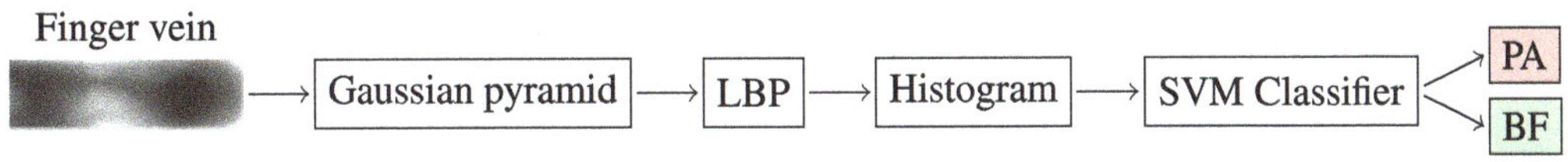

Fig. 14.5 General diagram of the proposed PAD algorithm. From the finger vein photo, the Gaussian pyramid is computed first, then LBP is applied and the corresponding histogram serves as input to the SVM classifier

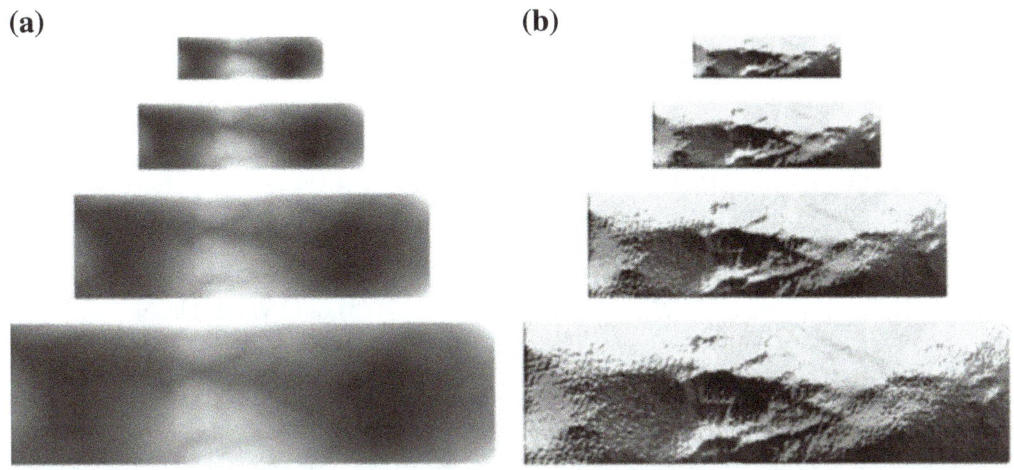

Fig. 14.6 Illustration of example pyramids for: **a** Gaussian pyramid of vein images and **b** LBP images of this Gaussian pyramid

with a Support Vector Machine (SVM). Each step is described in more detail in the following paragraphs.

Gaussian pyramids. For multi-resolution analysis, lowpass pyramid transforms are widely used [8]. In particular, the Gaussian blur lowpass filter can be used to down-sample the original image. This step can be repeated to get continuously smaller images, resembling a pyramid, as depicted in Fig. 14.6. In practice, one pixel of the down-sampled image corresponds to a fixed size area of the previous pyramid level, thereby losing information the further up we go into the pyramid. However, in our implementation, all levels of the pyramid have the same size, which is obtained by up-sampling the output image in each iteration. As a consequence, the higher level images appear blurrier.

It should be highlighted that, in our implementation, different pyramids with up to 16 levels are created. This allows us to determine how the PAD performance change when more levels of the pyramid are used.

Local Binary Patterns (LBP). Local binary patterns were introduced in [56] as a simple but efficient texture descriptor. Its computational simplicity and greyscale invariance are the most important properties of LBP. The algorithm compares neighbouring pixels and returns the result as a binary number, which is in turn stored as a decimal value. The process is illustrated in Fig. 14.7 for a radius of 1 pixel (3×3 block). It should be noted that the binary representation can also be flipped and the direction and starting point of reading the binary number does not matter as long

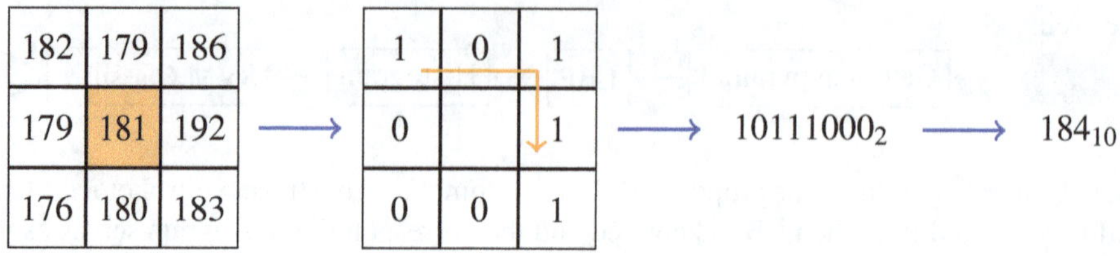

Fig. 14.7 LBP computation: Comparing the central pixel (orange) to each neighbouring pixel results in a binary representation. The binary values are converted to a decimal number, which is stored in the resulting LBP image instead of the original central pixel

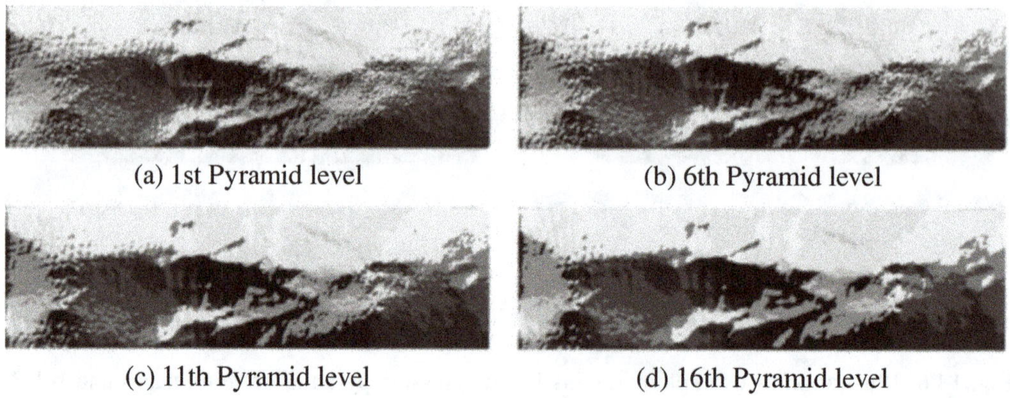

Fig. 14.8 Resulting bona fide LBP images of different Gaussian pyramid levels (i.e. PLBP images)

as it is fixed for the whole system (otherwise, the extracted feature would not be comparable). An example of the four selected PLBP images of the bona fide sample shown in Fig. 14.4 is presented in Fig. 14.8.

Classification. In order to reduce the dimensionality of the feature vector, a greyscale histogram is computed from the resulting LBP images. Subsequently, linear SVMs are used to classify the extracted histograms. These SVMs rely on a main parameter, C, which can be tuned for an optimal performance. Intuitively, the C parameter trades off misclassification of training examples against simplicity of the decision surface. A low C makes the decision surface smooth, while a high C aims at classifying all training examples correctly by giving the model freedom to select more samples as support vectors.

In addition, we benchmark two SVM approaches, as shown in Fig. 14.9 for the simple case of three pyramid levels. On the one hand, we use separate SVMs for each pyramid level (Fig. 14.9a). On the other hand, we utilise a single SVM for all pyramid levels (Fig. 14.9b). Both setups produce one label per pyramid level and then apply a majority vote on the corresponding SVM outputs in order to reach a final decision.

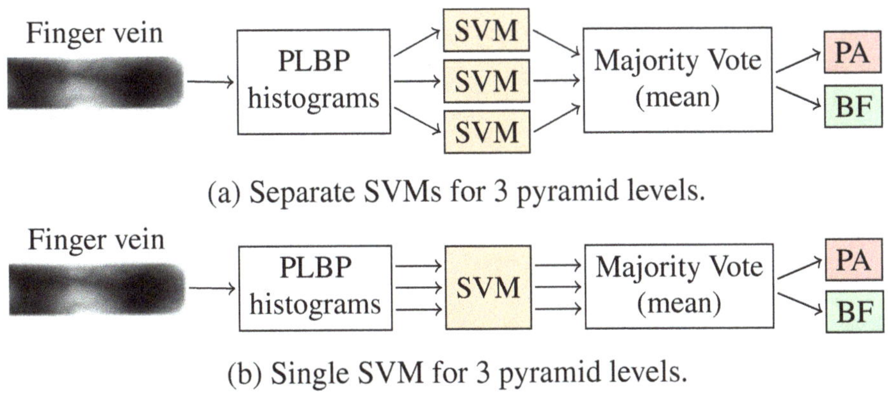

Fig. 14.9 Diagram of the two SVM approaches on the example of 3 pyramid levels

14.5 Experimental Evaluation

With the aim of analysing the suitability of the proposed method for finger vein-based PAD, several experiments were carried out using an identical experimental protocol. Our training and test sets are completely disjoint in order to avoid biased results. Furthermore, in order to allow reproducibility of the experiments, preprocessing and feature extraction are based on the bob toolkit [4, 5].

14.5.1 Experimental Set-Up

The captured dataset comprises 766 samples including 542 bona fides and 224 presentation attacks, stemming from 32 different PAI species. The PAs can be classified into three categories, namely: (i) 2D printouts, (ii) full fingers and (iii) overlays, whereby 2D printouts can also be used as an overlay during the presentation. A detailed listing of all PAIs from the database is presented in Table 14.4.

All samples were captured within the BATL project with our project partners at the University of Southern California. Note that the project sponsor has indicated that they will make the complete dataset available in the near future such that research results presented in this work can be reproduced.

We have additionally considered two test scenarios (see Table 14.5). The first one uses the same number of bona fides and PAs in the training set (69 samples each). To increase the robustness on the detection of bona fide presentations (i.e. minimise the BPCER), the second scenario adds additional 35 bona fide samples to the training set, thus reducing the test set. The partitioning for both scenarios is shown in Table 14.5. Both approaches, using a single SVM or separated SVMs, are compared using the same training and test sets for each scenario.

In more details, the training set comprises all different PAIs except from dragonskin overlays, since this thin and transparent material does not block NIR illumination as known from previous experiments [30]. As a consequence, all veins are visible

Table 14.4 Listing of all PAI species and the number of samples in parenthesis

2D printouts	Matte paper (10)
	Transparent (8)
Full fingers	3D printed (24)
	3D printed + silver coating (9)
	dragon-skin (6)
	dragon-skin + conductive paint (9)
	dragon-skin + conductive paint + nanotips (9)
	dragon-skin + graphite coating (9)
	latex + gold coating (8)
	play doh (28)
	in black, blue, green, orange, pink, purple, red, teal (3 each) and yellow (4)
	silicone (7)
	silicone + bare paint (13)
	silicone + graphite coating (9)
	silicone + nanotips (6)
	silly putty (3)
	silly putty metallic (6)
	silly putty "glowing in the dark" (6)
	wax (6)
Overlays	dragon-skin (9)
	monster latex (10)
	school glue (6)
	silicone (13)
	urethane (6)
	wax (4)

Table 14.5 Partitioning of training and test data

		# Samples	# PA samples	# Bona fide samples
Scenario 1	Train set	138	69 (50%)	69 (50%)
	Test set	628	155 (25%)	473 (75%)
Scenario 2	Train set	173	69 (40%)	104 (60%)
	Test set	593	155 (26%)	438 (74%)

and the sample has the same appearance as a bona fide. Using such samples to train the SVM would thus have a negative impact on its detection accuracy, increasing the BPCER. These PAIs are therefore used only for testing purposes.

In the first scenario, cross-validation is used during the training to automatically select a best-fitting C value as SVM parameter. As suggested by Hsu et al. [36], exponential growing sequences for C (2^x) were tested within the range $x = \{-20, ..., 20\}$. However, due to the increased number of training samples for the second scenario, and consequently, the training time required, only the range $x = \{-20, ..., 8\}$ has been used to cross-validate scenario 2.

Finally, all results are reported in terms of the APCER and BPCER over the test set (see Sect. 14.2), in compliance with the ISO/IEC 30107-3 standard on biometric presentation attack detection - part 3: testing and reporting [39].

It should be noted that establishing a fair benchmark with previous works in the state of the art are difficult since this is the first approach to carry out fingerprint PAD based on finger vein samples.

14.5.2 Results

The results in terms of APCER (dashed) and BPCER (solid) for scenario 1 are plotted in Fig. 14.10, in order to facilitate the visualisation and comparison across different pyramid levels. On the x-axis, the range of pyramid levels are given while the y-axis shows the error rates (in %). For the single SVM approach (Fig. 14.10a), both error rates reach a minimum when using 6 pyramid levels, namely, BPCER = 3.38% and APCER = 5.81%. On the other hand, for the separate SVM approach (Fig. 14.10b), the minimum of both error rates is reached at different levels, namely, BPCER = 2.54% for the fifth level and APCER = 6.45% for the fourth level. This means that, depending on the application at hand (i.e. which error rate should be optimised), different levels may be selected. As it may be observed from Fig. 14.10, the error rates of the separate SVMs somewhat stabilise for using five or more pyramid levels, whereas the single SVMs show much more peaks and no stabilisation.

Regarding the aforementioned decision of prioritising one error rate over the other one, it should be taken into account that a low BPCER results in user convenience (i.e. a low number of bona fide presentation will be wrongly rejected). On the other hand, a low APCER will grant a more secure system (i.e. the number of non-detected attacks will be minimised). One of the aims of the Odin program is achieving a low BPCER. To that end, we analyse the second scenario, for which more training samples for the bona fide class are utilised in order to make the classifier more robust. The corresponding plots with the APCER and BPCER for every pyramid level are presented in Fig. 14.11.

We can observe that the BPCER is significantly lower for all pyramid levels when compared to scenario 1, reaching minimum values of 0.68% for the single SVM and 2.28% for the separate SVMs. At the same time, the APCER stays similar to that of scenario 1, thereby showing the soundness of increasing the number of bona fide samples for training. Additionally, we can see that using only the first four levels produces higher peaks and higher error rates, thus making it unsuitable for PAD purposes. In turn, increasing the number of levels results in a decreasing BPCER, as can be seen for the levels greater than four. Taking into account the pyramid levels five to sixteen, the average APCER is slightly lower for the single SVM approach

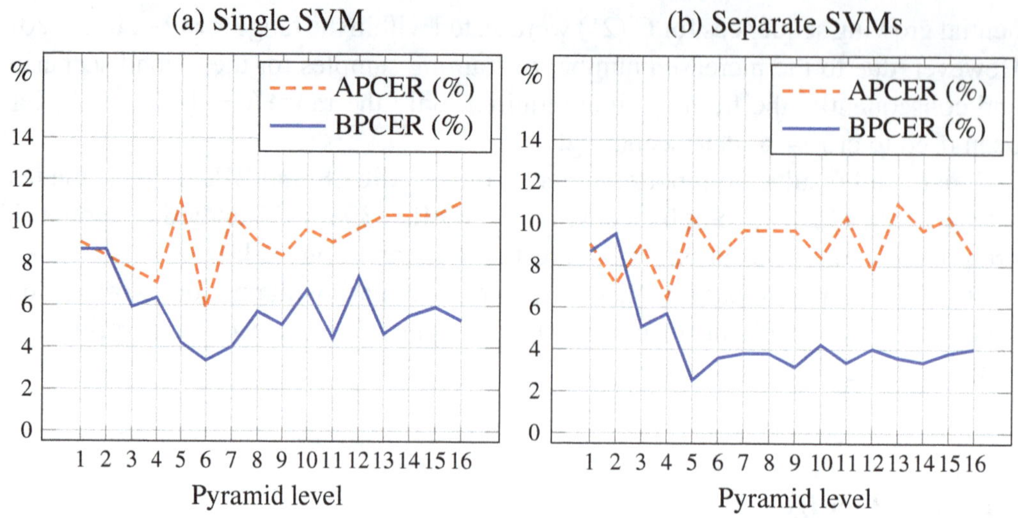

Fig. 14.10 Percentage of APCER and BPCER of **scenario 1** for both SVM classifiers

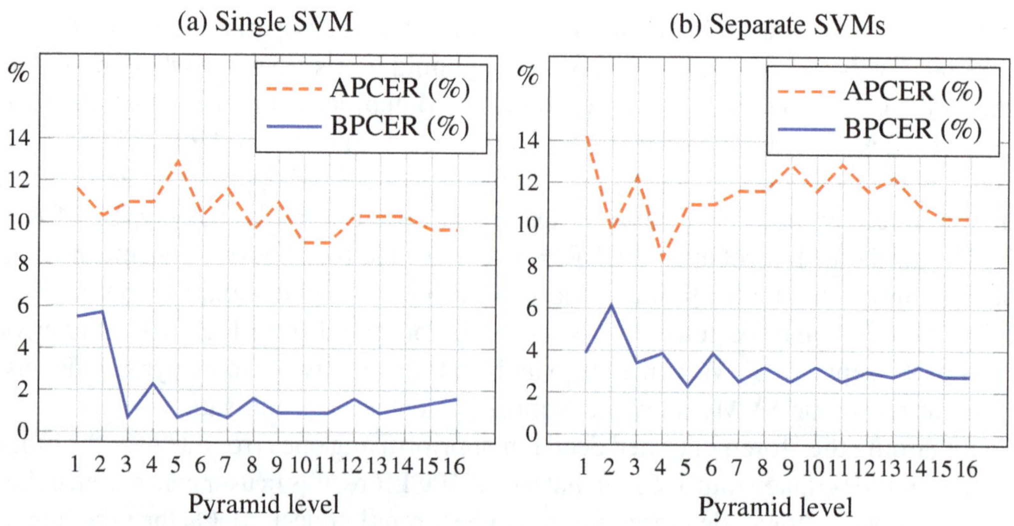

Fig. 14.11 Percentage of APCER and BPCER of **scenario 2** for both SVM classifiers

(10.32–11.50%), while the average BPCER improves significantly for the single SVM (1.12–2.87%). Therefore, we may conclude that the single SVM approach achieves a better PAD performance than the separate SVMs since the training set of the latter is not big enough to train one pyramid level independently of the others. The single SVM gets complimentary information when seeing all levels together and is thus able to reach a higher detection performance.

A comparison for both scenarios of the single SVM approach (level 7) to other handcrafted state-of-the-art implementations is given in Table 14.6. The *Luminosity* and *MC mean* algorithms operate on a very convenient threshold but classify only a fraction of presentation attacks correctly (APCER = 68.39% and APCER = 43.87%, respectively). The other algorithms use a support vector machine for classification

Table 14.6 Comparison of the proposed method to state-of-the-art implementations

Algorithm	Scenario 1		Scenario 2	
	APCER	BPCER	APCER	BPCER
Luminosity [30]	68.39	0.00	68.93	0.00
MC mean [30]	43.87	0.21	43.87	0.23
MC histogram [30]	13.55	9.51	12.90	8.22
BSIF [42]	28.39	5.71	26.45	4.57
LBP [56]	10.32	1.90	11.61	1.14
Proposed PLBP (lvl 7)	10.32	4.02	11.61	0.68

and present lower APCERs. However, in some cases, the BPCER raises to nearly 10%. In particular, the *MC histogram* achieves an APCER between 12 and 14%while the BPCER is between 8 and 10%. In contrast, the *BSIF* implementation results in a BPCER of around 5% at the cost of a higher APCER (26–29%). The results of the plain *LBP* implementation and the *proposed PLBP* implementation are identical regarding APCER but differ in the BPCER. Whereas for scenario 1 *LBP* provides a better BPCER of 1.9% compared to 4.02%, the *proposed PLBP* approach reduces its BPCER in scenario 2 to 0.68% in contrast to 1.14% for *LBP*. Therefore, we can see that our PLBP algorithm achieves the best results for scenario 2 while it is outperformed by *LBP* in scenario 1. The score files from all tests in this chapter are freely available.[7]

Even if the results are promising, reaching an APCER $\approx$ 10% for BPCER $\approx$ 1%, where also unknown attacks (i.e. only used for testing and not seen by the classifier at training) are considered, there is still room for improvement. In particular, a deeper analysis of the results shows that a remarkable number of misclassified PAIs are transparent overlays made of dragon-skin, silicone, monster latex, school glue or wax. In addition, two types of full fake fingers also managed to deceive the PAD algorithm in some cases, namely, glow-in-the-dark silly putty, and one of the samples acquired from a teal play doh finger. Some samples that were not detected are shown in Fig. 14.12. As we may observe, especially for the dragon-skin (c) and the school glue (f) overlays, the samples are very similar to the bona fide sample shown in Fig. 14.4. In particular, the vein structure can be clearly seen.

Finally, Fig. 14.13 shows the 11th level of PLBP images for (a) a dragon-skin overlay, (b) a teal play doh finger, (c) a school glue overlay and (d) a 3D printed finger with silver coating. Comparing these samples with the bona fide one from Fig. 14.8, we can see the high similarities for the transparent overlays in (a) and (c). However, the teal play doh and the 3D printed finger have different patterns (i.e. the 3D printed finger does not block the NIR light at all, only the silver-coated part is

[7] https://dasec.h-da.de/research/biometrics/presentation-attack-detection-for-finger-recognition/.

(a) Teal play doh (b) Silly putty (glows) (c) Dragon-skin overlay

(d) Silicone overlay (e) Monster latex overlay (f) School glue overlay

Fig. 14.12 Examples of undetected PAI species

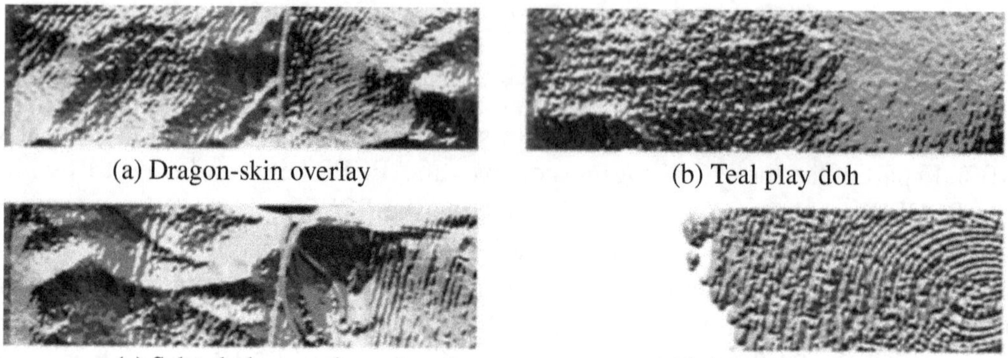

(a) Dragon-skin overlay (b) Teal play doh

(c) School glue overlay (d) 3D print + Ag

Fig. 14.13 Resulting LBP images of different PAIs for 11th Gaussian pyramid level (i.e. PLBP images)

visible). Hence, the SVMs always correctly classify the 3D printed PAIs, and only one error occurred for the teal play doh samples.

To sum up the findings in this section, we can state that the APCERs of around 10% show the limitations of vein-based still image PAD: thin transparent overlays cannot be detected since the extracted features look far too similar to the bona fide ones. However, this PAD technique already allows to successfully detect a wide range of PAIs, including full fake fingers and overlays fabricated from materials which block NIR light to a bigger extent than human flesh.

14.6 Summary and Conclusions

Although being relatively new in comparison with other biometric characteristics, such as fingerprints or handwritten signatures, finger vein recognition has enjoyed a considerable attention within the last decade. As with any other security-related technology, a wider deployment also implies an increase in security and privacy related concerns. This has, in turn, lead to the development of countermeasures to prevent, among others, presentation attacks.

In particular, the biometric community has focused on detecting finger vein images or videos presented to the capture device, in contrast to bona fide fingers. Highly accurate PAD methods have been developed in the literature, able to detect these PAIs with perfect error rates.

In parallel, multimodal capture devices able to acquire both finger vein and fingerprint images have been proposed and implemented. In contrast to the finger vein, which is harder to imitate, multiple recipes are available to an eventual attacker in order to carry out a PA and fool a fingerprint-based recognition system. These facts have motivated us to present in this chapter a novel approach to protect fingerprint sensors: finger vein PAD methods which are able to detect fingerprint PAIs.

In more details, due to the remarkable performance shown by LBP for different tasks, including PAD for several biometric characteristics, we chose this texture descriptor for our work. Even for some challenging PAIs, we can observe with the naked eye that the texture captured has a different appearance from the bona fide finger. In addition, different texture details were analysed utilising Gaussian pyramids and extracting the LBP features from each level of the pyramid. Subsequently, SVMs were utilised for classification purposes.

With a sensor developed for the Odin program, a database comprising 32 different PAIs was acquired and used for the present evaluation. After an extensive experimental evaluation, we found that using a single SVM for a concatenation of the features extracted from all the levels of the pyramid is the best performing approach. This scenario leads to operation points with BPCERs under 1% and an APCER around 10%. The latter shows the main limitation of vein-based still image PAD: thin transparent overlays cannot be detected. However, this PAD technique still allows to successfully detect a wide range of PAIs.

We thus believe that finger vein can be effectively used with fingerprint for both a more accurate recognition performance, as shown in previous works, and also for PAD purposes. In the end, an attacker who needs to deceive both the fingerprint and the vein sensors will face harder challenges in his path. In the forthcoming months, we will focus on improving the finger vein-based PAD, and on developing combined approaches with the finger photos captured with the sensor.

Acknowledgements This research is based upon work supported in part by the Office of the Director of National Intelligence (ODNI), Intelligence Advanced Research Projects Activity (IARPA) under contract number 2017-17020200005. The views and conclusions contained herein are those of the authors and should not be interpreted as necessarily representing the official policies, either expressed or implied, of ODNI, IARPA, or the U.S. Government. The U.S. Government is authorised to reproduce and distribute reprints for governmental purposes notwithstanding any copyright annotation therein.

We would also like to thank our colleagues at USC for the data collection efforts.

References

1. Adler A (2004) Images can be regenerated from quantized biometric match score data. In: Proceedings of Canadian conference on electrical and computer engineering (CCECE), pp 469–472
2. Akhtar Z, Kale S, Alfarid N (2011) Spoof attacks in mutimodal biometric systems. In: Proceedings of international conference on information and network technology (IPCSIT), vol 4, pp 46–51. IACSIT Press
3. Alegre F, Vipperla R, Evans N, Fauve B (2012) On the vulnerability of automatic speaker recognition to spoofing attacks with artificial signals. In: Proceedings of European signal processing conference (EUSIPCO), pp 36–40
4. Anjos A, Günther M, de Freitas Pereira T, Korshunov P, Mohammadi A, Marcel S (2017) Continuously reproducing toolchains in pattern recognition and machine learning experiments. In: Proceedings of international conference on machine learning (ICML)
5. Anjos A, Shafey LE et al (2012) Bob: a free signal processing and machine learning toolbox for researchers. In: Proceedings ACM international conference on multimedia (ACM MM), pp 1449–1452
6. BATL: Biometric authentication with a timeless learner (2017)
7. Bhogal APS, Söllinger D, Trung P, Hämmerle-Uhl J, Uhl A (2017) Non-reference image quality assessment for fingervein presentation attack detection. In: Proceedings Scandinavian conference on image analysis (SCIA), pp 184–196
8. Burt PJ, Adelson EH (1987) The Laplacian pyramid as a compact image code. In: Readings in computer vision, pp 671–679. Elsevier
9. Cappelli R, Maio D, Lumini A, Maltoni D (2007) Fingerprint image reconstruction from standard templates. IEEE Trans Pattern Anal Mach Intell 29:1489–1503
10. Chetty G, Wagner M (2005) Audio-visual multimodal fusion for biometric person authentication and liveness verification. In: Proceedings of NICTA-HCSNet multimodal user interaction workshop (MMUI)
11. Choi H, Kang R, Choi K, Kim J (2007) Aliveness detection of fingerprints using multiple static features. In: Proceedings of world academy of science, engineering and technology, vol 22
12. Chugh T, Cao K, Jain AK (2018) Fingerprint spoof buster: use of minutiae-centered patches. IEEE Trans Inf Forensics Secur 13(9):2190–2202
13. Chugh T, Jain AK (2018) Fingerprint presentation attack detection: generalization and efficiency. arXiv:1812.11574
14. Cooksey C, Tsai B, Allen D (2014) A collection and statistical analysis of skin reflectance signatures for inherent variability over the 250 nm to 2500 nm spectral range. In: Active and passive signatures V, vol 9082, p 908206. International Society for Optics and Photonics
15. Drahansky M, Dolezel M, Michal J, Brezinova E, Yim J et al (2013) New optical methods for liveness detection on fingers. BioMed Res Int 2013:197,925
16. Erdogmus N, Marcel S (2014) Spoofing face recognition with 3D masks. IEEE Trans Inf Forensics Secur 9(7):1084–1097
17. Espinoza M, Champod C (2011) Using the number of pores on fingerprint images to detect spoofing attacks. In: International conference on hand-based biometrics (ICHB), 2011, pp 1–5. IEEE
18. Galbally J, Cappelli R, Lumini A, de Rivera GG, Maltoni D, Fierrez J, Ortega-Garcia J, Maio D (2010) An evaluation of direct and indirect attacks using fake fingers generated from ISO templates. Pattern Recogn Lett 31:725–732
19. Galbally J, Gomez-Barrero M (2017) Presentation attack detection in iris recognition. In: Busch C, Rathgeb C (eds) Iris and periocular biometrics. IET
20. Galbally J, Marcel S, Fierrez J (2014) Biometric antispoofing methods: a survey in face recognition. IEEE Access 2:1530–1552
21. Galbally J, Marcel S, Fierrez J (2014) Image quality assessment for fake biometric detection: application to iris, fingerprint and face recognition. IEEE Trans Image Process 23(2):710–724

22. Galbally J, Marcel S, Fierrez J (2014) Image quality assessment for fake biometric detection: application to iris, fingerprint, and face recognition. IEEE Trans Image Process 23(2):710–724
23. Galbally J, Ross A, Gomez-Barrero M, Fierrez J, Ortega-Garcia J (2013) Iris image reconstruction from binary templates: an efficient probabilistic approach based on genetic algorithms. Comput Vis Image Underst 117(10):1512–1525
24. Ghiani L, Yambay D, Mura V, Tocco S, Marcialis GL, Roli F, Schuckers S (2013) LivDet 2013 fingerprint liveness detection competition 2013. In: International conference on biometrics (ICB), 2013, pp 1–6. IEEE
25. Ghiani L, Yambay DA, Mura V, Marcialis GL et al (2017) Review of the fingerprint liveness detection (LivDet) competition series: 2009 to 2015. Image Vis Comput 58:110–128
26. Gomez-Barrero M, Galbally J (2017) Inverse biometrics and privacy. In: Vielhauer C (ed) User-centric privacy and security in biometrics. IET
27. Gomez-Barrero M, Galbally J (2017) Software attacks on iris recognition systems. In: Busch C, Rathgeb C (eds) Iris and periocular biometrics. IET
28. Gomez-Barrero M, Galbally J, Fierrez J (2014) Efficient software attack to multimodal biometric systems and its application to face and iris fusion. Pattern Recogn Lett 36:243–253
29. Gomez-Barrero M, Kolberg J, Busch C (2018) Towards fingerprint presentation attack detection based on short wave infrared imaging and spectral signatures. In: Proceedings of Norwegian information security conference (NISK)
30. Gomez-Barrero M, Kolberg J, Busch C (2018) Towards multi-modal finger presentation attack detection. In: Proceedings of international workshop on ubiquitous implicit biometrics and health signals monitoring for person-centric applications (UBIO)
31. Gomez-Barrero M, Kolberg J, Busch C (2019) Multi-modal fingerprint presentation attack detection: looking at the surface and the inside. In: Proceedings of international conference on biometrics (ICB)
32. González-Soler LJ, Chang L, Hernández-Palancar J, Pérez-Suárez A, Gomez-Barrero M (2017) Fingerprint presentation attack detection method based on a bag-of-words approach. In: Proceedings of Iberoamerican congress on pattern recognition (CIARP), pp 263–271. Springer
33. Goodfellow I, Bengio Y, Courville A (2016) Deep learning. MIT Press
34. Hengfoss C, Kulcke A, Mull G, Edler C, Püschel K, Jopp E (2011) Dynamic liveness and forgeries detection of the finger surface on the basis of spectroscopy in the 400–1650 nm region. Forensic Sci Int 212(1):61–68
35. Howard AG, Zhu M, Chen B, Kalenichenko D, Wang W et al (2017) Mobilenets: efficient convolutional neural networks for mobile vision applications. arXiv:1704.04861
36. Hsu CW, Chang CC, Lin CJ et al (2003) A practical guide to support vector classification
37. Hussein ME, Spinoulas L, Xiong F, Abd-Almageed W (2018) Fingerprint presentation attack detection using a novel multi-spectral capture device and patch-based convolutional neural networks. In: 2018 IEEE international workshop on information forensics and security (WIFS), pp 1–8. IEEE
38. International Organisation for Standardisation (2016) ISO/IEC JTC1 SC37 Biometrics: ISO/IEC 30107-1. Information technology—biometric presentation attack detection—part 1: framework
39. International Organisation for Standardisation (2017) ISO/IEC JTC1 SC37 Biometrics: ISO/IEC 30107-3. Information technology—biometric presentation attack detection—part 3: testing and reporting
40. Jia X, Yang X, Cao K, Zang Y, Zhang N, Dai R, Zhu X, Tian J (2014) Multi-scale local binary pattern with filters for spoof fingerprint detection. Inf Sci 268:91–102
41. Jiang Y, Liu X (2018) Uniform local binary pattern for fingerprint liveness detection in the gaussian pyramid. Hindawi J Electr Comput Eng
42. Kannala J, Rahtu E (2012) BSIF: binarized statistical image features. In: 2012 21st international conference on pattern recognition (ICPR), pp 1363–1366
43. Keilbach P, Kolberg J, Gomez-Barrero M, Busch C, Langweg H (2018) Fingerprint presentation attack detection using laser speckle contrast imaging. In: Proceedings international conference of the biometrics special interest group (BIOSIG), pp 1–6

44. Kocher D, Schwarz S, Uhl A (2016) Empirical evaluation of LBP-extension features for finger vein spoofing detection. In: Proceedings international conference of the biometrics special interest group (BIOSIG), pp 1–5. IEEE
45. Kono M, Umemura S, Miyatake T, Harada K et al (2004) Personal identification system. US Patent 6,813,010
46. Krizhevsky A, Sutskever I, Geoffrey E (2012) ImageNet classification with deep convolutional neural networks. In: Advances in neural information processing systems, vol 25, pp 1097–1105. Curran Associates, Inc
47. Marasco E, Ross A (2015) A survey on antispoofing schemes for fingerprint recognition systems. ACM Comput Surv (CSUR) 47(2):28
48. Marcel S (2013) BEAT—biometrics evaluation and testing. Biom Technol Today 5–7
49. Marcel S, Nixon MS, Li SZ (eds) (2014) Handbook of biometric anti-spoofing. Springer
50. Memon S, Manivannan N, Balachandran W (2011) Active pore detection for liveness in fingerprint identification system. In: 2011 19th telecommunications forum (TELFOR), pp 619–622. IEEE
51. Nguyen DT, Park YH, Shin KY, Kwon SY et al (2013) Fake finger-vein image detection based on fourier and wavelet transforms. Digit Signal Process 23(5):1401–1413
52. Nguyen DT, Yoon HS, Pham TD, Park KR (2017) Spoof detection for finger-vein recognition system using NIR camera. Sensors 17(10):2261
53. Nikam SB, Agarwal S (2008) Texture and wavelet-based spoof fingerprint detection for fingerprint biometric systems. In: Proceedings of international conference on emerging trends in engineering and technology (ICETET), pp 675–680. IEEE
54. Nogueira RF, de Alencar Lotufo R, Machado RC (2016) Fingerprint liveness detection using convolutional neural networks. IEEE Trans Inf Forensics Secur 11(6):1206–1213
55. ODNI, IARPA: IARPA-BAA-16-04 (thor) (2016). https://www.iarpa.gov/index.php/research-programs/odin/odin-baa
56. Ojala T, Pietikäinen M, Harwood D (1996) A comparative study of texture measures with classification based on featured distributions. Pattern Recogn 29(1):51–59
57. Qian X, Hua X, Chen P, Ke L (2011) PLBP: an effective local binary patterns texture descriptor with pyramid representation. Pattern Recogn 44(10):2502–2515
58. Qiu X, Kang W, Tian S, Jia W, Huang Z (2018) Finger vein presentation attack detection using total variation decomposition. IEEE Trans Inf Forensics Secur 13(2):465–477
59. Qiu X, Tian S, Kang W, Jia W, Wu Q (2017) Finger vein presentation attack detection using convolutional neural networks. In: Proceedings of Chinese conference on biometric recognition (CCBR), pp 296–305
60. Raghavendra R, Avinash M, Marcel S, Busch C (2015) Finger vein liveness detection using motion magnification. In: Proceedings of international conference on biometrics theory, applications and systems (BTAS), pp 1–7. IEEE
61. Raghavendra R, Busch C (2015) Presentation attack detection algorithms for finger vein biometrics: a comprehensive study. In: Proceedings of international conference on signal-image technology & internet-based systems (SITIS), pp 628–632
62. Raghavendra R, Raja K, Surbiryala J, Busch C (2014) A low-cost multimodal biometric sensor to capture finger vein and fingerprint. In: Proceedings of international joint conference on biometrics (IJCB)
63. Raghavendra R, Raja K, Venkatesh S, Busch C (2018) Fingervein presentation attack detection using transferable features from deep convolution neural networks. In: Vatsa M, Singh R, Majumdar A (eds) Deep learning in biometrics. CRC Press, Boca Raton
64. Ratha N, Connell J, Bolle R (2001) Enhancing security and privacy in biometrics-based authentication systems. IBM Syst J 40
65. Senarathna J, Rege A, Li N, Thakor NV (2013) Laser speckle contrast imaging: theory, instrumentation and applications. IEEE Rev Biomed Eng 6:99–110
66. Simonyan K, Zisserman A (2015) Very deep convolutional networks for large-scale image recognition. In: Proceedings of international conference on learning representations (ICLR)

67. Sousedik C, Busch C (2014) Presentation attack detection methods for fingerprint recognition systems: a survey. IET Biom 3(1):1–15
68. Steiner H, Kolb A, Jung N (2016) Reliable face anti-spoofing using multispectral SWIR imaging. In: Proceedings of international conference on biometrics (ICB), pp 1–8
69. Sutskever I, Vinyals O, Le QV (2014) Sequence to sequence learning with neural networks. In: Proceedings of advances in neural information processing systems (NIPS)
70. TABULA RASA: Trusted biometrics under spoofing attacks (2010). http://www.tabularasa-euproject.org/
71. Tirunagari S, Poh N, Bober M, Windridge D (2015) Windowed DMD as a microtexture descriptor for finger vein counter-spoofing in biometrics. In: Proceedings of IEEE international workshop on information forensics and security (WIFS), pp 1–6
72. Tolosana R, Gomez-Barrero M, Busch C, Ortega-Garcia J (2019) Biometric presentation attack detection: beyond the visible spectrum. arXiv:1902.11065
73. Tolosana R, Gomez-Barrero M, Kolberg J, Morales A, Busch C, Ortega J (2018) Towards fingerprint presentation attack detection based on convolutional neural networks and short wave infrared imaging. In: Proceedings of international conference of the biometrics special interest group (BIOSIG)
74. Tome P, Marcel S (2015) On the vulnerability of palm vein recognition to spoofing attacks. In: Proceedings of international conference on biometrics (ICB), pp 319–325. IEEE
75. Tome P, Raghavendra R, Busch C, Tirunagari S et al (2015) The 1st competition on counter measures to finger vein spoofing attacks. In: Proceedings of international conference on biometrics (ICB), pp 513–518
76. Tome P, Vanoni M, Marcel S (2014) On the vulnerability of finger vein recognition to spoofing. In: Proceedings of international conference of the biometrics special interest group (BIOSIG), pp 1–10. IEEE
77. Vanoni M, Tome P, El Shafey L, Marcel S (2014) Cross-database evaluation with an open finger vein sensor. In: IEEE workshop on biometric measurements and systems for security and medical applications (BioMS)
78. Wu HY, Rubinstein M, Shih E, Guttag J, Durand F, Freeman W (2012)Eulerian video magnification for revealing subtle changes in the world. In: Proceedings of transaction on graphics (SIGGRAPH)
79. Yambay D, Czajka A, Bowyer K, Vatsa M, Singh R, Schuckers S (2019) Review of iris presentation attack detection competitions. In: Handbook of biometric anti-spoofing, pp 169–183. Springer
80. Yambay D, Ghiani L, Marcialis GL, Roli F, Schuckers S (2019) Review of fingerprint presentation attack detection competitions. In: Handbook of biometric anti-spoofing, pp 109–131. Springer
81. Zhou B, Khosla A, Lapedriza A, Oliva A, Torralba A (2016) Learning deep features for discriminative localization. In: Proceedings of international conference on computer vision and pattern recognition (CVPR)

Chapter 15
On the Recognition Performance of BioHash-Protected Finger Vein Templates

Vedrana Krivokuća and Sébastien Marcel

Abstract This chapter contributes towards advancing finger vein template protection research by presenting the first analysis on the suitability of the BioHashing template protection scheme for finger vein verification systems, in terms of the effect on the system's recognition performance. Our results show the best performance when BioHashing is applied to finger vein patterns extracted using the Wide Line Detector (WLD) and Repeated Line Tracking (RLT) feature extractors, and the worst performance when the Maximum Curvature (MC) extractor is used. The low recognition performance in the Stolen Token scenario is shown to be improvable by increasing the BioHash length; however, we demonstrate that the BioHash length is constrained in practice by the amount of memory required for the projection matrix. So, WLD finger vein patterns are found to be the most promising for BioHashing purposes due to their relatively small feature vector size, which allows us to generate larger BioHashes than is possible for RLT or MC feature vectors. In addition, we also provide an open-source implementation of a BioHash-protected finger vein verification system based on the WLD, RLT and MC extractors, so that other researchers can verify our findings and build upon our work.

Keywords BioHashing · Finger veins · Biometric template protection · Wide Line Detector · Repeated Line Tracking · Maximum Curvature · EU General Data Protection Regulation (GDPR) · UTFVP

15.1 Introduction

As our world is transforming into an interconnected network of individuals and devices, we are beginning to realise that current data protection mechanisms are

V. Krivokuća (✉) · S. Marcel
Idiap Research Institute, Martigny, Switzerland
e-mail: vedrana.krivokuca@idiap.ch

S. Marcel
e-mail: sebastien.marcel@idiap.ch

A. Uhl et al. (eds.), *Handbook of Vascular Biometrics*, Advances in Computer Vision and Pattern Recognition, https://doi.org/10.1007/978-3-030-27731-4_15

becoming inadequate to meet our growing security needs. Traditional security mechanisms, such as passwords and access cards, are no longer sufficient for establishing an individual's true identity, which is why we are turning to biometrics for stronger identity assurance. While the unique link between an individual and their biometric characteristics is the very fact that makes biometric authentication so reliable, it is this same aspect of biometrics that makes this authentication factor vulnerable. For this reason, the past decade has seen the emergence of a new field of research into developing effective biometric template protection strategies to secure biometric features during storage and transmission in an authentication system.[1] Research in this area is particularly important in light of the recent EU General Data Protection Regulation (GDPR),[2] which legally obliges users of biometric data to exercise caution in processing and storing this data to protect individuals' digital identities.

A recent review paper on biometric template protection by Sandhya and Prasad [1] shows that, between the years 2005 to 2016, the smallest amount of effort has been invested into developing protection mechanisms for finger veins. Nevertheless, finger vein recognition has increased in popularity over the past few years, with several companies having already deployed finger vein recognition systems for public use, e.g. M2SYS, Idemia, Hitachi and NEC. This suggests that there is an urgent need to direct our attention towards researching effective mechanisms for protecting finger vein templates.

Although the finger vein template protection field is still in its infancy, a number of methods have been proposed in the literature. For example, in one of the earliest approaches towards finger vein template protection [2], the finger vein pattern image is first transformed using the Number Theoretic Transform,[3] after which the transformed template is masked by a random filter. Image-based transformations are also applied towards protecting the finger vein template in [3], where block re-mapping and mesh warping are (separately) applied to the finger vein image to derive two versions of a cancellable finger vein template. Random projection is the template protection method of choice in [4], where the finger vein template consists of end points and intersections. Hybrid template protection strategies have been proposed for finger veins in [5, 6]. In [5], the finger vein image is first transformed into a template where the number of black (background) and white (vein) pixels is approximately equal, and then the Fuzzy Commitment scheme is applied to this template. In [6], the authors propose generating two BioHashes from the same finger vein template, then encrypting one BioHash using Fuzzy Commitment and the other using Fuzzy Vault, after which the two encrypted BioHashes are combined. Finally, [7–9] have focused on multi-biometric systems. More specifically, in [7], finger vein, fingerprint, finger knuckle print and finger shape features are fused, and then the

---

[1] https://www.iso.org/standard/52946.html.

[2] https://ec.europa.eu/commission/priorities/justice-and-fundamental-rights/data-protection/2018-reform-eu-data-protection-rules_en.

[3] This is essentially the Fourier transform, constrained to a finite field.

resulting feature vector is secured via Fuzzy Commitment. A similar approach is presented in [8], except here the authors also consider score-level and decision-level fusion, whereby Fuzzy Commitment is used to secure each individual feature vector, then the scores or decisions, respectively, of the resulting biometric cryptosystems are fused. In [9], the finger vein feature vector is protected using the Bloom filter approach, and the authors also investigate a multi-biometric system whereby the Bloom filter-protected finger vein template is fused with a Bloom filter-protected face template.

This chapter contributes towards research on finger vein template protection by investigating whether the BioHashing template protection strategy [10] is suitable for protecting finger vein templates, in terms of its effect on the recognition performance of the underlying recognition system. BioHashing is one of the most widely studied biometric template protection schemes in the literature. It involves the projection of a biometric feature vector into a random subspace defined by a user-specific seed, followed by binarisation of the resulting projected vector to produce a so-called BioHash. Although BioHashing has been applied to a number of biometric characteristics (e.g. fingerprints [10], face [11], palm prints [12], and iris [13]), the only mention of BioHashing on finger vein templates that we have come across is the BioHashing/Fuzzy Vault and BioHashing/Fuzzy Commitment hybrid scheme in [6], mentioned earlier. To the best of our knowledge, there does not yet exist any published research on applying BioHashing on its own to finger vein templates. This is where our contribution lies. We also provide an open-source BioHash-protected finger vein verification system, which can be used by other researchers to verify and build upon our work.

We have chosen to focus on BioHashing for three main reasons. First, one of the biggest and most well-known advantages of BioHashing is that, theoretically, there is the possibility of achieving a 0% error rate. While low error rates may be characteristic of two-factor template protection schemes in general, BioHashing is currently the most popular in this category. Second, finger vein images tend to be fairly large, so we were interested in seeing whether BioHashing could be used to produce significantly smaller finger vein templates. Finally, since BioHashing is one of the most well-known template protection schemes in the literature, we wished to provide an open-source implementation of this method for comparison purposes against other template protection techniques developed for finger vein templates.

Note that the new standard[4] for the evaluation of biometric template protection schemes, ISO/IEC 30136:2018, specifies a number of requirements that should be considered when assessing the robustness of a biometric template protection scheme. These include the recognition performance of a biometric system employing template protection compared to that of the same system without template protection; the irreversibility of a template protection scheme, which refers to the difficulty of recovering information about the underlying biometric characteristic from its protected template; diversity, renewability (or cancellability), and unlinkability, all of which relate to the possibility of generating multiple protected templates from

[4]https://www.iso.org/standard/53256.html.

the same biometric characteristic, such that the protected templates are effectively seen as different identities and can thus be used to (i) replace a compromised protected template, and (ii) enroll into multiple applications using the same biometric characteristic without the risk of cross-matching the protected reference templates. The standard also specifies the need to evaluate the possibility of impersonating an enrolled individual using information about their underlying biometric characteristic leaked from one or more of their protected templates, which may largely be attributed to the template protection scheme's compliance with the irreversibility and unlinkability properties. A thorough evaluation of a biometric template protection scheme must, therefore, take into account all of the aforementioned requirements. While the evaluation of recognition performance is relatively established, there are currently no solid, agreed-upon methods for assessing requirements such as irreversibility and diversity/cancellability/unlinkability (despite some guidelines provided by the new standard). Consequently, a thorough evaluation of a biometric template protection scheme necessitates a dedicated treatise of each requirement, which, in many cases, may involve the development and justification of new evaluation methodologies. In light of these reasons, this chapter focuses on evaluating only the recognition performance of BioHash-protected finger vein templates, and we reserve the analysis of the remaining requirements for future work.

The remainder of this chapter is structured as follows. Section 15.2 briefly describes the implementation of our BioHash-protected finger vein verification system. Section 15.3 presents experimental results on the recognition performance of this system and discusses memory constraints that should be considered when applying BioHashing to finger veins. Section 15.4 concludes the chapter and suggests areas for future work.

15.2 BioHash-Protected Finger Vein Verification System

Our BioHash-protected finger vein verification system[5] is an adaptation of the baseline finger vein verification system implemented in the PyPI package.[6] Our adapted system consists of four modules, as illustrated in Fig. 15.1.

The *preprocessor* locates, crops and horizontally aligns the finger in each finger vein image, as per [14, 15].

The *extractor* extracts the vein pattern from the cropped finger image. We used three well-known extractors: Wide Line Detector (WLD) [15], Repeated Line Tracking (RLT) [16] and Maximum Curvature (MC) [17]. The output of each extractor is a binary image, in which white pixels represent the finger vein pattern and black pixels represent the background. For each binary image, we then concatenate its rows to generate a finger vein feature vector.

[5]Code available at the following link: https://gitlab.idiap.ch/bob/bob.chapter.fingerveins_biohashing.

[6]https://pypi.python.org/pypi/bob.bio.vein.

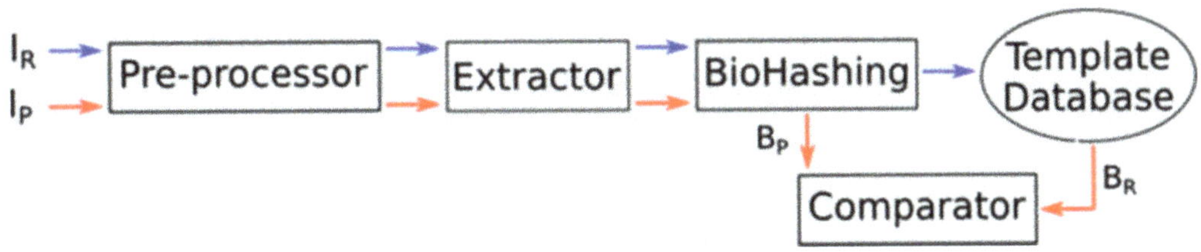

Fig. 15.1 Enrolment (blue arrows) and verification (red arrows) stages in our BioHash-protected finger vein verification system. I_R and I_P denote the reference and probe finger images, respectively. Similarly, B_R and B_P denote the reference and probe BioHashes, respectively

The finger vein feature vector obtained from the feature extraction stage is next *BioHashed*. Our implementation is based on the original BioHash method proposed in [10]. The steps are summarised below:

1. Generate a user-specific[7] random projection matrix of size $n \times l$ for each unique finger[8] in the database, where n represents the dimensionality of the finger vein feature vector and l denotes the desired BioHash length. To ensure that the same matrix can be generated for a specific finger during every verification attempt, the random matrix generation is seeded with a user-specific *seed*. (This seed should be stored on an external token, separately from the BioHash.)
2. Orthonormalise the random matrix.
3. Compute the dot product between the finger vein feature vector and each column of the orthonormalised random matrix. The result is an l-dimensional projected vector.
4. Binarise the projected vector using the mean of the vector as the binarisation threshold, such that all values greater than the mean are set to 1 and all values less than or equal to the mean are set to 0. The result is an l-dimensional binary vector, referred to as the "BioHash".

For the unprotected (without BioHashing) templates in our baseline finger vein verification system, *comparison* is performed on the extracted finger vein features separately for each of the three extractors (WLD, RLT and MC), using the comparison algorithm proposed in [16]. This method is based on a cross-correlation between the enrolled (reference) finger vein template and the probe template obtained during verification. For the protected (with BioHashing) templates in our BioHash-protected finger vein verification system, comparison is done by computing the Hamming distance between the reference and probe BioHashes.

[7]Note that "user" refers to an individual using the finger vein verification system. While the standardised term would be "biometric data subject" or "individual", we have chosen to retain the term "user" for consistency with [10].

[8]Each finger represents a different identity or "user".

15.3 Recognition Performance of BioHash-Protected Finger Vein Verification System

This section presents the results of the experiments we conducted to determine the recognition performance of our BioHash-protected finger vein verification system.

For the experiments reported in this paper, we employed the publicly available finger vein database UTFVP.[9] This database consists of four images for each of 60 subjects' left and right index, ring and middle fingers, which makes up 1,440 images in total. Each image has a height of 380 pixels and a width of 672 pixels. Associated with the database are a number of different evaluation protocols. We used the "nom" protocol,[10] for which the database is split into three sets ("world", "dev", and "eval"). We employed the "eval" set, which consists of fingers 29–60. The comparison protocol involved using the first two finger vein images from each finger for enrolment and the last two as probes.

We chose this database for two reasons. First, it is publicly available, which means that our results can be easily verified by other researchers. Second, it has been shown [18] that an EER of as low as 0.4% is achievable on this database, so we wanted to investigate the effects of BioHashing on such remarkable recognition performance.

15.3.1 Baseline Recognition Performance

To determine how effective our BioHash-protected finger vein verification system is for finger verification purposes, it was necessary to first establish the recognition performance of our baseline verification system, i.e. using unprotected finger vein features. We had three baselines, one for each of the three extractors.

Figure 15.2 illustrates the outputs of each of the three feature extractors on a finger image from UTFVP, and Table 15.1 shows the dimensionalities of the finger vein feature vectors from each extractor. Although the images in Fig. 15.2 have all been scaled to the same size for easier visual comparison of the extracted patterns, the three extractors actually produce images of different sizes, as is evident from Table 15.1. The MC extractor is the only one that outputs a binary image of the same size as the original image from the database, plus a little extra background padding for comparison purposes. On the other hand, both the WLD and RLT extractors output binary images that are much smaller than the original image. Our adopted WLD extractor reduces the image to a quarter of its original size in each dimension prior to feature extraction to speed up the processing, and the RLT extractor reduces each dimension of the image to a third of its original size. These dimensionalities will be shown to play an important role in the practical feasibility of applying BioHashing to finger vein patterns, a point which will be discussed further in Sect. 15.3.3.

[9] http://scs.ewi.utwente.nl/downloads/show,Finger%20Vein/.

[10] Defined by Idiap Research Institute. See https://www.beat-eu.org/platform/databases/utfvp/1/ for more details.

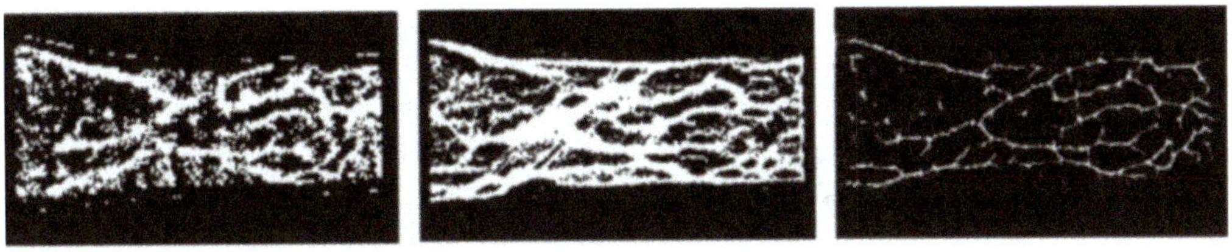

(a)WLD (b)RLT (c)MC

Fig. 15.2 Finger vein patterns extracted using three different feature extractors on the same finger image from UTFVP

Table 15.1 Sizes of the extracted binary finger vein pattern images and corresponding finger vein feature vectors

Extractor	Image size (pixels)	Feature vector dimensionality
WLD	94 × 164	15,416
RLT	234 × 409	95,706
MC	390 × 682	265,980

Figure 15.3 presents a visual comparison of the recognition performance of the three extractors in terms of Receiver Operating Characteristic (ROC) plots. We refer to this as the *baseline* recognition performance (i.e. the performance of the finger vein recognition systems prior to incorporating BioHashing).

Considering the recognition performance of the three extractor baselines in Fig. 15.3, it is evident that the MC extractor has the best performance. Looking at Fig. 15.2, this makes sense, because the MC extractor seems to produce the cleanest, thinnest finger vein patterns, which would be expected to contribute to more accurate recognition. The fact that the recognition performance of the WLD and RLT extractors is very similar may be attributed to the fact that the two extractors produce finger vein patterns of similar quality (thick, with a fairly noisy background), even

Fig. 15.3 Comparing baseline ROCs across the three feature extractors on the UTFVP database

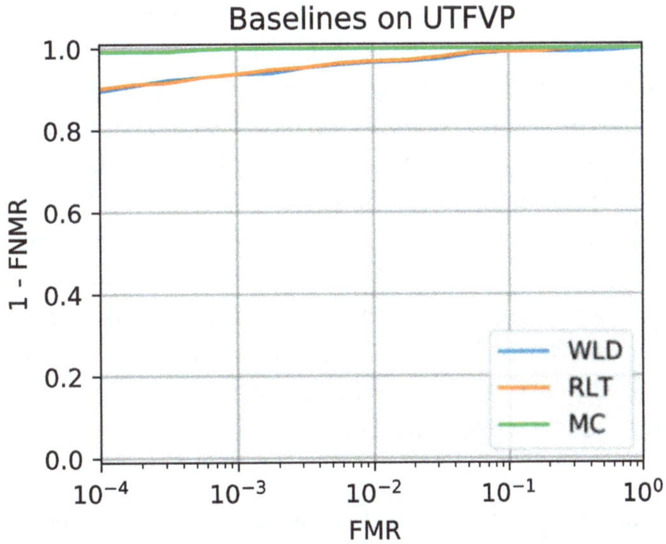

though the RLT-extracted pattern in Fig. 15.2 appears cleaner than the WLD-extracted pattern.

15.3.2 BioHashing Recognition Performance

This section presents experimental results on the recognition performance of our BioHash-protected finger vein verification system. We consider two scenarios: the Normal scenario and the Stolen Token scenario. The Normal scenario refers to the scenario where each user of the verification system employs their own secret seed and associated random projection matrix in the generation of their BioHash. This is the expected scenario for most cases in practice. The Stolen Token scenario refers to the scenario where a genuine user's secret seed is stolen and used with the impostor's own finger vein template to generate the impostor's BioHash. While it is hoped that such a scenario would not occur in practice, the fact that the user-specific seed is a valuable secret means that we must consider the scenario where that secret is leaked.

To determine the recognition performance of our BioHash-protected finger vein verification system in both the Normal and Stolen Token scenarios, we generated BioHashes of lengths $l = \{100, 200, 300, 400, 500\}$ (number of bits) for finger vein feature vectors resulting from each of our three feature extractors (WLD, RLT and MC). For the Normal scenario, the unique ID of the finger image was used as the seed,[11] and for the Stolen Token scenario, the same seed (seed $= 100$) was used to generate the BioHashes for all fingers. Table 15.2 indicates the dimensionality reduction resulting from applying BioHashing to the finger vein feature vectors (refer to Table 15.1 for the original finger vein feature vector dimensionality). Figure 15.4 shows the recognition performance of the three finger vein extractors in both the Normal and Stolen Token scenarios, in terms of ROC plots.

From Table 15.2, it is evident that generating BioHashes of 100–500 bits from finger vein feature vectors results in a *significant* dimensionality reduction for all three feature extractors. The greatest dimensionality reduction is observed for the MC extractor, and the WLD extractor shows the smallest dimensionality reduction. This makes sense, since MC finger vein feature vectors have the largest dimensionality and WLD finger vein feature vectors the smallest (see Table 15.1). While "dimensionality" does not necessarily equal "information", and thus "dimensionality reduction" does not necessarily imply "information loss", the size of the dimensionality reductions noted in Table 15.2 makes it highly probable that mapping finger vein feature vectors to BioHashes *does* result in some information loss. In particular, from the results in Table 15.2, we would conclude that BioHashing on MC finger vein feature vectors would incur the largest information loss and WLD feature vectors the smallest. This should be evident when comparing the recognition performance of the BioHash-protected finger vein recognition system to the baseline system (i.e. the system without BioHashing). We refer to Fig. 15.4 for this purpose.

[11] In practice, the seed should be randomly generated. We only used the finger ID as the seed so that our results are more easily reproducible.

Table 15.2 Dimensionality reduction (percentage of dimensionality lost) as a result of converting finger vein feature vectors to BioHashes of different lengths (l)

Extractor	$l = 100$	$l = 200$	$l = 300$	$l = 400$	$l = 500$
WLD (%)	99.35	98.70	98.05	97.41	96.76
RLT (%)	99.90	99.79	99.69	99.58	99.48
MC (%)	99.96	99.92	99.89	99.85	99.81

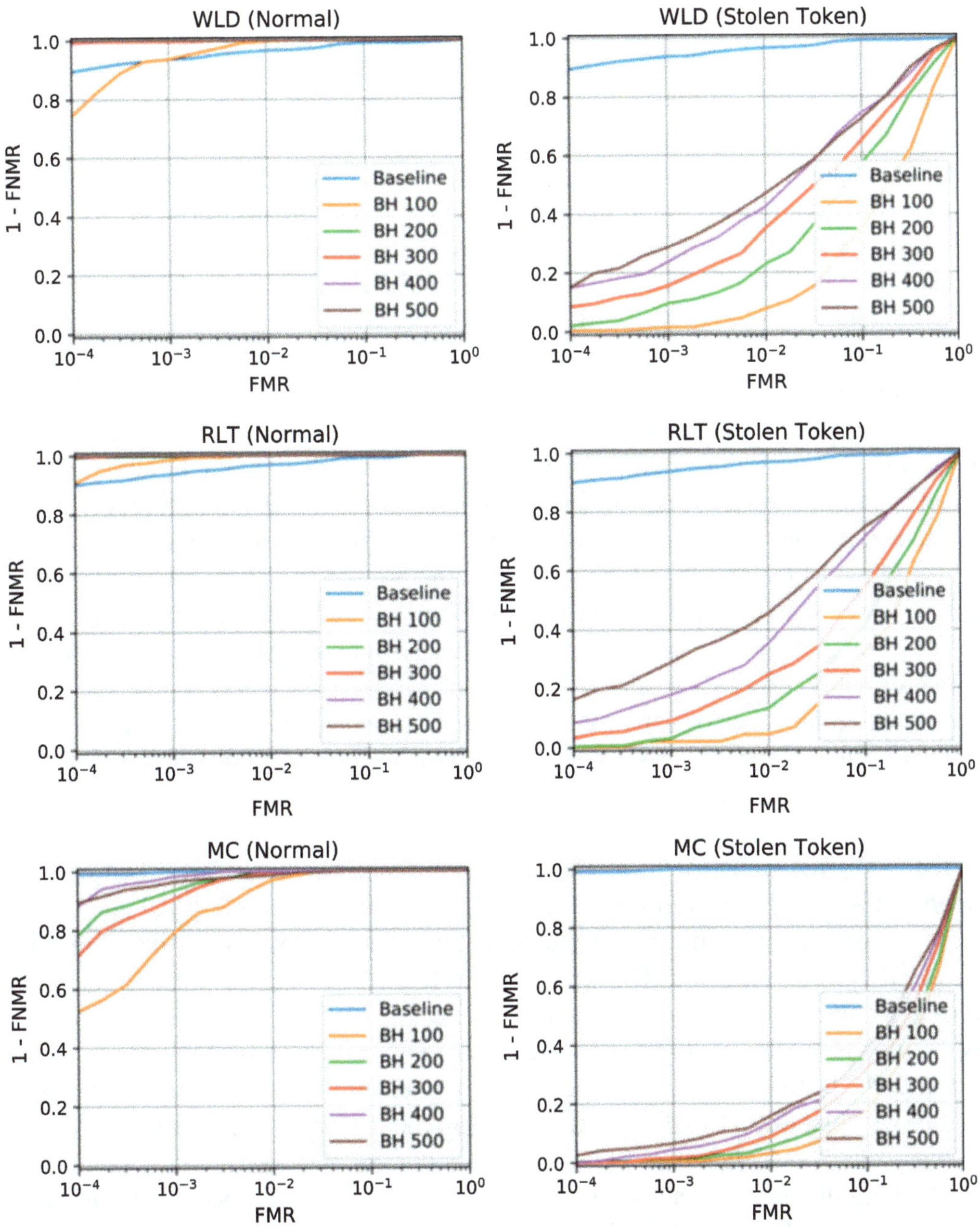

Fig. 15.4 Recognition performance of our BioHash-protected finger vein verification system in the Normal and Stolen Token scenarios

There a number of important observations from Fig. 15.4. First, in the Normal scenario, the BioHash-protected finger vein recognition performance for the WLD and RLT extractors is generally better than the baseline and has an error rate of approximately 0% at all FMR values, for $l > 100$. This is interesting, since the BioHashes are significantly smaller than the original finger vein feature vectors, as noted in Table 15.2. However, the additional entropy introduced by the user-specific projection matrices makes the resulting BioHashes more discriminative than the original finger vein feature vectors, so the superior performance of BioHashes is not surprising. The fact that the BioHashed MC finger vein patterns struggle to reach the baseline recognition performance as quickly as WLD or RLT BioHashes is probably because BioHashing on MC finger vein feature vectors results in the largest dimensionality reduction (see Table 15.2). It is interesting to note, however, that although the dimensionality reduction for both RLT and MC is greater than 99% for all BioHash lengths tested (refer to Table 15.2), RLT BioHashes perform much better than MC BioHashes. So, perhaps such a large dimensionality reduction is too severe for MC finger vein patterns. Nevertheless, we can see that the recognition performance improves as the BioHash length increases, and for all three extractors, the Normal scenario recognition performance in the BioHashed domain equalises or surpasses the baseline recognition performance as the FMR approaches 10^{-1}.

As for the Stolen Token scenario, from Fig. 15.4 we can see that the recognition performance for all three extractors is significantly worse than the baseline. Such a trend has been shown for other biometric characteristics in the literature (e.g. [19]), and it makes sense because in the Stolen Token scenario we are essentially performing a huge dimensionality reduction using the same projection matrix for each finger.[12] So, here we see the "real" effect (i.e. without the additional entropy introduced by the user-specific projection matrix in the Normal scenario) of the significant dimensionality reduction reported in Table 15.2. Since we cannot, in general, expect better recognition performance than the baseline when the dimensionality of our feature vectors is reduced via random projection, the best we can hope for is that the performance of our BioHash-protected finger vein verification system in the Stolen Token scenario is as close as possible to our baseline. From Fig. 15.4, we can see that, as in the Normal scenario, the recognition performance in the Stolen Token scenario approaches that of the baseline as the BioHash length increases.

If we were to rank our three extractors in the Normal scenario based on Fig. 15.4, we would place WLD and RLT first equal, followed by MC. This is an interesting turn of events, since the baseline ranking in Fig. 15.3 is the opposite. Our suspicion is that this is due to the thinness of the finger veins extracted by MC, which means that the MC feature vector may need a much higher resolution than the WLD or RLT feature vectors. So, a BioHash in the range of 100–500 bits might just be too small to represent the MC features.

Ranking the three extractors in the Stolen Token scenario, once again MC takes last place, with WLD and RLT fighting for first. It seems as if WLD has slightly better recognition performance than RLT for all but a BioHash length of 500, where

---

[12]Recall that each finger corresponds to a different identity.

RLT marginally takes over. We would expect that the smallest feature vector, that produced by WLD, would incur the smallest information loss as a result of the smallest dimensionality reduction in the projection to a 100–500 bit BioHash, while the greatest information loss would be incurred by the largest feature vector, that produced by MC. So, we would predict that the WLD extractor recognition performance would be closest to its baseline and MC furthest from its baseline in the Stolen Token scenario. This is, more or less, what we observe in Fig. 15.4.

If we had to draw a conclusion about the suitability of applying BioHashing to a finger vein verification system based on the recognition performance observed in Fig. 15.4 alone, we would probably have to say that BioHashing is *not* a suitable template protection scheme in this case. While we would assume that the system would operate in the Normal scenario most of the time, in which case BioHashing would be great for achieving a 0% error rate with the WLD or RLT feature extractors (or even the MC extractor, depending on what FMR the system needs to operate at), unfortunately we cannot ignore the possibility of the Stolen Token scenario. Since the recognition performance of all three extractors in the Stolen Token scenario is significantly worse than the baseline for the BioHash lengths tested, it seems too risky to recommend incorporating BioHashing into a finger vein verification system.

However, we have observed that the recognition performance of the BioHash-protected finger vein verification system improves as the BioHash length increases. So, this brings to mind a possible solution: Why not just try larger lengths? We discuss this point in Sect. 15.3.3.

15.3.3 Memory Constraints

This section investigates the possibility of increasing the BioHash length to gain better recognition performance for our BioHash-protected finger vein verification system in the Stolen Token scenario. Since we know that, theoretically, we cannot achieve better recognition performance than the baseline in the Stolen Token scenario, our first approach might be to choose the MC extractor, since Fig. 15.3 shows that it has the best baseline out of the three extractors tested. Even though the recognition performance of the BioHashed MC finger vein features in Fig. 15.4 was shown to be worse than the performance of the WLD and RLT features, our hope might be that if we choose a large enough BioHash length then perhaps it would be possible to push the performance of our BioHashed MC features up to the MC baseline performance. The question is, how large would this BioHash need to be in order for us to achieve such an improvement in the recognition performance?

Figure 15.5 shows a plot of the amount of memory required, in bytes, to generate the projection matrix for a single feature vector for each of our three extractors, as the BioHash length increases from 100 to 2,000. Remember that the projection matrix consists of n rows by l columns, where n denotes the number of bits in the binary feature vector (see Table 15.1) and l represents the BioHash length.

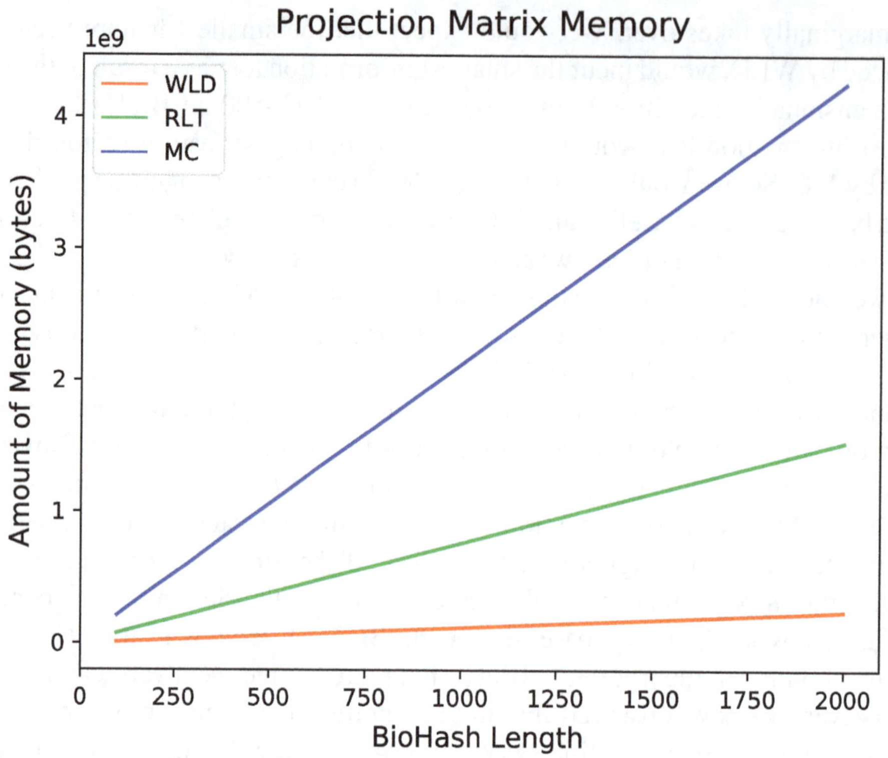

Fig. 15.5 Amount of memory required for the projection matrix as the BioHash length increases. Note that memory ranges from 0 to just over 4 GB in this plot

From Fig. 15.5, we can see that the amount of memory required for a projection matrix corresponding to a WLD feature vector grows quite gradually as the BioHash length increases, that for an RLT feature vector grows faster, and that for an MC feature vector the fastest. For example, it seems that for a 1,000-bit BioHash we would require less than 0.1 GB for a WLD projection matrix, about 0.75 GB for RLT, and over 2 GB for MC! This immediately suggests that anything close to or larger than a 1,000-bit BioHash would probably be impractical for MC features, possibly doable for RLT features but not for a much larger l, and manageable for larger BioHashes on WLD features.

We attempted 1,000-bit BioHashes for our three extractors. As expected, the result was a memory error for our MC feature vectors (i.e. insufficient memory available). This confirms our suspicion that, although MC has the best baseline, it may be impractical for BioHashing. We might consider re-scaling the MC-extracted finger vein pattern image so that we have a smaller feature vector to work with, but this is currently not a characteristic of our adopted MC extractor implementation. As for the WLD and RLT extractors, Fig. 15.6 compares their recognition performance on 1,000-bit BioHashes in the Stolen Token scenario (note that both extractors had an error rate of 0% in the Normal scenario, so this is not shown).

As expected from the Stolen Token plots in Fig. 15.4, the recognition performance of the two extractors in Fig. 15.6 is fairly close, with RLT doing slightly better at the larger BioHash length. Overall, however, this recognition performance may still be

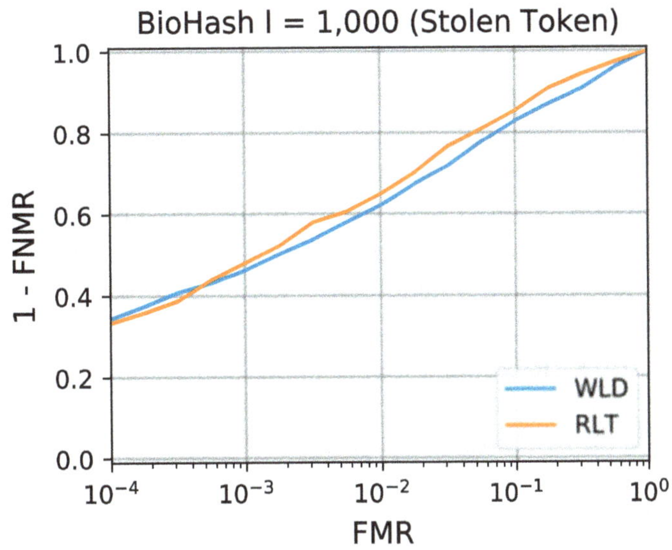

Fig. 15.6 WLD versus RLT when BioHash length is 1,000

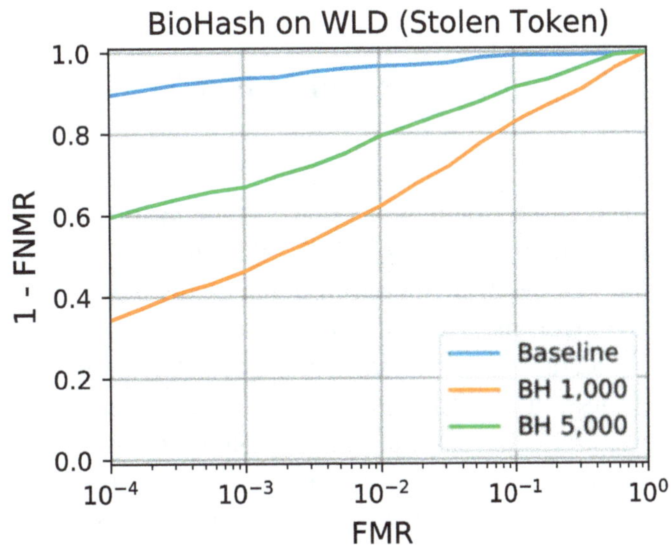

Fig. 15.7 1,000-bit versus 5,000-bit BioHashes on WLD compared to the baseline recognition performance

impractically low, so we might need to consider an even larger BioHash length to try to improve the performance.

We attempted a BioHash length of 5,000 for our WLD and RLT features. As expected, the RLT-based BioHash generation resulted in a memory error. This means that, with our current implementation of the RLT extractor, we cannot expect to gain a significant improvement in the recognition performance of RLT-based BioHashes in the Stolen Token scenario. The WLD-based BioHashes, on the other hand, had no memory issues. Figure 15.7 compares the recognition performance of our BioHash-protected finger vein verification system for 1,000-bit and 5,000-bit BioHashes on the WLD finger vein features in the Stolen Token scenario to the WLD baseline (note that both BioHash lengths had an error rate of 0% in the Normal scenario, so this is not shown).

Figure 15.7 confirms our previously observed trend (in Fig. 15.4) that the recognition performance of our WLD-based BioHash-protected finger vein verification system approaches the performance of the corresponding baseline in the Stolen Token scenario as the BioHash length increases. The final length will depend on how much of a drop in recognition performance is acceptable in the Stolen Token scenario. Technically, we can expect the BioHash recognition performance to be approximately the same as the baseline performance when the BioHash length is the same as the length of the original feature vector. The issue here is that, in this case, the BioHash is more or less fully invertible, meaning that it would be possible to recover the original feature vector if the user's secret seed and thus their projection matrix is leaked to an attacker. So, it is important to try to find a large enough BioHash length to ensure we have reasonable recognition performance in both the Normal and Stolen Token scenarios, while keeping the length small enough to ensure that the resulting BioHash is sufficiently privacy-preserving. The privacy-preserving properties of our BioHash-protected finger vein verification system must be investigated before we can fully justify any conclusions on whether or not BioHashing is a suitable template protection scheme for finger veins.

15.4 Conclusions and Future Work

This chapter presented the first investigation into the suitability of BioHashing as a finger vein template protection scheme for finger vein verification systems based on three feature extractors (WLD, RLT and MC), in terms of recognition performance only. Our experiments showed that, in the Normal scenario, it is possible to achieve a 0% error rate for BioHashes that are significantly smaller than the original finger vein feature vectors. BioHashes generated from WLD and RLT finger vein feature vectors were found to perform the best, while BioHashed MC features were shown to approach the baseline recognition performance as the FMR approached 10^{-1}. As expected, the recognition performance for all three extractors was worse than the baseline in the Stolen Token scenario due to the huge dimensionality reduction that is incurred in projecting a finger vein feature vector to a relatively small BioHash. While the recognition performance was shown to improve by increasing the length of the BioHash vectors, it was also demonstrated that the choice of length is constrained in practice by the amount of memory required for the projection matrix. Consequently, the WLD extractor was found to be the most promising for BioHashing purposes, since the relatively small size of WLD feature vectors allows for much larger BioHashes than would be possible for RLT or MC feature vectors. One issue with generating large BioHashes, however, is that, the larger the BioHash length, the easier it becomes to invert the BioHash to recover the original feature vector, thereby jeopardising the privacy of the verification system's users. To determine an optimal BioHash length that would ensure a reasonable balance between recognition performance and privacy preservation, we would need to conduct a full security and privacy analysis for the BioHashed WLD finger vein patterns. This will form part of our future work. Another area for future work could be to investigate the effect on BioHashing recognition performance when the three extractors are modified to produce feature vectors of the same size.

Acknowledgements The authors would like to acknowledge the following sources of funding for supporting this work: the Secure Access Control over Wide Area Network (SWAN) project and the Swiss Center for Biometrics Research and Testing.

References

1. Sandhya M, Prasad MVNK (2017) Biometric template protection: a systematic literature review of approaches and modalities. Springer International Publishing, Cham, pp 323–370
2. Hirata S, Takahashi K (2009) Cancelable biometrics with perfect secrecy for correlation-based matching. Springer, Berlin, Heidelberg, pp 868–878
3. Piciucco E, Maiorana E, Kauba C, Uhl A, Campisi P (2016) Cancelable biometrics for finger vein recognition. In: 2016 First international workshop on sensing, processing and learning for intelligent machines (SPLINE), July 2016, pp 1–5
4. Liu Y, Ling J, Liu Z, Shen J, Gao C (2017) Finger vein secure biometric template generation based on deep learning. Soft Comput 1–9
5. Favre M, Picard S, Bringer J, Chabanne H (2015) Balancing is the key: performing finger vein template protection using fuzzy commitment. In: 2015 International conference on information systems security and privacy (ICISSP), Feb 2015, pp 1–8
6. Yang W, Hu J, Wang S (2013) A finger-vein based cancellable bio-cryptosystem. Springer, Berlin, Heidelberg, pp 784–790
7. Lu L, Peng J (2014) Finger multi-biometric cryptosystem using feature-level fusion. Int J Signal Process Image Process Pattern Recognit 7(3):223–236
8. Peng J, Li Q, Abd El-Latif AA, Niu X (2014) Finger multibiometric cryptosystems: fusion strategy and template security. J Electron Imaging 23(2):023001
9. Gomez-Barrero M, Rathgeb C, Li G, Ramachandra R, Galbally J, Busch C (2018) Multi-biometric template protection based on bloom filters. Inf Fusion 42:37–50
10. Jin ATB, Ling DNC, Goh A (2004) Biohashing: two factor authentication featuring fingerprint data and tokenised random number. Pattern Recognit 37(11):2245–2255
11. Goh A, Ngo DCL (2003) Computation of cryptographic keys from face biometrics, pp 1–13. Springer, Berlin, Heidelberg
12. Connie T, Teoh A, Goh M, Ngo D (2005) Palmhashing: a novel approach for cancelable biometrics. Inf Process Lett 93(1):1–5
13. Chin CS, Jin ATB, Ling DNC (2006) High security iris verification system based on random secret integration. Comput Vis Image Underst 102(2):169–177
14. Lee EC, Lee HC, Park KR (2009) Finger vein recognition using minutia-based alignment and local binary pattern-based feature extraction. Int J Imaging Syst Technol 19(3):179–186
15. Huang B, Dai Y, Li R, Tang D, Li W (2010) Finger-vein authentication based on wide line detector and pattern normalization. In: 2010 20th International conference on pattern recognition, Aug 2010, pp 1269–1272
16. Miura N, Nagasaka A, Miyatake T (2004) Feature extraction of finger-vein patterns based on repeated line tracking and its application to personal identification. Mach Vis Appl 15(4):194–203
17. Miura N, Nagasaka A, Miyatake T (2007) Extraction of finger-vein patterns using maximum curvature points in image profiles. IEICE Trans Inf Syst 90(8):1185–1194
18. Ton BT, Veldhuis RNJ (2013) A high quality finger vascular pattern dataset collected using a custom designed capturing device. In: 2013 International conference on biometrics (ICB), June 2013, pp 1–5
19. Kong A, Cheung KH, Zhang D, Kamel M, You J (2006) An analysis of biohashing and its variants. Pattern Recognit 39(7):1359–1368

Chapter 16
Cancellable Biometrics for Finger Vein Recognition—Application in the Feature Domain

Simon Kirchgasser, Christof Kauba and Andreas Uhl

Abstract Privacy preservation is a key issue that has to be addressed in biometric recognition systems. Template protection schemes are a suitable way to tackle this task. Various template protection approaches originally proposed for other biometric modalities have been adopted to the domain of vascular pattern recognition. Cancellable biometrics are one class of these schemes. In this chapter, several cancellable biometrics methods like block re-mapping and block warping are applied in the feature domain. The results are compared to previous results obtained by the use of the same methods in the image domain regarding recognition performance, unlinkability and the level of privacy protection. The experiments are conducted using several well-established finger vein recognition systems on two publicly available datasets. Furthermore, an analysis regarding subject- versus system-dependent keys in terms of security and recognition performance is done.

Keywords Finger vein recognition · Template protection · Cancellable biometrics · Biometric performance evaluation · Block re-mapping · Warping

16.1 Introduction

Various methods exist to protect the subject-specific information contained in biometric samples and/or templates. According to several studies, e.g. Maltoni et al. [16], and ISO/IEC Standard 24745 [7] each method should exhibit four properties: *Security*, *Diversity*, *Revocability* and *Performance*. These shall ensure that the capture subject's privacy is protected and at the same time a stable and sufficient recognition

S. Kirchgasser · C. Kauba · A. Uhl (✉)
Department of Computer Sciences, University of Salzburg, Jakob-Haringer-Str. 2, 5020 Salzburg, Austria
e-mail: uhl@cs.sbg.ac.at

S. Kirchgasser
e-mail: skirch@cs.sbg.ac.at

C. Kauba
e-mail: ckauba@cs.sbg.ac.at

A. Uhl et al. (eds.), *Handbook of Vascular Biometrics*, Advances in Computer Vision and Pattern Recognition, https://doi.org/10.1007/978-3-030-27731-4_16

performance during the authentication process is achieved. The first aspect deals with the computational hardness to derive the original biometric template from the protected one (*security-irreversability*). *Diversity* is related to the privacy enhancement aspect and should ensure that the secured templates cannot be matched across different databases (*unlinkability*). The third aspect, *revocability*, should ensure that a compromised template can be revoked without exposing the biometric information, i.e. the original biometric trait/template remains unaltered and is not compromised. After removing the compromised data, a new template representing the same biometric instance can be generated. Finally, applying a certain protection scheme should not lead to a significant recognition performance degradation of the whole recognition system (*performance*).

One possibility to secure biometric information, cancellable biometrics, are introduced and evaluated on face and fingerprint data by Ratha et al. in [22]. The applied template protection schemes, *block re-mapping* and *warping*, have also been applied in the image domain and evaluated on iris [5, 14] and finger vein [20] datasets, respectively. Opposed to the latter study we want to investigate these schemes not in the image domain, but in the feature domain as several advantages and disadvantages exist in both spaces. These positive and negative aspects will be described in Sect. 16.2.

A detailed discussion on finger vein related template protection schemes, that can be found in literature, is given in Chap. 1 [26]. Thus, the interested reader is referred to this part of the handbook.

The rest of this chapter is organised as follows: The considered experimental questions are discussed in Sects. 16.2, 16.3 and 16.4 respectively. The employed non-invertible transform techniques are described in Sect. 16.5. Section 16.6 introduces the datasets utilised during the experimental evaluation, the finger vein recognition tool-chain as well as the evaluation protocol. The performance and unlinkability evaluation results are given and discussed in Sect. 16.7. Section 16.8 concludes this chapter and gives an outlook on future work.

16.2 Application in the Feature or Image Domain

If a template protection scheme is applied in the image/signal domain immediately after the image acquisition, the main advantage is that the biometric features extracted from the transformed sample do not correspond to those features computed from the original image/signal. So, the "real" template is never computed and does occur at no stage in the system and further, the sample is never processed in the system except at the sensor device. This provides the highest level of privacy protection for the capture subject. The main disadvantage of the application in the image/signal domain is that the feature extraction based on the protected image/signal might lead to incorrect features and thus, to inferior recognition performance. Especially in finger vein recognition, most of the well-established feature extraction schemes rely on tracking the vein lines, e.g. based on curvature information. By applying template protection methods like block re-mapping in the image domain right after the sample is captured, connected vein structures will become disconnected. These veins are then no longer detected as continuous vein segments which potentially causes problems during the feature extraction and might lead to an incomplete or faulty feature representation of the captured image. Consequently, the recognition performance of the whole biometric system can be negatively influenced by the application of the template protection scheme.

On the contrary, if template protection is conducted in the feature domain, the feature extraction is finished prior to the application of the template protection approach. Thus, the extracted feature vector or template is not influenced by the template protection scheme at this stage and represents the biometric information of the capture subject in an optimal way.

16.3 Key Selection: Subject- Versus System-Specific

There are two different types of key selection, subject- and system-specific keys. In the subject-specific key approach, the template of each subject is generated by a key which is specific for each subject while for a system-specific key, the templates of all subjects are generated by the same key.

Subject dependent keys have advantages in terms of preserving the capture subjects' privacy compared to system-dependent keys. Assigning an individual key to each capture subject ensures that if an adversary gets to know the key of one of the capture subjects, he can not compromise the entire database as each key is individual. A capture subject-specific key also ensures that insider attacks performed by legitimate registered subjects can not be performed straight forward. Such an attack involves a registered capture subject, who is been granted access to the system and has access to the template database as well. This adversary capture subject wants to be legitimated as one of the other capture subjects of the same biometric system. So he/she could just try to copy one of his/her templates over the template belonging to another capture subject and claim that this is his/her identity, thus trying to get authenticated as this other, genuine capture subject. If capture subject-specific keys are used, this is not easily possible as each of the templates stored in the database has been generated using an individual key. However, it remains questionable if such an insider attack is a likely one. In fact, it would probably be easier for an advisory who has access to the entire template database to simply create and store a new genuine capture subject that exhibits his/her biometric information together with a key he sets in order to get the legitimation he wants to acquire. Another advantage of capture subject-specific keys is that the system's recognition performance in enhanced by introducing more inter-subject variabilities and thus impacting the performed impostor comparisons. The additional variability introduced by the subject-specific key in combination with the differences between different biometric capture subjects leads to a better separation of genuine and impostor pairs which enhances the overall system's performance.

One drawback of using capture subject-specific keys is that the system design gets more complex, depending on how the capture subject-specific keys are generated and stored. In contrast to a system-specific key, which is valid for all capture subjects and throughout all components of the biometric recognition system, the individual capture subject-specific keys have to be generated and/or stored somehow. One possibility is to generate the key based on the capture subject's biometric trait every time the capture subject wants to get authenticated. This methodology refers to the basic idea of Biometric Cryptosystems (BCS), which have originally been developed for either securing a cryptographic key applying biometric features or generating a cryptographic key based on the biometric features [9]. Thus, the objective to employ a BCS is different but the underlying concept is similar to the one described earlier. The second option can be used to generate the capture subject specific key once and then store this key which is later retrieved during the authentication process. This key can either be stored in a separate key database or with the capture subject itself. Storing the keys in a key database of course poses the risk of the key database getting attacked and eventually the keys getting disclosed to an adversary. Storing the keys with the capture subject is the better option in terms of key security, however it lowers the convenience of the whole system from the capture subjects' perspective as they have to be aware of their key, either by remembering the key or by using smart cards or similar key storage devices.

16.4 Unlinkability

The ISO/IEC Standard 24745 [7] defines that irreversibility is not sufficient for protected templates, as they also need to be unlinkable. Unlinkability guarantees that stored and protected biometric information can not be linked across various different applications or databases. The standard defines templates to be *fully linkable* if a method exists which is able to decide if two templates protected using a different key were extracted from the same biometric sample with a certainty of 100%. The degree of linkability depends on the certainty of the method which decides if two protected templates originate from the same capture subject. However, the standard only defines what unlinkability means but gives no generic way of quantifying it. Gomez-Barrero et al. [4] present a universal framework to evaluate the unlinkability of a biometric template protection system based on the comparison scores. They proposed the so-called D_{sys} measurement as a global measure to evaluate a given biometric recognition and template protection system. Further details are given in Sect. 16.6.3 where the experimental protocol is introduced.

The application of the proposed framework [4] allows a comparison to previous work done on the aspect of key-sensitivity using the same protection schemes by Piciucco et al. [20]. Protected templates generated from the same biometric data by using different keys should not be comparable. Thus, the authors of [20] used the so-called Renewable Template Matching Rate (RTMR) to prove a low matching rate between templates generated using different keys on both protection schemes.

This can also be interpreted as a high amount of unlinkability as the RTMR can be interpreted as a restricted version of the D_{sys} measure.

16.5 Applied Cancellable Biometrics Schemes

The two investigated non-invertible transforms, block re-mapping and warping, are both based on a regular grid. Some variants of them have been investigated and discussed in [21, 22]. The input (regardless if a binary matrix or image) is subdivided into non-overlapping blocks using a predefined block size. The constructed blocks are processed individually, generating an entire protected template or image. As we aim to utilise the same comparison module for the unprotected and protected templates, there is one preliminary condition that must be fulfilled for the selected schemes: The protected template must exhibit a structure similar to the original input template. In particular, we interpret the feature vector (template) as binary image, representing vein patterns as 1s and background information as 0s. Based on this representation, each x-/y-coordinate position (each pixel) in the input image can be either described as background pixel or as vein pattern pixel. Thus, our approach can be used in the signal domain as well as in the feature domain and the template protection performance results obtained in image domain can be directly compared to results obtained in the feature domain. Note that in the signal domain the input as well as the protected output images are no binary but greyscale ones, which does not change the way the underlying cancellable biometrics schemes are applied (as they only change positions of pixels and do not relate single pixel values to each other). In the following, the basic block re-mapping scheme as well as the warping approach are described.

16.5.1 Block Re-mapping

In block re-mapping [22], the number of predefined blocks is separated into two classes, where the total number of blocks remains unaltered. The blocks belonging to the first class are randomly placed at different positions to the ones they have been located in the original input. This random allocation is done by assigning random numbers generated by a number generator according to a predefined key. This key must be stored, such that a new image acquired during authentication can be protected using the same number generator specification. The blocks belonging to the second class are dismissed and do not appear in the output. This aspect ensures the irreversibility property of the block re-mapping scheme. The percentage of blocks belonging to each of the two classes is set by a predefined value. The more blocks in the second class, the less biometric information is present in the output. Usually, the percentage of blocks in the first class is between 1/4 and 3/4 of the total blocks.

1	2	3	4
5	6	7	8

(a) Grid with blocks at their original positions.

5	2	7	3
4	1	3	5

(b) Block positions after re-mapping.

Fig. 16.1 Schematic block re-mapping scheme

Figure 16.1 shows the block re-mapping scheme which has been implemented in a slightly adopted version compared to the original one done by Piciucco et al. [20]. The main difference is the randomised block selection: We introduce an additional parameter, which controls the number of blocks that remain in the transformed template. To enable comparable results, we fixed the number of blocks that remain in the transformed templates to be at 75% of the original blocks. The required key information consists of the two set-up keys for the random generator and the block-size information for the grid construction. By comparing Fig. 16.1 (a) and (b) the following can be observed: While the blocks 4, 6 and 8 are present in (a) they do not occur in the protected, re-mapped image. All the other blocks are used to construct the re-mapped version (b) that has the same size as the original unprotected image or feature representation (a). It also becomes obvious that the blocks 3 and 5 are inserted multiple times into (b) in order to compensate for the absence of the non-considered blocks 6 and 8.

Due to the random selection, it is possible that some blocks are used more than once and others are never used. Otherwise, the re-mapping would resemble a permutation of all blocks, which could be reverted by applying a brute-force-attack testing all possible permutations or some more advanced attacks based on square jigsaw puzzle solver algorithms, e.g. [2, 19, 23].

The bigger the block size, the more biometric information is contained per block and thus, the higher the recognition performance is assumed to be after the application of block re-mapping. Of course, this argument also might depend on the feature extraction and comparison method as well as if it is done in signal or feature domain. Block re-mapping creates discontinuities at the block boundaries which influences the recognition performance if applied in the image domain as several of the feature extraction schemes try to follow continuous vein lines, which are not there any longer. This gets worse with decreasing block sizes. If block re-mapping is applied in the feature domain, this is not an issue as the feature extraction was done prior to applying the block re-mapping. However, due to the shifting process involved during comparison, the re-mapping of blocks can cause problems as a normalised region-of-interest is considered, especially for blocks that are placed at the boundaries of the protected templates. This might eventually lead to a degradation in the biometric systems performance because the information contained in those blocks is then "shifted out" of the image and the vein lines present in the blocks do not

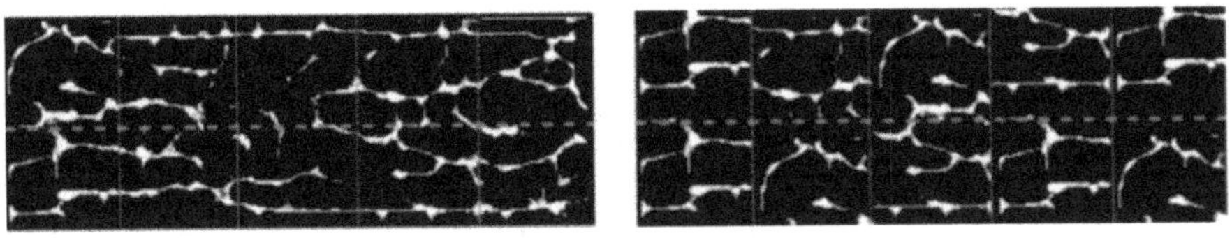

(a) Original template. (b) Re-mapped template.

Fig. 16.2 Finger vein templates displaying the variations that can occur during the re-mapping process using a block size of 64 × 64 pixel and MC as feature extraction method. The red dashed lines represent the grid

contribute to the comparison score anymore. In addition, blocks that share a common vein structure in the original template might be separated after performing the block re-mapping, posing a more severe problem due to the shifting applied during the comparison step. The vein structures close to the block borders are then shifted to completely different positions and cannot be compared any longer, leading to a decrease in the genuine comparison scores. Furthermore, it can also happen that the block re-mapping introduces new vein structures by combining two blocks that originally do not belong to each other. Both of the aforementioned possibilities have a potentially negative influence on the recognition performance. These problems due to the shifting applied during the comparison step are visualised in Fig. 16.2. It clearly can be seen that most of the vein structures visible in the original—left template, are not present in the protected—right template, but other structures have been newly introduced.

On the other hand, the larger the block size, the more of the original biometric information is contained per single block, lowering the level of privacy protection. Hence, we assume that a suitable trade-off between loss of recognition accuracy and level of privacy protection has to be found. Furthermore, the block size also corresponds to the irreversibility property of the transformation. The bigger the block size, the more information is contained per single block and the lower is the total number of blocks. The lower the number of blocks and the higher the information per block, the more effective are potential attacks on this protection scheme as discussed in the literature, e.g. [2, 19, 23].

16.5.2 *Block Warping*

Another non-invertible transformation in the context of cancellable biometrics is the so called "warping" (originally named "mesh warping" [27]). Warping can be applied in the image as well as in the template domain. Using this transformation, a function is applied to each pixel in the image which maps the pixel of the input at a given position to a certain position in the output (can also be the same position as in the input again). Thus, this mapping defines a new image or template containing the same information as the original input but in a distorted representation. The warping

(a) Basis grid, used to separate input information.

(b) Warped grid, built according to the initial grid.

(c) Positions of the blocks after block warping.

Fig. 16.3 Block Warping scheme including resize enhancement displayed schematically

(a) Original template.

(b) Warped template.

Fig. 16.4 Finger vein templates displaying the variations that can occur during the warping process using a block size of 32 × 32 pixel and PC as feature extraction method

approach utilised in this chapter is a combination of using a regular grid, as in the block re-mapping scheme, and a distortion function based on spline interpolation. The regular grid is deformed per each block and adjusted to the warped output grid. The number of blocks in the output is the same as in the input, but the content of each individual block is distorted in the warped output.

This distortion is introduced by randomly altering the edge positions of the regular grid, leading to a non-predictable deformation of the regular grid. Spline based interpolation of the input information/pixels is applied to adopt the area of each block with respect to the smaller or larger block area obtained after the deformation application (warping might either stretch or shrink the area of the block as the edge positions are changed). This distortion is key dependent and the key defines the seed value for the random generator responsible for the replacement of the grid edges. This key needs to be protected by some cryptographic encryption methods and stored in a safe place. However, if the key gets disclosed, it is not possible to reconstruct all of the original biometric data in polynomial time due to the applied spline based interpolation. Figure 16.3 shows the basic warping scheme, while in Fig. 16.4 an example of a original—left template and its protected—right template is given.

The application of interpolation does increase the template protection degree as the relation between original vein structures is distorted. However, these transformations might destroy dependencies between the vein lines which are necessary in the feature extraction step in order to enable the same recognition performance as on the original, unprotected data. On the one hand, the application of warping transformations increases the capture subject's privacy but on the other hand the recognition performance is likely to decrease. For more information about other warping methods, the interested reader is referred to [3], where a review of several different possible solutions including the use of parametric and non-parametric functions can be found.

16.6 Experimental Set-Up

In the following, the experimental set-up, including the datasets, the finger vein recognition tool-chain as well as the experimental protocol are explained.

16.6.1 Finger Vein Datasets

The experiments are conducted on two datasets: The first one is the University of Twente Finger Vascular Pattern Database (UTFVP) [25]. It consists of 1440 images, which were acquired from 60 subjects in a single session. Six fingers were captured, including the index, ring and middle finger of both hands with 4 images per finger. The finger vein images have a resolution of 672×380 pixels and a density of 126 pixels/cm, resulting in a width of 4–20 pixels for the visible blood vessels.

The second dataset we utilise here is the PLUSVein-FV3 Dorsal–Palmar finger vein dataset and which has been introduced in [10] and is partly discussed in Chap. 3 [12]. To enable a meaningful comparison with the UTFVP results, we only use the palmar subset. Region-Of-Interest (ROI) images containing only the centre part of the finger where most of the vein pattern information is located have been extracted from the captured images as well. Some example images of the PLUSVein-FV3 subsets are given in Fig. 16.5.

16.6.2 Finger Vein Recognition Tool-Chain

In this subsection an overview of the most important parts of a typical finger vein recognition tool-chain is given. There are several studies about finger vein recognition

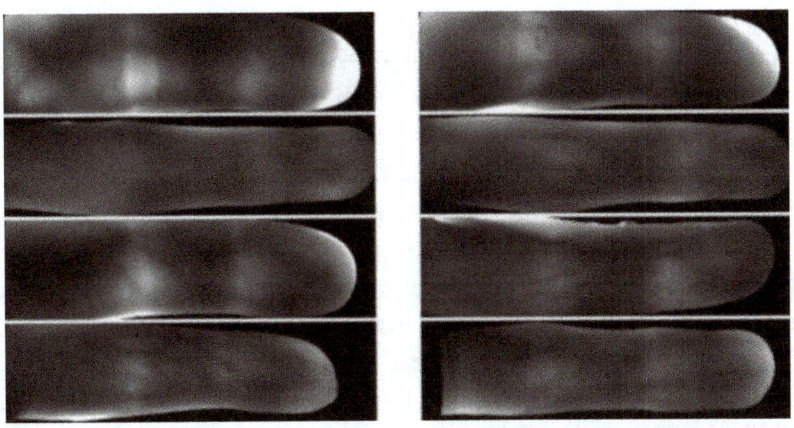

Fig. 16.5 Finger vein images of the PLUSVein-FV3 finger vein laser (first two rows) and LED subset (last two rows) showing 8 different fingers

systems, e.g. [8], that present and discuss different designs, but they all include a few common parts or modules. These main modules consist of: the finger vein scanner (image acquisition), the preprocessing module (preprocessing), the feature extraction module (feature extractor), the template comparison module (matcher) and the decision module (final decision). The system may contain an optional template protection module, either after the preprocessing module (image domain) or after the feature extraction module (feature domain). As the main focus of this chapter is on template protection applied in the feature domain, the system used during the experiments contains the template protection as part of the feature extractor. For feature extraction we selected six different methods: Gabor Filter (GF) [13], Isotropic Undecimated Wavelet Transform (IUWT) [24], Maximum Curvature (MC) [18], Principal Curvature (PC) [1], Repeated Line Tracking (RLT) [17] and Wide Line Detector (WLD) [6].

To calculate the final comparison scores an image correlation based comparison scheme as introduced by Miura et al. in [17] is applied to the baseline (unprotected) templates (features) as well as to the templates protected by block re-mapping and block warping. As the comparison scheme is correlation based, including a necessary pixel wise shifting, we selected a shift range of 80 pixels in x- and 30 pixels in y-direction, respectively. Further details on the deployed recognition tool-chain can be found in Chap. 4 [11] of this handbook.

16.6.3 Experimental Protocol and Types of Experiments

The necessary comparison scores are calculated using the correlation based comparison scheme described before and the comparison to be performed are based on the Fingerprint Verification Contests' (FVC) protocol [15]. To obtain the genuine scores, all possible comparisons are performed, i.e. the number of genuine scores is $60 * 6 * \frac{4*3}{2} = 2160$ (UTFVP) and $60 * 6 * \frac{5*4}{2} = 3600$ (PLUSVein-FV3), respectively. For the impostor scores, only a subset of all possible comparisons is performed. The first image of each finger is compared against the first image of all other fingers. This results in $\frac{60*6*(60*6-1)}{2} = 64{,}620$ impostor comparisons for each dataset (as both of them contain 60 subjects and 6 fingers per capture subject). As the employed comparison scheme is a symmetric measure, no symmetric comparisons (e.g. 1–2 and 2–1) are performed. The FVC protocol reduces the number of impostor comparisons in order to keep the computation time low for the whole performance evaluation while ensuring that every finger is compared against each other finger at least once. To quantify the recognition performance, several well-known measures are utilised: The equal error rate (EER, point where the FMR and the FNMR are equal), FMR_{100} (the lowest false Non-Match Rate (FNMR) for false match rate (FMR) $\leq 1\%$), FMR_{1000} (the lowest FNMR for FMR $\leq 0.1\%$) as well as the *ZeroFMR* (the FNMR for FMR $= 0\%$).

We conduct four sets of experiments:

1. In the first set of experiments the unprotected templates are considered. The first experiments provide a baseline to compare the recognition performance of the protected templates to
2. The second set of experiments deals with the protected templates, generated by applying one of the aforementioned cancellable biometrics schemes to the same templates that have been used during the first set of experiments. For score calculation, these protected templates are compared against each other. For both employed cancellable schemes, 10 runs using different system keys are performed to assess the recognition performance variability and key dependency of the recognition performance.
3. The third set of experiments compares capture subject specific and system-specific keys. Therefore, a different key (note: the key is controlling the random selection of blocks or the repositioning of the grid) is assigned to each finger, thus resulting in 360 virtual subjects (not only the 60 physical ones). Again, 10 runs with different keys per run are performed and averaged afterwards. These capture subject-specific key results are then compared to the system-specific key ones as obtained in the second set of experiments.
4. The last set of experiments is committed to the unlinkability analysis. The approach by Gomez et al. [4], introduced in Sect. 16.4 describes the extent of linkability in the given data, with a range of D_{sys} from [0, 1]. The higher the value, the more linkable are the involved templates. Thus, the resulting measure represents a percentage of linkability that is present. Of course, full unlinkability is given if the score is 0. D_{sys} is based on the local $D(s)$ value, which is calculated based on the comparison scores of several mated (genuine) as well as non-mated (impostor) comparison between templates protected by the same template protection system but using different keys, thus originating from different applications or systems. We utilise this measure to assess the unlinkability of the presented cancellable biometric schemes for finger vein recognition (block re-mapping and warping).

To comply with the principles of reproducible research we provide all experimental details, results as well as the used vein recognition SDK, settings files and scripts to run the experiments for download on our website: http://www.wavelab.at/sources/Kirchgasser19b/. The used datasets are publicly available as well, hence it is possible to reproduce our results for anyone who is interested to do so.

16.6.4 Selecting the Processing Level to Insert Template Protection

If template protection is done in the signal domain cancellable biometrics schemes are applied directly after the image acquisition and before the feature extraction. Otherwise, template protection is applied to the extracted binary vein features in order to protect the contained private biometric information right after the feature extraction is finished (feature domain).

The main purpose of this chapter and the experiments performed here is to provide a recognition performance comparison to the previous results obtained by Piciucco et al. [20]. The authors used the same cancellable methods on the UTFVP finger vein images, but as opposed to this chapter, not in the feature domain, but in the image domain. To ensure that our results are comparable with the previous ones by Piciucco et al. [20], we use the same block sizes during our experiments and select the same maximum offset for the block warping approach. Thus, we select block sizes of $16 \times 16, 32 \times 32, 48 \times 48$, and 64×64 for block re-mapping and block warping. For block warping, maximum offset values of 6, 12, 18, and 24 pixel are considered. In the following result tables block re-mapping is abbreviated using *remp_16* (block size: 16×16) till *remp_64* (block size: 64×64), while all warping experiments correspond to *warp_16_6* (block size: 16×16, offset: 6) till *warp_64_24* (block size: 64×64, offset: 24).

In contrast to the work of Piciucco et al. [20], we do not perform an analysis of the renewability and the key-sensitivity of the employed cancellable biometrics schemes. The key-sensitivity and renewability are expected to be similar for the schemes applied in the feature domain and in the image domain. Instead, we consider different issues like the comparison of capture subject vs. system-depended keys, and a thorough unlinkability analysis.

16.7 Experimental Results

This section presents and discusses all relevant results concerning the various template protection methods' impact on the recognition performance and unlinkability in the four sets of experiments that have been considered. As we aim to compare the experimental results to the corresponding results reported in [20], we first summarise their main results:

(a) The best performance results regarding EER were found for the block re-mapping scheme using a block size of 64×64.
(b) The best achieved *EER* was 1.67% for the protected data and 1.16% for the unprotected templates of the UTFVP dataset (using GF features).
(c) Block re-mapping outperformed block warping.

16.7.1 Baseline Experiments

Table 16.1 lists the performance results of the baseline experiments in percentage terms for the UTFVP and the PLUSVein-FV3 dataset. Overall, the performance on the UTFVP dataset is slightly superior compared to the PLUSVein-FV3 dataset for most of the evaluated recognition schemes.

Table 16.1 Baseline performance on the UTFVP and PLUSVein-FV3 database in terms of *EER*, FMR_{100}, FMR_{1000} and *ZeroFMR*. The best performing results are highlighted in bold numbers

Features	GF	IUWT	MC	PC	RLT	WLD
	UTFVP					
EER (%)	0.64	0.36	**0.09**	0.14	0.60	0.46
FMR_{100} (%)	0.60	0.27	**0.04**	0.13	0.32	0.27
FMR_{1000} (%)	1.00	0.55	**0.09**	0.13	1.15	0.60
ZeroFMR (%)	1.00	1.34	**0.23**	0.87	1.89	1.43
	PLUSVein-FV3 Laser					
EER(%)	0.74	1.49	**0.33**	1.47	1.71	1.38
FMR_{100}	0.63	1.66	**0.22**	1.50	1.91	1.44
FMR_{1000}	1.47	2.08	**0.44**	2.19	2.52	1.75
ZeroFMR	1.75	2.77	**0.72**	2.75	3.77	1.94
	PLUSVein-FV3 LED					
EER(%)	0.61	0.63	**0.28**	0.35	0.79	0.53
FMR_{100}	0.52	0.52	**0.27**	0.33	0.72	0.52
FMR_{1000}	0.63	0.97	**0.27**	0.38	1.16	0.55
ZeroFMR	1.00	3.05	**0.30**	0.66	1.77	0.69

On the UTFVP, the best recognition performance result with an *EER* of 0.09% is achieved by MC, followed by PC with an *EER* of 0.14%, then IUWT, WLD and RLT while GF has the worst performance with an *EER* of 0.64%. On both subsets of the PLUSVein-FV3 the best results are achieved by using MC as well, with an *EER* of 0.28% and 0.33% on the LED and laser subset, respectively. RLT performed worst compared to the other schemes on both subsets. Nevertheless, each of the evaluated recognition schemes achieves a competitive performance on all of the tested datasets. The other performance figures, i.e. FMR_{100}, FMR_{1000} and *ZeroFMR* are in line with the *EER* values and support the general trend that most of the applied feature extraction methods perform reasonably well on the given data sets using the baseline, unprotected templates.

16.7.2 Set 2—Protected Template Experiments (System Key)

As mentioned before, there are several parameters that have an essential influence on the recognition performance results obtained by applying the different cancellable biometrics schemes.

Table 16.2—feature domain and 16.3—signal domain, respectively, present the *EER* by using the mean ($\bar{x}$) and the standard deviation (σ) for both datasets. These results are calculated by randomly choosing 10 different keys and running the experiments first before the presented results are obtained by calculating $\bar{x}$ and σ of the performed computations.

Table 16.2 Recognition performance results (%) for template protection in the feature domain using system keys. The best performing results for each template protection method are highlighted in bold numbers

tempProt	*EER*											
	GF		IUWT		MC		PC		RLT		WLD	
	$\bar{x}$	σ	$\bar{x}$	σ	$\bar{x}$	σ	$\bar{x}$	σ	$\bar{x}$	σ	$\bar{x}$	σ
	UTFVP											
remp_16	13.76	1.58	6.29	0.51	8.41	1.09	8.31	0.56	5.77	0.71	6.71	0.37
remp_32	9.12	2.08	4.85	1.25	4.52	1.46	4.79	1.54	5.06	0.94	4.34	1.34
remp_48	7.18	4.20	4.07	2.33	3.62	2.61	4.55	3.38	4.26	2.07	3.59	1.98
remp_64	8.43	2.23	3.94	0.77	**3.27**	**0.83**	3.81	0.97	4.68	0.89	3.72	0.67
warp_16_6	3.36	0.74	0.74	0.18	0.78	0.23	**0.71**	**0.21**	1.20	0.24	1.16	0.25
warp_32_12	3.00	1.11	1.24	0.60	0.96	0.47	1.01	0.46	1.56	0.42	1.52	0.66
warp_48_18	2.45	1.15	1.15	0.60	0.87	0.42	0.92	0.47	1.44	0.45	1.34	0.67
warp_64_24	3.38	1.51	1.30	0.65	1.02	0.58	1.00	0.55	1.55	0.64	1.28	0.63
	PLUSVein-FV3 Laser											
remp_16	14.29	0.80	9.00	0.34	9.63	0.27	15.50	0.96	11.87	0.61	9.43	0.52
remp_32	12.02	1.12	7.72	0.97	10.24	0.57	12.38	2.07	11.54	1.42	6.60	0.94
remp_48	11.55	3.47	6.86	1.71	10.45	2.03	14.10	3.42	12.51	3.41	**5.52**	**2.04**
remp_64	10.79	5.10	7.20	2.19	10.60	0.88	14.82	6.78	15.90	11.24	5.60	2.90
warp_16_6	6.33	0.99	2.21	0.20	8.78	0.10	3.30	0.41	4.27	0.39	**2.02**	**0.18**
warp_32_12	6.20	2.26	3.00	0.75	8.80	0.10	4.29	1.38	5.09	1.67	2.66	0.70
warp_48_18	4.38	1.38	2.50	0.61	8.75	0.15	3.53	1.13	4.22	1.10	2.20	0.58
warp_64_24	4.59	1.59	2.86	0.73	8.73	0.30	3.76	1.38	4.16	1.22	2.32	0.68
	PLUSVein-FV3 LED											
remp_16	14.03	1.03	10.01	0.47	14.57	0.62	16.50	1.10	12.64	0.73	10.67	0.57
remp_32	11.84	1.68	8.12	1.14	9.72	2.00	12.81	2.51	12.18	1.85	6.79	1.05
remp_48	10.32	3.08	6.68	1.57	7.71	2.47	13.43	4.00	12.21	2.92	**4.42**	**1.27**
remp_64	10.08	5.76	7.21	2.20	9.73	8.87	14.48	7.78	16.11	11.32	5.14	3.08
warp_16_6	5.27	0.99	1.33	0.17	2.01	0.52	2.30	0.53	3.88	0.58	**1.00**	**0.17**
warp_32_12	5.67	2.29	2.51	0.92	3.32	1.92	3.76	1.66	4.87	1.86	1.84	0.72
warp_48_18	3.95	1.45	1.81	0.72	2.23	1.11	3.05	1.39	3.84	1.36	1.36	0.57
warp_64_24	4.07	1.69	2.48	1.15	2.27	1.06	3.51	1.66	3.90	1.65	1.55	0.90

At first we will discuss the results given by Table 16.2. Not surprisingly, the worst performance is observed for block re-mapping (*remp_16*, *remp_32*, *remp_48* and *remp_64*) using 16×16 as smallest block size while GF was applied (UTFVP). This trend is in line with the findings of Piciucco et al. [20], which have been observed in the signal domain. It has to be mentioned that the observed results are strongly depending on the particular feature extraction method. As in [20] only the GF method was used for feature extraction, a direct comparison can only be done based on the GF results using the UTFVP dataset. This direct comparison shows that our best results on GF are worse compared to the results presented in [20] as we used a different implementation of the scheme. However, the best results using UTFVP are obtained by MC using a block size of 64×64 (*EER* 3.27). In general *remp_48* and *remp_64* always resulted in the best performance for all datasets and not only on UTFVP (best *EER* of 5.52/4.42 for Laser/LED was achieved by applying WLD and *remp_48*). The only exception to this trend is given by RLT on the Laser/LED dataset. In this particular case, *remp_64* was performing worst, but this is a feature extraction type based observation.

In contrast to the block re-mapping based methods, the recognition performance of the warping based experiments (*warp_16_6* till *warp_64_24*) is better as observed for block re-mapping. This is in line with results reported for warping based experiments done in other biometric applications, e.g. [22] but opposed to the result of [20]. The best result on UTFVP is obtained for using PC and *warp_16_6* (*EER* 0.71). Nevertheless, there is not a big difference to the *EER* given by *warp_32_12*, *warp_48_18* and *warp_64_24*. It seems that the parameter choice has not a very high influence on the reported performance. For the other two datasets using WLD is resulting in the best *EER* values (Laser: 2.02, LED: 1.00).

As we want to compare the recognition performance of the feature domain template protected data to the same experiments which have been considering the transformations in the signal domain we will discuss the corresponding results now. The *EER* values applying template protection in the signal domain using system based keys are presented in Table 16.3.

The most important aspect using block re-mapping in the signal domain instead of applying the template protection schemes in the feature domain is a quite high-performance degradation in most of the conducted experiments. As mentioned in Sect. 16.2 it is likely that the feature extraction of the vein patterns after the template protection done in the signal domain might cause problems. This overall trend is confirmed by the observed *EER* results presented in Table 16.3. On UTFVP data, IUWT and PC resulted in the same trend that bigger block sizes are favourable in terms of performance (best average *EER*, 12.84, is given by IUWT using *remp_64*). For all other extraction schemes the *EER* values for *remp_16* or *remp_32* are better compared to *remp_64*. However, the performance difference is quite small.

Using warping, the influence on extracting the finger vein based features in the signal domain as compared to conducting the extraction in the feature domain is not so high as reported for block re-mapping. Hence, the overall performance trend using warping regardless of which dataset is considered, is similar to the results given in Table 16.2 (feature domain). IUWT again performs best in terms of *EER*. For *warp_16_6* the best performance can be reported. Surprisingly, the best average *EER*, 1.08, and the other performance values which are achieved applying IUWT on the template protected images are very similar for UTFVP and the LED dataset among each other.

Table 16.3 Recognition performance results (%) for template protection in the signal domain using system keys. The best performing results for each template protection method are highlighted in bold numbers

tempProt	EER											
	GF		IUWT		MC		PC		RLT		WLD	
	$\bar{x}$	σ	$\bar{x}$	σ	$\bar{x}$	σ	$\bar{x}$	σ	$\bar{x}$	σ	$\bar{x}$	σ
	UTFVP											
remp_16	14.66	0.66	15.43	0.80	15.04	0.58	15.67	0.62	16.09	1.04	15.02	0.58
remp_32	15.14	1.35	13.75	1.54	14.67	1.65	14.17	1.32	14.25	1.54	14.58	1.31
remp_48	17.88	1.63	13.24	1.16	16.03	1.25	13.91	1.16	15.29	1.37	15.34	1.31
remp_64	17.68	1.52	**12.84**	**1.11**	16.33	1.46	13.01	1.06	15.27	1.79	14.95	1.51
warp_16_6	4.13	0.48	**1.08**	**0.16**	2.28	0.39	1.23	0.20	1.35	0.16	2.00	0.34
warp_32_12	3.49	0.64	2.31	0.55	3.35	0.62	2.70	0.64	1.81	0.29	3.04	0.53
warp_48_18	3.93	0.81	2.53	0.72	3.44	0.84	2.79	0.82	2.33	0.61	3.05	0.76
warp_64_24	3.40	0.83	2.15	0.67	2.66	0.95	2.11	0.82	2.04	0.40	2.47	0.72
	PLUSVein-FV3 Laser											
remp_16	9.87	0.54	9.43	0.49	9.74	0.41	10.61	0.38	10.47	0.62	9.24	0.45
remp_32	9.44	0.77	**8.30**	**0.60**	8.46	0.35	10.07	0.71	9.53	0.60	8.42	0.59
remp_48	10.36	1.05	9.14	0.89	9.04	0.85	10.15	0.69	10.49	0.75	9.17	0.99
remp_64	11.40	0.87	9.67	0.81	9.04	0.76	11.16	1.28	10.78	0.63	9.38	0.99
warp_16_6	6.94	0.82	**2.61**	**0.20**	7.01	0.19	5.84	0.95	4.80	0.62	2.72	0.20
warp_32_12	8.38	1.01	3.99	0.52	6.63	0.19	9.37	0.92	6.58	0.67	3.83	0.56
warp_48_18	6.12	1.49	3.49	0.66	6.84	0.26	7.71	1.49	5.70	1.17	3.38	0.79
warp_64_24	6.00	1.60	3.39	0.65	6.96	0.27	7.52	1.66	5.67	1.39	3.07	0.70
	PLUSVein-FV3 LED											
remp_16	14.99	0.89	15.29	0.71	15.27	0.57	16.24	1.05	16.79	1.37	15.02	0.58
remp_32	15.88	1.43	13.75	1.54	15.49	1.60	15.20	1.34	15.28	1.60	14.58	1.31
remp_48	18.97	2.18	13.21	1.23	17.01	1.86	14.51	1.77	16.49	1.73	15.34	1.31
remp_64	19.15	2.51	**12.84**	**1.11**	17.23	2.31	13.90	1.77	15.46	2.59	14.95	1.51
warp_16_6	4.85	0.51	**1.08**	**0.16**	3.13	0.46	2.04	0.26	2.59	0.22	2.00	0.34
warp_32_12	5.06	0.86	2.33	0.58	4.63	1.02	4.05	0.86	3.09	0.38	3.04	0.53
warp_48_18	5.05	0.94	2.53	0.72	4.71	0.88	4.49	0.69	3.56	0.65	3.05	0.76
warp_64_24	4.46	0.92	2.15	0.67	3.93	1.09	3.71	0.82	3.38	0.51	2.47	0.72

16.7.3 Set 3—Subject Dependent Versus System-Dependent Key

In this subsection, the capture subject-specific key experiments and their results are described and compared to the performance values obtained by using a system-dependent key. For the capture subject specific key experiments, a different and unique key for each finger is selected, compared to only one system-specific key, which is the same for all fingers. This should lead to a better differentiation of single capture subjects as the inter-subject variability is increased. Considering the subject dependent template protection experiments the results are summarised in Tables 16.4—feature domain, and 16.5—signal domain, respectively. As expected,

Table 16.4 Recognition performance results (%) for template protection in the feature domain using subject-specific keys. The best performing results for each template protection method are highlighted in bold numbers

tempProt	EER											
	GF		IUWT		MC		PC		RLT		WLD	
	$\bar{x}$	σ	$\bar{x}$	σ	$\bar{x}$	σ	$\bar{x}$	σ	$\bar{x}$	σ	$\bar{x}$	σ
	UTFVP											
remp_16	3.28	0.20	4.82	0.38	4.70	0.29	7.68	0.47	3.19	0.24	5.79	0.31
remp_32	2.83	0.35	3.49	0.29	2.63	0.30	4.65	0.40	2.74	0.20	3.31	0.24
remp_48	2.93	0.28	3.18	0.41	2.27	0.25	3.41	0.36	2.90	0.33	2.31	0.15
remp_64	4.35	0.41	2.28	0.27	2.09	0.27	2.35	0.29	2.27	0.41	**1.90**	**0.27**
warp_16_6	2.74	0.23	0.72	0.18	**0.68**	**0.20**	0.82	0.13	1.00	0.10	1.24	0.16
warp_32_12	3.01	0.26	1.35	0.16	1.12	0.13	1.23	0.15	1.54	0.15	1.63	0.24
warp_48_18	2.20	0.24	1.16	0.19	0.90	0.16	1.08	0.16	1.26	0.20	1.33	0.15
warp_64_24	2.72	0.26	1.39	0.18	0.99	0.29	1.37	0.27	1.33	0.18	1.45	0.30
	PLUSVein-FV3 Laser											
remp_16	12.83	0.53	5.58	0.30	3.44	0.17	14.95	0.52	6.58	0.27	6.11	0.37
remp_32	9.50	0.40	3.46	0.28	3.60	0.23	10.96	0.45	6.58	0.38	3.81	0.21
remp_48	8.30	0.43	3.27	0.22	3.94	0.14	12.53	0.53	7.72	0.52	3.31	0.27
remp_64	5.15	0.31	**1.84**	**0.17**	3.93	0.26	11.09	0.93	6.93	0.62	2.52	0.15
warp_16_6	5.14	0.19	**1.81**	**0.10**	6.04	0.15	2.78	0.15	3.82	0.16	1.95	0.12
warp_32_12	6.07	0.28	2.41	0.16	5.83	0.12	4.54	0.33	5.02	0.27	2.41	0.15
warp_48_18	4.31	0.33	2.12	0.18	6.05	0.10	3.63	0.32	3.93	0.30	2.02	0.17
warp_64_24	4.42	0.35	2.26	0.24	4.71	0.23	4.35	0.22	3.96	0.40	2.18	0.19
	PLUSVein-FV3 LED											
remp_16	12.23	0.54	5.90	0.32	13.13	0.43	15.30	0.46	6.85	0.27	6.70	0.37
remp_32	9.08	0.42	3.67	0.36	8.02	0.38	11.00	0.65	6.79	0.28	3.81	0.25
remp_48	7.61	0.31	3.58	0.16	5.65	0.34	12.69	0.64	8.01	0.39	2.95	0.29
remp_64	4.64	0.33	**1.93**	**0.15**	5.51	0.40	10.35	0.80	7.32	0.73	2.15	0.26
warp_16_6	4.10	0.22	0.90	0.09	1.42	0.14	1.78	0.23	3.18	0.29	**0.85**	**0.09**
warp_32_12	5.85	0.41	2.00	0.21	3.36	0.28	4.22	0.27	4.83	0.19	1.65	0.23
warp_48_18	3.83	0.43	1.54	0.17	2.39	0.32	3.44	0.26	3.69	0.44	1.32	0.24
warp_64_24	3.88	0.30	1.85	0.29	2.54	0.43	4.00	0.31	3.66	0.33	1.50	0.44

it becomes apparent that the overall performance of all experiments using subject dependent keys is much better compared to the system-specific key results. This can be explained as the usage of subject dependent keys provides a better separation of genuine and impostor score distributions after applying the transformation.

The best feature domain based performance (see Table 16.4) is obtained on UTFVP using WLD during *remp_64* (*EER* 1.90) and MC during *warp_16_6* (*EER* 0.68), on the Laser dataset using IUWT (*EER* 1.84 for *remp_64*, *EER* 1.81 for *warp_16_6*) and finally on the LED dataset using IUWT/WLD (*EER* 1.93/0.85) applying *remp_64*/*warp_16_6*. According to the *EER* values highlighted in Table 16.5 (signal domain) the overall best recognition performance is achieved by applying the template protection schemes in the signal domain using subject-specific

Table 16.5 Recognition performance results (%) for template protection in the signal domain using subject-specific keys. The best performing results for each template protection method are highlighted in bold numbers

tempProt	EER											
	GF		IUWT		MC		PC		RLT		WLD	
	$\bar{x}$	σ	$\bar{x}$	σ	$\bar{x}$	σ	$\bar{x}$	σ	$\bar{x}$	σ	$\bar{x}$	σ
	UTFVP											
remp_16	0.98	0.15	0.59	0.09	0.78	0.10	0.98	0.13	1.13	0.13	0.53	0.04
remp_32	0.50	0.09	0.48	0.07	0.69	0.12	0.86	0.18	0.96	0.18	0.41	0.09
remp_48	**0.39**	**0.04**	0.46	0.07	0.54	0.05	0.77	0.14	0.52	0.10	0.45	0.08
remp_64	0.48	0.12	0.44	0.15	0.57	0.13	0.60	0.13	0.57	0.10	0.41	0.08
warp_16_6	1.39	0.16	0.57	0.07	0.64	0.12	**0.42**	**0.09**	0.80	0.06	0.43	0.10
warp_32_12	2.16	0.22	1.31	0.28	1.65	0.19	1.66	0.17	1.22	0.20	1.47	0.16
warp_48_18	2.15	0.19	1.55	0.14	1.64	0.20	1.70	0.15	1.51	0.14	1.76	0.16
warp_64_24	1.80	0.23	1.64	0.25	1.50	0.20	1.68	0.31	1.44	0.18	1.77	0.17
	PLUSVein-FV3 Laser											
remp_16	3.44	0.17	**0.96**	**0.11**	0.69	0.06	3.04	0.16	3.6	0.25	1.08	0.10
remp_32	3.21	0.33	1.29	0.20	0.96	0.08	4.29	0.26	4.34	0.29	1.38	0.20
remp_48	3.95	0.33	1.47	0.20	1.09	0.12	4.71	0.27	5.48	0.20	1.68	0.16
remp_64	4.09	0.31	1.88	0.19	1.11	0.10	5.45	0.40	4.89	0.38	2.17	0.24
warp_16_6	5.62	0.24	2.35	0.06	2.82	0.14	5.65	0.15	4.57	0.21	**2.12**	**0.10**
warp_32_12	6.74	0.27	2.87	0.10	2.88	0.12	8.46	0.26	5.74	0.26	2.65	0.11
warp_48_18	6.23	0.26	3.02	0.19	3.23	0.14	8.17	0.31	5.76	0.28	2.77	0.23
warp_64_24	5.71	0.30	2.81	0.14	3.87	0.20	7.61	0.31	5.54	0.34	2.45	0.12
	PLUSVein-FV3 LED											
remp_16	1.93	0.20	0.59	0.09	1.54	0.10	1.93	0.21	2.27	0.19	0.53	0.04
remp_32	1.06	0.16	0.48	0.07	1.51	0.20	2.53	0.27	2.14	0.21	0.41	0.09
remp_48	1.08	0.09	0.46	0.07	1.76	0.13	2.50	0.25	1.25	0.18	0.45	0.08
remp_64	0.88	0.16	0.44	0.15	1.46	0.23	1.87	0.25	1.21	0.21	**0.41**	**0.08**
warp_16_6	3.64	0.23	0.57	0.07	2.7	0.27	1.78	0.22	2.25	0.25	**0.43**	**0.10**
warp_32_12	4.81	0.28	1.31	0.28	4.05	0.22	3.95	0.24	2.83	0.23	1.47	0.16
warp_48_18	4.07	0.22	1.55	0.14	3.61	0.33	3.89	0.25	3.03	0.32	1.76	0.16
warp_64_24	3.72	0.30	1.64	0.25	3.37	0.25	3.77	0.29	3.06	0.13	1.77	0.17

keys. This observation is interesting because it seems that in most cases subject-specific keys have a more positive effect on the protected features' performance if the corresponding transformation was applied in the signal domain. However, there are also some cases where the subject-specific keys' signal domain performance is lower compared to the best results obtained in the feature domain, e.g. Laser dataset using WLD and *warp_16_6*. Compared to [20] the recognition performance presented in Table 16.5 using GF is outperforming the findings stated by Piciucco et al. no matter if block re-mapping or warping is considered. All other results obtained for UTFVP are better as well.

16.7.4 Set 4—Unlinkability Analysis

The unlinkability analysis is performed to ensure that the applied template protection schemes meet the principles established by the ISO/IEC 24745 standard [7], in particular the unlinkability requirements. If there is a high amount of linkability for a certain template protection scheme, it is easy to match two protected templates from the same finger among different applications using different keys. In that case, it is easy to track the capture subjects across different applications, which poses a threat to the capture subjects' privacy. The unlinkability is likely to be low (linkability high) if there is too little variation between protected templates based on two different keys (i.e. the key-sensitivity is low) or the unprotected and the protected template in general. Tables 16.6, 16.7, 16.8 and 16.9 lists the global unlinkability scores, D_{sys},

Table 16.6 D_{sys} unlinkability scores for the selected template protection schemes applied in feature domain using system dependent keys. The best results (low values, representing unlinkability) for each template protection method are highlighted in bold numbers

tempProt	Dsys											
	GF		IUWT		MC		PC		RLT		WLD	
	$\bar{x}$	σ	$\bar{x}$	σ	$\bar{x}$	σ	$\bar{x}$	σ	$\bar{x}$	σ	$\bar{x}$	σ
	UTFVP											
remp_16	3.43	0.52	3.02	0.58	3.91	0.97	**2.90**	**0.32**	3.09	0.46	4.35	0.53
remp_32	13.96	13.89	10.32	16.79	15.83	16.09	9.34	17.09	8.21	5.88	16.71	19.25
remp_48	18.72	22.27	14.92	23.90	21.49	25.76	13.86	23.66	10.65	17.60	18.54	26.33
remp_64	25.67	18.69	20.03	21.95	29.72	22.93	20.81	22.36	16.32	19.89	27.24	22.93
warp_16_6	56.35	8.94	85.01	6.92	82.61	6.31	79.54	8.02	81.66	6.00	74.87	8.19
warp_32_12	37.54	17.97	40.18	21.74	55.86	17.66	40.18	21.45	44.37	18.8	43.19	19.43
warp_48_18	**36.15**	**22.52**	39.08	27.65	52.76	22.89	37.17	26.75	42.92	25.3	41.56	25.20
warp_64_24	42.43	29.21	41.21	32.14	53.13	28.26	48.81	32.36	44.68	31.45	43.43	21.12
	PLUSVein-FV3 Laser											
remp_16	4.07	0.50	2.73	0.44	3.42	0.70	2.79	0.53	**2.64**	**0.49**	4.28	0.81
remp_32	20.16	17.10	13.77	18.96	21.00	20.97	10.40	18.23	8.80	9.95	17.13	21.00
remp_48	14.00	17.39	9.18	17.69	14.53	20.09	7.18	16.55	5.26	8.39	12.75	20.81
remp_64	19.58	22.01	14.37	22.48	24.51	22.42	10.06	18.07	7.38	10.77	17.77	21.53
warp_16_6	63.42	10.55	81.26	10.17	86.37	4.36	83.99	6.77	68.19	9.82	82.1	8.65
warp_32_12	34.62	17.86	35.90	20.96	53.34	17.51	44.14	18.82	**29.83**	**13.38**	46.36	18.48
warp_48_18	44.30	21.56	42.61	23.67	58.42	18.86	47.80	21.23	34.44	18.93	52.10	20.69
warp_64_24	33.33	26.48	35.28	28.94	43.99	28.59	34.27	27.20	28.83	24.97	47.23	17.95
	PLUSVein-FV3 LED											
remp_16	3.81	0.42	2.86	0.46	3.34	0.62	2.55	0.35	**2.34**	**0.45**	4.04	0.65
remp_32	19.67	17.36	13.07	18.9	21.71	20.47	10.62	18.32	8.69	10.20	17.03	21.01
remp_48	14.06	17.78	9.18	17.51	14.99	20.62	7.42	16.15	5.56	9.35	13.23	21.38
remp_64	19.44	22.26	13.58	22.05	23.53	22.61	10.13	17.94	7.71	10.23	16.91	21.19
warp_16_6	67.02	10.53	81.95	10.31	86.66	6.62	84.38	7.23	67.51	10.59	82.58	8.37
warp_32_12	37.51	17.38	35.27	20.74	56.52	16.52	44.58	18.94	**28.62**	**12.99**	47.66	18.31
warp_48_18	45.41	22.65	42.56	24.21	60.46	19.33	48.14	21.48	34.10	19.43	52.99	21.83
warp_64_24	32.81	26.35	32.99	28.49	45.09	28.34	33.88	27.47	27.70	24.25	48.52	19.11

Table 16.7 D_{sys} unlinkability scores for the selected template protection schemes applied in signal domain using system dependent keys. The best results (low values, representing unlinkability) for each template protection method are highlighted in bold numbers

tempProt	Dsys											
	GF		IUWT		MC		PC		RLT		WLD	
	$\bar{x}$	σ	$\bar{x}$	σ	$\bar{x}$	σ	$\bar{x}$	σ	$\bar{x}$	σ	$\bar{x}$	σ
	UTFVP											
remp_16	**2.97**	**0.63**	2.97	0.66	3.05	0.59	2.77	0.33	2.86	0.51	3.34	0.81
remp_32	6.03	12.42	6.17	12.76	6.07	12.19	5.80	12.48	5.84	12.55	6.46	12.39
remp_48	6.74	12.04	6.70	13.94	6.91	12.34	6.93	13.81	6.00	13.35	7.58	13.07
remp_64	6.43	11.24	6.56	13.61	6.37	11.53	6.63	13.79	6.16	12.94	7.30	13.04
warp_16_6	73.00	4.02	87.21	2.49	82.97	3.05	84.81	2.82	83.14	2.60	84.17	2.89
warp_32_12	42.85	14.28	50.90	14.94	52.36	12.40	47.03	15.45	55.01	12.49	49.88	14.39
warp_48_18	32.64	17.20	33.24	19.71	42.26	16.50	33.26	20.97	36.79	18.98	37.10	18.63
warp_64_24	26.00	17.83	**17.92**	**11.65**	28.71	14.28	23.11	20.41	26.72	19.19	26.40	18.45
	PLUSVein-FV3 Laser											
remp_16	2.68	0.44	2.30	0.34	2.41	0.40	**2.25**	**0.32**	2.57	0.38	3.59	1.03
remp_32	8.83	16.19	6.96	16.48	7.20	16.63	6.32	16.16	6.74	16.63	9.66	16.12
remp_48	9.12	15.05	7.27	15.86	8.52	14.69	6.71	15.86	6.30	16.13	8.90	15.21
remp_64	9.78	15.43	7.76	15.97	8.88	15.36	7.83	16.08	7.43	15.97	10.50	15.92
warp_16_6	76.36	5.87	89.06	2.95	87.14	1.66	77.23	2.55	80.01	2.64	86.3	1.51
warp_32_12	42.37	20.44	44.63	12.57	51.05	12.38	35.13	14.56	42.47	14.04	53.03	7.96
warp_48_18	29.59	16.50	31.37	18.84	41.96	18.63	24.50	16.14	27.83	19.52	47.16	23.77
warp_64_24	27.99	20.84	25.37	21.61	37.85	20.00	**20.92**	**17.16**	23.03	18.72	21.00	4.95
	PLUSVein-FV3 LED											
remp_16	2.97	0.63	3.00	0.5	3.00	0.56	**2.80**	**0.60**	2.86	0.51	3.34	0.81
remp_32	6.20	12.78	6.37	13.12	6.07	12.19	6.02	12.44	2.88	0.44	6.46	12.39
remp_48	6.74	12.04	7.05	14.79	6.91	12.34	6.99	13.62	6.38	14.16	7.58	13.07
remp_64	6.43	11.24	6.56	13.61	6.37	11.53	6.74	13.87	6.16	12.94	7.30	13.04
warp_16_6	78.42	5.77	90.04	3.05	88.48	1.96	78.32	3.05	81.22	3.46	88.02	1.94
warp_32_12	41.32	21.14	45.32	12.85	52.04	11.89	36.03	15.06	44.86	15.21	53.97	8.69
warp_48_18	30.55	17.05	31.34	19.79	41.58	19.25	23.99	15.12	28.66	20.12	48.86	24.97
warp_64_24	27.89	21.00	25.27	20.99	37.92	19.53	21.45	18.10	24.26	19.27	**20.95**	**6.01**

for all datasets using block re-mapping and warping, similar to the tables that have been used to describe the recognition performance. The D_{sys} ranges normally from 0 to 1, where 0 represents the best achievable unlinkability score. We shifted the range from [0, 1] to values in [0, 100] to improve the readability of the results.

The D_{sys} ranges reveal that there are several block re-mapping configurations leading to a low linkability score, indicating that the protected templates cannot be linked across different applications (high unlinkability). This can be observed not only for applying block re-mapping in the feature domain using system-specific keys but also for the application in all other feature spaces and key selection strategies. The lowest D_{sys} scores can be detected for the usage of *remp_16*. For most block sizes

Table 16.8 D_{sys} unlinkability scores for the selected template protection schemes applied in feature domain using subject dependent keys. The best results (low values, representing unlinkability) for each template protection method are highlighted in bold numbers

tempProt	Dsys											
	GF		IUWT		MC		PC		RLT		WLD	
	$\bar{x}$	σ	$\bar{x}$	σ	$\bar{x}$	σ	$\bar{x}$	σ	$\bar{x}$	σ	$\bar{x}$	σ
	UTFVP											
remp_16	3.43	0.52	3.02	0.58	3.95	0.96	**2.90**	**0.32**	3.09	0.46	4.35	0.53
remp_32	13.93	13.48	10.32	16.79	15.83	16.09	9.34	17.09	8.21	5.88	15.75	17.80
remp_48	18.72	22.27	14.92	23.90	21.49	25.76	13.86	23.66	11.82	17.72	18.78	25.23
remp_64	24.41	18.90	20.03	21.95	30.95	22.85	20.81	22.36	15.54	19.52	25.92	22.94
warp_16_6	58.04	1.07	83.14	0.75	82.94	0.85	79.15	0.62	79.77	0.73	74.92	1.05
warp_32_12	**31.73**	**11.71**	35.67	11.85	49.61	8.56	33.63	12.28	38.96	1.45	37.93	11.00
warp_48_18	39.17	10.46	41.63	10.63	53.54	7.86	40.12	10.94	44.94	1.53	44.28	9.66
warp_64_24	35.15	11.68	32.15	12.61	44.85	9.88	37.82	11.54	36.36	1.57	36.56	10.85
	PLUSVein-FV3 Laser											
remp_16	4.07	0.50	2.73	0.44	3.41	0.75	2.79	0.53	**2.65**	**0.51**	4.29	0.84
remp_32	20.38	17.60	13.77	18.96	21.00	20.97	10.40	18.23	9.08	10.21	17.95	21.35
remp_48	14.61	17.73	9.18	17.69	14.53	20.09	7.18	16.55	5.26	8.39	12.75	20.81
remp_64	19.58	22.01	14.37	22.48	24.51	22.42	10.48	18.53	7.38	10.77	17.77	21.53
warp_16_6	67.33	0.71	84.02	0.88	87.14	0.92	85.30	0.67	70.99	0.97	83.39	0.93
warp_32_12	32.71	12.16	34.82	13.06	49.23	9.01	41.37	10.71	29.76	0.94	44.48	10.19
warp_48_18	38.73	11.35	39.00	11.80	50.29	9.14	40.83	11.08	34.65	1.93	46.5	10.38
warp_64_24	31.46	13.65	32.65	13.16	41.79	11.84	31.79	13.04	**28.76**	**1.34**	43.25	10.12
	PLUSVein-FV3 LED											
remp_16	3.81	0.42	2.86	0.46	3.34	0.62	2.55	0.35	**2.34**	**0.45**	4.04	0.65
remp_32	19.67	17.36	13.07	18.90	21.71	20.47	10.62	18.32	8.69	10.20	17.03	21.01
remp_48	14.06	17.78	9.18	17.51	14.99	20.62	7.42	16.15	5.56	9.35	13.23	21.38
remp_64	19.44	22.26	13.58	22.05	23.53	22.61	10.13	17.94	7.71	10.23	16.91	21.19
warp_16_6	71.08	0.81	83.99	0.87	88.52	0.64	86.55	0.66	70.93	1.10	84.96	0.80
warp_32_12	34.39	11.73	33.42	12.73	51.79	8.49	41.2	10.74	**28.42**	**0.75**	45.48	9.75
warp_48_18	39.69	11.23	38.46	11.82	51.87	8.79	40.85	11.3	34.03	1.65	46.56	9.92
warp_64_24	31.96	12.91	31.72	13.33	43.29	10.78	31.66	13.12	28.79	1.73	44.34	9.68

48×48 or 64×64 the unlinkability values are higher compared to the schemes using lower block sizes. Thus, the linkability is increased.

For warping the situation is different. First, the obtained D_{sys} is mostly quite high which indicates a high linkability regardless the choice of key selection strategy or the domain. Second, *warp_32_12* or *warp_48_18* exhibit the lowest unlinkability scores, clearly the highest amount of linkability detected for *warp_16_6*. The reason for this is given by the applied warping scheme. If small block sizes are used the offset, which is responsible for the amount of introduced degradation during the transformation, is small as well. Thus, for an offset of 6 only a little amount of variation in the original image (signal domain) or extracted template (feature domain) is caused. Of course,

Table 16.9 D_{sys} unlinkability scores for the selected template protection schemes applied in signal domain using subject dependent keys. The best results (low values, representing unlinkability) for each template protection method are highlighted in bold numbers

tempProt	Dsys											
	GF		IUWT		MC		PC		RLT		WLD	
	$\bar{x}$	σ	$\bar{x}$	σ	$\bar{x}$	σ	$\bar{x}$	σ	$\bar{x}$	σ	$\bar{x}$	σ
	UTFVP											
remp_16	2.97	0.63	2.97	0.66	3.05	0.59	**2.77**	**0.33**	2.86	0.51	3.34	0.81
remp_32	6.16	12.79	6.17	12.76	6.07	12.19	5.80	12.48	5.84	12.55	6.67	12.74
remp_48	6.74	12.04	6.70	13.94	6.91	12.34	6.93	13.81	6.00	13.35	7.58	13.07
remp_64	6.43	11.24	6.56	13.61	6.37	11.53	6.63	13.79	6.16	12.94	7.30	13.04
warp_16_6	75.41	0.56	88.16	0.35	84.89	0.55	87.22	0.52	85.51	0.53	85.8	0.43
warp_32_12	46.76	8.57	54.42	7.20	55.75	6.54	51.39	7.64	58.88	6.22	54.15	6.97
warp_48_18	33.87	12.06	33.68	12.37	41.34	10.28	32.58	12.28	38.74	11.10	36.49	11.48
warp_64_24	29.82	13.06	**25.12**	**14.42**	34.74	12.11	25.41	14.21	30.16	13.12	29.96	13.16
	PLUSVein-FV3 Laser											
remp_16	2.68	0.44	2.30	0.34	2.41	0.40	**2.25**	**0.32**	2.57	0.38	3.59	1.03
remp_32	8.83	16.19	6.96	16.48	7.20	16.63	6.32	16.16	6.74	16.63	9.66	16.12
remp_48	9.12	15.05	7.27	15.86	8.52	14.69	6.71	15.86	6.30	16.13	8.90	15.21
remp_64	9.78	15.43	7.76	15.97	8.88	15.36	7.83	16.08	7.43	15.97	10.50	15.92
warp_16_6	78.38	0.56	90.26	0.46	87.71	0.51	78.41	0.58	80.34	0.48	88.56	0.43
warp_32_12	42.94	0.86	49.98	1.11	54.95	1.50	36.00	0.99	42.75	1.14	56.58	1.22
warp_48_18	29.25	0.95	29.10	0.97	37.86	1.20	21.38	0.70	25.02	1.17	37.98	1.07
warp_64_24	23.59	1.18	19.47	1.44	31.20	1.64	**15.97**	**0.98**	18.19	1.08	29.28	1.29
	PLUSVein-FV3 LED											
remp_16	2.97	0.63	3.00	0.5	3.00	0.56	**2.80**	**0.60**	2.86	0.51	3.34	0.81
remp_32	6.03	12.42	6.17	12.76	6.07	12.19	6.02	12.44	5.84	12.55	6.46	12.39
remp_48	6.74	12.04	7.05	14.79	6.91	12.34	6.99	13.62	6.38	14.16	7.58	13.07
remp_64	6.43	11.24	6.56	13.61	6.37	11.53	6.74	13.87	6.16	12.94	7.30	13.04
warp_16_6	79.05	0.78	91.02	0.59	88.45	0.89	79.88	0.75	81.45	0.75	89.16	0.66
warp_32_12	43.65	1.22	50.25	1.89	55.66	1.87	36.99	1.36	43.83	2.04	57.39	1.77
warp_48_18	29.85	1.36	30.02	1.48	38.58	1.67	22.22	1.12	26.28	1.99	38.75	1.39
warp_64_24	24.58	1.77	20.23	2.06	32.52	2.24	**16.28**	**1.25**	19.12	1.89	30.42	1.58

this results in a high linkability score as the transformed biometric information is minimally protected.

In Fig. 16.6 4 examples exhibiting score distributions and corresponding D_{sys} values are shown for block re-mapping: First row—*remp_16* (a) and *remp_54* (b), and warping: Second row—*warp_16_6* (c) and *warp_64_24* (d). The blue line represents the process of D_{sys} for all threshold selections done during the computation (see [4]). The green distribution corresponds to the so called *mated* samples scores. These comparison scores are computed from templates extracted from samples of a single instance of the same subject using different keys [4]. The red coloured distribution describes the *non-mated* samples scores, which are yielded by templates generated

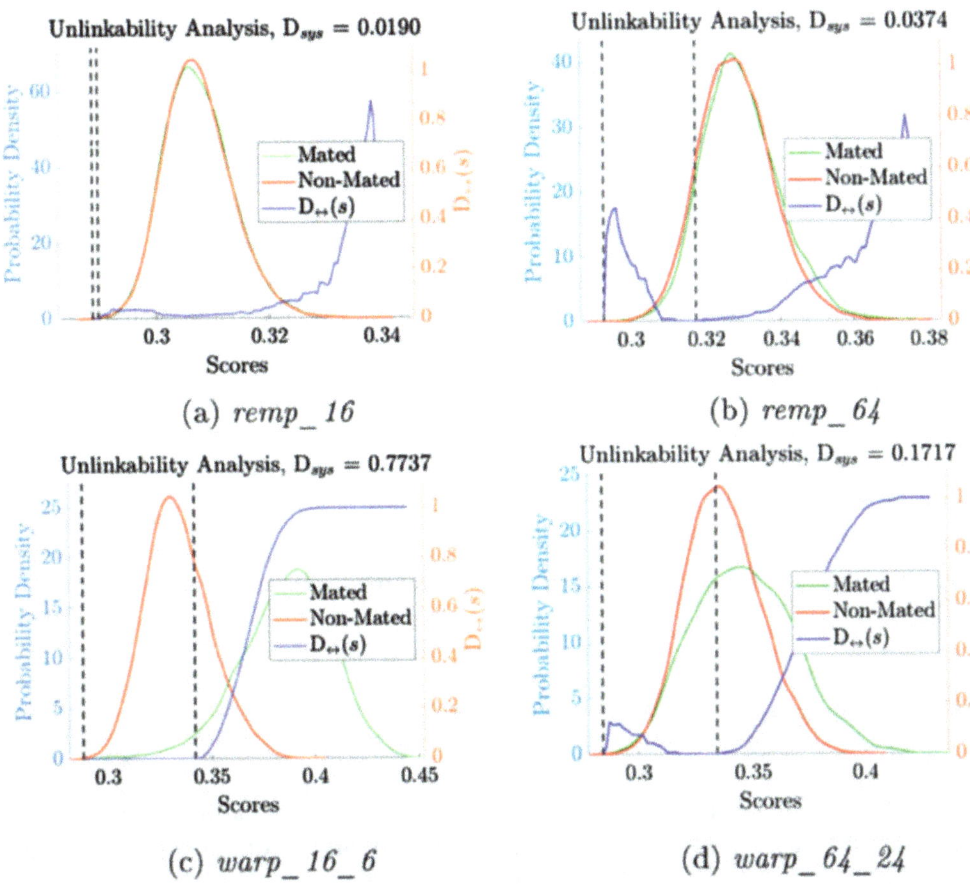

(a) *remp_16* (b) *remp_64*

(c) *warp_16_6* (d) *warp_64_24*

Fig. 16.6 Example images which display unlinkability scores. In all four examples signal domain, PC features on the PLUSVein-FV3 Laser dataset and subject-specific key selection was applied

from samples of different instances using different keys. According to [4] a *fully unlinkable* scenario can be observed if both coloured distributions are identical, while *full linkability* is given if mated and non-mated distributions can be fully separated from each other. For block re-mapping, (a) and (b) almost full unlinkability is achieved in both cases, while for the warping examples, (c) and (d) the distributions can be partly separated from each other. The worst result regarding the ISO/IEC Standard 24745 [7] property of unlinkability is exhibited by example (c) as both distributions are separated quite well, which leads to a high amount of linkability. Thus, in *warp_16_6* it is possible to decide with high probability to which dataset a protected template belongs. Furthermore, from a security point of view warping is not really a suitable template protection scheme using the given parameters. As the amount of linkability decreases using bigger block sizes and more importantly larger offsets it seems to be possible to select a parameter set-up that is providing both a good recognition performance and a quit low linkability at the same time.

According to these results, it is possible to summarise the findings taking the recognition performance and unlinkability evaluation into account:

(a) Only a very low amount of capture subject's privacy protection for configurations exhibiting a low *EER* is obtained for the application of warping schemes.
(b) A high *EER* is observed for the configurations that exhibit a high unlinkability (e.g. detected during the application of block re-mapping schemes in most cases).

Additionally, it must be mentioned that the template protection application in feature or signal domain shows differences regarding the unlinkability aspect. For both, block re-mapping and warping, it is better to apply template protection in the signal domain as the D_{sys} values are lower for almost all cases. If the recognition performance is taken into account as well the best obtained experimental setting is the template protection application in the signal domain using subject-specific keys.

However, the provided level of privacy protection, especially if it comes to unlinkability is clearly not enough for a practical application of warping based cancellable schemes in the feature domain and several signal domain settings using the selected parameters. Furthermore, the worse recognition performance restricts the use of block re-mapping schemes for real-world biometric systems in the most cases as well.

16.8 Conclusion

In this chapter, template protection schemes in finger vein recognition with a focus on cancellable schemes and their application in the feature domain were presented and evaluated. The focus was hereby on cancellable schemes that can be applied in both the signal and the feature domain in the context of finger vein recognition. Two well-known representatives of those schemes, namely, block re-mapping and block warping were evaluated in signal and feature domain on two different publicly available finger vein data sets: the UTFVP and the palmar subsets of the PLUSVein-FV3. These schemes are the same ones that have been applied in the image domain in the previous work of Piciucco et al. [20].

Compared to the previous results obtained in [20], none of the block re-mapping methods performed well in the feature and signal domain using system-specific keys. The experiments considering a capture subject-specific key instead of a system specific one lead to an improvement regarding the recognition performance, especially in the signal domain. Warping performed much better in both domains but further results on the unlinkability revealed that the privacy protection amount is very limited. Thus, an application in real-world biometric systems is restricted for the most experimental settings according to the fact that it is possible to track a subject across several instances generated with various keys.

Nevertheless, it was possible to observe the following trend that leads to an optimistic conclusion. Of course, both template protection schemes have their weaknesses, block re-mapping exhibits recognition performance problems, while warping lacks in terms of unlinkability, but according to the results it seems that the selection of a larger offset could reduce the unlinkability issue for warping in the signal domain. In particular, the larger the offset was selected the better the unlinkability performed, while the recognition performance was hardly influenced. According to this observation, we claim that warping is a suitable cancellable template protection scheme for finger vein biometrics if it is applied in the signal domain using subject-specific keys and a large offset to achieve sufficient unlinkability.

References

1. Choi JH, Song W, Kim T, Lee S-R, Kim HC (2009) Finger vein extraction using gradient normalization and principal curvature. Proc SPIE 7251:9
2. Gallagher AC (2012) Jigsaw puzzles with pieces of unknown orientation. In: 2012 IEEE Conference on computer vision and pattern recognition (CVPR). IEEE, pp 382–389
3. Glasbey CA, Mardia KV (1998) A review of image-warping methods. J Appl Stat 25(2):155–171
4. Gomez-Barrero M, Galbally J, Rathgeb C, Busch C (2018) General framework to evaluate unlinkability in biometric template protection systems. IEEE Trans Inf Forensics Secur 13(6):1406–1420
5. Hämmerle-Uhl J, Pschernig E, Uhl A (2009) Cancelable iris biometrics using block re-mapping and image warping. In: Samarati P, Yung M, Martinelli F, Ardagna CA (eds)Proceedings of the 12th international information security conference (ISC'09), volume 5735 of LNCS. Springer, pp 135–142
6. Huang B, Dai Y, Li R, Tang D, Li W (2010) Finger-vein authentication based on wide line detector and pattern normalization. In: 2010 20th International conference on pattern recognition (ICPR). IEEE, pp 1269–1272
7. ISO/IEC 24745—Information technology—Security techniques—biometric information protection. Standard, International Organization for Standardization, June 2011
8. Jadhav M, Nerkar PM (2015) Survey on finger vein biometric authentication system. Int J Comput Appl (3):14–17
9. Jain AK, Nandakumar K, Nagar A (2008) Biometric template security. EURASIP J Adv Signal Process 2008:113
10. Kauba C, Prommegger B, Uhl A (2018) The two sides of the finger—an evaluation on the recognition performance of dorsal vs. palmar finger-veins. In: Proceedings of the international conference of the biometrics special interest group (BIOSIG'18), Darmstadt, Germany (accepted)
11. Kauba C, Prommegger B, Uhl A (2019) An available open source vein recognition framework. In: Uhl A, Busch C, Marcel S, Veldhuis R (eds) Handbook of vascular biometrics. Springer Science+Business Media, Boston, MA, USA, pp 77–112
12. Kauba C, Prommegger B, Uhl A (2019) Openvein—an open-source modular multi-purpose finger-vein scanner design. In: Uhl A, Busch C, Marcel S, Veldhuis R (eds) Handbook of vascular biometrics. Springer Science+Business Media, Boston, MA, USA, pp 77–112
13. Kumar A, Zhou Y (2012) Human identification using finger images. IEEE Trans Image Process 21(4):2228–2244
14. Lai Y-L, Jin Z, Teoh ABJ, Goi B-M, Yap W-S, Chai T-Y, Rathgeb C (2017) Cancellable iris template generation based on indexing-first-one hashing. Pattern Recognit 64:105–117
15. Maio D, Maltoni D, Cappelli R, Wayman JL, Jain AK (2002) FVC2002: second fingerprint verification competition. In: 16th international conference on pattern recognition, 2002. Proceedings, vol 3. IEEE, pp 811–814
16. Maltoni D, Maio D, Jain AK, Prabhakar S (2009) Handbook of fingerprint recognition, 2nd edn. Springer

17. Miura N, Nagasaka A, Miyatake T (2004) Feature extraction of finger-vein patterns based on repeated line tracking and its application to personal identification. Mach Vis Appl 15(4):194–203
18. Miura N, Nagasaka A, Miyatake T (2007) Extraction of finger-vein patterns using maximum curvature points in image profiles. IEICE Trans Inf Syst 90(8):1185–1194
19. Paikin G, Tal A (2015) Solving multiple square jigsaw puzzles with missing pieces. In: Proceedings of the IEEE conference on computer vision and pattern recognition, pp 4832–4839
20. Piciucco E, Maiorana E, Kauba C, Uhl A, Campisi P (2016) Cancelable biometrics for finger vein recognition. In: 2016 First international workshop on sensing, processing and learning for intelligent machines (SPLINE). IEEE, pp 1–5
21. Ratha NK, Chikkerur S, Connell JH, Bolle RM (2007) Generating cancelable fingerprint templates. IEEE Trans Pattern Anal Mach Intell 29(4):561–572
22. Ratha NK, Connell J, Bolle R (2001) Enhancing security and privacy in biometrics-based authentication systems. IBM Syst J 40(3):614–634
23. Sholomon D, David O, Netanyahu NS (2013) A genetic algorithm-based solver for very large jigsaw puzzles. In: Proceedings of the IEEE conference on computer vision and pattern recognition, pp 1767–1774
24. Starck J-L, Fadili J, Murtagh F (2007) The undecimated wavelet decomposition and its reconstruction. IEEE Trans Image Process 16(2):297–309
25. Ton BT, Veldhuis RNJ (2013) A high quality finger vascular pattern dataset collected using a custom designed capturing device. In: 2013 International conference on biometrics (ICB). IEEE, pp 1–5
26. Uhl A (2019) State-of-the-art in vascular biometrics. In: Uhl A, Busch C, Marcel S, Veldhuis R (eds) Handbook of vascular biometrics. Springer Science+Business Media, Boston, MA, USA, pp 3–62
27. Wolberg G (1998) Image morphing: a survey. Vis Comput 14(8):360–372

Chapter 17
Towards Measuring the Amount of Discriminatory Information in Finger Vein Biometric Characteristics Using a Relative Entropy Estimator

Vedrana Krivokuća, Marta Gomez-Barrero, Sébastien Marcel, Christian Rathgeb and Christoph Busch

Abstract This chapter makes the first attempt to quantify the amount of discriminatory information in finger vein biometric characteristics in terms of Relative Entropy (RE) calculated on genuine and impostor comparison scores using a Nearest Neighbour (NN) estimator. Our findings indicate that the RE is system-specific, meaning that it would be misleading to claim a universal finger vein RE estimate. We show, however, that the RE can be used to rank finger vein recognition systems (tested on the same database using the same experimental protocol) in terms of their expected recognition accuracy, and that this ranking is equivalent to that achieved using the EER. This implies that the RE estimator is a reliable indicator of the amount of discriminatory information in a finger vein recognition system. We also propose a Normalised Relative Entropy (NRE) metric to help us better understand the significance of the RE values, as well as to enable a fair benchmark of different biometric systems (tested on different databases and potentially using different experimental protocols) in terms of their RE. We discuss how the proposed NRE metric can be used as a complement to the EER in benchmarking the discriminative capabilities of different biometric systems, and we consider two potential issues that must be taken into account when calculating the RE and NRE in practice.

V. Krivokuća (✉) · S. Marcel
Idiap Research Institute, Martigny, Switzerland
e-mail: vedrana.krivokuca@idiap.ch

S. Marcel
e-mail: sebastien.marcel@idiap.ch

M. Gomez-Barrero · C. Rathgeb · C. Busch
Hochschule Darmstadt, Darmstadt, Germany
e-mail: marta.gomez-barrero@h-da.de

C. Rathgeb
e-mail: christian.rathgeb@h-da.de

C. Busch
e-mail: christoph.busch@h-da.de

A. Uhl et al. (eds.), *Handbook of Vascular Biometrics*, Advances in Computer Vision and Pattern Recognition, https://doi.org/10.1007/978-3-030-27731-4_17

Keywords Finger veins · Relative entropy · Nearest neighbour estimator · Biometric template protection · Security · Privacy · Discriminatory information · Kullback–Leibler divergence · VERA · UTFVP · Wide Line Detector · Repeated Line Tracking · Maximum Curvature

17.1 Introduction

There is no doubt that biometrics are fast becoming ubiquitous in response to a growing need for more robust identity assurance. A negative consequence of this increasing reliance on biometrics is the looming threat of serious privacy and security concerns in the event that the growing biometric databases are breached.[1] Fortunately, the past decade has seen notable efforts in advancing the field of biometric template protection, which is dedicated to protecting the biometric data that is collected and used for recognition purposes, thereby safeguarding the privacy of the data subjects and preventing "spoofing" attacks using stolen biometric templates. Unfortunately, we are still lacking solid methods for evaluating the effectiveness of the proposed solutions. An important missing ingredient is a measure of the amount of discriminatory information in a biometric system.

A few approaches, for example, [1–3], have focused on estimating the "individuality" (or discrimination capability) of biometric templates in terms of the inter-class variation alone (i.e. the False Match Rate or False Accept Rate). Along the same lines, the best-known attempt to measure the amount of information in a biometric system is probably the approach proposed by Daugman [4]. This method computes the Hamming distance between every pair of non-mated IrisCodes, and the resulting distance distribution is then fitted to a binomial distribution. The number of degrees of freedom of the representative binomial distribution approximates the number of independent bits in each binary IrisCode, which in turn provides an estimate for the discrimination entropy of the underlying biometric characteristic. This approach was adopted to measure the entropy of finger vein patterns in [5]. However, as explained in [5], while this method of measuring entropy is correct from the source coding point of view, the issue with calculating the entropy in this way is that it only provides a reasonable estimate of the amount of biometric information if there is no variation between multiple samples captured from the same biometric instance. Since this intra-class variation is unlikely to be zero in practice, the discrimination entropy would probably overestimate the amount of available biometric information [6, 7].

In an attempt to extend the idea of using entropy as a measure of biometric information while more practically incorporating both inter- and intra-class variation, several authors have adopted the *relative entropy* approach. Adler et al. [8] defined the term "biometric information" as *the decrease in uncertainty about the identity*

[1] For a real-life example, see: http://money.cnn.com/2015/09/23/technology/opm-fingerprint-hack.

of a person due to a set of biometric measurements. They proposed estimating the biometric information via the *relative entropy* or *Kullback–Leibler (KL) Divergence* between the intra-class and inter-class biometric feature distributions. Takahashi and Murakami [6] adopted a similar approach to [8], except that they used *comparison score* distributions instead of *feature* distributions, since this ensures that the whole recognition pipeline is considered when estimating the amount of discriminative biometric information in the system. Around the same time, Sutcu et al. [9] adopted the same method as that employed in [6], with an important difference: they used a Nearest Neighbour (NN) estimator for the KL divergence, thereby removing the need to establish models for the comparison score distributions prior to computing the relative entropy.

This paper adopts the approach proposed in [9] to estimate the amount of discriminatory information in finger vein biometrics. We show that the Relative Entropy (RE) metric is equivalent to the Equal Error Rate (EER) in terms of enabling us to rank finger vein biometric systems according to their expected recognition accuracy. This suggests that the RE metric can provide a reliable estimation of the amount of discriminatory information in finger vein recognition systems. We additionally propose a Normalised Relative Entropy (NRE) metric to help us gain a more intuitive understanding of the significance of RE values and to allow us to fairly benchmark the REs of different biometric systems. The new metric can be used in conjunction with the EER to determine the best-performing biometric system.

The remainder of this chapter is structured as follows. Section 17.2 explains the adopted RE metric in more detail. Section 17.3 presents our results for the RE of finger vein patterns and shows how this metric can be used to rank finger vein recognition systems in comparison with the EER. Section 17.4 proposes the new NRE metric and presents NRE results on various finger vein recognition systems. Section 17.5 discusses how the NRE could be a useful complement to the EER in benchmarking the discrimination capabilities of different biometric systems, and we also present two issues that must be considered when calculating the RE and NRE in practice. Section 17.6 concludes this chapter and proposes a primary direction for future work.

17.2 Measuring Biometric Information via Relative Entropy

Let us say that $G(x)$ represents the probability distribution of *genuine* (mated) comparison scores in a biometric recognition system, and $I(x)$ represents the probability distribution of *impostor* (non-mated) comparison scores. The RE between these two distributions is then defined in terms of the KL divergence as follows:

$$D(G||I) = \sum_{i=1}^{n} G(x_i) \log_2 \frac{G(x_i)}{I(x_i)} \tag{17.1}$$

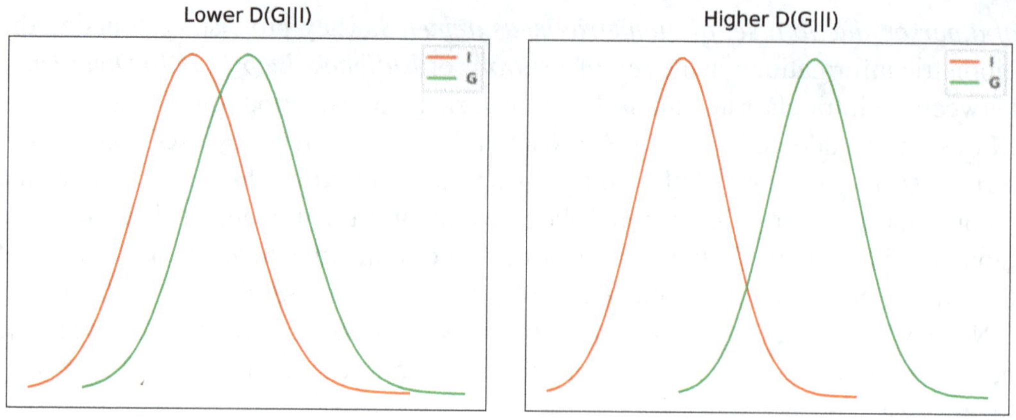

Fig. 17.1 Examples of G and I relationships producing lower and higher $D(G||I)$ values

In information-theoretic terms, $D(G||I)$ tells us the number of extra bits that we would need to encode samples from G when using a code based on I, compared to simply using a code based on G itself. Relating this to our biometric system, we can think of $D(G||I)$ as providing some indication of how closely our genuine score distribution corresponds to our impostor score distribution. The worse the match, the *higher* the $D(G||I)$ value and the easier it is to tell the two distributions apart. Consequently, the higher the RE, the easier it should be for our biometric recognition system to differentiate between genuine users and impostors based on their corresponding comparison scores, and thus the better the expected recognition accuracy. Figure 17.1 shows a simple illustration of what the relationship between G and I might look like for lower and higher $D(G||I)$ values.

One issue with using Eq. (17.1) to estimate the RE is evident when we consider what is represented by n. Technically, n is meant to denote the total number of comparison scores, and it is expected that the G and I distributions extend over the same range of scores. This, however, is not usually the case, since the overlap between the two distributions should only be partial. One consequence of this is that we will have at least one division by 0, for the range where $I(x) = 0$ but $G(x) \neq 0$. The result will be $D(G||I) = \infty$. This makes sense theoretically, since if a score does not exist in I then it is impossible to represent it using a code based on I. For our purposes, however, an RE of ∞ does not tell us much, since we already expect only partial overlap between G and I. So, we would like our RE metric to generate a finite number to represent the amount of information in our biometric recognition system.

Another issue with Eq. (17.1) is that this approach requires us to produce models for the genuine and impostor score distributions, G and I. Since the number of scores we have access to is generally not very large (this is particularly likely to be the case for genuine scores), it may be difficult to generate accurate models for the underlying score distributions.

In light of the issues mentioned above, Sutcu et al. [9] proposed approximating the RE using the NN estimator from [10]. Let $s_g^1, \ldots, s_g^{N_g}$ and $s_i^1, \ldots, s_i^{N_i}$ represent the comparison scores from the sets of genuine and impostor scores, respectively. Further, let $d_{gg}(i) = \min_{j \neq i} ||s_g^i - s_g^j||$ represent the distance between the genuine score s_g^i and its nearest neighbour in the set of genuine scores, and let $d_{gi}(i) = \min_j ||s_g^i - s_i^j||$ denote the distance between the genuine score s_g^i and its nearest neighbour in the set of impostor scores. Then the NN estimator of the KL divergence is defined as

$$\hat{D}(G||I) = \frac{1}{N_g} \sum_{i=1}^{N_g} \log_2 \frac{d_{gi}(i)}{d_{gg}(i)} + \log_2 \frac{N_i}{N_g - 1} \tag{17.2}$$

Using Eq. (17.2), we can estimate the RE of a biometric system using the genuine and impostor comparison scores directly, without establishing models for the underlying probability densities. Moreover, using the proposed KL divergence estimator, we can circumvent the issue of not having complete overlap between the genuine and impostor score distributions. For these reasons, this is the approach we adopted to estimate the amount of information in finger vein patterns.

17.3 Relative Entropy of Finger Vein Patterns

We used the NN estimator approach from [9] to estimate the RE of finger vein patterns.[2] Section 17.3.1 describes our adopted finger vein recognition systems, and Sect. 17.3.2 presents our RE results for finger vein patterns.

17.3.1 Finger Vein Recognition Systems

We used two public finger vein databases for our investigation: VERA[3] [11] and UTFVP[4] [12]. VERA consists of two images for each of 110 data subjects' left and right index fingers, which makes up 440 samples in total. UTFVP consists of four images for each of 60 data subjects' left and right index, ring and middle fingers, which makes up 1,440 samples in total. Both databases were captured using the same imaging device, but with slightly different acquisition conditions. Figure 17.2 shows an example of a finger image from each database.

Finger vein patterns were extracted and compared using the `bob.bio.vein` PyPI package.[5] To extract the vein patterns from the finger images in each database, the fingers were first cropped and horizontally aligned as per [13, 14]. Next, the finger vein pattern was extracted from the cropped finger images using three well-known

[2]Code available at https://gitlab.idiap.ch/bob/bob.chapter.fingerveins_relative_entropy.

[3]https://www.idiap.ch/dataset/vera-fingervein.

[4]http://scs.ewi.utwente.nl/downloads/show,Finger%20Vein/.

[5]https://pypi.python.org/pypi/bob.bio.vein.

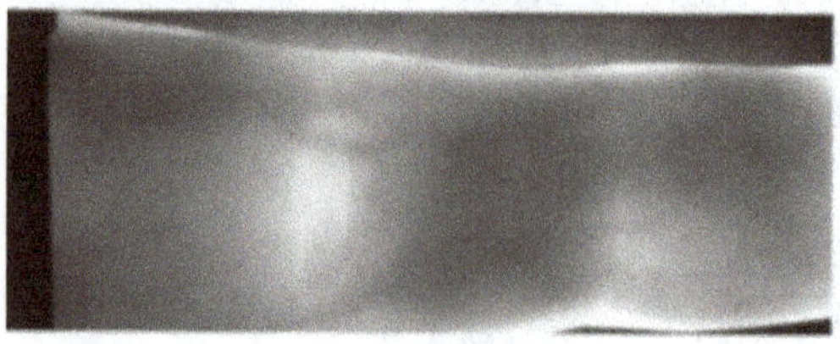

(a) VERA

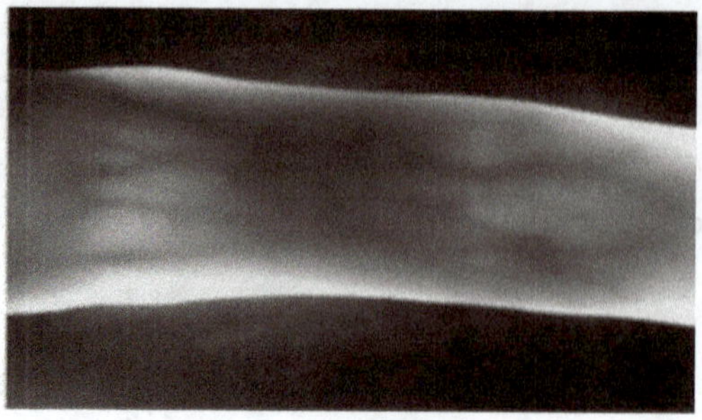

(b) UTFVP

Fig. 17.2 Examples of finger images from the VERA and UTFVP databases. Note that the UTFVP images are larger in size, as shown in this figure

feature extractors: Wide Line Detector (WLD) [14], Repeated Line Tracking (RLT) [15] and Maximum Curvature (MC) [16].

The comparison between the extracted finger vein patterns was performed separately for each extractor, using the algorithm proposed in [15]. This method is based on a cross-correlation between the enrolled finger vein template and the probe template obtained during verification. The resulting comparison scores lie in the range [0, 0.5], where 0.5 represents maximum cross-correlation and thus a perfect match.

17.3.2 Relative Entropy of Finger Veins

We used Eq. (17.2) to calculate the RE of finger vein patterns[6] for each of the three feature extractors (WLD, RLT, and MC) on both the VERA and UTFVP databases. One issue we faced when implementing this equation was dealing with the case where the $d_{gg}(i)$ and/or $d_{gi}(i)$ terms were zero. If $d_{gi}(i) = 0$ (regardless of what value $d_{gg}(i)$ takes), this would result in $\hat{D}(G||I) = -\infty$, whereas $d_{gg}(i) = 0$ (regardless of what value $d_{gi}(i)$ takes) would result in $\hat{D}(G||I) = \infty$. This is one of the issues we wanted to circumvent by using the NN estimator in the first place! Neither the paper that proposed the NN estimator for KL divergence [10], nor the paper that proposed using this estimator to calculate the RE of biometrics [9], suggests how to proceed in this scenario. So, we decided to add a small value (ϵ) of 10^{-10} to every $d_{gg}(i)$ and $d_{gi}(i)$ term that turned out to be 0. The choice of ϵ was based on the fact that our comparison scores are rounded to 8 decimal places, so we wanted to ensure that ϵ would be smaller than 10^{-8} to minimise the impact on the original score distribution.[7]

[6] Note: $RE = \hat{D}(G||I)$.

[7] This choice of ϵ may not necessarily be optimal, but it seems sensible.

Table 17.1 Relative Entropy (RE) and Equal Error Rate (EER) for different extractors on the VERA and UTFVP databases. The RE and EER ranks refer to the rankings of the three extractors (separately for each database) in terms of the highest RE and lowest EER, respectively

DB	Extractor	RE	EER (%)	RE rank	EER rank
VERA	WLD	11.8	9.5	2	2
VERA	RLT	4.2	24.3	3	3
VERA	MC	13.2	4.3	1	1
UTFVP	WLD	18.9	2.7	2	2
UTFVP	RLT	18.0	3.2	3	3
UTFVP	MC	19.5	0.8	1	1

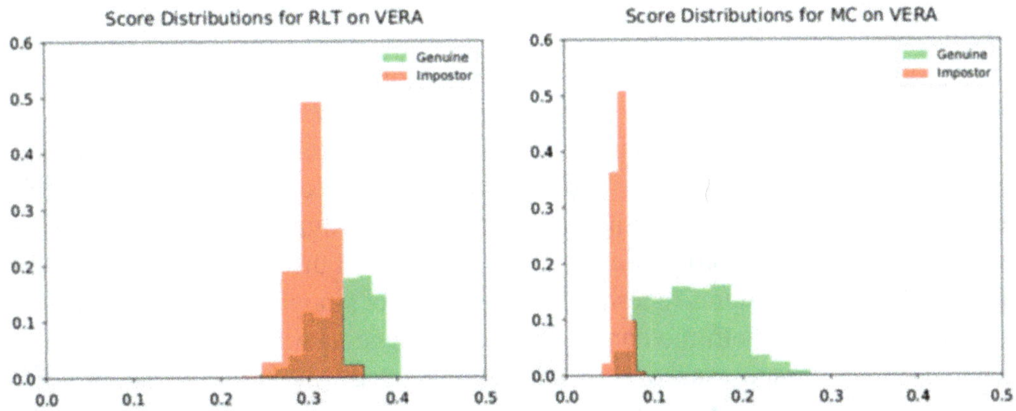

Fig. 17.3 Genuine and impostor score distributions corresponding to the lowest (left) and highest (right) RE values for the VERA database from Table 17.1

For this experiment, a comparison score was calculated between a finger vein template and *every other* finger vein template in the database. The resulting RE values are summarised in Table 17.1, along with the corresponding EERs.[8]

We can interpret the RE results in Table 17.1 as providing an indication of how many bits of discriminatory information are contained in a particular finger vein recognition system. For example, we can see that using the RLT extractor on the VERA database results in a system with only 4.2 bits of discriminatory information, while the MC extractor on the same database contains 13.2 bits of discriminatory information. Figure 17.3 illustrates the genuine and impostor score distributions for these two RE results.

Since our results show the RE to be dependent upon both the feature extractor and database adopted, it would be misleading to claim a universal finger vein RE estimate; rather, it makes more sense for the RE to be system-specific.

[8]Note that we have chosen to compare the RE to the EER, because the EER is a widely used metric for evaluating the overall recognition accuracy (in terms of the trade-off between the False Match Rate (FMR) and False Non-Match Rate (FNMR)) of a biometric recognition system. The comparison seems appropriate, since RE aims to provide us with an idea of a biometric system's overall discrimination capability.

Intuitively, we can see that, the higher the RE, the greater the amount of discriminatory information, and thus the greater the expected recognition capabilities of the underlying system. This intuition is confirmed when we compare the REs and EERs of the different systems in Table 17.1, in terms of the RE-based versus EER-based rankings. From this analysis, it is evident that the ranking of the three extractors for each database is the same regardless of whether that ranking is based on the RE or the EER. In particular, MC has the highest RE and lowest EER, while RLT has the lowest RE and highest EER. This implies that the most discriminatory information is contained in finger vein patterns that have been extracted using the MC extractor, and the least discriminatory information is contained in RLT-extracted finger veins. These results suggest the possibility of using the REs of different finger vein recognition systems to rank the systems according to the amount of discriminatory information and thus their expected recognition accuracies. Consequently, it appears reasonable to conclude that the RE estimator is a reliable indicator of the amount of discriminatory information in a finger vein recognition system.

While RE quantifies the amount of discriminatory information in a biometric system, it is difficult to gauge what exactly this number, on its own, means. For example, what exactly does x bits of discriminatory information signify, and is a y-bit difference in the REs of two biometric systems significant? Furthermore, benchmarking different biometric systems in terms of their RE is not straightforward, since the RE estimate depends on both the comparison score range as well as on the number of genuine (N_g) and impostor scores (N_i) for each database and experimental protocol. Consequently, REs reported for different biometric systems usually do not lie in the same $[RE_{\min}, RE_{\max}]$ range.[9] To help us better understand the meaning of the RE metric in the context of a biometric system, as well as to enable fair cross-system RE benchmarking, Sect. 17.4 adapts Eq. (17.2) to propose a *normalised* RE metric.

17.4 Normalised Relative Entropy

This section proposes a normalised version of the RE (NRE), based on the NN estimator in Eq. (17.2). The reason for this normalisation is to help us interpret the RE in a more intuitive way, and to enable fair benchmarking of different biometric systems in terms of their RE.

We propose using the well-known "min–max" normalisation formulated by Eq. (17.3):

$$NRE = \frac{RE - RE_{\min}}{RE_{\max} - RE_{\min}} \tag{17.3}$$

[9]For the finger vein systems we used, the comparison scores for both the VERA and UTFVP databases lie in the same range of [0, 0.5]. However, the N_g values across the two databases are different as are the N_i values. Consequently, the $[RE_{\min}, RE_{\max}]$ range is not the same for both databases, meaning that we cannot fairly compare the RE results across the two databases.

In Eq. (17.3), $RE_{\min}$ and $RE_{\max}$ refer to the minimum and maximum possible RE values, respectively, for a particular biometric system. Thus, we need to begin by establishing $RE_{\min}$ and $RE_{\max}$. In this formulation, we assume that comparison scores are similarity values, such that small scores indicate low similarity and large scores indicate high similarity. Keeping this in mind, the minimum RE would occur when all d_{gi} values are zero and all d_{gg} values are as large as possible. Therefore, for each genuine score, there would need to be at least one impostor score with exactly the same value, and all the genuine scores would need to be spread apart as far as possible. Let us say that all scores lie in the range $[s_{\min}, s_{\max}]$, and that the number of genuine scores for a particular database and experimental protocol is denoted by N_g. Then, the maximum possible d_{gg} value would be $\frac{s_{\max}-s_{\min}}{N_g}$. By adapting Eq. (17.2), our equation for the minimum RE thus becomes

$$RE_{\min} = \frac{1}{N_g} \sum_{i=1}^{N_g} \log_2 \frac{0}{\frac{s_{\max}-s_{\min}}{N_g}} + \log_2 \frac{N_i}{N_g - 1} \tag{17.4}$$

If we now tried to solve Eq. (17.4), we would get $RE_{\min} = -\infty$, because of the 0 d_{gi} term. Since this is an impractical result for measuring the (finite) amount of information in a biometric system, we replace the 0 with ϵ. Furthermore, we can see that the division by N_g gets cancelled out by the summation across N_g, so we can simplify Eq. (17.4) as follows:

$$RE_{\min} = \log_2 \frac{\epsilon}{\frac{s_{\max}-s_{\min}}{N_g}} + \log_2 \frac{N_i}{N_g - 1} \tag{17.5}$$

Equation (17.5) thus becomes the final $RE_{\min}$ equation.

The maximum RE would occur when all d_{gi} values are as large as possible and all d_{gg} values are zero. The only way this could occur would be if all the genuine scores took on the largest possible value, $s_{\max}$, and all the impostor scores took on the smallest possible value, $s_{\min}$. In this case, the genuine and impostor score sets would be as different as possible. By adapting Eq. (17.2), we thus get the following equation for the maximum RE:

$$RE_{\max} = \frac{1}{N_g} \sum_{i=1}^{N_g} \log_2 \frac{s_{\max} - s_{\min}}{0} + \log_2 \frac{N_i}{N_g - 1} \tag{17.6}$$

If we tried to solve Eq. (17.6), we would get $RE_{\max} = \infty$ due to the 0 term in the denominator. So, once again we replace the 0 term with ϵ. Furthermore, just like we did for Eq. (17.4), we can simplify Eq. (17.6) by removing the N_g division and summation. Our final equation for $RE_{\max}$ thus becomes

$$RE_{\max} = \log_2 \frac{s_{\max} - s_{\min}}{\epsilon} + \log_2 \frac{N_i}{N_g - 1} \tag{17.7}$$

We can now use Eq. (17.3), with Eq. (17.5) for $RE_{\min}$ and Eq. (17.7) for $RE_{\max}$, to calculate the NRE of a particular biometric system.

Due to the "min–max" operation in Eq. (17.3), the NRE will lie in the range [0.00, 1.00]. We can thus interpret the NRE as follows. An NRE of 0.00 would suggest that the system in question contains zero discriminative information (i.e. recognition would actually be impossible), whereas an NRE of 1.00 would indicate that the system contains the maximum amount of discriminative information possible for that system (i.e. the recognition accuracy would be expected to be perfect).

Figure 17.4 illustrates what the impostor and genuine comparison score distributions might look like for a minimum NRE system and a maximum NRE system, when the comparison score range is [0, 0.5] (i.e. the score range corresponding to our finger vein recognition systems).

In general, therefore, we can look at the NRE as providing an indication of the proportion of the maximum amount of discriminatory information that the corresponding biometric system contains. An NRE of 0.50, for example, would indicate that the biometric system achieves only 50% of the maximum attainable recognition accuracy. Therefore, the higher the NRE, the better the expected recognition accuracy of the biometric system we are measuring.

Table 17.2 shows the NRE results for our aforementioned finger vein recognition systems. Note that, for these finger vein systems: $s_{\min} = 0$; $s_{\max} = 0.5$; $N_g = 440$ for VERA; $N_g = 4,320$ for UTFVP; $N_i = 192,720$ for VERA; $N_i = 2,067,840$ for UTFVP.

Note that the first column of Table 17.2 refers to the finger vein recognition system constructed using the specified database and feature extractor. We have pooled the databases and extractors into "systems" now to indicate that the NRE values can be benchmarked *across systems* (as opposed to, for example, in Table 17.1, where the databases were separate to indicate that RE-based benchmarking of the different extractors should be *database-specific*).

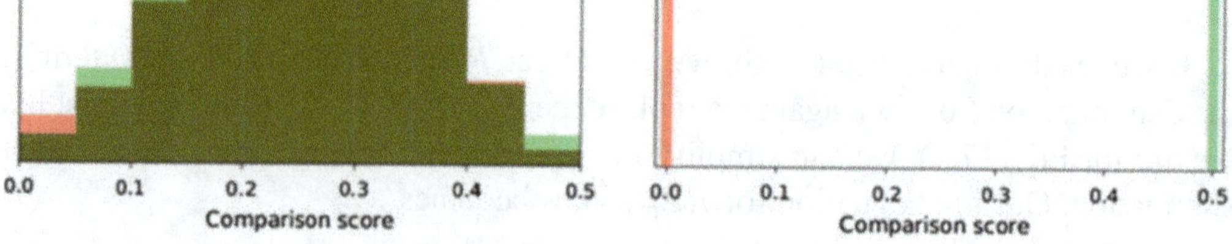

Fig. 17.4 Illustration of impostor and genuine score distributions for a minimum and a maximum NRE system, when the comparison score range is [0, 0.5]

Table 17.2 Relative Entropy (RE) and Normalised Relative Entropy (NRE) for different finger vein recognition systems

System	RE	NRE
VERA-WLD	11.8	0.48
VERA-RLT	4.2	0.34
VERA-MC	13.2	0.50
UTFVP-WLD	18.9	0.58
UTFVP-RLT	18.0	0.56
UTFVP-MC	19.5	0.59

As an example of how the NRE results from Table 17.2 can be interpreted, let us compare the NRE of VERA-RLT to that of UTFVP-MC. The NRE of 0.34 for VERA-RLT tells us that this system achieves only 34% of the maximum attainable discrimination capability. Comparatively, the UTFVP-MC system contains 59% of the maximum amount of discriminative information. So, we could conclude that the UTFVP-MC finger vein recognition system contains 25% more discriminatory information than the VERA-RLT system.

Using the NRE also helps us gauge the significance of the differences in the REs across different biometric systems. For example, if we look at the RE on its own for the UTFVP-WLD and UTFVP-MC systems in Table 17.2, we can see that the latter system's RE is 0.6 bits larger than the former system's RE. It is difficult to tell, however, whether or not this is a significant difference. If we then look at the NREs of the two systems, we can see that their difference is only 0.01. This indicates that the 0.6-bit difference between the two systems' REs is not too significant in terms of the proportion of the maximum discriminatory information the two systems contain. On the other hand, the 15.3-bit difference in the REs between the VERA-RLT and UTFVP-MC systems seems much more significant, and we may be tempted to conclude that the latter system contains about five times more discriminative information than the former system. Looking at the two systems' NREs, we do see a fairly significant difference, but we would have to conclude that the UTFVP-MC system contains not five times, but two times, more discriminative information than the VERA-RLT system.

In this section, we have shown how the NRE can be used for RE-based benchmarking of different finger vein recognition systems, for which comparison scores were evaluated on different databases. The main reason for using the NRE in our case was thus to conduct fair cross-database system benchmarking. Our proposed NRE metric, however, can also be used to fairly benchmark the REs of systems based on different biometric modalities, tested on different databases using different experimental protocols. For example, part of our future work will involve benchmarking the NRE of our best finger vein recognition system, UTFVP-MC, against NREs of systems based on different types of biometrics. This makes the proposed NRE metric a flexible tool for both quantifying and benchmarking the amount of discriminative information contained in different biometric systems.

17.5 Discussion

In this section, we begin by presenting a discussion on an important aspect of the NRE, which supports its adoption in the biometrics community. We then discuss two potential issues that may arise when calculating the NRE, and we suggest the means of dealing with them. Sections 17.5.1, 17.5.2 and 17.5.3, respectively, tackle these three discussion points.

17.5.1 NRE as a Complement to EER

So far, we have shown how the RE can be used to measure the amount of discriminatory information in finger vein recognition systems. We also proposed the NRE metric to fairly benchmark the REs across different biometric systems. In this section, we discuss how an NRE estimate could complement the EER to provide a more complete picture of the performance of a biometric recognition system.

In Sect. 17.2, we explained how, in the context of a biometric recognition system, the RE metric provides some indication of how closely our genuine score distribution matches our impostor score distribution. Let us explore the meaning of this by considering Eq. (17.2). Equation (17.2) tells us that we are attempting to estimate the relative entropy of a set of genuine comparison scores (G) in terms of a set of impostor comparison scores (I). In other words, we wish to quantify the "closeness" of these two sets[10] of scores. The d_{gi} and d_{gg} terms represent the distance between a genuine score and its closest score in the set of impostor and genuine scores, respectively. Larger d_{gi} values will result in *larger* RE results, whereas larger d_{gg} values will result in *smaller* RE results.[11] We can thus see that larger REs favour a larger inter-class variance (i.e. greater separation between genuine comparison trials and impostor trials) and a smaller intra-class variance (i.e. smaller separation between multiple biometric samples from the same biometric instance). This makes the RE suitable as a measure of the performance of a biometric recognition system: the larger the RE value, the better the recognition accuracy. The best (highest) RE would, therefore, be obtained in the case where all the d_{gi} values are as large as possible, while the d_{gg} values are as small as possible, and vice versa for the worst (lowest) RE.

The RE metric thus informs us about two things: how far genuine scores are from impostor scores, and how far genuine scores are from each other. Consider the case where we have a set of impostor scores, I, and a set of genuine scores, G. The larger the intersection between I and G, the smaller the d_{gi} values and thus the lower the RE. Conversely, the smaller the intersection between the two sets, the greater the d_{gi} values and thus the higher the RE. So far, the RE metric appears to tell us the same thing as the EER, since a smaller EER indicates less overlap between genuine and

[10]Note: We are purposely using the word "set" as opposed to "distribution", since the NN estimator in Eq. (17.2) works directly on the scores as opposed to distributions representing the scores.

[11]Assume constant N_g and N_i values.

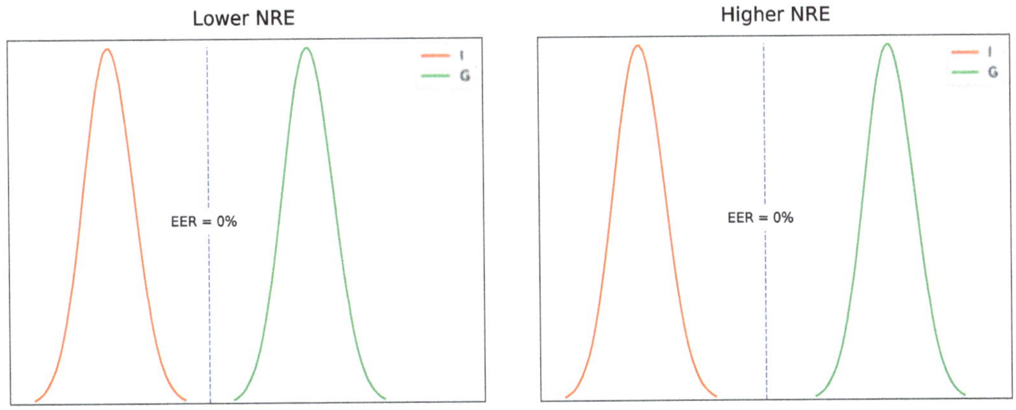

Fig. 17.5 Two biometric systems with the same EER of 0%, but where the system on the right has greater separation between the impostor and genuine comparison scores, and thus a higher NRE than the system on the left

impostor comparison scores, while a larger EER indicates more overlap. Where the two metrics differ, however, is in the scenario where I and G are completely separated. In this case, the further apart the two sets of scores are the higher the resulting RE. The EER, however, would be 0% regardless of whether the separation is small or large. Imagine if we had to benchmark two biometric systems, both of which had complete separation between the genuine and impostor comparison scores, but where for one system the separation was much larger than for the other, as illustrated[12] in Fig. 17.5. If we considered only the EER, it would indicate that the two systems are the same (i.e. both have an EER of 0%). The NRE,[13] however, would clearly indicate that the system with greater separation is better in terms of distinguishing genuine trials from impostors, since the NRE value would be higher for that system. In this case, complementing the EER with an NRE estimate would provide a more complete picture of the system comparison. This could come in useful particularly in situations where the data used for testing the biometric system was collected in a constrained environment, in which case an EER of 0% could be expected. The NRE, on the other hand, would provide us with more insight into the separation between the genuine and impostor score distributions.

Another example of a scenario in which the NRE metric would be a useful complement to the EER is when we have two biometric systems for which I is the same and the separation (or overlap) between I and G is the same, but G differs. In particular, in the first system the genuine scores are closer together, while in the second system the genuine scores are further apart from each other. Figure 17.6 illustrates

[12]Note: The only reason for using probability density plots in this figure is to present a cleaner illustration of our point. Probability density functions are *not* used to represent genuine and impostor score distributions for the NRE calculation.

[13]When benchmarking different biometric systems, the NRE should be used instead of the RE to ensure that the benchmarking is fair. The only exception to this rule would be in the case where the different systems had the same comparison score range, and the same N_g and N_i values, in which case the resulting REs would lie in the same $[RE_{\min}, RE_{\max}]$ range.

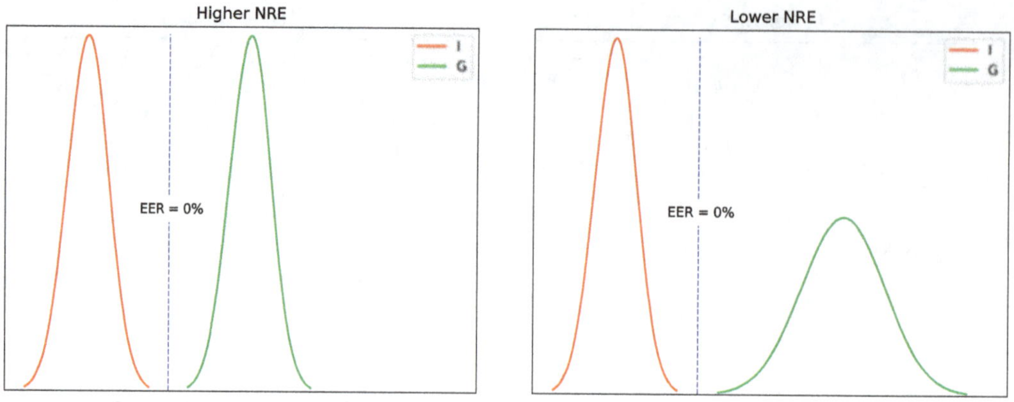

Fig. 17.6 Two biometric systems with the same I, the same separation between I and G and thus the same EER, but with different G. In particular, G for the system on the right has a larger variance, and thus the NRE is lower to reflect this

this scenario.[14] In this case, since the separation between I and G for both systems is the same, the EER would also be the same, thereby indicating that one system is just as good as the other. The NRE, however, would be smaller for the second system due to the larger d_{gg} values. The NRE would thus indicate that the larger intra-class variance in the second system makes this system less preferable in terms of biometric performance when compared to the first system, for which the genuine scores are closer together and thus the intra-class variance is smaller. Using both NRE and EER together, we could thus conclude that, although both systems can be expected to achieve the same error rate, the system with the smaller intra-class variance would be a superior choice.

When choosing between the EER and NRE metrics for evaluating the performance of a biometric system, we would still recommend using the EER as the primary one, since it is more practical in providing us with a solid indication of our system's expected error rate. The NRE, however, would be a useful complement to the EER when we are trying to decide on the best of n biometric systems that have the *same* EER.

17.5.2 Selecting the ϵ Parameter

As mentioned in the introductory paragraph of Sect. 17.3.2, ϵ is a parameter chosen to deal with zero score differences (i.e. $d_{gg} = 0$ or $d_{gi} = 0$) in order to avoid an RE of $\pm\infty$ (which would be meaningless in the context of measuring the amount of discriminatory information in a biometric system). It is clear from Eqs. (17.2), (17.3), (17.5) and (17.7), however, that the choice of ϵ could potentially have a significant effect on the resulting RE and, therefore, NRE, particularly if the number of zero score

[14]Note: In Fig. 17.6, the EER for both systems is 0%; however, it could also be possible for both systems to have the same non-zero EER. In this case, I and G would partially overlap.

differences is large. While the number of zero score differences will be dependent on the biometric system in question and this number is, therefore, difficult to generalise, we wished to see what effect the choice of ϵ would have on the RE and NRE of our best finger vein recognition system, that obtained when using MC-extracted finger veins from the UTFVP database. Figure 17.7 shows plots of the RE and NRE versus ϵ, when ϵ is selected to lie in the range $[10^{-12}, 10^{-8}]$. For convenience, Table 17.3 summarises the RE and NRE values from Fig. 17.7.

From Fig. 17.7 and Table 17.3, we can see that, while the choice of ϵ does affect the RE and NRE to some degree (more specifically, the RE and NRE decrease as ϵ decreases[15]), this effect does not appear to be significant. So, we may conclude that, as long as the ϵ parameter is sensibly chosen (i.e. smaller than the comparison scores, but not so small that it is effectively zero), then the RE and NRE estimates should be reasonable.

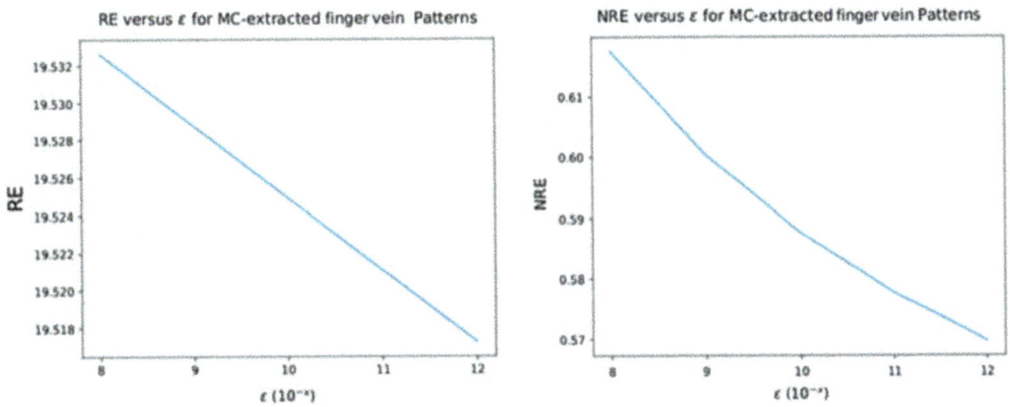

Fig. 17.7 RE versus ϵ and NRE versus ϵ, when ϵ takes on different values in the range $[10^{-12}, 10^{-8}]$, for MC-extracted finger vein patterns in the UTFVP database

Table 17.3 RE and NRE for MC-extracted finger veins from UTFVP, when ϵ is varied in the range $[10^{-12}, 10^{-8}]$. Note that, for consistency with Table 17.2, RE and NRE values are rounded to 1 d.p. and 2 d.p., respectively

ϵ	RE	NRE
10^{-8}	19.5	0.62
10^{-9}	19.5	0.60
10^{-10}	19.5	0.59
10^{-11}	19.5	0.58
10^{-12}	19.5	0.57

[15]In general, the RE, and thus the NRE, would be expected to *decrease* with a decrease in ϵ when there are more d_{gi} than d_{gg} zero score differences. Alternatively, the RE, and thus the NRE, would be expected to *increase* with a decrease in ϵ when there are more d_{gg} than d_{gi} zero score differences.

17.5.3 Number of Nearest Neighbours

The method proposed in [9] to estimate the RE of biometrics uses only the *first* nearest genuine and impostor neighbours of each genuine score. An issue with this approach is that it makes the RE estimate highly dependent on any single score, even if that score is an outlier. This might be particularly problematic if we do not have a large number of scores to work with, which is often the case.

It seems that a safer approach would be to use k nearest neighbours, where $k > 1$, then average the resulting $d_{gg}(i)$ and $d_{gi}(i)$ values over these k neighbours prior to estimating the RE. This would introduce some smoothing to the underlying score distributions, thereby stabilising the RE estimates. While the effect of k on the RE, and therefore NRE, is difficult to generalise since it would, in practice, be dependent on the biometric system in question, we wished to test the effect of the choice of k on the RE and NRE of our best finger vein recognition system, that obtained when using MC-extracted finger veins from the UTFVP database. Figure 17.8 shows plots of the RE and NRE versus k, when k increases from 1 to 5. For convenience, Table 17.4 summarises the RE and NRE values from Fig. 17.8. Note that, for this experiment, $\epsilon = 10^{-10}$, as for the RE and NRE experiments in Sects. 17.3 and 17.4.

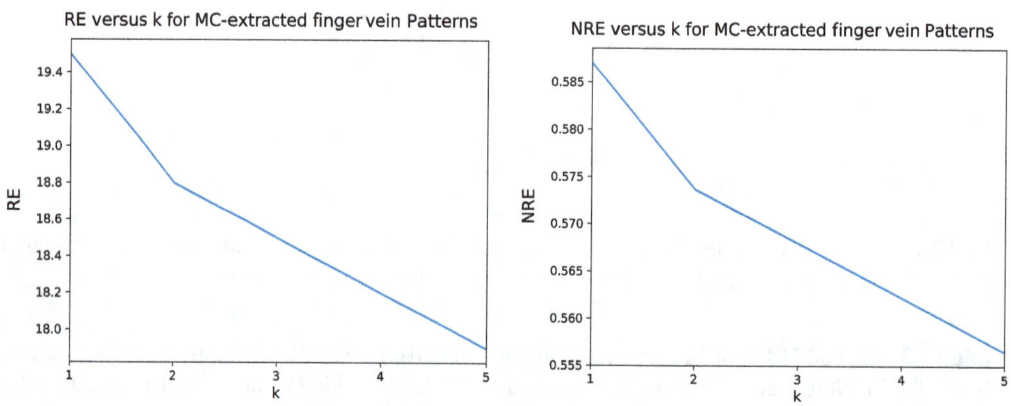

Fig. 17.8 RE versus k and NRE versus k, when k increases from 1 to 5, for MC-extracted finger vein patterns in the UTFVP database

Table 17.4 RE and NRE for MC-extracted finger veins from UTFVP, when k increases from 1 to 5. Note that, for consistency with Tables 17.2 and 17.3, RE and NRE values are rounded to 1 d.p. and 2 d.p., respectively

k	RE	NRE
1	19.5	0.59
2	18.8	0.57
3	18.5	0.57
4	18.2	0.56
5	17.9	0.56

From Fig. 17.8 and Table 17.4, it is evident that increasing k tends to decrease both the RE and NRE, but the decrease is not drastic for $k \leq 5$. This decrease makes sense, since a larger k means a greater degree of smoothing, which decreases the effects of individual comparison scores. Another consequence of using a larger k would be that the effect of the ϵ parameter on RE and NRE would be expected to be less pronounced. This is because a larger k means that a larger number of neighbouring scores are averaged when calculating the RE and NRE, so we are less likely to encounter zero average scores than in the scenario where only *one* nearest neighbouring score is considered. Keeping the aforementioned points in mind, it is important to sensibly tune the k and ϵ parameters depending on the biometric system in question (e.g. if there are outlier scores, use $k > 1$, and select ϵ based on the score precision, as discussed in Sect. 17.5.2). Furthermore, we urge researchers adopting the RE and NRE measures to be transparent about their selection of these parameters to ensure fair system comparisons across the biometrics community.

Note that the NN estimator on which Eq. (17.2) is based [10] *is* actually a k-NN estimator, where k denotes the number of nearest neighbours. It is not clear, however, whether the proposed k-NN estimator is based on *averaging* the k nearest neighbouring scores, as we have done for Fig. 17.8 and Table 17.4, or whether the authors meant that *only* the kth neighbour should be used. If their intention is the latter, then our averaging approach represents an effective new way of stabilising the k-NN estimator for RE measures.

17.6 Conclusions and Future Work

This chapter represents the first attempt at estimating the amount of information in finger vein biometrics in terms of score-based Relative Entropy (RE), using the previously proposed Nearest Neighbour estimator. We made five important contributions.

First, we showed that the RE estimate is system-specific. In our experiments, the RE differed across finger vein recognition systems employing different feature extractors and different testing databases. For this reason, we refrain from claiming a universal finger vein RE estimate, since this would be misleading.

Second, we showed that the RE can be used to rank different finger vein recognition systems, which are tested on the same database using the same experimental protocol (in our case, the difference was the feature extractor employed), in terms of the amount of discriminative biometric information available. The ranking was shown to be comparable to an EER-based ranking, which implies that the RE estimate is a reliable indicator of the amount of discriminatory information in finger vein recognition systems.

Third, we proposed a new metric, the Normalised Relative Entropy (NRE), to help us gauge the significance of individual RE scores as well as to enable fair benchmarking of different biometric systems (in particular, systems tested on different databases using different experimental protocols) in terms of their RE. The NRE lies in the range [0.00, 1.00] and represents the proportion of the maximum amount of discriminatory information that is contained in the biometric system being measured. The higher the NRE, the better the system is expected to be at distinguishing genuine trials from impostors.

Fourth, we discussed how the NRE metric could be a beneficial complement to the EER in ranking different biometric systems in terms of their discrimination capabilities. The NRE would be particularly useful in choosing the best of n biometric systems that have the same EER.

Finally, we discussed two potential issues in calculating the RE and NRE, namely, the effects of the ϵ parameter and the number of nearest neighbours (k) used for computing the genuine–genuine and genuine–impostor score differences. We showed that, as long as ϵ is sensibly selected, its effect on the RE and NRE is unlikely to be significant. We also showed that increasing the number of nearest score neighbours may be expected to slightly decrease the RE and NRE, but the upside is that using a larger number of nearest neighbours would help to dilute the effects of outliers among the genuine and impostor comparison scores. We concluded by suggesting that ϵ and k be tuned according to the biometric system being evaluated and that researchers be transparent in terms of reporting their selection of these two parameters.

At the moment, our primary aim for future work in this direction is to use our proposed NRE metric to benchmark finger vein recognition systems against systems based on other biometric modalities, in terms of the amount of discriminatory information contained in each system.

Acknowledgements The authors would like to acknowledge the following sources of funding for supporting this work: the Secure Access Control over Wide Area Network (SWAN) project, the German Federal Ministry of Education and Research (BMBF) and the Hessen State Ministry for Higher Education, Research and the Arts (HMWK) within the Center for Research in Security and Privacy (CRISP).

References

1. Ye Y, Zheng H, Ni L, Liu S, Li W (2016) A study on the individuality of finger vein based on statistical analysis. In: 2016 international conference on biometrics (ICB), pp 1–5, June 2016
2. Yanagawa T, Aoki S, Ohyama T (2007) Human finger vein images are diverse and its patterns are useful for personal identification. MHF Prepr Ser 12:1–7
3. Jeffers J, Arakala A, Horadam KJ (2010) Entropy of feature point-based retina templates. In: 2010 20th international conference on pattern recognition, pp 213–216, Aug 2010
4. Daugman J (2004) How iris recognition works. IEEE Trans Circuits Syst Video Technol 14(1):21–30
5. Krivokuca V, Marcel S (2018) Towards quantifying the entropy of fingervein patterns across different feature extractors. In: 2018 IEEE 4th international conference on identity, security, and behavior analysis (ISBA), pp 1–8, Jan 2018
6. Takahashi K, Murakami T (2010) A metric of information gained through biometric systems. In: Proceedings of the 2010 20th international conference on pattern recognition. IEEE Computer Society, pp 1184–1187
7. Sutcu Y, Tabassi E, Sencar HT, Memon N (2013) What is biometric information and how to measure it? In: 2013 IEEE international conference on technologies for homeland security (HST), pp 67–72, Nov 2013

8. Adler A, Youmaran R, Loyka S (2006). Towards a measure of biometric information. In 2006 Canadian conference on electrical and computer engineering, pp 210–213, May 2006
9. Sutcu Y, Sencar HT, Memon N (2010) How to measure biometric information? In : 2010 20th international conference on pattern recognition, pp 1469–1472, Aug 2010
10. Wang Q, Kulkarni SR, Verdu S (2009) Divergence estimation for multidimensional densities via k-nearest-neighbor distances. IEEE Trans Inf Theory 55(5):2392–2405
11. Vanoni M, Tome P, El-Shafey L, Marcel S (2014) Cross-database evaluation using an open finger vein sensor. In: 2014 IEEE workshop on biometric measurements and systems for security and medical applications (BIOMS) proceedings, pp 30–35, Oct 2014
12. Ton BT, Veldhuis RNJ (2013) A high quality finger vascular pattern dataset collected using a custom designed capturing device. In: 2013 international conference on biometrics (ICB), pp 1–5, June 2013
13. Lee EC, Lee HC, Park KR (2009) Finger vein recognition using minutia-based alignment and local binary pattern-based feature extraction. Int J Imaging Syst Technol 19(3):179–186
14. Huang B, Dai Y, Li R, Tang D, Li W (2010) Finger-vein authentication based on wide line detector and pattern normalization. In: 2010 20th international conference on pattern recognition, pp 1269–1272, Aug 2010
15. Miura N, Nagasaka A, Miyatake T (2004) Feature extraction of finger-vein patterns based on repeated line tracking and its application to personal identification. Mach Vis Appl 15(4):194–203
16. Miura N, Nagasaka A, Miyatake T (2007) Extraction of finger-vein patterns using maximum curvature points in image profiles. IEICE Trans Inf Syst 90(8):1185–1194

Index

Numerals

3D finger vein reconstruction, 71–73, 88

3D printed part, xi, 77, 79, 93, 101, 106, 267

A

Acquisition

conditions, xii, 8, 12, 119, 179–182, 184–186, 188, 189, 192–197, 399, 511

Adaptive Histogram Equalisation (AHE), 23, 69–71, 125, 126

Additional filter, 85, 92

Age related macular degeneration, 326

Airport security, 155

Anatomy Structure Analysis based Vein Extraction (ASAVE), 116, 119, 128, 132

Anchors, xiii, 355–357, 364, 376, 377, 379–382, 384

Anti-vandalism, 160, 169

Area under curve, 414, 425, 427

Automated label training, 208

Automated Teller Machines (ATM), 11, 78, 145, 148, 153, 154, 167–172, 181

Automatic brightness control algorithm, 89, 103

Automation, 119, 120

Availability, 29, 35, 77, 78, 113, 114, 173, 210

B

Bifurcations and crossings, 317, 319, 322, 335, 339

Binarisation, vii, xiv, 15, 17, 22, 32, 127, 128, 130, 189, 228, 232, 233, 238, 242, 255, 280, 286, 359, 467, 469

Binary search tree, 237, 238, 255, 256

Binary vascular structure, 15, 16, 23

BioHash, xiv, 465–470, 472–478

BioHashing, xiv, 33, 465, 467–472, 474–476, 478

Biometric Crypto Systems (BCS), 31–33, 484

Biometric Graph (BG)

biometric graph comparison (BGC), xiii, 22, 228, 355, 356, 358, 361, 365, 368

biometric graph matching (BGM), 20, 25, 356

Biometric identification, 145, 226, 229, 232, 356

Biometric performance evaluation, 242

Biometric recognition system, 39, 117, 118, 181, 270, 271, 278, 436, 481, 484, 509, 510, 513, 518

Biometric template protection, vii, xiv, 78, 384, 466, 467, 468, 484, 508

BiowatchID, 4, 10, 40

Blind spot, 6, 13, 25, 311, 315, 317, 319–321, 329, 336–340, 348, 349

Block remapping, xiv, 32, 466, 481–483, 485–488, 490–492, 494, 495, 498, 500, 502–504

Bloodstream mask, 330

Blood vessel segmentation, 24, 403

Bloom filter, 32, 225, 235–238, 240, 242, 249–252, 254–256, 467

Brightness control board, 98–100, 106

C

Camera

holder bracket, 92–94

Cancelable biometrics, 31

A. Uhl et al. (eds.), *Handbook of Vascular Biometrics*, Advances in Computer Vision and Pattern Recognition, https://doi.org/10.1007/978-3-030-27731-4

Column Principal Component Analysis (CPCA), 232–234, 237, 238, 240–242, 245–248, 250–256
Compactness, 160, 163
Comparison
scores, 10, 19, 21, 114, 119, 129, 130, 132, 134, 189, 193, 232, 235, 236, 239, 241, 253, 271, 273, 275, 276, 278, 281–284, 357, 378, 409, 484, 487, 490, 491, 502, 507, 509–519, 521, 523, 524
Compliance, 160, 162, 454, 468
Contactless, xii, 7, 10, 19, 38, 40, 44, 90, 145, 146, 147, 148, 151, 155, 184, 396
Contrast Limited Adaptive Histogram Equalisation (CLAHE), 27, 123–126, 136, 189, 279, 400
Convolutional Neural Networks (CNN), vii, xii, 16, 18, 20, 21, 23, 35, 37, 183, 201–205, 211–213, 217–220, 351, 395, 397–399, 402–404, 406, 407, 416–419, 425, 427, 436, 440–446, 508
COTS finger vein scanners, 78, 82, 83, 90
CPCA-Tree, 237, 238, 240, 242, 250–256
Cross-entropy loss function, 206
Curvature, 15, 16, 20, 22, 24, 30, 31, 37, 70, 71, 73, 115, 116, 121, 126–129, 136, 137, 171, 183, 189, 203, 208, 213, 229, 241, 245, 276, 280, 281, 358, 400, 421, 422, 465, 468, 482, 490, 512

D
Data augmentation, 210, 405, 444
Datasets, vi, x, xi, xiii, 3, 5, 7, 9, 12–14, 18, 19, 21, 27–30, 36, 42–44, 63, 64, 66, 69–71, 74, 77–80, 83–87, 106, 113–116, 119, 120, 122, 138, 256, 264, 338, 379, 395, 397, 400–402, 411, 412, 443–445, 481, 482, 489, 491, 493, 495, 500
Deep learning, xiii, 17, 18, 26, 35, 39, 44, 203, 207, 340, 396, 397, 399, 439–441, 444
Deformation
deformation tolerant feature point matching (DTFPM), 116, 129, 132, 183, 281, 284, 286, 288–290, 292–300
DET plot, 121, 134, 135, 137, 138, 247, 282
Device EYRINA, 309, 316
Diabetic retinopathy, 7, 38, 39, 43, 309, 322, 324, 325, 329, 338
Dimensionality reduction, 20, 32, 272, 472–475, 478
Discriminatory information, vii, xiv, 18, 507–509, 513, 514, 516–518, 520, 523, 524
Diseases, vii, xi, xiii, 3, 8, 9, 38, 43, 44, 86, 309, 312, 323–329, 333, 334, 340, 350, 358, 445
Dissimilarity vectors, 355, 357, 377–379, 384
Diversity, 467, 468, 481, 482
Dorsal, xi, 3, 6, 10, 15, 21–23, 27–29, 34, 36, 38, 40–42, 44, 77, 79, 81–90, 101, 103–106, 118, 261, 263, 265, 284–290, 292, 296–301, 356, 359, 369, 489
Druses, 317, 324, 326, 327, 329–331, 333–335
Durability, 160, 169, 171

E
Edge detector, 15
Efficient identification, xii, 79
Emission spectrum, 93, 94, 96
Encoder–decoder network, 207, 399, 405, 417
Enhanced Maximum Curvature (EMC), 127
Enhancement, xi, 12, 14, 17, 20, 22–24, 26, 27, 33, 41, 64, 113, 114, 116–127, 136, 182, 189, 279, 286, 400, 446, 482, 488
Entry control, 151
Environmental conditions, 40, 169, 179–181, 186, 195
Equal Error Rate (EER), 28, 63, 69–71, 74, 105, 118–121, 132, 134, 135, 137, 189, 192–195, 210, 211, 213, 217, 241, 242, 248, 251, 253, 254, 273–278, 283–301, 374, 376, 391, 414, 438, 439, 443, 446, 470, 490, 492–495, 497, 504, 507, 508, 509, 513, 514, 518–520, 523, 524
External influences, 77, 78, 262, 266, 300–302, 312
Exudates, 317, 324, 325, 329–331, 333–335, 338, 350
EyeDentify, 11, 312, 313, 315, 316
Eye recognition, 309
EyeVerify, 12

F

F1-score, 413, 417, 418, 421, 422
False accept(ance) rate, 149, 197, 413, 414, 508
False reject(ion) rate, 149, 180, 323, 413
Feature
  extraction, vii, xi, xiv, 9, 12, 13, 15–23, 26, 27, 31–33, 35, 37, 38, 45, 105, 113–122, 126, 128–132, 136, 138, 183, 189, 193, 201, 202, 204, 208, 229, 234, 241, 243, 245, 250, 261–263, 270, 274–276, 278, 280, 282, 283, 284, 286, 288–302, 397, 400, 403, 413, 424, 426, 452, 469, 470, 482, 483, 486–488, 490–495
  level fusion, 18, 20, 21, 118, 119, 135, 229, 272–274, 276, 278, 282
Financial services, ix, xii, 12, 145, 153, 154, 157, 169, 181
Finger deformation, 19
Finger guide, 80, 87, 88, 100
Finger masking, 116, 123
Finger placement unit, 88–90, 94, 100–102
Fingerprint Recognition, ix, 11, 16, 44, 63, 180, 435, 437, 448
Fingerprint Verification Contests (FVC), 30, 132, 133, 137, 138, 210, 256, 283, 490
Finger rotation
  compensation normalisation, 123
Finger vein
  capture device, xii, 65, 66, 261, 262, 266, 268, 269, 272, 276, 298, 300, 301, 446, 449
  datasets, xi, 28, 63, 77–80, 83–86, 104–107, 115, 122, 134, 261–266, 269, 270, 276, 278, 302, 489
  image restoration, 14, 125
  patterns, 15, 63, 66, 68, 72, 74, 201–206, 220, 275, 465, 466, 468, 470, 471, 474, 476, 478, 508, 509, 511, 512, 514, 521, 522
  recognition, xii, xiv, 5, 7, 8, 11, 12, 14, 15, 17–19, 27, 28, 30–32, 40, 41, 44, 64–66, 77–82, 88, 105–107, 113, 115, 117–119, 130, 138, 179, 189, 201–204, 209, 210, 220, 261–264, 270, 273, 278–280, 298, 300–302, 436, 437, 439, 457, 466, 471, 472, 474, 481, 482, 489, 491, 504, 507, 509, 511, 513, 514, 516–518, 521–524
    based on deformation information, 130
  ridge enhancement, 125
  scanner, xi, 10, 19, 64, 65, 71–73, 77–80, 82–85, 87–92, 101, 105–107, 114, 185, 266, 490
    design, xi, 71, 78, 80, 85, 89–92, 105, 106, 114, 161, 165, 205, 266, 269
  segmentation, vii, xii, 116, 124, 206, 220
  template protection, 31, 465, 466
Flapper gate, 152
FMR100, 134, 137, 189, 192–196, 210, 278, 283, 287–292, 297, 298, 300, 376, 391, 490, 493
FMR1000, 134, 137, 189, 192–196, 210, 278, 283, 287–292, 297, 298, 300, 376, 391, 490, 493
FNMR1000, 134
Fourier, 15, 17, 25, 27, 33, 35, 123, 124, 131, 230, 231, 255, 256, 279, 436, 439, 466
Fovea, 6, 311, 319, 322, 326, 329, 333, 336, 339, 344, 349, 377
Fujitsu, vii, xii, 4, 10, 11, 41, 146, 148, 150–152
Fundus
  camera, 6, 42, 311–314, 316–318, 334, 339, 340, 343
  image, xiii, 13, 24, 29, 30, 38, 39, 42, 43, 205, 321, 358
  imaging, vii, xiii, 24, 42
  photography, 6, 7, 38, 43
Fused label training, 217, 220
Fusion, xii, xiii, 9, 12, 15–23, 26, 27, 37, 38, 113, 116, 118–121, 124, 135, 136, 138, 201, 202, 204, 205, 209, 218, 220, 229, 239, 243, 251, 261–266, 269–278, 282–284, 288–302, 446, 467
Fuzzy commitment, 32, 466, 467
FVC protocol, 133, 138, 490
FV-USM, 28, 84–86, 114, 122

G

Gabor
  filter, 14, 15, 19–25, 27, 32, 33, 37, 124, 125, 128, 136, 189, 203, 208, 213–216, 229, 273, 275, 279, 280, 396, 398, 400, 490
  Gabor filtering (GF), 86, 128, 203, 208, 280, 490
Gaze detection, 26
General Data Protection Regulation (GDPR), 319, 466

Government and municipal, 156
Graph comparison, xiii, 22, 228, 355, 356, 358, 361, 365, 368, 377, 391
Graph registration, 355, 361, 363, 364, 375, 383
Grey level grouping with circular Gabor filtering, 124

H
Haemoglobin, 5, 64, 78, 80, 449
Hamming distance, 34, 116, 233, 275, 336, 469, 508
Handvein
  recognition, 376
Hard exudates, 325, 333
Health care, 154, 155
High throughput, 160, 172
High frequency emphasis filtering, 21, 27, 123, 189, 279
Hitachi, 4, 10, 41, 42, 65, 82, 161, 162, 436, 466
Hong Kong Polytechnical University (HKPU), 28, 84, 86, 87, 114, 122
Human eye, 4, 310, 314

I
Identification, 13, 24, 41, 79, 145–147, 149, 153, 156, 157, 172, 204, 225–227, 229, 232, 235, 241–243, 271, 312, 316, 318, 356
Illumination
  control, 72, 79, 85, 86
  control system, 85
Illuminator
  bracket, 89, 90, 94, 97
  control board, 89, 90
  peak wavelength, 87, 88
Image descriptors, 397–400, 406
Image domain, 481–483, 485, 486, 490, 492, 504
Image mosaicing, 403, 405
Image quality, 12, 35, 37–39, 77, 78, 89, 91–93, 96, 97, 103, 116, 126, 160, 182, 184, 267, 279, 329, 331, 334, 370, 437, 440–442, 444
Image sensor, 5, 64, 65, 80, 81, 88, 92, 103, 182, 184, 185, 262, 264–267
Indexing, 13, 79, 225, 226, 232, 235–243, 249–256, 336
Information amounts, 335
Infrared filter, 67, 72, 86, 88
Intensity variation normalisation, 125
Interclass variance, 238, 518
Iris recognition, 8, 173, 232, 396, 398, 399, 401
ISO/IEC 30136:2018, 467
Isotropic Undecimated Wavelet Transform (IUWT), 121, 129, 490, 493–502

K
Key point
  descriptors, 130, 281
Kullback–Leibler divergence, 132

L
Laptop
  PC, 148, 150
Laser diodes, 88, 95, 96, 267
Learned binary codes, 17
LeeRegion, 121, 123, 136, 210
Lens, 6, 42, 67, 85–89, 91–98, 185, 267, 310, 312, 314–316, 396, 410–412, 447–449
Light transmission, 64, 65, 77, 79–82, 85, 86, 88–96, 99, 102, 103, 106, 184, 185, 262, 264, 267, 449
Liveness detection, 8, 9, 36, 436
Local Binary Patterns (LBP), 16, 17, 20, 22, 23, 31, 34, 35, 38, 44, 116, 130–132, 183, 203, 275, 397, 400, 439–444, 449–451, 456–458, 450
Login, 145, 149, 150, 157

M
MATLAB, 30, 31, 39, 71, 114, 115, 117, 119–121, 126, 130, 131, 136, 138, 139, 208
Maximum Common Subgraph (MCS), 356, 361, 365–368, 372, 373, 376, 379
Maximum Curvature (MC), 15, 30, 31, 70, 71, 105, 115–117, 121, 126–128, 136, 137, 189–195, 203, 208, 213–216, 218–220, 229, 241, 245, 276, 280, 282, 284–286, 288–301, 400, 421, 422, 455, 456, 465, 468–476, 478, 487, 490, 493, 494, 496–502, 512–514, 517, 521, 522
Memory, 122, 228, 465, 475–478
Minutiae
  cylinder codes, 16, 32
Mobility, 160, 166
Morphological post-processing, 15, 24, 131, 137

Multi-algorithm fusion, 262, 265, 266, 284, 292–294, 296, 298–301
Multichannel Gabor filtering, 124
Multimodal
recognition, 20
Multi-perspective
finger vein
biometrics, 118, 262, 263, 266
capture device, 261–263, 265, 266, 268, 269, 276, 298, 300
fusion, 19, 288, 293, 296, 299
Multitask learning, 397, 406–408

N
Narrow bandpass filter, 93, 96
Nearest neighbour estimator, 523
Near-Infrared (NIR)
blocking filter, 41, 78, 88, 92
illumination, 5, 8, 41, 78, 81, 201, 266, 447, 449, 452
laser modules, 77, 90
light
source, 5, 65, 80, 88, 449
emitting diodes, 79
long-pass filter, 267
pass-through filter, 80, 88, 89, 91–94, 101, 107, 185
Neural network, 16, 18, 24, 35, 41, 183, 204, 205, 220, 349–351, 395, 397, 399, 427, 437, 441, 442, 444
Non environmental conditions, 179
Non invertible transformation, 31, 487
Normalised cross correlation, 70, 116
Normalised relative entropy, 507, 509, 514, 517, 523
Normal scenario, 472, 474–478

O
Ocular biometrics, 398–401
On the move, xi, 8, 9, 26, 27, 39, 42, 43, 45
Open source
design, 106, 107
Ophthalmology, 6, 9, 310, 316, 322–324, 338
Optical output power, 88, 96
Optic disc, 6, 318, 345, 350, 358, 364, 377

P
Palm
vascular, 3, 4, 5, 12, 13, 19–21, 23, 31, 33, 36, 38, 44
Palmar, 6, 10, 15, 27–29, 41, 77, 79, 81, 82, 84–86, 89, 90, 101, 103, 105, 106, 118, 261–265, 283–290, 292, 296–302, 489, 504
PalmSecure, 10, 11, 33, 41
Palm vein
authentication, xii, 145–157
recognition, ix, xii, 12, 19, 31, 33, 240, 275
sensor, 19, 20, 147–149
Payment systems, 152–153
Peak wavelength, 80, 87, 88, 93, 94, 96, 97, 185
Performance
evaluation, 74, 78, 114–116, 118, 122, 134, 137, 138, 146, 180, 183, 192–196, 241, 440, 442, 443, 490
Periocular recognition, 45
Phase Only Correlation (POC), 19, 25, 131, 132, 273
PLUS OpenVein
scanner, 88–90
toolkit, 115–118, 120, 122, 137, 138
PLUSVein-3D-FV, 123
PLUSVein-FV3
dataset, 85, 492
Portability, 66, 160, 166, 175
Precision, 4, 41, 231, 232, 413, 414, 417, 418, 421, 422, 523
Preprocessing, 9, 12, 14, 21, 23, 25, 30, 44, 69, 71, 114–117, 119–123, 126, 136–138, 182, 189, 270, 272, 276, 278–280, 285, 286, 299, 325–327, 329, 449, 452, 490
Presentation attack
presentation attack detection (PAD), xi, xiii, 9, 34, 35, 40, 435–443, 446, 449, 454
Principal Curvature (PC), 71, 105, 107, 115, 116, 121, 128, 137, 189–197, 203, 280, 282, 284, 286, 288, 289–300, 488, 490, 493–503
Privacy, vi, vii, x, xi, xiii, 3, 8, 9, 30, 43, 44, 115, 154, 229, 257, 257, 436, 457, 478, 481–483, 487, 488, 499, 504, 508
Probability map, 206, 210, 402, 403, 405, 406, 409, 416–418, 421, 422, 424, 427
Proximity graphs, 371, 372

R
Radiation half-angle, 94, 96, 97

RANSAC, 27, 361, 364
Recall, 12, 243, 248, 413, 414, 417, 418, 421, 422, 474
Receiver Operating Characteristic (ROC), 121, 134, 135, 137, 138, 202, 282, 414, 426, 427, 471, 472
Recognition accuracy, vii, xiii, 14, 26, 38, 41, 43, 105, 107, 181, 188, 196, 197, 213, 218, 221, 261, 262, 275, 278, 298, 300, 356, 368, 384, 396, 487, 507, 509, 510, 513, 514, 516, 518
Recognition performance, xii, xiv, 14, 21, 40, 43, 77–79, 89, 90, 104–106, 113–115, 118, 134, 137, 179, 180, 182, 184, 193, 195, 197, 201, 202, 206, 210, 211, 213, 219, 221, 233, 243, 245, 261, 263–266, 271, 278, 283–291, 293, 298, 299, 301, 324–329, 355, 361, 364, 376, 395, 396, 399, 408, 424, 458, 465, 467, 468, 470–478, 481–483, 486–498, 500, 503–505
Reflected light, xi, 5, 6, 20, 21, 28, 29, 41, 44, 64, 77, 79, 80, 81, 85, 88–91, 97–100, 103, 106, 118, 145, 184, 314
Region of Interest (RoI), 12–15, 18–23, 29, 41, 137, 189, 240, 241, 265, 278, 279, 284–286, 359, 370, 400, 402, 403, 405, 410, 423, 448, 449, 486, 489
Relative entropy, xiv, 336, 507–509, 511–514, 517, 518, 523
Repeated Line Tracking (RLT), 15, 30, 31, 70, 71, 115–117, 121, 127, 203, 208, 209, 213–220, 421, 422, 465, 468–478, 490, 493–502, 512–514, 517
Reproducible research, vi, x, 14, 27, 44, 491
Retina
  code, 12, 25, 318
  recognition, vii, xiii, 6, 8, 9, 12, 13, 24, 29, 33, 45, 318
Retinex, 121, 125
Revocability, 32, 481, 482
ROC curve, 135, 414, 426, 427
ROC plot, 137, 138, 471, 472

S

Sample quality, xi, 3, 9, 12, 13, 34, 37, 38, 45
Scale-Invariant Feature Transform (SIFT), 16, 17, 20, 22, 25, 44, 105, 117, 119, 121, 129, 130, 132, 189–195, 275, 276, 281, 282, 286, 288–301, 397, 400, 424, 425, 427, 442, 444
Scanner control software, 103
Scanner design, xi, 77, 79, 80, 83, 85, 88–94, 96, 97, 104–107, 114
Scanner housing, 83, 93, 95, 102
Scanner parts, 79, 89, 91
Scattering, 8, 14, 20, 24, 81, 124, 125, 181–183, 202
Sclera Blood Vessels, Periocular and Iris (SBVPI) dataset, 395–398, 400–402, 409, 410, 412, 414, 415
ScleraNet, 395, 395, 398, 400, 402, 403, 406–409, 416, 424, 425, 427
Sclera recognition, ix, xi, xiii, 3, 7, 12, 13, 26, 27, 34, 43, 45, 395–403, 409, 411, 412, 416, 418, 425, 427
Sclera segmentation, xiii, 13, 26, 27, 29, 43, 395–397, 399, 400, 403, 404, 409, 414–417, 423
Score distributions, 179, 190–194, 235, 239, 250, 336, 497, 502, 509, 510–513, 516, 518, 519, 522
Score normalisation, 135, 136, 272, 275
Score level fusion, xii, xiii, 18, 27, 113, 116, 119, 135, 138, 261, 262, 264, 265, 269, 272, 275, 276, 278, 282, 297, 301, 446
SDUMLA-HMT, 28, 83, 84, 86, 114, 122
Security, x, xiii, 4, 11, 31, 45, 115, 145, 147–149, 151–157, 159, 179, 181, 204, 323, 377, 384, 436, 457, 466, 478, 481, 482, 484, 503, 508
Segmentation, vii, xii, xiii, 13, 15, 16, 22, 24–27, 29, 30, 39, 43, 101, 116, 124, 183, 201, 202, 204–207, 209, 210, 219, 220, 274, 275, 338, 395–400, 402–406, 409, 412–427
Semantic segmentation, vii, xii, 16, 26, 205
Sensor
  construction, 13
Singular Value Decomposition (SVD), 16, 35
Skeleton, 13, 20, 22, 25, 27, 131, 357–360
Skip connections, 405
Slit lamp, 314
Spectral minutiae
  spectral minutiae representation (SMR), xii, 23, 32, 225, 228–234, 237, 238, 239, 242, 243, 247, 248, 250
Speeded Up Adaptive Contrast Enhancement (SUACE), 121, 126
Spoofing, 8, 9, 34–36, 85, 86, 122, 153, 508

Stolen Token scenario, 465, 472–478
Structural Similarity (SSIM), 38, 39, 351, 355, 356, 357, 377–379, 384
Subject key, 483, 484, 491, 496, 497, 502–505
Subject related influences, 302
SURF, 17, 20, 26, 130, 276, 424, 425, 427
Surface conditions, 7, 201
Survey, 14, 24, 26, 43, 149, 225, 398, 400, 438
Synthetic images, 340, 349, 350
Synthetic retinal images, 309, 340, 348, 351
Synthetic sample data, 30
System specific key, 483, 484, 491, 496, 497, 500, 504

T

Tablet, 11, 41, 148, 150
Techsphere, 4, 10
Template protection, vi, vii, xi, xiii, xiv, 3, 9, 31–33, 43, 78, 79, 226, 228–230, 232–234, 355, 376, 377–379, 384, 385, 465–468, 475, 478, 481–485, 490–492, 494–505, 508
Texture, 12, 13, 17, 18, 21–26, 35, 36, 38, 39, 44, 86, 87, 98, 218, 240, 276, 277, 285, 286, 298, 341–345, 348, 396, 398, 399, 437, 439, 440, 442, 443, 446, 449, 450, 458
Thinning, 15, 16, 128, 131, 359, 360
Transillumination, xi, 5, 6, 8, 10, 20, 21, 27–29, 36, 40–42, 44, 66, 79, 80, 118, 181, 184, 185

U

Universal design, 159–161, 167
Universality, 160, 173
University of Twente Finger Vascular Pattern (UTFVP)
  dataset
Unlinkability, xi, xii, 133, 137, 492, 494
Usability, xii, 83, 107, 159–162, 164–168, 170, 173, 175, 176, 227, 334
USB finger vein scanner, 82
Use case, xii, 138, 145, 147, 149, 159–163, 166, 167, 169, 171–173

V

Vascular
  bed, 318, 340, 341, 343, 346
  biometrics, 227–229, 335, 356–359, 368, 383, 396, 400, 410, 421
  graph, 355, 356, 358, 369, 371
  network, 6, 15, 16, 20, 22, 24, 25, 32, 37, 44, 344, 356
  pattern, vi, ix, 3, 5, 9, 16, 23–26, 64–69, 73, 77, 78, 80, 81, 94, 97, 113, 129, 136, 160, 175, 181, 197, 226, 228, 229, 240, 255, 262, 266, 281, 309, 324, 325, 327, 328, 340, 355, 356, 360, 369, 372, 378, 396, 398, 402, 410, 421, 481, 489
  pattern based biometrics, 78, 80, 113
  segmentation, 13, 15, 396–400, 404, 415, 419–422, 425–427
Vein
  authentication, xii, 41, 82, 145–157
  recognition framework, xi, 17, 113, 115–117, 119, 122, 127, 130, 134–135, 138
  recognition schemes, 18, 77, 105, 114, 115, 122, 179, 182, 263, 264
VERA
  finger vein spoofing dataset, 36
  palm vein dataset, 36
Verification (true accept) rate, 414
Vertical finger movement, 79, 96, 97

W

Warping, xiv, 32, 466, 481, 482, 485, 487, 488, 490–492, 495, 498, 500–505
Wide line
  wide line detector (WLD), 31, 71, 115, 127, 465, 468, 490, 512
Wrist vein
  recognition, xi, 3, 5–7, 13, 23, 41, 44

Y

Yannan Tech, 10

Z

ZeroFMR, 134, 137, 210, 278, 283, 287–292, 298, 300, 490, 493
ZeroFNMR, 134

www.ingramcontent.com/pod-product-compliance
Lightning Source LLC
LaVergne TN
LVHW062155200926
848484LV00007B/1916